MORESHET

Journal for the Study
of the Holocaust
and Antisemitism

D1238447

Claims Conference

This publication has been supported by a grant from the Conference on Jewish Material Claims Against Germany

MORESHET

Journal for the Study
of the Holocaust
and Antisemitism

Dr. Graciela Ben Dror
Editor

Moreshet, Mordechai Anielevich Memorial
Holocaust Study and Research Center, Givat Haviva

Alfred P. Slaner Chair in Antisemitism and Racism,
Tel Aviv University

19 | 2022

Moreshet, Mordechai Anielevich Memorial was established in 1961 by: **Yehuda Bauer, the late Yisrael Gutman, Abba Kovner, Shalom Cholawsky, Ruzka Korczak, Akiva Nir, Yehuda Tubin, and Haika Grossman**

MORESHET
Journal for the Study of the Holocaust and Antisemitism

Editor
Dr. Graciela Ben Dror

Guest Editor
Prof. Marcos Silber

Editorial Board
Prof. Yehuda Bauer, Dr. Graciela Ben Dror, Prof. Aviva Halamish, Dr. Ariel Hurwitz, Prof. Guy Miron, Prof. Dalia Ofer, Prof. Dina Porat, Prof. Marcos Silber, Prof. Roni Stauber, Prof. Eli Tzur, Dr. Rafi Vago, Prof. Yechiam Weitz.

Moreshet Director .... Yaakov Asher

Editorial Coordinator ..... Judith Wolff
English Language Editor ..... Naomi Landau

Published by
Moreshet, Mordechai Anielevich Memorial
Holocaust Study and Research Center, Givat Haviva

Alfred P. Slaner Chair in Antisemitism and Racism
Tel Aviv University

This publication has been supported by grants from

The Havatzelet Cultural and Educational Institutions

and from the Eta and Sass Somekh Family Foundation

Copyright © 2022 ISBN 978-1-885881-65-6

All rights reserved to Moreshet-Havatzelet
Editorial Offices and Administration
Givat Haviva, Doar Na Menashe 37850, ISRAEL
Tel: 972–4–6309248
E-mail: judymoreshet@gmail.com
The complete catalogue of Moreshet articles: www.moreshet.org

Design
Amy Erani www.multieducator.net

Table of Contents

Moreshet, Journal for the Study
of the Holocaust and Antisemitism • Volume 19

Eastern Galicia 1941 - 1944,
80 Years after "Operation Barbarossa"

Holocaust Research

Historiography and Holocaust Memory

Documentation and Testimony

Book Reviews

From the Editors

We are pleased to present our readers with Volume 19 of *Moreshet, Journal for the Study of the Holocaust and Antisemitism*. Moreshet, Mordechai Anielevich Memorial, was established 60 years ago, in 1961. The journal *Moreshet, Journal for the Study of the Holocaust and Antisemitism* was founded two years later, in 1963. It has appeared consistently ever since. Over the last six decades 102 issues have been published in Hebrew, with an English version from 2003. The momentum that began in the new millennium has grown steadily ever since, making *Moreshet* a leading peer review journal in its field, with the most rigorous and professional reviewing by an external panel of experts on the specific topic in question.

Since 2011, the journal has been published under the academic sponsorship of The Alfred P. Slaner Chair for the Study of Racism and Antisemitism, which is currently held by Prof, Dina Porat. Over the years, *Moreshet Journal* has also received the support of the Conference on Jewish Material Claims against Germany, and we are deeply grateful to the Claims Conference for its ongoing important patronage.

It is our privilege to have been associated with the growing stature of Moreshet in the scholarly community of Holocaust research worldwide. The contributors to this issue, leading scholars from several countries from three continents, reflect this development.

We devote this issue to the Holocaust in Eastern Galicia (1941 – 1944), on the 80th anniversary of the Barbarossa Operation marking the beginning of the "Final Solution", the planned and organized mass murder of the Jews by Nazi Germany and its implementation with the help of the local population, beginning in these areas and then in Europe. Eastern Galicia, that today constitutes the bulk of Western Ukraine, was in the south-East of the Second Polish Republic during the interwar period. It was a very heterogeneous region. According to the 1931 census, out of 6,200,000 inhabitants, 3,256,300 declared their religion as "Greek Catholic" (a Christian religion that unites Catholicism with the Byzantine rite for liturgies, laws, and cultural identity), the vast majority identifying as "Ukrainian". 2,281,400 declared themselves Roman-Catholics (Poles in their vast majority), and 616,200 Jews.

As is well known to our readers, on 1 September 1939 Germany invaded Poland, and on 17 September the Soviet Union attacked Poland from the east. Following the Hitler-Stalin-Pact, the Soviet Union annexed Poland's prewar Eastern territories, including Eastern Galicia.

On the one hand, the Jewish population in Eastern Galicia under the new Soviet administration suffered from new ideological and economic pressures. The new regime nationalized industrial and commercial enterprises owned by the Jewish middle class. New taxation created serious economic and social difficulties. Governmental pressure to accept the new citizenship offered by the fledgling Soviet state created new challenges. The summer of 1940 saw the beginning of a wave of deportations of the suspicious middle class, including tens of thousands of Galician Jews, to the interior of the Soviet Union, to Siberia and the Urals.

On the other hand, the Soviets generally considered Jews as a potentially more loyal element than Poles and Ukrainians. During the first stages of the Soviet occupation, secular and educated Jews found new opportunities for employment in public administration. Women also found new employment opportunities in the Soviet economy, changing the gender distribution of the Jewish workforce. The impression that Jews welcomed the new regime (generally owing to their expressions of relief at not having fallen into German hands) exacerbated Polish–Jewish and Ukrainian-Jewish tensions and fed the myth of Żydokomuna. As a motive or a pretext, the myth fed the deadly anti-Jewish violence in the short period of interregnum between the Soviet and the German occupations, under the German regime, and immediately after the liberation from the Nazi occupation. The power of the myth persisted notwithstanding the increasing import of Ukrainian Communists from regions that had been part of the USSR before the war who gradually replaced the Jews in the state apparatus. Even though on the eve of the Barbarossa Operation the percentage of Jews in the state apparatus had considerably diminished in favor of the rising participation of ethno-national Ukrainians, "the Jews" were still identified as the main participants in the local Soviet system.

The Barbarossa Operation began on 22 June 1941, when Germany invaded the Soviet Union. Within a few weeks around 620,000 Jews in East Galicia had fallen into the hands of the German forces. From the beginning Jewish men, women, and children were hit by a wave of violence and mass murder in virtually every city, town, and village. **Yehuda Bauer's** article, the first article in this issue, provides a comprehensive picture of the region from the beginning of the Barbarossa Operation onward. He focuses his detailed description on the large numbers of people whose task was to murder the Jews of the parts of the Soviet Union that were occupied by Nazi Germany. They included not only the *Einsatzgruppen*, but also various types of police forces and military personnel who offered complete, planned-out assistance in the murder process and in the onset of the operation in the areas that were occupied from 1941 onward.

Anti-Jewish violence consisted not only of mass murder by units of the German police, primarily the Einsatzgruppen, but also by the non-Jewish local population. Both elements of violence have been discussed extensively in the research literature. **Kai Struve's** article focuses on the atrocities of the Waffen-SS Division "Wiking" in several localities in eastern Galicia during the first weeks after the German attack on the Soviet Union on 22 June 1941. Struve's article discusses their relevance for understanding the motives and nature of different segments of violence and murder from both the German and local sides.

Anna Zapalec focuses her study on the situation of the Jews in Drohobycz, one of the most important and prosperous Jewish communities in Eastern Galicia, during the first months of the German occupation. Based on hitherto unknown documentation, she discusses the development of the local anti-Jewish German policy, the living conditions of Jews during the earlier months of the German occupation, the rapid deterioration in the situation of the Jews, the growing distress, the ongoing pauperization, the increasing mortality, and starvation. She emphasizes the reactions of the Jewish population to the German policy, from a top-down perspective. She sheds light on the tactics the local Judenrat used to deflect the German measures and also refers to the attitudes of the non-German gentile population.

Alina Molisak introduces us to literary reflections of victims of this anti-Jewish murderous violence in Galicia. She focuses on Michał Borwicz, Zuzanna Ginczanka, and Mieczysław Frenkel. The three were already well-known in the artistic milieu before the outbreak of the war, and related their experiences either during the war (Ginczanka in poetry) or shortly after (Borwicz in essays and Frenkel in short stories). The topography of their texts deals primarily with Lwów/Lviv and its surroundings. Molisak focuses on the presentation of interethnic Jewish-Polish-Ukrainian relations, on the experience recorded in literature – as a testimony of personal experience – and on literary descriptions of the Holocaust experience.

Yuri Radchenko focuses on the Ukrainian side of the Jewish-Polish-Ukrainian triangle. In his article, he points out the case of Julian Temnyk, a member of the Organization of Nationalists in Ukraine, (OUN-M), who joined the SD in Drohobych. Radchenko describes how as a member of this structure he played an active role in the extermination of local Jewish communities. In 1943-44 Temnyk served in the division SS "Galizien". Using unpublished sources from German, Ukrainian, Canadian, American, and Israeli archives, he examines Temnyk's political views, his involvement in Nazi crimes, and his postwar fate in Western Europe and Canada. This close examination of Temnyk's career and experiences relates to the debate over whether Holocaust perpetrators were "Ordinary Men."

The question of ordinary men as bystanders is addressed in **Omer Bartov**'s article. Discussing the case of Buczacz in 1941-1944, he examines how a local study can shed light on the categories of Perpetrators, Victims, and Neighbors. He convincingly claims that conventional histories of the Shoah tend to make clear distinctions between perpetrators, victims, and bystanders. Yet when we carefully examine such cases as the Soviet and German occupations of Buczacz in 1939-1941 and 1941-1944, respectively, as well as the years immediately preceding the war and in its immediate aftermath, we realize that both the reality and the subjective perception of events were far more complex. This is especially so in areas such as Eastern Galicia and many other regions in the vast swath of territory stretching between the Baltic and the Balkans, where most towns had a multiethnic and multi-religious population with a history of growing mutual tension and resentment.

Additionally, quite apart from the fact that each ethnic group in Buczacz and many other towns in Galicia tended to see itself as the other groups' victim throughout this period, the events of the Holocaust specifically also blur these categories, especially that of bystanders. He convincingly claims that there were no bystanders, but only degrees of engagement, not least because the killing was both intimate and public, and no one was in a position, or likely to choose, to merely stand by and watch.

Tamir Hod also focuses on Ukrainian perpetrators. He explores the Everyday Life of the Ukrainian Collaborators at Treblinka and at Belzec extermination camps, which were two of the three camps established in order to murder the Jewish population of the General Governorate in Poland (the third was Sobibor), Belżec being the place of extermination of Galician Jewry. Because of the limited manpower at the Germans' disposal they recruited a cadre of largely Ukrainian collaborators – soldiers who had fought with the Red Army and were taken prisoner by the Germans. In his article, Hod highlights the everyday life of these collaborators during their service in the extermination camps in order to refute their claim of forced collaboration. Through this examination of the free-time activities of the collaborators, the conversations between them, their possibility of escape, and other aspects of their everyday lives, we gain a better understanding of what was behind the choice of collaboration. Hod's comparison between the Treblinka and Belzec extermination camps sheds additional light on the factors that influenced the collaborators' everyday life. In his study, insights at the micro level – the realm of everyday life –facilitate understanding of the macro level – in this case, the decision to actively collaborate with the Germans in mass murder.

Ronnen Harran's article "The Liquidation of the Jewish Communities of Eastern Galicia: A Systematic or a Random Process?" deals with the extermination of the Jewish communities in the Eastern Galicia region – the approximate 180 large and small communities located in the District of Galicia (*Distrikt Galicien*), which was declared in August 1941 by the German occupation authorities and appended to the General Governorate as a fifth district. Harran characterizes the liquidation of the Jewish communities in the General Governorate as a whole (and in the District of Galicia in particular) as a multi-stage process consisting of the following stages: 1) local executions (shootings beside murder pits) from the beginning of the occupation onward; 2) establishment of a ghetto and concentrating local Jews within it; 3) removal of the Jews from the small communities in the surrounding area and concentrating them in a nearby ghetto; 4) deportation of most of the Jews who were concentrated in the ghetto to a concentration camp (or another ghetto); 5) establishment of a "residual ghetto" (*Restghetto*) for the purpose of assembling and concentrating the Jews who had managed to escape and hide in the local area; and 6) liquidation of the residual ghetto (typically through local execution). The primary research question guiding Harran's article is: Was the liquidation of the Jewish communities, in its various stages, organized and systematic, or was it conducted in a random or arbitrary order that can be characterized only as chaotic? And if a system, or not, in place and in time, can be identified in the liquidation Aktions, then what were the priorities of the perpetrators? What was the operational rationale behind this order? To identify trends and patterns in the overall implementation of this campaign, the article offers an analysis of the different stages of community liquidation, which involved hundreds of local events, by means of spatial-temporal analysis dealing simultaneously with the spatial dispersion of the events throughout the district, the region's administrative division into counties (*Kreise*), and the distribution of the events over time, from the onset of the German occupation in the summer of 1941 to the completion of the liquidation of the remainders of the Jewish communities in the summer of 1943.

Joanna Tokarska-Bakir goes a step further in deconstructing the deceiving nature of the bystanders and perpetrators categories and also analyzes the continuation of anti-Jewish violence immediately after the German occupation. The author meticulously recounts the historical events of the murder of a Jewish family in South-Eastern Poland, the Schlaf family, in 1945 by local Poles. Based on a meticulous reading of new archival materials and on a sophisticated analytic framework, Joanna Tokarska Bakir elucidates the social, cultural, political, and psychological contexts of the murder, its memory, and its aftermath. She scrupulously reconstructs the crime, paying special attention to discursive linguistic tools to repress the memory of the crime and absolve the perpetrators. Contextualizing the murder in the socio-political and cultural realities of postwar Poland and its memory at the local level in the long run, the author scrutinizes the conflicting versions of the event and manages to overcome contradictions and lacunas suggesting possible explanatory directions to understand the motives of the perpetrators and the social dynamics of its preservation in the local knowledge.

This masterful micro-historical case study adds an important aspect to the study of the Holocaust and its aftermath in Poland, detecting the very local and communal dynamics and mechanisms that facilitate interethnic violence in times of social and political liminality and its long-term legacies.

This issue includes groundbreaking studies from leading scholars working today in the field of the Holocaust in Eastern Galicia. It also includes an unpublished study by **Aharon Weiss**, a pioneer historian of the Holocaust in Eastern Galicia. It is a section from his groundbreaking and thus far unpublished 1973 dissertation *The Jewish Police in the General Government and Upper Galicia during the Holocaust*. Although almost five decades have passed since its completion, Weiss's doctoral dissertation continues to be relevant. Though brief, the section of his dissertation "The Judenrat and the Jewish Police in Lwów, 1941-1944," is still a significant study of the institutions and their activities in Lwów. Weiss's work on Lwów in this context is pioneering, as no other scholar has investigated this topic thus far. **Noam Leibman**'s introductory remarks point out the importance of Weiss' study while adding a historiographical review of the development of the topic during the last decades.

In dealing with the historiography of the Holocaust in Eastern Galicia, **Rossolinski-Liebe** has conducted an incisive study of the participation of the Organization of the Ukrainian Nationalists, the Ukrainian Insurgent Army and members of the Ukrainian police and administration in the murder of several thousand Jews. The article explores how, why and which methods and conceptualizations were used and draws on historians from different countries and backgrounds to investigate this aspect of the Holocaust.

Per Anders Rudling takes the case of Sambir to discuss the politics of memory in Ukraine. After describing the atrocities and murder of Sambir's Jews, by Germans and their Ukrainian collaborators, especially members of the Ukrainian Insurgent Army (UPA), the author analyzes the politics of memory. He points out the post war erasure of the prewar Jewish presence. At the center of this analysis is the post-soviet dispute over the creation of a memorial at the site of the already devastated Jewish cemetery. He focuses on the placing of three oversized Christian crosses on a mass grave in a Jewish cemetery in Sambir commemorating UPA soldiers, and the ensuing attempts to remove them. He emphasizes that the monument unveiling event in Sambir reveals that the main idea is to present the Ukrainian Insurgent Army (UPA) as enemies and opponents of the Nazis, when in fact it was actively involved in the mass murder of Jews. Rudling maintains that the case shows the appropriation of the perceived moral capital of the suffering of the Jews for political purposes. The use of the monument to create a national myth is more about contemporary Ukrainian politics and nationalist mythmaking than an honest, open discussion about the dark past.

The current volume also contains two important testimonies from the region of Eastern Galicia. One was given in France in 1946 by Gedaliah Lachman, a Jew from the region of Skala Podolska, who fled from place to place in Eastern Galicia and survived the war; its documentation can be found in the Moreshet Archive. The second testimony was documented by the *Yahad in Unum* (YIU) organization in France, which was founded by Father Patrick Desbois. We want to thank *Yahad in Unum* for sending us this document and for their permission to print it in English for the first time in this special *Moreshet Journal* issue dedicated to that area. This testimony of Petro A., a male born in Ukraine in 1929, was collected on July 6, 2019 by the team of Father Desbois and Dr. Michal Chojak in Eastern Galicia, in the villages of Travotoly and Lavrykivtsi, in Tarnopil region. Have we seen the last Ukrainian witness who, with his own eyes, saw a Jewish family murdered by the Germans, or the tireless search for isolated Jews in the region until the last Jew in hiding was murdered?

The last section of this issue reviews four recently groundbreaking books on the Holocaust in Eastern Galicia written by Omer Bartov, Patrick Desbois, John Paul Himka, and Wendy Lower. The books reflect different methodological tools, thematic approaches, and research paradigms. The four reviewers, Jan Burzlaff, Havi Dreifuss, Oded Heilbronner, and Nicolas Dreyer, hailing from three countries and leading institutions of research, also reflect different methodological, thematic, linguistic and generational differences. This section completes an updated analysis about the Holocaust in Eastern Galicia that this issue attempts to present.

A NOTE ON NAMES AND PLACES: Eastern Galicia or Western Ukraine? Lwów, Lvov or Lviv? Sambor or Sambir? Stanisławów, Stanislav, Stanyslaviv or Ivano-Frankivs'k? As in many regions in Eastern Europe, the name reflects an ethno-national and linguistic belonging, identification, and point of view. Each name reflects different associations, perspectives and cultural sea-chests. They are not neutral names. The editors discussed whether unifying and standardizing the names in this issue (using the current name, as is often used nowadays, or the name used in those times, as often used in other studies) would make the arguments and perspectives of the articles clearer. Our opinion is that it will be clearer respecting the decision of the respective authors.

One more personal remark: we both, as editors, who belong to a generation without grandfathers, and to families originating from Eastern Galicia, whose grandfathers or their close relatives perished during those years, feel a special duty and wish to honor them while offering this issue to you, the reader.

Dr. Graciela Ben Dror, Editor
Prof. Marcos Silber, Guest Editor

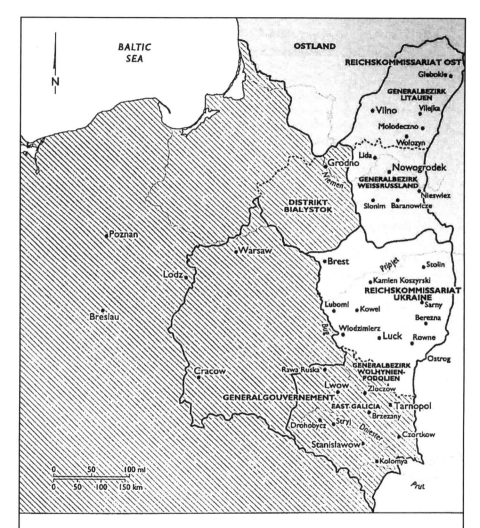

The German Occupation, 1941–1944
The kresy are now under separate German administrations. Part is in the
Ostland (shaded dark gray). East Galicia is in the Generalgouvernement.
The German Reich (striped area) includes the Bialystok district, but the
district also has a separate administration.

East Galicia, 1941–1944

Yehuda Bauer

The Holocaust in the Kresy*

German preparations for the attack on the Soviet Union, called Operation Barbarossa, have been treated in detail by many historians. Preparations included the so-called Commissar Order, which mandated the murder of political officers in the Red (Soviet) Army and also a general setting up of special murder units. These units, the *Einsatzgruppen* (EGs – Task Forces), were in the Central Reich Security Office (RSHA), under Reinhard Heydrich, Himmler's chief subordinate and commander, in effect, of the Nazi terror machine. The RSHA was composed of the Criminal Police (KRIPO); the Security Police (SIPO), which included the Gestapo; and the Security Service (SD), which was the intelligence unit of the Nazi Party.

No written orders were given to the EGs, apparently, just oral instructions, but there was definitely talk of getting rid of Jews, though probably no direct order to kill all Jews. Heydrich himself talked to the EG officers, and so did other high RSHA functionaries. On July 2, 1941, ten days after Operation Barbarossa began, Heydrich issued an order to kill Communist Party officials and "others", such as Jews; on the surface, the context appeared to be the fight against communism. Because in the Soviet Union all public functions, as well as trade and industrial or quasi-industrial production, were in the hands of the government and the party, killing party officials in fact meant killing anyone that the German authorities decided was in their way – first and foremost the Jews. The idea behind this order was that the Bolshevik Soviet Union was controlled by Jews, so the major enemy of the Germans were the Jews, who ran that state (and all other countries opposed to Germany). Getting rid of Jewish males was a key way of destroying Bolshevism and ensuring German security. In the early stages of Operation Barbarossa, which began on June 22, the EGs murdered Jewish men wherever they could. We have here the primacy of ideological motivation: the German war against the Soviets was an ideological undertaking, and economic planning was embedded in the ideology. Within that context, the killing of Jews as the supposed mainstay of the Soviet regime became a primary aim.

This interpretation is a matter of controversy. Christian Gerlach, in his book *Kalkulierte Morde*, on the German policies in Belorussia – a masterpiece of historical writing – puts it almost the other way round[11]. Economic factors, in his view, were decisive in the planning and execution of German policies, because Germany needed the vast resources of the Soviet Union for the conduct of the war. Antisemitic and racist motivations formed the background to these policies, he says. Gerlach relied on German documentation, and that documentation undoubtedly reflects the economic factors as being primary importance.

However, Gerlach does not ask what exactly the Germans wanted to achieve in the war, and why they needed resources. After all, there was no objective need for physical conquest, which in even the most pro-German scenarios would have inevitably destroyed many of the very resources that the Germans wanted to acquire; they could easily have procured raw materials and agricultural products in return for manufactured goods that Germany produced. The Stalinist regime, fearful of a German attack, was willing, between 1939 and 1941, to supply the Germans with everything they wanted, in vast quantities. The Germans did not need to fight the Soviets for that. Today, a much larger number of Germans on a much smaller territory engage in exactly that kind of economic exchange, and they prosper. The "need" for expansion was purely ideological and had nothing to do with economic reality. The ideologists saw Germany as the future major power that would control Europe, and through Europe and with allies, the world. Control of Europe required control of the riches of the Soviet Union. According to this quasi-religious-fundamentalist ideology, the forces that stood against Germany were controlled by the archenemy of the Aryan race: the Jews. If this interpretation is correct, then World War II, with its tens of millions of victims on all sides, was the product of an ideology whose core was antisemitism. Once that ideology dictated territorial expansion by force, economic factors motivated by that ideology became tremendously important. I would therefore argue not only that the Holocaust was ideologically motivated but that World War II itself, instigated and initiated by Nazi Germany, was basically an ideological project, one in which antisemitism played a major role. On this central issue, despite all my admiration for Gerlach's work, I am of a radically different opinion from that advanced by him and by others.

The military campaign, which began on June 22, 1941, started off with major German victories. The German army attacked on three fronts. In the south, the forces, under Gerd von Rundstedt, comprised forty-two divisions, of which five were Panzer (armored) divisions and three were motorized; they attacked south of the Pripjet Marshes, in the direction of Kiev. North of the Pripjet Marshes, the main German forces were concentrated on the central front; forty-nine divisions, under Fedor von Bock, including nine Panzer divisions and six motorizes divisions, were grouped in two Panzer armies; Panzer Group 3 was under Hermann Hoth, and Panzer Group 2 was under Heinz Guderian. The German forces at the northern front were commanded by Wilhelm von Leeb; they consisted of twenty-nine divisions, including three Panzer divisions and two motorized ones, which formed Panzer Group 4, under Erich Hoepner. The German attacked with 3 million men (not counting the Romanians and, later. The Hungarians, Finns, and others), 3,580 tanks, 7.184 artillery pieces, and 1,830 airplanes. The kresy were mostly overrun within a couple of weeks by the German armies attacking from the center and the south fronts; only a small area in the northeast held out until August. Much has been written about the lack of understanding by the Soviet High Command, and especially by Stalin, of German plans and German might[2]. In the early stages, Soviet counterattacks were beaten off, with tremendous Soviet losses, but the Germans, too, suffered major losses, and by July the German High Command expressed serious concerns about the attrition in terms of dead and wounded soldiers and materiel. In Belorussia and the Baltic States, the Soviet armies were beaten, surrounded. And liquidated, despite repeated counterattacks.

In the kresy, Brest-Litovsk was taken on June 22, Grodno on June 23, Vilno on June 24, Baranowicze on June 25, Bialystok on June 27, and Minsk on June 28 – there the German army was already beyond the kresy. In the south, Rowne, in Vilhynia, was finally taken on June 28, Lwow on July 1, and in mid-July the German army reached the prewar Polish-Soviet border. The Soviet general responsible for defending the Ukrainian areas, Mikhail P. Kirponos, was more successful than his northern comrades; he managed an orderly withdrawal after a major tank battle on June 24-26 in the Rowne area. But elsewhere the disorder and, often, the panic were great.

Before the war, Soviet units were prevented, on Stalin's orders, from taking precautionary military measures. Despite repeated and detailed warnings of an imminent invasion, Stalin and his cronies thought that the Germans would not start a two-front war by invading the Soviet Union and that the warnings were Anglo-American attempts to embroil the Soviet Union in a war with Germany, which would weaken both contestants. Even after the invasion had begun, the political leaders tried, during the first couple of days, to avoid a full-scale war by holding back Soviet forces. When they finally accepted that a full-scale invasion was under way, they ordered Soviet forces to attack without proper preparation and without sufficient fuel, spare parts for tanks, or even ammunition. The result was the slaughter of Soviet soldiers and the destruction of whole divisions.

In the first couple of days, more than 2,000 Soviet airplanes were destroyed, either on the ground or in air battles, which eliminated air support for Soviet units for months and left the German Luftwaffe free to do as it pleased. Soviet units were badly led, which was largely the result of Stalin's purges of very high proportion of military commanders in 1937-1938. Nevertheless, in most places, Soviet soldiers tried to fight back and tenaciously defended their positions. The massing of Soviet soldiers in the frontier areas made it easy for the Germans to cut through them or encircle them and destroy them. But the Soviets continued to fight as the invaders conquered the kresy, and their resistance became stronger and more organized. Still, it was three years before the Red Army reoccupied the kresy.

Soviet soldiers made a determined and suicidal defense of the fort ar Brest-Litovsk. The Brest fortifications had been built around 1837, and the Soviets had strengthened them. The town of Brest was conquered on the first day of the Barbarossa invasion, but the fort held out for a month, although it was completely cut off from the retreating Soviet armies. At the end, the decimated garrison was led by Efim M. Fomin, a Jewish NCO, a former violinist. When the ammunition finally gave out and the defenders surrendered, the Germans murdered them all – there were no survivors.

After the first day or two of the invasion, Soviet authority in the kresy collapsed. In some towns hurried attempts were made to recruit people into the army, but as the military framework buckled, most of these recruits were sent home again, or they just left of their own accord. Quite a number of Jews had been called up recently, in the spring, and these soldiers now became part of the hundreds of thousands who fought and either died or were taken prisoner. They had practically no chance to survive. The German orders stated that all Jewish soldiers were to be handed over to the SS, the special Nazi units in charge of intelligence, Policing, and extermination mentioned above; as a result, Jews were taken from prisoner-of-war enclosures and murdered. Their comrades often told the Germans who the Jews in their units were, although they knew perfectly well what the fate of these Jews would be. Only rarely did Jews succeed in hiding their identity. In any case, only a small percentage of all Soviet POWs, Jews and non-Jews alike, survived their first year in captivity; an intentionally murderous policy of starvation, exposure to extreme weather, deprivation of medical assistance, and skimpy housing reduced the survival rate drastically. The dead numbered in the millions; there are only a few testimonies relating to Jewish survivors.

The Communists Party and the Soviet government managed to evacuate their officials almost everywhere, often at the very last moment[3]. In July, when eastern Belorussia and Ukraine up to Kiev were the scenes of bitter military struggles. The party left certain trusted cadres behind in order to organize future urban and partisan resistance, but most were soon caught and killed. Many industrial establishments were either evacuated or, if that was impossible, destroyed. Most of the evacuees were easterners from pre-1939 areas and party stalwarts. Jews were among them, but the proportion of Jews among these cadres was quite low – we do not know the exact percentage – so not many Jews were saved in this way. In a few places Soviet officials tried to persuade Jews to leave with them, but in most towns and cities Jews as such were not evacuated.[4] In the panic of war, some Jews, especially young men, tried to escape. Most were overtaken by German troops and had to return to their homes, others were killed trying to escape into the Soviet interior, and yet others, especially in the south, were stopped as the old Polish-Soviet borders by Soviet frontier troops, accused of spreading panic, and sent back. Only a relative few managed to reach the unoccupied areas, and they usually carried on eastward into Soviet Asia: Uzbekistan, Turkmenistan, Kirgizstan, and Kazakhstan.

Beginning on June 14, a week before the invasion, the Soviet launched their fourth main wave of deportations of "class enemies". Quite a number of Jews were deported to Siberia – which saved the lives of many of them – but in the last few days before Operation Barbarossa the main Soviet target was Ukrainian nationalists, or people suspected. When the invasion came, Lavrenti Beria, Head of the dreaded NKVD, the Soviet secret police, gave orders to either evacuate the prisoners, by rail or on foot, or kill them. Those orders were followed. Some were deported, mostly on foot – not too many prisoners survived that ordeal. But most of them were murdered – an estimated 30,000 – in the prisons that held them. The Germans arrived immediately afterward; they and the Ukrainian nationalists in their tow accused the Jews of having committed the crime, although Jews were among the victims as well. To this day, Ukrainian nationalists accuse the Jews of the slaughter, although those responsible were clearly Russians and Ukrainians from the east; only a smattering of Caucasians, Jews, and others were among the NKVD cadres. Utilizing the fury of the Ukrainian nationalists, the Germans encouraged them to engage in massive killings, in early July, especially in Lwow, where some 5,000 Jews, at least, were killed, but also elsewhere; when the Ukrainians did not show enough initiative, the Germans stepped in and themselves murdered Jews.

In most of the kresy there was a brief interval between the collapse of the Soviet regime and the entry of German troops, just as there had been between the collapse of the Polish regime and the entry of Soviet troops. Pogroms unrelated to the kind of mass murder that occurred in Lwow broke out, especially in the south, and some people were killed, but the main purpose of the attackers was to steal Jewish property.[5] Occasionally in some shtetlach, Jews made successful attempts to defend themselves, and here and there, local Ukrainian groups or individuals defended Jews. In Kurzeniec, Belorussian townspeople kept peasants from surrounding villages from robbing the Jews, But that was because they saw Jewish property as their own future spoils and did not want to share.[6] After a while, in many cases, the Germans officers stopped the pogroms to establish some kind of order. One commander, General Karl von Roques, issued an order on July 27 for army personnel not to participate in pogroms.[7]

Many young Jews fled before the advancing German armies. Testimonies suggest that people thought the Germans would endanger the lives of young men but probably not harm women, children, and old people. However, the German advance in the kresy was so swift that the chance of escaping was very low. Escape was largely, too, a matter of luck. Thus, in Belorussia, during the first days of the invasion, whoever fled in the direction of Minsk was caught in the huge pincer movement that captured Minsk on June 28; people who fled in the direction of Mogilev had a better chance of escaping because the German advance in that direction was slower and the Soviet resistance stiffer. In the south, German forces advanced at a slower pace than in the north, and areas in eastern Volhynia were easier to flee from. But Soviet border guards on the former Polish-Soviet border prevented the mainly Jewish refugees from crossing into "old" Soviet areas – at least during the first few days of the war. The guards turned the refugees back, accusing them of anti-Soviet behavior, cowardice, and spreading panic; the great Red Army, they said, would soon turn the Germans back, so the refugees should return home. Testimonies indicate that the old border was not open until after June 26, and then people could run for their lives.[8] Shmuel Spector has calculated that about 5 percent (12,000-13,000 people) of the Jewish population of Volhynia managed to flee into the Soviet unterior.[9] In East Galicia and Belorussia the percentage was probably smaller. Those who fled, mostly young men, had a terrible decision to make: leaving their families behind. Sometimes their parents encouraged them to run, and sometimes the parents tried to prevent their escape, fearing what would happen to them in the Soviet interior and fearing, too, that they would be killed by Germans along the way.[10]

Those who reached the Soviet interior did not necessarily survive. German aerial bombardments took their toll, and life for a refugee in eastern Ukraine or Soviet Central was extremely difficult. Some refugees were overrun by the Germans later on in eastern Ukraine, others died from disease and malnutrition, and some were recruited into the Red Army – often into labor battalions that had a high casualty rate – and if recruited as Red Army soldiers, they became part of the Soviet war effort and often died or were severely wounded in action. All these dangers notwithstanding, their chances of survival were higher than if they had stayed behind in the kresy.

Many (not all) accept that the Holocaust, the genocide of the Jews, was not preplanned but was prefigured by the potentially genocidal ideology that motivated the National Socialist regime. As late as 1941, there seems to have been no actual murder plan but instead a development of genocidal intent, For the Nazi leadership, as we have seen, the invasion of the Soviet Union was an ideological necessity, and it was the Bolshevik regime that had to be destroyed as having been set up by a Jewish conspiracy. The Soviet Union was, in that ideological construct, run by the Jews, and beginning with the murder of Jewish men served the double purpose of, first, depriving the Bolsheviks of a central part of their leadership by eliminating Jewish intellectuals and, second, helping to prevent any possible Jewish resistance to German measures. The first wave of massacres was conducted primarily by the four EG units, numbering together about 3,000 men (plus a few women secretaries), by a number of battalions of Order Police (ORPO), numbering several thousand men, and by additional German troops, usually rear units of the army who were responsible for "pacifying" the recently conquered areas, which were put under temporary military command.

On September 1, 1941, the areas of the kresy were handed over to civilian administration, but some rear army units stayed there to strengthen the German presence. The EGs and the ORPO were both part of the SS, and the collaboration of the army and the emerging civilian authorities with the SS murdering teams was very smooth. The EGs were part of the RSHA, whereas the ORPO was run by Kurt Daluege as a separate SS formation – again, however, in full collaboration with Heydrich's units. The organization was complicated, because Himmler also set up a parallel command structure run by the *Höhere SS-und-Polizeifuhrer* (Higher SS and Police Commanders). These HSSPFs were put in charge of all the SS and police in their respective areas, of which there were two: HSSPF North, and HSSPF South. The relationship between the HSSPFs and Heydrich's RSHA was not always smooth, and the EGs remained, in fact, under Heydrich's command. For the areas of the kersy, the two EGs responsible were "B" and "C", originally under Arthur Nebe ("B"), a brutal police commander (who in 1944 mutated into an anti-Hitler conspirator), and Dr. Dr. Otto Rasch ("C"; he had two doctorates). In addition, Himmler had, under his personal command, a special force of three SS regiments, one cavalry and two motorized, called the *Kommandostab Reichsfuhrer SS* (KRFSS), who were heavily involved in the murder of Jews alongside all the other units. The cavalry regiment especially, under Hermann Fegelein, who later became Hitler's brother-in-law – a relationship that. However, did not protect him from being executed for cowardice during the last days of the Thousand-Year Reich. Fegelein was charged with annihilating the Jews in the area of the Pripjet Marshes, between Belorussia and Ukraine. In July and August 1941, Fegelein's regiment murdered more than 14,000 Jews; some units also participated in the mass murder of Jews in the town of Pinsk, in the same area.

The number of German forces involved in the mass murder ran into the tens of thousands, far more than the 3,000 men of the EGs. The areas to be covered were vast, the EGs had to follow the advancing armies, and in many places, especially those that were small or out-of-the-way, they simply did not have enough men to do the job, even though the Germans could easily augment their strength, and did when they needed to. Thus, during the first sweep of the kresy, in July and August 1941, the Germans murdered tens of thousands of Jews, largely men, concentrating on intellectuals, but the bulk of the Jewish population was left alive.[11] Many of the prewar Jewish leaders who had survived the Soviet period without being deported to Siberia were now murdered. They included teachers, rabbis, political activists, medics, lawyers, engineers, and so on, which made future resistance of any kind much more difficult to organize. A case in point is the town – not shtetl – of Brest-Litovsk. Some 5,000 men were murdered there right at the beginning of the German occupation, disrupting families, forcing a change in gender roles, and upsetting any possible efforts at organizing Jewish life. That the community nevertheless managed to organize is a matter of some wonderment.[12]

In accordance with the precedents established in German-occupied Poland since September 1939, the Germans immediately nominated Jewish councils – Judenräte – which were to be responsible for executing all German orders promptly and obediently. Penalty for disobedience was death. In fact, however, in many places, if not most, the Jews themselves chose the Judenräte. The Jews had no idea what the Germans would later do, and they naturally needed people to represent them with the new, threatening occupation power. In other places, especially in Ukrainian areas, local Ukrainian collaborators took over the administration of towns and townships and proposed to the Germans the nomination of Jews whom they thought would be pliant instruments in their own and the German's hands. Sometimes both these elements mixed. In Kurzeniec, for instance, a German army officer appeared with the occupiers and called for a Judenrat to be established. By common consent, the individual chosen to head the Judenrat was a former sports teacher, a refugee from Vienna named Schatz, whose great advantage was that his mother tongue was German.[13] But in most cases the Judenrat heads were former Jewish community heads or acknowledged leaders of pre-Soviet Jewish political groups. It was as if the Jewish communities, whose internal bonds had been destroyed by the Soviets, were being revived, as if they had risen from the dead. They seemed at first to restart from where they had been when the Soviet occupation had destroyed them. The resurrection was a chimera, however; it immediately became clear that the new Judenrat were to be quite different from the prewar communal authorities, with different tasks and responsibilities. They would have to supply forced labor to the Germans and the local collaborators; they would have to worry about food supply, medical help, and, if possible, even education and social welfare; before the war, Jewish communal administrations had taken care of social welfare only partially. The main problem now would be to keep the community alive physically.

During the first sweep of the EGs, the Germans established rudimentary local police forces that would collaborate with them, but they did not yet equip them with weapons. In some cases, the local police were really a continuation of the ordinary police forces from the Soviet period, usually minus their communist or pro-communist commanders. During the first months of occupation, such local police forces were established in all the towns and villages, and the first mobile local police forces were called the *Schutzmannschaften* (Protective Police Forces), but the Germans usually referred to them as Hiwis (*Hilfswillige*, or "Willing Helpers"). By the winter of 1941-1942, they were beginning to be equipped with firearms and were participating actively in the murder of Jews, often taking over the actual murders from Germans, though in all cases without exception acting under German supervision and under German command. It was the recruitment of local police that enabled the Germans to murder the Jews speedily and efficiently.

From the end of July, the Germans murdered women and children as well as men.[14] Again, there seems to have been no actual order to do so. Once EG "A", under Dr. Walther Stahlecker, which was responsible for murdering people in the Baltic region, began to kill Jewish women and children, other units elsewhere quickly took up the practice, whether they copied what EG "A" did or whether they started doing it on their own initiative. A consensus arose, on the basis of the shared ideology, that the present generation of Jews in the Soviet Union would be the last one there, which is why women and children were now included in the developing policy of total extermination. On August 26-27, around 16,000 Hungarian Jews, together with local Ukrainian Jews, were executed near Kamenets-Podolskyi, Ukraine, under the leadership of the HSSPF Friedrich Jeckeln and with the help of, among others, Hungarian troops who held the perimeter of the murder site. On September 23, after the occupation of Kiev, explosions in German-occupied buildings in the city, engineered by Soviet demolition groups, prompted the murder of more than 33,000 Jews – women, men, and children. Germans led by a unit of EG "C" murdered them at Babyi Yar, on the outskirts of Kiev. After that, women and children were not only included but became the main targets. The German administrators and the army realized that they needed Jewish workers, at least for the time being, so the criterion for being left alive (temporarily) was fitness to work. Men now had a greater chance of survival than women or children.

On September 1, 1941, the German civilian administration took over from the military government. That meant a division of the kresy into two *Reichs-kommissariate* (administrative areas), one of Ukraine, under Erich Koch, an old Nazi Party hack from East Prussia, and one of the combined Baltic and Belorussian area, which the Germans called Ostland, under Hinrich Lohse. Ostland was further divided into so-called *Generalkommissariate*, and Belorussia, now called Weissruthenien, a portion of the former Soviet Belorussia, came under Wilhelm Kube, another party old-timer. Koch, who ruled from Kiev, divided his domain into counties (*Generalbezirke*), one of which was Volhynia-Podolia (German:

Wolhynien-Podolien), which consisted of Volhynia and the southern part of the former Bielorussia and included Brest-Litosk and Kamenets-Podolskyi. The *Generalkommissar* of Volhynia-Podolia was Heinrich Schoene, who had his seat at Brest and then at Lutsk; he subdivided his region into twelve *Gebiete* (areas). The other Ukrainian area in the south, East Galicia, had a different structure. It became a part of the *Genearlgouvernement*, the German-occupied territories of Poland, which had a civilian administrator. Kube, the other *Reichskommissar*, ruled first from Rowne and then from Minsk; he subdivided his domain into eleven Gebiete, each headed by a *Gebietskommissar*.

The areas to the rear of the advancing German armies were ruled by a civilian administration in conjunction with the SS – which included, as have seen, the Order Police (ORPO). The SS-and-Police centers that were established were largely manned by former EG personnel. They were organized in the same way as the RSHA that controlled them. Thus, the sections of the area and local command posts reflected the internal RSHA organization, which meant that the Security Police (SIPO), which included the Gestapo in section 4, and the Security Service (SD) dealt with the Jews. The local command posts were called *Aussenstellen* (area posts); Baranowicze, for instance, was an Aussenstelle of the Minsk command, and Buczacz was controlled from the Czortkow Aussenstelle.

The cooperation between the civilian administrators, the SIPO units and the ORPO battalions was perfect. Some of the civilian administrators were, in fact, recruited from the Police and the SS; the Gebietskommissar (area governor) Wilhelm Traub in Nowogrodek was an example. In many cases, it was the local civilian governor who initiated the murder of the Jews, and he did that with SIPO, ORPO, available army rear command units, and usually considerable numbers of local collaborationist police and militias. He could then boast that he had made his area *Judenfrei* or *Judenrein* – "free" or "clean" of Jews. There is no evidence from German documentation that this setup was planned; rather, it seems to have developed in response to the ideologically motivated challenges of a genocidal policy directed at the population of the occupied areas – at Belorussians, Poles, Ukrainians, Roma (Gypsies), Czechs, and others – but Jews were the main target, Within that context, economic considerations were very important.

The annihilation of the Jewish population has been described as proceeding in waves, or stages. In the kresy, however, the dates of the various murder "actions", or *Aktionen* – they were called *aktzies* in Yiddish – occur with no clear regularity. Even the harsh Russian winter, which made it difficult to prepare the mass graves into which the shot Jews tumbled, did not always prevent "actions" from taking place. In many places the first major "actions" took place in the late summer, fall, and early winter of 1941. Total annihilation was the fate of the Jews of Hancewicze (Belorussia) in August 1941 and of Horodyszsze (also Belorussia) in the fall. In Kosow Huculski (East Galicia), 2,000 of more than 4,000 Jews were murdered in October. In Nowogrodek, 4,000-5,000 of 6,500 or so Jews were murdered on December 8. In Volhynia, about 25 percent of the Jewish population was murdered in September-October.[15]

Before the early winter, German assessments of the Jew's importance for the economy were contradictory, as we can see from German documentation. On September 17, 1941, an EG "C" report says that killing all the Jews "would render the task of both the economic reconstruction of Ukrainian industry and the reconstruction of municipal administrative centers nearly impossible". But another report by the same EG "C" from November 1941 says that "Jews, needless to say, gave their wholehearted support to the Communists... Only one option presents itself in Volhynia: to exterminate the Jews totally... After all, there is no doubt that they are insignificant as a labor force, but cause great damage as the carriers of the bacillus of communism". And yet, on April 10, 1942, the Germans argued against the immediate annihilation of Jews because they were "most vital as professional workers and craftsmen".[16] There was a consensus that the Jews had to be killed but there was an argument about the timing. As time wore on, some of the Jewish labor was deemed to be of some importance, and occasionally mass murders were postponed. Workers, men and women alike, were separated from their families; the families were murdered, and the workers were left alive for a while; however, it was clear that all Jews.

Most of the Jews of the kresy were murdered between March and December 1942. In March, 3,000 Jews out of 12,000 were murdered in Baranowicze. A second "action" took place in September, and the final annihilation came in December. Only a small number of Baranowicze Jews survived in closed forced-labor camps. In many places, the fact that Jews were needed for forced labor postponed their annihilation. In Buczacz, there was a lull in "actions" between the summer of 1941 and October 1942. The summer of 1942 saw the annihilation of the Jews in large number of shtetlach. In Krzemieniec (Volhynia), where no major "actions" had taken place since the summer of 1941, all the Jews were murdered in one big massacre in August 1942. Nor had there been any "actions" in Sarny and Rokitno (Volhynia) until both shtetlach were annihilated, all at once, on August 26-27, 1942. The Jews of Kurzeniec were murdered on September 9; before that, smaller "actions" claiming dozens of victims rather than hundreds or more had taken place in the spring.

By the end of 1942, most of the shtetlach in the kresy had been decimated. Jewish labor was still needed, however, and some of the Jews who could still work survived in camps run, in most cases, by the SS or the local civilian administration; in exceptional cases, the army ran the camps. When the Germans had specific labor became essential. In 1942 they began building a major road, Military Road 4 (Durchgangsstrasse 4) between Lwow and the Crimea to supplement the existing Soviet roads, which could not carry heavy tanks and other similar traffic. The planned route was divided into sections, and labor camps were set up to be run by the Todt labor organization, which was building roads and other essential projects within the Nazi empire.

The conditions in these camps were such that the Jewish workers were dying off in huge numbers, requiring the labor force to be constantly replenished from still-existing ghettoes.[17] By early 1943 the shtetlach had been annihilated, and no more Jewish labor could be recruited. The workers died, and the road, whether for that or for other reasons, was never completed. To all who argue for an interpretation of German policies that puts the main emphasis on economic factors we need only show what happened on Military Road 4: the Germans killed off the workers they needed in order to build an essential road. Why? Because their radical antisemitic ideology put the murder of Jews above all economic considerations.

A similar policy was followed elsewhere: saving Jews for labor and then letting them die. In Czortkow and Tluste in East Galicia, for instance, the Germans tried to grow Kox-Agis, a plant out of which they hoped to extract a kind of rubber; rubber was absolutely essential for the German war machine. They established a number of forced-labor camps and put Jews to work. According to one testimony, they established nine camps, especially around the shtatl of Tluste, which had 5,000 Jews in its ghetto in 1942. Jewish men and women were recruited from a number of shtetlach in the general area — for example, from Czortkow, Buczacz, and Kopyczynce. In some of camps the conditions were almost sufferable, depending on the local commanders, some of whom were older army men, although the SS had formally taken over the camps in September 1942. By 1943 the Germans apparently realized that their plan to grow Kox-Agis was a failure, but they maintained seven (some say nine) of the camps as agricultural enterprises until 1944 because they needed certain agricultural products. Nevertheless, they murdered the Jews in most of these camps. Some of the Jews managed to flee, and there was some physical resistance in the camps, too. In at least one camp, the commander, an army man, protected the Jews until the arrival of the Soviets, saving around a hundred people.[18] Here we can see a combination of economic motives with ideological ones: the ideological motives are evident in the fact that the Jews were murdered despite being economically useful.

Christian Gerlach argues that in Belorussia extermination went faster than it went elsewhere because Jewish labor was unimportant.[19] This may be so in general terms, but labor was needed locally nevertheless. After the Baranowicze ghetto had been liquidated in December 1942, the remaining Jews were employed at the airfield and as suppliers of essential labor to the SD itself, including "private" work done for corrupt SD commanders. In Nowogrodek, craftsmen were still employed until the late summer of 1943 because there was no one else to do the work. The work was still essential when the Jews were murdered. Again and again, we can see that ideologically motivated murder took precedence over economic considerations of any kind.

By early 1943, all the Jews who still survived under German control in the kresy were working in labor camps. Aa the year wore on, they were murdered. Almost none still survived in early 1944, when the Red Army approached the area. There were some differences between the provinces: Fritz (Friedrich) Katzmann, the SS commander in East Galicia, gave out an order, on April 21,

1943, to kill all the Jews in the area. I have not seen a similar explicit order for Volhynia or Belorussia, although German commanders everywhere were enjoined to do away the Jews as quickly as feasible, and some meetings were held of high officials where the consensus was the same: namely, that the Jews should be done away with.

The problem of the establishment of ghettoes has been discussed in the historical literature. In East Galicia, ghettoes were established not only in the big city of Lwow but also in larger towns, such as Stanislawow (today, Ivano-Frankivsk), Tarnopol (Ukr.: Ternopil), Stryj, and Kolomya. The same happened in other areas: ghettoes were established in Brest, Slonim (Belorussia), Rowne (Vohlynia), and elsewhere in fall of 1941. But the Germans soon discovered that the establishment of ghettoes had its downside. Because they did not supply the ghettoes with enough food, typhoid epidemics broke out, and the epidemics did not stop at the ghetto walls or fences. Administrative work multiplied, too. In Galicia, Fritz Katzmann ordered that no more ghettoes were to be established without compelling reasons to do so. The same discoveries and responses were repeated elsewhere in the kresy, and no ghettoes were established in many shtetlach, or else ghettoes were established only when annihilation became imminent and the Germans wanted to concentrate the Jews to make the murders easier to accomplish. There were no ghettoes in the small communities of Kosow, Zabie (East Galicia), Kurzeniec (Belorussia), or Rokitno (Volhynia); many similar instances could be listed. But in these and other places, where there were no ghettoes with walls or barbed wire fences, Jews were still forced to concentrate in certain areas, streets, or houses. The establishment or otherwise of ghettoes was therefore a purely pragmatic issue and took place or did not at the German's convenience.

Contrary to many other genocides, the genocide of the Jews did not, as a rule, include rape by Germans, because of the strict order, motivated by Nazi racism, for Germans not to have sexual relations with Jews. Occasional sexual harassment apparently occurred in the kresy anyway, although it is difficult to document because of the understandable reluctance of Jewish women survivors to talk about it. Rape by collaborators is documented in some instanced.[20]

From the testimonies, we gain an overall impression of the German's genocidal policies regarding the Jews that reinforces the impression found in recent literature – namely, that there was close cooperation between the Berlin Center and local initiaives.[21] The local initiatives were the result of a consensus that had developed during the thirties and during the early stages of the war: that somehow – "so oder so", as Hermann Goering put it at the famous November 12, 1938, meeting of top Nazi officials in the wake of the November 9 pogrom known as *Kristallnacht* – the Jews had to "disappear", as Heinrich Himmler, head of the SS, put it later. I use the crucial term "consensus" in its widest possible meaning, as embracing a social attitude shared by most Germans and ranging from a mild anti-Jewish feeling to sadistic murderousness. The mild anti-Jewish prevented any meaningful opposition to the genocidal intent pushed by the Center, with Hitler himself as the main radicalizing factor.

When we examine the biographies of the local perpetrators, we see the many of them were radical Nazi Party members with impeccable antisemitic credentials – which is why they were sent to the "east" in the first place. For the RSHA as a whole. This association between antisemitism and geographical posting has been worked out very convincingly by Michael Wildt.[22] Sir Ian Kershaw, for his part, has called the "work" the local initiators did "working toward the Fuhrer", which meant that they knew they were acting in the spirit of the Fuhrer, who would have approved of what they were doing if the relevant information had reached him. For whatever reason, then – whether to advance their careers, make material gains, or fulfill deeply felt ideological commitments – these individuals initiated radical anti-Jewish actions knowing they would be patted on their backs by appreciative superiors, local, reginal, or at the Center. This is clearly reflected in Himmler's appointment diary for 1941-1942. The SS head took many trips to inspect his east European empire, meeting with local commanders, approving radical actions, and initiating more. Here and there, individuals who were found to be too "soft" were replaced by more radical ones. The general social consensus enabled them to take murderous action against the Jews in the reasonably justified belief that their work reflected the wish of German society at large. This does not mean that all of German society or all Germans would have been happy had they known about the gruesome details of the mass murders; as David Bankier, Bernward Dörner, and many others have shown, Germans knew generally about the elimination of the Jews, but the details were less known. A minority of Germans, and no one can tell how many, were distinctly unhappy about the murder of Jews, Poles, and others. In the east, including the kresy, individual Germans tried to help and even rescue Jews, but they were an infinitesimally small minority indeed.[23]

The general murderous policy allowed plenty of room for the expression of extreme sadism and brutality. Psychologists tell us that the potential for this kind of behavior is potentially present with most, perhaps all, humans, but social context determines whether it is expressed in action or not, and whether individuals will approve of it when others commit it.

On the whole, therefore, the murder of the Jews was accomplished smoothly, if messily, in the kersy. In East Galicia, Jews were transported to the death camp of Belzec, just beyond the northern border of the province, in the Lublin area of the Generalgouvernement; elsewhere, the Jews were shot where they would fall into pits or mass graves. Shooting was quick, but caused a mess that locals had to clear up by covering the pits, dealing with bodies that had somehow been left outside, and so on. Also, it meant that in most cases, local inhabitants were either direct witnesses of the mass murder or heard the shots and knew where the mass graves were located. They still do, or their descendants do. For decades afterward, local inhabitants dug for the gold that Jews were supposed to have owned and been buried with – in areas where the Jews were at least as poor as their neighbors. Antisemitism is a very hardy weed indeed.

In considering these overall developments, it is crucial to bear in mind the correlation between the development of the war situation and the genocide of the Jews. Mass murders began during the first rapid German advances and were carried out into the fall of 1941 while the German euphoria still held sway – although a few German generals were already aware of the problems ahead and painfully aware of the considerable German losses in men and materiel, After the first big Soviet counteroffensive in the winter threw the German forces cack from the gates of Moscow, the murder continued unabated. It continued in the spring of 1942, during the great German advances, nor did it stop when the Germans were defeated at Stalingrad in the winter of 1942-1943. It is important to bear these facts in mind when trying to explain the continued mass slaughter of Jews both during the euphoria of victories and in the face of German setbacks. This found expression in the desire of the Nazi leadership to accomplish the annihilation of the Jews even if Germany was defeated, as Hitler's testament shows. The murder of the Jews was a primary objective in victory or defeat and was pursued under each and every circumstance. The progress of the war certainly influenced the fate of the Jews, but not in a correlation with victories. Rather, as the tide of war turned and as German brutalities multiplied, some among the local population began to show more support for the few Jews who were trying to escape or hide (although with others, as will be shown, the opposite happened: the locals wanted to get rid of the Jews because they feared that survivors would incriminate them with the Soviets for having participated in mass murder).

The attitude of the local population was, in any case, absolutely crucial to the survival or otherwise of Jews. During the German advance, when the Ukrainians, Belorussians, and Poles thought that the Soviet Union was collapsing and the Germans were there to stay, any help to Jews would have been taken as opposition to the new, all-powerful masters. The conquered ethnicities had a massive incentive, in any case, to avoid all contact with an unpopular minority destined to be killed. When the Germans withdrew that first winter, from the immediate vicinity of Moscow, the local population wavered, In 1942, during the greatest German victories, attitudes toward Jews hardened again. They softened after Stalingrad, when the return of the Soviet regime became possible, then probable, and finally certain. People feared that the Soviet security service might ask what they did or did not do regarding the victims of the Germans, primarily the Jews. Their anticipation of the Soviet response might have meant either a friendlier attitude toward the surviving Jews or a burning desire to get rid of witnesses who might accuse them of murder and robbery, especially if property that had clearly belonged to Jews was discovered in their possession. We shall see how the attitudes of peasants and, to a lesser extent, townspeople changed in accordance with who they thought would prevail in the armed struggle. The peasants in many of these areas might have been living in primitive conditions, but news spread. As time went on, Soviet partisans, in areas where they were active, informed the local population ever more reliably. Their news had an effect on attitudes toward Jews.

The Soviet partisan movement was late to arrive in the kresy. At first, Soviet soldiers escaping from encirclement or from POW camps made it to the thick forests of Belorussia and Polesie, the border region between Belorussia and Ukraine. Genuine pro-Soviet and Communist Party elements formed a few detachments. The majority of the others, the outlaws, were actually something between ordinary robbers and people fleeing the German occupiers, Ethnically, they were a mixed bunch, with a predominance of Russians, and most of them were anti-Jewish. Because they robbed, killed, and raped Jewish escapees, Jews mostly stayed away from the forests, at least until the spring of 1942. It was only then, and specially from May 1942 on, that an organized Soviet partisan movement emerged, and murderous antisemitism among the partisans diminished. By the summer, significant partisan units had established themselves in a few of the forested areas, and by the winter of 1942 they had spread throughout Belorussia and northern Ukraine. But by then most of the Jews were dead. The small minority that still survived had a chance of finding refuge in the forests as armed partisans or as largely unarmed groups of families and individuals sheltering there. Both groups depended on the goodwill of the surrounding peasantry. In the end, partisans both killed thousands of Jews and rescued thousands of Jews.

All this was true mainly in the north. No Soviet partisan movement developed in central and southern Volhynia, and only small partisans units of this kind developed in East Galicia until close to liberation. Jews Fleeing into the woods in these regions had little chance of survival. Ukrainian nationalist partisans in the south and Polish nationalist guerrillas in the north engaged in killing of Jews, making Jewish survival even more difficult.

Liberation came with the Soviet reconquest of parts of Volhynia in February 1944; by March, Soviet forces had also penetrated East Galicia, though German counterattacks forced the Red Army out of some areas they had already liberated. On June 22, 1944, the great Soviet offensive started, and it smashed the German central front completely. By mid-July, the kresy had become "Nazi-frei". Only pitiful remnants of the former Jewish population were left. The Soviets had come too late.

Endnotes

* We want to thank Yale University Press for its permission to publish Chapter Four, "The Holocaust in the Kresy" from Yehuda Bauer`s book *The Death of the Shtetl,* Yale University Press, New Haven and London, 2009, pages 56-72, 180-182.

1   Christian Gerlach, *Kalkulierte Morde: Die Deutsche Wirtschafts- und Vernichtungspolitik in Weissrussland, 1941 bis 1944* (Hamburger Edition, 1999).

2   This is not the place to examine the reasons for the very quick German advance, nor for the lack of preparedness of the Soviets. But I would argue for the interpretation that says that Stalin's policy seems to have based on the recognition of the fact that the Soviet armies were no match for the German armies. As a result, in 1941 Stalin was desperately trying to avoid war; he knew it was ultimately inevitable, but he hoped to gain time to make the Red Army ready. He was very suspicious of the British, and he feared they would make a deal with Hitler to free the Germans to attach the USSR, perhaps with British help. So he tried to avoid what in his eyes could be interpreted by the Germans as provocation; the result was orders to the Soviet military that prevented any real preparations for the German onslaught. Even on June 22, he still thought that the invasion was at the initiative of German military commanders and against Hitler's wishes. He thought this despite detailed information that he had received from Soviet intelligence, which was actually even more detailed than the famous intelligence reports that were sent to the Kremlin by Britain, The United States, and Soviet spies in Japan and elsewhere. However, knowing Stalin's preconceived notions, the Soviet intelligence chiefs for their own lives if they insisted too much on reports that did not fit Stalin's concepts. See Gabriel Gorodetsky, *Grand Delusion: Stalin and the German Invasion of Russia* (Yale University Press, New Haven, 1999); and below in the text.

3   On June 26, the Soviet government established an Evacuation Council that organized the evacuation of factories and equipment in order to relocate them in the Soviet interior.

4   Thus, one testimony says that a Soviet officer offered to take Jews on his truck, because if they stayed, the Germans would slaughter them. Shoah Foundation Testimonies (SF)-37869, Edmund Dickman of Bukaszowce in East Galicia.

5   In Tuczyn (Volhynia), seventy Jews were killed in a pogrom; in Ludvipol (also in Volhynia), peasants "stormed into each Jewish house they took a liking to". In Miedlyrzecz (Ukr.: Mezhirichi; in Volhynia) the "peasants, satchels in hand, appeared in the townlet together with the Germans... they broke Jewish stores and the Soviet cooperative stores open". Shmuel Spector, *The Holocaust of Volhynian Jews* (Yad Vashem, Jerusalem, 1990), p. 65. Similar events can be documented from all over the kresy.

6   Yehuda Bauer, "Kurzeniec, a Jewish Shtetl in the Holocaust", *Yalkut Moreshet* (Tel Aviv; English edition) 1 (2003), p. 139. The villagers nevertheless tried to loot and rob, and in this case the Jews put up resistance, with the help of some of their neighbors.

7   Spector, Holocaust, p. 69. This was done after quite a number of German soldiers had participated in the looting – e.g., in Tuczyn and Stepan (Volhynia).

8   Yehuda Bauer, "Sarny and Rokitno", in *The Shtetl*, ed. Steven T. Katz (Boston University Press, Boston, 2007), p. 263.

9   Spector, *Holocaust*, p. 55.

10 One wrenching story is recorded in ibid, p. 50: Two brothers decided to board a Soviet evacuation train. "Mother chased after the rolling train, tearing hair out of her head, screaming after me to stay. But my brother gripped my hand strongly and didn't let go until the train moved away from the station".

11 Spector calculates that about 15,000 Jews were killed in Volhynia in thirty-seven localities in July-August 1941, or 6 percent of all the Jews – the victims being the Jewish leadership groups and young men. The perpetrators included, apart from the EG units, the 213th Defense Division, a rear army unit of the regular Wehrmacht, and ORPO battalions. Spector, *Holocaust*, p. 79.

12 Yehuda Bauer, *Rethinking the Holocaust* (Yale University Press, New Haven, 2001), pp. 153-154.

13 Bauer, "Kurzeniec", p. 140.

14 Ibid, p. 139: One of the first places where women and children were murdered was Vilejka, a few miles north of Kurzeniec, where at least 400 people fell victim to a sub-unit (*Einsatzkommando* 9) of EG "B".

15 Spector, *Holocaust*, pp. 106-107.

16 Spector. *Holocaust*, pp. 107-109.

17 There are a number of survivor testimonies relating experiences in these hellholes – e.g. SF – 37869, Edmund Dickman.

18 Martha Goren, "*Kolot min Haya'ar Hashachor*" (unpublished manuscript, 2007), chap. 8, pp. 18ff. Goren gives the commander's name as Epner. Another army commander, by the name of Patti (the name is quite clear), in Tluste, also protected Jews. This person seems to be identical with a man called Vathie by Mojzesz Szpigiel (U.S. Holocaust Museum Archive, Reek 37, 301/3492). Goren also says that when the Wehrmacht retreated from the area, their attitude toward the surviving Jews was friendly.

19 Gerlach, *Kalkulierte Morde*, Passim.

20 For rape by Lithuanians in Stolpce (Belorussia), see U.S. Holocaust Memorial Museum (USHMM), Reel 7, 564ff., testimony of Berko Berkowicz. For Zaloszcze (East Galicia), see Sarah Kataiksher, Yad Vashem Archive (YVA) 033/477 ("most of the women were raped, and then murdered" [hot men aich di gresste teil fun froien geshendet un nachher sei geschossen]). Similar testimonies exist for Baranowicze and Krzemieniec. In Stolin, a Ukrainien was executed after Jews proved to the Germans that he had raped Jewish girls. *Sefer Zikaron liKehillat Stolin Vehasviva*, ed. A. Avatichi and Y. Ben Zakai (Irgun Yotz'ei Stolin, Tel Aviv, 1952), p. 220.

21 For rape by Lithuanians in Stolpce (Belorussia), see U.S. Holocaust Memorial
    Museum (USHMM), Reel 7, 564ff., testimony of Berko Berkowicz. For Zaloszcze
    (East Galicia), see Sarah Kataiksher, Yad Vashem Archive (YVA) 033/477 ("most of
    the women were raped, and then murdered" [hot men aich di gresste teil fun froien
    geshendet un nachher sei geschossen]). Similar testimonies exist for Baranowicze
    and Krzemieniec. In Stolin, a Ukrainien was executed after Jews proved to the
    Germans that he had raped Jewish girls. *Sefer Zikaron liKehillat Stolin Vehasviva*, ed.
    A. Avatichi and Y. Ben Zakai (Irgun Yotz'ei Stolin, Tel Aviv, 1952), p. 220.

22 Michael Wildt, *Generation des Unbedingten* (Hamburg Edition, Hamburg, 2003).

23 David Bankier, *The Germans and the Final Solution* (Basil Blackwell, Oxford, 1993);
    Bernward Dörner, *Die Deutschen und der Holocaust* (Propyläen, Munich, 2007).

Kai Struve

German Pogroms:
Atrocities of the Waffen-SS Division 'Wiking' in Eastern Galicia in July 1941

During the first weeks after the German attack on the Soviet Union on June 22, 1941, the Jews in the newly occupied territories were hit by a wave of violence and mass murder. In most of those western territories, that the Soviet Union had incorporated only between September 1939 and July 1940 as a result of the Hitler-Stalin-Pact, this violence consisted not only of mass executions by units of the German police forces, primarily the Einsatzgruppen of the Security Police, but also of violence and murder from among the non-Jewish local population, usually described as pogroms. Both elements of violence have been discussed extensively in the research literature. The following article will argue that, nevertheless, some misperceptions about both continue to prevail. While for the German side the role of antisemitic hatred seems to be underestimated, it tends to be overemphasized for crimes from the side of the local population.

The article will analyse a series of pogrom-like massacres where the core group of perpetrators did not come from the local population, but from the Waffen-SS Division Wiking. Parts of this unit committed atrocities in Zolochiv (Pol.: Złoczów), Zboriv (Pol.: Zborów), Ozerna (Pol.: Jezierna), Ternopil' (Pol.: Tarnopol), Skalat (Pol.: Skałat), and Hrymailiv (Pol.: Grzymałów). Here, between 4,300 and 7,000 Jews perished in the four days between July 3 and 6, 1941. Previous research has interpreted most of these atrocities only or primarily as pogroms by the local population, mostly their Ukrainian part. In fact, in all localities Ukrainian militias and civilians did also participate in these acts of violence. But the core group of perpetrators came from the Waffen-SS. Only because of their participation were these excesses much more deadly than attacks on Jews from the local population in other localities in the same period.

In the first part of the article, I will give a short sketch of the state of research on pogroms in summer 1941 and, more specifically, in western Ukraine. In the next part, I will describe the atrocities in the above-mentioned cities and towns in more detail. Finally, in the last part of the paper I will discuss which conclusions can be drawn from these cases for notions of violence and murder originating from the local population and from the Germans.

Research on the Pogroms and the Crimes of the Waffen-SS

In the last two decades the debate on pogroms has been strongly influenced by Jan Tomasz Gross' book on the town Jedwabne in north-eastern Poland, where Polish inhabitants murdered most of their Jewish neighbours about two weeks after the German occupation of the region.[1] Gross' study emphasized an image of violence from the local side as a largely spontaneous massive outbreak of antisemitic hatred from among the population where, as he summarized his description of events in Jedwabne, "half of the population[…] murdered the other half," referring to the fact that about one half of Jedwabne's inhabitants were Christian and the other half Jewish.[2] More recent research has not only shown that immense acts of violence from the local side also took place in many other localities of the region, but also that intense activities of different German police units and the involvement of Polish underground forces played an important role.[3] Nevertheless, the most influential, general view of the violence from the local side in the initial phase of the German-Soviet war not only in this, but also in other regions of the western Soviet Union, is that of a largely spontaneous outbreak of antisemitic hatred from among the non-Jewish population.[4]

By contrast, based on a close analysis of perpetrators, motifs, and contexts of anti-Jewish violence in more than thirty cities and towns and some villages in eastern Galicia I have argued that, in fact, anti-Jewish violence from the local side was a more diverse phenomenon and that a more complex notion of it is needed.[5] Though antisemitism among the local population had strongly increased in the period of Soviet rule after September 1939, in the form of a stereotypical view of Jews as supporters of Soviet rule, deadly violence from the local side on a larger scale occurred only under two conditions: either groups of organized anti-Soviet insurgents and/or German forces were involved. In Western Ukraine an anti-Soviet insurgency in support of the German attack had been organized by the Bandera wing of the "Organization of Ukrainian Nationalists" (OUN-B). They had an underground force of several thousand men at their disposal and in the spring of 1941 they prepared detailed plans for taking over local power as a basis for Ukrainian state-building after the beginning of the German attack of the Soviet Union.[6]

One central context of violence from the local side was reckonings of these insurgent groups with those whom they considered to have been supporters of Soviet rule and "traitors" or enemies of Ukrainian state-building. In many localities they did not kill only Jews but also Ukrainians and Poles, who in their view had committed crimes by cooperating and supporting the Soviets. However, based on the stereotypical view of Jews as supporters of Soviet rule, mostly Jews were murdered. Usually, such killings happened in smaller localities where no German or Hungarian forces – Hungarian troops had occupied the southeastern part of Galicia – were present. Testimonies of Jewish survivors often describe these acts of violence as pogroms. However, in all cases that I could analyse more closely, there are clear indications that these killings were not the result of spontaneous outbreaks of violence, but planned, targeted acts of murder of certain individuals or families.

Another important context was the attacks on Jews during the retrieval of corpses of prison inmates whom NKVD personnel had murdered before their retreat in a large number of cities and towns in Western Ukraine. In eastern Galicia as a whole probably about 10,000 prison inmates had been killed and several thousands more in Volhynia.[7] The largest massacre had taken place in Lviv (Pol.: Lwów). Here about 2,500 inmates had been murdered in the days before the German occupation of the city on June 30, 1941.[8]

The following events in Lviv after the city had been occupied by German troops on June 30 strongly influenced the overall description of violence from the local side, not least because of a large number of photos that exist from the pogrom of July 1 in this city, among them an iconic series of photos that German war reporters produced with propagandistic purposes.[9] In Lviv, as in some other, similar cases, there was a strong spontaneous participation of inhabitants in the attacks on Jews. However, at the center of the pogrom-like violence on July 1 was the fact that the local Ukrainian militia had received an order by the German military authorities to take Jews to three prison buildings as forced laborers, where they had to retrieve the corpses of inmates from cells, basements, and mass graves. Soon, locals who did not belong to the militia also began to drive Jews to the prisons while mistreating and beating them when they took them from their apartments, on the street, and at the prison buildings. It is likely that Einsatzgruppe C contributed to the escalation of violence and to the fact that many more Jews were brought to the prisons than were actually needed for the work. On June 29, Reinhard Heydrich had sent a written instruction to the commanders of the Einsatzgruppen that they should allow for and, if necessary, intensify "self-cleansing attempts of anti-communist and anti-Jewish circles" that he also described as "local popular pogroms" (*"örtliche Volkspogrome"*).[10] Probably several hundred Jews were killed on that day in Lviv,[11] and very similar excesses took place in Boryslav (Pol. Borysław) and Sambir (Pol. Sambor). But also in other localities, the prison buildings and the retrieval of murdered inmates were at the center of anti-Jewish violence from the local side.[12]

The six cases that will be discussed in the next chapter have strong overlaps with these two major contexts. In Zolochiv and Ternopil' the violence was closely related to a mass murder of prison inmates by the Soviets. In all these localities, Ukrainian militias and, to a different extent, other inhabitants also participated in the violence. However, these cases were specific, by the fact that the central role here belonged to members of the Waffen-SS Division Wiking. This was also the reason for the enormous number of victims in these localities, compared to those where acts of anti-Jewish violence took place without a larger involvement of Wiking men. This allows for distinguishing the atrocities of the SS Division Wiking as a third major context of violence against Jews.[13]

The fact that pogroms had taken place in Western Ukraine in the summer of 1941 was mentioned already in early publications on the German-Soviet war and the mass murder of Jews, though the massive involvement of the Waffen-SS Division Wiking rather surprisingly has remained largely unrecognized. The pogroms in Western Ukraine were discussed in a more concrete and comprehensive way in a scholarly publication for the first time by Philip

Friedman in 1959. Among the localities that appeared in his study were Ternopil', Zolochiv, and Skalat. He refers to Ternopil', and in a footnote also to Zolochiv, as localities where the violence against Jews was related to Soviet mass killings of prison inmates. For these localities he assumes a certain control of the Germans. He mentions Skalat among those localities where pogroms – which he describes as "mainly unorganized, wild outbursts of the urban or rural populace," without direct German involvement – took place. He did not distinguish the Waffen-SS as a specific group of perpetrators.[14] Though often mentioned in research literature, further substantial research of pogroms in the summer of 1941 started only during the 1990s. A pioneering study was Andrzej Żbikowski's attempt at an overview of pogroms in eastern Poland at that time. He mentions Ternopil' and Ozerna as localities where pogroms by Ukrainians took place. However, in the text he also refers to Ternopil' as a locality where "SS men" were among the perpetrators, but without giving any details. For Zolochiv he notes that Ukrainians and Germans participated.[15]

The pogroms were treated in a more detailed manner in Dieter Pohl's important study on the Holocaust in Eastern Galicia. Here he assumes some role by Sonderkommando 4b in pogroms in Zolochiv and Ternopil', but lists these places together with Skalat among the Ukrainian pogroms, as well.[16] He mentions atrocities committed by Division Wiking, but relates to them only for Zboriv and for the road from Lviv to Zolochiv.[17]

Zboriv was the only locality among those mentioned above that earlier research clearly identified as the site of a crime of the Waffen-SS against Jews, as the Einsatzgruppen reports, one of the most important and widely used sources on German crimes in the occupied Soviet territories, mentioned that a Waffen-SS unit had "liquidated" 600 Jews in Zboriv as "retaliation" for Soviet atrocities.[18]

The events in Zolochiv and Ternopil' received relatively large attention in the controversy about the so-called "Wehrmacht exhibition" in Germany during the second half of the 1990s. In this controversy, photos from Lviv, Zolochiv, Ternopil', and Boryslav raised close attention because it was disputed whether they actually showed victims of pogroms during the first days of German rule, or prison inmates who had been murdered by the Soviets during the last days of their rule after June 22, 1941. The question at stake here was if the exhibition ascribed responsibility to the Wehrmacht for crimes that actually had been committed by Soviet forces.[19]

In this context Bernd Boll, one of the authors of the exhibition, published a study about the events in Zolochiv.[20] Actually, this was one of the first detailed local studies of one of the pogroms.[21] His close description of the atrocities showed the central role of Division Wiking rather clearly. But his discussion of the events remained on the one hand influenced by the concept of "Ukrainian pogroms" and on the other hand focused critically on the Wehrmacht and their general attitude towards pogroms, but not on the role of the Waffen-SS. In addition, the article does not connect the events in Zolochiv to atrocities of Division Wiking in other localities, not even in Zboriv. A close reading of the article allows the identification of members of Wiking as a core group of perpetrators, but the author does not highlight this significant fact nor does he include it in the discussion of the results of his study.[22] Even more surprisingly, the discussion about Ternopil' in the context of the "Wehrmacht exhibition" remained totally unaware of the fact that the main group of perpetrators of the massive atrocities in this city came from Division Wiking and not from the Ukrainian population.[23] For Zolochiv, Marco Carynnyk in a short article, published in 2005, more clearly hinted at the role of Division Wiking.[24]

Besides the strong influence of the concept of "Ukrainian pogroms," another reason why the massive atrocities of Division Wiking were not recognized by scholars was due to the fact that also more generally the Waffen-SS and their specific character among the German armed forces did not raise much attention in research until after the turn of the century.[25] Since then research has shed some additional light on crimes of the Waffen-SS combat units in southern and western Europe, but not on the eastern front. A recent survey of the state of research on the Waffen-SS referred to the eastern front only regarding the murder of 600 Jews in Zboriv in July 1941 by the Division Wiking and considered it still "unconfirmed."[26] However, a major exception here is Martin Cüppers' study about the "Kommandostab Reichsführer SS" and its SS Brigades. Still, these units did not operate subordinated to the Wehrmacht, but were one of the forces that Heinrich Himmler had at his disposal for securing the German rear areas in addition to the Einsatzgruppen and the Order Police battalions of the Higher SS- and Police

Leaders in the occupied Soviet territories.[27] Nevertheless, in a more general and summarizing chapter on crimes of the Waffen-SS, in addition to Zboriv and Zolochiv, Martin Cüppers also mentions Ternopil' as one of the localities of mass crimes by Division Wiking, based on information of the Einsatzgruppen reports about "passing troops" having killed 600 Jews in Ternopil'.[28]

More hints of atrocities of Division Wiking in Galicia in the beginning of July 1941 appeared in studies about the non-German volunteers from Finland, Norway, Denmark, and the Netherlands, but did not attract attention in international research. Division Wiking was the first unit of the Waffen-SS that included so-called "Germanic volunteers" from the Nordic countries and from the Netherlands. However, in June 1941 the "Germanic volunteers" counted for only about eight to ten percent of the division's personnel of nearly 20,000 men.[29]

Some information on atrocities in these studies came from memoirs and other sources of the non-German volunteers who, apparently, during the post-war decades were less careful to hide them than the German members of the division. Already in 1945 the former Finnish volunteer Sakari Lappi-Seppälä reported about shootings of several dozen Jews and POWs east of Lviv at the road to Zolochiv.[30] But it was only after the turn of the century that this and other reports were more systematically analyzed, supplemented by interviews with former volunteers, German documents and post-war judicial investigations in a book of the Norwegian journalist Egil Ulateig. He included here a number of sources about crimes of Division Wiking that indicated that its members were not only responsible for the murder of Jews in Zolochiv and Zboriv, but also in Ternopil' and Hrymailiv, as well as of Soviet POWs in other localities, though he did not truly recognize the scale of the massacres, especially in Ternopil'.[31] Mostly based on these and the information that had appeared in Boll's and Cüpper's studies, Terje Emberland and Matthew Kott also addressed the involvement of Wiking and its Scandinavian volunteers in atrocities in their fundamental study on "Norwegians in the Greater German project."[32]

There are also diaries and other materials from Dutch volunteers that include information on crimes against Jews and POWs at the beginning of July 1941.[33] However, only recently Lars Westerlund published a comprehensive analysis of the involvement of the volunteers in crimes that, among other sources, is based on more than 80 diaries, testimonies, and memoirs of former volunteers, mostly from Finland.[34]

The following chapter will summarize findings on atrocities of Division Wiking that the author has presented more extensively and with a more comprehensive documentation of sources, including a close analysis of testimonies of Jewish survivors, in an earlier publication. These findings will be supplemented here with results of the studies on the "Germanic volunteers."[35]

Atrocities of the Waffen-SS Division Wiking

The Division Wiking of the Waffen-SS had been newly deployed only in December 1940 from the SS infantry regiment "Germania" that was augmented by two new regiments "Westland" and "Nordland." In addition, SS artillery regiment 5 was attached to the new division. Division Wiking was trained and equipped as a combat unit.[36]

Formally, the Waffen-SS was a separate part of the SS that developed from different armed units of the SS at the end of 1939 after several SS regiments had participated, militarily subordinated to the Wehrmacht, in the campaign against Poland. By deploying SS combat units, Reichsführer SS Heinrich Himmler aimed to develop his own armed forces, thereby extending his influence into the military realm as well. After SS military units had participated in the campaigns in Poland, France, and in the Balkans a strong extension of the SS military activities began with the German-Soviet war. Five well equipped SS Divisions as well as the somewhat smaller "Leibstandarte Adolf Hitler" participated in the invasion of the Soviet Union. As combat units, they functioned within the German armed forces like the divisions of the Wehrmacht. The Waffen SS Division Wiking and Leibstandarte Adolf Hitler belonged together with seven army divisions to Tank Group 1 under the command of general colonel Ewald von Kleist. Tank Group 1 was subordinated to Army Group South and moved into the Soviet Union between the 6th Army and the 17th Army in northern Galicia.[37]

During the war, combat units of the Waffen-SS massively increased from about 96.000 men in 1941 to about 600.000 in 1944. This growth also resulted from the fact that, in contrast to the Wehrmacht, the Waffen-SS recruited ethnic Germans from various parts of Europe and also, increasingly, non-Germans.[38] As mentioned above, Division Wiking was the first unit of the Waffen-SS that included so-called "Germanic volunteers" from the Nordic countries and from the Netherlands.

The SS military units saw themselves as a military elite of the national socialist state. Their recruits were volunteers, at least until 1941. The German members of the division belonged to a generation that had been socialized in schools, the Hitlerjugend, and other organizations in the period of Hitler's rule. The officers often had already served for many years in the SS. The strongly ideological motivation of its members was additionally fueled by programs of "ideological education" (*"weltanschauliche Erziehung"*) within the SS. The need for a brutal, ruthless fight against bolshevism as well as racist and antisemitic subjects were central parts of the educational program.[39] Among the "Germanic volunteers," as well, many had sympathies for radical right-wing ideas and sympathies for Nazi ideology.[40]

Only some parts of Division Wiking, among them the artillery regiment and some units of regiment "Germania," participated in the attack on the Soviet Union on June 22, 1941 and the following days. The bulk of the division crossed the border only on June 30, when the battle in the border region had already ended. On July 1 large parts of the division came through Lviv, the day of the pogrom and of a public display of the victims of the Soviet mass murder in the prison buildings.

In Lviv some of the Wiking members visited the prisons, as many German soldiers did, in order to see the victims of the Soviet atrocities. Many of the Germans and the locals who often searched for relatives felt horrified by the view of the decomposing bodies in the prisons. The Soviet prison massacre confirmed their view that the Soviet Union was ruled by an evil, brutal regime for which many blamed the Jews. There are hints that some members of Division Wiking already participated in anti-Jewish violence on that day, but, apparently, not on a large scale.[41]

After most of the division had passed through Lviv some parts of regiment "Westland" became involved in an exchange of fire east of Lviv with retreating Soviet forces. It spent the night near the village Slovita (Pol.: Słowita) on the main road eastwards towards Zolochiv and Ternopil'. In the morning of July 2 the commander of "Westland," SS-Standartenführer Hilmar Wäckerle, was shot by a sniper while inspecting the territory. As an act of retaliation "Westland" shelled the village Novosilky (Pol.: Nowosiołki) where they believed the sniper had hidden and killed many inhabitants.[42]

But the death of Wäckerle was also an additional trigger for unleashing excessive violence both against Soviet POWs and against Jews. Rumors spread that Jews were responsible for Wäckerle's death. On July 2 several Wehrmacht units did not only complain that parts of Division Wiking caused traffic jams by not observing traffic rules on this major road eastwards, but that they lacked discipline in other respects as well. The 295th Infantry Division reported "that the SS is shooting Russian soldiers and civilians whom they consider suspicious indiscriminately en masse." The "Russian soldiers" the report referred to were POWs and the "suspicious civilians" Jews. A report of the Fourth Army Corps to the command of the 17th Army put it more bluntly: While blocking the road with vehicles in order to reserve it for their own unit, "individual members of the division go hunting for Jews."[43]

Zolochiv

However, the first larger massacre took place in the first city along the road that Division Wiking reached, i.e. Zolochiv. Zolochiv had been occupied after heavy fighting by the 9th Tank Division on July 1. Soon afterwards two mass graves were found in the yard of a large Soviet prison in an old castle on the outskirts of the city. Later 649 corpses were exhumed here. On July 2 a new Ukrainian city administration was established and recognized by the Wehrmacht's city commandant (*Stadtkommandant*), and a local Ukrainian militia was also created. As in most other localities the militia had been organized by OUN-B and, as it seems, OUN-B also had a strong influence in the local administration.[44]

Initial units of Division Wiking arrived in Zolochiv in the late afternoon of July 2. They camped in army barracks at the outskirts of the city. Immediately after their arrival they forced several dozen Jews whom they captured in the surrounding quarter to do repair and cleaning work at the barracks. They mistreated and later shot most of them.[45] During July 3 other parts of Division Wiking also arrived in the city.

Already on July 2 some acts of violence against Jews from the local side took place. On July 3, the violence escalated into mass murder. This was clearly the result of the involvement of Division Wiking. In Zolochiv, as in Lviv and other localities, the central context was that Jews were brought in large numbers to the prison building where they were forced to retrieve the corpses of the prison inmates from the mass graves.

On July 2, announcements were posted in the city that the Jews should assemble on the morning of July 3 in the marketplace. But apparently, only a small number of them showed up, and later the Waffen-SS men, together with members of the Ukrainian militia, started searching apartments and driving Jews to the prison building.[46] Soon civilians also participated in taking Jews out of their apartments and bringing them to the castle. All this was accompanied by an increasing level of violence. Jews were attacked and beaten and a number of them were also killed in the streets and in their apartments. However, the actual mass murder took place in the yard of the prison building. Here Jews had to take out the corpses of the murdered inmates from the mass graves. They were beaten and many killed both by soldiers of Division Wiking, members of the militia and by civilians.

Apparently, Division Wiking soldiers also encouraged the militia and the local population to engage in violence. Nevertheless, most were killed when Division Wiking members started to shoot the Jews with machine guns in one of the mass graves in the prison yard from which they had taken out the corpses of the murdered inmates. Only men were shot. Women who also had been brought to the prison yard were released at about the same time, maybe on an order from a Wehrmacht officer who appeared at that time at the castle. The shooting ended when heavy rain set in at about 6:00 pm.[47]

This was not the end of violence and murder. More Jews were driven to the prison building on the morning of July 4. As on the day before, they were beaten and many killed. Meanwhile, the command of the 295th Infantry division passing the city, maybe on the initiative of the division's Chief of Staff, Helmuth Groscurth, had sent one of its regiment commanders, Otto Korfes, into the city with the task of stopping the violence. In a testimony in 1960 Korfes reported that, when he arrived at the prison building, he found two members of the SS there who together with 12 to 14 civilians threw German hand grenades into a pit into which they had driven 60 to 80 Jews. Korfes stopped this. At that time, a large number of German soldiers were in the castle.[48]

In contrast to the command of the 295th Infantry Division, apparently, the Wehrmacht's city commandant did not intervene in order to stop the violence. There are indications that the excessive violence on July 3 and 4 may have not only resulted from the forced recruitment of Jews for the work in the prison, but that it also took place in the context of a more general search for "Russians and Jews" by parts of Division Wiking. It is unlikely that this occurred without the order or consent of the Wehrmacht's city commandant.[49]

It is difficult to determine the number of victims of the massacre because no comprehensive enumeration has been carried out. All numbers are only estimates. Reports of surviving Jews mention 2,500 to 3,500 victims. However, these numbers seem to be too high in view of the fact that before June 1941 Zolochiv had about 7,000 Jewish inhabitants (of 16,000) though at the beginning of July the number of Jews in the city probably was higher because many refugees from Lviv had come to Zolochiv. Nevertheless, in view of the fact that mostly men were killed on July 3 and 4 and that the reports do not indicate that nearly the whole male Jewish population was exterminated, the number was probably lower. A report of the Einsatzgruppen mentioned "three to 500 liquidated Jews" as "retaliation" for the Soviet atrocities.[50] Otto Korfes estimated the number of Jews killed at the castle at 500 to 600. But many had also been killed in other places. Therefore, a number of about 1,000 victims seems to be more likely.[51]

Zboriv

Zboriv is located about 25 km southeast of Zolochiv, halfway to Ternopil'. Here, on July 4, another massacre was carried out by Division Wiking. In the summer of 1941 Zboriv had about 2,000 Jewish inhabitants. As mentioned above, the massacre in Zboriv is the only one that in the earlier literature had been clearly identified as a crime of the Waffen-SS and not as a Ukrainian pogrom, based on information in the Einsatzgruppen reports: "In Zboriv 600 Jews liquidated by the Waffen-SS as a retaliation measure for Soviet atrocities."[52] In fact, there had been no Soviet atrocities in Zboriv. Only the corpse of one Ukrainian who probably had belonged to the anti-Soviet underground and had been shot and buried in the garden of the court building was found here. In contrast to

Zolochiv, where the local Ukrainian militia and civilians were actively involved in violence and mass murder, their role in Zboriv seems to have been much smaller. Nevertheless, they also supported the Waffen-SS and helped to identify Jews and their houses, but the sources do not report killings by locals.

On the morning of July 4, SS men began to take out male Jews from their houses and bring them to a certain place in the town. Ukrainians showed them the houses of Jews. When brought to the place, the Jews were beaten, brutally mocked and mistreated. Later they were driven into a bomb crater and shot there with machine guns. The arrests and shooting ended in the evening. Jewish women were forced to cover the mass grave.

Another mass murder of about 100-150 Jews took place the next day after the body of the murdered Ukrainian had been discovered in the yard of the court building. The Jews were brought to that place and shot. Memoirs of Jews mention 850 victims while the Einsatzgruppen reports have, as cited above, 600. In any case, a large part of the town's male Jewish population was murdered during these two days.[53]

Ozerna

The next town on the road to Ternopil' was Ozerna. In 1931, about 700 Jews had lived here. It is likely that in 1941 their number was higher because of refugees. German troops came to Ozerna on July 2. Arrests and mass murder of a large part of the male Jewish population took place only on July 4 and 5, when parts of Division Wiking came through the town. On the morning of July 5, the Wiking men brought 180-200 male Jews whom they had arrested the day before to a field north of the town. Here they shot them with machine guns in a pit. The sources do not mention Ukrainians as perpetrators in the killings, but, as in the other localities, Ukrainians pointed out the houses of Jews. There are also reports that the SS burned down two synagogues after they had locked Jews inside.[54]

Ternopil'

The largest massacre conducted by Division Wiking took place in Ternopil', which was a bigger city than the others. According to the census of 1931 it was home to about 40,000 inhabitants, approximately 40 percent of which were

Jews. Ternopil' had a large Soviet prison. In contrast to other prisons, most of its inmates were evacuated into the Soviet interior. However, according to Soviet documents 560 inmates were shot. 197 corpses remained in the cellars of the prison building and the others were buried in a mass grave in the prison yard.[55]

The 9th Tank Division occupied Ternopil' on the afternoon of July 2. The initial units of Division Wiking arrived in the afternoon and evening of July 3. Others came through the city on July 4.[56] For Ternopil', the sources allow for a better reconstruction of the local military administration and its relation with Division Wiking than for the other localities. Colonel Erwin Sander, who served at that time with the 14th Army Corps under General Gustav von Wietersheim, was the city commandant (*Stadtkommandant*) from July 4 to 7. The headquarters of the 14th Army Corps to which both the 9th Tank Division and Wiking were subordinated were located in Ternopil' from the afternoon of July 3 to July 8.[57] At least one platoon of the 3rd company of regiment "Nordland" was assigned to the city commandant.[58]

The massacre of Jews began on the morning of July 4. The sources clearly show that the SS troops systematically searched the city. Jeanetta Margules remembered that at about 9:00 am machine guns were put up at street junctions and SS units appeared in the streets.[59] Other memoirs report similar observations. Often the SS men were attended by the Ukrainian militia or civilians who showed them apartments and houses of Jews. They took male Jews from their dwellings and brought them to a number of assembly points. Here they were shot. Sara Frydman remembered that "a drunken German" forced himself with a pistol in his hand into her apartment cursing the Jews as being responsible for the war. His intent to shoot her husband failed because his pistol had no more bullets. Then he drove him to the market square. She followed with her child and saw that several hundred Jews had already been assembled there. Some Jews had to scrub SS men's cars while they were brutally beaten. Groups of Jews were driven to the interior of a large store at the marketplace and were shot there.[60]

The Finnish Wiking Division member Olavi Liesinen remembered that an order had been given to assemble Jewish men between the ages of 16-60 at a square in the town. According to his testimony he was shocked by what he then observed while waiting at their trucks to continue their march. 500-600 youngsters and men were shot by five German Wiking men with submachine guns while wives, children and other relatives of the victims watched.[61]

Many others were shot in their apartments or on the streets. Soon streets were strewn with corpses. The violence was most intense on July 4, but also continued on July 5. Otto Schorman remembered the scenes on the streets that he observed from the window of his apartment: "The SS men were shooting Jews as if it was a hunting expedition."[62] Nevertheless, it was brutal, excessive violence. Synagogues were burned down, and before this occurred Jews were forced to take out Torah scrolls and to dance on them. Jews may have also been burned inside a synagogue.[63] According to an Einsatzgruppen report, members of the Waffen-SS threw hand grenades into apartments of Jews and caused fires.[64]

A major site of violence and murder was the prison building where Jews were brought to and forced to retrieve the corpses of murdered inmates. They also had to transport the corpses to cemeteries at the outskirts of the city. The transport and burial of the corpses was another context of violence and mass murder. Here Jews were also killed in the days after July 5.[65]

In the prison the retrieval of the corpses was supervised by the Waffen-SS, apparently by order of the city commandant. Jews were beaten and mistreated during the work and many beaten to death or shot. Here and at other locations, Wehrmacht soldiers and Ukrainians also participated in violence and murder. A report of Einsatzgruppe C mentions that in Ternopil' 70 Jews had been killed with hand grenades by Ukrainians, which probably refers to the prison yard.[66] If Ukrainians had been the perpetrators, they clearly had received and had been encouraged to use the hand grenades, like in Zolochiv, from the SS.

Ten corpses of Wehrmacht soldiers were found among the murdered prison inmates. This may have contributed to the escalation of the violence. However, the first corpses seem to have been found only when the killings of Jews had already started on the morning of July 4.[67]

As indicated above, Sonderkommando 4b under SS-Standartenführer Günther Herrmann have also sometimes been assumed to be perpetrators or involved in the massacres east of Zolochiv. In fact, it was the first part of Einsatzkommando C that moved from Lviv further to the east on the same road as Division Wiking. However, it seems to have moved through Zolochiv only on July 4 when the pogrom had already been largely concluded.[68] By contrast, in Ternopil', Sk 4b, or at least parts of it, were in the city during the pogrom of July 4. A report of the Einsatzgruppe C claimed that, as a result of a "persecution of Jews (*Judenverfolgungen*) inspired by the Einsatzkommando, liquidations of 600 Jews" had taken place.[69] In fact, as the events in the other localities prove, Division Wiking did not need additional "inspiration" for massive violence. Sk 4b also reported 127 executions by the commando in Ternopil'. However, these executions took place only in the days after July 5.[70]

With regard to Ternopil' as well, it is impossible to establish an exact number of victims. Many memoirs of surviving Jews mention about 5,000. A demographic study that appeared in a Ukrainian publication in the US in 1983 mentioned 2,300 victims without giving a source or a more detailed explanation. Małgorzata Bolchower, who came to Ternopil' on July 8, heard people speaking about 3,000 Jews who had been killed during the days before. Salomon Hirschberg remembered that the Ukrainian local health authority registered during the weeks after the pogrom, based on reports of the families, more than 4,000 deaths.[71]

The enormous massacre in Ternopil' still did not end Division Wiking's bloody raid through Galicia. Moving towards the front line at the former Polish-Soviet border, parts of Wiking's Westland Regiment devastated at least two more small-town Jewish communities on the road from Ternopil' to Husiatyn, where they became involved in their first major battle.

Skalat

Skalat suffered from two raids of Waffen-SS units. According to the memoirs of Abraham Weissbrod, several hours after the first German troops had arrived early in the morning on July 5, an "SS brigade" stopped in the town at about 10:00 am. The commander told his men: "Ten minutes to butcher the Jews." What happened then Weissbrod describes as follows: "Sweaty, begrimed from the long ride, in shirt sleeves with the cuffs rolled up, they ran about like wild wolves, firing their guns. First they assaulted Jews they encountered on the streets. The first victim was Efraim Diener, whose beard they cut along with part of his face." They drove a Jewish couple into a river and shot them there. "Other soldiers raided homes, ostensibly searching for weapons and hidden Bolsheviks, while robbing, defacing and destroying the contents of the homes. The allotted ten minutes sufficed to turn the town upside down, to leave some twenty Jews killed and an equal number wounded."[72]

However, a much more devastating raid took place during the following day when another part of "Westland" came into the city. On the morning of July 6, SS men and members of the local Ukrainian militia searched the houses of Jews and drove male Jews to the marketplace where they finally assembled several hundred people. They forced Jews to wash their cars. The Jews were mocked and beaten, and many were also killed. Not only did the SS men wound and kill Jews; so too did members of the militia and inhabitants of the town. In the afternoon and evening groups of Jews were brought from the market place to the ruins of a castle in the town that had four large towers. They were led up to the towers and forced to jump down while they were shot at with machine guns. Abraham Weissbrod ascribed these killings to Ukrainians.[73] However, the central role that the Waffen-SS had during the massacre in the city clearly proves that this massacre was organized by them and that they at least provided the weapons and probably also took part in the shooting themselves. Another report describes the shooting of Jews at the same location by SS men.[74]

Estimates about the number of deaths on July 5 and 6 in different testimonies range from 350 to 500. At that time about 4,600 Jews lived in Skalat, and constituted about half of the town's population.[75]

Hrymailiv

In Hrymailiv, that is located about 15 km south of Skalat, a mass murder of Jews had already taken place on July 5. This town was also occupied by German troops in the early morning hours of that day. For Hrymailiv, the sources show clearly that on the morning of July 5 OUN-B-led insurgents came to the town from nearby villages in order to establish a new local Ukrainian administration.[76] Here too, after the first German troops parts of Division Wiking arrived, and some of them stayed until the next day. The SS men searched the town together with the OUN-B insurgents. Already during that search many Jews were killed in their houses and on the streets. Those whom the SS men and the Ukrainians had assembled were driven into a pond and shot. A Dutch volunteer of the 2nd Company of "Westland" described what happened in his diary:

Left Tarnopol and stopped in a village. […] We grabbed a few Jews and had them clean our car until it was shining. Before we shaved them, leaving one side of the beard untouched and the other cut with scissors. With others we burned them off with petrol. So it went. With a sabre and a wooden stick, we gave them hell and made them sweat. Later we delivered them to the commander. There they were swept up through a gate alongside a pond, and then prrt prrt with an MP and a bunch of Jews fell into the pond. I saw the pond the next morning. It was chock-full; dead, half dead etc. Roar and stench. I put a handkerchief in front of my mouth because I had to vomit.[77]

Here too, the SS men offered weapons to Ukrainians to shoot Jews.[78] On July 6, other Jews were forced to take the corpses out of the pond and bury them in the Jewish cemetery. These Jews and maybe others were shot there. During these two days, according to different sources, between 350 and 500 of about 2,200 Jews who lived at that time in Hrymailiv were killed.[79]

Conclusion: German and Local Violence

A summation of the above mentioned likely numbers of victims in the different localities results in between about 4,280 and 6,950 Jews who were killed during the violent excesses of Waffen-SS Division Wiking between July 3 and 6, 1941.

Victims of massacres of the Waffen-SS Division Wiking, July 3-6, 1941

Hrymailiv	350-500
Ozerna	180-200
Skalat	250-400
Ternopil'	2,300-4,000
Zboriv	600-850
Zolochiv	600-1,000
TOTAL	**4,280-6,950**

Jews who had been shot alongside the roads and whose numbers are difficult
to establish have not been included here. There are indications that Jews were
killed by the combat units of the Waffen-SS in other localities of the region as
well, though on a smaller scale.[80]

In these six cities and towns more Jews were killed than in the several dozen
other localities in the entire region of Galicia that I could identify as places where
Jews were murdered by local perpetrators during the first half of July. Their
number was between 3,000 and 4,300. Furthermore, the localities where the SS
Division Wiking was involved had a much higher rate of victims among the Jewish
population than nearly all other cities and towns. Here between eight and thirty
percent of the Jewish population were killed. In Lviv, for example, the number of
victims of the pogrom on July 1 was clearly below .5 percent. In Boryslav, where one
of the bloodiest pogroms except for those in these six cities and towns took place,
the share of victims among the Jewish inhabitants was 1.5-2.8 percent.[81]

In contrast to the Einsatzgruppen and the other German police units,
Division Wiking had no police function, but was a part of the combat troops
and their operations were subordinated to the Wehrmacht's Tank Group 1.
Orders and instructions for mass killings of alleged supporters of Soviet rule that
the police units had did not apply to them. Their mass murder of Jews during
their move through Galicia was an outbreak of antisemitic hatred in exceptional
emotional circumstances created by the invasion of the Soviet Union. Before they
had their first serious encounter with the Soviet army they began their war against
the Soviet Union by shooting Jews whom they identified with Soviet rule. The
excessive nature of the killings by SS Division Wiking is also established by several
reports of the rape of Jewish women by members of the Waffen-SS during the
pogroms in Ternopil', and probably also in Zolochiv.[82]

The rather surprising fact is that the atrocities of the Waffen-SS had been
either missing from or had been described as Ukrainian pogroms in earlier
research. This is especially striking for the huge massacre in Ternopil'. The
identification as Ukrainian pogroms had been facilitated by the fact that, in all
these localities, Ukrainian militias and civilians also participated in the violence
and that some memoirs of surviving Jews focus more on crimes of their Christian
neighbors than on the SS men, probably because they were especially shocked

by their deeds and because they could more clearly identify them as opposed to the German perpetrators. Nevertheless, many reports identify Germans or SS men as the main perpetrators. A close analysis of these reports supplemented with the German sources and the information from diaries and memoirs of the Scandinavian and Dutch members of the division leave no doubt about the central role of the SS men in these localities.

Apparently, the reason the massacres of the Waffen-SS largely escaped the attention of researchers for so long is also related to somewhat stereotypical, pre-existing notions about the nature of the violence of the Germans and the local Ukrainians. In many reports of surviving Jews the atrocities appear as wild outbursts of violence shortly after the German occupation. Such forms of mass violence correspond, as explained above, to the concept of "pogrom" that, however, in Holocaust research usually is not associated with the Germans, but with the local population, whereas the view of the Germans is that they conducted mostly rather well organized mass executions.

This view of violence from the German side is based on two dominant and, in a way, complementary models of explanation for the German mass murder of Jews by mass executions after the invasion of the Soviet Union. More strikingly than others, the case of the atrocities of the Wiking Division suggests that these explanations may need some addition.

One model argues that the extension of mass executions of Jews during the first months of the German-Soviet war was the result of a dynamic process between the centre and the SS and police officers on the ground. According to this model, Himmler and Heydrich made clear that more executions of "Bolsheviks and Jews" were better than less, as Heydrich described the targets of "cleansing activities" in a letter to the Einsatzgruppen on July 1, 1941.[83] When specific units took more radical measures, Himmler usually approved of them and reprimanded those who lagged behind. However, when necessary either Himmler or his direct emissaries also conveyed instructions to extend the mass murder, as was clearly the case when women and children were included in mass executions after August 1941.[84]

The second influential model refers to the internal workings of the German killing units. Here the dominant interpretation is that primarily institutional and situational conditions transformed "ordinary men" into mass murderers, as Christopher Browning's most influential study on Police Battalion 101 has argued.[85] According to this model most members of the German killing units rather reluctantly approached their bloody trade, but, nevertheless, engaged in it because they acted in an institutional setting that for most of them made it psychologically more difficult to refuse than to participate in mass killings.[86]

The conclusion that can be drawn from the case of the SS Division Wiking is not that these models are wrong. Nevertheless, they divert attention from a factor that the atrocities of Division Wiking also clearly reveal as important: that of antisemitic hatred among the German perpetrators on the ground. The two basic models described above produce an overall image where antisemitism creates a framework of action, but direct mass murder is mostly the result of careerism among the officers, who wanted to meet the expectations of their superiors, and of the institutional setting of the killing units. However, the massacres of Waffen-SS Division Wiking clearly reveal the scale of antisemitic hatred among one of the highly ideologized units of the German armed forces.

Though Wehrmacht soldiers also participated in several localities in eastern Galicia in violence against Jews during the first days of the war, these were mostly acts of individual soldiers. There were no outbreaks of violence on a comparable scale from Wehrmacht units that were on average much less indoctrinated with the racist ideas of the national socialist regime.

Yet, the crimes of Division Wiking bore a strong similarity to a massacre that took place further to the north, in the territory of Army Group Centre, i.e. a pogrom of Police Batallion 309 in Białystok on June 27. In Białystok members of Police Battalion 309, many of them drunk, searched the Jewish quarter, allegedly for dispersed Soviet soldiers, and killed probably between 2,000 and 2,200 Jews, among them about 700 who were burned alive in a synagogue. Others were killed in their apartments or on the streets. Police Battalion 309 was subordinated to the Wehrmacht's 221st Security Division. In contrast to the Order Police battalions of the Higher SS- and Police Leaders in the occupied Soviet territories, the Police battalions within the Security Divisions of the Wehrmacht rarely participated in the mass murder of Jews. On June 27, this was also not an organized mass execution as those of the Einsatzgruppen and the Order Police battalions of the Higher SS- and Police leaders, but wild excessive violence during a search of the mostly Jewish quarters of Białystok. Apparently, the background was that about 25 soldiers of the 221st Security Division had been murdered and their bodies mutilated after they had been caught by Soviet troops. Parts of the Police Battalion saw the corpses shortly before they arrived in Białystok.[87] Most members of Order Police Battalion 309 were, similar to the members of the Division Wiking, volunteers who had joined the Order Police in 1940. However, most were born between 1909 and 1912 and therefore belonged to an older generation than most members of Division Wiking. Nevertheless, voluntary service for the police of the Third Reich, as well as ideological education that the members of the newly formed police battalions also received, allows us to assume high identification with the National Socialist regime.[88] Apparently, the thesis that it was mostly the institutional setting of the killing units that transformed "ordinary men" into mass murderers cannot explain such excesses. [89]

Antisemitic hatred related to stereotypical images of Jews as the core group of supporters of Soviet rule also drove the mass executions of the Einsatzgruppen even though they did not assume the form of wild outbursts of violence. This is already clearly visible in mockery and mistreatments during the early executions of "Einsatzkommando Tilsit" in the Lithuanian border regions in the days after June 24.[90] Similar elements are discernible in early mass executions in Western Ukraine, especially in executions by Sonderkommando 4a in Sokal', Luts'k and other localities after June 27.[91] The role of antisemitic hatred would also deserve more attention in the close analysis of later German mass executions of Jews and the treatment of Jews in general.

In contrast to violence from the German side, the acts of deadly violence against Jews from the local side during the early weeks of the German-Soviet war are usually seen as mostly spontaneous outbreaks of antisemitic hatred. In fact, as I have argued above, the anti-Jewish violence from the local side in the summer of 1941 in the western Soviet Union was a more complex and diverse phenomenon. Usually, it became deadly only in those localities where groups of organized anti-Soviet insurgents and/or Germans were involved. In smaller localities, deadly violence from local elements without German involvement consisted mostly of the targeted killings of certain persons and, in the case of Jews, also often of entire families, by anti-Soviet insurgents and not spontaneous outbreaks of violence.

Overall, this article argues for more complex notions of the violence against Jews both from locals and Germans during the initial weeks of the German-Soviet war in the western regions of the Soviet Union. Its findings suggest that on the one hand antisemitic hatred among the forces of SS and Police should be considered a more important factor for the extension of the mass murder of Jews and that on the other hand many acts of deadly violence from the local side were not spontaneous outbursts of antisemitic hatred, but planned killings of certain individuals and families. However, both segments of violence were to a large extent based on a stereotypical, antisemitic identification of Jews as supporters of Soviet rule.

Endnotes

1   Jan T. Gross, *Neighbors: The Destruction of the Jewish Community in Jedwabne, Poland* (Princeton, 2001) (first published in Polish in 2000).

2   Ibid., p. 7.

3   Edmund Dmitrów, "Oddziały operacyjne niemieckiej Policji Bezpieczeństwa i Służby Bezpieczeństwa a początek zagłady Żydów w Łomżyńskiem i na Białostocczyźnie latem 1941 roku," in Paweł Machcewicz and Krzysztof Persak (eds.), *Wokół Jedwabnego*, (Warsaw, 2002), Vol. 1, pp. 273-351; Andrzej Żbikowski, *U genezy Jedwabnego. Żydzi na kresach północno-wschodnich II Rzeczypospolitej, wrzesień 1939-lipiec 1941* (Warsaw, 2006), pp. 191-211; Alexander B. Rossino, 'Polish Neighbors' and German Invaders: Anti-Jewish Violence in the Białystok District during the Opening Weeks of Operation Babarossa," *Polin* 16 (2003), pp. 431-451; Mirosław Tryczyk, *Miasta śmierci. Sąsiedzkie pogromy Żydów* (Warsaw, 2015), pp. 47-102.

4   See, for example, Jeffrey Kopstein's and Jason Wittenberg's recent study, which conceptualizes violence against Jews in the summer of 1941 as rather uniform outbreaks of "ethnic riots." Kopstein and Wittenberg, *Intimate Violence: Anti-Jewish Pogroms on the Eve of the Holocaust* (Ithaca, 2018). See also Wendy Lower's "Pogroms, Mob Violence and Genocide in Western Ukraine, Summer 1941: Varied Histories, Explanations and Comparisons," *Journal of Genocide Research* 13(3) (2011), pp. 217-246, which describes the locals' attacks on Jews as "mob violence."

5   Kai Struve, *Deutsche Herrschaft, ukrainischer Nationalismus, antijüdische Gewalt. Der Sommer 1941 in der Westukraine* (Berlin, 2015).

6   Ivan K. Patryljak, *Vijs'kova dijal'nist' OUN(B) u 1940-1942 rokach* (Kiev, 2004). On the antisemitic bias of these plans, see Marco Carynnyk, "Foes of Our Rebirth: Ukrainian Nationalist Discussions about Jews, 1929-1947," *Nationalities Papers* 39 (2011), pp. 315-352: pp. 329-332.

7   The total of 10,000 victims in eastern Galicia is my estimate based on a close analysis of events in most localities where murdered inmates had been found, Struve, *Deutsche Herrschaft*, pp. 214-216. Other estimates are higher. According to Oleh Romaniv and Inna Fedushchak, in Galicia and Volhynia about 22,000 prison inmates were murdered, including approximately 17,000 in Galicia. Romaniv and Fedushchak, *Zakhidnoukraïns'ka trahediia 1941* (Lviv, 2002), p. 63. On the Soviet atrocities see also Ksenya Kiebuzinski and Alexander Motyl (eds.), *The Great West Ukrainian Prison Massacre of 1941: A Sourcebook* (Amsterdam, 2017).

8   On the number of victims in Lviv, see Kai Struve, "Masovi vbyvstva v'iazniv l'vivs'kykh tiurem: shcho vidomo pro mists ta kil'kist' zhertv?" *Ukraina Moderna*, September 9, 2018 (http://uamoderna.com/md/struve-lonckoho).

9   Gerhard Paul, *BilderMACHT: Studien zur Visual History des 20. und 21. Jahrhunderts* (Göttingen, 2013), pp. 182-189.

10 For Heydrich's letter of June 29, see Peter Klein (ed.), *Die Einsatzgruppen in der besetzten Sowjetunion 1941/42: Die Tätigkeits- und Lageberichte der Chefs der Sicherheitspolizei und des SD* (Berlin, 1997), p. 319.

11 On the events of June 30 and July 1 in Lviv, see Struve, *Deutsche Herrschaft*, pp. 253-379; John-Paul Himka, "The Lviv Pogrom of 1941: The Germans, Ukrainian Nationalists, and the Carnival Crowd," *Canadian Slavonic Papers/Revue canadienne des slavistes* 53 (2011), pp. 209-243.

12 On Sambir and Boryslav, see Struve, *Deutsche Herrschaft*, pp. 433-442 and pp. 464-484.

13 The analysis of this context is based on a larger chapter in Struve, *Deutsche Herrschaft*, pp. 561-631, where more extensive documentation of sources can be found. A major new contribution to the research on these atrocities is Lars Westerlund, *The Finnish SS-Volunteers and Atrocities against Jews, Civilians and Prisoners of War in Ukraine and the Caucasus Region, 1941-1943: An Archival Survey* (Helsinki, 2019). Westerlund largely confirms the findings of my study and provides additional evidence from diaries and other sources from Scandinavian and Dutch volunteers. It more clearly shows that, during this period, Division Wiking also murdered large numbers of Soviet POWs, but it sometimes lacks a critical analysis of sources. For example, it seems somewhat doubtful that the villages specified as Urych and Podhorolyce (or other towns and villages with similar spelling) are correctly identified as locations of crimes of Division Wiking. Some rather dubious and sensationalist quotes that are unconfirmed by other sources also appear in the chapter on Lviv, on p. 100 (Halik Kohanski) and p. 108 (Unto Boman). The photo on p. 105 is not of corpses of murdered Jews but rather victims of the Soviet mass murder of prison inmates, most likely in Zolochiv. See Struve, *Deutsche Herrschaft*, p. 581, fn. 85.

14 Philip Friedman, "Ukrainian-Jewish Relations during the Nazi Occupation," *Journal of Jewish Social Science* 12 (1958/59), pp. 259-294: here pp. 273-275.

15 Andrzej Żbikowski, "Lokalne pogromy Żydów w czerwcu i lipcu 1941 roku na wschodnich rubieżach II Rzeczypospolitej," *Biuletyn Żydowskiego Instytutu Historycznego* 1992(2-3), pp. 3-18: pp. 12-14. His list does not include Hrymailiv, Skalat, or Zboriv.

16 Dieter Pohl, *Nationalsozialistische Judenverfolgung in Ostgalizien 1941-1944. Organisation und Durchführung eines staatlichen Massenverbrechens* (Munich, 1997), pp. 54-67. See pp. 62-64 for references to the above mentioned localities.

17 Ibid., p. 70.

18 In 1956, Gerald Reitlinger already suggested that the perpetrators had belonged to SS-Division Wiking. Reitlinger, *The SS. Alibi of a Nation, 1922-1945* (Melbourne, 1957), p. 157. However, Yaakov Lozowick believed that the perpetrators came from the 1st SS Brigade of the "Kommandostab Reichsführer SS." Yaakov Lozowick, "Rollbahn Mord: The Early Activities of Einsatzgruppe C," *Holocaust and Genocide Studies* 2 (1987), pp. 221-241: p. 228. See also Thomas Sandkühler, "Endlösung," in

Galizien. Der Judenmord in Ostpolen und Rettungsinitiativen von Berthold Beitz 1941-1944 (Bonn, 1996), pp. 120-121. For the report see Mallmann et al. (eds.), *Die "Ereignismeldung UdSSR" 1941: Dokumente der Einsatzgruppen in der Sowjetunion* (Darmstadt, 2011), p. 104 (Report no. 19, July 11, 1941). Thomas Sandkühler also mentions Hrymailiv, based on a post-war West German judicial investigation, and concludes that 150-300 Jews were murdered there on July 5 by an OUN-led Ukrainian militia. He (mistakenly) assumes some involvement of Sonderkommando 4b but not of a Waffen-SS unit. Sandkühler, "Endlösung," p. 120.

19 For a critique of the photos from western Ukraine in the exhibition, see Bogdan Musial, "Bilder einer Ausstellung. Kritische Anmerkungen zur Wanderausstellung 'Vernichtungskrieg. Verbrechen der Wehrmacht 1941 bis 1944'," *Vierteljahreshefte für Zeitgeschichte* 47 (1999), pp. 563–591. Only one photo from Zolochiv in the exhibition clearly showed victims of the Soviet mass murder of prison inmates. The others likely showed victims of anti-Jewish violence during the initial days of German rule or victims of both incidents of mass murder. For documentation of the controversy in the catalogue of a revised version of the exhibition, see Hamburger Institut für Sozialforschung (ed.), *Verbrechen der Wehrmacht. Dimensionen des Vernichtungskrieges 1941-1944. Ausstellungskatalog* (Hamburg, 2002), pp. 687-729.

20 Bernd Boll, "Złoczów, July 1941: The Wehrmacht and the Beginning of the Holocaust in Galicia. From a Criticism of Photographs to a Revision of the Past," in Omer Bartov, Atina Grossmann, and Mary Nolan (eds.), *Crimes of War: Guilt and Denial in the Twentieth Century* (New York, 2002), pp. 61-99.

21 Another was a study of the Lviv pogrom by Hannes Heer, the main author of the exhibition. This study is rich in sources but presents an exaggerated and misleading interpretation of the Wehrmacht's role in it. Hannes Heer, "Einübung in den Holocaust: Lemberg Juni/Juli 1941," *Zeitschrift für Geschichtswissenschaft* 49 (2001), pp. 409-427. For a critique of Heer's thesis, see Struve, *Deutsche Herrschaft*, pp. 13-14, 376.

22 On the involvement of the Waffen-SS Division Wiking, see Boll, "Złoczów, July 1941," pp. 74-75.

23 See Klaus Hesse, "NKWD-Massaker, Wehrmachtsverbrechen oder Pogrommorde? Noch einmal: die Fotos der 'Tarnopol-Stellwand' aus der 'Wehrmachtsausstellung'," *Geschichte in Wissenschaft und Unterricht* 51 (2000), 712-726. Bogdan Musiał, who had been one of the most important critics of the Wehrmacht exhibition, also did not pay attention to the role of the Waffen-SS in Zolochiv and Ternopil, although he deals with these cases extensively in a larger study on the Soviet prison massacres and the subsequent anti-Jewish violence. See Bogdan Musial, *"Konterrevolutionäre Elemente sind zu erschießen." Die Brutalisierung des deutsch-sowjetischen Krieges im Sommer 1941* (Berlin, 2001), pp. 179-185, 239-241. Delphine Bechtel lists Zolochiv and Ternopil among the Ukrainian pogroms and, as the title suggests, holds that the massacre in Zolochiv belongs to the same category of crimes as that committed in Jedwabne. Delphine Bechtel, "De Jedwabne a Zolotchiv: Pogromes

locaux en Galicie, juin-juillet 1941," in Delphine Bechtel and Xavier Galmiche (eds.), *La Destruction des Confins* (Paris, 2005), pp. 69-92. A study by Witold Mędykowski falls even back behind the state of knowledge that had been reached by Boll's article on Zolochiv. Indeed, his chapter on Zolochiv fails even to mention the Waffen-SS. For Ternopil, although several of the sources that he cites mention the SS, this does not influence his interpretation of the events as a Ukrainian pogrom like many others. Witold Mędykowski, *W cieniu gigantów. Pogromy 1941 r. w byłej sowieckiej strefie okupacyjnej* (Warsaw, 2012), pp. 250-259, 262-268.

24 Marko Tsarynnyk (Marco Carynnyk), "Zolochiv movchyt'," *Krytyka* 10 (2005), pp. 14-17.

25 The few earlier studies either offered a general overview of the history of the Waffen-SS or focused on structure, ideology, and recruitment, but not on the question of crimes and atrocities during the war. See Bernd Wegner, *Hitlers Politische Soldaten: Die Waffen-SS 1933-1945*, 8th Edition (Paderborn, 2008) (first published in 1982). See also George H. Stein, *The Waffen SS. Hitler's Elite Guard at War, 1939-1945* (Ithaca, 1966).

26 Jan Erik Schulte, Peter Lieb, and Bernd Wegner, "Die Geschichte der Waffen-SS – Forschungsschwerpunkte und Ausblicke," in *Die Waffen-SS. Neue Forschungen* (Paderborn, 2014), pp. 11-22: p. 19. This volume includes summaries of several larger recent studies about the Waffen-SS, which also address crimes committed in southern and western Europe. See also Klaus-Jürgen Bremm, *Die Waffen-SS. Hitlers überschätzte Prätorianer* (Darmstadt, 2018), p. 128, which contains comparable and extremely limited information on crimes on the eastern front.

27 Martin Cüppers, *Wegbereiter der Shoah. Die Waffen-SS, der Kommandostab Reichsführer-SS und die Judenvernichtung 1939-1945* (Darmstadt, 2005).

28 Ibid., pp. 339-342. Mallmann et al., *Die "Ereignismeldungen UdSSR,"* p. 151 (no. 28, July 20, 1941). Another earlier report stated that "dwellings of Jews had been set on fire by members of the Waffen-SS with hand grenades," Mallmann et al., *Die "Ereignismeldungen UdSSR"*, (no. 24, July 16, 1941), p. 133.

29 Westerlund, *The Finnish-SS Volunteers*, p. 22. In contrast to the extensive research on the Scandinavian and Dutch volunteers in the SS, no scholarly study has been undertaken of the Waffen-SS Division Wiking as such. The existing literature was written by veterans of the division and, not surprisingly, does not report crimes. See, for example, Peter Strassner, *Europäische Freiwillige. Die 5. SS-Panzerdivision Wiking* (Coburg, 2000) (the first edition was published in 1968).

30 Sakari Lappi Seppälä, *Haudat Dnjeprin varrella. SS-miehen päiväkirjan lehtiä* (Helsinki, 1945), pp. 86-91. These crimes, and suggestions of some other sources about the brutal behavior of Division Wiking, are noted in an early extensive and rather apologetic study of the Finnish volunteers. Mauno Jokipii, *Panttipataljoona. Suomalaisen SS-pataljoonan historia* (Helsinki, 1968), pp. 192, 759-760. See also Westerlund, *The Finnish SS-Volunteers*, p. 116.

31 Egil Ulateig, *Jakten på massenmorderne. En dokumentarbok* (Oslo, 2006), pp. 69-86, 164-176.

32 Terje Emberland and Matthew Kott, *Himmlers Norge. Nordmenn i det storgermanske prosjekt* (Oslo, 2012), pp. 239-242. However, in contrast to Egil Ulateig they seem to also believe in the veracity of testimony given by former Division Wiking member Hans-Wilhelm Isenmann in Soviet custody in 1944 and 1945. Isenmann recounts participation in mass executions of Jews in Lviv and in several places east of the former Polish-Soviet border. No other sources confirm the participation of Division Wiking in mass executions in Lviv. Apparently, Isenmann also confessed here to German crimes that had not been committed by Division Wiking, but rather by Einsatzgruppe C. See Emberland and Kott, *Himmlers Norge*, pp. 242-243; Ulateig, *Jakten*, pp. 80-81, 267-268. Interrogation protocols can be found at the State Archive of the Security Services of Ukraine (HDA SBU) 55663, vol. 12. I am grateful to Ray Brandon for the information on this source. On the crimes of Division Wiking based on previous studies, see also Sigurd Sørlie, *Sonnenrad und Hakenkreuz. Norweger in der Waffen-SS 1941-1945* (Paderborn, 2019) (translated from the Norwegian version, which was first published in Oslo in 2015), pp. 276-277, 294-300. On volunteers from Denmark, see Claus Bundgård Christensen, Niels Bo Poulsen and Peter Scharff Smith, "Dänen in der Waffen-SS 1940-1945. Ideologie, Integration und Kriegsverbrechen im Vergleich mit anderen 'germanischen' Soldaten," in Schulte, Lieb, and Wegner, *Die Waffen-SS*, pp. 196-215.

33 Some of these diaries are analyzed in Evertjan van Roekel, *Jongens von Nederland. Nederlandse vrijwilligers in de Waffen-SS* (Antwerp, 2011), pp. 93-99. However, this study does not relate the accounts of the Dutch volunteers to other sources on crimes in the region located east of Lviv and, therefore, is unable to estimate its real scale. On the diaries of Dutch volunteers with translations of relevant excerpts into English, see also C. Kleijn and S.J.P. Reurs, *Report on Dutch Sources concerning the Involvement of SS-Division Wiking in War Crimes and Crimes against Humanity in Ukraine in Summer of 1941* (Amsterdam, 2018) (available on https://arkisto.fi/news/2312/328/The-Finnish-SS-volunteers-and-atrocities-against-Jews-Civilians-and-Prisoners-of-War-in-Ukraine-and-the-Caucasus-Region-19411943).

34 Westerlund, *The Finnish SS-Volunteers*. On the diaries, see pp. 55-57. This state-sponsored investigation originated in a debate sparked by a critical study of the attitudes and motives of the Finnish volunteers that levelled sharp criticism at Mauna Jokipii's earlier account. See André Swanström, *Hakaristin ritarit. Suomalaiset SS-miehet, politiikka, uskonto ja sotarikokset* (Helsinki, 2018).

35 Struve, *Deutsche Herrschaft*, pp. 561-630.

36 On the deployment of the division see Westerlund, *The Finnish-SS Volunteers*, pp. 61-75. See also Strassner, *Europäische Freiwillige*, pp. 27-28.

37 On the deployment and operations of German troops in the initial phase of the war, see Ernst Klink, "Heer und Kriegsmarine," in Horst Boog et al. (eds.), *Der Angriff auf die Sowjetunion* (Stuttgart, 1983), pp. 451-652: pp. 470-480.

38 On personnel and the development of the Waffen-SS, see Wegner, *Hitlers Politische Soldaten*, p. 210; Bremm, *Die Waffen-SS*, p. 96.

39 Jean-Luc Leleu, *La Waffen-SS. Soldates politiques en guerre* (Paris, 2007), pp. 413-440; Jürgen Förster, "Die weltanschauliche Erziehung in der Waffen-SS," in Jürgen Matthäus et al., *Ausbildungsziel Judenmord? "Weltanschauliche Erziehung" von SS, Polizei und Waffen-SS im Rahmen der 'Endlösung'* (Frankfurt, 2003), pp. 87-113.

40 As already noted, the motives and attitudes of the volunteers are central to the controversies in the respective countries. For a summary of these debates and a differentiated discussion of findings on the Norwegian example, see Sørlie, *Sonnenrad*, pp. 12-24, and for a critical evaluation of earlier views in the Finnish case, see Swanström, *Hakaristin*.

41 See the discussion in Westerlund, *The Finnish SS-Volunteers*, pp. 104-111. The sources that Richard Rhodes cites as proof of the intensive involvement of Wiking men in atrocities in Lviv likely relate to Zolochiv or Zboriv. Richard Rhodes, *Masters of Death: The Die SS Einsatzgruppen and the Invention of the Holocaust* (New York 2003), p. 63. See also Struve, *Deutsche Herrschaft*, p. 364.

42 Lars Westerlund, *The Finnish SS-Volunteers*, pp. 112-117. Another source identifies neighboring Velyka Vilshanytsia (in Polish: Olszanica) as the village that had been destroyed in retaliation. Yaroslav Dovhopolyi, To ne ti nimtsi," Zaxid.net, September 25, 2012, http://zaxid.net/home/showSingleNews.do?to_ne_ti_nimtsi&objectId=1266107 (accessed June 2021).

43 For this and the quotes, also see Boll, "Złoczów, July 1941," p. 75. On the killings of Jews and POWs in this region, see Westerlund, *The Finnish SS-Volunteers*, pp. 118-124. As mentioned above, the report of Finnish volunteer Sakari Lappi Seppälä, which was published in 1945, describes the murder of several dozen Jews in this region.

44 See the July 16, 1941 report of Einsatzgruppe C, in Mallmann et al. (eds.), *Die "Ereignismeldungen UdSSR,"* p. 133. For a more extensive account regarding Zolochiv, see Struve, *Deutsche Herrschaft*, pp. 566-585; Westerlund, *The Finnish-SS Volunteers*, pp. 125-134.

45 S. Altman, "Haunting Memories," in Eliezer Boneh, Baruch Karu, and I.M. Laski (eds.), *The City of Zloczow* (Tel Aviv, 1967), pp. 29–146: pp. 33-36.

46 The clearest and most detailed account can be found in the memoirs of Shlomo Wolkowicz. See Wolkowicz, *Das Grab bei Zloczow. Geschichte meines Überlebens. Galizien 1939-1945* (Berlin, 1996), pp. 43-49. Samuel Tennenbaum's memoirs add important details about his personal experiences but are not always reliable with regard to the general developments in Zolochiv. Tennenbaum, *Zloczow Memoir* (New York, 1986), pp. 164-170. See also Szlojme Mayer, *Der Untergang fun Zloczów* (Munich, 1947, pp. 5-15 (in English translation, see https://www.jewishgen.org/yizkor/Zolochiv/Zolochiv.html#TOC, accessed June 2021), which focusses intensely on Ukrainian perpetrators and overemphasizes their initiative.

47 Shlomo Wolkowicz had fallen into the pit immediately after the shooting began but survived beneath the corpses. During the night, he was able to free himself from the corpses and escape. Wolkowicz, "Das Grab," pp. 49-52. Chaim Wittelsohn and Abram Rozen (Abraham Rosen) also escaped from among the corpses during the night. Chaim Wittelsohn, report of July 14, 1945, Jewish Historical Institute Archive (AŻIH) 301/531, p. 1; Abram Vol'fovich Rozen, testimony of September 16, 1944, State Archive of the Russian Federation (GARF) 7021/67/80.

48 For Korfes' testimony, see Ausschuss für deutsche Einheit (ed.), *Der Oberländer Prozess. Gekürztes Protokoll der Verhandlung vor dem Obersten Gericht der Deutschen Demokratischen Republik vom 20.-27. und 29.4.1960* (Berlin, 1960), p. 107. Korfes reported that he met with Groscurth late in the morning of July 4 at the castle, after the violence had already stopped. See Ausschuss für deutsche Einheit (ed.), *Der Oberländer Prozess*, p. 108. No documentary basis exists for Lars Westerlund's presentation of Groscurth as having personally appeared at the castle and stopped the violence. Westerlund, *The Finnish SS-Volunteers*, pp. 129-130. Groscurth was an important member of the military opposition in the Third Reich. See also Helmut Groscurth, *Tagebücher eines Abwehroffiziers 1938-1940. Mit weiteren Dokumenten zur Militäropposition gegen Hitler*, edited by Helmut Krausnick and Harold C. Deutsch (Stuttgart, 1970). Groscurth does not mention the atrocities in Zolochiv in his diaries. Also available is a short film from the Zolochiv prison yard in the morning of July 4 with brutal scenes of beatings recorded by a German and released for the first time in 2000 the documentary *Der Skandal um die Wehrmachtsfotos* by Tina Mendelsohn and Jochen Trauptmann. A copy of this footage is located in Bundesarchiv-Filmarchiv, Berlin.

49 For the quote, see Altman, "Haunting memories," pp. 33-34. German documents also mention "Russians and Jews" as victims of the pogrom in Zolochiv. Struve, *Deutsche Herrschaft*, p. 571.

50 Mallmann et al., *Die "Ereignismeldungen UdSSR,"* p. 133 (Report no. 24, July 16, 1941).

51 For a more extensive discussion of the numbers, see Struve, *Deutsche Herrschaft*, pp. 584-585. For Korfes' estimate, see Ausschss für deutsche Einheit, *Der Oberländer Prozess*, pp. 107-108.

52 Mallmann et al., *Die "Ereignismeldungen UdSSR"*, p. 104 (Report no. 19, July 11, 1941).

53 For a more detailed description and sources, see Struve, *Deutsche Herrschaft*, pp. 586-588. See also Solomon Berger, *The Jewish Commonwealth of Zborow* (New York, 1967), pp. 84-85, and reports by Josef Gershon Leviner, Leib Kronish, Chula Broida, and Sima Zeiger in Eliahu Zilberman (ed.), *The Memory Book of the Community of Zborov* (Haifa, 1975) (Hebrew).

54 On Ozerna, see Struve, *Deutsche Herrschaft*, pp. 589-570. See also the reports of Helena Heliczker, September 30, 1947, AŻIH 301/2798, p. 1; Dora Mantel-Lempert, "A kapitel yezierner umkum," in Yitzhak Sigelman (ed.), *The Jezerna Memory Book* (Haifa, 1971), pp. 213-225 (Hebrew), pp. 214-216. See also Westerlund, *The Finnish-SS Volunteers*, pp. 135-136, which cites diaries and recollections of Finnish Wiking men that probably refer to Ozerna.

55 See the documents in Romaniv and Fedushchak, *Zakhidnoukraïns'ka trahediia*, pp. 370, 395.

56 Struve, *Deutsche Herrschaft*, p. 592.

57 Kriegstagebuch der Führungsstaffel (Ia) Gen. Kdo XIV. A.K., 22.4.-15.12.41, Bundesarchiv-Militärarchiv (BArch-MA) RH 24-14/33, Bl. 27, 35.

58 See interrogation of SS-Untersturmführer Lösken, SS- und Polizeigericht VI Krakau, 22. January 1942, BArch-MA RW 2/150, p. 38. See also Westerlund, *The Finnish SS-Volunteers*, p. 141; Ulateig, *Jakten*, pp. 172-173.

59 Jeanetta Margules, *Moje przeżycia na tle getta żydowskiego w Tarnopolu*, AŻIH 302/158, p. 2. An edited version of these 1946 memoirs that avoids mentioning the Soviet crimes in Ternopil was published as Żaneta Margules, "Moje przeżycia podczas wojny," *Biuletyn Żydowskiego Instytutu Historycznego* 36 (1960), 62-94. An English translation appeared in B.F. Sabrin (ed.), *Alliance for Murder. The Nazi-Ukrainian Nationalist Partnership in Genocide* (New York, 1991), pp. 61-76.

60 Sara Frydman, Report of May 12, 1948, AŻIH 301/3551, p. 3.

61 Westerlund, *The Finnish SS-Volunteers*, p. 146. For more reports in the diaries and testimonies of Dutch and Finnish Wiking soldiers about Ternopil in Westerlund, *The Finnish SS-Volunteers*, pp. 143-146; Ulateig, *Jakten*, pp. 173-174.

62 Otto Schorman, The Brown Terror, AŻIH 302/295, p. 7.

63 Aaron Ohrenstein, testimony, Munich, February 21, 1961, State Archives of Baden-Württemberg, Ludwigsburg, EL 317 III, Vol. 1392; Markus Horowitz, "Tarnopol unter Herrschaft der Gestapo", ibid., Vol. 1390.

64 Mallmann et al. (eds.), *Die "Ereignismeldungen UdSSR,"* p. 133 (Report no. 24, July 16, 1941).

65 Struve, *Deutsche Herrschaft*, pp. 611-615. For the days following July 5, see also the memoirs of Jeanetta Margules, *Moje przeżycia*, pp. 3-10.

66 Mallmann et al., *Die "Ereignismeldungen UdSSR,"* p. 86 (Report no. 14, July 6, 1941). For a more detailed analysis of the events in the prison yard, see Struve, *Deutsche Herrschaft*, pp. 603-611. Several photos from the prison building are reproduced and analyzed in Hamburger Institut für Sozialforschung (ed.), *Verbrechen der Wehrmacht*, pp. 109-120. Parts of a short film that usually is described as showing scenes from the Brygidki prison in Lviv probably are, in fact, from Ternopil, "Opfer russischer Massaker im Baltikum und in Südrussland", (https://collections.ushmm.org/search/catalog/irn1004505, 10:53:40 to 10:55:18 min.). I thank Taras Nazaruk and Andrii Usach for a discussion of the likely locations of this film; see also Hamburger Institut für Sozialforschung (ed.), *Verbrechen der Wehrmacht*, p. 116.

67 Struve, *Deutsche Herrschaft*, pp. 603-604.

68 Only Einsatzkommando 6, which followed later, reported to have shot 16 Communists, "including three female Jews," on July 8. Mallmann et al., *Die "Ereignismeldungen UdSSR,"* p. 104 (Report no. 19, July 11, 1941), see also Struve, *Deutsche Herrschaft*, pp. 568-569.

69 Mallmann et al., *Die "Ereignismeldungen UdSSR,"* p. 104 (Report 19, July 11, 1941).

70 See also Struve, *Deutsche Herrschaft*, pp. 597-598, 614-615.

71 For a more detailed discussion of numbers and sources, see ibid., pp. 616-618.

72 Abraham Weissbrod, *Death of a Shtetl* (New York, 1995) (first published in Yiddish in 1948), p. 4.

73 Ibid., pp. 8-9.

74 Isidor Butel (Isaac Birnbaum), "The Day I Survived the Pogrom in the Bashtis," in Weissbrod, *Death of a Shtetl*, pp. 89-90.

75 For a more detailed analysis of the events in Skalat, see Struve, *Deutsche Herrschaft*, pp. 621-625.

76 The events in Hrymailiv were investigated by the Soviet NKGB in 1944. For several interrogation protocols referring to the beginning of July 1941, see HDA SBU 31025, pp. 27-63. I would like to thank John-Paul Himka for providing me with a copy of these materials.

77 Westerlund, *The Finnish-SS Volunteers*, p. 153; Kleijn and Reurs, *Report on Dutch Sources*, p. 19; also quoted in van Roekel, *Jongens van Nederland. Nederlandse vrijwilligers*, p. 99. For two photos of the pond from a series of nine photos from the album of a Finnish SS volunteer, see Westerlund, *The Finnish SS Volunteers*, pp. 116-117. Unfortunately, this source mistakenly identifies them as being from Husiatyn. They were first published, without information on their location, in Ulateig, *Jakten*, after p. 161. I am indebted to Lars Westerlund for providing me with additional information regarding these photos.

78 See the 2009 testimony of Stanislav M. (born in 1913) who refused to participate in the shooting: http://www.yahadmap.org/#village/hrymayliv-grymailiv-grimailov-grymailov-grzymalov-ternopil-ukraine.85.

79 Struve, *Deutsche Herrschaft*, pp. 626-628.

80 Near the town of Mykulintsi (in Polish: Mikulińce) south of Ternopil, on July 5 following a larger battle, the SS Division Wiking shot what appears to be 200 or more Soviet POWs. In the same town, between one and several dozen Jews were killed at the beginning of July. However, a more detailed analysis would be required to determine how many were killed by the Waffen-SS and how many by local Ukrainian forces, Westerlund, *The Finnish SS-Volunteers*, pp. 148-152; Ulateig, *Jakten*, pp. 159-161. At the beginning of the 1960s, West German prosecutors investigated possible crimes committed against Jews in Mykulyntsi in July 1941, Bundesarchiv B 162/3912. In Zbrarazh (in Polish: Zbaraż) northeast of Ternopil, at the beginning of July 1941, German troops shot at least twenty Jews and burned down a synagogue. This pattern of violence resembles those in the other described localities, but further research is necessary to clearly identify Waffen-SS troops as perpetrators. See Marek Szmajuk, testimony of June 4, 1946, AŻIH 301/2571,

p. 2; Icchok Liljen, testimony of May 11, 1948, AŻIH 301/3554. With regard to Pidvolochys'k (in Polish: Podwołoczyska) on the former Polish-Soviet border east of Ternopil, there are indications that a Waffen-SS unit shot about 70 local Jews as well as Soviet POW Jakub Gilsohn, AZIH 301/1745; Westerlund, *The Finnish SS-Volunteers*, p. 40. We also have information regarding crimes of Regiment Westland against Soviet POWs and Jews in the former Polish-Soviet border town of Husiatyn. Here, the regiment found itself in a fierce battle with Soviet forces and suffered heavy casualties. Some civilians, mostly female victims of a Soviet atrocity, were found here. On the killings of Soviet POWs, see Westerlund, *The Finnish SS-Volunteers*, pp. 154-156. The Waffen-SS may have also conducted a search in the town and shot a larger number of Jews. I am grateful to Jan Ulvenlöv for information about his ongoing research on Husiatyn. A Swedish police interrogation of volunteer Kurt Lundin conducted at the end of 1943 mentions Husiatyn both as a location of a large massacre of Soviet prison inmates and a massacre of Jews by the Waffen-SS, but very likely Lundin mixes this town with other localities. Bert Hoppe and Hildrun Glass (eds.), *Die Verfolgung und Ermordung der europäischen Juden durch das nationalsozialistische Deutschland, 1933-1945, Vol. 7: Sowjetunion mit annektierten Gebieten I: Besetzte sowjetische Gebiete unter deutscher Militärverwaltung* (Munich, 2011), pp. 502-505. Violent excesses against Jews by German troops with strong indications that Jewish women were raped, but without murders took place in Busk. There are also hints that a major massacre of Soviet POWs occurred here. It is possible, but no clear proofs could be established, that the Division Wiking was also responsible for these crimes, see Kai Struve, "La violence contre les Juifs au cours de l'été 1941 en Ukraine occidentale: les cas de Jovkva, Kamianka Strumylova et Busk", *Revue d'Histoire de la Shoah* 213 (2021), pp. 15-44.

81 Struve, *Deutsche Herrschaft*, pp. 668-671.

82 Regarding Ternopil, see Anna Terkel, AŻIH 301/367, p. 1; Sara Frydman, Report of May 12, 1948, AŻIH 301/3551, p. 3. For more sources see Struve, *Deutsche Herrschaft*, p. 602. Regarding Zolochiv, some clues appear in Mayer, *Der Untergang*, pp. 6, 11, although he also refers to Ukrainians as perpetrators.

83 Klein, *Die Einsatzgruppen*, p. 320.

84 Such a model has been put forward most clearly by Jürgen Matthäus in "Controlled Escalation: Himmler's Men in the Summer of 1941 and the Holocaust in the Occupied Soviet Territories," *Holocaust and Genocide Studies* 21 (2007), pp. 218-242; and Klaus-Michael Mallmann, "Die Türöffner der "Endlösung." Zur Genesis des Genozids," in Gerhard Paul and Klaus-Michael Mallmann, *Die Gestapo im Zweiten Weltkrieg. Heimatfront und besetztes Europa* (Darmstadt, 2000), pp. 437-463.

85 Christopher Browning, *Ordinary Men: Reserve Police Battalion 101 and the Final Solution in Poland* (New York, 1992). For a newer study using material about Police Battalion 45, which was active in Ukraine, see Harald Welzer, *Täter. Wie aus ganz normalen Menschen Massenmörder werden* (Frankfurt, 2005).

86 On the sociological development of such a model, see Stefan Kühl, *Ganz normale Organisationen. Zur Soziologie des Holocaust* (Berlin, 2014).

87 Wolfgang Curilla, *Die deutsche Ordnungspolizei und der Holocaust im Baltikum und in Weißrussland 1941-1944* (Paderborn, 2006), pp. 508-518; Stefan Klemp, *"Nicht ermittelt." Polizeibataillone und die Nachkriegsjustiz – Ein Handbuch* (Essen, 2005), pp. 261-267; Christian Hartmann, *Wehrmacht im Ostkrieg. Front und militärisches Hinterland 1941/42* (Munich, 2009), pp. 271-275.

88 Browning, *Ordinary Men*, pp. 4-6.

89 Browning's "ordinary men" thesis is often juxtaposed with Daniel Jonah Goldhagen's thesis on the perpetrators as "ordinary Germans," which he developed based partly on the same sources used by Browning regarding Police Battalion 101. Goldhagen emphasizes the radical antisemitism of German society as the central explanation for the Holocaust. Daniel Jonah Goldhagen, *Hitler's Willing Executioners. Ordinary Germans and the Holocaust* (New York, 1996). Here, I argue that differences existed between various German units on the ground that need to be taken into account.

90 Christoph Dieckmann, *Deutsche Besatzungspolitik in Litauen 1941-1944* (Göttingen, 2011), pp. 379-391.

91 Struve, *Deutsche Herrschaft*, pp. 234-245, also pp. 230-231 (on Dobromyl), pp. 362-366, 397-400 (on Lviv).

Anna Zapalec

The Situation of the Jews in Drohobycz in the Early Months of the German Occupation (July–December 1941)

Drohobycz had a rich history, being one of the earliest urban settlements in the lands of the Polish-Lithuanian Commonwealth. Its geographic situation on the main trade route from the west of Europe to the Black Sea fostered the town's growth. Its wealth drivers also included the mining and sales of salt, as did the discovery of crude oil in areas around Drohobycz and Borysław in the late 19th century. The development of the mining and refinery industries changed the economic, social, and urban landscape of Drohobycz, adding new districts of industrial character to the old part of the city.[1]

Prior to the outbreak of the Second World War, Drohobycz (today's Drohobych in Ukraine) was the main city of a county (Polish: *powiat*) located in Lwów Voivodeship (Lviv Province). According to 1931 census data, the city had a population of 32,261, including 12,931 residents of the Mosaic persuasion (40 percent), 10,629 Roman Catholics and Armenian Catholics combined (32.9 percent), and 8,104 people of Greek Catholic and other Eastern Catholic creeds (25.1 percent), followed by other denominations with considerably lower numbers of adherents. Compared to the county as a whole, Drohobycz stood out for its number of Jewish residents, though generally it was a smaller urban center than the nearby city of Borysław (Boryslav), with a population of 41,496.[2] We do not have exact population figures for Drohobycz in 1939.[3] The troubles in the months directly preceding the outbreak of the war fueled the influx of Polish and Jewish population into Eastern Galicia from various directions, and once the hostilities began, war refugees started to arrive in large numbers as well.[4] Memoiristic sources provide differing data with regard to the number of the city's Jewish residents before and immediately after the outbreak of the war; greater certainty can be ascribed to the figures stated in the Judenrat's (Jewish Council's) documentation dated 1942, assessing that there were 15,600 Jews in Drohobycz before the war. Due to the migration processes that took place in Eastern Galicia in September 1939 and in the ensuing months, the number should be considered quite probable, even if in need of further confirmation.[5]

The first time that the Germans marched into Drohobycz was in September 1939, but a few days later they withdrew from the city, which was followed by the entry of the Soviet troops on September 24, as a consequence of the Molotov-Ribbentrop Pact formed before the war (August 23, 1939). That initiated the construction of Soviet power structures in the city: provisional bodies at first, subsequently superseded by civilian administration, the communist party, and the security police apparatus. Between 1939 and 1941, Drohobycz was promoted in administrative terms, as it became the center of a new *oblast* as early as December 1939, encompassing several prewar counties within its new borders: Drohobycz, Mościska, Rudki, Sambor, Stryj, Turka, Żydaczów, partly Przemyśl, Dobromil, and Lesko. The area underwent all the changes typical of the Sovietization process, as did other formerly Polish lands annexed by the USSR in 1939. In general, this period also contributed to the impoverishment of the city's inhabitants, including its Jewish population, due to the nationalization of craftsmen's workshops, stores, and other businesses, which effectively put a halt to private commercial activity. Some of the most damaging Soviet actions were repressions against individuals and social groups considered hostile to the communist rule. They affected people of various ethnic nationalities, including Jews and their social and political organizations. The most thorough data on the number of persecuted Polish citizens in the Drohobych Oblast pertains to mass deportation campaigns conducted in 1940 and 1941, when thousands of families (including Jewish ones) were transported deep into the Soviet Union – to Siberia, northern Kazakhstan, and other remote areas. In the successive bouts of deportation from the Drohobych Oblast, 10,593 people were dispatched in February, 3,628 in April, and 7,328 in June 1940. The latter batch probably included the greatest number of Jewish war refugees. No figures, however, are available with respect to those dispatched in the final deportation campaign in May and June 1941, and consequently it is still impossible to determine the total number of Jews from Drohobycz County (or the city itself) among all the deportees from the area. A somewhat greater quantity of detailed data is available for people arrested between 1939 and 1941, as an alphabetical list of those arrested in the Lwów and Drohobycz areas has been published, with biographical notes, for 5,822 Polish citizens. It is further known that the city's prison held at least 3,800 inmates as of June 10. The subsequent days of June saw numerous arrests by the NKVD, so the number of those imprisoned prior to the outbreak of the German-Soviet war in June 1941 may have been even greater.[6]

The Beginning of the German Occupation

The Soviet rule in Drohobycz lasted until the end of June 1941, when the city was retaken by the Germans, this time after pushing the Soviets out. Before this happened, by the order of Lavrentiy Beria of June 24, the local People's Commissariat for State Security (Russian: *Narodnyy Komissariat Gosudarstvennoy Bezopasnosti*, NKGB)[7] evacuated some of the prisoners deep into the USSR while releasing individuals detained for lesser offences. Prisoners accused or convicted of military or economic sabotage, or counter-revolutionary and anti-state activities, were shot in prison. The existing literature of the subject refers to the execution of several hundred or even as many as one thousand individuals in Drohobycz during those days.[8]

As was the case in a number of towns and villages in the east, the start of the German occupation in Drohobycz involved a pogrom of the Jews. Unfortunately, much of the information pertaining to those events is still difficult to ascertain. One of such difficulties refers to the exact date when they began. Some of the Jewish witnesses said that assaults on Jews had begun still before the German troops entered the city. They were certainly still underway on July 1, when the Germans were already there. In preserved Jewish memories, local Ukrainians are usually indicated as the main perpetrators, although Polish participation is occasionally mentioned as well. Peasants of Drohobycz County also reportedly came to the city in large numbers. Captured Jews were forced to exhume the bodies of the inmates of the NKVD investigative prison that had been shot in the courtyard of the NKVD/NKGB building at Stryjska Street which used to house the municipal court before the war. Jews were blamed for collaborating with the NKVD and contributing to the deaths of those executed by shooting. They were repeatedly rounded up and forced to take part in the exhumations, during which they were maltreated and beaten up. Jewish homes were plundered. According to witness testimonies, the German commandant of the city eventually issued an order banning the killing and the plundering. Sporadic assaults against the Jewish population continued for two days, nonetheless. Many people were harshly beaten or wounded. During the pogrom, some were killed on the spot, others died of wounds in hospital. Those whom Polish or Ukrainian acquaintances helped to hide during the pogrom were very lucky.[9] The sources and the literature on the subject mention different numbers of Jews killed during the pogrom.[10] However, according to the local Judenrat's death records for the period, 13 pogrom victims were interred in the Jewish cemetery. Moreover, based on witness testimonies, it has been established that 18 Jews were buried in the courtyard of the NKGB/NKVD building. These should be considered pogrom victims, killed during the removal of the bodies of the executed inmates of the NKVD investigative prison, which is confirmed by the testimony of one of the Jews who witnessed the event. In the Judenrat's documentation, the total number of Jews killed during the pogrom was thus 31.[11]

Soon after the Germans took over Drohobycz, the city was reached by the so-called expeditionary group (Ukrainian: *pokhidna hrupa*) of the Organization of Ukrainian Nationalists (*Orhanizatsiya Ukrayinskykh Natsionalistiv*, OUN). Its members were tasked with forming the Ukrainian power structures and militia. On July 3, they called a gathering of the Ukrainian residents of Drohobycz in the People's Center, where one of the local OUN activists informed those in attendance that the independence of Ukraine had been announced on June 30 in Lviv, and its government was headed by Yaroslav Stetsko. On July 6, a large Ukrainian rally was held in the square outside Saint George's Church, and the Act of Renewal of the Ukrainian State was solemnly read out.[12]

Throughout July, the highest authority in Drohobycz was its German military commandant, and a garrison (*Ortskommandantur*) was stationed in the city. Nevertheless, the military authorities had only tentative control over the city, which experienced various unrest and disturbances provoked by the Ukrainian militia. During that time, a considerable influence on the situation in Drohobycz was exerted by OUN members billeted in that city. Moreover, from July 8, a special squad of the German Security Service (*Sicherheitsdienst*

Einsatztrupp) was present; it reported to a special operations group (*Einsatzgruppe z.b.V*). This was the unit attributed with the murders of Jews committed on July 12, when 23 were killed in a forest outside Drohobycz, and July 20, when another 20 were executed by shooting.[13]

During this military occupation, an office of the Security Service (German: *Sicherheitsdienst*, SD) was set up. A City Council was formed, with the Ukrainian Osyp Kostshembski as mayor: on the one hand, he implemented the orders of the German authorities while on the other he had to take into account the postulates of the OUN representative in the city. As early as the second half of July 1941, the German authorities appointed a Jewish Council (*Judenrat*), and soon thereafter the Jews were ordered to wear armbands bearing the Star of David. Further decrees were issued to restrict the Jewish population's freedom of movement, e.g. by specifying the hours when they were allowed to do their shopping in the marketplace, and they were required to perform various work for the occupying administration, among other burdens imposed on them.[14]

On August 1, the District of Galicia (*Distrikt Galizien*) was formed as part of the General Government (*Generalgouvernement*). At the same time, a German civilian administration replaced the military one in Drohobycz, and the city became the center of a German county (*Kreis Drohobycz*) of 4,480 square kilometers in total area, as part of the District of Galicia. Eduard Jedamzik was appointed the first *Kreishauptman*. As an urban center, Drohobycz was now administered by City Commissar (*Stadtkommissar*) Vetterman. These appointees were replaced later on during the occupation. The local Gestapo was headquartered at 15 Adam Mickiewicz Street. A Ukrainian Auxiliary Police (*Ukrainische Hilfspolizei*) was formed as well. There was also a criminal police (*Kripo*) station, staffed mostly with *Volksdeutsche* and Poles. In September 1941, a border guard station (*Grenzpolizeikommissariat*) was set up, and from November 1941 onward, a kind of municipal police called Service Units of Security Police (*Schutzpolizei-Dienstabteilung*) was a permanent presence.[15]

In July, some Ukrainian commercial organizations, such as Maslosayuz, Narodna Torhivla, and others, resumed operations. The Ukrainians hoped that their social and economic organizations would be able to operate unrestrictedly and play a significant role under the German occupation. However, as early as late July, the German authorities formed the local division of the Central Office for Agriculture (*Landwirtschaftliche Zentralstelle*, LZ). Moreover, contrary to the Ukrainian expectations, in mid-September the Germans put a stop to uncontrolled OUN activity in Drohobycz by arresting some of the organization's activists.[16]

Creation of the Jewish Residential District and Organization of the Judenrat

The Judenrat was required to carry out the orders and instructions of the German authorities. At the same time, it was responsible for all the matters involved in the functioning of the Jewish Community, and one of its primary responsibilities was to supply Jewish workers for forced labor required by the German military, or along the roads, in the cemetery, and at any other location where the German authorities would deploy them.[17] Practically no documents have survived that could provide an insight into the organizational structure of the Judenrat and its operations between July and September but we have relatively detailed documentation for the months that followed, primarily reports of the various departments and sections of the Jewish Council. What is worth mentioning here is a document passed as late as February 1942, "The Organizational System of the Jewish Community in Drohobycz," stating that the Judenrat, composed of 12 members, was the "decision-making and auditing body of the Jewish Community." The first among many responsibilities falling within its competences was to "receive orders from the German Authorities[18] and supervise their implementation" while the chairman was to be personally responsible for it.[19] The structures of the various administrative bodies of the Judenrat and the practicalities of their operation developed gradually over the early months of the German occupation. The major departments, sections, and subsections reporting to the Judenrat were formed, to shoulder responsibility for the most vital aspects of the social, economic, and cultural lives of the Jewish Community in Drohobycz. They were appointed at different times, e.g. the Social Welfare Department started operations in July 1941, the Legal Department in September, the Division for Workers' Matters and Social Insurance and the Personnel Subsection in October, the Organizational Department in November, and many other units followed. It was not until late November that the newly formed Organizational Department of the Judenrat proceeded to draft the organizational bylaws and the rules regulating the operation and competencies of the various departments, sections, and institutions. Specific documents were passed in 1942.[20]

A Jewish residential district (ghetto) was formed at the start of the German occupation, but initially it was not closed off to the remainder of the city. It included primarily the part of Drohobycz called Łan, inhabited solely by Jews before the war. It spread on both sides of Sobieski Street, all the way to the court building in one direction and to Skotnicka Street in the other, and then reached the rear of the Little Market Square and the Adam Mickiewicz School. The ghetto also included several streets inhabited by non-Jewish residents, who were subsequently resettled elsewhere and replaced with Jews expelled from other parts of the city.[21] A number of changes in the community's life followed, such as the discontinuance of courses in Jewish history, religion, and the Hebrew language as a consequence of the circular issued by the School Council on October 20.[22]

In July 1941, one of the first institutions formed by the Judenrat was the Jewish Service for the Maintenance of Order (Polish: Żydowska Służba Porządkowa, ŻSP; German: *Jüdischer Ordnungsdienst*, OD), i.e. a Jewish police force. As of October 1941, 25 policemen served in this formation. During that time, an investigations department was formed as part of it to deal with crime. The primary responsibilities of the Jewish police thus included criminal cases in addition to ensuring orderly conduct at and operation of the Labor Office (German: *Arbeitsamt*), patrolling the ghetto streets, checking Jews' identity documents in the streets with a view to spotting individuals deliberately avoiding work, ensuring public order outside stores, soup kitchens, the Social Welfare Department's office, and during the issuance of bread and the payment of wages. Furthermore, the Jewish police assisted in inventory-taking and enforcement procedures; they were also summoned in emergencies by the Judenrat Presidium or heads of the various departments. They counteracted illegal dealing in goods, which intensified in Drohobycz in the second half of October. Given that it was during that time that the situation in terms of essential supplies became dramatic in the ghetto, verging on famine, the operations of the Jewish police against the "black market," giving fines and confiscating goods "in a rigorous manner," must have incited much controversy and resentment against this formation.[23] We find evidence of that in the Drohobycz Judenrat's Complaints Section, which received complaints against the operations of the ŻSP, often caused by the policemen's brutal conduct.[24]

In the first half of December, the ŻSP had a force of 29 officers in permanent positions, two individuals on a trial period, and one assisting in legal matters. By the end of December, the number of Jewish policemen reached 35. During that time, their responsibilities included those indicated before, i.e. criminal matters, supervision over compliance with the employment requirement, public order maintenance outside stores and soup kitchens as well as during the payment of wages and the issuance of bread, etc.[25]

Jewish Population Numbers

The outbreak of the German-Soviet war in June 1941 compelled a largely unknown number of Jews to leave the city in flight from the advancing German troops; others were evacuated along with the Soviet institutions and offices or withdrew with the Soviet army as its servicemen. At the start of the German occupation, there may have been 13,600 or more Jews in Drohobycz.[26]

In the early months of the German occupation, the number of Jews and the migration dynamics were influenced by a combination of such factors as e.g. the pogrom and killings in July and November 1941, deregistration of residents, growing mortality rates caused by deteriorating living conditions, e.g. hunger, as well as some people leaving the city, and on the other hand children continued to be born and ever new groups of Jews came to Drohobycz, including refugees from other towns. The Demographic Records Department of the Judenrat kept an alphabetical file. All population changes and movements were recorded: new registrations and deregistrations of residents, births, and deaths. It bears adding here that the statistical and registration data were not used only by the Judenrat for their own purposes but also by the German authorities. For example, all changes in the number of males aged 12-60, who were subject to the employment requirement, were communicated to those units within the Drohobycz Judenrat that were responsible for dispatching Jews to work outside the Jewish residential district and for paying wages for such work, but also forwarded to the German Labor Office.[27]

The rate and dynamics of the changes in Drohobycz's Jewish population in the period under review are demonstrated by the numbers recorded by the Demographic Records Department: prior to November 2, 1941, 825 Jews had been registered as new residents of Drohobycz, 180 had been deregistered, and 111 individuals had moved house. Between November 2 and 17, 96 new residents were registered, 45 deregistered, and 55 died. In the ensuing weeks, specifically by December 2, 95 residents were registered, 51 deregistered, and 55 died; between December 2 and 17, 25 Jews were newly registered residents, 6 deregistered, 70 died, 36 were proclaimed absent, and 29 were added to the overall number of Jews. Between December 18 and January 6: 34 were newly registered, 0 deregistered, 35 died, 144 were removed from the records due to permanent absence, and 20 were added to the overall number of Jews.[28] These statistics, however, did not record the casualties of November 22, when a large group of people were executed by shooting.

In the fall, the Judenrat Secretariat issued a great number of passes to leave Drohobycz to groups of Jews who sought to reach the central and western parts of the General Government. Seventy such passes were issued in the first half of November 1941 alone. Previously, anyone wishing to move out of town had to obtain the consent of the German county office to leave Drohobycz and travel to their new place of residence.[29]

The Judenrat's statistics cited above indicate that considerable changes in the numbers of Jewish population took place in Drohobycz in the early months of the German occupation. Between July and November 1941, a sizable quantity of newcomers were registered as residents in the city. In the ensuing months, this figure steadily decreased, which should be associated with the regulations restricting the freedom of movement, as Jews were prohibited from leaving their place of residence (effective September 5, 1941), and in the latter half of October noncompliance with this prohibition became punishable by death.[30] Consent (if any) for leaving the city had to be obtained from the German authorities. According to the data accumulated by the Demographic Records Department of the Drohobycz Judenrat, as of January 6, 1942, the number of Jewish population in the city was 13,156.[31]

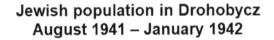

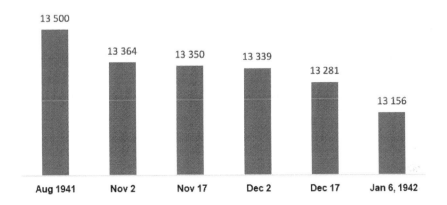

Compiled by the author. Sources: *Sprawozdanie Wydziału Ewidencji Ludności za czas do 2 listopada 1941 roku* [undated, filed November 4, 1941], GARF, f. 7021, op. 59, d. 5, l. 13; *Sprawozdanie Wydziału Ewidencji Ludności za czas do 17 listopada 1941 r.* [two-week reporting period], GARF, f. 7021, op. 59, d. 11, l. 19; *Sprawozdanie Wydziału Ewidencji Ludności za czas do 2/XII 1941*, GARF, f. 7021, op. 59, d. 11. l. 37; *Sprawozdanie Wydziału Ewidencji Ludności za czas do dnia 17/XII 1941*, GARF, f. 7021, op. 59, d. 13, l. 18; *Sprawozdanie Wydziału Ewidencji Ludności za czas do 6/I 1942 r. Drohobycz, 07.01.1942*, GARF, f. 7021, op. 59, d. 2, unnumbered leaf. The Jewish population figure for Drohobycz in August 1941 is probably rounded off. It still requires greater precision and confirmation: *Graphische Darstellung der Bewegung der jüdischer Einwohnerzahl in Drohobycz, Drohobycz, 11.11.1942*, GARF, f. 7021, op. 59, d. 12, l. 61.

Supplies of Food and Other Essentials

We have no detailed data on the provisioning of the ghetto during the early months of the German occupation of Drohobycz. Data of higher precision has been preserved for the period from October 1941 onward. It indicates that, in October, bread was baked at Rosner's bakery (26,544 kg) and Bittnerowa's [Mrs. Bittner's] bakery (14,853 kg). This can be compared with the November figures: 21,176 kg at Rosner's and 7,953 kg at Bittnerowa's, with additional information that the former paid his employees on his own while the latter's staff were paid wages by the Judenrat's Provisioning Department. The stores that sold bread were located at Stolarska Street (Store No. 1) and Kowalska Street (Store No. 9). Initially, salt, sugar, yeast, and candles could be purchased there as well; later, they only sold bread. Groceries were offered in Store No. 2 at Kowalska Street.[32]

In October, 41,397 kg of bread were issued or sold, in addition to 4,520 packets of coffee, 5,300 kg of sugar, 20,983 eggs, 540 kg of herring, 850 kg of live fish, 1,642 kg of sea fish, and smaller quantities of other products (coffee, salt, yeast, and candles). As regards the Jewish district, most of the supplies were allotted to the Jewish population by the *Gebietelandwirt* and the *Stadtverwaltung* (municipal administration). Some products, such as sea fish, eggs, herrings, or peat, were purchased by the Judenrat on the free market from Ukrainians.[33]

During the first three weeks of October, the situation with regard to food supplies was still relatively stable, as the flour allotment was granted regularly, 8,500 kg per week. But even then, a decrease in provisioning with essential foodstuffs could be observed when compared to September, and the personal bread ration for Jews was consequently reduced from 125 g to 100 g a day. Only those who worked could count on an additional allotment of 100 g, and eventually the Judenrat made the decision to increase the bread rations for working individuals to 250 g a day. Unfortunately, with no other option available, they did it at the expense of non-workers, to whom a mere 70 g of bread was issued every day. As indicated by the report of the Provisioning Department, this is how several hundred kilograms of flour were saved every week in order to boost the allotments granted to the hospital, the soup kitchens, and the workers; some of it was also kept as a reserve.[34]

A truly drastic situation with respect to provisioning, however, arose after October 24, when deliveries of flour to the ghetto stopped altogether. Judenrat officials' efforts gained a meager allotment of 1,550 kg of flour, used up to issue bread rations to Jewish workers for 30 days, to Judenrat employees for 29 days, and to all the remaining Jewish population merely until October 26. Then the reserve was drawn upon. The Jews were left without an allotment of flour till November 8, except for November 3, when the Judenrat received a metric ton of flour to bake bread intended for manual laborers. It was still possible to issue the sugar rations for September and October, 400 g per person. Things were worse as regards the supplies of milk, as the Provisioning Department received only between 40 and 50 liters daily in September and early October, truly a drop in the ocean compared to the demand. Supplies of 300 liters daily were secured for only a few days in October, between the 6th and the 10th, then they began to decrease dramatically and finally ceased completely on the 22nd. As of October 24, the German authorities ceased to issue not just bread but any food to the Jews, and so did the Ukrainian organizations, even though such goods were purchased from them. There were no supplies of heating fuel for the imminent winter, either.[35] Because of this difficult situation, the Provisioning Department ended up being one of the most criticized by the ghetto's population, especially for its allocations of bread rations to working people. For example, accusations of diminishing the weight of bread rations were voiced against the council.[36] On November 8, the German authorities resumed the deliveries of flour to the Jews, but the new weekly allotment was 6,900 kg, and then 8,300 kg in each of the last two weeks of that month. Nonetheless, it made it possible to increase the personal allotments of flour to 350 g in the second week of November, 400 g in the third, and 450 g in the fourth. The bread ration for workers was reduced to 200 g.[37]

November 13 marked the launch of the potato allocation campaign. The German authorities promised 675 metric tons of potatoes for this purpose, which meant allotting a 50 kg purchase per person. Given the approaching winter, it was a matter of key importance to ensuring basic sustenance for the Jewish population. Special organizational structures were formed in the ghetto for this campaign and advance payments were collected. Ultimately, however, only a small quantity of potatoes from the Landwirtschaftliche Zentralstelle reached the ghetto, a mere 30.35 tons.[38] This situation demonstrates graphically under what extreme conditions the provisioning of the ghetto with foodstuffs for the winter had to be undertaken. In November, the Judenrat managed to distribute some quantities of other products: 29,129 kg of bread, which, given the Jewish population number at the time, translated into a meager 2.2 kg per person on the average for the whole month; 2,400 kg of sugar out of the 2,700 kg allotment received, i.e. about 180 g per person, while the rest was kept as a small reserve; 670 candles; 700 kg of live fish; 132 kg of yeast; 2,000 kg of salt; 7,350 matches; and 41 cubic meters of peat. These figures go to show that generally the provisioning situation in the face of imminent winter was dramatic. There was still no supply of any kind of heating fuel whatsoever.[39]

The provisioning improved somewhat in mid-December, when the ghetto received 178,185 kg of potatoes extra, though it was still not the quantity that the German authorities had promised. Most of the allotment was distributed to 2,687 families; a small amount was used as social aid and for the "winter aid" campaign. In December, such aid was still not received by 800 families and 800 single residents. There was, however, some improvement in the deliveries of milk, as the ghetto received 643 liters of it, in addition to 37,933 kg of flour. Moreover, 50,272 kg of bread was issued, as was 2,440 kg of sugar and smaller quantities of other products (matches, salt, and vinegar). Unfortunately, in as cold a month as December, the population had no heating fuel, even though a firewood allotment was formally granted. Despite some of the money being paid to the company responsible for supplying the wood, that did not expedite the delivery as it was expected in January 1942 at the earliest.[40]

Poverty and Hunger

For a lot of people, the start of the occupation brought about the loss of their sources of income. Some lived on their savings, others sold or bartered their clothing and other belongings. Over time, they fell into deeper and deeper poverty, and many people ran out of savings and supplies. Such people faced starvation.[41] The available sources show the destitution of a considerable portion of the Jewish population already in the early months of the German occupation. This is particularly evident in the documentation of the Social Welfare Department, which was formed in July 1941 and aided those harmed the most in the pogrom. Initially, the department had only two employees. Their number grew over time, so that, as of December 31, 1941, a total of 71 people worked in it and in the institutions reporting to it – such as the soup kitchens and the emergency care and sanitary sections.[42] A passage from the *Report dated November 3, 1941 of the Audit and Complaints Section and the Fiscal Appeals Commission at the Jewish Council in Drohobycz for the period from September 29* [date barely legible on the microfilm] *to November 2, 1941* is worth quoting here for its assessment of the material situation of the Drohobycz Jewry:

If I were to propose a title for this report, I believe "Hunger death in its [march]"[43] would be most appropriate.

This phenomenon has been completely unknown to our community before. What has been prophesied in our books for the time of God's curse on humanity, [and] what we can read in various modern authors about the calamity of hunger in Bolshevik Russia is unfortunately beginning to come true here, among the Jewish population, as well.

The very fact of the Jews being allotted a ration of 70 g of bread a day – and actually, due to the shortage of bread, much less than this for several days at the least – causes practically the whole Jewish population to starve, especially when we consider that other foodstuffs, such as potatoes or meat, are available only at luxury prices – beyond the reach of the wide public.

Whoever has had an opportunity to watch, day after day, the hosts of poor Jews filling the courtyard, corridors, and offices of the Social Welfare Department, whoever looks at these people's swollen faces and sunken eyes knows that these are symptoms of disease caused by hunger, and he must ring the bells to sound the alarm, because the danger is here in our midst.

The mortality rate among the Jewish population of our city is highly abnormal compared to the prewar times, when it was 16 to 17 a month on the average, while in recent months cases of natural death have reached a figure that is several times higher.

Indeed, from Oct. 26 to Nov. 6, 1941,[44] i.e. over a period of just 11 days, 30 people died, of which the deaths of 9 were caused by starvation.

And we are facing a harsh winter, approaching soon, while most of our population have no heating fuel, no clothing, no footwear, no hot meals, and often no roof over their heads, and worst of all, no funds to acquire any of the above.[45]

Aid was most urgently needed by orphaned and abandoned children as well as Jewish refugees and evictees who continued to come to Drohobycz from various directions, e.g. from smaller towns, believing that they would find better living conditions here. Some stayed in Drohobycz only for a while, stopping here on their way to other places or in an attempt to reach the Hungarian border. Many requested aid from the Social Welfare Department of the Drohobycz Judenrat, which, however, it had very limited means to grant.[46] Between the final days of September and November 2, the Department distributed food to those in greatest need: only 858 rations of bread, i.e. 107 loaves, at a total cost of 171.40 zloty, or 0.20 zloty per ration. Between September 23 and October 11, 45 bread rations were issued daily, subsequently boosted to 65 rations. This, however, was insufficient to provide aid to all those in need: in order to meet the assessed demand, at least 300 rations of bread would have had to be issued daily, i.e. about 40 loaves. The situation was difficult to improve because it was not up to the Judenrat.[47] Consequently, efforts were made to provide aid through the soup kitchen, which had been set up on August 15. Generally, a price was charged for lunch, but the poorest received meals for free. Between late September and November 2, 30,948 lunches were served (including 8,932 free meals), i.e. considerably more than in the early months of its operation, when about 22,000 lunches were served. The nutritional value of these meals, however, was low as they comprised a watery soup and sometimes a piece of bread. Given the ever growing demand, there were plans to launch another kitchen at Stryjska Street, and a third one, primarily for children, in the prayer house at Garbarska Street.[48] By December, however, the only new soup kitchen opened was one for people of middle wealth whose standard of living had drastically deteriorated (it started operations on November 19). The children's kitchen remained just a plan.[49]

As early as in November 1941, the chairman of the Social Welfare Department called for increased funding for the improvement of the quality of the meals and appealed for free lunches:

> I am of the opinion that, at least with respect to the kitchen's own income, the decisions should not be made by the Finance Department but rather by the head of the Social Welfare

Department, who deals directly with people's poverty and knows exactly the local realities – he has a better orientation than the Finance Department as to how many and which people deserve free lunches.

In this matter, no percentage standard calculated by the Finance Department should be decisive as destitution and hunger are not governed by any percentage standards.[50]

At the same time, cash aid was provided to the poorest, so that 250 people were disbursed allowances ranging from 5 to 50 zloty, and 140 patients received medical consultations free of charge at the outpatient clinic while 81 were admitted to the Jewish hospital for free. On November 1, the so-called "winter aid" campaign was launched, intended to go on till the end of March 1942; it included the aid effort described above and was augmented with a collection of clothing, underwear, and footwear for the poorest, conducted among the Jewish community of Drohobycz. There were also plans to provide the less affluent and poor residents with free potatoes and heating fuel, and also to arrange rooms where those in need, especially children left without care, could find warm shelter on cold and frosty days.[51] It is difficult to determine which of these plans were actually implemented, and to what extent. The Judenrat had to collect funds for this campaign within the Jewish community.

The dramatic situation of the poorest Jewish population is confirmed in the memories of one of the female Jewish residents of Drohobycz, who remembered the following scene:

> The whole day the poor would knock on the door. Give us a piece of bread, give us something hot to drink. They didn't even have a place to heat up some water. It was terrible misery. Cold, and in winter the cold made things even worse. It was terrible.[52]

In the first half of December, the Social Welfare Department allotted 1,401 rations of bread to those in greatest need, 1/8 of a loaf each, i.e. 175 and 3/8 of a loaf in total. During that time, People's Kitchen 1 was frequented by 1,455 people for lunch: in total, 18,273 lunches were served, including 8,844 free meals. At People's Kitchen 2, during the first two weeks of December, 4,796 lunches were served to 400 people, including 39 free meals. Furthermore, 183 people were referred for free medical consultation and 36 for hospitalization. Additionally, small amounts were disbursed for the purchase of medications and outpatient treatments; there were also attempts to extend aid to families facing death from starvation and those whose loved ones had been executed by shooting in the German *Aktion* of November 22.

A frequent observation during the early weeks of December was:

> the growing impoverishment and misery of the hungry population waiting endlessly outside the Welfare office, demanding comprehensive aid and assistance, which led to the incessant formation of lines while, for obvious reasons, the petitioners' demands could not be satisfied even in fifty percent.[53]

Quite a few cases of hunger death had already been recorded: 31 people died from starvation between 1 and 15 December alone. To turn this situation around, the Judenrat initiated various efforts aiming to prevent hunger deaths, e.g. placed starving Jewish children with families that could help them; distributed potatoes among the poorest, though a very small percentage of families received such aid due to the shortage of this basic foodstuff; initiated the setup of Kitchen 3 and another one to feed children.[54] Still before the end of December, the so-called food campaign was launched to save families living in poverty. Food was collected from the most affluent Jews, which made it possible to distribute aid to 230 families. Also with the poorest in mind, potatoes were handed out, to 155 people in total. This aid, however, was limited in scope as the Social Welfare Department did not receive the full quantity of potatoes that was promised for the project.[55]

To recapitulate the relief effort undertaken by the Social Welfare Department during the first six months of the German occupation, the foodstuffs issued until the end of December 1941 came to "9,853 and 1/8 of a bread ration, which equals 1,231 and 5/8 of a loaf, worth 1,970.60 zloty in cash" while two Jewish soup kitchens in Drohobycz served 157,074 lunches, including 61,624 provided free of charge. A total of 970 medical consultations were paid for and hospitalization was covered for 254 patients. Through the efforts of the Women's Circle formed at the Department, 3,000 pieces of various clothing and footwear were collected, and some of these gifts were handed out to 666 people in need, while 20 pieces of underwear were forwarded to the epidemic hospital. A total sum of 12,952.39 zloty was disbursed in allowances and other financial aid. However, in the Social Welfare Department's assessment, all this aid and assistance was insufficient in comparison with the number of people expecting support. There was a shortage of bread, foodstuffs required to cook lunch, heating fuel, and cash to grant allowances to a greater number of people.[56]

It should be pointed out here that during the German occupation some of the Jews tried to acquire food outside the ghetto, from Ukrainians or Poles. Initially, the Drohobycz ghetto was not closed off, so the Jews took the risk and left their residential district to purchase food from their peasant acquaintances who had come to the city. Food smuggling is not particularly conspicuous in the documents of the Drohobycz Judenrat, but such information is supplied by Jewish survivors' memories. Regina (Majzels) Leiter, who lived in Drohobycz, later reminisced:

> My father owned a large hide and leather store before the war. First the Germans ordered him to close his store and then they robbed it clean. We had some hides stashed at home. One by one, we exchanged them for food. I would leave the house, my armband on my sleeve, and go to peasants who knew me well and would take the hide in exchange for food, even though Jews were not allowed to come into contact with the Aryan population.[57]

Work

In the first half of November, about 1,200 people from the ghetto were sent to work in various businesses and workshops by the orders of the German Labor Office. Additionally, registration of volunteers in the municipal workshops (*Städtische Werkstätte*) began, whereupon 316 volunteers reported immediately, and the number kept growing in the following weeks. Those were, however, mostly unqualified workers, wishing to secure minimum safety for themselves or looking for a new occupation. Some Jews ended up in German institutions and enterprises. The Judenrat offered an option to buy one's way out of the employment requirement for about 120 zloty per month. This was beyond the reach of many people and a large group tried to avoid work because usually it was hard labor and Jewish workers were often treated brutally in the workplace. The Judenrat would initiate criminal proceedings for unjustified failure to report for work where such appearance was ordered by the Labor Office (*Arbeitsamt*). In the first half of November, such proceedings were initiated against 1,200 individuals, of whom about 40 percent received a punishment. Minors who persistently failed to report for work were whipped, or alternatively punished with a lighter sentence, a few hours in jail.[58]

Many people, however, sought employment to improve their existence and ward off hunger, and later also to use the fact of being employed to secure at least some protection against German repressions, as initially these did not apply to people who had a job. Dozens of people looked for employment at the Judenrat offices, especially after the Germans' November *Aktion* in which a large group of Jews classified as unfit to work were shot dead. Afterwards, even those whose poor health or age disqualified them as workers began to look for employment as well. Some were indeed hired by the Judenrat, as its offices were in the ongoing process of organization and extension.[59] In mid-December 1941, various Judenrat offices, institutions, and enterprises employed 507 people, and there were further 250 Jewish employees in Judenrat-controlled enterprises.[60]

During the period between mid-November and mid-December, the total number of non-permanent workers dispatched for forced labor increased. On the average, 1,400 workers, including 250 women, worked daily. The municipal workshops hired 435 individuals to be employed in the following sections: brush making, tailoring, carpentry, and sewing bedclothes and underwear. The workshops did not, however, start operations before the end of December and only 68 Jews were employed there, performing administrative and cleaning work. It is worth pointing out that, from the beginning of December, 55 Jews worked on a farm in Chyrawka near Rychcice (some 5 km away from Drohobycz). A small number of Jews were also employed in German enterprises, where 14 held permanent positions while 12 were hired on a temporary basis.[61]

Mortality and Its Drivers

More and more people died with every passing month. This is indicated by the reports of the Sanitary Department and the Section for Kehilla Matters (subsequently also the documents of the Cemetery Commission and Records Department) of the Drohobycz Judenrat. The deceased were buried at the old Jewish cemetery.[62] For example, according to the data compiled by the Section for Kehilla Matters, between October 16 and October 31, 30 people were interred at the old cemetery, "including 13 men, 14 women, and 3 children."[63] We read in the report for that period:

> […] The mortality rate for people over 60 years of age is 63 percent. Having no immunity to the current living conditions, these people are dropping like flies, and 90 percent of the deceased have ended their lives in most abject destitution, to the extent that many did not even have sheets for their burial garments. […]
>
> The matter of transporting corpses to the cemetery is critical. Having no horse of our own, we have to depend in each case on local wagoners, who demand more money with every passing day, on account of the fodder prices going up and up and up.
>
> We have no other choice than to make a hand-drawn hearse, as has actually been done in other cities, and the cost of procuring such a buggy will be 1,000 zloty at the least. […]
>
> At the cemetery, we prevent further theft and damage by permanent watch on duty, [and] oversight by the Ż.S.B. [ŻSP?], while Chevra Kadisha members assist in burials, [and] curb the unruliness of the cemetery functionaries and the neighbors, whose behavior has recently verged on the absurd. Those guilty have been taken to court.[64]

Table 1. Mortality in the Jewish population in Drohobycz and adjacent areas during the period July through December 1941, according to Judenrat statistics

Month	Total no. of deceased	Sex of deceased	Cause of death
July 4 – August 30 1941 [65]	48	24 men 18 women 6 children	34 died of natural causes 13 victims of pogroms[66] 1 suicide
September[67]	34	11 men 17 women 6 children	Precise data not available; some of the deceased died due to hard living conditions
October[68]	50[69]	25 men 20 women 5 children	90 percent of deaths in the second half of the month were caused by starvation
November[70]	106[71]	64 men 35 women 7 children	Most died of starvation
December[72]	111	Data on the sex of deceased incomplete	Most died of starvation
TOTAL	349		

Prepared on the basis of Judenrat statistical tables: GARF, f. 7021, op. 59, d. 12, ll. 41-52.[73]

In December 1941, acts of vandalism were perpetrated at the cemetery. Damage was reportedly done to the "cemetery wagons; buildings containing the sepulchers of rabbis and the Lindenbaum family were demolished, as was the wooden fence under construction, at several places."[74]

Medical Care

There was a small Jewish hospital in Drohobycz before the war, at Leon Reich Street, and it continued in operation during the German occupation. Until July 22, 1941, it also had patients of other ethnic nationalities, especially women in the obstetrics ward. Afterwards, only Jews were admitted. The daily average of patients in August 1941 was 20, but it more than doubled by December, coming to 45. This increase did not, unfortunately, translate into growing receipts and the hospital's income decreased from month to month between July and December 1941. The fee for one day in hospital was 10 zloty. People referred by the Judenrat were charged less, 8 zloty, and those referred by the Social Insurance Institution paid 6 zloty. In addition to the fees paid by the patients, the hospital's budget received subsidies from the Judenrat in cash and in kind, fees for outpatient treatments, and small amounts from the Social Insurance Institution and the Jewish Social Aid. In the second half of December 1941, the Provisioning Department of the Judenrat increased its allotments of bread and potatoes to the hospital, which made it possible to improve the patients' diets during that period: they received 150 g of bread and were also served a second breakfast and a tea time meal.[75] Between July 1 and the end of December 1941, the hospital treated 445 patients in total,[76] the largest number in its obstetrics and gynecology ward (147). During that period, 52 people died in hospital.[77]

The Jewish hospital in Drohobycz had an outpatient clinic, located at Kolejowa Niżna Street. In October 1941, it had 42 employees, including 21 doctors, who provided 2,970 consultations of various types during that month, of which 475 were given to paupers dependent on welfare care. In December, the figure shot upward, as a total of 3,825 medical consultations were given in Drohobycz and outside the city. The number of paupers to whom medical assistance was extended increased as well, coming to 766 in total.[78]

Table 2. Medical consultations at the Jewish outpatient clinic in October and December 1941

Area of medical consultation	October		December	
	In town	Out of town	In town	Out of town
Surgery	609	---	852	8
Dentistry	532	---	929	---
Internal medicine	247	68	685	302
Pediatrics	35	7	73	51
Opthalmology	103	---	155	2
Laryngology	51	---	108	9
Dermatology	98	---	325	---
Neurology	63	---	60	5
Gynecology	95	---	174	1

Physiological medicine	---	---	28	---
Physical therapy	---	---	58	---
Medical panels	1067	---	---	---
TOTAL	**2895**[79]	**75**	**3447**	**378**

Source: *Sprawozdanie pracy ambulatorium żydowskiego za miesiąc październik 1941*, GARF, f. 7021, op. 59, d. 5, ll. 9, 25; *Sprawozdanie ambulatorium za grudzień 1941 r.* [Outpatient Clinic Report for December 41], GARF, f. 7021, op. 59, d. 2, l. 42.

On December 7, 1941, the first case of epidemic typhus was reported in Drohobycz. The patient was a Jewish worker who worked at the POW camp. To prevent the outbreak of an epidemic, all the Jews who worked at that camp between November 25 and December 15 were placed under observation. The Judenrat arranged an isolated area for infectious diseases in the Jewish hospital and also a sanitary station with a storage facility at 7 Jan Sobieski Street; inspections were carried out at the soup kitchens, businesses, and workshops. Soon, an epidemic hospital was arranged in the building until then occupied by the outpatient clinic. A disinfecting apparatus was acquired. The epidemic hospital was headed by Dr. Eisenberg. The outpatient clinic was transferred to the upper story of the Talmud Tora building at Szkolna Street. It was supposed to be its temporary location until such time as new and better rooms were found for it. In mid-December 1941, the outpatient clinic had a staff of 57, including 28 physicians, 7 dentists, and 6 nurses.[80] In total, 12,845 medical consultations were given there between August 29 and December 31, 1941.[81]

Repressions against and Murders of Jews

The early months of the German occupation saw a rapid impoverishment of the Drohobycz Jewry. Evictions from their current apartments and houses were one of the causes. At the same time, there were not enough housing units where those evicted could be accommodated.[82] Moreover, the material situation of the Jewish population was affected by the fact that, from the start of the German occupation, the Judenrat was required to supply furnishings for the dwellings of the various officials and functionaries of the German authorities, complete with bedclothes and tableware, which the Jews had to hand over from their households. Moreover, special collections were held to gather things to be used as bribes for German officials in certain matters of great importance to the Jewish community or to save someone from repressions.[83] All these circumstances contributed to the ongoing pauperization of the Jewish populace.

On November 22, 1941, the German security policy (*Schutzpolizei*) and the Ukrainian police conducted their first *Aktion* against the Jews: they shot around 400 people classified as unfit for labor in a mass execution in the woods outside the village of Bronica, having previously requested a list of such individuals from the Drohobycz Judenrat.[84] Some light on this event is shed by a short reference in the report of the Judenrat's Division for Workers' Matters and Social Insurance, prepared soon after the *Aktion*. We read in it: "On November 21 and 22, this year, the Labor Office was used to summon several hundred persons for an unknown purpose. According to the completed records, 151 of these persons have not returned to date."[85]

In the second half of December 1941, another *Aktion* was ordered by the Germans in Drohobycz, requiring the Jews to hand over their fur coats and skis.[86] On December 29, the Jewish Service for the Maintenance of Order conducted a series of searches against Jews suspected of failing to comply with the German authorities' order. The storerooms for the confiscated fur coats were arranged in the Sokol Society building and the Old People's Home.[87] As a consequence of the *Aktion*, many Jews were deprived of their warmest clothing during the winter.

Moreover, Adela Bar-Eli – a Drohobycz resident – mentions the existence of the so called "*Raubkomission*," composed of one German and several members of the Ordnungsdienst, who would come to Jewish homes and take away the bedclothes, some of the household furnishings, and other items required by German functionaries and officials.[88]

Conclusion

To summarize the situation of the Jewish population in Drohobycz in the early months of the German occupation, one should primarily mention the pogrom of the Jews carried out in the city. The ensuing weeks of July 1941 brought about more Jewish victims, resulting from killings perpetrated by a German special squad. The community was also shocked by the German *Aktion* of November 1941, when a large group of Jews were driven away from the city and executed by shooting.

The early months of the German occupation were thus marked with murders on Jews which began soon after the occupying forces marched into the city. To give a complete picture of the Jewish population's tragic situation, one should also mention the repressions, such as forced labor for the benefit of the occupying Germans, the marking of Jews with the Star of David, concentrating them in a Jewish district, evictions, a ban on leaving one's place of residence, and the restriction of other freedoms. These were the circumstances surrounding the formation and activities of the Judenrat, who managed the affairs of the Jewish Community in Drohobycz and at the same time had to implement the orders of the German authorities. Those orders were often adverse to the proper functioning of the Jewish Community as indeed all the aspects of the functioning of that community and the fate of the Jews themselves were up to the German authorities, because the latter made the decisions on the food allotments, the working and living conditions, and ultimately the lives and deaths of individual Jews.

The earliest months of the German occupation were also a period characterized by attempts made by the various departments of the Judenrat, and above all its Social Welfare Department, to save the poorest, whose number in town continued to increase. The ongoing pauperization and the dramatic provisioning situation in the Jewish quarter drove mortality upward, especially in the final months of 1941, when deaths caused by starvation became prevalent.

The developments described above demonstrate the condition of the Jewish community still before *Aktion Reinhardt*, which began in Drohobycz as early as the early spring of 1942; the Jews of that city were among the first to be deported from the District of Galicia to the extermination camp in Bełżec.

Endnotes

1 More in Filip Sulimierski et al. (eds.), *Słownik geograficzny Królestwa Polskiego i innych krajów słowiańskich*, Vol. 2 (Warsaw, 1881), pp. 150-157; Mścisław Mściwujewski, *Królewskie wolne miasto Drohobycz* (Lwów, 1929); Stanisław Nicieja, *Kresowe trójmiasto: Truskawiec-Drohobycz-Borysław*, 2nd ed. (Opole, 2018).

2 *Drugi powszechny spis ludności z dnia 9 grudnia 1931 r. Mieszkania i gospodarstwa domowe. Ludność. Stosunki zawodowe* [Second national census of December 9, 1931], *Statystyka Polski*, Series C, Book 68: *Województwo lwowskie bez miasta Lwowa* (Warsaw, 1938), p. 36.

3 According to the calculations made by Volodymyr Kubiyovych, a Ukrainian ethnographer and geographer, in January 1939 the city had a total population of 34,600, including 13,800 Jews. See Kubiïovych, *Ethnic Groups of the South-Western Ukraine (Halyčyna – Galicia) 1.1.1939. National Statistics of Halyčyna – Galicia* (Wiesbaden, 1983), p. 22 (Ukrainian). In the literature on the subject, it has even been asserted that in 1939 the population of Drohobycz reached 37,000, without further specification as to whether this figure refers to the first or the second half of the year. See Ruslana Popp [Rusłana Popp], "Drohobych during the Second World War: The Ethno-Social Processes," in Janusz Gmitruk and Wojciech Włodarkiewicz (eds.), *Wrzesień 1939: wojna na dwa fronty* (Warsaw, 2010), p. 635 (Ukrainian).

4 Information on this topic can be found in various Jewish testimonies, e.g. "Testimony of Rutka Hirschberg", Archive of the Jewish Historical Institute (Archiwum Żydowskiego Instytutu Historycznego, AŻIH) in Warsaw, 301/1129, p. 1; "Testimony of Kazia Schneckendorf", *Yad Vashem Archives* (YVA), O.3/1356. According to the data compiled by the NKVD of the Ukrainian Socialist Soviet Republic, in January 1940 a total of 31,000 refugees were present in the Drohobych Oblast, but just how many of them stayed in the city is difficult to assess (cited in Popp, "Drohobych during the Second World War," p. 637).

5 *Graphische Darstellung der Bewegung der jüd*[ische] *Einwohnerzahl in Drohobycz, 11.11.1942* [Graphical representation of movements in the number of Jewish residents in Drohobycz], State Archive of the Russian Federation (GARF), f. 7021, op. 59, d. 12, l. 61. Tatiana Berenstein calculated the Jewish population of Drohobycz prior to September 1, 1939 to be around 14,000. See Berenstein, "Eksterminacja ludności żydowskiej w dystrykcie Galicja (1941-1943)," *Biuletyn Żydowskiego Instytutu Historycznego* 61(1) (1967), Table 4. One of the letters of the County Committee for Jewish Social Aid in Drohobycz mentions that the city had a Jewish population of 13,500 before the war (*List do Żydowskiej Samopomocy* [w Krakowie], *Drohobycz, 24.02.1942* [Letter to the Jewish Aid organization in Krakow], AŻIH, 211/362, p. 21). Samuel Rothenberg, a Holocaust survivor, reminisces that the city's total population before the war was 38,000, including 19,500 Jews, but this figure seems decidedly overstated. See Rothenberg, *List o zagładzie Żydów w Drohobyczu*, ed. with intr. and notes by Edmund Silberner (London, 1984), p. 7.

6   For more on this subject, see Dieter Pohl, *Nationalsozialistische Judenverfolgung in Ostgalizien 1941-1944. Organisation und Durchführung eines staatlichen Massenverbrechens*, 2nd ed. (Munich, 1997), p 42; *List dr Leona Tannenbauma z Drohobycza do Prezesa Żydowskiej Samopomocy Społecznej, Drohobycz, 09.03.1942* [Letter from Dr. Leon Tannenbaum of Drohobycz to the Chairman of the Jewish Social Aid], AŻIH, 211/362, p. 42; Włodzimierz Bonusiak, "Rządy radzieckie w Drohobyczu – aparat okupacyjny 1939-1941," in Włodzimierz Bonusiak (ed.), *Drohobycz: miasto wielu kultur* (Rzeszów, 2005), pp. 128-141; Ivanna Luchakivska [Iwanna Łuczakiwśka], "The Establishment of Soviet Authorities in the Drohobycz Area (1939-1941)," in Bonusiak (ed.) *Drohobycz: miasto wielu kultur*, pp. 142-156 (Ukrainian); Edyta Czop, "Deportacje z obwodu drohobyckiego w 1940 r.," in Bonusiak (ed.) *Drohobycz: miasto wielu kultur*, pp. 176, 183, 186; Rothenberg, *List o zagładzie Żydów*, p. 8; Katarzyna Thomas, "Rzeczywistość wojenna Drohobycza w latach 1939-1945," in Agnieszka Kasperek, Agnieszka Żmuda, and Sławomir Jacek Żurek (eds.), *J. Karski: świadek, emisariusz, człowiek* (Lublin, 2015), pp. 215-218.

7   From March 12, 1941, under the order of the NKGB and the NKVD of the USSR of March 3, prisons were supervised by NKGB state security bodies. Consequently, the prerogatives of the NKGB and the NKVD were separated. See Ivan Bilas, *The Repressive Penal System in Ukraine 1917-1953. A Publico-Political and Historico-Juristic Analysis in Two Volumes*, Vol. 1 (Kyiv, 1994), p. 128 (Ukrainian).

8   Ewa Orlof, "Losy więźniów z obwodu drohobyckiego w czerwcu 1941 roku," in Bonusiak, *Drohobycz: miasto wielu kultur*, pp. 151, 195-197. In 1990 in Drohobych, the remains of the 486 prisoners murdered in June 1941 were exhumed. Only 22 individuals were identified by name. See Popp, "Drohobych during the Second World War," p. 640.

9   According to some accounts, the first German soldiers were seen in the streets of Drohobycz late on the evening of June 30, but the city was not occupied until the following day: July 1, 1941. More on the circumstances of the pogrom and relevant research findings can be found in Katarzyna Thomas, "O pogromie w Drohobyczu w 1941 roku w świetle materiałów z Archiwum Yad Vashem," *Studia Żydowskie. Almanach* 5 (2015), pp 119-131; Andrzej Żbikowski, "Lokalne pogromy Żydów w czerwcu i lipcu 1941 r. na wschodnich rubieżach II Rzeczypospolitej," *Biuletyn Żydowskiego Instytutu Historycznego* 162-163 (2-3) (1992), pp. 12, 14; Witold. W. Mędykowski, *W cieniu gigantów: pogromy 1941 r. w byłej sowieckiej strefie okupacyjnej* (Jerusalem, 2018), p. 269; Dariusz Libionka, *Zagłada Żydów w Generalnym Gubernatorstwie. Zarys problematyki* (Lublin, 2017), p. 72; Aleksandr Kruglov and Martin Dean, "Drohobycz," in M. Dean (ed.), *Encyclopedia of Camps and Ghettos, 1933–1945*, Vol. 2: *Ghettos in German-Occupied Eastern Europe* (Bloomington, 2012), p. 774; Thomas, "Rzeczywistość wojenna Drohobycza w latach 1939-1945," pp. 218-219. Pogroms in Eastern Galicia are also discussed in Kai Struve, "Wstrząsy w strefie starcia imperiów. Galicja Wschodnia latem 1941 roku," in Andrzej Zięba (ed.), *OUN, UPA i zagłada Żydów* (Krakow, 2016), pp. 149-152, 161, 163-171; Struve, "Rytuały przemocy? Pogromy latem 1941 roku," in Zięba, *OUN, UPA i zagłada Żydów*, pp. 203-221. Some of the witnesses' accounts of

the pogrom can be found in Ukrainian in Volodymyr Yatsiv, "Drohobych: the City of Oil Fields in the War Periods of 1929-44," in Adolf Hladylovych et al. (eds.), *Drohobych County – the Land of Ivan Franko*, Vol. 3 (New York, Paris, Sydney, and Toronto, 1986), pp. 92-93; Testimony of Rutka Hirschberg, AŻIH, 301/1129, p. 1; Testimony of Jakub Gerstenfeld, AŻIH, 301/1177, pp. 2-3; Anonymous testimony, AŻIH, 301/847, p. 1; Testimony of Regina Wilder, AŻIH, 301/1277, p. 1; Testimony of Kazia Schneckendorf, YVA, O.3/1356; Testimony of Feliks Milan, Eastern Archive of the KARTA Center in Warsaw (*Archiwum Wschodnie, AW*), 8 I/0700, pp. 3-4; Testimony of Adela Bar-Eli (copy of YVA, O.3/7656), Archive of the Institute of National Remembrance in Warsaw (*Archiwum Instytutu Pamięci Narodowej*, AIPN), BU 2323/1214, pp. 2-8; Testimony of Towa Sztok (digital copy of YVA, O.3/3014), AIPN, BU 2323/954, p. 2; Rothenberg, *List o zagładzie Żydów*, p. 8. One of the sources contains a statement that, despite the German authorities' directive to keep peace and order in the city and cease the murders and plunder, the situation was not entirely under control. The assaults were discontinued only after the Germans executed (by shooting) 10 young Ukrainians involved in plunder and robbery in Drohobycz. See Testimony of Kazia Schneckendorf, YVA, O.3/1356.

10 Hersz Bettman, a witness to the pogrom, reminisces that, during the removal of prisoners' bodies from the grave in the courtyard of the NKGB building, 24 Jews were killed and buried there (Testimony of Hersz Bettman, YVA, O.3/2187, p. 2). The literature varies with regard to the number of Jews killed during the pogrom. Aleksandr Kruglov and Martin Dean assert that 47 people were killed (Kruglov and Dean, "Drohobycz," p. 775), whereas Katarzyna Thomas writes that, during the pogrom, "according to incomplete data, about 460 individuals" may have lost their lives (Thomas, "O pogromie w Drohobyczu w 1941 roku," p. 125).

11 *Śmiertelność ludności żydowskiej w Drohobyczu i okolicy za czas od 4 lipca 1941 r. do 15 sierpnia 1941 r.* [Mortality in the Jewish population in Drohobycz and adjacent areas during the period from July 4, 1941 to August 15, 1941], GARF, f. 7021, op. 59, d. 12, l. 41; *Śmiertelność ludności żydowskiej w Drohobyczu i okolicy za czas od 1 lipca do 31 grudnia 1941 r.* (II połowa 1941 r.) [Mortality in the Jewish population in Drohobycz and adjacent areas between July 1 and December 31, 1941 (2nd half of 1941)], GARF, f. 7021, op. 59, d. 12, l. 52.

12 Yatsiv, "Drohobych: the City of Oil Fields," pp. 93-94; Pohl, *Nationalsozialistische Judenverfolgung in Ostgalizien*, p. 47.

13 Pohl, *Nationalsozialistische Judenverfolgung in Ostgalizien*, pp. 47, 54, 64, 70; Kruglov and Dean, "Drohobycz," pp. 774-775; Yatsiv, "Drohobych: the City of Oil Fields," p. 94.

14 Yatsiv, "Drohobych: the City of Oil Fields," pp. 94-95; Kruglov and Dean, "Drohobycz," p. 775; Testimony of Rutka Hirschberg, AŻIH, 301/1129, p. 1; Testimony of Kazia Schneckendorf, YVA, O.3/1356, p. 8; Testimony of Janusz Fleischer, YVA, O.3/1314, p. 7.

15 Kruglov and Dean, "Drohobycz," p. 774; Yatsiv, "Drohobych: the City of Oil Fields," p. 95. The figures for Kreis Drohobycz are from a 1943 statistical publication:

Amtliches Gemeinde- und Dorfverzeichnis für das Generalgouvernement auf Grund der Summarischen Bevölkerungsbestandsaufnahme am 1. März 1943 (Krakow, 1943).

16 Dmytro Bilyy, "In Drohobych under German Occupation," in Hladylovych et al., *Drohobych County: The Land of Ivan Franko*, p. 110 (Ukrainian); Yatsiv, "Drohobych: the City of Oil Fields," p. 95.

17 Testimony of Adela Bar-Eli (copy of YVA, O.3/7656), AIPN, BU 2323/1214, p. 8.

18 Capitalized in original.

19 GARF, f. 7021, op. 59, d. 5. Quoted in *Ustrój Gminy Żydowskiej w Drohobyczu, Drohobycz, 10.02.1942 r.* [The organizational system of the Jewish Community in Drohobycz], GARF, f. 7021, op. 59, d. 10, ll. 3-8; *Zarządzenie Judenratu w Drohobyczu, Drohobycz, 12.03.1942* [Judenrat order on the formation and structure of departments to perform the responsibilities of the Jewish Community in Drohobycz], GARF, f. 7021, op. 59, d. 10, ll. 13-18.

20 *Pismo Wydziału Organizacyjnego Żydowskiej Rady w Drohobyczu z 26 listopada 1941 r. do Naczelników wydziałów Żydowskiej Rady w Drohobyczu* [Letter from the Organizational Department of the Jewish Council in Drohobycz to the Heads of the departments of the Jewish Council in Drohobycz, dated November 26, 1941], GARF, f. 7021, op. 59, d. 10, l. 40.

21 Testimony of Janusz Fleischer, YVA, O.3/1314, p. 7; Testimony of Kazia Schneckendorf, YVA, O.3/1356, p. 9; Andrzej Chciuk, *Atlantyda: opowieść o Wielkim Księstwie Bałaku* (Łomianki, 2015), p. 108.

22 *Sprawozdanie Sekcji dla Spraw Kahalnych z czynności za czas od 16 do 31 października 1941 r.* [Report on the activities of the Section for Kehilla Matters for the period from October 16 to 31, 1941], GARF, f. 7021, op. 59, d. 5, l. 21 verso.

23 Żydowska Służba Porządkowa – *Sprawozdanie za miesiąc październik 1941 r., Drohobycz, 5 listopada 1941 r.* [Jewish Service for the Maintenance of Order: Report for the month of October; Drohobycz, November 5, 1941], GARF, f. 7021, op. 59, d. 5, l. 26.

24 *Sprawozdanie z 3 listopada 1941 r. Sekcji Kontroli i Zażaleń oraz Komisji Odwoławczej-Podatkowej przy Radzie Żydowskiej w Drohobyczu za czasokres od dnia 29 września do 31 października 1941 r.* (Report dated November 3, 1941 of the Audit and Complaints Section and the Fiscal Appeals Commission at the Jewish Council in Drohobycz for the period from September 29 [date barely legible on the microfilm] to October 31, 1941), GARF, f. 7021, op. 59, d. 5, ll. 28-30 verso.

25 Żydowska Służba Porządkowa – *Sprawozdanie za czas od 16/XI do 15/XII 1941, Drohobycz, 22.12.1941* [Jewish Service for the Maintenance of Order: Report for the period from Nov. 16 to Dec. 15, 1941], GARF, f. 7021, op. 59, d. 13, ll. 33-36; Żydowska Służba Porządkowa – *Sprawozdanie za czas od 16/XII – 31 XII 1941, Drohobycz. 08.01.1942* [Jewish Service for the Maintenance of Order: Report for the period from Dec. 16 to Dec. 31, 1941], GARF, f. 7021, op. 59, d. 2, l. 38.

26 *Graphische Darstellung der Bewegung der jüdischer Einwohnerzahl in Drohobycz, Drohobycz, 11.11.1942*, GARF, f. 7021, op. 59, d. 12, l. 61. The document specifies the number

of Jews in Drohobycz in August 1941: 13,500. In late June and early July 1941, the number of Jewish residents of Drohobycz may actually have been greater, given the fact that several dozen Jews were murdered in July, which influenced the Jewish population statistics for August. Furthermore, we do not have precise information on the number of Jews who left the city before the appointment of the Judenrat and consequently were not included in the population change statistics compiled by that body.

27 *Sprawozdanie Wydziału Ewidencji Ludności za czas do 2 listopada 1941 roku* [Report of the Demographic Records Department for the period ending November 2, 1941; undated], GARF, f. 7021, op. 59, d. 5, l. 13.

28 *Sprawozdanie Wydziału Ewidencji Ludności za czas do 2 listopada 1941 roku* [Report of the Demographic Records Department for the period ending November 2, 1941; undated, filed November 4, 1941], GARF, f. 7021, op. 59, d. 5, l. 13; *Sprawozdanie Wydziału Ewidencji Ludności za czas do 17 listopada 1941 r.* [Report of the Demographic Records Department for the [two-week] period ending November 17, 1941], GARF, f. 7021, op. 59, d. 11, l. 19; *Sprawozdanie Wydziału Ewidencji Ludności za czas do 2/XII 1941* [Report of the Demographic Records Department for the period ending Dec. 2, 1941], GARF, f. 7021, op. 59, d. 11, l. 37; *Sprawozdanie Wydziału Ewidencji Ludności za czas do dnia 17/XII 1941* [Report of the Demographic Records Department for the period ending Dec. 17, 1941], GARF, f. 7021, op. 59, d. 13, l. 18.

29 *Sprawozdanie Sekretariatu Rady Żydowskiej za I połowę listopada 1941 r., Drohobycz, 17.11.1941* [Report of the Secretariat of the Jewish Council for the first half of November 1941], GARF, f. 7021, op. 59, d. 11, l. 16.

30 Berenstein, "Eksterminacja ludności żydowskiej," pp. 14-15.

31 *Sprawozdanie Wydziału Ewidencji Ludności za czas do 6/I 1942 r., Drohobycz, 07.01.1942* [Report of the Demographic Records Department for the period ending on June 2, 1942], GARF, f. 7021, op. 59, d. 2, unnumbered leaf. In one of its reports, the County Committee for Jewish Social Aid in Drohobycz indicates that there were 12,781 Jews in town in January 1942. That number allegedly included at least 1,000 war refugees and inhabitants of Drohobycz County. It bears pointing out that the documentation of the various Judenrat departments reflect differences in reference to the total number of the Jewish population in Drohobycz compared to the Demographic Records Department's figures. See *Wydział Aprowizacji. Kartoteka kart chlebowych i spożywczych na podstawie spisu ludności od sierpnia 1941 do końca czerwca 1942* [Provisioning Department. Register of bread and grocery cards based on the census records between August 1941 and the end of June 1942], GARF, f. 7021, op. 59, d. 12. In the present article, the Demographic Records Department's data has been chosen as the most reliable because this department kept statistical records and had them verified ex officio.

32 *Sprawozdanie z działalności Wydziału Aprowizacyjnego za październik 1941 r.* [Report on the activities of the Provisioning Department for October 1941], GARF, f. 7021, op. 59, d. 5, l. 12 verso; *Sprawozdanie z działalności Wydziału Aprowizacyjnego za miesiąc listopad 1941 r.* [Report on the activities of the Provisioning Department for November 1941], GARF, f. 7021, op. 59, d. 11, l. 30.

33 *Sprawozdanie z działalności Wydziału Aprowizacyjnego za październik 1941 r.*, GARF, f. 7021, op. 59, d. 5, l. 11.

34 Ibid.

35 Ibid., l. 12.

36 *Sprawozdanie z 3 listopada 1941 r. Sekcji Kontroli i Zażaleń oraz Komisji Odwoławczej-Podatkowej przy Radzie Żydowskiej w Drohobyczu za czasokres od dnia 29 września* (date barely legible on the microfilm) *do 31 października 1941 r.*, GARF, f. 7021, op. 59, d. 5, l. 30 verso.

37 *Sprawozdanie z działalności Wydziału Aprowizacyjnego za miesiąc listopad 1941 r.*, GARF, f. 7021, op. 59, d. 11, l. 29 verso. It is noteworthy that Hersz Bettman mentions in his testimony that he received 200 grams of bread as payment for work; he would go to the Judenrat to collect it (Testimony of Hersz Bettman, YVA, O.3/2187, p. 2).

38 A different document specifies a somewhat greater quantity of potatoes allotted in November: 31,734 kg. See *Sprawozdanie z działalności Wydziału Aprowizacyjnego za miesiąc grudzień 1941 r.* [Report on the activities of the Provisioning Department for December 1941], GARF, f. 7021, op. 59, d. 2, ll. 30-31.

39 *Sprawozdanie z działalności Wydziału Aprowizacyjnego za miesiąc listopad 1941 r.*, GARF, f. 7021, op. 59, d. 11, l. 29.

40 *Sprawozdanie z działalności Wydziału Aprowizacyjnego za miesiąc grudzień 1941 r.*, GARF, f. 7021, op. 59, d. 2, ll. 30-31.

41 Testimony of Adela Bar-Eli (copy of YVA, O.3/7656), AIPN, BU 2323/1214, p. 19.

42 *Sprawozdanie półroczne Wydziału Opieki Społecznej Rady Żydowskiej w Drohobyczu (za czas od 1/7-31/12 1941)* [Semiannual report of the Social Welfare Department of the Jewish Council in Drohobycz for the period from July 1 to December 31, 1941], GARF, f. 7021, op. 59, d. 10, l. 66.

43 The word is barely legible on the microfilm.

44 These are the dates specified in the source, despite the fact that the report formally covers the period between late September and November 2, 1941.

45 *Sprawozdanie z działalności Wydziału Opieki Społecznej za czas od 29 września do 2 listopada 1941 r.* [Report of the Social Welfare Department for the period from September 29 (date barely legible) to November 2, 1941], GARF, f. 7021, op. 59, d. 5, l. 3.

46 Ibid.

47 Ibid, l. 4.

48 Ibid., ll. 4-5.

49 *Sprawozdanie półroczne Wydziału Opieki Społecznej Rady Żydowskiej w Drohobyczu (za czas od 1 lipca – 31 grudnia 1941)*, GARF, f. 7021, op. 59, d. 10, l. 66 recto and verso; *Wydział Opieki Społecznej. Dożywianie w kuchniach ludowych za czas od 15*

sierpnia 1941 do 30 maja 1942 r. [Social Welfare Department. Food aid in people's kitchens for the period from August 15, 1941 to May 30, 1942], GARF, f. 7021, op. 59, d. 12, l. 21.

50 *Sprawozdanie z działalności Wydziału Opieki Społecznej za czas od 29 września do 2 listopada 1941 r.*, GARF, f. 7021, op. 59, d. 5, l. 5.

51 Ibid., ll. 5-6.

52 Testimony of Adela Bar-Eli (copy of YVA, O.3/7656), AIPN, BU 2323/1214, p. 20.

53 *Sprawozdanie z działalności Wydziału Opieki Społecznej za czas od 1 grudnia – 15 grudnia 1941 r.* [Report of the Social Welfare Department for the period from December 1 – December 15, 1941], GARF, f. 7021, op. 59, d. 13, ll. 8-10.

54 Ibid., l. 10 verso. The death by starvation figures are from *Sprawozdanie Wydziału Sanitarnego za pierwszą połowę grudnia 1941 r., Drohobycz, 17.12.1941* [Report of the Sanitary Department for the first half of December 1941], GARF, f. 7021, op. 59, d. 13, l. 24.

55 GARF, f. 7021, op. 59, d. 10; untitled document without date or pagination, follows leaf 67 in the file.

56 *Sprawozdanie półroczne Wydziału Opieki Społecznej Rady Żydowskiej w Drohobyczu (za czas od 1 lipca – 31 grudnia 1941)*, GARF, f. 7021, op. 59, d. 10, ll. 66-67. The destitution of the Jewish population in late 1941 and early 1942 is confirmed by other sources. See *List dr Leona Tannenbauma z Drohobycza do Prezesa Żydowskiej Samopomocy Społecznej, Drohobycz, 20.01.1942*, AŻIH, 211/362, pp. 10-11.

57 Testimony of Regina (Majzels) Leiter, YVA, O.3/1651, p. 6. Leiter was a great granddaughter of Dow Ber Meisels, the Chief Rabbi of Krakow who supported the Polish national liberation movement in the ninieteenth century. Her family lived in Drohobycz. Her parents and sisters – Golda, Jochewet, and Brajdel – all died during the German occupation. Regina Leiter was the only family member to survive the war (ibid., pp. 6-9).

58 *Sprawozdanie z działalności Oddziału dla spraw robotniczych i ubezpieczenia społecznego za czas od 1 do 15 listopada 1941, Drohobycz, 19.11.1941* [Report on the activities of the Division for Workers' Matters and Social Insurance for the period from November 1 to 15, 1941], GARF, f. 7021, op. 59, d. 11, ll. 12-14.

59 *Referat Personalny – sprawozdanie za czas od 20 października do 20 grudnia br.* [Personnel Subsection: Report for the period from October 20 to December 20, 1941], GARF, f. 7021, op. 59, d. 13, ll. 25, 30.

60 *Sprawozdanie Oddziału dla spraw robotniczych i ubezpieczenia społecznego za czas od 16 listopada 1941 r. do 15 grudnia 1941 r.* [Report of the Division for Workers' Matters and Social Insurance for the period from November 16 to December 15, 1941], GARF, f. 7021, op. 59, d. 13, l. 19.

61 Ibid.

62 *Sprawozdanie z 3 listopada 1941 r. Wydziału Sanitarnego za miesiąc październik 1941 r.* [Report of the Sanitary Department for October, dated November 3, 1941], GARF, f. 7021, op. 59, d. 5, l. 17.

63 *Sekcja dla Spraw Kahalnych. Sprawozdanie z 1 listopada 1941 r. z czynności za czas od 16 do 31 października 1941 r.* [Section for Kehilla Matters. Report on activities for the period from October 16 to 31, dated November 1, 1941], GARF, f. 7021, op. 59, d. 5, l. 20.

64 Ibid.

65 Table: Śmiertelność ludności żydowskiej w Drohobyczu i okolicy za czas od 4 lipca 1941 r. do 15 sierpnia 1941 r., GARF, f. 7021, op. 59, d. 12, l. 41; Table: Śmiertelność ludności żydowskiej w Drohobyczu i okolicy za czas od 16 sierpnia 1941 r. do 31 sierpnia 1941 [Mortality in the Jewish population in Drohobycz and adjacent areas during the period from August 16 to August 31, 1941], GARF, f. 7021, op. 59, d. 12, l. 42.

66 Although the commentary on the July-August 1941 statistics also mentions 18 individuals buried in the courtyard of the NKVD/NKGB investigative prison, they are not accounted for in the official mortality figure for July and August, as the Judenrat reached the number solely on the basis of witness accounts. These individuals were described as "victims of excesses," but they were in fact pogrom victims and were buried in the inner courtyard of the NKGB building in July 1941.

67 Table: Śmiertelność ludności żydowskiej w Drohobyczu i okolicy za czas od 1 września 1941 r. do 15 września 1941 [Mortality in the Jewish population in Drohobycz and adjacent areas during the period from September 1 to September 15, 1941], GARF, f. 7021, op. 59, d. 12, l. 43; Table: Śmiertelność ludności żydowskiej w Drohobyczu i okolicy za czas od 16 września 1941 r. do 31 września 1941 [Mortality in the Jewish population in Drohobycz and adjacent areas during the period from September 16 to September 31, 1941], GARF, f. 7021, op. 59, d. 12, l. 44.

68 Table: Śmiertelność ludności żydowskiej w Drohobyczu i okolicy za czas od 1 października 1941 r. do 15 października 1941 [Mortality in the Jewish population in Drohobycz and adjacent areas during the period from October 1 to October 15, 1941], GARF, f. 7021, op. 59, d. 12, l. 45; Table: Śmiertelność ludności żydowskiej w Drohobyczu i okolicy za czas od 16 *października 1941 r. do 31 października 1941*, [Mortality in the Jewish population in Drohobycz and adjacent areas during the period from October 16 to October 31, 1941] GARF, f. 7021, op. 59, d. 12, l. 46.

69 The Sanitary Department's report for October 1941 provides a figure of 43 deceased. Establishing the cause of this discrepancy has proved impossible. The Judenrat's tables specify a higher number: 50 deceased in October. Source: *Sprawozdanie z 3 listopada 1941 r. Wydziału Sanitarnego za miesiąc październik 1941 r.*, GARF, f. 7021, op. 59, d. 5, l. 17.

70 Table: Śmiertelność ludności żydowskiej w Drohobyczu i okolicy za czas od 1 listopada 1941 r. do 15 listopada 1941 [Mortality in the Jewish population in Drohobycz and adjacent areas during the period from November 1 to November 15, 1941], GARF, f. 7021, op. 59, d. 12, l. 48; Table: Śmiertelność ludności żydowskiej w Drohobyczu i okolicy za czas od 16 listopada 1941 r. do 30 listopada 1941 [Mortality in the Jewish population in Drohobycz and adjacent areas during the period from November 16 to November 30, 1941], GARF, f. 7021, op. 59, d.12, l. 49.

71 Somewhat higher figures are provided in the monthly report of the Judenrat Sanitary

Department for November 1941: 109 deceased, including 74 men and 35 women. Starvation was the cause of death for 67 of them. See *Sprawozdanie Wydziału Sanitarnego za listopad 1941, Drohobycz, 02.12.1941* [Report of the Sanitary Department for November 1941], GARF, f. 7021, op. 59, d. 11, l. 42. The number of deceased indicated in the Judenrat statistics did not include those killed in the *Aktion* conducted on November 22, in which the Germans executed a group of people by shooting in the woods outside the village of Bronica. These victims were not recorded in the statistics of the Cemetery Commission and Records Department.

72 *Sprawozdanie Wydziału Metryki i Komisji Cmentarnej za czas od 1 do 15 grudnia 1941 r.*, [Report of the Cemetery Commission and Records Department for the period from December 1 to 15, 1941], GARF, f. 7021, op. 59, d. 13, l. 3. Identical figures for the first half of December appear in *Śmiertelność ludności żydowskiej w Drohobyczu i okolicy za czas od 16 grudnia 1941 r. do 31 grudnia 1941 r.* [Mortality in the Jewish population in Drohobycz and adjacent areas for the period from December 16, 1941 to December, 1941], GARF, f. 7021, op. 59, d. 12, ll. 50-51; *Sprawozdanie z czynności Wydziału Metryki i Komisji Cmentarnej za czas od 16 do 31 grudnia 1941 r.* [Report of the Cemetery Commission and Records Department for the period from December 16 to 15, 1941], GARF, f. 7021, op. 59, d. 2, l. 3. Somewhat lower figures for the first half of December are provided by the report of the Sanitary Department: *Sprawozdanie Wydziału Sanitarnego za pierwszą połowę grudnia 1941 r., Drohobycz, 17.12.1941*, GARF, f. 7021, op. 59, d. 13, l. 24.

73 Numbers for the deceased in Drohobycz that differ somewhat from those provided by the table are given for July-August, September, and November 1941 in the February 1942 letter sent by the County Committee for Jewish Social Aid in Drohobycz to the Jewish Social Aid organization in Krakow. According to the information provided there, a total of 50 people died in July and August, 30 in September, and 103 in November. There is no way of identifying the County Committee's source for these figures, but they were definitely not the product of their own statistics. For this reason, the table is based on the Judenrat's data. See *List do Żydowskiej Samopomocy* [in Krakow], *Drohobycz, 24.02.1942*, AŻIH, 211/362, p. 22.

74 *Sprawozdanie z czynności Wydziału Metryki i Komisji Cmentarnej za czas od 16 do 31 grudnia 1941 r.*, GARF, f. 7021, op. 59, d. 2, l. 4.

75 *Wydział Zdrowia. Działalność szpitala żydowskiego za czas od 1 lipca 1941 do 30 czerwca 1942* [Health Department. Activities of the Jewish Hospital during the period from July 1, 1941 to June 30, 1942] GARF, f. 7021, op. 59, d. 12, l. 10; *Jewish Hospital in Drohobycz, https://sztetl.org.pl/en/towns/d/814-drohobycz/101-organizations-and-associations/80873-jewish-hospital-drohobycz* (accessed June 27, 2021).

76 This number includes three patients at the epidemic hospital.

77 *Wydział Zdrowia. Działalność szpitala żydowskiego za czas od 1 lipca 1941 do 30 czerwca 1942*, GARF, f. 7021, op. 59, d. 12, l. 10.

78 *Sprawozdanie pracy ambulatorium żydowskiego za miesiąc październik 1941*, [Report on the activities of the Jewish Outpatient Clinic for October 1941], GARF, f. 7021, op. 59, d. 5, l. 9. The same document is reproduced on leaf 25 of the same file.

79 The sum total of the various figures is 2,900. It has proven impossible to identify the table rubric containing the error. Given that the quoted document consistently specifies the total number of all medical consultations as 2,970 in various tabular statements, this figure is also cited in the text of this article.

80 *Sprawozdanie Wydziału Sanitarnego za pierwszą połowę grudnia 1941 r., Drohobycz, 17.12.1941*, GARF, f. 7021, op. 59, d. 13, l. 24 verso; GARF, f. 7021, l. 59, d. 13, l. 20 [report from December 1941, title barely legible].

81 The last three digits are barely legible. Source: *Wydział Zdrowia. Działalność ambulatorium żydowskiego za czas od dnia 29 sierpnia 1941 do 30 czerwca 1942* [Health Department. Report on the activities of the Jewish outpatient clinic for the period from August 29, 1941 to June 30, 1942], GARF, f. 7021, l. 59, d. 12, l. 12.

82 *Sprawozdanie z 3 listopada 1941 r. Wydziału Mieszkaniowo-Komunalnego za czas od 16 do 31 października 1941 r.* [Report of the Department of Housing and Communal Services for the period from October 16 to 30, 1941, dated November 3, 1941], GARF, f. 7021, op. 59, d. 5, l. 15; *Sprawozdanie Wydziału Mieszkaniowego za czas od 1/XI do 15/XI 1941* [Report of the Housing Department for the time from November 1 to 15, 1941], GARF, f. 7021, op. 59, d. 11, l. 8.

83 Testimony of Adela Bar-Eli (copy of YVA, O.3/7656), AIPN, BU 2323/1214, p. 10.

84 Kruglov and Dean, "Drohobycz," p. 775; Testimony of Jakub Gernstenfeld, AŻIH, 301/1177, p. 3; Testimony of Renata (Edikus) Fleischer, YVA, O.3/2553, pp. 3-4.

85 *Sprawozdanie z działalności Oddziału dla spraw robotniczych i ubezpieczenia społecznego za czas od 16 listopada do 15 grudnia 1941 r.*, GARF, f. 7021, op. 59, d. 13, l. 19.

86 *Sprawozdanie Sekretariatu Rady Żydowskiej za grudzień 1941 r., Drohobycz,* [?] *styczeń 1941* [Report of the Secretariat of the Jewish Council for December 1941, Drohobycz, January [day illegible], 1941], GARF, f. 7021, op. 59, d. 2, l. 1.

87 Żydowska Służba Porządkowa – *Sprawozdanie za czas od 16/XII – 31 XII 1941*, Drohobycz. 08.01.1942, GARF, f. 7021, op. 59, d. 2, l. 41.

88 Testimony of Adela Bar-Eli, AIPN, BU 2323/1214, pp. 10-11.

Alina Molisak

Lviv and Galician Spaces during the Holocaust: Borwicz, Frenkel, and Ginczanka

Many refugees sought shelter in Lviv after the outbreak of the Second World War. This problem primarily concerned Jews. In March 1941, more than 39,000 so-called "refugees" registered in the city, including 26,000 Jews who arrived in Lviv after September 1939.[1]

One of those in search for shelter was Michał Borwicz,[2] a writer and literary critic from Kraków, as well as Zuzanna Ginczanka,[3] a poet from Równe who lived in Warsaw in the 1930s and who now viewed Lviv as an opportunity for survival. Mieczysław R. Frenkel[4] was connected with Lviv in a different manner as in the interwar period he was a member of the local literary community. I point to these three authors who were already well-known in the artistic milieu before the outbreak of the war as I would like to draw particular attention to their texts. Their works are connected not only by the specificity of their experience, a shorter or longer stay in Lviv under Soviet rule (after September 17, 1939), but also by their later experience of German occupation. An additional binding element is the fact that the authors wrote their works either during the war (Ginczanka) or shortly after (Borwicz, Frenkel).[5] All of the authors touch on the time of the Holocaust and the relations between the ethnic groups that inhabited the territories occupied by the German army – the topography of these texts deals primarily with Lviv and its environs[6]. The main thread that I want to draw attention to is the relationship between Poles, Jews, and Ukrainians at that time. It should also be noted that before World War II, the city itself was inhabited by many ethnic groups - as emphasized by Christoph Mick: "The Polish census of 1921 questioned respondents about their nationality. Out of 219,388 inhabitants of Lvi'v, 136,519 (62.4 percent) considered themselves Poles, 19,855 (9.2 percent) considered themselves Ruthenians, 60, 431 (27.6 percent) Jewish and 1,626 (0.8 percent) German."[7]

It should be remembered, of course, that relations between these ethnic groups were not without controversy — Ukrainian aspirations to establish their own state met with violent Polish opposition (1918); there was antisemitism and violence against Jews, which sometimes assumed brutal forms (pogroms in Galicia during the First World War, a pogrom in Lviv in 1918). The late 1930s were also a time of interethnic conflicts in Poland, mainly related to the nationalist ideology of the authorities of the time. Without losing sight of such a complicated historical context, I want to point to interesting literary texts that were written after the outbreak of the Second World War.

1. The Space of Language

As I mentioned, Borwicz spent the time between September 1939 and September 1943 in Lviv, which first remained under Soviet and, after the outbreak of the German-Russian war, under Nazi control. This allows us to situate most of his texts published shortly after 1945 – even when they refer to more general issues and phenomena – in the space of Galicia. The years Borwicz spent in Lviv under Soviet rule are described in a very interesting memoir *Inżynierowie dusz* (Soul Engineers) that he later wrote in exile in France.[8] The next period –when Lviv was under German occupation – received more of his attention as immediately after the war, Borwicz issued very significant publications, closely related to his personal experience, showing reflections of a broader nature, and gathering recollections of a very careful and penetrating view of the events of the time.

In his introduction to late memoirs *Spod szubienicy w teren* (From the Gallows to the Field), Borwicz indicates that he made his first extensive records of the occupation years while still in the Janowska concentration camp in Lviv. Borwicz emphasizes that it was thanks to these "notebooks, very shortly after the war, in 1946, two of my publications appeared ... *Uniwersytet zbirów* [The University of Criminals] and *Literatura w obozie* [Literature in the Camp]."[9] When announcing the eclectic character of the volume, in which Borwicz included texts written at different times and published in the émigré press, he notes that the memoir part chronologically covers his later fate, namely the unsuccessful hanging, escape from the Janowska camp, reaching Krakow, and later underground and partisan activity. This personal history is supplemented by sections devoted to the postwar fate of the Polish Socialist Party (PPS) party milieu and by texts concerning his return after years to subjects linked to the experience of violence in occupied Lviv, which was connected with Borwicz's appearance as a witness during later trials against Nazi perpetrators. Borwicz's memoir about his stay in the Janowska camp bears the symbolic title *Uniwersytet zbirów*. We may understand this description of a peculiar "education" as an ironic reference to the idea of *Bildung*, an important concept in German culture. However, both this small publication and the texts included in *Literatura w obozie* mainly focus on his observations and experiences connected with his stay in a closed, secluded space, in which violence and suffering became part of everyday life. I wish to especially highlight Borwicz's work published just after the war as we may view it to be similarly precursory to Victor Klemperer's well-known book *LTI – Notizbuch eines Philologen*.[10] Borwicz titled his essay related to the inciting of anti-Jewish aggression and violence during the Holocaust years as *Organizowanie wściekłości* (The Organization of Rage).[11]

When describing Polish-Jewish relations from the early stages of the war, Borwicz indicates that "the Polish popular masses, shocked (in the literal sense of the word) by the defeat, became even more susceptible to anti-Jewish slogans; such a reception … was later to be widely used by all antisemitic demagogues, against all Jews."[12]

One of Frenkel's Lviv stories speaks of hatred that was not only the result of modern propaganda but also stemmed from a tradition of antisemitism passed down from generation to generation that only gained in intensity with time. The narrative entitled "Sądny dzień" (Judgment Day) notes the common activity of Jews in hiding and seeking refuge in the space of Catholic churches: "In churches, sacristans with candles in their hands go around the choir after vespers, climb the winding stairs to the towers; in the evening, you can see from the street how the light is coming out of the increasingly higher hatches; it is the sacristans, fearing reprisals, who search the nooks and crannies, looking for Jews."[13] Not only were church employees reluctant to assist the persecuted. Others, called "spectators," are characterized by highly negative emotions, which stem – among other things – from the fact that "the mute fear in the eyes of the pursued evokes paroxysms of laughter … among those taught for hundreds of years hatred [for the Jews] passed from father to son like a will or an estate."[14]

Moreover, Borwicz highlights the very different aspects of language, indicating how Nazi propaganda was systematically applied in cultural spaces. He also stresses that these forms of aggression were accepted by parts of the societies of Central and Eastern Europe: "The 'organization of anger of non-Jews against Jews, regulated by the pedantic instructions of the Nazi police authorities, continued throughout the war and intensified week after week in all countries occupied by Germany. The murders were accompanied by a methodical campaign of hatred against the murdered."[15] Furthermore, Borwicz diagnoses the consequences of both the instrumental use of language to create anti-Jewish violence and the results of such propaganda, which accompanied the killing of Jews, depriving them of their right to exist. Borwicz regards the Holocaust as an epoch of radical change and destruction of morality:

> the oppressed were infected by the oppressors …; the occupier used such means and such methods that reversed the healthy way of thinking and feeling. It shattered natural notions and brakes. It mutilated not only those who were baited but also the ones who baited. The oppressor did it so profoundly that the mutilated did not notice their own disability.[16]

Borwicz uses the name "laboratories of poisons" to describe various pseudo-scientific institutions (operating before the outbreak of the war and almost during its entire duration, generously subsidized), and abundant publications of researchers (with professorial titles), which proved everything that was demanded of them.[17] Borwicz indicates that antisemitism functioned in many forms. The tradition of European antisemitism was superimposed on its successive forms: from pseudo-scientific books to the "reptile" press published intensively in local languages (to reach as many recipients as possible). Borwicz recognizes that such activities were one of the main means of destroying the conquered.[18] In Borwicz's opinion, these "laboratories of poisons" produced effective psycho-manipulation, which allowed the Germans to focus attention on Jews as the most essential figure of the enemy, and after the outbreak of war, even to accuse Jews of causing it and its consequences: the destruction and the suffering. The effectiveness of verbal aggression was reinforced by the utter destruction of logic, the dismantling of rational thought, the use of all available tools of influence to strengthen antisemitism: pictures, photomontage, posters, slogans, brochures, leaflets, the press, loudspeakers mounted on street poles and lamps ("szczekaczki"), and the cinema. Moreover, he foregrounds the adjustment of the means of propaganda to specific social groups.[19]

Borwicz's account of Polish-Jewish relations indicates the successive stages of persecution of the Jewish population and brings forth certain analogies used against the Polish population, namely "nur für Deutsche," teaching bans, and confinement in concentration camps. Borwicz believes that such repressions that affected the Polish population as direct witnesses of the persecution of Jews should have resulted in rational thinking "evoking reflexes of only sympathy and compassion."[20] However, the events and attitudes that Borwicz himself could observe proved that this was not the case, both in the Nazi-occupied Lviv and later, when he was in hiding after escaping from the Janowska concentration camp. Borwicz precisely indicates not only effective propaganda and the strengthening of antisemitic beliefs but also the process accompanying the separation of the Jewish population from the rest, the process of the gradual perception of Jews no longer as "aliens" but as an increasingly "abstract" group. In the personal dimension, the face of a specific neighbor "disappeared," and Jews ceased to be viewed as familiar individuals who had previously functioned in common spaces. People started to see "the Jewry" only as a generalization.[21]

The susceptibility and effectiveness of antisemitic propaganda is evidenced, among other things, by a note in one of the volumes of the Ringelblum Archive, in which a reporter describes the mood of the Polish population in German-occupied Galicia with these words:

> The trains were filled with smugglers-Aryans. The content of their conversations was most often the Jewish question, and they were so marked by antisemitism and some outright fanatical hatred of Jews that it surprised me. "There is only one benefit from the Germans for us – that was the conclusion of all the discussions on the subject – how to deal with the Jews."[22]

In characterizing the non-Jewish inhabitants of the occupied territories, Borwicz notes that,

> consciously or unconsciously prepared to absorb the German poison, they became its disseminators – perhaps subjectively even out of "conviction." In turn, they influenced others who had no benefit from it. In this way, a psychic climate was created which doubtlessly facilitated the adoption of suggestions spread by the occupant.[23]

Notably, Borwicz emphasizes the characteristic of the population subjected to the influence of propaganda: the conscious or unconscious readiness to accept and embrace the views. Such an attitude of non-Jewish inhabitants of this part of occupied Europe proves the existence of already well-established antisemitic views.

Describing the peculiar hierarchization of inhabitants the Germans implemented in the conquered territories, Borwicz accurately captures the workings of a certain mechanism of influence on local communities:

> A thoroughly perfidious system aimed at demoralizing the persecuted. The deeper the demoralization, the easier the task of the Nazi henchmen. The second aim was to breed burning mutual hatred between the victims, which would make it impossible for them to jointly fight against the source murderer.[24]

The lasting effect of this social segregation and hierarchization was the significant strengthening of antisemitic attitudes, a peculiar legitimization of anti-Jewish violence, not only perpetrated by the Nazis but also that which could be perpetrated by everyone else. As a result,

> In this system, the Jews were a vent for others' bitterness. By giving them the opportunity to cooperate in the pursuit and torment of the Jews, Hitlerism wanted to create for the rest of its victims a useful substitute for its own purposes of "importance" or "superiority." An illusion intended to obscure [for non-Jewish victims] the fact that they themselves are the poor victims.[25]

This gave rise to a way of thinking and perceiving wartime reality similar to clan structures: the dominant belief was in the priority of personal gain (or the gain of a small group of one's own), achieved at any price. Or, as Borwicz assesses it, with the help of antisemitism, Nazis "bred unscrupulousness."[26]

We may also find interesting remarks on interethnic relations during the occupation years in Borewicz's later memoirs *Spod szubienicy w teren* written in emigration. In the abovementioned records, Borwicz also recalls various meetings just after his arrival in Krakow, after his escape from the Janowska concentration camp. Let us note the synthetic account of the statement of Maria Hochberg-Mariańska, who as Borwicz notes, "was active during this period mainly in the thorny area of helping Jews in hiding."[27] Borwicz characterizes her attitude in the following way:

> During meetings she speaks with her usual directness the truth about
> the disproportion between the needs and the proper range of help,
> she bitterly argues about failures, about negligence. She persistently
> organizes and fixes the problems of those in her charge. She runs,
> solicits, and prevents; she reaches, delivers, and comforts.[28]

We should note these words because they testify to the disproportion already perceived at that time, to the different – even in the circles of those who helped – treatment of the conspirators in hiding and the Jews in need of help. Borwicz indicates the fundamental dilemma and probably the greatest difficulty in saving Jewish lives: "For the average fugitive, the permanent difficulties began only after successful escape and – in most cases – were summed up with a question as simple as it was hopeless: "Where to run? How to hide?"[29] While Polish escapees from concentration camps or prisons could – at least to a large extent – count on a network of acquaintances or relatives, Jews escaping from closed ghettos or camps had much fewer chances of obtaining help, especially selfless help.

As Borwicz himself stresses, even when writing about himself:

> The basic feature of living on "Aryan papers" was the concern
> about concealing one's Jewish origin. At stake was one's own life so
> any carelessness could end with death. At the same time, so many

different factors awaited the unmasking of the person in hiding that this concern seeped into every movement, into every step.[30]

Borwicz recalls that his involvement in the leftist underground and his various functions were conducive to numerous travels and contacts, especially in the resistance movement in the Polish provinces. However, Borwicz very clearly indicates that "there happened no dangerous accusation of me being guilty of the crime … of Jewish origin. As a result, I did not experience blackmail, buying off, bargaining, wandering, or all the other adventures from the notorious repertoire of Jews with Aryan papers."[31] He clearly articulates here the fundamental difference that is most often marginalized or passed over in Polish memory, namely the fundamental difference between the Polish fate and the Jewish fate in an era when Jewish existence was equal to a death sentence.[32]

2. The Space of Matter

During the Holocaust, Jews were deprived of their properties, houses, and workshops, their movable assets were taken away from them, in fact they were deprived of everything that had any value.[33] It is important to note an important aspect of these actions for it denotes not the category of possessions but actually the chances for survival: "Taking away things and money was taking away life."[34]

Moreover, in the essays in the volume *Organizowanie wściekłości*, Borwicz underlines that Nazi propaganda gained acceptance reinforced through everyday experiences. One such experience was the seizing of property left behind by the captured Jews. Poles who settled in previously Jewish apartments and workshops usually justified this gesture by the fact that it could improve their existence in this exceptional situation. In the chapter entitled "Funkcje łupu po ofiarach" (The Functions of Loot After Victims), Borwicz observes that "the Germans were practical. The mass murder of Jews was preceded and accompanied by the imposition of (enormous) tributes."[35] Borwicz lists the forms of Jewish property seizure such as requisitions of movable property or deprivation of property. At the same time, Borwicz notes that "it is quite understandable that this total plunder of material possessions from the several-million-strong mass of the murdered could not have happened without scattering waste along the way."[36] According to

Borwicz, the local population – Poles and Ukrainians – came into possession of what he calls "waste," meaning less valuable Jewish objects or those that did not fall into the hands of the occupants. However, when enumerating those forms of anti-Jewish violence, Borwicz notices two more, very important ways in which non-Jewish communities made money out of the situation. The first strategy involved situations where Jews gave their belongings for safekeeping to acquaintances in the hope that they would be able to use their property to save their lives. The second strategy involved the seizure of so-called "post-Jewish" apartments, stores, and workshops.[37] According to Borwicz, the seizure of Jewish belongings or property was accompanied by an internalized conviction – derived both from Nazi propaganda and from earlier antisemitism – that "it will be better when there will be no Jews."[38] According to Borwicz, those who "got rich or took the place of the Jews" preferred not to understand "that together with these crumbs of post-German plunder, they are swallowing the poison of depravity, which in many places will lie down for many years."[39] For Borwicz, this long-lasting change of mentality among the non-Jewish population during the occupation was one of the worst consequences that accompanied the Holocaust. Borwicz writes that "those who benefited from the "revival" of Poland became adherents of racism."[40]

In Frenkel's volume of short stories, which contains thirty-five texts, we can find many in which the narrative concerns the interethnic relations of the time and the problem of depriving Jews of their property[41] I would like to draw attention to a few of them.

The protagonists of the story "Wydani bez reszty" (Utterly Given Away) about hiding Jews and getting rich are the Humenik couple. He, a Ukrainian from Volhynia, is a rather corrupt official in *Hausverwaltung* under German occupation. Dubna is a Russian housewife. They view occupation as a chance to improve their financial situation. They are hiding a Jewish couple, but when a policeman (from Silesia) visits their house due to Dubna's greed – she had cheated a market vendor – they are relieved that the Jews have taken poison. "When the Humeniuks and an undercover policeman were looking at a suit taken off a hanger, the Jews took the opportunity and ate the poison."[42] The husband's brief arrest is the only consequence.

The second story "Gdzie kogoś biją tam trzeci korzysta" (While a Dog Is Beaten Over a Bone, a Third Runs Away with It),[43] takes place in a rural setting. What testifies to the widespread knowledge and social control is the fact that "well into the evening the cottages became crowded, news spread from chimney to chimney that rich Jews-Herods came from Lviv, and with their huge amounts of luggage, they got off at Antosiowa's farmyard."[44] The Polish heroine of this story took in a trunk full of things for safekeeping, which she hid in the attic. It was to wait there for the arrival of the tenants, ladies from Lviv. Before she hides the possessions entrusted to her, she carefully and critically examines them, assessing their usefulness from a peasant's perspective. When the owners of the trunk do not show up, she decides to check what is happening with them; first she sends her son and then she herself pays a visit to the tenement house where – under the pretext of selling cheese – she learns that the apartment of her potential tenants is occupied by a German. It turns out that "there were no Jews. The janitor didn't find them. … In a town like this for people to not know anything about each other."[45] The protagonist is convinced that "the townspeople must have "really" fished off the Jews, the villagers got only these scraps."[46] However, when the Jewish owner of the trunk shows up at Antosia's house, the latter reacts strongly: "No … you have nothing at my place, nothing, everything is gone, I swear on my health; they stole it, they took it, they sent policemen to my house, they will murder me, they will put me in "jail."[47] When refusing to return even one pair of winter shoes and chasing the Jewish woman out of the house for the night, "Antosia fixed the kerchief on her head, pulled it sharply over her forehead so that people would not recognize who walks with her, and taking her to the gate … whispered: "If you show your face again, I'll call the mayor and the police, and send you to the police."[48]

In the already mentioned short story "Sądny dzień," the narrator characterizes the general plight of the Jews in Lviv in the following manner:

> The enemy watches and catches. The caretakers of houses, the fat, fat tradeswomen, the scum of basements, the scum of all classes … watch every step of their neighbors and report them, bring the police, ambush them together, greedy for loot, greedy for what is not theirs, for easy money.[49]

In many texts describing the tragic fate of the Jewish population, Frenkel emphasizes a kind of impunity and general acceptance – or even envy – felt toward those who were able to get rich. The common belief that those who help Jews receive a lavish reward is also evidenced by the narrator's remark in another story: "The peasants suspected Praxeda of getting enriched on her debt collectors, for only a fool would help such wayfarers for free; the peasants could not get over her benefits."[50]

Zuzanna Ginczanka indicates obsession with possession, accumulation by blackmail, or simple robbery of Jewish movables in an excellent poem from 1942. Published for the first time in 1946, its title references a European classic by Horace "Non omnis moriar."[51] Ginczanka foregrounds the Jewish movables that were the object of desire of the greedy Lviv caretaker, Chomin's wife, who in the poem becomes the figure of a blackmailer and shmaltsovnik.[52] Here is a direct apostrophe:

> Niech więc rzeczy żydowskie twoja dłoń wyszpera,
> Chominowo, lwowianko, dzielna żono szpicla,
> Donosicielko chyża, matko folksdojczera.
> Tobie, twoim niech służą, bo cóżby obcym.[53]

> You, Chomin's wife, the snitch's daring wife,
> Volksdeutcher's mother, swift informant, please
> Allow your hand to dig up Jewish things.
> May they serve you and yours, and not some strangers.

Ginczanka's poetic text, rich in intertextual references to both European and Polish culture, is brimming with irony.

Frenkel's short story, in which we encounter a similarly bitter ironic reference to Jewish things, is entitled "Handel dewocjonaliami" (Trade with Devotional Articles). An execution of Jews happens in a suburban space, viewed by young bystanders as a performance: "Through open bushes the boys from Żłoby and Krzywczyce watched from a distance the executions of Jews. … Girls also came to look at the "Jewish spectacle."[54] While Frenkel locates specific crime scenes here, he records a more general reflection later in this narrative:

> Near the execution sites, kids from the surrounding streets and
> alleys would rummage through piles of things abandoned by
> the victims or their torturers. ... They collected pocketknives,
> tin cigarette cases, identification cards in celluloid covers, cigar
> boxes, birth certificates, photographs, glasses in cardboard cases,
> photos of entire groups, empty trinkets. ... They stuffed their
> cotton pants' pockets with them, the girls collected them in
> baskets, brought them home in abundance, the elders looked
> through the trophies.[55]

Even the most dilapidated pieces of clothing could find buyers "The last Jewish
rags, soaked with their blood, were washed by grandmothers and sold on the
market, without surcharge for the documentary value of the item."[56] The
young behave like little collectors, they exchange their trophies, and when they
cannot observe the shootings for some time – they themselves organize games
of catching Jews and murdering them. The bitter irony is most evident in the
words of one of the adult characters in the story:

> Melker, the ex-streetcar-driver, hid under his table a full box of
> Jewish documents, personal effects of the deceased. This "goody-
> goody" promised himself a lot from this collection. / "You see, Sir,
> the war will end one day. Rich Jews will come from America and
> pay big money for this last sign of life of the murdered. Then –
> bam! A basket of Jewish relics will be brought to the market, and
> they will sell out like hotcakes. They will make a man rich. Let
> them lie under the table, there will be plenty of room. They will
> pay off, Sir, they will pay off someday."[57]

3. The Space of Encounter

Using a category used in many studies (after M. L. Pratt), we may point to
the peculiar "contact zones" in the years of German occupation.[58] One such
contact zone during the war years was the urban space, a place where non-
Jewish inhabitants and Jews in hiding could come into contact. The risk of

encountering someone from prewar times was very common and was connected with the uncertainty of the other side's reaction.

In Frenkel's story "W grobowcu" (In a Tomb) about hiding in the Lychakiv Cemetery, we can find an accurate diagnosis of those times and of the postwar years:

> No Jew will be offended if an old acquaintance does not recognize him, does not bow, does not smile with a fleeting reassuring smile. If the acquaintance recognizes the Jew, he will be angered by his Semitic vitality. For a while, he will weigh the fate of this Jew in his hand, he will wonder whether to hand him over to the authorities …. Years later, in the company of friends, this acquaintance will show off his humanitarian deed and mention the risk-taker Jew, who touched the land of the free with the foot of a slave but luckily came across him, the noble man.[59]

The interethnic relations in this perspective follow a pattern, which sometimes is framed – according to the needs in later years – as a gesture that is to testify to the kindness and empathy of non-Jewish communities.

In a significant section of his essay "Szantażyści" (The Blackmailers), Borwicz writes about attitudes that he probably had the opportunity to observe repeatedly.[60] Borwicz recognizes the importance and scale of the phenomenon directly relating to the relationship between the Polish or Ukrainian population and the Jews in hiding: "Scraps of property left behind by murdered Jews were not the only source of income. There were other sources. Many Jews … lived with "Aryan papers." As a result, a whole lot of people were busy tracking them down and exposing them."[61] Borwicz clearly perceives the emergence of unethical behavior, manifested precisely in the peculiar zone of interethnic contact, which – according to the diagnosis – were quite common. Borwicz clearly indicates that:

> It is not … about declared spies and agents. There appeared blackmailers. These individuals were not concerned with "race" in any way. They did not hand over the discovered Jews to the Gestapo, but they made them pay for their discretion. They were

tireless leeches, having at their disposal thousands of fanciful ways. They had their own organizations, their own street duty, their own relays, their own messengers and contacts.[62]

Reporting on his daring escape from the Janowska concentration camp, Borwicz describes in detail all the preparations and the course of exiting the space of confinement.[63] Notably, the passage when Borwicz recalls his meeting with his helpers and rides in a crowded streetcar immediately after his escape, already with a false *Kennkarte*, at which point he also experiences the following emotions: "For a moment, the fear that – from the shoal of animated heads murmuring at each other – the mouth of a spy or the eyes of a denouncer will reach me."[64] The awareness of constant danger accompanied all those in hiding as they assumed new versions of identity. Noteworthy, it was the behavior of the local population that often led to the unmasking of a person with the false ID. We may regard both gestures and oral or written denunciations as a form of collaboration with the occupation authorities.

In the mentioned memoir *Spod szubienicy w teren*, Borwicz also describes his life during the war, including travels, a stay in the occupied Krakow, and later involvement in the activities of left-wing guerilla forces.[65] During a train trip to Krakow, shortly after his escape, repeating in his mind the new data from the false papers, Borwicz sees such a scene:

> In Przemyśl, German policemen were going through suitcases, shining flashlights in the eyes. In Tarnów, there is a commotion: a Jewish woman has been caught on the train. The passengers get off the train to get a closer look at what can still be seen. When they return, they begin an excited conversation about it: "Who would expect that they are still here," says one of the passengers with disgust.[66]

Frenkel also accurately characterizes the attitude of Polish society by insightfully writing about a fundamental issue that has received little attention to date: the phenomenon of indifference to the Holocaust. He characterizes Polish society in general, but his diagnoses stem from his observations of what happened in Galicia at the time. In the short story "Handel dewocjonaliami," Frenkel distinguishes the most common attitudes using the apt metaphor of "Polska przyziemna," which means "mundane Poland," but for the fragment below to work best, it requires the use of the literal translation of "Poland close to the ground" and "grounded:"

> Grounded Poland has always been more visible than underground Poland. There were only some rumors about underground Poland, while the grounded one was seen, heard, it was palpable, people separated themselves from underground Poland because they were not ready for its dimensions. They made a virtue out of lack. With a previously unseen indifference they watched the murders and tortures like those boys on the sands. The meager Polish *łyk* [townsperson] calculated this way: first the German will conduct fascist adaptations, arrange the country, then the German will be driven by the Anglo-Saxons, and we shall have a treat anyway.[67]

However, we may perceive differently the activities of groups hiding in the forests or small units participating in the resistance. In such cases, it is not the city or the train journey but the forest that becomes the space of interethnic contact. Borwicz writes about it in one of his later texts:

> Let us note that the Home Army absorbed almost all the main currents of the Polish resistance. As a result, its ranks also included antisemitic elements associated with the right wing. There is no doubt that the influence exerted by these elements was fatal. In the conditions of conspiracy, where controversy reigned and control was lacking, it often happened that local commanders committed reprehensible acts. It is the name of National Armed Forces (but not only) that we associate with the tragedy of Jewish "forest bands." These were small groups of Jewish resistance fighters who had no contact with recognized leaders (certainly through no fault of their own) or even with individual Jews who had fled into the forests – and who had to somehow obtain a minimum of supplies. It should

be noted that non-Jewish partisans used the same methods on a much larger scale; in the latter case, these methods were considered military, and therefore permissible, since they were equated with requisitions. In the case of the Jewish groups, their acquiring of food became a convenient pretext for fighting them – and indeed this chapter is particularly tragic.[68]

We may understand the space of the forest as at least ambiguous, as a hope of rescue, a chance of hiding, but also as an area associated with danger to life because it was in such places that the hiding Jews encountered both Polish and Ukrainian guerillas or even local peasants who knew the area.[69] The space of the forest - which is worth emphasizing - can be understood in two aspects: rescue and death. The Jews hiding in the forest were threatened not only by partisans, but also by the local non-Jewish population. Those who carried food to the bunker could be easily spotted and thus contribute to the detection of the hiding place. The local peasants were well acquainted with the surrounding woods, hence the gangs blackmailing the Jews easily obtained the last valuables and money.

4. Spaces of Ethics and Morality: Concluding Remarks

Summarizing, let us focus on another phenomenon undoubtedly connected with the experience of the Second World War and the Holocaust, which has already been the subject of much attention,[70] but which remains important for my reflections, namely the issues related to moral attitudes. Although this is a very general issue, the reflections formulated by Borwicz or written down in Frenkel's stories are closely connected with the observations and insights made by both writers when they were living in the territory of the Lviv district (*Distrikt Galizien*). That is why I take the liberty of recalling these statements and diagnoses. Borwicz indicates a peculiarly "discreet" – and, I might add, often later tabooed – formula for collaboration: "Anyway, there was but half a step from a blackmailer to a registered spy. The one who established contacts with the German police – because of his "anti-Jewish" activities – sometimes after a time began receiving stable pay and orders from them."[71] Writing about the organization of hatred and the influence of propaganda, Borwicz does not limit his remarks only to the war situation but draws attention to the scale of "shifts in moral concepts:" "Shifts all the more dangerous because they happen daily, because they are inculcated into the minds of simple people, because they concern practical and seemingly "innocuous" valuations."[72]

In fact, in Frenkel's story "Handel dewocjonaliami," the narrator describes the following attitudes of the non-Jewish population of Lviv and its surroundings:

> Pseudo-patriots hated each person who betrayed sympathy for the victims of the German invasion. Such an "uncle to the Jews" risked at best the name of a madman, at worst a visit of Gestapo. How could a fascist of native breeding not eulogize the genius who seized most generously his homeland to subject it to thorough pest control? The collaboration of these men with the invader was of great and positive importance to the invader as it sanctioned his conduct.[73]

Clearly, those who felt empathy for the excluded and condemned Jews had to fear not only reprisals from the Nazis but also the threat of their friends and neighbors. Not only was the attitude of the rescuers exceptional and rare but in the eyes of many members of their own community, it was met with no recognition or acceptance, but rather stigmatization.

Noting the prevalence of antisemitism, Borwicz emphasizes the persistence of the ideology, making it clear that supporters of anti-Jewish violence included members of various ethnic groups: "Some epigones of Hitlerism wish to keep the commandments "do not kill" and "do not steal," which are of Jewish origin, but with one limitation: that they should not apply to Jews. Attempts of this kind characterize criminals of all nationalities."[74] Referring to the wave of postwar violence, Borwicz adds, "In those affected by the venom of "anti-Jewishness" – [this state in which they find themselves after the war] utterly distorts … the manner and categories of both thought and action."[75]

Writing about the attitudes of the non-Jewish population, about the "bystanders" who did not react to antisemitic aggression, Borwicz diagnoses:

> they do not speak out against [the antisemitic campaign], convinced that its individual sinews and tentacles have become too

intertwined with the mass of other notions so that a strike against the anti-Jewish psychosis would have to entail disorientation in a whole clutch of old cliches, mistakes, and superstitions. They fail to appreciate that it is this very connection that is the most dangerously destructive factor.[76]

Referring to the opinions of Polish scholars, who write about the "antisemitic social code" (Janion) or the "culturally inscribed anti-Jewish code" (Libionka), Elżbieta Janicka emphasizes that the category of antisemitic culture would mean more in the sense that antisemitism is not just one of the currents or codes of a culture, but it is a generator of communal identity – first religious, then national – established according to ethno-religious criteria, which is also an axio-normative community.[77] Such an assessment is close to Borwicz's perspective, who directly observed both the violence against Jews and attitudes of indifference so evident in the years of occupation.

We should remember how early Borwicz made his diagnoses, how quickly he realized (and conveyed to readers) that descriptions and narrations concerning Jewish fate during the war will be subject to very different ways of shaping, in accordance with various meanders of successive leaders of the Polish society who would run diverse peculiar politics of memory (even until today). Recalling his own intensive involvement in the work of the Jewish Historical Commission, he writes many years later:

> I made the choice spontaneously, out of deep conviction and a sense of duty. On top of that, with a sober and clear program for myself; to do as much and as well as possible in this field, but also as quickly as possible, namely before the solidification of top-down pressures and oppressions makes honest work in this field impossible.[78]

Highlighting how we organize and shape memory, Bożena Keff recently emphasizes that the taboo is not so much the subject of the Holocaust and Polish-Jewish relations – even if it is rarely mentioned – as it is showing certain situations that concern the attitude of Poles toward Jews during the occupation. This refers to clearly defined, direct situations such as antisemitic statements, shmaltsovniks, informers, lootings, violence, and murders.[79] That is why today we should recall texts written a long time ago – which are very accurate descriptions of experiences, diagnoses of key events – that tell a lot about the Holocaust and interethnic relations in the space of occupation (as we can see here also in Lviv and Galicia), that later became partly marginalized and forgotten. What should motivate us even more to recall such texts and events is the current prevalence of nationalist exclusivism that foregrounds Polish martyrdom and mentions the memory of Jews only when it can ennoble the attitudes of Poles.

Endnotes

1   Quoted after Ringelblum Archive, *Relacje z Kresów*, Vol. 3 (Warsaw, 2000), p. 503.

2   So far, Judith Lyon-Caen has most fully reconstructed the biography of Michał Borwicz (Maksymilian Boruchowicz). See Judith Lyon-Caen, "Michel Borwicz: Między Polską a Francją, między literaturą a historią," *Zagłada Żydów, Studia i materiały* 13 (2017), pp. 261–274. Stefan Gąsiorowski also wrote about him. See Stefan Gąsiorowski, "Michał Borwicz in Kraków from 1911–1939" [introduction to] *Scripta Judaica Cracoviensia* (17) (2019), pp. 95–104.

3   The author of Ginczanka's biography is Izolda Kiec, who also published Ginczanka's poems in her own edition. See Izolda Kiec, *Ginczanka. Nie upilnuje mnie nikt*, (Warsaw, 2020). Agata Araszkiewicz and Irena Grudzińska-Gross also wrote about Ginczanka (here I primarily point out texts related to the subject of the article). See A. Araszkiewicz, *Wypowiadam wam moje życie, Melancholia Zuzanny Ginczanki*, (Warsaw, 2001); I. Grudzińska-Gross, "Something or Other: The Portait of Zuzanna Ginczanka," https://www.biweekly.pl/article/2120-something-or-otherthe-portrait-of-zuzanna-ginczanka.html?print=1 (accessed August 3, 2012).

4   Little is known about Mieczysław Frenkel's biography. Frenkel was an artist associated with the Lviv milieu, a critic, and an essayist and was active in the Union of Polish Writers. Frenkel published in *Sygnały* and *Wiadomości Literackie*. After the war, he lived in Zabrze. He published prose books, such as *Minuta milczenia* (1932), *To jest morderstwo* (1958, 2nd edition in 1960), *Ślepy pasażer* (1961) and a collection of essays titled *Marszruty i manowce półwiecza* (1960). In 1986, a Spanish translation of the short stories about Lviv during the war and the Holocaust was published under the title *La rapsodia de Lwow: esto es un asesinato* (Buenos Aires, 1986). It should be noted that Bożena Keff has established that although the short stories in the volume *To jest morderstwo* (This is Murder) were ready for publication as early as 1949, the book was not published until 1959.

5   It is important to note the poor and even silent reception of these works over the decades. Frenkel's short stories had a minimal impact; after his escape from Poland to France, Borwicz was hardly mentioned (suffice it to say, to this day his important works published in French and Yiddish have not been translated into Polish). Ginczanka was recalled thanks to the efforts of researchers such as Izolda Kiec and Agata Araszkiewicz, but only in the 1990s.

6   In this article I use the term "Galicia" to describe the space present in the analyzed texts; treating this concept, however, as a cultural phenomenon. It is not so much about geographical and historical boundaries and names – for these have changed – but about a certain civilizational and cultural category.

7   Christoph Mick, *Lemberg, Lwów*, Lviʹv, 1914- 1947 (Bloomington, 2016), pp. 210-211.

8   Michał Borwicz, "Inżynierowie dusz," *Zeszyty Historyczne* 3 (84) (Paris, 1963), pp. 121–163. I wrote about these very interesting reminiscences of Borwicz in the

article "1939–1941 – eine besondere Epoche in Lwow/Lwiw," in Kerstin Schoor, Ievgeniia Voloshchuk, and Borys Bigun (eds.), *"Blondzhende Stern": Jüdische SchriftstellerInnen aus der Ukraine als Grenz-gängerInnen zwischen den Kulturen in West und Ost* (Göttingen, 2020), pp. 250–270.

9   Michał Borwicz, *Spod szubienicy w teren*, (Paris, 1980), p. 5. Borwicz also mentions a volume of poems written during the war years, titled *Ze śmiercią na ty*, which was also published in 1946.

10 Victor Klemperer's book was first published by Aufbau Verlag in Berlin in 1947.

11 It should be remembered that Borwicz's reflections entitled *Organizowanie wściekłości* were published by Liga Walki z Rasizmem (League for Fighting Racism), "a social organization established in the spring of 1946 in Warsaw, whose aim was to fight racism, and above all, all signs of antisemitism in Polish society …. The League was active mainly in academic circles, in Krakow and Łódz. For a period, it published a magazine titled *Human Right* and a few books. After the Kielce pogrom (July 4, 1946), the League published its protest in the form of posters and leaflets. In the second half of 1946, Władysław Bartoszewski was arrested, the magazine ceased to be published, and many League members either left Poland or withdrew from public activity." https://collections.ushmm.org/findingaids/RG-15.343_01_fnd_pl.pdf (accessed May 17, 2021).

12 Michał Borwicz, "Les rapports entre la clandestinité polonaise et la clandestinité juive," *Le Monde Juif* 1 (53) (1969), pp. 11–17.

13 Mieczysław R. Frenkel, "Sądy dzień," in *To jest morderstwo* (Katowice, 1960), p. 100. Here I use the book's second edition.

14 Ibid., p. 100.

15 Michał Borwicz, *Organizowanie wściekłości* (Warsaw, 1947), p. 8.

16 Ibid.

17 Ibid., pp. 14–15.

18 Ibid., p. 16.

19 Ibid., p. 20.

20 Ibid., pp. 10–11.

21 Ibid., pp. 12–13.

22 Quoted after the Ringelblum Archive, *Relacje z Kresów*, p. 698. A refugee from Warsaw was the author of this account. He had been in Lviv since September 1939, and after the Lviv ghetto was established he decided to escape from the city "without an armband," meaning without any symbols distinguishing him as a Jew.

23 Borwicz, *Organizowanie wściekłości*, p. 32.

24 Ibid., pp. 26–27.

25 Ibid., p. 27.

26 Ibid., p. 27.

27 Borwicz, *Spod szubienicy w teren* (Paris, 1980), p. 42.

28 Ibid., p. 42.

29 Ibid., p. 43.

30 Ibid., p. 54.

31 Ibid., p. 54.

32 See Bogdan Wojdowski, "Judaizm jako los," *Puls* 3 (1993). I wrote about it in: "'Judaism as fate:' On the Essay by Bogdan Wojdowski," *Polin: Studies in Polish Jewry* 28 (2016), pp. 441–456.

33 Among those who wrote about it was (e.g.) Bożena Shallcross, *The Holocaust Object in Polish and Polish–Jewish Culture* (Bloomington, 2011).

34 Bożena Keff, *Strażnicy fatum: literatura dekad powojennych o Zagładzie, Polakach i Żydach: dyskurs publiczny wobec antysemityzmu* (Warsaw, 2020), p. 48. Keff draws attention to the historical and cultural context in the passage cited above, writing of "peasant serfdom and post-servitude culture," within which material goods "had an overwhelming significance … This is manifested in the fetishization of objects, things, and possessions." However, we can note that analogous gestures of taking things and money away from Jews were not only the experience of the peasants in society but also turned out to be quite a common practice in the occupied territories.

35 Borwicz, *Organizowanie wściekłości*, p. 30.

36 Ibid., p. 30.

37 Kazimierz Wyka made similar observations very early, even before the end of the war, which he only published in his 1957 essay "Życie na niby."

38 Borwicz, *Organizowanie wściekłości*, pp. 30–31.

39 Ibid., p. 31.

40 Ibid.

41 On the last page of Frenkel's volume of short stories we find the date and place where the texts were written: "Lviv, 1944–1945." See Frenkel, *To jest morderstwo*, p. 328.

42 Ibid., p. 97.

43 Frenkel refers to the well-known Polish saying "gdzie dwóch się bije tam trzeci korzysta," which is known in English as "while two dogs are fighting for a bone, a third one runs away with it."

44 Frenkel, *To jest morderstwo*, p. 143.

45 Ibid., p. 147.

46 Ibid., p. 148.

47 Ibid.

48 Ibid., p. 149.

49 Ibid., p. 100.

50 The title of the story is "Szantaż" (Blackmail). See Frenkel, *To jest morderstwo*, p. 120.

51 The poem (1942) was published by Julian Przyboś from the author's manuscript in 1946. See *Odrodzenie* 12 (1946), p. 5.

52 Agnieszka Haska writes about the postwar trial of Chominowa in "'Znałam tylko jedną Żydóweczkę ukrywającą się' Sprawa Zofii i Mariana Chominów," *Zagłada Żydów: Studia i Materiały* 4 (2008).

53 Zuzanna Ginczanka, "Non omnis moriar," *Zeszyty Literackie* 3 (131) (2015), pp. 103–105. The English translation of the quoted section is taken from: https://www.biweekly.pl/article/2120-something-or-otherthe-portrait-of-zuzanna-ginczanka.html.

54 Frenkel, *To jest morderstwo*, p. 245. The locations indicated were Krzywczyce, the rural part of which the Germans annexed to Lviv in 1942 (the Weinberger district), and suburban Żłoby, which was also located on the eastern outskirts of Lviv.

55 Ibid., p. 251.

56 Ibid., p. 248.

57 Ibid, p. 252.

58 Mary Louise Pratt introduced the concept of "the contact zone." She writes: "I use this term to refer to social spaces where cultures meet, clash and grapple with each other, often in contexts of highly asymmetrical relations of power, such as colonialism, slavery, or their aftermaths as they lived out in many parts of the world today." See M. L. Pratt, "Arts of the Contact Zone," *Profession* (1991), p. 91.

59 Frenkel, *To jest morderstwo*, p. 186

60 Borwicz, *Organizowanie wściekłości*, p. 36.

61 Ibid., p. 36.

62 Ibid.

63 Borwicz wrote about this in his memoir *Spod szubienicy w teren* (Paris, 1980).

64 Ibid., p. 35

65 Borwicz was associated first with the Polish Socialist Party and then with the Polish Socialist Party – Freedom, Equality, Independence.

66 Borwicz, *Spod szubienicy w teren*, pp. 37–38.

67 Frankel, *To jest morderstwo*, p. 251.

68 Borwicz, "Les rapports entre la clandestinité polonaise et la clandestinité juive," *Le Monde Juif* 1 (53) (1969), pp. 11–17.

69 Olga Kaczmarek has written interestingly about the category of "forest" in the Polish Holocaust imagery. See Olga Kaczmarek, "Las," in Paweł Dobrosielski, Justyna Kowalska-Leder, Iwona Kurz, and Małgorzata Szpakowska (eds.), *Ślady Holokaustu w imaginarium kultury polskiej* (Warsaw, 2018), pp. 219–244.

70 I am referring to Primo Levi, Jean Amery, Karl Jaspers, and Emil Fackenheim, among others.

71 Borwicz, *Organizowanie wściekłości*, p. 37.

72 Ibid., p. 28.

73 Frenkel, *To jest morderstwo*, p. 250.

74 Borwicz, *Organizowanie wściekłości*, p. 74

75 Ibid., p. 78.

76 Ibid., p. 78.

77 Elżbieta Janicka, "Pamięć przyswojona. Koncepcja polskiego doświadczenia zagłady Żydów jako traumy zbiorowej w świetle rewizji kategorii świadka," https://core.ac.uk/download/pdf/230557985.pdf, p. 19.

78 Michał Borwicz, "Trzydzieści lat temu. Ze wspomnień 'lekkiego kalibru,'" *Zeszyty Historyczne* 33 (1975), p. 203.

79 Bożena Keff, *Strażnicy fatum*, (Warsaw, 2020), p. 85.

Yuri Radchenko

"I saw him in SS uniform…": The OUN-M, the SD, and the Holocaust in Drohobych County (the Case of Julian Temnyk)

Introduction

In the summer of 1992, *Visti kombatanta*, the bimonthly journal of war veterans in the Ukrainian diaspora in the West, published another issue. Among its various sections were eulogies in memory of former soldiers and officers of the Ukrainian military units of the German army during World War II. One of these eulogies was in memory of Julian Temnyk, a Galicia native whose comrades in arms from the various units in which he served spared him no compliments:

> In Toronto, at the age of 96 toil-filled years, Julian Temnyk, the last of the Mohicans in the struggle for Ukrainian liberation –the Ukrainian Galician Army, the Ukrainian Military Organization, the OUN,[1] and the 1st Ukrainian Division of the Ukrainian National Army[2] – has passed away.[3]

The funeral was attended by many guests, including numerous representatives of the Brotherhood of Former Soldiers of the SS Galician Division and of another veterans' organization known as the Ukrainian Rifleman's Association. Temnyk was buried at Mount Peace Cemetery.[4] Although various publications have paid substantial attention to other aspects of his biography, very little has been written about his life during World War II. To quote one incarnation of Temnyk's biography: "During World War II – [he served as a] heavy anti-aircraft artillery commander in the Ukrainian Division."[5]

Another biography reads as follows:

> In 1943, Julian Temnyk volunteered to serve in the Ukrainian Division, and four months after he was married (May 6) to Daria Horodys'ka he

began anti-aircraft artillery training. He became the commander of the third battery. Over time, he attended courses for artillery officers and became the head of a staff unit of an artillery company.[6]

The accounts say nothing about the period between 1941 and 1943. During this time, Temnyk served in the SD in Drohobych, taking part in the extermination of the Jews of Drohobych and Sambir. However, a small amount *has* been written about Temnyk's role in the Holocaust as it pertained to another SD member: Sturmscharführer Paul Behr. Behr himself murdered a number of Jews in Drohobych. He invited his "pet Jew" Munion (Mundek) Badian hunting, where he shot him to death. He also murdered a Jewish woman and her two children – the wife and children of Abraham Schleier. Together with Temnyk, Behr is also known to have murdered and robbed a few family members of Ida Rubinstein.[7] Still, the details of Temnyk's involvement in the Holocaust, and many other parts of his life, remain unknown. After the 1940 split in the OUN, Temnyk joined the faction of Andrii Melnyk's supporters (OUN-M). Contemporary studies show that the "Melnykites" actively participated in the Holocaust while serving in the Einsatzgruppen, in the Security Police (*Sicherheitspolizei*), and in the SD in the occupied territory of Ukraine.[8] Still, the extent of OUN-M members' participation in the Holocaust has yet to be fully researched. This is particularly interesting in light of the fact that, in 1943, some of the Ukrainians who collaborated with the Nazis between 1941 and 1943 tried to establish their own separate partisan regiment.[9] What was Julian Temnyk's life like before the war? What were the political forces that shaped his worldview up to the onset of his work in the SD in Drohobych? To what extent did he participate in the Holocaust? Temnyk is known to have taken part in the persecution of Jews where he had lived before the war. Did his victims include anyone he knew or any friends from before the war? What happened to him after the war? The present article will answer these questions and more.

Temnyk's Life Story until his Service in the SD in Drohobych

On June 3, 1896, like many other future OUN-M and OUN-B activists, Temnyk was born to a peasant family in Berezhnytsia in the Sambir district.

His parents (Iwan and Rozalia) were able to give their children an education, and Julian graduated from the gymnasium in Sambir. Temnyk was brought up in the spirit of Ukrainian patriotism, and at the age of 18 he wanted to serve in the Legion of Ukrainian Sich Riflemen, which was part of the Austro-Hungarian army. However, he was not accepted due to the unit's limit of 2,000 soldiers. Ultimately, Temnyk was conscripted into a "regular" unit in the Austro-Hungarian army. Between October 1, 1914 and January 10, 1915 he underwent basic training, and from the end of training until July 25, 1917 he fought against the Russian army on the Eastern front. On July 27, 1917, like many other soldiers in the Austro-Hungarian army, he was taken prisoner by the Russians and was jailed in a camp in Tsaritsyn along with Yevhen Konovalets and Andrii Melnyk. He escaped on December 18, 1917,[10] and the future leaders of the OUN and a number of additional comrades who escaped Russian imprisonment a few days later, on Catholic Christmas Eve (December 24, 1917), may have followed in Temnyk's tracks. The Russian army was already almost completely destroyed, and the group with which Melnyk and Konovolets left the camp during the celebrations crossed the frozen Volga River and continued through the snowy wilderness to Voronezh, to Kursk, and finally to Kyiv.[11]

It can be assumed that Temnyk's close relationship with Melnyk and Konovolets had an influence on his subsequent decision to join Melnyk's faction when the OUN split in 1940. Following these events, Temnyk used the experience he had accrued while in the Austrian army in the service of the Ukrainian enterprise – the Western Ukrainian People's Republic – by joining the Ukrainian Galician Army, in which he served as a commander of the 13th Regiment of the 7th Lviv Brigade. In this capacity, he fought against the Poles and was injured in battle in the defense of Przemyśl. Later, he took part in the Galician Army's Chortkiv offensive against the Polish army. After the collapse of the Western Ukrainian People's Republic and the transfer of Eastern Galicia and Volhynia to Polish control, Temnyk fled to Czechoslovakia in fear of persecution at the hands of the Polish authorities. In Prague he attended a technological school, but later, in 1924, he returned to Galicia, where he worked as an agronomist-engineer. It is unknown exactly when he joined the OUN and whether he was officially a member of the party by 1939. Nonetheless, between the two world wars he engaged in the development of Ukrainian cooperative and cultural organizations in his native regions.[12]

At the onset of World War II, some local OUN activists launched a series of uprisings in Galicia and Volhynia under the leadership of Lopatyns'ky (Volodymyr Tymchii) and uncoordinated with the leadership of the movement. The OUN partisans conquered settlements and established their rule there.[13] At the same time, OUN fighters frequently attacked the Polish and Jewish populations. When German forces entered Sembira in September 1939, Temnyk worked on setting up a Ukrainian OUN police force. He succeeded in seizing the local archive, where OUN men searched for lists of Polish intelligence personnel who had fought against the Ukrainian nationalists. In a report from Krakow dated September 27, 1940, Temnyk wrote:

> When the German forces arrived in Sembira, I was charged with organizing Ukrainian self-defense in Sembira and in the district. The building that had previously housed the Polish police became the headquarters of the Sembira police. During a scouring of the police records, a file containing classified documents was found in the desk of police commander Radwanski. Along with the other police personnel, we began to check the documents that had been drawn up by Polish counterintelligence. In the documents, we found exact lists of undercover police [agents – Y.R.] from Sembira and Chyrów and the information they had conveyed. I checked these documents throughout the entire night, from 7 in the evening until 8 in the morning, and I can hereby state that they did not contain information on Krakow or the surrounding area – specifically, there was no document whatsoever regarding Juroslaw Branowsky [a well-known OUN member who was suspected of collaborating with Polish intelligence – Y.R.].[14]

When the German forces left Sembira in 1939 Temnyk also appears to have left, returning to the region where he was raised only in the summer of 1941.

Serving in the SS

The outbreak of war between Germany and the Soviet Union on June 22, 1941 provided OUN-M activists in the occupied Ukrainian territories with a window of opportunity. In the summer of 1941, in the footsteps of the German army, Melnykites and Banderites began to establish a police force and self-rule in the occupied territories. These organizations took part in the pogroms of the summer of 1942 in Galicia and Volhynia. The exact date on which Temnyk returned to Drohobych is not known. It can be assumed that this occurred after the German army reached the town on July 1, 1941. During this period, the town contained approximately 2,000 Jews who had become victims of pogroms and mass murder. Beginning in the autumn of 1941, local Security Police and SD forces under the authority of the SD units in Lviv (Drohobycz/KdS Lemberg) operated in Drohobycz. Their commander was Sturmbannführer Hans Block. Security Police and SD units played an important role in the Holocaust in different parts of Ukraine: in the Generalgouvernement (in Buczacz, for example),[15] in Reichskommissariat Ukraine (in Kyiv),[16] and in the area of military government (Kharkiv).[17] Between 1941 and 1944, many Melnykites served in the ranks of the Einsatzgruppen, in police units, and in the SD. Some, like Oleska Babyi, also managed to serve in the German military apparatus.[18] Many of those who would later serve as soldiers in the Ukrainian Legion of Self-Defense served in the SD.[19] For example, military officers (Sotnyk) Kaschuk and Yarymenko served in the SD in Volhynia; Popadynets' served in the SD in Stanislawow; and Yarish served in the SD in Przemyśl.[20] Melnykites who served in the SD took part in the Holocaust and also persecuted Ukrainians who espoused different political views (such as Banderites). For example, the SD in Stanislawow, in which a Melnykite named Shchebunchak served, participated in the murder of local Jews. Moreover, between September 12 and 15, 1941, a group of Banderites, including Stephan Bandera's brother Andrii was arrested there.[21]

The exact date on which Temnyk began serving in the SD is unknown. However, his personal SS file indicates that in 1942, he was already on active duty. In a questionnaire he completed while in the SS, he specified that his religion was Catholicism and that he spoke German, Ukrainian, Polish, and Russian. He appears to have learned Russian while being held prisoner by the Russians in

1917. On May 3, 1943, Temnyk got married, left his position with the SD, and began to serve in the SS Galician Division, where, on January 1, 1944, he received the rank of Obersturmführer.[22] Temnyk served in this unit (apparently with the same rank) until the surrender of Nazi Germany in May 1945.

What crimes did Temnyk take part in during the period of German occupation? The testimonies of Holocaust survivors from Sembira indicate that he actively participated in at least a few events of extermination of local Jews. One such "event" occurred in Sembira between September 4 and 6, 1942. According to the 1931 census, Buczacz was home to 6,068 Jews. Sembira, like Lviv, was occupied by the Germans on June 30, 1941, and pogroms were carried out against the Jews. In the summer of 1941, a Jewish registry was compiled, and Jews were required to wear bands bearing the Star of David around their arm. From time to time, the Germans and their collaborators would assign the Jews a physical task that was to be completed without payment, during which they would beat the Jews savagely. In March 1942, a ghetto was set up in Sembira, into which 6,686 Jews were moved. From time to time, mass murders were carried out against Jews living in the ghetto, including the abovementioned events of August 1942 in which Temnyk took part. These crimes were perpetrated under the direction of SS-Obersturmführer Robert Gschwendtner from the staff of SS-Brigadeführer Fritz Katzmann, the SS and Police Leader for the Galicia District. Among the units that took part in these "*Aktionen*" was a company of the German gendarmerie, the Ukrainian police, the Jewish police, and a team from the Security Police of Drohobych led by Hauptscharführer Jozef Gabriel. The murderers assembled the Jews from the town and from nearby localities (Strii, Sembira, Felsztyn, Střelecký, Tarshow, Tershiv, and many more) in the stadium, where they performed a "selection" to choose 150 (or according to some sources, 600) Jews to work at Janowska concentration camp. The others were shot to death. The selection process was directed by Janowska camp commandant Untersturmführer Gustav Willhaus. A large portion of the Jews of Sembira were loaded onto trains by the Germans and their collaborators and deported to Bełżec death camp.[23] Paul Blum from the city of Strii, who had attended the gymnasium with Temnyk, saw him "commanding a Ukrainian unit that took part in the extermination [in

Sembira] together with the SS."[24] Another witness, Yitzhak Khilch, testified in 1964 that Temnyk took part in an Aktion in Sembira on August 4 and 6, 1942:

> I remember that Temnyk the Ukrainian, a native of the region whom I met before the war, participated in those Aktions. My brother-in-law, Heinrich Gluek, saw him [Temnyk] in SS uniform. I know that Temnyk moved to the Gestapo in Drohobych. I also know that at the end of the war, Temnyk moved to Germany and later to Canada.[25]

During the war, Sembira was the site of numerous extermination Aktions that were organized by the Germans and their collaborators. For example, between February and June 1943, the Security Police in Drohobych conducted four Aktions in conjunction with the Ukrainian police: on February 13, April 14, May 20-22, and June 5, 1943. The final Aktion was actually the liquidation of the ghetto. The Jews who survived were jailed in the local prison and taken to the forest to be executed by shooting. Throughout 1943 as a whole, some 3,000 Jews were murdered in Sembira and more than 600 were sent to the camps at Majdanek and Janowska.[26] It can be assumed that Temnyk and those in his command took part in these mass murders.

After the War

Like many other soldiers and officers of the SS Galician Division after the war, Temnyk was held prisoner by the British in Rimini, Italy. Later, he moved to Britain with his wife, and in June 1952 they immigrated to Canada. In Canada, Temnyk remained in close contact with immigrant Melnykites. For example, he joined and later headed the Ukrainian Riflemen Association. In 1966, Temnyk became the chairman of the association's executive committee, and in 1975 he became its honorary leader. He was also known to have been an active member of Prosvita (the society for Ukrainian culture and education) and the "Ukrainian National Union," which had close ties to the OUN-M.[27] During his time living in Canada, he never changed his name and he attended ceremonies of the Ukrainian veteran associations. For example, he was one of the prominently active members in the celebrations marking the 50th anniversary of the Ukrainian Rifleman's Association that took place in Montreal on November 14, 1970. The event was attended by 35 veterans who had been active between 1914 and 1920 and many guests from the Ukrainian diaspora. It was hosted by Temnyk, who at the time was serving as chairman of the executive committee and lifetime secretary of the association; Mykhailo Seleshko, a well-known member of the OUN-M, and representatives of the Ukrainian Greek-Catholic Church and the Ukrainian Orthodox Church. During the ceremony, Ukrainian veteran Yaroslav Kobylians'kyi entered to a march carrying the banner of the organization and proclaimed to Temnyk:

> Chairman of the Executive Committee, Sir! My strength is depleted due to my advanced age and my 50 years of service to the homeland. I pass this flag on to you, and you, in turn will pass it on to the young, so that the young generation will carry it proudly, as we have.

After accepting and kissing the flag, Temnyk responded: "Mister Chairman – like my predecessors, I will carry this flag with pride and sincerity, and I will not disgrace it to my final day – may God help me!" The ceremony was followed by a brief concert and a reception. The event concluded with a brief but content-laden military-style speech "to which the attendees listened from beginning to end with great interest, and to which they responded with thunderous applause."[28]

During the Ukrainian Rifleman's Association's 50th anniversary celebrations, exchanges occurred between the old generation and the new generation of the Ukrainian diaspora. According to a Canadian journalist of Ukrainian descent with ties to the OUN-M, the gathering was characterized by a friendly and ideological atmosphere:

> The mother tongue, representatives of the church, the riflemen, and the organized young generation convinced the heroes of the struggle for liberation that their goal had not been lost, that a free and independent Ukraine would return to life, and that its free children would worship freely.[29]

Apparently, in the final years leading up to his death, Temnyk ceased his political activity. During his time in Canada he established a large family; at the time of his death on August 26, 1992, he had two daughters (Oskana and Khrystia) and seven grandchildren.[30] However, his war crimes during World War II were not forgotten. They were investigated by the judicial authorities of the Federal Republic of Germany and the Israeli police based on the testimony of Holocaust survivors. In the 1960s, the West German investigative authorities tried to have Temnyk extradited to stand trial in Germany, but without success.[31] This was not an exceptional situation. A similar example was that of Ivan Iuriiv, who served in Sonderkommando 10a and was active in the OUN-M. Iuriiv, too, lived a politically and socially active life in Canada without concealing his identity and died peacefully in his own bed.[32]

Motivations for Collaboration during the Holocaust

One of the most important aspects of the research on the Holocaust and collaboration with the Nazis is the motivations of the collaborators. Why did non-Jewish local populations agree to collaborate with the Germans and to play an active role in murdering the Jews? Based on the findings of studies by Christopher Browning, Alexsandre Prusin, and Daniel Goldhagen,[33] I distinguish among five categories of collaborators (primarily policemen and members of the self-defense) in Ukraine who helped the Nazis murder Jews:

1. Political activists
2. Career professionals
3. Unwilling conformists
4. Regular perpetrators
5. Marginal criminal elements

The first category usually included members of the different anti-Soviet parties: the OUN, the National-Labor Alliance of the New Generation,[34] former soldiers and officers of the "white" armies, and the army of the Ukrainian People's Republic. It also included unaffiliated antisemites. Although this category usually contained only a small number of individuals in comparison to other groups, it cannot be defined as homogenous; rather, it can be divided into three subcategories. The first subcategory included those whose motivations were shared by Nazi Germany and who actively collaborated, but who were also capable of crossing over to the opponents of the Third Reich the moment disagreement arose. Crossing this line frequently forced political activists to maneuver between opposition to and limited collaboration with the Nazis. Examples of such individuals included OUN-B members, who in the summer of 1941 actively collaborated in the persecution and extermination of Jews but in the autumn of the same year, with the onset of the clash with the Nazis, started to oppose Germany – initially through propaganda and subsequently also by military means. The second subcategory consisted of "political activists" who – despite the Nazi policy of occupation toward the Ukrainians, the Russians, and other non-Jews – continued to collaborate. Their primary motivation was the desire to help their fellow countrymen. Such individuals related to the murder of Jews with indifference or active participation. They blamed the Germans' murder of Ukrainians on "Soviet agents" or "zealous Nazis." This subcategory included some members of the OUN-M and members of the National-Labor Alliance of the New Generation. The third subcategory consisted of those who supported the ideas of National Socialism, who constituted a small minority of the Christian population and were a minority within a minority among the political activists. During the period preceding the war, they could have been members of the National Fascist Party and, at the same time, of a larger fascist party that was already in power or enjoyed the support of Nazi Germany. For example, prior to the war, German supporters of Nazism could join units of the SA, the Nazi party in Germany, or the youth movement of the Fascist party in Italy. After the Nazis seized control of Belgium, for example, such "political activists" could join the Rexist Party of Leon Degrelle.

The second category included those who, during the 1930s, held junior and mid-level positions in the Soviet state and party machinery. These individuals were usually able to surmise which way the winds were blowing and were willing to serve any regime. The third category, that of unwilling conformists, consisted of people who, when asked to collaborate with the Nazis, had few if any options for making a behavioral choice. This category primarily contained prisoners of war, who were frequently forced to choose between collaboration, service in the punitive Nazi units, and death from illness or the abuse of the camp police. Regular perpetrators, the fourth category, were people with the smallest amount of social mobility within the Soviet population: kolkhozists and unskilled laborers. The fifth and final group, marginal criminal elements, consisted of regular criminal offenders who, prior to the war, had already been sentenced to a number of prison terms and held no defined political perspective whatsoever.

Until 1945, the ideology of the Melnykites was extremely antisemitic in character. For example, one of the booklets it published in 1941 read:

> The Organization of Ukrainian Nationalists…brings you Ukrainian youth liberation, freedom, and a stellar nationalist life on your land, which will contain:
>
>> Not even a single *katsap*
>> Not even a single Jew
>> Not even a single Pole.[35]

Under the terms of the Ribbentrop-Molotov Agreement, the Germans treated the Ukrainians and the OUN in the territory of the Generalgouvernment in a positive manner, but they tried not to overly publicize this fact. This contradiction in German policy found partial expression in one of the reports of the Melnykites from the spring of 1941. According to the report, the treatment "of the Ukrainians by the German authorities is tolerant and positive overall." The report also stated that the occupation authorities in the Generalgouvernment "regard the Ukrainians as a loyal element."[36] At the same time, the report noted that "on the ground things are conducted differently." There, "everything depends on the local German military, civil, and political authorities." The report also asserted that the Germans' negative impression of the Ukrainians was being created by "Poles disguised as Germans – Volksdeutsche."[37] During the same period, the OUN-M issued instructions containing a positive depiction of the German "military" and "paramilitary" units by movement members:

> One of the modern forces in the current period constitutes various frameworks in the service of the Germans. Although most of them are not under our authority and the security and the policing service take up a great deal of time, training that would raise the skill level

[of those serving in them – Y.R.] occurs within this framework. At the same time, this service would cultivate the attributes of a Ukrainian soldier-revolutionary. The period of transition in the security and the auxiliary police units must be taken advantage of to acquire extensive knowledge and to strengthen character.[38]

On June 22, 1941, the pendulum in the territory of the Generalgouvernement swung toward increased cooperation between the Germans and the Ukrainians, who were usually represented by the OUN-M. As noted above, during the war between Germany and the Soviet Union many Melnykites viewed the police and the self-government as elements that could be used to influence the policy of the German occupiers. Writer Ulas Samchuk, an active member of the OUN-M, attended a parade of the local police in the village of Tyliavka, Volhynia in Augusts 1941. The parade was commanded by fellow student Arion Kokharchyk. A few years later, Samchuk recounted the event with enthusiasm:

> I stood at the entrance to our school, and a procession of our boys wearing regular home attire with yellow and blue bands on their arms passed before me. They tried to maintain a goosestep. It was a unique sight: a police parade being received by a writer. But it was not a parade of police, rather of heart, happiness, and enthusiasm.[39]

During the war, the OUN-M did not propagate anti-German slogans. Indeed, even in 1943, members of the Ukrainian peasant movement called for "supporting the German army," for in doing so, Melnyk's propagandists maintained, they too were "building their state."[40] In only one booklet, published in 1944, did the OUN-M refer to Nazi Germany as "temporary occupiers."[41] In the autumn of 1941, for the first time, the Germans began arresting and executing not only Banderites but also Melnykites. At the time, OUN-M representatives met with different envoys of the German occupation apparatus to clarify the matter. In the course of one of these meetings, a low-level German official told Samchuk that the Melnykites needed to "keep quiet," like the Czechoslovakian collaborators: "Look at the Czechs. They could have more claims against us, but look at how they act. And they are profiting as a result."[42]

Much can be learned about the OUN-M's attitude toward Nazi Germany from a booklet titled "Our Attitude toward the Germans," which was written in 1942 by party activist M. Kasyan. The booklet contains antisemitic clichés, such as characterizations of the Soviet regime as "Jewish."[43] Although the Germans had conquered Ukraine based on their desire to become an empire, argued Kasyan, they could also be useful at this stage, first and foremost in the rehabilitation of their economy:

> In order to mobilize resources to manage this extended war, the Germans are being forced to rebuild our economy, which was destroyed during the war. This is consistent with our national interests. We need to play an active role in it and help the Germans.[44]

Despite the author's cool and at times even negative attitude toward Germany, he cast the calls for opposition as destructive:

> Are those calling for an uprising correct? No, they are mistaken. Now, we need to demonstrate calm, confidence, and intransigence in defending our rights and our national interests. They can tell us that we will die doing so. No, we will not die. The German state will collapse faster than the Ukrainian People will die. People die, but ideas are eternal.[45]

Even Melnyk's partisan units, which were established in 1943 and had few members, were rapidly integrated into the Ukrainian Insurgent Army under Bandera's command or appended to the Ukrainian Legion of Self Defense, which operated under the authority of the German occupation authorities.[46]

The Russian collaborators associated with the National-Labor Alliance of the New Generation espoused a similar approach. For example, Vladimir Sokolov (Samarin), deputy editor of the newspaper *Rech*, which was published in occupied Oriol and was known for its unbridled antisemitic propaganda, wrote the following in his memoirs after the war:

> Prisoners of war and members of the civilian population were intentionally killed according to a calculated plan that was drawn up ahead of time. Opponents of the Bolsheviks remained on guard

and gritted their teeth. They were faced with two winds: German Hitlerism and Bolshevism. What is worse than that?[47]

Based on his life trajectory, Julian Temnyk can be characterized as belonging to the category of "political activist," first joining the OUN and then siding with the faction of Andrii Melnyk. Nonetheless, throughout his entire life he remained a loyal member of the movement. His lot during World War II and the Nazi occupation – collaboration with the Germans and participation in the Holocaust – was characteristic of many mid-level officials at the time. For Temnyk, serving in the SD and in the SS Galician Division and taking part in the anti-Jewish measures wearing the uniform of the German army were an indivisible part of his political aspirations, the realization of which, in his view, needed to precede the establishment of the mono-ethnic, pro-German, sovereign Ukrainian state.

Conclusions

In the mid-2010s, the Ukrainian Institute of National Memory embarked upon a new project: a "Virtual Remembrance Site for Ukrainian Immigrants." The project's goal was to create a registry of the cemeteries containing the graves of Ukrainian political refugees who had emigrated from Ukraine. In the course of the project, Julian Temnyk's grave was also photographed, and information about him was posted on the project's website[48] and Facebook group.[49] These biographical listings, however, say nothing about Temnyk's service in the SD or his role in the Holocaust.

For the most part, the life course of Julian Temnyk was typical of mid-level OUN commanders. He began as a Ukrainian patriot who, while still a young man, was ready to fight alongside Austro-Hungary for the independence of Ukraine. He later took advantage of his military experience, fighting in the ranks of the Ukrainian Galician Army for the independence of the Western Ukrainian People's Republic. After the failure of the Ukrainian leaders of the Ukrainian People's Republic and the Western Ukrainian People's Republic, Temnyk was forced to flee Galicia. It is difficult to determine whether he engaged in political activity after returning to Eastern Galicia, which was controlled by the Poles. It is more reasonable to assume that during this period, he acted like other Ukrainian war veterans, such as Andrii Melnyk and Ivan Iuriiv, who for a time formally withdrew from political activity and focused instead on the cultural and the economic arenas. It is not known for certain when exactly Temnyk joined the ranks of the OUN. However, by September 1939, he had already managed to play an active role in the OUN uprising in Western Ukraine, and in 1940 he joined the Melnykites. The main reason for the latter act was apparently his personal relationship with the "head of the OUN."

During the war between Germany and the Soviet Union, Temnyk played an active role in the murder of Galician Jewry and the theft of their property. He personally knew many of the victims he murdered, as well as those who had survived, from before the war. Many, for example, had been his fellow students. The existing documentation indicates that Temnyk took part in exterminating Jews, at least in Drohobych and Sembira. His activities within the territory of the Generalgouvernment between 1939 and 1941, when Melnykites took part in the theft of Jewish property, have yet to be sufficiently explored. Nothing is known about Temnyk's actions in the summer of 1941, when the OUN-B and the OUN-M carried out a series of pogroms in Galicia and Volhynia. One of these pogroms was conducted in Drohobych, where Temnyk arrived in 1941. His actions while serving in the SS Galician Division also remain virtually unexamined. One question that remains unanswered, for example, is whether or not Temnyk helped suppress the Slovak National Uprising of 1944. Another pertains to his involvement in the "anti-partisan" activities in Ukraine and in the Balkans. In any event, the present study proves that the members of the SS Galician Division also included war criminals who took part in the Holocaust; this fact is not recognized by some opinion journalists and propagandists in Ukraine.[50]

Temnyk's life after the war establishes that he remained a political soldier of the OUN-M until his dying day. The German prosecutor's attempts to demand his extradition in order to try him for his crimes during the war ended in failure. Temnyk lived a full life in Canada without having to live in hiding. In 1992, like many war criminals who never faced trial, he died at home, in his bed, after the Soviet Union had already disintegrated and Ukraine received independence. As noted above, many chapters of his life have not been researched. All of these problematic topics can be investigated through research in the Ukrainian archive in Canada and the archives in Germany. The study of similar biographies could help us better understand the uniqueness of the Holocaust and the nature of the collaboration with the Nazis at the local level.

Endnotes

1 The OUN (Organization of Ukrainian Nationalists), the radical wing of the Ukrainian nationalist movement, was established in 1929 in Vienna. In February 1940, the OUN split into two mutually hostile factions. One faction, whose members were primarily young adults, was led by Stepan Bandera. The second faction, which consisted primarily of older movement members, was led by Colonel Andrii Melnyk. Bandera's supporters were frequently referred to as *Banderivtsi* (Banderites) or members of OUN-B, whereas Melnyk's supporters were known as *Melnykivtsi* (Melnykites) or members of OUN-M.

2 This was the name of the Galician SS Division during the final days leading up to the surrender of Nazi Germany.

3 "Ti, shcho vidiishly. Inzh. Yulian Temnyk 3.VI.1896–26.VIII.1992," *Visti Kombatanta* 5(6) (1992), p. 131.

4 Ibid.

5 *Za chest', za slavu, za narod. Zbirnyk na iuvilei Ukraiins'koii Strilets'koii Hromady v Kanadi 1928-1978* (Toronto, 1978), p. 500; Mykhailo Marunchak, *Biohrafichnyi dovidnyk do istoriii ukraiintsiv* (Winnipeg, 1986), p. 622.

6 "Ti, shcho vidiishly. Inzh. Yulian Temnyk 3.VI.1896–26.VIII.1992," p. 132.

7 Klaus, "Who shot Munio Badian?" http://remembertogetheracrossborders.eu/who-shot-munio-badian/ .

8 Yuri Radchenko, "The Organization of Ukrainian Nationalists (Mel'nyk Faction) and the Holocaust: The Case of Ivan Iuriiv," *Holocaust and Genocide Studies* 31(2) (2017), pp. 215–239; Yuri Radchenko, "The OUN-M, Collaboration and the Holocaust as Reflected in 'Biographies of Ukrainian Nationalists'," *Yad Vashem Studies* 47(2) (2019), pp. 43-82; Yuri Radchenko, "The Biography of the OUN(m) Activist Oleksa Babii in the Light of his 'Memoirs on Escaping Execution' (1942)," *Journal of Soviet and Post-Soviet Politics and Society* 6(1) (April 2020), pp. 239-279.

9 Radchenko, "The Biography of the OUN(m) Activist Oleksa Babii", pp. 263-271

10 German Federal Archive (Bundesarchiv Berlin – BAB), 175-B.

11 Dmytro Herchanivs'kyi, "U rosiis'komu poloni," in *Andrii Mel'nyk. 1890-1964. Spohady Dokumenty. Lystuvannia* (Kyiv, 2011), pp. 88-90.

12 "Ti, shcho vidiishly. Inzh. Yulian Temnyk 3.VI.1896–26.VIII.1992," p. 132.

13 Ivan Patryliak, *Ukraiins'ke natsionalistychne pidpillia ta povstans'kyi rukh v 1939-1944 rr.: struktura, chysel'nist', diial'nist'*, ipn.gov.pl/download/1/69461/Ukrainskiepodziemienarodowe.pdf.

14 Zynovii Knysh, *Spohady i materiialy do rozkolu OUN u 1940-1941 rokakh* (Toronto, 1969), p. 185.

15 Omer Bartov, *Anatomy of a Genocide: The Life and Death of a Town Called Buczacz* (New York, 2018).

16 Alexander Prusin, "Community of Violence: the SiPo/SD and Its Role in the Nazi Terror System in Generalbezirk Kiew," *Holocaust and Genocide Studies* 21(1) (2007), pp. 1-30.

17 Yuri Radchenko, "'Ioho choboty ta esesivs'ka forma buly zabryzkani kroviu…': taiemna pol'ova politsiia, politsiia bezpeky ta SD, dopomizhna politsiia u terori shchodo ievreiiv Kharkova (1941-1943 rr.)," *Holokost i suchasnist'. Studiii v Ukraiini i sviti* 2(10) 2011), pp. 46-86.

18 Radchenko, "The Biography of the OUN(m) Activist Oleksa Babii."

19 On the Legion itself, see Yuri Radchenko and Andrii Usach, "'For the Eradication of Polish and Jewish-Muscovite Rule in Ukraine: An Examination of the Crimes of the Ukrainian Legion of Self-Defense," *Holocaust and Genocide Studies* 34(3) (2020), pp. 450–477.

20 "Do spravy t. zv. Ukraiins'koho lehionu samooborony," Archive of Yaroslav Stetsko (copy from the archive of Andrii Usach).

21 Radchenko, "The Organization of Ukrainian Nationalists (Mel'nyk Faction) and the Holocaust: The Case of Ivan Iuriiv," p. 72.

22 BAB 175-B; Übernahmen und Beförderungen von Offz. Und Offz Anwärten der 14 Gal. SS Freiw. Division. A copy of this document is located in the personal archive of Andrii Usach.

23 Il'ia Al'tman (ed.), *Kholokost na territorii SSSR: Entsiklopediia* (Moscow, 2011), p. 887.

24 Bundesarchiv Ludwigsburg (BAL), 162/ 27837, Bl. 3.

25 BAL, 162/ 27837, Bl. 3.

26 Al'tman, *Kholokost na territorii SSSR*, p. 888.

27 Mykhailo Marunchak, *Biohrafichnyi dovidnyk do istoriii ukraiintsiv*, p. 622.

28 Illia Homontko, "50-richnyi iuvilei ukraiins'kykh kombatantiv," *Novyi Shliakh*, February 27, 1971.

29 Ibid.

30 Marunchak, *Biohrafichnyi dovidnyk do istoriii ukraiintsiv*, p. 622.

31 BAL, 162/ 27837, Bl. 29-30.

32 Radchenko, "The Organization of Ukrainian Nationalists (Mel'nyk Faction) and the Holocaust: The Case of Ivan Iuriiv," p. 232.

33 Aleksandr Prusin, "Ukrainskaia politsiia i Kholokost v general'nom okruge Kyiv, 1941-1943: deistviia i motivatsii," *Holokost i suchasnist'. Studiii v Ukraiini i sviti* (2007), pp. 31-59; Daniel Goldhagen, *Hitler's Willing Executioners: Ordinary Germans and the Holocaust* (New York, 1997); Christopher Browning, *Ordinary Men: Reserve Police Battalion 101 and the Final Solution in Poland* (New York, 1998).

34 The National-Labor Alliance of the New Generation (*Narodno-trudovoi soiuz novogo pokoleniia*, or NTSNP) was a right-wing Russian extremist group consisting of "whites" (opponents of the Bolshevik Revolution). The organization was founded in June 1930 in Belgrade. Its ideology was characterized by an antisemitic approach, and its members collaborated with the Nazis during World War II.

35 "Ukrainian youth!" pamphlet, OUN Archive, RG 1, List 1, File 194, p. 221. *Katsap* is a derogatory term for Russians.

36 OUN Archive, RG 1, List 2, File 47, Page 13.

37 Ibid.

38 OUN Archive, RG 1, List 2, File 47, Page 30.

39 Ulas Samchuk, *Na bilomu koni. Spomyny i vrazhennia* (Winnipeg, 1972), p. 148.

40 "Ukrainian peasant!" State Archive of the Security Services of Ukraine, RG 13, File 376, Vol. 9, http://avr.org.ua/index.php/viewDoc/1793/.

41 Thomas Fisher Rare Book Library (Toronto, Canada), The Peter J. Potichnyj Collection on Insurgency and Counter-Insurgency in Ukraine, Box 75, *We Accuse*.

42 Ulas Samchuk, *Na bilomu koni. Spomyny i vrazhennia* (Winnipeg, 1972), p. 198.

43 M. Kasyan, "Go Easy On the Germans," OUN Archive, RG 1, File 281, Page 3.

44 Ibid., p. 6.

45 Ibid., p. 8.

46 Iurii Kaliberda and Andrii Fed'ko, *Zbroini formuvannia OUN Mel'nyka u 1943-1944 rokakh na Volyni*, http://www.rusnauka.com/15_DNI_2008/Istoria/33427.doc.htm.

47 Vladimir Samarin, "Grazhdanskaia zhizn' pod nemetzkoi okkupatsiei, 1942-1944," in Oleg Budnitskii and Galina Zelenina (eds.), *"Svershilos'. Prishli nemtsy!" Ideinyi kollaboratsionizm v SSSR v period Velikoi Oteshestvennoi voiny* (Moscow, 2012), p. 272.

48 Temnyk Iuliian Ivanovich, June 3, 1896 – August 26 1992, http://necropolis.uinp.gov.ua/burial?id=2375485090592457769

49 Ukrainian necropolis in Canada, https://www.facebook.com/permalink.php?story_fbid=3867035140049584&id=916109341808860

50 Mariia Shchur, "Dyviziia 'Waffen SS' 'Halychyna'. Shcho tse za z'iednannia i chomu tryvaiut' superechky?" https://www.radiosvoboda.org/a/dyvizia-halychyna-superechky/31230015.html

Omer Bartov

Perpetrators, Victims, and Neighbors: The Fate of the Jews in Buczacz, 1941-1944

I.

This article presents the main arguments and findings of my recent book, *Anatomy of a Genocide: The Life and Death of a Town Called Buczacz*.[1] The book provides a heavily documented narrative of events in this locality, but it largely refrains from discussing the theoretical and methodological concepts that undergird it and does not sketch out the main contribution such local studies make to our understanding of the Holocaust as a whole. In the following I articulate these ideas, briefly summarize the gist of the book, and argue for its contribution to a new understanding of the Holocaust.

I began thinking about this book in the early 1990s. At the time, the disintegration of the communist system was initially presented by some observers as the "end of history."[2] But such assertions were quickly followed by two genocides in Bosnia and Rwanda, in which people were often killed by their own neighbors.[3] Ironically, it was during that same decade that the Holocaust came to be recognized by the international community as a major event in World War II and, indeed, in the history of the twentieth century.[4] Yet the conventional understanding of the Holocaust at the time set it apart from other genocides, presenting it as a highly organized undertaking of industrial murder which succeeded in distancing the killers from their victims and compartmentalized the process of extermination in a manner that left little room for either responsibility or choice. The victims, as the former commandant of the extermination camps Sobibór and Treblinka, Franz Stangl, chillingly remarked many years later, allegedly appeared to the perpetrators like lemmings running to their inevitable deaths.[5]

The intimate nature of the violence in Bosnia and Rwanda, and the sense that the prevailing representation of the Holocaust had largely taken the perpetrators off the hook by making them into mere pawns in a vast, impersonal machine, caused me to rethink the reigning paradigms of Holocaust historiography, briefly put, decision-making at the top and the incremental implementation of a highly bureaucratized, continent-wide genocide.[6] Instead, I wanted to find out whether there was after all an intimate encounter between the perpetrators and their victims, and if so, what was the nature of that encounter? Was there a degree of mutual recognition of a shared humanity, and if there was, how did it affect the contours of the event as a whole?

To be sure, by that time, notwithstanding the almost compulsive scholarly and public focus on the extermination camps, especially on Auschwitz, it was already known that about half of the victims of the Holocaust had been killed elsewhere. Indeed, as it turned out, a vast majority of those victims were murdered where they lived, in their own synagogues and cemeteries, parks and streets, or in nearby woods and ravines. But research on such killings told us precious little about cases in which there had been any significant contact between the killers and the victims before the slaughter began.[7]

In order to investigate this question, I chose to closely examine how events unfolded in Buczacz, a fairly characteristic town in Eastern Europe, the region where the majority of the Jews had lived before the war and where most of them were murdered.[8] Buczacz had the distinction of being the birthplace and literary focus of the Hebrew-language author and Nobel Prize laureate Shmuel Yosef Agnon.[9] It was also the hometown of Emanuel Ringelblum, the renowned historian of Polish-Jewish relations and founder of the Warsaw Ghetto's "Oyneg Shabes" archive, as well as of the "Nazi hunter" Simon Wiesenthal.[10] Finally, my own mother spent the first years of her life in Buczacz, before immigrating to Palestine in 1935 at the age of eleven along with her parents and two brothers. None of the rest of my family that remained in the region survived the Holocaust.

In 1995, by way of launching my research, I interviewed my mother about her childhood. What struck me in her account was that she had little to say about antisemitism, fear, or animosity. She grew up speaking Yiddish at home, studying at the local Polish public school, and conversing in Ukrainian with her girlfriends. She had fond memories of going with them to the forest to pick wild berries and mushrooms. It was a good childhood, which ended, in fact, as soon as she arrived in Palestine.

It is true, as I subsequently learned, that childhood friendships across ethnic and religious lines at that time often, albeit not always, unraveled in adulthood. But my mother's story indicated that my initial question concerning the encounter between the perpetrators and the victims was insufficient, since it left out the impact of long-term interethnic relations on such local genocides once the killing began. In other words, rather than beginning at the end, when – as in the case of another closely documented site – one half of a town set out to murder the other half,[11] I sought to go back further in time in order to understand how communities of ethnic and religious coexistence were gradually transformed into communities of fraternal violence.

II.

In Buczacz, a town of about 15,000 people on the eve of World War II, three ethnic and religious groups had lived side-by-side since the sixteenth century: Poles, Jews, and Ukrainians (known for much of this period as Ruthenians). Initially a private town owned by the noble Buczacki family, in 1612 Buczacz was inherited by the powerful Potocki clan, serving as one of a chain of borderland strongholds to ward off invasions from the east and the south. Indeed, the town was devastated during Bohdan Khmelnytsky's 1648 Cossack uprising and was sacked in 1676 by Ottoman Sultan Mehmed IV's invading armies.[12] But in the course of the eighteenth century, governed for much of the period by the eccentric Count Mikołaj Potocki, Buczacz flourished. Many of the city's most outstanding edifices were constructed at that time, including its splendid baroque city hall, the impressive Greek Catholic Basilian Monastery, the remodeled Roman Catholic Church, and the massive Great Synagogue, whose thick walls were meant to protect the local congregation from anti-Jewish violence.[13]

Even as Buczacz prospered, the Polish-Lithuanian Commonwealth had partly crumbled, and by the end of the eighteenth century had entirely vanished from the map. In the first partition of Poland in 1772, the Habsburg Empire annexed the kingdom's southern territories and renamed them Galicia. This newly acquired land now became Austria's easternmost and poorest province, which also boasted the largest concentration of Jews in the empire. While the Polish aristocracy maintained its influence in the region, the larger part of the province, known as eastern Galicia, had a majority Ukrainian population. It was there that Buczacz now found itself, and over the nineteenth century the town's Jewish community kept growing, amounting to two-thirds of the city's residents in the 1880s, and stabilizing at about 50 percent of the population by 1914. The Poles comprised the city's second largest group, whereas the countryside had a majority Ukrainian population, as well as many mixed Polish-Ukrainian villages and even families.[14]

But the vast, multiethnic, and multi-religious Austro-Hungarian Empire, as it came to be known in the last decades of its existence, also went the way of all empires and vanished from the map at the end of World War I. The old province of Galicia was now taken over again by a resurrected Poland, even as its eastern districts remained majority Ukrainian and its towns were densely populated by Jews. It was only under German and Soviet rule that this four-centuries-long coexistence was violently and irreversibly undone. This means that for many generations, the only reality known to the people of the region was one of an ethnically mixed society. To be sure, throughout this period each group preserved (and transformed) its unique customs, religion, language, and often socioeconomic niche. But at the same time there was always lively and regular social and economic interaction between the groups, with individuals often speaking other groups' languages and making acquaintances, business partners, and friends across ethnoreligious lines.

This is not to say that we can anachronistically describe pre-World War II Galician society as pluralistic or multicultural. Most people adhered strongly to their religious and ethnic identities, even before they acquired national-political attributes, and collective memories of the bloody events of the seventeenth century never entirely disappeared. There was also, of course, always a degree of socioeconomic envy and resentment, and religious prejudice was ubiquitous, although its intensity greatly varied over time and space. Indicatively, even in the case of the numerous intermarriages between Roman Catholic Poles and Greek Catholic Ukrainians, the sons of such unions traditionally followed the father's religion, while the daughters followed the mother's, thereby perpetuating ethnoreligious differences within families over generations. Nonetheless, it must be stressed that during the two centuries between the Ottoman wars and World War I, Buczacz specifically and eastern Galicia as a whole experienced very little communal violence of any sort.[15]

Why, then, did these same groups perpetrate such extreme violence on each other in World War II? Clearly, the violence must be attributed in part to the invasion of external forces. But the fact of the matter is that interethnic violence began in the region long before the Germans arrived on the scene, and that its seeds were sown decades before the first round of killings in World War I. Indeed, the most direct roots of violence in Galicia can be traced to the rise of nationalism in the region during the second half of the nineteenth century, which was often grafted onto previous religious and ethnic affinities. As the nationalizers began to gain supporters among the masses, the question was increasingly asked: Who belongs to this land, and who does not? Or, to whom does the land belong, and who is an alien, a colonizer, or an invader?

According to the Polish nationalist narrative, popularly articulated in Nobel Prize laureate Henryk Sienkiewicz's 1884 novel *By Fire and Sword*, benevolent Polish noblemen had come to the "wild lands" of the east to civilize and bring prosperity to their primitive inhabitants and to ward off invasions by savage Cossacks, Tatars, and Turks. Consequently, Polish nationalists preferred to depict the mostly rural Greek Catholics of Galicia as Ruthenians who were unconnected to the Ukrainians living under Russian rule, and who would therefore eventually become part of the larger Polish nation.[16] Ukrainian nationalists, for their part, presented themselves as the representatives of the colonized indigenous population, oppressed and exploited by the Polish landlords and their Jewish lackeys, who leased their estates, monopolized the production and sale of alcohol, and robbed the honest peasants of their last penny and drop of dignity.[17] The popular Ukrainian-Galician author Ivan Franko, who became a herald and leader of pre-World War I Ukrainian nationalism, dedicated many of his stories and novels to the fraught relations between the three groups, consistently describing Ukrainian villagers as the victims of Polish arrogance and Jewish greed and machinations.[18]

Jewish nationalism arrived late in Galicia, largely under the impact of Polish and Ukrainian nationalists, not least because the only issue on which these two groups could agree was that in their future vision of their respective nation-states the Jews had no place. But in Galicia Jewish nationalism increasingly meant Zionism, which borrowed from its Polish and Ukrainian counterparts the notion of an ethno-territorial nation but trained its sights on another land and therefore opted out of the competition over ownership of Galicia (which explains why not a few antisemitic Poles and Ukrainians supported Zionism). The eventual struggle of Zionism with the Arab inhabitants of Palestine was an ironic extension of this East European story but cannot be discussed here.[19]

Nonetheless, the growing nationalism and antagonistic rhetoric of the three groups did not generally translate into physical violence before World War I, as the empire, which had allowed the emergence of the nationalists, managed to balance them one against the other and to keep them from going for each other's throats. All this changed dramatically with the outbreak of war in 1914. World War I put an end to the old social order; the extraordinary violence of the fighting and the massive destruction of property were accompanied by extensive population displacement and numerous instances of cruelty and brutality against civilians. Especially targeted were those Jews who came under Russian occupation, as occurred in Buczacz in 1914-15 and again in 1916-17, during which time Cossacks and other Russian troops killed, raped, maimed, robbed, and humiliated the Jewish inhabitants, often to the merriment and material benefit of their Gentile neighbors.[20]

Many of the soldiers in the multiethnic Austro-Hungarian army had little loyalty to the empire. What Galician Polish and Ukrainian recruits fought for was the creation of their own future national political entities, whose establishment went directly against the interests of imperial Vienna. Only the Jews were still known as "*Kaisertreu*," or loyal to the emperor, not least because they feared what would happen to them once the empire collapsed. This in turn was seen by their neighbors as either siding with their enemies or gutlessly evading the fighting altogether, the plentiful evidence of Jewish sacrifice for the empire notwithstanding.[21]

With the collapse of Austria-Hungary in 1918, the Poles and Ukrainians turned on each other, fighting a bitter war, replete with many massacres of civilians, over the territory of Galicia. By 1919 the Ukrainian gambit to create an independent West Ukrainian People's Republic (ZUNR) had gone up in flames and the region became part of Poland. The fraternal fighting had not prevented either force from also perpetrating violence on Jewish communities, the most notorious instance of which was a pogrom by Polish soldiers in Galicia's capital of Lwów (Lemberg) in November 1918.[22]

The six years of extreme violence that ended up with Poland's annexation of Galicia had filled the hearts of its inhabitants with terror, fear, and resentment. The unfulfilled Polish promises to grant Ukrainian autonomy further fueled the conflict between these two groups, and the memories of wartime horrors remained seared in the minds of the youths who would become the activists and fighters of the 1930s and 1940s. The Polish authorities attempted to redress the demographic conundrum of a Ukrainian majority in eastern Poland by providing preferential treatment to colonists arriving from the heartland of the country, thereby heightening local interethnic tensions. At the same time Ukrainian efforts to promote their national identity in schools, reading clubs, and a variety of patriotic associations were severely repressed. This in turn led to the establishment in 1929 of the underground terrorist Organization of Ukrainian Nationalists (OUN), which was dedicated to the creation of a Pole-free and Jew-free independent Ukraine, became associated with other east European fascist movements, and subsequently gained the support of the Nazi regime. OUN activists in Buczacz in the 1930s resurfaced as members of the administration and police once the Germans occupied the region in the summer of 1941.[23]

The Jewish population of Buczacz, drastically decimated in World War I, only partially recovered in the postwar period, and then experienced growing poverty in the 1930s as a result of the Great Depression and Ukrainian boycotts intended to limit Jewish economic influence. Polish state antisemitism greatly increased after the death of the authoritarian leader Józef Piłsudski in 1935 and the rise of extreme right parties advocating the removal of the Jews from Poland. Yet by that time restrictions on immigration to the United States, western Europe, and Palestine made it all the more difficult to leave. Letters sent overseas on the eve of the war express a sense of despair at being trapped in a land where Jews are not wanted with nowhere to go. Some young, mostly working-class Jewish men and women turned to communism, but failed to find any adherents among the rest of the population. A few of those who survived formed small resistance groups under the German occupation; most of them were killed before the end of the war.[24]

III.

As previously agreed between Adolf Hitler and Joseph Stalin, on 17 September 1939, just over two weeks after the Germans invaded Poland from the West, the Red Army marched into Galicia. In an attempt to rapidly integrate this region into the Soviet Union, the new authorities nationalized the economy, thereby causing severe food shortages; organized fraudulent elections so as to create the impression of public support for the annexation; and, most harmfully, launched a campaign of deportations, and incarcerations, and executions of their real and imaginary opponents. The first wave targeted mostly the Polish elites, the second included Jews belonging to objectionable socioeconomic groups and political parties, and the third consisted in mass arrests of Ukrainian nationalist activists. Notably, initially many Ukrainians had greeted the Soviets as liberators from Polish oppression, and many Jews were relieved not to have come under German-Nazi rule. Subsequently, both Poles and Ukrainians recalled their respective deportations as national tragedies, whereas Jews perceived them as inadvertent rescue from a far worse fate under Hitler. Additionally, although proportionately Jews were more likely to be deported, their Gentile neighbors blamed their own deportations on Jewish collaboration with the Soviets.[25]

As the Red Army began retreating from Galicia in the face of the massive German invasion in late June 1941, the NKVD (Soviet secret police) executed thousands of Ukrainian activists incarcerated in local jails. This in turn led to mass violence throughout Galicia by local Ukrainian nationalists and rabble against Jewish citizens accused of precipitating these executions even before the Germans arrived. The new authorities, themselves wedded to the idea of "Judeo-Bolshevism," at first encouraged and participated in the violence, before casting it in their own more thorough and systematic mold.[26] In Buczacz, as soon as the Soviets began leaving, a Ukrainian "Sich" militia was formed, numbering about a hundred men and commanded by prewar nationalist activists. The militia unleashed a series of reprisal actions against former Soviet administrators, as well as widespread anti-Jewish violence. The older political and religious elites were powerless in the face of these young armed nationalists and hooligans and expressed the hope that once German order was established it would put a stop to the arbitrary killings, rapes, and looting. Ukrainian leaders also hoped that the Germans would allow Ukrainian autonomy and eventual independence. And while Hitler had no intention of allowing a Ukrainian state, German authorities on the ground were delighted to enlist local support in implementing their policy of removing the Jews, which neatly coincided with the agenda of such organizations as the OUN.[27]

The Germans marched into Buczacz on July 5, 1941, and after a few weeks of chaos took control of the city. As part of this process, they converted the local "Sich" into an auxiliary police force, eventually creating a battalion of over 300 men whose main goal was to assist them in carrying out the mass murder of the local Jewish population. In August the so-called Jewish "intelligentsia" of Buczacz, about 450 mostly male professionals, were led to the nearby Fedor Hill and shot by a German Security Police (*Sicherheitspolizei* – Sipo) force from Tarnopol, assisted by the local Ukrainian police. The following month a new Sipo outpost was established in the nearby town of Czortków, whose task was to exterminate the entire Jewish population in the region. This outpost, numbering between 20-30 Gestapo, Criminal Police, and SS men, including several ethnic Germans from Lithuania and Czechoslovakia, assisted by the Ukrainian auxiliary police battalion along with local detachments of uniformed German gendarmerie, Ukrainian police, and Jewish police (*Ordnungsdienst* – OD), murdered approximately 60,000 Jews in the Czortków-Buczacz area, mostly between August 1942 and June 1943. About half of the victims were loaded onto trains in extremely brutal roundups, during which hundreds were shot on the streets, and transported to the Bełżec extermination camp, where they were gassed. Once this camp shut down in late 1942, the rest of the victims were shot in or near their towns. In the case of Buczacz, the burial pits were dug on Fedor Hill and Baszty Hill – the site of the Jewish cemetery – located on either of the sides of the town and a brief walk from the main square, well within earshot of all inhabitants. This was the pattern of the murder of all 500,000 Jews in Galicia, approximately half of whom were shot where they lived.[28]

When the German Sipo personnel and local Buczacz gendarmes were not busy killing the Jews, they were having a mighty good time. Living in bucolic settings, without any danger to their personal security, and enjoying unlimited access to food, alcohol, tobacco, and sex, they had absolute power over life and death, and were only loosely controlled by their superiors in Lemberg. Not only could they act as they pleased, at times they also brought their family members, wives, children, even parents, as well as mistresses, to share with them the pleasures of genocidal colonial rule, and recalled that period even decades later, when some of them were eventually brought to trial, as the best time of their lives.[29]

The Germans also got to know their victims, often intimately, before they murdered them. Since the bulk of the killings began only a year after their arrival, in the meantime they used the Jews not merely as forced labor in such projects as road construction but also as their maids, babysitters, dentists, barbers, tailors, housecleaners, secretaries, and so forth. They knew many of the Jews by name, just as the few Jews who survived remembered them. Other Germans in Buczacz, such as the local civilian administrators, train and postal officials, engineers and foremen brought there to repair the train bridge and tunnel blown up by the retreating Soviets, as well as these men's wives, similarly became acquainted with the Jewish population, at times even befriended them, but also partook of the property left behind by those who were murdered and, in some cases, either observed the killings or participated in them. And, of course, the Germans had numerous contacts with the non-Jewish population, as civil servants, doctors, policemen, lovers, or friends. It was, as many recalled, a lively social scene, even as regular roundups and mass killings were occurring right under people's windows.[30]

In Buczacz alone approximately 10,000 Jews from the town and surrounding communities were killed, over half of them in situ, between October 1942 and June 1943, when the city was declared *Judenfrei*, or free of Jews. The remaining Jews, some of whom were hiding with villagers, while others were employed in agricultural labor camps, were mostly killed in the period leading to the takeover of Buczacz by the Red Army in March 1944. Large numbers of them were murdered by their own putative rescuers or denounced and killed either by the Germans, or, most commonly, by the Ukrainian police. Still, when the Soviets arrived, some 800 Jews came out of hiding, a relatively high number attributed both to less vehement antisemitism among the peasants in the Buczacz area (and the greater willingness of some Polish villages to help Jews), and to the attacks by small Jewish resistance groups on several "professional denouncers," which succeeded in intimidating those who hoped to make a profitable business from handing Jews over to the Germans. But in April 1944 the Red Army made a tactical retreat from Buczacz and most of the surviving Jews, too weak to escape and unable to return to their exposed shelters, were murdered. By the time the Soviets returned for good in July 1944 fewer than one hundred Jews out of a prewar population of 8,000 were still alive in the city and its vicinity.[31]

<h2 style="text-align:center">IV.</h2>

In reconstructing the normalization and routinization of genocide on the local level, one must make ample use of first-person, most often Jewish accounts. Such testimonies often have little to say about the Germans and repeatedly refer to choices made by Christian neighbors and villagers. To be sure, considering the unrelenting determination of the Germans to exterminate the Jews, choices were limited. And yet, for those who survived, they made the difference between life and death. Most Jewish survivors owed their lives to a neighbor, an acquaintance, or an unknown villager, who offered them shelter, or even just handed them some bread and milk. Conversely, not a few Christians who took Jews in for pay, whether to buy them food or to enrich themselves, ended up betraying them when the Jews ran out of money, or when the putative rescuers grew impatient to lay their hands on Jewish property, or because they feared that their neighbors, who resented them for profiting from their Jews, were about to denounce them. In rare instances, even Germans let Jews go. One remarkable Wehrmacht officer protected some 600 Jews from local bandits, raiding villagers, and disbanded paramilitary units in the nearby town of Tłuste during the last weeks of the German occupation, keeping his promise to stay until merely a few hours before the Red Army marched in. We know of his heroic act only from accounts by the Jews he saved.[32]

The killing in the region did not end with the murder of the Jews. As German rule in the region began to disintegrate, units of the radical faction of the OUN, known as Banderites after the name of their leader, Stepan Bandera, along with the newly formed Ukrainian Insurgent Army (UPA), which had already been engaged in an ethnic cleansing campaign of the Polish population in the nearby province of Volhynia, crossed over to Galicia in early 1944 and set about massacring entire Polish communities. The underground Polish Home Army (AK) and other armed peasant battalions in the area responded in kind, and a brutal civil war between the two groups ensued. The Germans paid scant attention to these mutual massacres as long as they did not interfere with their own operations, and in some cases actually helped Polish civilians escape to the west. The fighting continued beyond the return of the Red Army, with the OUN-UPA also engaging in a bitter insurgency against the Soviets, brutally suppressed by the NKVD, which deported thousands of insurgents and their families to gulags and settlements in Siberia and Central Asia. By then a population exchange agreed between the USSR and the communist authorities in Poland ensured that Galicia was entirely emptied of its remaining Polish inhabitants. For the first time in recorded history, this centuries-old multiethnic region had finally been transformed, through genocide, ethnic cleansing, deportations, and population policies, into a purely Ukrainian land. Ironically, the goal of Ukrainian nationalists going back to the late nineteenth century had been accomplished through the combined policies of the region's German and Soviet occupiers.[33]

For the next four decades the prewar and wartime history of Buczacz, as that of Eastern Galicia as a whole, was thoroughly distorted and largely erased. Under Soviet rule there was no room to speak of the particular horror of the extermination of the Jews, nor of the collaboration of much of the Ukrainian population, whereas the anti-Soviet insurgency was presented as the work of a few fascist bad apples. A local guidebook for Buczacz merely commented that 7,000 innocent Soviet citizens were murdered there by the "Hitlerites," insisting that the population as a whole never submitted to their hated rule. Once Ukraine gained independence in 1991, a new version of events emerged. Now the OUN and UPA were presented as national heroes who continued the task first taken up by Khmelnytsky to liberate their land from foreign oppression. Statutes of Stepan Bandera sprouted everywhere.[34]

Conversely, in provincial towns such as Buczacz no mention was made of the murder of their own Jews or of the fact that before the war at least half of the population was Jewish. Even in the local high school, where Ringelblum and Wiesenthal had once studied, the town's Jewish past remains unmentioned. And while the Roman Catholic church has now been beautifully restored, the single remaining Jewish edifice in Buczacz, the study house, was bulldozed in 2001 to make room for a shopping center. No signs have been put up to mark the sites of the mass graves surrounding the town. Somewhat more optimistically, on the initiative of several young people in town, a bust of Agnon has been put up and a literary center was created on the street named after him, where he is erroneously thought to have lived in his childhood.[35]

What the local Ukrainian population remembers of those years of war and occupation is a saga of oppression and a bitter struggle for liberation. Ukrainians speak of themselves as victims of the interwar Polish regime; as the principal target of Soviet repression in 1939-1941; of being robbed and sent to forced labor in the Reich by the Germans; and of suffering for many years in gulags and deportation after the failed postwar insurgency. What they prefer to forget are the numerous Ukrainian policemen who facilitated the roundups and mass executions of their Jewish neighbors. Even those who recalled their Jewish friends with sympathy and sorrow, insisted that local Poles and Ukrainians only tried to help them however they could. Such types as Volodymyr Kaznovskyi, a former district attorney turned police chief under the Germans, have been erased from the local collective memory. Instead, Fedor Hill, where thousands of Jewish victims are buried, is adorned by a large memorial to the heroes and martyrs of the struggle for Ukrainian liberation, while a statute of Bandera looks down on the city from another hill.[36]

V.

What can be learned about the Holocaust as a whole and genocide more generally from this study of the deep roots of interethnic coexistence and the particular manner in which genocide unfolded in Buczacz under German rule? Let me offer some concluding thoughts on the value of such local studies of genocide.

First, research on Buczacz serves as a corrective to the understanding of the Holocaust as largely carried out in a detached manner, whereby the encounter between perpetrators and victims was greatly limited. On the local level, in hundreds of towns such as Buczacz, that was hardly the case. Indeed, the genocidal encounter between killers and their targets was intimate rather than detached, because often the victims had become known to the perpetrators for many months before they were killed.

Second, the perception that much of the killing took place in secret, remote, and well-concealed extermination camps, is refuted by the finding that in such cases as Buczacz the roundups were public, watched by the entire local population and the German civilians in the town. Even train deportations were accompanied by extreme brutality and hundreds were shot on the street. The killings in situ occurred within everyone's earshot and were watched by many residents and German civilians, some of whom deliberately walked up to the pits out of sheer curiosity, as they subsequently testified.

Third, the category of bystanders is largely emptied of meaning in such cases of local genocide. In these small towns no one simply stood by; rather, there were only degrees of engagement, ranging from total collaboration in the killing to altruistic rescue. Most people were somewhere in-between, and often moved along the scale depending on the circumstances. People might take over the property of friends and neighbors killed in front of their eyes simply because otherwise someone else would appropriate it. Once they did so, they became part of the profit-making enterprise that genocide invariably is.

Fourth, local genocide exposes the ambiguity of goodness, whereby survival depended on help from one's neighbors, just as it was usually neighbors, or even the rescuers themselves, who were most likely to denounce those in hiding. Sheltering Jews was dangerous and expensive but could also bring in a nice profit, as well as allow for labor and sexual exploitation. The Germans often depended on locals to identify Jews, discover their hideouts, and go into the woods to kill them. Yet almost all Jews who survived were rescued by Christian acquaintances or strangers, in some cases by extremely poor peasants.

Fifth, in examining the longue durée of local violence we find that those who were or perceived themselves as being victimized under one set of circumstances, could swiftly become the perpetrators of violence under other conditions. Local Poles and Ukrainians related differently to changing rulers, but locally attributed much of their suffering to the other group, whose members they often knew intimately. Yet both groups tended to see the Jews as siding with the other, as well as with external forces. At the same time, they denied participation in the mass murder of the Jews and occasionally suggested that the victims had responded to their own genocide so passively because they perceived it as expiation for their past sins. The Jews, for their part, spoke after the event of their neighbors as being "worse than the Germans," not because they actually were, but because of a deep sense of betrayal by their fellow townsmen. It was this kind of reasoning that motivated Banderites to massacre Poles and Jews and led Poles and the few remaining Jews to join Soviet "extermination battalions" charged with eradicating the Ukrainian insurgency.

Sixth, and following from the previous point, we can conclude that the local dynamics and relations between these groups largely determined the nature, perception, and memory of the events of World War II. Not only did each group see itself as the other groups' victim, but there was also a widespread sense that any other group's relative success had come at the expense of one's own people. This was an old sentiment, which bred growing resentment and rage. It is also for this reason that in studying local genocide one must begin long before violence was unleashed and trace the process whereby interethnic coexistence began to fray and transform into mutual fear, hostility, and rage.

Seventh, the study of local genocide can only be comprehensive by making full use of all available personal accounts in the form of diaries, letters, testimonies, courtroom records, interviews, and memoirs. Such first-person evidence, when effectively woven together with other documentary records, makes it possible to create a nuanced, complex, three-dimensional picture of an event that is often described and remembered only through a partisan lens by the protagonists, and is just as often depicted by historians largely from the perspective of the perpetrators' far neater but hardly more objective archival documents.[37]

Eighth, these first-person narratives also teach us that the terminology we often take at face value has different meanings for each group of historical protagonists. Such terms as collaboration and liberation are good examples.

What Christians saw as Jewish collaboration with the Soviets was perceived by Jews as the chance to participate for the first time in the state apparatus, become policemen, carry arms, attend secondary school. What Jews saw as Ukrainian collaboration with the Germans, Ukrainians saw as the hitherto denied opportunity to work toward an independent Ukraine. What Jews saw as liberation by the Red Army in 1944, Ukrainians saw as reoccupation. Jewish survivors perceived Jewish Red Army officers as a veritable miracle; Ukrainians saw them as proof of Judeo-Bolshevism. Ukrainians saw Poles in "extermination battalions" as Soviet collaborators, Poles saw this as revenge for the massacres of the OUN-UPA forces.

Ninth, within the larger historiographical context, the study of local genocide sheds a critical light on recent work that has tended to portray Eastern Europe as a whole as the victim of two titanic and evil external forces, Stalinist Russia and Nazi Germany.[38] Once we look in more detail into events on the local level, we quickly realize that much of the violence was the product of local dynamics, at times serving the interests of one or the other external invader and at other times quite independent of them. Hence, while the Soviets and the Germans would have tried to pursue their own goals in any case, the manner in which they did so, and the extent of their success, depended on the local scene. In the Czortków-Buczacz region, for instance, the twenty-odd members of the Sipo outpost charged with murdering 60,000 Jews would have been hard put to accomplish this task so swiftly without ample local collaboration both in the form of police detachments and because widespread hostility and resentment toward Jews made it exceedingly difficult to evade the perpetrators.

Tenth, this also implies that by examining local events from "below," we are in fact providing the basis for rewriting the history of the Holocaust as a whole, since Buczacz stands for hundreds of towns and cities throughout the vast swath of Europe's eastern borderlands, from the Baltics to the Balkans. By shifting our gaze from the "top" and the "center," from the perspective of the decision-makers and bureaucrats of the "final solution," we come much closer to the reality of genocide on the ground in all its gruesome detail, but also in all its human complexity and malleability. We also come to understand that while the Holocaust was unique in certain respects, especially its modern bureaucratic organization, logistical apparatus, and extermination facilities, in other respects it resembled many other genocides both before and after World War II, where governmental forces and agencies combined with local elements to produce extensive killing by long-term neighbors. It was precisely the intimate nature of the genocide that contributed to the ubiquity of gratuitous violence, as those who had known each other for generations strove to eradicate the humanity of their victims even before they killed them.

Finally, what the study of such local genocides ought to teach us is that the sense of security that many of us enjoy and expect in our own neighborhoods, and the vast distance we perceive between our current existence and that of the populations of Eastern Europe in World War II or other sites of communal genocide, may well be questioned. For this perception of security is founded on nothing more than a thin crust of social order and respect for the law that can easily be shattered. Once we identify certain groups within our midst or on our borders as being outside the bounds of human solidarity; once we direct the forces of law and order against those marked for discrimination, isolation, incarceration, expulsion, or death, we are no longer bystanders but actively participating in the dismantling of the order on which we rely. To be sure, we wish to exclude ourselves from such identifications; yet if and when we too become targets of the state and its agencies, we have nothing to fall back on. For the thin crust of security in which we trust is merely based on our internalized sense that we can always ultimately rely on the state apparatus to protect us from each other. One night, upon hearing a suspicious noise outside our door, we call the police. But when the police arrive, they arrest us. At that instant we realize that this whole apparatus, while still perfectly in place, can be turned against us – as so many Black citizens of the United States have long known. From this point on it is only a matter of time before one of our neighbors, who had previously always said hello to us when we returned from work, will break into our home wielding an axe, and demand our property. Once the social fabric that ties us all together begins to fray, there is no telling where it may end up. What occurred in Buczacz should serve as a warning.

Endnotes

1 Omer Bartov, *Anatomy of a Genocide: The Life and Death of a Town Called Buczacz* (New York, 2018).

2 Francis Fukuyama, "The End of History?" *The National Interest* 16 (1989), pp. 3–18.

3 See, e.g., Philip Gourevitch, *We Wish to Inform You That Tomorrow We Will Be Killed With Our Families: Stories from Rwanda* (New York, 1998); Elizabeth Neuffer, *The Key to My Neighbor's House: Seeking Justice in Bosnia and Rwanda* (New York, 2001).

4 See, e.g., https://www.holocaustremembrance.com/stockholm-declaration; http://www.europarl.europa.eu/pdf/divers/eprs_briefingholocaust_en.pdf.

5 Gitta Sereny, *Into that Darkness: From Mercy Killing to Mass Murder* (New York, 1974).

6 See, e.g., Hans Mommsen, *From Weimar to Auschwitz*, trans. Philip O'Connor (Princeton, 1992); Christopher Browning, *The Path to Genocide: Essays on Launching the Final Solution* (New York, 1992).

7 See, e.g., Christopher Browning, *Ordinary Men: Reserve Police Battalion 101 and the Final Solution in Poland* (New York, 1992).

8 Omer Bartov, "Eastern Europe as the Site of Genocide," *The Journal of Modern History* 80(3) (2008), pp. 557-593.

9 See, e.g., S. Y. Agnon, *A City in Its Fullness*, eds. Alan Mintz and Jeffrey Saks, multiple translators (New Milford, CT, 2016).

10 Samuel Kassow, *Who Will Write Our History? Emanuel Ringelblum, the Warsaw Ghetto, and the Oyneg Shabes Archive* (Bloomington, 2007); Tom Segev, *Simon Wiesenthal*, trans. Ronnie Hope (New York, 2010).

11 Jan T. Gross, *Neighbors: The Destruction of the Jewish Community in Jedwabne, Poland* (Princeton, 2001).

12 For sources see Bartov, *Anatomy of a Genocide*, pp. 6-13. See also Nathan Hannover, *Abyss of Despair: The Famous 17th Century Chronicle Depicting Jewish life in Russia and Poland during the Chmielnicki Massacres of 1648-1649 (Yeven metzulah)*, trans. Abraham J. Mesch (New Brunswick, 1983).

13 Bartov, *Anatomy of a Genocide*, pp. 13-15.

14 Ibid., pp. 15-17, 22-4, 34-5. See also Abraham J. Brawer, *Galizien, wie es an Österreich kam: Eine historisch-statistische Studie über die inneren Verhältnisse des Landes im Jahre 1772* (Leipzig andVienna, 1910).

15 Bartov, *Anatomy of a Genocide*, pp. 17-19, 22-5. See also Oskar Kofler, *Żydowskie dwory: Wspomnienia z Galicji Wschodniej od początku XIX wieku do wybuchu i wojny światowej*, ed. Ewa Koźmińska-Frejlak (Warsaw, 1999).

16 Bartov, *Anatomy of a Genocide*, pp. 26-8. See also Henryk Sienkiewicz, *With Fire and Sword*, trans. W. S. Kuniczak (New York, 1991).

17 Bartov, *Anatomy of a Genocide*, pp. 19-22. See also John-Paul Himka, *Galician Villagers and the Ukrainian National Movement in the Nineteenth Century* (New York, 1988).

18 See, e.g., Ivan Franko, *Turbulent Times: A Trilogy*, trans. Roma Franko (Toronto, 2006).

19 Bartov, *Anatomy of a Genocide*, pp. 25, 33-6. See also Joshua Shanes, *Diaspora Nationalism and Jewish identity in Habsburg Galicia* (New York, 2012); Omer Bartov, "The Return of the Displaced: Ironies of the Jewish-Palestinian Nexus, 1939-1949," *Jewish Social Studies* 24(3) (2019), pp. 26-50.

20 Bartov, *Anatomy of a Genocide*, pp. 47-52, 57-62. See also S. Ansky, *The Enemy at his Pleasure: A Journey through the Jewish Pale of Settlement during World War I*, trans. Joachim Neugroschel (New York, 2003); and Antoni Siewiński's account in Omer Bartov (ed.), *Voices on War and Genocide: Three Accounts of the World Wars in a Galician Town* (New York, 2020), pp. 21-137.

21 Bartov, *Anatomy of a Genocide*, pp. 54-5, 65-8, 71. See also Derek Penslar, *Jews and the Military: A History* (Princeton, 2013).

22 Bartov, *Anatomy of a Genocide*, pp. 64-81. See also William Hagen, "The Moral Economy of Popular Violence: The Pogrom in Lwów, November 1918," in Robert Blobaum (ed.), *Antisemitism and Its Opponents in Modern Poland* (Ithaca, 2005), pp. 124-47.

23 Bartov, *Anatomy of a Genocide*, pp. 102-114, 122-8. See also, e.g., Per Anders Rudling, "The OUN, the UPA and the Holocaust: A Study in the Manufacturing of Historical Myths," *The Carl Beck Papers in Russian and East European Studies* 2107 (2011); Marco Carynnyk, "Foes of Our Rebirth," *Nationalities Papers* 39(3) (2011), pp. 315-352.

24 Bartov, *Anatomy of a Genocide*, pp. 82-90, 93-102, 116, 121-2. See also Emanuel Melzer, *No Way Out: The Politics of Polish Jewry, 1935-1939* (Cincinnati, 1997). See also Moshe Wizinger's account in Bartov, *Voices on War and Genocide*, pp. 285-428

25 Bartov, *Anatomy of a Genocide*, pp. 129-57. See also, e.g., Jan T. Gross, *Revolution from Abroad: The Soviet Conquest of Poland's Western Ukraine and Western Belorussia*, 2nd ed. (Princeton, 2002).

26 See, e.g., Kai Struve, *Deutsche Herrschaft, ukrainischer Nationalismus, antijüdische Gewalt: Der Sommer 1941 in der Westukraine* (Berlin, 2015); John-Paul Himka, "The Lviv Pogrom of 1941: The Germans, Ukrainian Nationalists, and the Carnival Crowd," *Canadian Slavonic Papers* 53(2-4) (2011), pp. 209-243.

27 Bartov, *Anatomy of a Genocide*, pp. 158-62, 167-9. See also, e.g., Karel Berkhoff and Marco Carynnyk, "The Organization of Ukrainian Nationalists and Its Attitude toward Germans and Jews: Iaroslav Stets'ko's 1941 'Zhyttiepys,'" *Harvard Ukrainian Studies* 23(3) (1999), pp. 149-184.

28 Bartov, *Anatomy of a Genocide*, pp. 163-7, 169, 175-85. See also, e.g., Dieter Pohl, *Nationalsozialistische Judenverfolgung in Ostgalizien 1941-1944: Organisation und Durchführung eines Staatlichen Massenverbrechens* (Berlin, 1997); Thomas Sandkühler, *"Endlösung" in Galizien: Der Judenmord in Ostpolen und die Rettungsinitiativen von Berthold Beitz, 1941-1944* (Bonn, 1996). For a Ukrainian insider's view, see the account by Viktor Petrykevych in Bartov, *Voices on War and Genocide*, pp. 139-282.

29	Bartov, *Anatomy of a Genocide*, pp. 185-6, 188-213. See also, e.g., Ernst Klee et al. (eds.), *"The Good Old Days": The Holocaust as Seen by Its Perpetrators and Bystanders*, trans. Deborah Burnstone (New York, 1991).

30	Bartov, *Anatomy of a Genocide*, pp.186-8, 213-29. See also, e.g., Gordon Horwitz, *In the Shadow of Death: Living Outside the Gates of Mauthausen* (New York, 1990).

31	Bartov, *Anatomy of a Genocide*, pp. 229-30, 232-45. See also Israel Cohen (ed.), *The Book of Buczacz* (Tel Aviv, 1956), pp. 233-302 (Hebrew). English translation at: https://www.jewishgen.org/yizkor/buchach/buchach.html

32	Bartov, *Anatomy of a Genocide*, pp. 245-62. See also, e.g., Jan Grabowski, *Hunt for the Jews: Betrayal and Murder in German-Occupied Poland* (Bloomington, 2013); Mordercai Paldiel, *The Path of the Righteous: Gentile Rescuers of Jews during the Holocaust* (Hoboken, 1993).

33	Bartov, *Anatomy of a Genocide*, pp. 265-88. See also, e.g., Timothy Snyder, "The Causes of Ukrainian-Polish Ethnic Cleansing 1943," *Past and Present* 179 (2003), pp. 197-234; Grzegorz Motyka, "Der Krieg im östlichen Galizien," *Karta* 30 (2000), pp. 36-37.

34	Bartov, *Anatomy of a Genocide*, pp. 291-3, 296-8; Omer Bartov, *Erased: Vanishing Traces of Jewish Galicia in Present-Day Ukraine* (Princeton, 2007). See also, e.g., John-Paul Himka, "The Organization of Ukrainian Nationalists and the Ukrainian Insurgent Army: Unwelcome Elements of an Identity Project," *Ab Imperio* 4 (2010), pp. 83-101; Grzegorz Rossoliński-Liebe, "Debating, Obfuscating and Disciplining the Holocaust: Post-Soviet Historical Discourses on the OUN–UPA and Other Nationalist Movements," *East European Jewish Affairs* 42(3) (2012), pp. 199-241.

35	Bartov, *Anatomy of a Genocide*, pp. 293-5. See also: https://www.nashholos.com/ukrainian-jewish-heritage-agnon-literary-center/; http://odessareview.com/returning-agnon-ukraine/

36	Bartov, *Anatomy of a Genocide*, pp. 164-7, 179-82, 248, 289-91, 293-8. See also Grzegorz Rossoliński-Liebe, *Stepan Bandera: The Life and Afterlife of a Ukrainian Nationalist: Fascism, Genocide, and Cult* (Stuttgart, 2014); John-Paul Himka, "Ukrainian Memories of the Holocaust: The Destruction of Jews as Reflected in Memoirs Collected in 1947," *Canadian Slavonic Papers* 54(3-4) (2012), pp. 427-442.

37	Omer Bartov, "Wartime Lies and Other Testimonies: Jewish-Christian Relations in Buczacz, 1939-1944," *East European Politics and Societies* 25(3) (2011), pp. 486-511.

38	Timothy Snyder, *Bloodlands: Europe between Hitler and Stalin* (New York, 2010).

Tamir Hod

The Everyday Life of Ukrainian Collaborators at Treblinka: Belzec as a Case for Comparison
(a Topic Forgotten after John Ivan Demjanjuk's Acquittal in Israel)

Introduction

In the concluding chapter of my doctoral dissertation on the Demjanjuk Affair in Israel, I maintained that valuable historical information that had been gathered for the purpose of the trial has not been addressed in a fitting manner.[1] It was Demjanjuk's acquittal, I argued, that caused the affair to be forgotten – including the important historical information involved. I recommended that this information be revealed, as its historical importance is not contingent on the outcome of the trial.[2] Archival documents that were assembled for the purpose of the legal proceedings against Demjanjuk (the trial and the appeal), as well as protocols documenting the legal proceedings themselves, relate extensively to the topic of collaboration during the Holocaust. These sources pertain to the activity of Nazi collaborators in the camps of Operation Reinhard in general and in Treblinka in particular.[3] Although the collaborators included representatives of various Slavic peoples, the Ukrainian presence in this group was especially prominent. Reports from the period, including documentation of the names and nationalities of the collaborators, are indicative of the central role played by the Ukrainians in the calamitous tragedy that was Operation Reinhard, during which approximately 1.7 million Jews were murdered, primarily in the camps of Belzec, Sobibor, and Treblinka.[4]

The aim of this article is to focus on the everyday life of the Ukrainian collaborators at Treblinka and to make use of this examination to address the claim, made by many, that they had had no other choice. Studies have been conducted on what occurred in the camps of Operation Reinhard, including the activities of collaborators; however, none have concentrated on what we refer to here as the "free time" of the Ukrainians who operated at Treblinka.[5] This focus is accomplished through the examination of a combination of sources that were assembled for and during the Demjanjuk Trial, in addition to supplementary sources that became available after the conclusion of the trial in Israel.[6] The final section of the article contains a brief discussion of the Belzec extermination camp for the sake of comparison. This comparison between two extermination camps is intended to highlight factors that may have influenced the everyday lives of the collaborators. These factors include the fact that Belzec was the first Operation Reinhard camp to be established, whereas Treblinka was the third. In the case of Treblinka, therefore, experience had already accrued, including with regard to the treatment of collaborators. Another factor was the German command, which usually differed between the camps. We can also surmise that the demographic aspects of the areas in which the camps were located had influence on the collaborators. Many of the primary resources utilized in this article were translated into English and Hebrew for use in the trials on the matter that were conducted in Israel and the United States.

Definition of the Major Concepts:
The Operation Reinhard Camps,
the Ukrainian Collaborators, and Everyday Life
Operation (Aktion) Reinhard and the Extermination Camps

Belzec, Sobibor, and Treblinka, established in that order, were constructed as a primary means of achieving the Final Solution to the Jewish Question within the territory of the General Governorate (*Generalgouvernement*) in occupied Poland, whose Jewish population is estimated to have exceeded 2.5 million. Management of the operation was entrusted to Odilo Globocnik, SS and Police Leader in the Lublin District. The preparations for the operation got underway in 1941, and the operation received its name after the attempted assassination of Reinhard Heydrich and his subsequent death in June 1942.[7] Operation Reinhard was named after Belzec and Sobibor were already in operation.

The Belzec camp began its extermination operations on March 17, 1942 (until December 1942); Sobibor began its extermination operations in April 1942 (until October 1943); and Treblinka began its extermination operations on July 23 (and was closed in November 1943).[8] Every camp that was built constituted an improved model of the camp that preceded it. Treblinka, then, was considered to be the "super camp" of Operation Reinhard, as reflected in its number of victims, among other things.[9] Also relevant is the fact that the camp at Treblinka was set up for the extermination of the Warsaw Ghetto, the largest of all the Jewish ghettos. All three were classified as extermination camps, meaning that prisoners were kept alive solely to assist in the extermination process. In all three camps, the staff consisted of 30 SS men, between 80 and 120 Ukrainians from the auxiliary forces, and hundreds of Jews holding different positions. Under Globocnik's command were more than 150 police and SS men in the Lublin District, almost 200 police and SS men who were transferred from other areas in the General Governorate, and 92 members of the staff of the *Aktion T4* "Euthanasia" campaign (which was almost completely halted in August 1941).[10] All in all, Globocnik had approximately 450 men at his disposal,[11] and it was clear that for an operation of the scale planned, more manpower would be needed. A solution was found in Soviet prisoners of war – Russians, Lithuanians, Estonians, and especially Ukrainians – who had been captured by the Germans during the initial phases of Operation Barbarossa.

The Ukrainian Collaborators

Philip Morgan begins his book *Hitler's Collaborators* with the assertion that the issue of collaboration during the Holocaust is more polemic, unpleasant, and divisive than any other topic.[12] It is a phenomenon with many shades of grey that was present in all the populations that lived under the influence of Nazi rule. Per Anders Rudling maintains that, in the course of World War II, no less than a quarter of a million Ukrainians collaborated with the Germans,[13] engaging primarily in acts of murder and informing on and turning in others during the summer of 1941 in Soviet territory that had been conquered by Nazi Germany. Alongside this immense number, however, it must be noted that there were also 2,659 Ukrainian Righteous Among the Nations who helped Jews, even if they represented only a minority of the Ukrainian population and were not reflective of the actions of all.[14] The story around which this article revolves, however, is that of the almost 5,000 collaborators who took part in Operation Reinhard, many of whom were Ukrainian and almost all of whom participated in some of the cruelest acts known in human experience.

In a recently published comprehensive study on the life and times of Dr. Mengele,[15] historian David Marwell discusses researchers who have engaged with the testimonies of Auschwitz survivors from which it can be concluded that all the Jews at Auschwitz underwent Mengele's selection. This, Marwell notes, would mean that Dr. Mengele worked 24 hours a day, when the fact is that Mengele did his job like the other members of the medical staff at the camp. Based on these testimonies, Zadnek Zofka has concluded that the name "Mengele" actually parted ways with the man himself and became synonymous with all the doctors at Auschwitz.[16] The diversity of sources at our disposal regarding the collaborators at Treblinka leaves no room for doubt regarding the prominent representation of Ukrainian prisoners of war among the collaborators. At the same time, the collaborators, too, became synonymous with Ukrainians, regardless of their actual ethnic origins.[17] According to historian David Rich, it can be estimated that 50% of the collaborators were Ukrainian,[18] and historian Peter Black places the number at 45%.[19] In any event, the figures must be approached cautiously, as the percentage of Ukrainians may have been slightly lower. This perception is due to the approach of the Germans at the time, who preferred Ukrainian collaboration over collaboration with other national groups, leading many to lie about their ethnic origins in order to improve their chances of being selected.[20] The use here of the term "Ukrainian collaborators" is derived from both the existing data and dozens of testimonies of survivors, murderers, and inhabitants of the villages and towns that were located in close proximity to the camps of Operation Reinhard.

As noted, the German command staff was in need of increased manpower to achieve the goals of Operation Reinhard and was able to recruit it from among the Soviet prisoners of war. The collaborators who were chosen were trained at a training camp at Trawniki, not far from Lublin. The camp was meant to train the collaborators to hold the different positions they were destined to hold throughout their service. Collaborators, then, were referred to using such labels as "Trawniki Men" or "Trawnikis," "*Wachmänner*" (plural of *Wachmann*, or guards), and sometimes also "Black Ruskis."[21] Karl Streibel, who personally visited a number of the prisoner of war camps in search of potential collaborators, was appointed commander of the training camp.[22] Streibel visited camps such as Chelm and Rivne, which were characterized by terrible conditions. During the initial months of Operation Barbarossa, almost three million Red Army soldiers were taken prisoner, and many died due to the harsh conditions in which they were held. The chance of survival in such camps was approximately 15%. The SS officials who entered the prisoner of war camps to recruit collaborators offered those who joined food, cigarettes, wages, assistance for families suffering hardship, and the like.[23] As a result of these enticements, it appears, a decisive majority willingly volunteered to collaborate.[24]

As noted in the introduction, this article examines collaborators' claims that they had no choice but to volunteer, due primarily to the impossible conditions in the prisoner of war camps. Former Wachman Feodor Fedorenko, who served at Treblinka, stated before a Soviet court: "I did not want it. I was happy with my family and I had a good life."[25] "The victims thought of themselves," he continued, "and I thought of myself."[26] This suggests that the main reason the auxiliary forces took part in the undertaking was actually to save their own lives. However, familiarity with the Ukrainian populations' attitude toward the Jews, particularly in the mixed cities that were conquered by the Germans during Operation Barbarossa, supports the possibility that there were other reasons, aside from survival, that led the Ukrainians to volunteer to serve Nazi Germany.[27] Yitzhak Arad's book on Operation Reinhard identifies several of these reasons:[28]

1. Ukrainian nationalists' bitter hatred of the Communist regime and their hope that the Nazi regime would grant them independence in exchange for their cooperation.

2. Antisemitism: A combination of traditional hatred for the Jews and an emphasis of the linkage that had been established between them and Communism.

3. The difficult economic conditions of the prisoners of war, even before the outbreak of the war, and hope that collaboration would extricate them and their families from this situation.

4. *Volksdeutsche* – Ethnic Germans living outside the borders of Germany. The Trawnikis, for example, had immigrated

to Ukraine in the eighteenth century, and tens of thousands
of them volunteered to serve in the auxiliary forces. Their
belonging to the German nation and command (of some) of
the German language ushered them into command positions
within the collaborator units.

The above factors typically functioned in concert with one another, which
may explain conduct that often reached levels of cruelty displayed by the SS
men.[29] They also explain why the Germans had no problem placing rifles and
pistols in the hands of those who had just fought against them and training
them as fighters to help fulfill one of the main goals of the Nazi regime: the
extermination of the Jewish People. This is reflected in the following testimony
of one of the collaborators who underwent training at Trawniki:

> In the Wachmann school, we underwent military training. We
> learned the structure of the rifle; underwent foot drills and tactical
> training; learned the German language and German commands;
> and learned and sang German songs. In addition, we heard lectures
> on political topics, we discussed the situation on the front, and we
> praised the German army… *I had a carbine, and when I went home
> on leave I was given a pistol.*[30]

Their training at the Trawniki training camp lasted approximately two to three
months, during which the volunteers learned all that was required to become
useful and efficient collaborators. An integral part of the training involved a
demonstration of shooting Jewish prisoners from the nearby labor camp. It should
also be noted that the Trawnikis carried out a large variety of tasks in addition to
their service in the Operation Reinhard camps, including policing activity in the
ghettos of the Lublin District, assistance in deporting Jews to the extermination
camps, guarding the trains, and more.[31] Trawnikis also played a meaningful and
brutal role in suppressing the Warsaw Ghetto Uprising.[32] During their training,
they lived not as prisoners but rather as soldiers in training. Therefore, after duty
hours, they could be found enjoying time off in the nearby town, which often
resulted in marriages between Trawniki men and local girls.[33]

Everyday Life

This article deals primarily with the hours during which the collaborators were not guarding at the camp, escorting transports from the ghettos to the extermination camps, or operating the diesel engine at Treblinka (as in the case of Ivan the Terrible). With regard to the "routine" activities of the collaborators, sources that were assembled for the purpose of the Demjanjuk Trial, and many other sources, establish that the *Wachmänner* in the Operation Reinhard camps took part in all the work in the camp. This information lends support to what has already been established in various studies: that the work of the Wachman did not begin and end with manning the guard towers that surrounded the camps. According to the testimony of one collaborator:

> There was no German, *Zugwachmann*, *Oberwachmann*, or *Wachmann* who did not take part in unloading the train, in leading people to the "dressing rooms" and to the gas chambers, and in shooting the prisoners in the "clinic," because this was our service...usually, the *Wachmänner* took part in exterminating people when they were drunk and could harm the victims as they pleased, as the Germans not only did not punish them but rather encouraged them.[34]

My examination of the everyday life of the collaborators in the Treblinka extermination camp focuses on three topics: (1) money, gold, and property; (2) the collaborators' style of "free-time" activity, which included drinking alcohol, abusing victims after working hours, and relations – consensual and coerced alike – with women inside and outside the camp; and (3) attempts to escape from the camp. Each of these topics has the potential to shed light on the "mood" that permeated the world of the collaborators at Treblinka and therefore on the phenomenon of collaboration and the reasons for which many collaborators chose this path.

Between Economic Hardship and Greed

The most prominent factors that influenced the activities of the Ukrainians at Treblinka were money and gold. Their desire to amass as much as possible sometimes benefitted the Jews in an indirect manner. On several occasions, camp inmates sought to bribe the Ukrainians to help them escape or acquire weapons. Usually, the collaborators simply took what they were offered without providing the assistance requested. At the same time, however, they did not inform on those who did the bribing out of fear that the Germans would confiscate the bribe and punish them. In some cases, both the briber and the bribed paid with their lives.[35] The Jews' encounter with the Ukrainians' hunger for money and valuables began on the trip to Treblinka. Chil Rajchman, a survivor of Treblinka, offered the following description:

> Every time the train stops I ask the Ukrainians going down to the platform for a bit of water. They do not respond, but if you give them a gold watch they will bring you a bit of water. Many people parted with their valuables without receiving the few sips of water that were agreed upon.[36]

In the camp, the Ukrainians did not need to wait for such an offer from the Jews. A vast amount of money and property was collected from the Jews during Operation Reinhard, the scope of which is reflected in the detailed report that Globocnik sent to Himmler upon the conclusion of the operation.[37] In addition to the immense amount of property that was collected and sent to the Reich, the collaborators found ways to line their pockets with a substantial amount of money, gold, and jewelry. The Ukrainians benefited from this possibility throughout almost the entire period of their service in the camp, although the phenomenon reached its height during the first month of the camp's operation. During this period, the camp was commanded by Dr. Immfried Eberl. The number of transports continued to increase, and the camp could not contend with them all and with the cargo they carried. During this period, the collaborators could pocket money and gold as they pleased.[38] Eberl was discharged from this position and replaced by Franz Stangl in August 1942, which was an event that had an impact on all the inhabitants of the camp.

According to the testimonies at our disposal, some collaborators were made rich by their service in the camps of Operation Reinhard. One Wachmann told his interrogators: "The Germans and the Ukrainians had so much money that it was not so valued. I think that everyone became millionaires at Treblinka."[39] A Wachmann named Stepanović recounted: "From the property that was stolen from the Jews, I had two watches, a piece of fabric for an outfit for my wife, and children's shoes."[40] This was property that Stepanović took with him when he left the camp to go home on leave. At the end of the war, he still had 300 grams of gold that he had stolen from the Jews.[41] In 1965, a collaborator named Nikolaevich, who served in Treblinka and other camps, testified as follows:

> For this service, the Germans gave us money, gave us clothing and shoes, and fed us for free. But overall, the *Wachmänner* did not receive money, as there was no need for it – they had enough money and gold, which they would take in different ways from those who were condemned to die.[42]

The testimony of Kozminski, who also served at Treblinka, proves that the collaborators did indeed accrue large amounts of valuables and property – so much that they did not even bother to pick up their wages: "Not all the *Wachmänner* would take their wages, as everyone had the ability, in all kinds of ways, to acquire a great deal of the money, gold, and valuables left behind by those who had been exterminated."[43]

In many instances, money and property were passed on to the Ukrainians by the Jews who worked sorting the belongings. These Jews passed on the valuables in exchange for provisions they needed to survive, such as bread, salami, and, in certain cases, vodka. In some cases, the Jews were caught and paid with their lives. From their perspective, however, the risk was worth it.[44]

The information that substantial property was moving through Treblinka made its way beyond the camp fences. In her testimony, Holocaust survivor Sonia Lewkowicz recounted that after they escaped from the camp, they were pursued by inhabitants of the region who thought they were carrying money, gold, and valuables. Lewkowicz described how the Poles did more than try to rob Jews; they also tried to hurt them. In any event, even when the Jews promised to compensate them in exchange for help, the help was never given.[45] One reason that the locals knew about the substantial amount of property was the collaborators' frequent visits to the villages and the towns that were located near Treblinka, particularly to the village of Wolka Okrglik. In this context, Arad's book on Operation Reinhard contains the following testimony:

In the neighboring villages near the camp the Ukrainian fascists were welcomed by some of the local farmers. Their daughters, as it was widely known, became the girlfriends of the murderers and enjoyed the benefits of their generous hearts. It is no wonder that, even if it was wartime, one could see in the neighboring villages extensive construction on the farms and the village women wearing furs and clothes of expensive material whose source was well known…[46]

In 1989, a crew of the American television program *60 Minutes* took advantage of the fall of the Iron Curtain, which had kept the Soviet Bloc cut off from the West, to interview residents of the village of Wolka Okrglik. Interest in the village had been aroused by the Demjanjuk Trial, which was underway at the time. The local residents explained to the correspondents the type of leisure activity in which the Ukrainians engaged in the village, which, as noted, was facilitated primarily by the significant amount of money they carried.[47] Beginning on July 23, 1942, when the first transport arrived from the Warsaw Ghetto, and over the following months, the extermination process at Treblinka fulfilled all the needs of many of the collaborators in the camp.

In summation, we can conclude that the collaborators and their family members greatly benefited from the abundance with which their jobs in the camps provided them. What was initially claimed to be a choice between life and death turned out to boil down to the maximum possible exploitation of the situation while benefiting from the jobs for which they had been recruited. Even if it is possible that, in some situations, the events corrupted the souls of the collaborators, it is impossible to ignore the reasons for collaboration that influenced the *Wachmänner*'s choice in the first place. These factors apparently made the contemptible work easier.

Different and At Times Perverse Ways to Spend Their Free Time

One desire that can compete with the collaborators' avarice for money and gold was their incessant hunger for sex, often of a perverse and disturbing nature that was devoid of humanity. Avraham Broide of Grodno, who survived Treblinka, maintained that the Ukrainians in the camp and the surrounding area lived a "wild life." In his testimony, Jacob Wiernik depicted the everyday life of the Ukrainian *Wachmänner*, explaining that they were usually drunk and sought ways to acquire more and more money in order to buy brandy in the nearby villages. The Germans did not like this situation but were apparently unable to stop it.[48] Once the collaborators' desire to eat and drink had been fulfilled, they began to look for other ways to pass the time. A regular pastime, according to Wiernik's testimony, was to find the prettiest Jewish women who had arrived in the last transport, drag them to their quarters, and brutally rape them. After they finished abusing the women, the victims were taken to the gas chambers and murdered alongside the Jews with whom they had arrived at the camp.[49] The description found in Wiernik's testimony recurs in other testimonies in different versions, each more brutal than the last, as in the case of the testimonies of Pinhas Epstein and Eliyahu Rosenberg, who testified at the Demjanjuk Trial.[50] The perverse sexual conduct of the Ukrainian Trawnikis was not unique to the Treblinka extermination camp; it occurred in all the camps of Operation Reinhard, as well as during the liquidation of the Warsaw Ghetto Uprising.[51]

In the early spring of 1943 (apparently in March or April), a group of 25 non-Jewish Ukrainian women arrived at Treblinka to engage in service work in the living quarters of the Germans and the Ukrainians. During the day, they cooked, washed clothing, cleaned, and straightened the rooms in the camp's staff quarters.[52] In their free time, they conducted various types of relationships with the *Wachmänner* serving in Treblinka. Such relationships were conducted even when they had a husband, a wife, or children at home, as was true in the case of Ivan the Terrible and others.[53] After the war, these Ukrainian women who served at Treblinka were interrogated in the Soviet Union. Like the male collaborators, they too were required to specify with whom they served and to provide the interrogators with as many details as possible. The testimony of one of these women – a Ukrainian woman by the name of Kirpa Alexandra Terentivna – is especially interesting. In addition to the fact that she had a personal relationship with Ivan the Terrible, the information she provided about him reinforced doubts regarding Demjanjuk's connection to the affair. She also effectively described the personal relationships that existed between the *Wachmänner* and this group of Ukrainian women:

Alexander Jager...the SS commander of the Wachmann force, who lived with my friend Anastasia Tymofenko...from March to September 1943...Robertus...was an SS *Zugwachmann*. For a time, he lived with the same Anna Tymofenko. Vasily Yilenchuk was an SS Wachmann, he lived with my friend Milenia Tretyak Efimovna... Alexander Volchenko...was an SS *Zugwachmann*, and I lived with him like a husband until May 1943...Ivan Marchenko Ivanovich... was an SS *Oberwachmann*from May to September 1943; he lived with me like his wife from May to September 1943.[54]

During the operation of the Treblinka extermination camp, between 100 and 120 auxiliary personnel served there, including Ukrainians and others. In many cases, the *Wachmänner* found what they were seeking outside the camp fence. That is to say, the Ukrainian collaborators were given leave. Some chose not to make the long trip home to their families and preferred instead to spend time in the villages near Treblinka. Avraham Broide testified that the Ukrainian guards "would drink alcohol with no limit and organized orgies at the brothels in the area. They had no lack of money..."[55] In the abovementioned episode of *60 Minutes* dealing with the village of Wolka Okrglik, residents spoke about the frequent visits made by the Ukrainians to purchase alcohol and to have relations with some of the women of the village. They even spoke of a married woman, 'Miss Dodek,' who would have relations with Ivan the Terrible on a regular basis. This was done with her husband's permission, in exchange for money and alcohol.[56] Although we know of instances of romantic relations between Ukrainians and local girls, the relations were characterized by mutual exploitation – a number of local young women gave their bodies to the *Wachmänner* in exchange for money, gold, clothing, and other valuables. In one case, which was by no means unique, a farmer from one of the villages in the area forced his daughter, who was only 12 years of age, to sleep with one of the Ukrainians in exchange for money. When a group from the Polish underground heard about this, they beat her father severely.[57] In another instance, two Polish girls arrived to the area after hearing about the new "economic possibilities" that the Treblinka camp provided for the inhabitants of the area, rented a room, and began receiving Ukrainians. Members of the underground succeeded in identifying the location of their activity, executed one of them and shaved the head of the other, as a means of deterrence.[58]

The claim of "lack of choice," which emerged at the stage that those who chose to collaborate were contending with impossible conditions in the camps of Chelm and Rivne, does not truly pass the test of reality. Indeed, the sexual abuse of Jewish women moments before they were murdered can be regarded as a distinct example of action that historian Gideon Greif has referred to as "unnecessary suffering" – that is, cases in which a person's impending death was known and would occur in any event, but in which his murderers went further by adding unnecessary suffering.[59] Cases of collaborators engaging in sexual relations with 12-year old girls may also not be regarded as the lack of choice.

The Possibility of Escape

Richard Rashke, who researched the case of Demjanjuk and other collaborators in the United States, discussed the choice made by many Ukrainians to collaborate with the Nazis.[60] In his view, if, as a young man, he would have been faced with a choice between joining the auxiliary forces or dying in the Chelm or Rivne camps, he would have chosen the former. The story changes, however, after it became clear to these *Wachmänner* what was expected of them. In this case, he maintains, the relatively comfortable living conditions of the Ukrainian guards should have enabled them to escape.[61] Prof. Cornelius Nestler of University of Köln holds a similar view. In a lecture delivered in Jerusalem, Nestler, who took part in Demjanjuk's prosecution in the trial that was conducted in Munich, presented all of Demjanjuk's opportunities for escape from Sobibor. He too maintained that he would not have chosen differently if faced with the choice of collaborating or remaining in the prisoner of war camp. However, the moment it became clear what their job was, they needed to find a way to escape. For their collaboration from this point onward, they needed to be put on trial for taking part in the extermination of the Jewish People during Operation Reinhard.[62]

Rashke and Nester were both fortunate enough to not have to check their hypothetical positions in practice, no matter how well-based they were. In most cases related to the events of the Holocaust I accept Michael Burleigh's assertion that the condemnation – by "armchair moralists, especially in countries that were not occupied" – of choices that were made during the war are not taken seriously today.[63] Similar in this context is Ka-Tzetnik's reservations about being treated by psychiatry professor Jan Bastiaans, "…as Professor Bastiaans had never been in Auschwitz. And even those who had been there did not know Auschwitz. Not even someone who had been there two long years, like I was."[64] What could be done, as cases of escape indeed occurred, is to compare different periods and examine why during a certain time we find a substantial number of escapes, in contrast to other periods, during which the *Wachmänner* preferred to retain their positions and enjoy the benefits.

When we examine the scope of the phenomenon of escape by the collaborators who served in Treblinka we encounter two main problems. One is the fact that the collaborators were systemically defined as "Trawniki men," regardless of where they served, and were under the authority of their home base and of the command in Lublin. Attempted escapes by collaborators, like other offenses, were tried in the SS court in Lublin. Even the SS reports containing cases of escape typically referred simply to "Trawniki men," and not to the name of the camp where the escapees were stationed at the time. The court sentenced the escapees in accordance with the circumstances of the escape. If the defendant did not return from leave at home or from leave spent elsewhere, their punishment was no more than a few weeks or months imprisonment in a labor camp. If the defendant escaped with a weapon and joined the partisans who were operating in the area, the trial would end in a death sentence.[65] The second problem relates to the date of the escape of the collaborators. In a few cases, the number of escapes was found to have increased significantly during the final weeks of the war. During this period, escapes were not recorded in an organized manner, if at all. The chaos that characterized this period enabled collaborators who were tried in the Soviet Union on charges of betraying the homeland to say that they had tried to escape, even if such an attempt had never been made.[66]

The sources that were collected for the purpose of the Demjanjuk Trial, along with the studies that were conducted after the trial, point to isolated instances of escape during the initial months of operation of the extermination camp at Treblinka. This information is provided by SS documents and the testimonies of those who were connected to the camp and the surrounding area.

Eugenia Samuel, a woman who lived near Treblinka, recounted that those who tried to escape included not only Jews but also Ukrainians. In her testimony, she noted that her uncle provided these Ukrainians with weapons that helped them survive during their escape.[67] In an interview with Gitta Sereny, Pan Zebecki, a local Pole who worked at the train station at Treblinka, described the events he witnessed in detail, including the escape attempts of Ukrainians:

> Amongst the Ukrainians there were several who we knew wanted to get away. But you see, that too was dangerous; they were in just as much danger as everybody else. One of the Ukrainian guards did escape, with the help of his Polish girlfriend from that little village near us. Stangl himself came to the village then, and asked the village chief – the mayor… Who this Ukrainian had visited…Then they went to the father of this girl and took him to the camp. His old mother hanged herself that night; actually, the man was allowed back home the next day.[68]

Stangl's visit to the camp was extremely significant with regard to the everyday life of the Ukrainians. Stangl employed various means to create order in the camp. One of the changes included strict discipline on the part of the Ukrainian guards. *Wachmänner*, he determined, would cease going on leave with a weapon in their possession. This was the result of a number of incidents in which Trawnikis got drunk in the nearby villages and then began shooting in every direction. To contend with possible threats from the partisans and the Polish underground, collaborators would therefore buy their own personal weapon. After Stangl discovered one of the Polish weapons dealers who sold pistols and rifles to Ukrainians, both the weapons dealer and his family were brought to the camp and gassed to death.[69] The new camp commander also intensified the supervision of the property that was taken from victims in order to prevent it from falling into the wrong hands. Within the camp, he limited the number of bullets available to each Wachmann to five, in an attempt to prevent shooting incidents that spiraled out of control.[70] Stangl's command style resulted in a significant increase in the number of escapes from the camp.

That is to say, the number of escapes increased when control over the events in the camp was restored. As noted, the first month of the camp's operations was characterized by total chaos. In a study on the escape of Jews from Treblinka, Naama Galil found that "in light of the chaos and bedlam that was typical of the camp during the first month of its operations, the phenomenon of prisoner escapes there was widespread."[71] According to the testimony of Treblinka survivor Dodek Lewkowicz, escaping the camp was a relative possibility during this period: "It is true that at the beginning it was relatively easy to escape."[72] Later in his testimony, he explains that not many did so, as "escaping was like a person taking cover from the rain and standing under a drainpipe, because a Jew had nowhere to go, and no one would let him into their home…"[73]

In light of the information at our disposal concerning the living conditions of the Ukrainian collaborators, it can be assumed that if the Jews could have escaped during the period in question, doing so would have been much easier for the Ukrainians, and they would have taken advantage of the situation. In the course of his de-naturalization trial in 1978, Treblinka Wachmann Feodor Fedorenko testified that during his time in the camp, some 20 *Wachmänner* went on leave and never returned. Of these 20, four were captured and shot to death.[74] Although all four paid with their lives, these numbers are indicative of a particularly high escape-success rate, certainly in comparison to the Jewish prisoners.[75] The assumption that the Ukrainians would have taken advantage of the chaos to escape therefore proves to be incorrect, for, as we have seen, the number of escapes increased only later. In my opinion, a possible explanation for this phenomenon lies in the economic possibilities with which this period presented the Ukrainian collaborators. During the meeting at which he appointed Stangl commander of Treblinka, Globocnik angrily maintained that although hundreds of thousands of Jews had already been sent to Treblinka, the anticipated goods were not exiting the camp.[76] The collaborators were the major benefactors of this reality and apparently did not want to give up this state of affairs, even at the price of remaining at the camp and engaging in brutal acts of murder.

The period during which the phenomenon of escape increased to dimensions which the command in Lublin could not ignore appears to have begun in 1943, as reflected in the files holding the regular reports from the headquarters in Lublin. The reports contain the date of the escape, the name of the escapee, a precise description, and the personal information of the escapee and his family members. In certain cases, the report was also updated to indicate that the escapee had joined the partisan forces in the area. Reports of escapes increased concurrently with reports of operations of partisan units in the area surrounding the camp.[77] The clearest evidence that the number of escapees during this period was on the rise appears to be the establishment of a special unit of secret agents, consisting primarily of Ukrainians and Russians, to contend with instances of escape by those with whom they served.[78]

Reports regarding the escape of *Wachmänner* who served at Treblinka continued to be recorded during the autumn of 1943 until the cessation of the camp's operations. On October 22, five *Wachmänner* escaped near Chelm while returning from escorting a transport.[79] On November 7, 1943, another Wachmann escaped.[80] According to historian Peter Black, more than 30 percent of the Trawniki men escaped from their service in Nazi Germany (1,500 out if 5,082), many during the final weeks of the war. Historian Sergei Kudryashiv, who offers a lower estimate of escapes amounting to nine percent of all the Trawniki men (459 guardsmen), notes that their numbers may have been higher, as he too found that many escaped only in the final stages of the war and therefore were not documented.[81] In addition, in his book on the Trawniki men, Baldwin proposes four primary reasons that prompted collaborators, including the *Wachmänner* at Treblinka, to escape:

1. **The changing tide of the war** – Fear of the possibility that the Germans would lose the war and that they would be forced to answer to the Soviet legal authorities. In this case, they had no doubt that they would be treated as traitors and that they would pay a heavy price. Some thought that escaping and returning home would conceal the fact that they had volunteered for the auxiliary forces.[82]

   ✦ Here, I state only that the fears of those who returned to the Soviet Union and did not emigrate elsewhere were proven to be correct.[83]

The punitive cost of collaboration was a heavy one, ranging from 25 years imprisonment to the death penalty.[84] The testimony of Treblinka survivor Sonia Lewkowicz reflects the fears of the Ukrainian *Wachmänner*. According to Lewkowicz, "the Ukrainians also knew that their end would be a very bitter one when the Russians came, so anyone with brains fled."[85]

2. **Fear of the day they would become a target** – Fear that one day, the Germans would do to them what they did to the Jews. The moment their work was complete, there would be no need for the collaborators. In addition, the Germans would want to do away with them as witnesses to and partners in the murders.[86] In this case, too, Sonia Lewkowicz's testimony establishes that the collaborators had good reason to fear: "There was one case in which the Germans burned a Ukrainian and threw him into a bonfire. That is what Eliyahu Rosenberg told me. From this, we can understand that the Ukrainians did not really feel safe there…They knew that something was awaiting them too."[87]

3. **The personality of the escapee:** Some of the collaborators lacked discipline from the outset and sought only to extricate themselves from the situation. As soon as they could leave, they did so.[88]

4. **Moral reasons:** Some *Wachmänner* objected to the gruesome treatment and murder of civilians.[89]

Three of the reasons presented by Baldwin are indicative of the personal interests that constituted a major factor in the decision of *Wachmänner* to escape and when to do so. As the escapes occurred primarily as the camps were winding down their operations, the fourth reason appears to have pertained to the decision of only an extremely small number of collaborators, who until that point had taken part in some of the cruelest acts known to humanity. In addition to the four reasons offered by Baldwin, I propose adding another one relating to the change in the Jews' reaction to the actions of the Nazi regime: April 1943 witnessed the major uprising in the Warsaw Ghetto; on August 2, an uprising broke out at Treblinka; and on October 14 an uprising broke out at Sobibor. All these events, which occurred in parallel to the increasing activity of Jewish and non-Jewish partisans, also took the lives of Ukrainian collaborators. The advance of the Red Army, in addition to the Jewish struggle, made it clear to the *Wachmänner* that the reality had changed. The ability of collaborators to escape from Treblinka and other locations appears to be a factor that can be used to effectively identify the considerations underlying the decision to serve in the SS in Operation Reinhard. When these prisoners of war volunteered, they did not know the purpose of their activity. The desire to be rescued from the fate that awaited those who remained in the prisoner of war camps left no other choice. During their training at the Trawniki camp, their understanding of what was expected of them became clear. Service in the extermination camps was the height of the cruelty in the collaboration. Even when the conditions allowed escape with high chances of success in order to avoid participating in the murders, the collaborators chose to stay. Escapes by *Wachmänner* increased when the conditions in the camp were detrimentally impacted and when they felt they were in mortal danger. The cruel acts they were forced to perform did not constitute a major factor motivating them to escape from the camp.

"There is a crack, a crack in everything. That's how the light gets in."[90] (Leonard Cohen)

"Nevertheless, perhaps for reasons that go back to our origins as social animals, the need to divide the field into 'us' and 'them' is so strong that this pattern, this bipartition – friend/enemy – prevails over all others."[91]

Primo Levi dealt with a great deal in the "grey zone" that was the outcome of the tragic, complex reality of the Holocaust. With honesty and daring, his writing shows how, in certain cases, one could find both enemies and friends among the humans who populated Auschwitz. His proposal to not divide the world into black and white becomes challenging when discussing the acts of the Ukrainians in the Treblinka extermination camp and the surrounding area. Despite the challenge, it should be noted that even in the great despair that was Treblinka, we find isolated incidents of humanity – a crack through which light could get in. The two instances in question actually saved the lives of Jewish prisoners Sonia Lewkowicz and Isadore Helfing. The small scope of this section can be viewed as symbolic of the gap between the good and the bad at Treblinka.

Sonia Lewkowicz[92]

Sonia Lewkowicz was born in 1922 in Dabrowa, Poland. She arrived at Treblinka on December 7, 1942 along with another 7,000 Jews. Between her arrival and the month of March, she worked in Camp 1 in the Ukrainian laundry. From March until the uprising that broke out in August, she worked in the laundry in Camp 2, where the gas chambers were located. In her testimony, she recounted an incident that occurred just prior to the uprising that broke out in the camp. At that point, Lewkowicz had already been in the extermination camp for eight months. In addition to the long duration of her time in the camp and its significance, this was a period during which almost no transports arrived at the camp and, therefore, there was almost nothing to eat. Lewkowicz testified as follows:

> A Ukrainian from the camp called me over and said – Do you want to eat some honey? The honey was synthetic, and he gave me a bowl of it…He planned on escaping, and later he really escaped. It was a very difficult time. There were no transports, and there was almost nothing to eat. So I took the bowl with the honey from him, and later they told me that that Ukrainian was already outside, that he had escaped.[93]

As we have no details regarding the identity of this Wachmann and Lewkowicz does not expand further, we have no way of knowing how he behaved during his service in the camp. After all, according to the testimonies presented above, every Wachmann was required to carry out all the jobs that were done at Treblinka. Nonetheless, this specific incident, especially during the period in question, undoubtedly improved Lewkowicz's situation.

Isadore Helfing[94]

Another case, as noted, is the story of Isadore Helfing, who was born in Kielce, Poland in 1922. When he arrived at the camp, he was put to work sorting the belongings of Jews who had been sent to be exterminated. He held this job for almost ten months, and at some point he was sent to work removing bodies at the rear of the gas chambers. Two weeks after he was transferred to this job, he understood that if he continued doing it he would be liable to take his own life, as many of those around him had done. One day when he was sent to fill up water, he managed to escape and to return to the area of living quarters where he had worked as a sorter. In this area, there were stables that served the SS officers and the Ukrainian collaborators. When asked by a Jewish man if he knew anything about horses, Helfing said that he did, even though he had never even stood beside a horse. He was accepted to work in the stables with the same Jewish man under the supervision of two Ukrainians. In Los Angeles, Helfing gave the following testimony:

> At the time of the preparations for the uprising [that occurred on August 2, 1943], we were told that we had to kill the Ukrainian that was responsible for us and take his rifle. When I heard this I had a hard time. This Ukrainian happened to be good to us. He…brought me and my partner all kinds of Polish kielbasas, and white bread – at that time it was a big deal, white bread…And so my condition improved, and I was able to see the possibility of surviving…He once definitely saved my life, when I was ill with typhus… He knew that the Nazi officers were coming to the stables and that if they saw me in my condition, I would immediately be sent to the gas. He hid me in the stables in a place where no one would see me, claiming that I had to do a job of some kind. In this way, he actually saved my life.[95]

Helfing believed that on the day of the uprising he had been very lucky, and not only because he managed to escape alive. Quite extraordinarily, the same Ukrainian who saved his life was not at the stables that day. Helfing did not know what became of this Wachmann or what his name was. In this instance, we also do not know what this collaborator did during his time in the camp. In light of our lack of all the details regarding these rescuers, we focus on the act of rescue itself and its meaning for the survivors and their families.

A Forgotten Past: Belzec as a Comparative Discussion

One of the nicknames given to the Belzec extermination camp was the "forgotten camp,"[96] stemming primarily from the paucity of sources we have regarding what happened there. Researchers who have viewed the various sources pertaining to the camp quickly discovered their narrow scope. This study is based primarily on the testimonies of residents of the surrounding area, isolated testimonies of SS men who served in the camp for a period or who visited it in the course of their service, the trial of Trawniki men, and the Belzec Trial that took place in Stuttgart between 1963 and 1965 and involved eight SS men from the camp's staff.[97] The Belzec Trial ended with the acquittal of seven of the defendants and a four year prison sentence for Josef Oberhauser, who served as the adjutant of Christian Wirth, the first commander of the camp.[98] Prominently absent from the trial were the testimonies of survivors. Three Jews who were prisoners at Belzec were still alive at the end of the war, and two of them, Rudolf Reder and Chaim Hirschman, gave testimony immediately following the war's end. Hirschman delivered a partial testimony and was then murdered by Polish nationalists.[99] One way to understand the lack of witnesses from Belzec in comparison to Treblinka is the fact that in the Eichmann Trial, an event that is considered a crossroads in Israeli society's attitude toward the events of the Holocaust and their survivors, no Jews were found to testify to the former camp, in contrast to four who were selected from the survivors of Treblinka. The June 7, 1961 issue of *Haaretz* contained an article bearing the headline "Documents Will Testify about Belzec Because No One Survived." The text of the article itself explained that according to the report of the Polish commission, only one person survived, and his whereabouts were unknown.[100] It was later discovered that Rudolf Reder was living in Toronto and had changed his name to Roman Robak.[101] Over the years, survivors of Treblinka have given numerous testimonies about what they experienced at the extermination camp, including their views on the actions of the Ukrainian collaborators. Five of them also testified at the Demjanjuk Trial.[102] The last survivor of Treblinka, Samuel Willenberg, passed away in 2016.

Close to half a million Jews and a few tens of thousands of Roma were murdered at the Belzec camp, which began operating on March 17, 1942. Belzec was the first of the Operation Reinhard camps and in this capacity served as a prototype for the camps to follow. It was located on the railway line from Lviv to Lublin, from which the first transports were sent to the camp.[103] The reasons for the selection of the site were the same for all three camps: the Germans sought a remote location that was far from large population centers but close to a village or town (to ensure regular supplies) and to a railway line and train station. In the case of Belzec, an effort was also made to take advantage of the trenches that had been dug against Soviet tanks in the area by turning them into pits for the burial of murder victims.[104]

News of the events in the camp spread soon after it began its extermination operations. The Oyneg Shabbos Archive contains reports that the Germans had set up a death camp near the town of Belzec.[105] The reports were initially received with great skepticism. Among the inhabitants of the ghetto at this point, there were many who found it difficult to accept the possibility that Jews were being murdered en masse.[106] This skepticism waned as reports of the events in the camp multiplied. There was also an increase in the cases of Jews trying to jump off trains as they made their way to Belzec.[107] The difficulty of accepting the possibility of mass extermination, as well as the method of deception that was established by Christian Wirth, influenced the victims' inability to internalize what was about to occur until they reached the threshold of the gas chambers. This is testified to by Kurt Franz, who served at the Belzec extermination camp:

> I heard with my own ears how Wirth, in a quite convincing voice, explained to the Jews that they would be deported further and before that, for hygienic reasons, they must bathe themselves and their clothes would have to be disinfected. Inside the undressing barrack was a counter for the deposit of valuables…I can still hear, until today, how the Jews applauded Wirth after his speech. This behavior of the Jews convinces me that the Jews believed Wirth.[108]

In his testimony, Belzec survivor Rudolf Reder described a similar reality. In this case, the speaker was SS officer Fritz Eirman:

Eirman spoke in a loud and very clear voice: "You are now going to bathe. Then you will be sent to work." That's all. Everyone was pleased, happy that they were going to work, and applauded. I remember the words he repeated every day, usually three times a day, during the four months I spent there. It was a moment of hope and delusion. For a moment, the people sounded relieved. There was complete serenity. The crowd walked forward in silence…[109]

The village of Belzec was located not far from the extermination camp. Despite the claims of some local inhabitants that they did not know what was happening in the camp on the other side of the fence, there were some who testified that the screams and the odors that enveloped the area could not be ignored. The village was home to Ukrainians, Poles, and Jews, and close relationships naturally formed between the Ukrainian residents and the Trawnikis.[110] As in the case of Treblinka, here too the *Wachmänner* frequently visited the villages in the area, and information was relayed regarding what was going on in the extermination camp. If any of the residents were truly unaware of what was occurring, this changed immediately following the liquidation of the camp. A few years after the extermination camp ceased operating, area residents were still digging in the locations where the murders took place, as a rumor had circulated that many of the Jews had been buried while hiding expensive valuables on their person.[111]

The sources at our disposal indicate that the everyday life of the Ukrainian *Wachmänner* at Belzec did not differ significantly from that of their fellow Ukrainians at Treblinka. Their similar lifestyle was reflected primarily in their common quest for valuables and the use of their resources to enjoy themselves in the nearby villages. A resident of one of the villages testified that Germans and Ukrainians would visit his village frequently from the nearby camp. The Ukrainians bought vodka using dollars and gold and did business with the residents. Collaborators often visited the village when they were drunk. On one occasion when they visited the local bakery, the baker asked why they were always drunk. "If you were to serve in that camp," he answered, "you would also be drunk."[112] One employee of the train station testified to rumors regarding the vast wealth of the camp staff. These rumors travelled fast, attracting young women to the area seeking to take advantage of the economic potential.[113] Historian Robert Kuwałek, who for several years directed the museum at Belzec, found that the Ukrainian guards were part of the landscape of the town of Belzec and tended to boast about their status and their wealth, which included property stolen from the victims. The Ukrainian *Wachmänner* energetically courted the girls of the town, and some married local girls.[114] One Belzec resident, Aniela Bober, testified that the Ukrainians would arrive with articles of clothing they had taken from Jews and would sell them. A few of her friends, she noted, had relations with the Trawnikis, which angered the people of the village.[115] Robert Kuwałek asked one of the young women who married a Trawniki why she did so. Her answer was as follows: "…I was young, I was foolish, and my father told me that if [I was going] to be a prostitute, it was best to do so officially…"[116] A resident who lived near the train station and knew one of the Ukrainian guards said that the Wachmann's wife would come to visit once every two weeks and that on each visit she came with empty suitcases and left with suitcases full of gold and clothing.[117]

Another topic that is relevant to both camps is the choice of whether to escape and when to do so. As shown in the case of Treblinka, some *Wachmänner* chose to escape, and it was possible to identify the periods during which this phenomenon increased. In the case of Treblinka, this occurred after Irmfried Eberl was replaced by Franz Stangl, and after the tide of the war had turned and Germany no longer held the upper hand. Instances of escape from Belzec occurred throughout the duration of its operations, although most cases occurred after the extermination of the Jews had concluded. At this stage, we find cases of groups of *Wachmänner* deciding to flee together.[118] The explanations offered by Baldwin for all the cases of escape – the proximity of the Red Army, the declining discipline, fear that they would become targets, and moral concerns – are certainly also applicable here. However, in the case of Belzec, I would add another reason – avarice for property and money and loss of the ability to acquire them. As noted, the money, gold, and valuables that the Trawnikis stole from the victims are what afforded them such a comfortable life during their service in the extermination camps. Many came from lives of poverty and had nothing until they were recruited by the SS. In Belzec, the extermination ceased in 1942. The cessation of transports meant the cessation of theft by the Trawniki men. Therefore, in March 1943, three months after the cessation of the extermination operations, we find mention of an escape of 12-15 Trawnikis who decided to leave the camp.[119] The explanation offered for this escape was a punishable offense committed by one of the escapees, who feared the punishment he would receive. It is doubtful whether this also explains the decision of the others to join him. In this case, we see that both the period in which the camps operated, and the amount of time that elapsed between the cessation of the exterminations and the liquidation of the camp, had impact on the decision of whether or not to escape.

Another difference between the two camps with regard to the everyday life of the Trawnikis was a man named Christian Wirth. Wirth had headed the administrative side of the German Euthanasia campaign. In actuality, Wirth is the one who came up with the extermination system that was used in the camps of Operation Reinhard. At first, Wirth was the direct commander of the Belzec extermination camp and determined its working procedures. He was then appointed chief inspector of all the camps of Operation Reinhard, meaning that in practice he commanded the entire operation.[120] From the perspective of the Trawnikis, there was a difference between the direct command (camp commander) of a man like Wirth and the indirect command of such a man as inspector of all the camps. In the ranks of the SS, it should be noted, there were many who despised the Ukrainians, due both to their decision to collaborate and to their origins. At the same time, the SS men understood that this force was required in order to achieve the goals of the operation.[121] SS officers treated the collaborators with varying levels of cruelty, but Wirth's exceeded that of all others. In the mid-1960s, Nazi war criminal Erwin Lambert, a senior perpetrator of the Euthanasia campaign and Operation Reinhard, stood trial twice: in the Treblinka Trials and in the Sobibor Trials. In his testimony, he addressed the difference between Wirth and Stangl, the latter of which commanded Treblinka for almost one year. His testimony may contain elements indicative of the reality with which the collaborators had to contend in both camps:

Stangl dealt with me like a fair man. He also treated the Ukrainian workers in my unit fairly. I did not discern Stangl treating the

Jewish work units unfairly. I would like to say that in their appearance, the difference between Wirth and Stangl was like the difference between night and day. Wirth was a cruel man not only toward us Germans, but also toward the Jews. He was a savage…I met Wirth later in Italy. There, especially, I came to realize how inconsiderate and cruel this man was. I have no words to describe the extent of Wirth's cruelty.[122]

During the period in which Wirth was in command of the extermination camp at Belzec, there were many instances in which he was cruel to the Ukrainian collaborators. In one instance, when a Wachmann failed to start the motor that caused the gas to flow into the extermination chambers, Wirth beat and severely injured him.[123] Later, the same Wachmann was transferred to serve in Treblinka. In cases when *Wachmänner* committed disciplinary offenses, Wirth would deny them food and water for a few days. Wirth spared no means when *Wachmänner* did not behave by the rules. In a particularly unusual incident, he arrested two Trawnikis suspected of telling area residents what went on in the camp, and he sent them to the gas chambers along with the Jews that had arrived the same day. Later, his deputy Gottlieb Hering, who took part in the punishments discussed above, appears to have inherited not only his position but also his legacy. Two *Wachmänner* who were caught stealing the belongings of Jews who had arrived at the extermination camp were forced to wear coats bearing the yellow badge; they were then taken to the shooting pits and shot to death. Their companions from the auxiliary forces were compelled to watch.[124] Trawnikis were tried for disciplinary matters and were given different sentences at each camp; however, Wirth's treatment of the Ukrainians appears to have exceeded all others in its cruelty.

This section presents several elements for comparison between the two extermination camps. The topics in question enable us to learn about the everyday lives of the Ukrainian collaborators. The location of the camp, the attributes of its operations, and the figures that served there were directly related to the differences between them. At the same time, with regard to these two camps, the differences between them appear to have been influenced primarily by the surviving witnesses who recounted what occurred during the period in question. Although only a small number of witnesses survived Treblinka (approximately 70 at the end of the war), this number significantly exceeds the number of Jewish witnesses that survived Belzec. We are therefore missing a significant vantage point on the everyday life of the Ukrainian collaborators at Belzec.

Conclusion: "It may be too late to do justice, but it is never too late to discover the truth."[125]

In the Eichmann and the Demjanjuk trials, two narratives were advanced simultaneously: an historical narrative and a legal narrative. Some of the testimonies that were delivered by Holocaust survivors had important historical value but made no legal contribution. The possibility of these "two narratives" proceeding together after the trial ended depended, it turns out, on the results of the trial. In the case of Eichmann, the trial ended with a ruling that found him guilty and with a death sentence. The Demjanjuk trial (and appeal) ended with an acquittal on grounds of reasonable doubt. The testimonies and the documents that were presented during the Eichmann Trial are studied and researched in schools and in academia. On the other hand, it is as if many important historical sources that were presented during the Demjanjuk Trial, including the testimonies of survivors of Treblinka, were "deported" along with Demjanjuk. The aim of this article is to examine one of the many topics about which we can learn from the "historical story" of the Demjanjuk Trial. In this case, the topic was the everyday life of the Ukrainian collaborators at Treblinka.

The Ukrainian collaborators were selected from among millions of Red Army soldiers who were taken prisoner by the Germans during World War II. The conditions in the prisoner of war camps were appalling, and the chances of survival were slim. The commanders of Operation Reinhard visited these camps and recruited volunteers while promising them wages, food, and other benefits. It would be reasonable to assume that many would have agreed to this generous offer, especially if it meant saving one's own life. Also to the credit of the volunteers is the understanding that they apparently had no clear knowledge of the nature of the collaboration. At this stage, then, the claim of having "no choice" would apparently resonate among many.

Shortly after the beginning of their training as collaborators at Trawniki, it started to become clear what would be required of them in the course of their service. Once they were sent to the extermination camps, they knew that the task at hand was the murder of civilians. The sources in our possession show that many of the *Wachmänner* not only did not suffer from the reality they encountered but rather enjoyed it. Their service afforded them living conditions they had never known until the moment they volunteered for the SS forces. Their enjoyment of the status of collaborators had extremely perverse expressions, including murder, the rape of female prisoners, sexual relations with minors (12 year old girls), and a long list of other aberrations.

It would be reasonable to assume that once these prisoners of war, who had volunteered in order to save their own lives, discovered what was required of them, they would try to escape. The benefits enjoyed by the Trawnikis – which included the ability to go on leave, typically armed – made escape possible, albeit not simple. One Wachmann who stood trial after the Holocaust recounted that, in Treblinka, twenty fellow collaborators escaped and only four were captured. This is a high success rate by all accounts. Escape attempts did indeed occur, but primarily after conditions changed for the worse and a genuine threat was posed to the lives of the collaborators. Up to this point, however, the large majority were not interested in parting with the good life the war had given them.

The comparison with Belzec shows that the differences between the everyday lives of the collaborators in both camps were insignificant. The type of leisure activity was the same, and the reasons for choosing whether to escape or to remain in the camp were also not fundamentally different. Another meaningful issue about which we can learn through comparison is the historical importance of survivors' testimonies. When Claude Lanzmann filmed *Shoah*, he visited the area around Treblinka, and a few locals he met refused to speak to the camera and recount what had occurred out of fear of exposing their connections to the collaborators. We are aware of the close connection that existed between the *Wachmänner* and the locals at Treblinka and at Belzec, based also on what is presented in this article. This connection also included the conveying of information about what was occurring in the extermination camps. Unlike the case of Belzec, our information with regard to Treblinka is not exclusively dependent on local inhabitants' agreement to testify. In the case of Treblinka, we have testimonies of Holocaust survivors who managed to escape from the camp, and these testimonies help us complete the picture to the best of our abilities. After the war, survivors of Treblinka wrote memory books and testified in trials in Israel and elsewhere, including Demjanjuk's de-naturalization trial in the United States and the Demjanjuk Trial in Israel. These testimonies are important, disconcerting, and difficult testimonies regarding the actions of collaborators and other issues. They can be used in the teaching of history, even when the trial itself ended in acquittal. After all, no one denies the existence and the actions of the Ukrainian collaborators. **The testimonies we have may no longer help achieve justice, but there is no limitation on their ability to assist in seeking the truth.**

Endnotes

1   The research on which this article is based was made possible by the Norbert and Liza Schechter z"l Fund. The article is dedicated to Yitzhak Arad. For an extensive discussion, see Tamir Hod, "The Demjanjuk Affair in Israel, 1986-1993: History, Memory, Law," doctoral dissertation, Ben-Gurion University in the Negev, 2018 (Hebrew).

2   Ibid., p. 282.

3   These include numerous sources that were collected for other Holocaust trials that have been conducted over the years, including: the Nuremberg Trials, the Eichmann Trial, the Treblinka and Belzec trials that were held in Germany, the trial of collaborators in the Soviet Union, and the de-naturalization trials of collaborators in the United States. They also include the protocol of the Demjanjuk Trial, during which survivors of Treblinka and experts in various fields testified about the events in the camps during Operation Reinhard.

4   See, for example, Israel State Archive (hereinafter ISA), gimel-lamed-3/21585 (the Demjanjuk Trial – S.S. documents), which contains personal information regarding collaborators during Operation Reinhard. The testimonies of survivors of Treblinka regarding the collaborators typically use the term "the Ukrainians" or "the Ukrainian guards." Also see these other testimonies: Eliyahu Rosenberg, Yad Vashem Archive (hereinafter YVA), 0.33-39; Avraham Broide, YVA 0.3-4183, p. 8.

5   See, for example, Yitzhak Arad, *Operation Reinhard: Belzec, Sobibor, Treblinka* (Jerusalem, 1988; 2nd edition 2013) (Hebrew), and Josh Baldwin, *Trawniki Guards: Foot Soldiers of the Holocaust* (Atglen, PA, 2020), pp 12-21.

6   One reason for the emergence of "new" sources was the collapse of the Communist Bloc, which facilitated access to sources that had been inaccessible until that point.

7   Arad, *Operation Reinhard*, pp. 53-63; Raul Hilberg, *The Destruction of the European Jews*, Vol. 3 (Jerusalem, 2012), pp. 836-841 (Hebrew); Witold Chrostowski, *Extermination Camp Treblinka* (London, 2004), pp. 6-21.

8   In actuality, on October 19, 1943, Globocnik sent Himmler an official telegram informing him of the conclusion of Operation Reinhard: "Reichsführer! On October 19, 1943, I concluded Operation Reinhard, which I conducted in the General Governorate, and I dismantled all the camps. ... In one of his visits, the Reichsführer spoke of the chance of awarding several Iron Crosses for special actions in this difficult position after the work was concluded...I would be very grateful to you, Reichsführer, for an affirmative decision on this matter..." ISA alef-6/3106, The Eichmann Trial (Criminal Case 61/40), Globocnik's January 10, 1944 report to Himmler. Despite its different date, the letter announcing the conclusion of the operation is located in this file.

9   Only estimates can be made regarding the number of victims that were killed in the new camp at Treblinka. The number of victims released by the Central Commission for the Investigation of German Crimes in Poland after the war stood at 731,600. ISA alef-65/3102, Eichmann Trial (Criminal Case 61/40), Report of the Polish

Commission on War Crimes at Treblinka, p. 10. In his book on Operation Reinhard, Yitzhak Arad offers a figure of 800,000-850,000 victims. Arad, *Operation Reinhard*, p. 547. Another report, issued in Poland on November 22, 1945, assessed the number of victims as totaling almost 1.5 million. This figure is taken from YVA 0.3-546, p. 5.

10 The "Euthanasia" operation, *Aktion T4*, was meant to cleanse the Aryan race; it resulted in the murder by gassing of tens of thousands of Germans suffering from physical and intellectual disabilities and incurable illnesses. A few of the prominent figures in Operation Reinhard had accrued experience during this campaign.

11 Arad, *Operation Reinhard*, p. 54; Chrostowski, *Extermination Camp Treblinka*, p. 6.

12 Philip Morgan, *Hitler's Collaborators: Choosing Between Bad and Worse in Nazi-Occupied Western Europe* (Oxford, UK, 2018), p. 1.

13 Per Andres Rudling, "'Not Quite Klaus Barbie, but in That Category': Mykola Lebed, the CIA, and the Airbrushing of the Past." In Norman J.W. Goda (ed.), *Rethinking Holocaust Justice: Essays across Disciplines* (New York, 2018), pp. 158-187.

14 This figure is taken from the Yad Vashem website: https://www.yadvashem.org/he/righteous/statistics.html

15 David G. Marwell, *Mengele: Unmasking the "Angel of Death"* (New York, 2020).

16 Ibid., p. 78.

17 See Arad, *Operation Reinhard*, pp. 53-63; Hilberg, *The Destruction of the European Jews*, Vol. 3, pp. 836-841; Chrostowski, *Extermination Camp Treblinka*, pp. 6-21. See also Chil Rajchman, *The Last Jew of Treblinka: A Memoir* (New York, 2021); Jankiel Wiernik, *A Year in Treblinka: An Inmate Who Escaped Tells the Day-to-Day Facts of One of His Tortuous Experiences* (New York, 2015). Wiernik's book was first published in 1944 and constitutes one of the earliest comprehensive reports of what was occurring in the extermination camp. Wiernik testified at the Eichmann Trial and built the model of the camp that is currently located in the Ghetto Fighter's House museum and that was displayed at both the Eichmann Trial and the Demjanjuk Trial.

18 Baldwin, *Trawniki Guards*, p. 53.

19 Ibid., p. 54.

20 Ibid.

21 Arad, *Operation Reinhard*, p. 61. A resident of one of the villages near Belzec who worked at the train station through which Jews passed on their way to the extermination camp recounted that inhabitants of the region nicknamed the Ukrainians "Black Ruskis," largely because of their black uniforms. See the testimony of Josef Swietojanski, United States Holocaust Memorial Museum (hereinafter USHMM) Archive, RG-50.488*0013, p. 2. The testimony was recorded in 1998.

22 On an extensive account of the recruitment of collaborators and on the Trawniki camp, see Gehoffrey P. Megagee (ed.), *The United States Holocaust Memorial Museum: Encyclopedia of Camps and Ghettos 1945-1933* (Vol. 1, Part b, pp. 893-897); Ian Baxter, *The SS of Treblinka* (Stroud, Gloucestershire, 2010).

23 Baldwin, *Trwaniki Guards*, p. 10; Chris Webb & Michal Chocholaty, *The Treblinka Death Camp: History, Biographies, Remembrance* (Stuttgart, 2014), p. 210.

24 The year 2019 witnessed the release of a documentary film titled *School of Executioners*, which surveys the recruitment of the collaborators during Operation Reinhard, their training in the camp at Trawniki, and the different activities in which they engaged during their service. See Ella Tukhareli and Aleksey Kitaytsev, *School of Execurioners*, 2019.

25 Ibid., minute 35.

26 See the report from the court: Alison Smale, "Soviet Wife of Accused War Criminal Testifies," *AP News*, June 11, 1986 (accessed June 17, 2021). On the case of Feodor Fedorenko, see, for example, Michael L. Bazyler and Frank M. Tuerkheimer, *Forgotten Trials of the Holocaust* (New York, 2014), pp. 247-273.

27 These events have appeared in various studies. See Havi Dreifuss (Ben-Sason), *"We Polish Jews"?: The Relations between Jews and Poles during the Holocaust – The Jewish Perspective* (Jerusalem, 2009), pp. 126, 128 (Hebrew); Yehuda Bauer, *The Death of the Shetl* (Jerusalem, 2009), p. 115 (Hebrew); Saul Friedlander, *Nazi Germany And the Jews: The Years Of Extermination: 1939-1945* (Tel Aviv, 2007; Third Edition, 2010), pp. 221-223 (Hebrew).

28 Arad, *Operation Reinhard*, pp. 658-60.

29 During the Demjanjuk Trial, Treblinka survivors testified to the cruel actions of the Ukrainian Wachmann. Justice Zvi Tal told me how he used to wait for the breaks in the proceedings to weep in his office, far from the television cameras.

30 Testimony of *Gregorczuk Paweł* Stepanović, ISA gimel-lamed-1/21586 (Demjanjuk Trial, Prosecution Exhibit k), p. 8.

31 On this topic, see Baldwin, *Trawniki Guards*, pp. 15-23, as well as the film *School of Executioners*.

32 On the actions of the Trawniki men during the liquidation of the Warsaw Ghetto, see Havi Dreifuss (Ben-Sason), *Warsaw Ghetto – The End: April 1942 to June 1943* (Jerusalem, 2017), pp. 500-501 (Hebrew).

33 Testimony of a local resident in the documentary film *School of Executioners*.

34 Testimony of Riabzev Prokofiy Nikolaevich, ISA gimel-lamed/21586 (Demjanjuk Trial, Prosecution Exhibit k), p. 76.

35 Chrostowski, *Extermination Camp Treblinka*, p. 66.

36 Rajchman, *The Last Jew of Treblinka*, p. 27.

37 ISA alef-6/3106 Eichmann Trial (Criminal Case 61/40), Globocnik's January 10, 1944 report to Himmler.

38 Gitta Sereny spoke extensively with Franz Stangl, the second commander of Treblinka extermination camp, when he was on trial. In one conversation, Stangl told her about the meeting at which Globocnik appointed him as camp commander. Globocnik was furious that hundreds of thousands of Jews had already been sent

to Treblinka and that, thus far, neither money nor property had returned. On this occasion, he asked Stangl to clarify where it had all gone. See Gitta Sereny, *Into That Darkness: From Mercy Killing to Mass Murder* (London, 1974), p. 133.

39 Arad, *Operation Reinhard*, p. 262.

40 Testimony of *Gregorczuk Paweł* Stepanović, ISA gimel-lamed-1/21586 (Demjanjuk Trial, Prosecution Exhibit k), p. 10.

41 Ibid.

42 Testimony of Riabzev Prokofiy Nikolaevich, ISA gimel-lamed/21586 (Demjanjuk Trial, Prosecution Exhibit k), p. 77.

43 Testimony of Anani Grigorievich Kozminsky , ISA gimel-lamed/21586 (Demjanjuk Trial, Prosecution Exhibit k), p. 96.

44 Chrostowski, *Extermination Camp Treblinka*, p. 66. The testimony of Treblinka survivor Eliyahu Rosenberg is also indicative of the "weakness" of the Ukrainians. In planning the uprising that broke out on August 1943, it was determined that a few groups would entice the Ukrainian guards to descend from the guard towers. The method that was always effective involved flashing them paper currency in dollars, after which "the Ukrainians would descend from the tower… In exchange for twenty dollars, we received a piece of salami, 100 cigarettes, a loaf of bread, and a bit of alcoholic beverage." Testimony of Eliyahu Rosenberg, YVA 0.33/39 (Memoirs, Testimonies, and Diaries), p. 7.

45 Testimony of Sonia Lewkowicz, ISA gimel-lamed-3/21534 (Demjanjuk Trial — Sonia Lewkowicz), p. 67. This file contains the testimonies that Lewkowicz delivered over the years. This included testimony recorded by Yitzhak Arad in 1979 for his study on the Treblinka uprising.

46 Arad, *Operation Reinhard*, pp. 263-264.

47 See Jeane Solomon-Langley, "Ivan the Terrible," *CBS 60 Minutes*, February 25, 1990.

48 Wiernik, *A Year in Treblinka*, p. 32.

49 Ibid.

50 See the testimonies of Treblinka survivors at: State of Israel v. Ivan (John) Demjanjuk: Decision, Israeli Ministry of Justice, Jerusalem 1988. Epstein's testimony can be viewed at minutes 2:30-6:00.

51 See Dreifuss (Ben-Sasson), *Warsaw Ghetto – The End*, pp. 500-501.

52 Women from this group who were interrogated in the Soviet Union after the war provided a great deal of information on what occurred at Treblinka. See ISA gimel-lamed-1/21586 (Demjanjuk Trial – Prosecution Exhibit k), various testimonies.

53 Ibid., p. 45. Kirpa Terentivna, Ivan the Terrible's lover, recounted that he had left at home a wife named Katarina, two sons, and a daughter,

54 Ibid., p. 47.

55 Testimony of Avraham Broide, YVA 0.3/4183 (Testimonies), p. 8.

56 The testimony of the Dodeks added to the doubt regarding the possibility that Demjanjuk was Ivan the Terrible.

57 Sereny, *Into That Darkness*, p. 156.

58 Ibid.

59 From the author's conversations with Gideon Greif.

60 See Richard Rashke, U*seful Enemies: John Demjanjuk and America's Open- Door Policy For Nazi War Criminals* (New York, 2013). Rashke makes this argument in a lecture marking the publication of his book: https://www.youtube.com/watch?v=G_l4lg0yFIU&t=888s

61 Ibid.

62 The lecture was held on February 2, 2012 at the Hebrew University of Jerusalem and was recorded by the author of this article.

63 Michael Burleigh, *The Third Reich: A New History* (New York, 2000), p. 418.

64 Quote taken from Tom Segev, *The Seventh Million: The Israelis and the Holocaust* (New York, 1991) p. 8. Prof. Bastiaans was a psychiatrist who lived in Beer Sheva and specialized in the elderly and Holocaust survivors.

65 Baldwin, *Trawniki Guards*, p. 80.

66 Ibid., p. 83.

67 Testimony of Eugenia Samuel, USHMM Archive RG-50.488*0008, Testimony Abstract.

68 Sereny, *Into That Darkness*, pp. 155-156.

69 Chrostowski, *Extermination Camp Treblinka*, pp. 66-67.

70 YVA TR15/565 (Demjanjuk Case), pp. 39, 182.

71 Naama Galil, "Prisoner Escapes from the Treblinka Extermination Camp July 1942–August 1943," master's thesis, University of Haifa, 2017, p. 18 (Hebrew).

72 Testimony of Dodek Lewkowicz, YVA 0.3/526 (Testimonies), p. 7.

73 Ibid.

74 Bazyler and Tuerkheimer, *Forgotten Trials of the Holocaust*, p. 252.

75 Galil, "Prisoner Escapes from the Treblinka Extermination Camp."

76 Sereny, *Into That Darkness*, p. 133.

77 The file in question contains a collection of regular reports that also reflect updates on escapes, robbery, fires, and cases of physical and psychological harm. See ISA gimel-lamed-3/21583 (Demjanjuk Trial – SS Documents).

78 Ibid., p. 8.

79 Baldwin, *Trawniki Guards*, p. 93.

80 Ibid., p. 94.

81 Ibid., p. 80.

82 Ibid., p. 83.

83 While many collaborators returned to the Soviet Union, many others chose to immigrate to the United States and elsewhere. On the entry of collaborators into the United States, see Eric Lichtblau, *The Nazis Next Door: How America Became a Safe Haven For Hitler's Man* (New York, 2014); Allan A. Ryan, *Quiet Neighbors: Prosecuting Nazi War Criminals in America* (San Diego, 1984).

84 The files containing documentation of the interrogations of collaborators usually also contain their sentence. See ISA gimel-lamed-1/21586 (Demjanjuk Trial – Prescution Exhibit k).

85 Testimony of Sonia Lewkowicz, p. 56.

86 Baldwin, *Trawniki Guards*, p. 83.

87 Testimony of Sonia Lewkowicz, p. 56.

88 Baldwin, *Trawniki Guards*, p. 83.

89 Ibid.

90 This quote is from the song "Anthem" by Leonard Cohen, which appears on the album *The Future*.

91 See Primo Levi, *The Drowned and the Saved* (New York, 1986), p. 25.

92 The account of the case of Lewkowicz is taken from the Testimony of Sonia Lewkowicz, ISA gimel--lamed-3/21534 (Demjanjuk Trial – Sonia Lewkowicz).

93 Ibid., p. 56.

94 See the filmed 1983 testimony of Isadore Helfing, USHHM Archive RG-50.005.50.

95 Ibid.

96 See, for example Rafael Ostroff and Lili Haber (eds.), *Belzec: The Nazi Extermination Camp (Testimonies)* (Israel, 2020), p. 9 (Hebrew).

97 For an extensive discussion, see Udi Tsin, *Belzec – According to Robert Kuwałek, Director of the Belzec Museum* (undated, in Hebrew), https://meyda.education.gov.il/files/noar/belzets.pdf (accessed July 16, 2021). Tsin edited two of Kuwałek's lectures from 2005, added important information about the camp, and posted it online.

98 The trial has been written about in detail by Tuvia Friedman, *The Belzec Extermination Camp: A Documentary Collection* (Haifa, 1982) (Hebrew).

99 Tsin, *Belzec – According to Robert Kuwałek*, p. 4.

100 Author not specified, "Documents Will Testify about Belzec Because No One Survived," *Haaretz*, June 7, 1961, p. 1 (Hebrew).

101 Friedman, *The Belzec Extermination Camp: A Documentary Collection*, p. 2.

102 For an extensive discussion, see Hod, "The Demjanjuk Affair in Israel."

103 On Belzec, see, for example, Webb, *The Belzec Death Camp*.

104 Arad, *Operation Reinhard*, pp. 139-148.

105 Samuel Kassow, *Who will write our history? A New Look at Oneg Shabbat – the Important Jewish Archive in the Warsaw Ghetto* (Jerusalem, 2014), p. 315 (Hebrew).

106 Dreifuss, *Warsaw Ghetto – The End*, p. 81.

107 In one example, two girls jumped from the train and one was shot in the leg. The girls were picked up by the mother superior of a convent who cared for them with great devotion. See Nahum Bogner, *At the Mercy of Strangers: The Rescue of Jewish Children with Assumed Identities in Poland* (Jerusalem, 2000), p. 177 (Hebrew).

108 Arad, *Operation Reinhard*, p. 142.

109 Ostroff and Haber, *Belzec: The Nazi Extermination Camp (Testimonies)*, p. 63.

110 These descriptions appear in detail in Friedman, *The Belzec Extermination Camp: A Documentary Collection* and in Tsin, *Belzec – According to Robert Kuwałek*. At the end of the 1990s, a few inhabitants of Belzec and the surrounding area testified to what occurred at the camp and in the town of Belzec. See, for example, the testimony of Tadeusz Jarosz, USHMM RG-50.488*0009.

111 Testimony of Tadeusz Jarosz, USHMM RG-50.488*0009.

112 Baldwin, *Trawniki Guards*, p. 37.

113 Webb, *The Belzec Death Camp*, pp. 67.

114 See Tsin, *Belzec – According to Robert Kuwałek*, pp. 1-5.

115 Testimony of Aniela Bober, USHMM RG-50.488*0113, p. 4.

116 Tsin, *Belzec – According to Robert Kuwałek*, p. 3.

117 Testimony of Tadeusz Jarosz, USHMM RG-50.488*0009.

118 On escapes and their timing, see Baldwin, *Trawniki Guards*, pp. 84-88.

119 Ibid., p. 85.

120 See Arad, *Operation Reinhard*, pp. 286-289.

121 In testimony delivered for his trial (the Treblinka Trials that were held in Dusseldorf), SS officer Franz Suchomel described the work of the *Wachmänner* and recounted a directive that prohibited the Germans from engaging in such work. See YVA TR.15/56 (Demjanjuk Trial), Testimony of Suchomel, p. 116. A similar interview appears in the film *School of Executioners*.

122 Testimony of Erwin Lambert, YVA TR.15/56, p. 236.

123 Baldwin, *Trawniki Guards*, p. 71.

124 Ibid.

125 Tukhareli and Kitaytsev, *School of Executioners*. This film concludes with the above statement by John Loftus, the federal prosecutor in the office of special investigations in the US Justice Department.

Joanna Tokarska-Bakir

"They Told 'Em to Prostrate into a Star." Kisielów, March 1945, Eight O'clock in the Evening

In the ethnographic region of Polish Podkarpacie (Subcarpathia) referred to in this article, one enduring custom is the archaic ritual of "leading Judas."[1] Still celebrated before Easter here, the ritual consists of parading a straw man, dressed up as a Jew with sidelocks, around the village on a wagon, followed by the flogging and burning of the figure.[2] Before the last world war, such an effigy was often hung on Jewish houses and then their inhabitants were forced to pay for its removal. There are no longer any Jews in Podkarpacie, but the ritual custom continues to be practiced – "out of respect for tradition."

After the war, the region stood out for its level of violence against Holocaust survivors, endorsed by the National Military Organization (*Narodowa Organizacja Wojskowa*, NOW, aka National Military Union, *Narodowe Zjednoczenie Wojskowe*, NZW), an underground organization, commonly referred to as *narodówka*. In the first half of 1945, that violence peaked in Leżajsk (February 18/19, 1945, 14 victims),[3] Kisielów (March 1, 1945, 6-8 victims), and Kańczuga (March 31, 1945, 9-16 victims).[4]

The task that I have set for myself in this paper, based on my research in the holdings of the Institute of National Remembrance (*Instytut Pamięci Narodowej*, IPN), is to reconstruct the crime in Kisielów, whose victims were the Schlaf family, and take a look at the variants of the memory of that crime.

"In our Kisielów, near Zarzecze, the Jews survived the whole war, in hiding," is what some Kisielów residents told a journalist with reference to the Schlafs.

"Nobody touched 'em 'cause they was our own' village Jews. And later, after the war, when they came back home, there were those who went over to their house and shot 'em all. Good God, there were children there too. She'd given birth during the war. And then they told 'em to prostrate into a star and shot 'em all."

"What do you mean: prostrate?"

"They told 'em to lie down on the ground and form a star."

"Who killed them: the partisans or bandits?"

"How can we call 'em partisans? Bandits. They were partisans but they also got around on their own account, stealing and killing."[5]

So far, on the subject of the Kisielów killing, we have the article by Piotr Lipiński[6] and a paragraph-long narrative in the book by Mirosław Surdej:[7]

On March 1, 1945, a group of NZW soldiers, from that part of Radwan's detachment[8] that reputedly included Bronisław Gliniak [i.e. "Radwan"], Ewald Sroczyński [noms de guerre "Dąb"and "Rzeka"], Józef Drabik ["Dziadek"/"Kruk"/"Pług"], his son Zygmunt Drabik ["Zabawa"], Bronisław Kaduk ["Szpak"], his brother Tadeusz Kaduk ["Latawiec"], Stanisław Baran ("Kosiba"), Zbigniew Skocel ["Góral"], and Herakliusz Lubomirski,[9] among others, shot the Jewish family of Schlauf [actually: Schlaf] in Kisielów (…). The motive remains unknown; however, it appears that, as in other similar cases, it should be sought in an accusation of collaboration with the communists. Even if the underground organizations had proof of such collaboration, the completely unjustifiable method of collective liability was used here. The fact that the victims included children calls for particular condemnation.[10]

Given the standards of historical writing prevailing at the IPN, the manner in which the Kisielów killing is addressed here might seem quite decent, but a closer look reveals a dual coding technique. The author suggests that there are acts that are not reconcilable with a soldier's honor, and in this way tries to save the heroic image of the NZW, whose members committed this crime.[11] On the one hand, he says that there is no proof of "collaboration with the communists" on the part of the victims of the Kisielów killing, but on the other, he uses the conditional mode to smuggle through the suggestion of such collaboration, which, given the widespread practice of using it to justify the postwar murders of Jews, is probably intended as a mitigating circumstance. The author omits no opportunity to assume the role of defender of murdered children, which, as we will see, is a popular eristic ploy in the Polish cultural discourse.

Although a number of authors have written about it,[12] it is nonetheless worth offering a brief reminder of the mode of operation of the political force field in which Jewish Poles found themselves when returning from the camps or hiding places after the war. The notion of Judeo-Bolshevism (Polish: żydokomuna),[13] an idea of tremendous impact, created a fatal connotation between the returning survivors and the invasion of Poland by its eastern neighbor, which was underway at that time. To make things worse, the Red Army and "the communists" were the only force which the Jews could turn to for protection from violence. Equating their attempts to secure such protection for themselves with collaboration is a serious methodological error and – from a moral point of view – amounts to relativization of crime.[14]

Józef Schlaf's Letters

In March 1961, Józef Schlaf (1922-1995), a classical philologist from Warsaw,[15] sent letters to the Office for Complaints and Petitions at the Ministry of Internal Affairs and to the Head of the County Office of Public Security (*Powiatowy Urząd Bezpieczeństwa Publicznego*, PUBP) in Jarosław. In one of them, we read:

> In 1945 in the village of Cieszacin Mały (Kisielów), Jarosław county, my family was murdered: Saul Schlaf [b. 1898, son of Gitla and Mosze], Tauba Schlaf [aka Tonka, née Szyfman, b. 1900 in Rożniatów], Józef Schlaf [aged 14], Fajga Schlaf [daughter of Tauba's relatives] and two other children [Chaim, aged 16, and Estera, aged 4 or 7, both of them the Schlafs' children].[16] For years I have been demanding information from the security authorities as to whether the perpetrators of this crime have been apprehended and punished."[17]

Józef Schlaf's letter (AIPN, Rz 043/502, fol. 12)

The answer that the authorities gave, first internally (in correspondence exchanged between the County Command of the Civic Militia (*Milicja Obywatelska*, MO, regular police force in Jarosław, the chiefs of the Security Service at the Provincial Command of the Civic Militia in Rzeszów, and the Department of Complaints and Petitions at the Ministry of Internal Affairs) and subsequently possibly also to the petitioner, was not unambiguous. It went as far as saying that "the facts stated in Citizen Józef Schlaf's letter are known by our Section and consist of (…) the truth." It was not, however, clear whether the perpetrators of the murder had been punished. The name of Marian Madera of Zarzecze, Przeworsk county, is mentioned, with a remark that the matter was clarified in an inquest conducted in 1955 through 1956 by the Security Service (*Służba Bezpieczeństwa*, SB) Investigations Department in Rzeszów. This claim, however, is contradicted by a note in the margin: "not clarified," and by another annotation stating that "there is no inquest case on Marian Madera in the files."[18]

In one of his subsequent letters, Schlaf made the authorities aware that Marian Madera ("Goryl") also used another name:[19] "One of the active murderers of the Schlaf family was allegedly a Marian Ossoliński [aka Madera], currently sojourning in Brzozów county."[20]

It is rather strange that the Civic Militia in Jarosław should need to be reminded of the man whose fame as a bandit had decidedly spread beyond the county borders. The indictment against Ossoliński, dated June 30, 1956, was 20 pages long[21] and charged him with participation in dozens of killings, including the massacre in Kańczuga. When giving his testimony about the killing of the family of the Ukrainian cleric Mykoła Płachta of Surochów on April 24, 1945, Madera said during the trial:

> On orders from Radwan (…) we led the priest's family out of the basement (…), where subsequently [Edward] Makara[22] and another man whose pseudonym was Cienki[23] shot the priest and his wife[24] and wounded their son. After an hour (…) we heard a child cry. When I walked over to that place, I noticed that, seated between his parents (…) was their ten-year-old son, and it was he who was crying. I didn't want him to suffer so I shot him with my TT pistol.[25]

This statement resembles the reminiscences of Stefan Mazur, the MO man who killed Abram Fisz, the month-old son of Rywka Fisz, both of whom he shot during the Kielce pogrom of July 4, 1946. When asked by the judge if he had felt no pity for the baby, Stefan Mazur replied: "Naturally [I did], but even though I felt pity, what could I do, given that the mother was gone? What can you do? Should the baby be left to carry on crying?"[26] As mentioned above, acting "in the best interests of" children is a popular eristic ploy in the Polish cultural discourse, intended to camouflage narcissism, ruthlessness, and cruelty.[27]

Group photo of the Schlaf family, taken in 1936 at a wedding in Jarosław (from the collection of Józef Schlaf; courtesy of Arthur Kurzweil). The following three portraits are extracted from it.

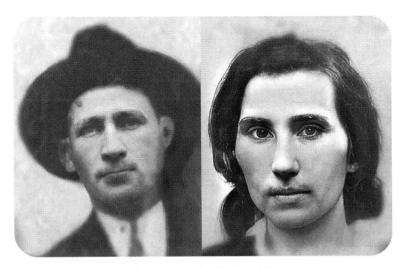

Saul and Tauba/Tonka Schlaf

Józef Schlaf, the survivor

Resumption of the Inquest into the Schlafs' Case

Apart from the name of Madera/Ossoliński, in the letter cited above Schlaf also supplied the authorities with a description of "new circumstances obtained from Kisielów":

> While my family were being murdered, all the people in the street were chased into Szczerbińska's shop, which was in our house.[28] The only person who remained in the street was the village head (*sołtys*) Józef Kilian [actually: Kilisan],[29] whom the bandits did not touch, and he was outside the whole time while the murder was in progress. When the pack of bandits left, having taken some of the property (cattle), that man, Kilian, took all the movable property, including the milk separator. (…) Reputedly, Kilian's mother still has some of the pillaged objects at her home.[30]

Józef Kilisan, *sołtys* of Kisielów-Cieszacin, was an important figure in the village. He knew every nook and cranny in the area, and had something to say about every villager. While he was one of the few who did not belong to the underground resistance movement, he obviously supported it, for example by supplying the wagons that were used to transport the loot from the raids.[31] We learn from his testimonies that in 1945, just as during the occupation, a night watch was kept in the village, and the *sołtys* would often lead it on patrols of the area to check that there were no strangers around.[32] The leader of the partisan detachment, Bronisław Gliniak ("Radwan"), who hailed from Wiązownica, a village beyond Jarosław, was not considered a stranger. Their "own village Jews," who had recently returned from exile, however, *were*. By standing outside the Schlafs' house while they were being murdered, Kilisan in a way legitimized this crime.

As a result of the pressure exerted by the sender of the letter, the inquest into the killing in Kisielów was resumed. The conclusion reached by Captain Mieczysław Pasierb of the Jarosław MO, namely that the perpetrators of the murder of the Schlaf family had not to date been held accountable, is dated February 11, 1962.[33] Consequently, a new case was launched with a view to operational identification of the perpetrators, codenamed "Murderers."[34] It produced a sizable body of documentation which offers insights into the secrets of the village's life. Only the final part of our analysis will enable us to understand why such a detailed inquest produced such mediocre results.

The inquest began with an attempt to verify the information about the eye witnesses who had been in the shop in the Schlafs' house at the time of the raid. The first of the ten witnesses who were interrogated was Stanisława Płocica-Nowosiad[35] of Kisielów, who said that, on March 1, 1945,[36] around eight in the evening, she had accompanied the Schlafs' daughter home, and a quarter of an hour later she heard a wagon approach from the direction of Cieszacin. The perpetrators "came on two wagons from Zarzecze in high spirits, and one of them [probably Eugeniusz Podbilski] was playing the accordion."[37]

Eugeniusz Podbilski • Photograph from the military identity document from the period when he was in hiding using the name Świrski (AIPN, Rz 0_50_1850, fol. 75, 103)

Nowosiad testified that, during the raid, those present in the apartment

> were also Katarzyna Hałys (…), Jerzy Zapalski of Cieszacin Mały, Julia Płocica, married name Bielecka,[38] a resident of Kańczuga, Kazimiera Mączyńska (…), and two minor boys, i.e. Edward Machaj, aged 5,[39] and Cezary [or Czesław] Szczerbiński, aged 4, of Kisielów. Present in the next room in the same building were also Jerzy S[zczerbiński] and his wife; he was ill at the time and was residing in that house as a lodger.[40]

The woman goes on to say that the assailants surrounded the Schlafs' house, forced their way into the apartment, "ordered all those present to lie down with their faces to the floor,"[41] and then shot seven Jews. Nowhere, in any of the inquest documents, is there anything to confirm the six-pointed star into which the bodies of the murdered were aligned.[42] On the other hand, this peculiar lead, which survived in the local memory, is hard to reject without looking through the materials accumulated in the trials (see Note 21). It may have been omitted by the perpetrators in the interrogations in the 1960s and earlier because "the star of David" formed by the victims' bodies would be an obvious indication of the antisemitic nature of the crime, for which the sentence would be incomparably harsher than for robbery murder.

The narrator of this testimony, who tried to run away, was hit on the head with a revolver. Before she lost consciousness, she heard that "those present in the apartment pleaded that they were Catholics and begged for their lives to be spared but the armed individuals paid no attention to this." She also says that the perpetrators spoke German and Russian and she did not recognize anyone, which, however, is hard to believe, given that she was the sister-in-law of one of the assailants,[43] and her husband was his subaltern.[44]

Józef Drabik (AIPN, Wr 024_2821, Folder 2, fol. 235)

The name of Józef Drabik,[45] aka "Dziadek," commander of the local NZW outpost, soon came up in the interviews conducted by the MO officers. His participation in the crime was corroborated by another eyewitness, Katarzyna Hałys,[46] who also remembered that:

> one of those committing the murder addressed the terrorized Jews with a demand to hand over their dollars and jewelry (…), to which one of those murdered replied "We have no jewelry on us." Then the perpetrators proceeded with physical violence and beat up the Jews, who were lying on the floor. When the beating produced no results, as the Jews were not giving away any money or jewelry, the perpetrators began to break their fingers and kick their faces. As a result of such torture one could hear the wails and pleadings of those still alive, who were asking the perpetrators to leave them alive.[47]

Katarzyna Hałys's husband, Felicjan, remembered that, two days before the murder, Schlaf had come to him, complaining that Józef Drabik ("Dziadek") had demanded two cubic meters of wheat in exchange for a promise of "peace and quiet in the future." Schlaf did not give him any wheat.[48]

Drabik's helper in the NZW was his son, Zygmunt, the terror of the neighborhood, with a telling pseudonym: "Zabawa" (Fun).[49] While – by the 1960s, when the Kisielów inquest was initiated – he had managed to do his time in prison for the deaths of several dozen Red Army soldiers,[50] he was never convicted for participating in the Schlafs' murder, just like the other perpetrators.

Zygmunt Drabik (AIPN, Wr 024_2821, Folder 2)

In the meantime, the MO men in Kisielów confirmed that those present at the crime scene had included Jerzy Zapalski[51] and Anna Baran,[52] both of whom had taught the Schlafs' children, and a five-year-old boy, Edward Machaj, who was playing in their house at the time of the raid.[53] In his testimony Zapalski says that, in the evening, everyone was in the Szczerbińskis' store, through which one could access the Schlafs' apartment. Suddenly, a tall man with a rifle walked in. He was wearing a green military overcoat and a field *rogatywka* cap. He was followed by another man, with an automatic weapon. The assailants removed the Schlafs to a separate room and demanded dollars, which were given to them. Even though they already had their loot, the bandits murdered the residents and pillaged clothes and household goods, including a feather stuffed duvet and children's shoes.[54] They also killed two pigs and a cow and took them away.

The Schlafs must have attached great importance to their children's education, given that no fewer than three teachers congregated at their home. In addition to Zapalski and Baran, Kazimiera Mączyńska was also present, a teacher of Polish and a member of the NZW, serving as commandant of the organization's female district.[55] After Ewald Sroczyński, who headed the raid in Kisielów, later testified that Mączyńska supplied intel on the Schlaf family, she explained to the investigators that "that family provided her with greater aid than Polish families in consideration of her teaching their children and consequently she would never have brought about their murder. She believed her presence in the home of those murdered and the sending of the children home, where they would get killed, to be a coincidence – sheer chance."[56] Mączyńska's role was never fully clarified. All that can be gathered from various witness testimonies is that, when the assailants separated the ethnic Poles from the Jews, a few minutes before the murder they had a whispered conversation with her, apparently agreeing on some details. Then, however, they shoved her back into the store while yelling at her: "You Jew teacher; we'll show you what it means to teach Jewish kids!" Other witnesses took this to be a botched attempt at deflecting attention away from the partisans being in cahoots with Mączyńska.

When they were on their way out, one of the perpetrators addressed Zapalski and Szczerbiński: "You know what Saul Schlaf has been shot for? For throwing out a runaway."[57] The "runaway" was reputedly Józef Szewczyk of Zamość, whom the Germans had resettled to the Schlafs' homestead after removing the Jews. A rather strange explanation given that the Polish underground was not known for standing up for the Germans' protégés.

As can be gathered from this, except for the Szczerbińskis, who immediately left Kisielów (and headed for Bytom), and the little Edward, who was playing in the Schlafs' house that evening, all the individuals present at the crime scene were connected in one way or another with the perpetrators. These ties proved stronger than their solidarity with the victims, to whom they were tied by bonds that were indeed numerous[58] but not important enough for anyone to risk defending them.

The situation described above contradicts to some extent the social psychologists' hypothesis that antisemitic violence occurred in situations of considerable social distance.[59] As indicated above, the Schlafs' was an open home: they accommodated a village store under their roof that everyone used and also entertained teachers and their neighbors' children. They were referred to as "our own village Jews."[60] In confrontation with a hateful ideology and banditry, however, such protection proved insufficient.

The Kinship System and the Pact of Silence

As the investigative officers had considerable knowledge of the underground past of Kisielów's residents, they extracted the suspects' names from them soon enough. Getting specific information with respect to participation in the crime proved more difficult. The first to be identified were the Machaj brothers, Władysław and Stanisław, referred to by the locals as "the Millionaires."[61] They were relatives of the five-year-old Edward who was playing with the Schlafs' children.

Then the name of the Machajs' brother-in-law Gienek came up, i.e. Eugeniusz Podbilski,[62] who was an MO man in Zarzecze in the spring of 1945; he is the one who played the accordion as the pack of bandits approached on a wagon. A more distant relation of the Machaj brothers, Franciszek, married the daughter of Józef Drabik ("Dziadek"), commandant of the NZW outpost in Cieszacin, and he himself was a member of the unit reporting to Tadeusz Kaduk.[63]

Why are the dense crisscross relations by blood and marriage that I describe in the biographic endnotes to this article so important for the reconstruction of the crime? Because they suggest that even in the event that any of the *narodówka* partisans or eye witnesses suddenly felt less convinced that murdering Jews was the right thing to, they would still be bound by the ties of family loyalty. These connections are of key importance to understanding the pact of silence that prevented the secret from getting out for so many decades.

Bronisław Kaduk (AIPN, Rz 00_90_218, fol. 7)

The murder remained a public secret: the village knew the perpetrators' names from the start. Stanisława Płocica-Nowosiad, who was hit on the head with a revolver during the raid, told people left and right that it was Bronisław Kaduk who had done it to her.[64] She could not, however, complain to the authorities about it because she was bound by loyalty to his commander, to whom she was a sister-in-law. Moreover, her husband and other relatives were still members of the NZW.[65]

Bronisław Kaduk,[66] who was known for his impetuous character, had a twin brother named Tadeusz, of equal notoriety.[67] It would have been unwise to get on their bad side. Both were NZW team leaders. Tadeusz used to play a violin known to have been part of the loot robbed from the Jews in Kańczuga during a raid that both Kaduk brothers took part in.[68] On that occasion, three Jewish families were murdered: the Rozenholces, the Rajewelts, and the Szlelcers, in addition to a man named Cwancyngier. The perpetrators walked from house to house in search of Jews. In total, sixteen were killed, including several children and a pregnant woman.[69]

As late as 2010, when a *Gazeta Wyborcza* journalist asked him about the Jews, an old Tadeusz Kaduk snarled, annoyed by the interruption in his tale of the good old partisan days: "What do I care about the Jews? Each of us had some Jews around at some point."[70]

The Pig-Slaughter Feast

The system of relations by marriage also had its role in the developments after the crime in Kisielów. The partisans got on a wagon and drove to Józef Skowron's place in Mirocin.[71] Why? Because his wife, Anna Skowron, was the sister of Stanisław Kotliński of Radwan's group[72] while Stefania, the wife of their brother, Jan Kotliński, was sister to Tadeusz and Bronisław Kaduk.[73]

The wagoner who drove them was Stanisław Henderscheder, Bronisław Kaduk's father-in-law.[74] He needed no fewer than three wagons (purveyed by *sołtys* Kilisan), which, in addition to the Schlafs' belongings, were also loaded with two killed pigs and a cow. Some time after the crime, the Skowron brothers, Józef and Władysław,[75] had a falling out, and Władysław decided he was no longer bound by secrecy and loyalty. This would indicate that the disclosure of the crime in Kisielów was caused – in a way – by a leak in the kinship system.

In addition to kinship, one can hardly overlook the envy that the goods stolen from the Schlafs must have attracted, especially in light of the fact that they included livestock. There is no hiding a pig-slaughter feast in any village, not in a time of hunger. Even though in this case the ritual included some unorthodox elements, because the animals were shot rather than slaughtered, all the other parts of it were rather traditional: lots of blood first, then gorging and revelry. Władysław Skowron narrates:

> It may have been March because there was still manure in the yard, and the farm work had not been done in the fields yet (…). In the evening around 10 o'clock, some men that I didn't know came to Mirocin; they stopped on the road outside my house and tied the horses to a post at the fence.

Before Władysław Skowron pointed the newcomers to his brother Józef's house, the decision was made to dress one of the stolen pigs in his farmyard, on a pile of manure. "I saw with my own eyes how one of them ripped the pig open with a bayonet and they all dressed it together," he said.[76] They were helped in that work by his neighbor, Jan Kotliński.[77] The innards were removed, the meat divided, then loaded back onto the wagon and driven to Skowron's brother's place, where it was cooked and eaten.

> While at Józef Skowron's, I saw how those men drank vodka, cooked meat and had a rather loud feast of it. (…) After drinking a certain amount of vodka, the men grew bolder in conversation and said that they had just come from Kisielów. The man who used the pseudonym Rzeka or Dąb said the following: "We finally did a good job with the Jews in Kisielów." "We shot them all and felled them to the ground like so many sheaves."[78]

The description of the contents of the wagons that Skowron gave 20 years later is so detailed that it leaves hardly any doubt as to his feelings about it:

> Other than the pig, there were such things on the wagon as clothes, fur coats, bedspreads, quilts, a feather stuffed duvet, pillows, boots,

and head scarves, all covered with a tarpaulin. The pillaged things were divided between Jan Kotliński and Józef Skowron. I saw personally how Jan Kotliński carried a large fur coat over his arm, hemmed with black cloth, which he hid in the barn. Someone stole this coat from him; he even suspected his brother, Stanisław Kotliński, and there was bad blood between them for some time. Besides, the following day in Józef Skowron's yard I saw two green bedspreads that Józef Skowron's wife, Anna, was airing.[79] From the things on the wagon, from the robbery, Skowron's wife received two green bedspreads, some sheets, a duvet, fur vests hemmed with black cloth, red fur jackets with sleeves, and 'Tibet' [flower-patterned] head scarves.[80]

Władysław Skowron concludes his testimony with a statement that Jan Kotliński had recently threatened him "from his farmyard [saying] that, if I talked about what I knew during an interrogation, then he and the others would take revenge on me (…) and he says that no trace of me will be left."[81]

When accosted by MO men, Anna Skowron, Władysław's sister-in-law, did not admit to having received two "green bedspreads." She claimed to have bought them from a woman named Kinkowa in Jarosław, while the "red fur jacket" she had also acquired legally from Kaduk. She added that her brother-in-law, Władysław, had also enriched himself "on the Jews." How did she know? Well, some time after the raid of the Schlafs' place she saw in Władysław's yard "three duvets hung out while previously [his wife Zofia] had always aired only two."[82] The neighbors' perceptiveness – not an isolated instance, as indicated by the earlier mentions of the milk separator at Kilisan's place – demonstrates the reach and strength of rural social control, confirming the conjecture that Kisielów-Cieszacin-Zarzecze must have been aware of the crimes.

Symbolic violence extended even into the highest echelons of the prewar social hierarchy in the area. The pressure to join the underground did not even omit Count Tadeusz Dzieduszycki of the Zarzecze manor. It may be mere bragging, but Tadeusz Kaduk claims that he had the count in his ZWZ platoon.[83] We do not, however, know Dzieduszycki's subsequent fate (in the context of the parceling of the estate) and why his manor was pillaged by Radwan's detachment in the spring of 1945.

Count Ewald

Tadeusz Kaduk, the owner of a "formerly Jewish" violin, was pressured by the MO investigators as early as 1962. That was when the name of his commander, whose pseudonyms were "Dąb" and "Rzeka," came up, but the investigators did not catch up with the suspect until four years later. He was, in Kaduk's words, a certain "count from the Poznań region,"[84] a tall bulky man with curly blond hair. While his status as a "count" proved rather dubious (his mother's last name was Grzęda ["perch"]), being a career military man, he nonetheless certainly had hardly any difficulty in impressing peasants. He lived in one of the outbuildings of the Dzieduszyckis' manor palace.

This is how the inquest files came to include one on Ewald Sroczyński,[85] who, in addition to owning a beer and soft drink bottling plant in Pleszew, became a county-level chairman of the Society of Fighters for Freedom and Democracy (*Związek Bojowników o Wolność i Demokrację*, ZboWiD) as early as the 1960s.[86] Eyewitnesses, e.g. Jerzy Zapalski, recognized Sroczyński in several photographs.[87]

Ewald Sroczyński, noms de guerre "Dąb" and "Rzeka"
(AIPN, Po 0_8_579, fol. 43)

When interrogated, he immediately admitted to having been in charge of the killing in Kisielów but, being aware of the Security Office operatives' inclination to accuse commanders, he tried to shift the responsibility to his superior, the Commandant of the NZW Forest Troops, Kazimierz Mirecki, nom de guerre "Tadeusz" (abroad since 1945), and to Kazimiera Mączyńska, who had allegedly prepared intel on the Schlafs.[88]

It came to my attention that a Jewish family was residing in Kisielów, whom "Tadeusz" [Kazimierz Mirecki] ordered to liquidate.[89] The liquidation progressed in the following manner: 10 members of the AK organization were placed at my disposal, most of whom were Radwan's militant group. All the men placed at my disposal were armed with firearms. I don't recall the exact date; in early March 1945, toward the evening, said group and I rode on several wagons to the village of Kisielów, heading for the house that was the residence of the Jews, whose names I don't remember. After securing the perimeter around the house with organization members, "Radwan," organization member Horacjusz Lubomirski, "Góral" – Zbigniew Stencel [elsewhere: Zbysław Skacel] – and myself walked into the house where the Jews were staying. Other than the Jews, there were other individuals in the apartment, Kazimiera Mączyńska among them. While separating the other individuals from the Jews, to make it look as though Citizen Mączyńska had nothing to do with our operation, I deliberately pushed her into the room where the other individuals were. We conducted a search of the Jews' apartment. I recall that the search resulted in finding 10 dollars, which were retained by organization member Horacjusz. After completing the search I ordered the Jews present in the room to lie down on the floor. When the Jews did so, I gave the order to open fire at the Jews. The following took direct part in the shooting: myself,[90] Radwan, Horacjusz, and Góral. During the murder, all of their belongings were taken from the Jews, including swine livestock, among other items.[91]

In the context of what we know about those events, what is striking in Ewald Sroczyński's testimony is the mysterious names of the perpetrators. And these are not just any names, because one is Horacjusz Lubomirski and the other Zbysław Skacel ("Góral") of Nisko,[92] "currently abroad." In Surdej's monograph on the NZW, the former's name is mentioned only once, with no further clarification,[93] as is the pseudonym "Góral."[94] What is known about Gliniak ("Radwan"), whom Sroczyński mentions as the third participant of the raid, is that he had been an emigrant for 15 years. Sroczyński's ploy thus seems to be an attempt to shift responsibility away from himself and blame those to whom nothing could be done anymore, which was the standard method of protecting one's buddies. It could also be a way of catering to the Security Office, which loved to besmirch landed noblemen and high-ranking commanders. Sroczyński, who had collaborated with the security police on exposing his NZW comrades since 1945 (since 1953 as Secret Collaborator "Halny"), would probably have accepted any scenario suggested to him. As for the actual perpetrators of the Kisielów crime, he mentions only the name of Bronisław Kaduk, long safe by then in his role as Secret Collaborator "Szpak," and Stanisław Baran ("Kosiba"), off the hook for some years due to an amnesty.

One way or another, the long-term effort to slow down the investigation accomplished its purpose. When – five years after Józef Schlaf's letter demanding action from the authorities – Ewald Sroczyński was finally interrogated, the case codenamed "Murderers" was coming to its conclusion. After 20 years, the crime was about to be covered by the statute of limitations.[95] The year was 1968 – not an auspicious time for classifying it as ethnic cleansing or genocide.[96]

One can imagine a hypothetical scenario, otherwise difficult to verify, in which convicting those guilty of the Kisielów murder would have been inconvenient to one or more of the investigators. An officer at the Rzeszów WUBP, Henryk Drabik, is a likely candidate (regrettably, we do not know if and how he was related to the Drabiks of Zarzecze), who in 1956 discontinued the case against Bronisław and Tadeusz Kaduk (both accused of the Kańczuga killing), even though it was not covered by amnesty.[97] Another lead: the Sroczyński file includes mysterious memos by the Agency of Internal Security (*Agencja Bezpieczeństwa Wewnętrznego*, ABW) from 2003, referring to missing documents in the folder, over 50 sheets in all.[98] The name of the person who looked through them has been painstakingly redacted. The depletion coincides with the time when Piotr Lipiński, a *Gazeta Wyborcza* reporter, approached the IPN for the Ewald Sroczyński file. There is no way of knowing whether or not the ABW has conducted an inquest into this matter.

Contexts: The Karol Urban Story

We still need a broader context to understand how the murder in Kisielów could happen at all. The region was an area of harsh Polish-Ukrainian conflict, preceding the so-called Operation Vistula, which resulted in a considerable portion of the Ukrainian population being expelled from the new Polish state and resettled in the Ukrainian SSR, on the other side of the recently moved border.

What happened in the Przemyśl area after the west-bound Red Army left it is graphically shown by an early-spring 1945 report found in what is known as Stalin's Special File on Poland, supplied by the NKVD.

> In the territory of Rzeszów Province, the bandit groups have attacked and terminated 25 Civic Militia stations in the communes of Hyżne, Lubaczów, Kuryłówka, Tryńcza, Kańczuga, Leżajsk, and other places. In all actuality, there are no local authorities in those counties.[99]

Kisielów partisans remember that the last order that came from the High Command in London after the dissolution of the Home Army (AK) in January 1945 provided guidelines to the effect that the military organization should be formally dissolved, the weapons hidden, and the soldiers were expected to "enter the state life mode – take official posts so that the leading positions in the state are in AK members' hands, and everyone is their own commander."[100] This suggestion produced chaos and a host of small detachments operating on their own.

One of the people who took the High Command's call literally and joined the Security Office, while at the same time forming a partisan micro-unit, was the Home Army soldier Karol Urban ("Lira"),[101] who subsequently subordinated himself to Radwan.[102] From March 1945, he worked at the Jarosław PUBP, while heading the militant group "Hiki-Piki." In the testimony that he gave when interrogated after being arrested in May 1945, we get a taste of the doublethink generated by his conflicted self:

> Currently the most harmful party is the *narodówka*, who is liquidating PPR members, the People's Party members, and killing Soviets. They are the Polish fascists. They robbed the Społem [co-operative store] in Jarosław, the bank in Przeworsk, the manor in

Ożanna and the manor in Zarzecze. The *narodówka* is an *endek* [National Democratic] party. The main commander of the *narodówka* is now Leut. Rzeka [Ewald Sroczyński of Zarzecze].[103]

The circumstances surrounding the arrest of Karol Urban tell us more about the esprit of the time than bulky treatises:

I was arrested by members of the Security [Office] in Jarosław, on May 2, 1945, on homicide charges for killing the Jewish woman Friedmanowa and a male Jew that was keeping her company, in the restaurant owned by Friedmanowa.

When asked why he killed Friedmanowa (i.e. Mrs. Friedman), Urban gives a straight answer: "I didn't have a specific reason; I just did it under the influence of vodka; I was very drunk at the time."[104] And then he goes on to describe how drunk is very drunk:

As I was drunk, I have a foggy recollection of running after someone, someone running away from me; whether I shot my revolver I can't recall, but I must definitely have defended myself; I also bolted into some building; there used to be a restaurant in there – a *Volksdeutscher* had a restaurant in there – I also remember running around that house, and I recall getting a bullet in my arm, and I dropped my gun then. When leaning over to pick it up, I was hit again, in my side. Whether I shot anyone then I don't remember.[105]

Alcohol, Weapons, and Military Parades

The connection between alcohol and weapons as the "motive" underlying men's conduct in Poland in 1945 still awaits proper research. It surfaces in the credible reports by the command representatives who carried out inspection visits to Radwan's detachment in the spring of 1945: "[the detachment] is billeted in Zarzecze and Cieszacin, over 100 people. The commander and the detachment [are] always [found] in an unsober state."[106] Even harsher opinions can be found in reports of the Freedom and Independence (*Wolność i Niezawisłość*, WiN) organization, where the groups based in Jarosław county, such as "the bands of the ilk of those headed by Radwan and Ulewa (NSZ)," are described as ones that "practice brigandry" and it is postulated that influence be exerted over them by the central bodies of the National Party (SN).[107] The surviving correspondence exchanged by the commanders of the still operational AK troops, who occasionally joined their forces with the NZW in their fight against the communists, includes admonitions that are well exemplified by the following: "I request (…) that they be punished because they represent the AK. You, for your parts, need to be cautious because (…) they can cause a lot of stink."[108]

Given the popularity of raids on distilleries, it would be hard to overestimate the ubiquity of alcohol in the everyday life of Radwan's detachment. A raid in April 1945 brought the partisans 500 liters of pure spirit, of which Stanisław Machaj alone received 30 liters.[109] Bronisław Kaduk's testimony indicates that the perpetrators drank three liters of moonshine prior to the killing in Kańczuga.[110] Kaduk explains that he was unable to attack the third Jewish house because he had "vomited strongly" after the murder in the second one.[111] Ewald Sroczyński, who headed the group responsible for the killing in Kisielów, also mentions that they worked up their courage with liquor before driving out. "How much we drank I don't remember," he says.[112]

What is striking in various memoirs from that period is the close coexistence of ethnic cleansing and feasts, as though the feasting merry-makers had a premonition that the moment of triumph was transient. "You live today, you rot tomorrow," says the alcoholic Marian Madera/Ossoliński to the people whose place he breaks into in search of drinking companions. In Kisielów, Radwan feasted in the community center known as "the people's house," built before the war for the contributions of members of the PSL Wyzwolenie, the agrarian party whose members included much of the generation of the parents of the nationalists under review.[113] In keeping with the Polish custom, the village often held name-day celebrations, involving considerable amounts of alcohol.

Another striking feature is the need for religious blessing after a slaughter of victims. On May 3, 1945, the anniversary of the Constitution of the Third of May, a field mass and a military parade were held in Ożanna.[114] The festivities were meant as a dare to the communists who had ruled the country for over a year. This is how Maj. Józef Baran ("Lucjan") describes the celebrations:

> The forest troops were in the next village, the one from which "Wołyniak" had chased the Ukrainians away. The guests from Leżajsk brought vodka, barrelfuls of beer, bread, sausages, and other smoked meats. A field altar was erected in the forest; a monk-priest came from the Leżajsk monastery, and a lot of people from the villages in the area. (…) The mass began. The priest delivered a patriotic homily. (…) The speeches were followed by a military parade, which (…) I received in the company of the priest and the whole gathered population.[115]

After the parade, as Mirosław Surdej writes, everyone was invited to a "luncheon arranged in the formerly Ukrainian (*poukraińskie*) houses."[116] In the Polish language, this word is one of a series comprising such descriptions as *pożydowskie* ("formerly Jewish") or *poniemieckie* ("formerly German"), and is always a euphemism for plunder and robbery.

The feasting went on well into the night, and then a drunk Józef Zdzierski ("Wołyniak") gathered 40 soldiers and attacked the nearby MO station and robbed the Społem Cooperative's store.[117] "No force could stop him from doing it," Maj. Baran lamented.[118] A similar upsurge of strength and power was experienced by the Kisielów killers: in the middle of the night, drunk after the pig-slaughter feast, they drove out in wagons to rob a state-owned farm of its pigs, which they slaughtered immediately afterward.[119]

In Search of Motives

Does all of this mean that the postwar killing of Jews in the Rzeszów region should be put down to the alcohol-induced white fever that tended to overtake the *narodówka* soldiers corrupted by the war? Quite the contrary, those were acts undertaken in cold blood, combined with conspicuous social assent and highly realistic expectation of loot. We have already spoken of loot; let us discuss assent now. Here is a report submitted by one of the NZW soldiers: "On Friday, April the 26ᵗ, 1946, I detained a suspect. Visually, and upon checking his documents, it turned out that he was a Jewish communist. I led the detained Jew away and executed him by shooting."[120] A trace of another murder can be found in the NZW files at the State Archives in Rzeszów. They include the documents of Szlama Piwko, born in 1916, an inmate of the German concentration camp in Waldenburg (now Wałbrzych), camp ID number 64602. "The fact of this certification being in the NSZ files may suggest that he died at the hands of NZW soldiers, and his documents were subsequently forwarded to the District Command," Mirosław Surdej writes.[121] The problem is not that NZW soldiers, often simple folk, were unable to distinguish between Jews and communists. It is rather that such non-distinction was a skill that they acquired in the organization.[122] In the industry producing victims in postwar Poland, the ideology of Judeo-Bolshevism became serious competition to the blood libel.[123]

The Kisielów perpetrators were religious people, as indicated by numerous records of personal searches revealing that they had rosaries and scapular medals on them (Zygmunt Drabik) and the fact that they went to confession (Stanisław Górski). The Zarzecze partisans were in good relations with the parish priest, who, since 1936, had been Fr. Józef Hajduk.[124] The priest harbored the bandits and was aware of their raids. We do not know if he approved of the latter but he probably gave the penitents absolution (we know that the perpetrators went to confession around Easter).[125] They were also aided by the local organist, Jan Witkiewicz,[126] Fr. Brzóska in Zasanie, the monks of the Virgin Mary Monastery in Jarosław, and the Leżajsk monks, already mentioned here.[127]

The need for confession may be indicative of pangs of conscience. The perpetrators' testimonies are punctuated with images that haunt them, such as a mother over a cradle completely buried in straws,[128] a water well filled with bodies of murdered victims,[129] or corpses of Soviet soldiers floating down the San river.[130] There were so many murdered victims that – as one NZW report indicates – "[only] major episodes are itemized as it would be difficult to write about specific Ukrainian individuals dispatched into the San."[131] Given how few Jews were left around after the Holocaust, the scale of the murders perpetrated on them in Jarosław county is not at all smaller in comparison to those referred to in that report.[132]

In order to live normal lives, the perpetrators had to justify their acts somehow. This is what gave rise to the motif of a list that Jews were reportedly creating to avenge themselves on the Poles. This excuse was in common use in 1945 in Leżajsk, Klimontów Sandomierski, Ostrowiec, and in the Podhale region. Here is what a participant of the Kańczuga killing, Marian Madera/Ossoliński, said:

> During the briefing, one of the members of the illegal organization told me that we were to drive wagons to Kańczuga, Przeworsk county, with the purpose of liquidating a citizen of Jewish nationality whose

name I don't remember, and who was involved in writing a list of prewar non-commissioned and commissioned officers, who were allegedly [subsequently] exiled to Siberia.[133]

Folk visions of the Final Judgment often feature the motif of the so-called black book in which the devil or a wizard keeps a record of a person's bad deeds.[134] The motif of keeping a log of sins haunted those who worked on such lists themselves. This is expressly mentioned by Janina Dusiło,[135] whom her neighbors invited to Easter breakfast in 1945. During the meal, out of the blue, Zygmunt Drabik and Edward Makara of the liquidation group in Radwan's detachment walk into the room. The soldiers join those present at the table but, when offered vodka, Drabik refuses to drink and begins to toy with his pistol instead. He asks the host, a tailor by trade, to make an alteration to his overcoat. When the host explains that the partisans have taken away his sewing machine, the partisan pulls a piece of paper from his pocket: "Look, this is how many sentences I still have to carry out; all of these will go to their death."[136] To conclude, he fires a series into the ceiling and walks away. The tailor is killed on the same day in the afternoon.

As Maxim Gorky wrote, still before he joined the Bolsheviks: "In our Russia, the conscience is unique, rabid as it were. A conscience terrified to the point of losing its senses, a conscience that has fled to the woods, into the gorges, into the thicket, and is hidden there. Here you are, going about your business, when out it jumps and grabs your soul."[137] A comparison with the Russians would probably be offensive to some Poles, so it is better to put a period here.

Photo by Katarzyna Sosnowska

Endnotes

1 Joanna Tokarska-Bakir, "Wieszanie Judasza czyli tematy żydowskie dzisiaj," in Tokarska-Bakir, *Rzeczy mgliste. Eseje i studia* (Sejny, 2004), pp. 73-94; English version: "'The Hanging of Judas' or Contemporary Jewish Topics," in Israel Bartal, Antony Polonsky, and Scott Ury (eds.), *Polin: Studies in Polish Jewry, Volume 24 Jews and Their Neighbours in Eastern Europe since 1750* (Oxford, 2011), pp. 281-400. The text is based on ethnographic interviews conducted toward the end of the 20th century in Cieszacin Wielki by Alina Cała and Krystyna Gieryszewska, among others.

2 Joanna Tokarska-Bakir, "A Chronic Blunder," in Tokarska-Bakir, *Jewish Fugitives in the Polish Countryside, 1939-1945: Beyond the German Holocaust Project* (Frankfurt am Main, 2021; forthcoming).

3 For more on the killing in Leżajsk see Mirosław Surdej, *Okręg Rzeszowski Narodowej Organizacji Wojskowej – Narodowego Zjednoczenia Wojskowego w latach 1944-1947* (Rzeszów and Warsaw, 2018), pp. 334-341.

4 For more on the killing in Kańczuga see Surdej, *Okręg Rzeszowski Narodowej Organizacji Wojskowej*, pp. 306-309. The first author to have written about this crime was Witold Piecuch, "Wielka noc w Kańczudze," *Gazeta Wyborcza*, March 2-3, 2002. See also Piecuch, "To są groby konkretnych ludzi," *Gazeta Wyborcza*, Rzeszów edition, May 12, 2016.

5 Piotr Lipiński, "Nikt ich nie tykał," *Gazeta Wyborcza*, August 30, 2002.

6 Ibid.

7 Surdej, *Okręg Rzeszowski Narodowej Organizacji Wojskowej*.

8 "Radwan" was the nom de guerre of Bronisław Gliniak, son of Jan and Maria (née Portas), b. February 11, 1924, in Wiązownica, Jarosław county; from 1942 a soldier of the National Military Organization (NOW, aka NZW), from mid-1943 a team leader in the detachment led by Franciszek Przysiężniak (nom de guerre "Ojciec Jan"). He was the brother-in-law of Kazimierz Mirecki, commandant of the Rzeszów District of the NZW, and president of the district board of the National Party (*Stronnictwo Narodowe*, SN). In 1945, an NZW sabotage unit was formed in Zarzecze in which Gliniak first served as a runner for Sub-lieutenant Ewald Sroczyński ("Dąb"/"Rzeka"; more on him further on in the text), and then became its commander (Detachment 3 "Orlęta" [Young Eagles]). He took credit for the bloodiest crimes in the region. From mid-November 1945 he was an émigré (Archive of the Institute of National Remembrance [henceforth: AIPN], Rz 050_86, fol. 43), and he died in 1969 in Chicago. On the pacifications of Ukrainian villages by Radwan's groups, see Rafał Wnuk, Sławomir Poleszak, Agnieszka Jaczyńska, and Magdalena Śladecka (eds.), *Atlas polskiego podziemia niepodległościowego, 1944-1956* (Warsaw and Lublin, 2007), pp. 178, 182.

9 Lubomirski is probably erroneously associated with this crime; I have found no evidence of his presence in the area; see Note 93.

10 Surdej, *Okręg Rzeszowski Narodowej Organizacji Wojskowej*, p. 305.

11 Surdej's book, which ends with a call to fight for the "good name" of NZW soldiers, somehow manages to ignore its own conclusions from its analysis of the murders perpetrated by detachments of that formation. Furthermore, it contains no criticism of the extremely jingoistic program of the National Party, of which those murders were a consequence. Page 34 provides a commentary that gives the reader an idea of the author's personal views. First he quotes a passage from a 1944 report by the Mielec office of the Government Delegation for Poland which criticizes "fascistizing," which is what the Delegation called the appointment to certain functions in the Home Army (*Armia Krajowa*, AK) of "people of ONR [*Obóz Narodowo-Radykalny*, National Radical Camp] and NSZ [*Narodowe Siły Zbrojne*, National Armed Forces] background, [and] the removal of the previous holders of those functions for their democratic convictions." Commenting on this opinion, Surdej writes that this formulation "emanates the mode of thinking characteristic of 'left-wing' activists, dividing the world of politics into two camps – 'democratic' and 'fascist'" (Surdej, *Okręg Rzeszowski Narodowej Organizacji Wojskowej*, p. 34).

12 See Andrzej Żbikowski, "Morderstwa popełnione na Żydach w pierwszych latach po wojnie," in Feliks Tych and Monika Adamczyk-Garbowska (eds.), *Następstwa zagłady Żydów. Polska 1944-2010* (Lublin, 2011), p. 73. In the same book, see also Alina Skibińska, "Powroty ocalałych i stosunek do nich społeczeństwa polskiego," pp. 39-70.

13 Paul Hanebrink, *A Specter Haunting Europe. The Myth of Judeo-Bolshevism* (Cambridge, MA, 2018).

14 In an attempt to prove the victims' dubious collaboration with the County Office of Public Security in his description of the killing in Leżajsk (Surdej, pp. 306-309), the author relies on the memories of A. Maksymowicz (1992), a former combatant in the military organization involved in those events, and on the brochure *Żołnierze Wyklęci* by I. Kozimal (Rzeszów, 2015), a publication so overtly one-sided that it offends common sense and withstands no criticism.

15 See Józef Schlaf, "W sprawie obywatelstwa Myrona z Eleuterai," *Meander* 18(10) (1963), p. 455. I would like to thank Katarzyna Sosnowska for making this article available to me, along with biographical materials on and photographs of Józef Schlaf. According to a registration sheet issued in Lwów (Lviv) in September 1945 (now in the 1945-1950 Records and Statistics Department of the Central Files of the Jews in Poland in the Archives of the Jewish Historical Institute in Warsaw), Józef Schlaf (Szlaf), son of Estera and Eliasz, was a commissioned officer of the Polish Army in Lublin in 1945 and before the war a registered resident of Przemyśl, born January 13, 1921. I would like to thank Alina Skibińska, Marta Janczewska, and Agnieszka Żółkiewska for finding his sheet.

16 In his letter dated September 11, 1962, Józef Schlaf adds that, in addition to their own three children, two or three children from the extended family of Tauba Schlaf of Rożniatów co-resided with the Schlafs (AIPN, Rz 0_43_502, fol. 17). According

to Józef Schlaf, the number of victims killed was thus six. However, according to another eyewitness testimony, given by Stanisława Płocica-Nowosiad, there were seven victims (which was also confirmed by Secret Collaborator "Liść"; AIPN, Rz 0_43_502, fol. 157). Płocica-Nowosiad is on record as saying that, on the day of the murder, the following were present in the Schlafs' apartment: "Schlaf, Saul (head of the family); Schlaf, Tauba (wife); Schlaf, Chaim; Schlaf, Josef; Schlaf Eścia [Estera], and two other Jews, one allegedly from Siennowo, the other from Jagieła" (AIPN, Rz 0_43_502, fol. 127). The investigation materials contain sporadic mentions of eight victims (e.g. AIPN, Rz 0_43_502, fols. 131, 229, 241). In the context of Kisielów, the Yad Vashem registers mention Saul and Tauba Schlaf and their three children: Josef, Chaim, and Ester. The dates of their death are misstated: 1942 and 1944. I would like to thank Yael Godfeld of Yad Vashem for her assistance in gaining access to these documents. With the assistance of Jarosław Dulewicz, using the JRI-Poland database I have found out that Saul Schlaff/Kurzweil (the way in which his name is written suggests that his parents were not registered as married and he was considered a child born out of wedlock), was registered in 1900 as the son of Moses and Gella Jutte Kurzweil. The family lived in Kisielów but probably hailed from the village called Wielkie Oczy. Moses and Gella had other children: Elias (1891), Pessel (1893), Hersch (1895), Ester (1898), and Chaim (1905), all born in Kisielów. Saul's parents did not register their marriage until 1915. Marriage certificate data: Izrael Moses Schlaff, b. 1862, Wielkie Oczy/Kisielów (this suggests that he was originally from Wielkie Oczy and resided in Ksielów), son of Gdal Schlaff and Freida Genss, married Gelle Jutte Kurzweil, b. 1866 in Kisielów, daughter of Hersch Kurzweil and Pessla Gans. In 1929, Saul Schlaff married Tauba Werner, b. 1901 in Wołkowyja/Rożniatów (the family came from Wołkowyja and lived in Rożniatów), daughter of Mala Werner (there is no mention of a father, which probably means that she was born out of wedlock). This information comes from Fonds 2136: Vital Records of the Israelite Religious Commune in Jarosław.

17 AIPN, Rz 043/502, fols. 12, 13. Józef Schlaf sent more letters demanding information in 1962 (see e.g. fol. 46, letter dated March 15, 1962), and in the autumn of that year he delivered one personally (fol. 15). Fol. 54 contains a mention that such letters had been arriving since 1946.

18 AIPN, Rz 043_502, fol. 13.

19 Marian Ossoliński (Osoliński) aka Madera, noms de guerre "Goryl" and "Tępir," son of Michał and Felicja (née Pelczarska), b. September 8, 1923, in Borysław, Lwów Province; locksmith; from 1939 to 1941 a member of the Borysław Komsomol (AIPN, Rz 0_61_411, fol. 103); from 1943 a member of the AK; he claims that from 1945 he was first in the NSZ detachment led by Stanisław Baran ("Kosiba"), and subsequently in Radwan's detachment, and took part in the killings of Jews in Kisielów and Kańczuga, among other incidents (AIPN, Rz_00_90_218, fol. 30). A deserter from the Polish Army, he went into hiding in Brzozów near Sanok; revealed himself on March 7, 1956, handing over a pistol and two grenades; admitted to participating in the killings in Kisielów (AIPN, Rz 043/502) and Kańczuga

(shooting one man, his wife, and his daughter in the former, and two women in the latter; fol. 109; the indictment describes the latter crime differently: the victims shot are identified as Fejwel Jakubes, aged 33, and Berek Zwanziger, aged 26, and a third man of unknown name), to killing the family of the Ukrainian priest Płachta in Piwoda, and to burning down the village of Serednia or Terebnie, Jarosław county (AIPN, Rz_0_61_411, fols. 86-97, etc.).

20 AIPN, Rz_0_43_502, fol. 16.

21 AIPN, Rz_052_303, fols. 59-78. Due to the fact that I wrote this paper during the Covid-19 pandemic, I was unable to gain access to the trial files, which reportedly are very copious. On April 26, 1990, they were permanently transferred to the State Archives in Rzeszów. This information was revealed by a search for the name Marian Madera/Ossoliński in IPN holdings (AIPN, Rz_0182_5), referring to entry 10968 in the archival log of cases in the operational records of the Provincial Command of the Civic Militia referring to the work of its operative in Cieszacin.

22 Edward Makara, nom de guerre "Czarny," of Jarosław; NZW soldier, first in Radwan's group, subsequently in the Standby Special Ops Force (*Pogotowie Akcji Specjalnej*, PAS), killed by the Internal Security Corps (*Korpus Bezpieczeństwa Wewnętrznego*, KBW) in Sieniawa on June 5, 1946 (AIPN, Rz_050_86, fol. 43).

23 Stanisław Chmura, nom de guerre "Cienki," b. 1923 in Jarosław, killed on June 28, 1946 (AIPN, Rz_05_17).

24 Ossoliński adds that Edward Makara raped Płachta's wife before she died (AIPN, Rz 107_1592, Folder 2, fol. 27; quoted in Surdej, *Okręg Rzeszowski Narodowej Organizacji Wojskowej*, pp. 310-311). A different version of Ossoliński's testimony: "in the evening hours of the same day, at the place where the sentence was enforced on the priest and his family, I heard a cry, so I headed over there along with two other members of the band. When we got there I found that the Ukrainian priest's son had not been killed by Makara but was wounded and was still yelling, so I fired a shot at him from the TT pistol that I had on me in order to finish him off. (…) Let me clarify that the Ukrainian priest's wife (…) was raped by Edward Makara, Jan Perzyński, and another member of the band before the killing. Radwan found out about this and the following day after their killing he ordered Makara and the others who had raped her to bury the priest, his wife, and his son" (AIPN, Rz_0_61_411, fol. 101).

25 AIPN, Rz_107_1592, Folder 2, fol. 27 (quoted in Surdej, *Okręg Rzeszowski Narodowej Organizacji Wojskowej*, pp. 310-311).

26 Quoted in Joanna Tokarska-Bakir, *Pod klątwą. Społeczny portret pogromu kieleckiego* (Warsaw, 2018, Vol. 1), p. 291.

27 See also the announcement of the Kielce Diocese Curia signed by Father Piotr Dudziec, condemning the Kielce pogrom of July 4, 1946: "Having no precise knowledge, without going into the background, the direct causes that brought about this sad incident, and its development, it needs to be stated that it is a fact

that a tragedy has taken place, all the more terrible for the fact that it took place before the eyes of young people and children" (AIPN, Prosecutor's main file on the "Kielce pogrom" case, ref. S58/01/ZK, Folder 2, fol. 384).

28 The fact that the Schlafs' house also included the store owned by Szczerbiński (who reputedly was Jewish as well and came from the Poznań region) and the fact that the person standing outside was *sołtys* Józef Kilisan, who, after the murder, decided to bury the victims in the field owned by the murdered Schlaf, was later confirmed by Stanisława Płocica-Nowosiad, whose brother, Stanisław Płocica, helped the *sołtys* to bury them (AIPN, Rz_0_43_502, fols. 30-32, 63).

29 Different spelling: Józef Kilisan, son of Franciszek and Franciszka (née Celińska), b. January 1, 1913, in Cieszacin Mały. When interrogated in 1947, he gave a detailed description of the underground organizations in the village, even though he claimed that they were all part of the NSZ rather than the NZW (AIPN, Rz_107_894, fols. 65-67; Rz_050_1083, fols. 2-3). In the report filed by Secret Collaborator "Jastrząb," his last name is again spelled Kilian (AIPN, Rz_00_141_760, fol. 5).

30 AIPN, Rz_0_43_502, fol. 16.

31 Testimony of Bolesław Rusinek (AIPN, Rz_050_1083, fol. 20).

32 AIPN, Rz_107_894, fol. 65.

33 AIPN, Rz_0_43_502, fol. 35.

34 AIPN, Rz_0_43_502, fol. 42.

35 Stanisława Płocica-Nowosiad, daughter of Józef and Józefa (née Hada), b. August 11, 1921 (AIPN, Rz 0_43_502, fol. 127).

36 There is also mention of a different date, March 5 (AIPN, Rz 0_43_502, fol. 124).

37 This information was supplied by Krzysztof Kucza (AIPN, Rz 0_43_502, fols. 47, 99). Eugeniusz Podbilski, son of Franciszek and Stanisława (née Górska), b. December 11, 1924, in Młodowice (Młachowice), Przemyśl county; married to Helena Machaj; from June 1943 to May 1944, blue policeman (officer of the Polish Police under German rule) at Krzywcza, Przemyśl county (Kucza claimed that Podbilski used to go about in a German uniform; fol. 50); subsequently a member of the AK; after the war, using the name Jan Przytuła, he joined the Civic Militia (MO), from which he deserted and joined the NZW-NSZ-PAS forces; took part in the murders in Kańczuga and Kisielów, among other killings; together with Jan Toth ("Twardy") and Bogumił Męciński, he took part in the robbery of the National Bank of Poland in Przemyśl on June 26, 1945, where 12 million złoty was stolen (the team members were accused of pocketing the loot; AIPN, Po 0_8_579. See also Surdej, *Okręg Rzeszowski Narodowej Organizacji Wojskowej*, p. 112.); on January 29, 1953, he was tried for his membership in the PAS and sentenced to a total of 12 years' imprisonment (AIPN, Rz 050/1850, fol. 75). Being an MO man, Podbilski played a key role in the murder at Kańczuga because the Jews trusted him. See Tadeusz Górski's testimony from 1949: "Podbilski called the Jew outside, and then he immediately put a gun to his head and told him to raise his hands, and ordered me to frisk him" (AIPN, Rz_0_61_411, fol. 10).

38　Julia Płocica-Bielecka, daughter of Józef and Józefa (née Hado), sister to Stanisława, b. 1923 in Kisielów (AIPN, Rz 0_43_502, fol. 88).

39　Edward Machaj (b. 1940, son of Jan; brother of Józef Machaj, b. 1925) testified that he was near the Schlafs' house and was forced by the perpetrators to lie down in a ditch; he subsequently revoked this testimony (AIPN, Rz 0_43_502, fol. 67).

40　AIPN, Rz 0_43_502, fol. 127.

41　AIPN, Rz 0_43_502, fol. 29.

42　All that is repeated is the perpetrators' *modus operandi*, in which they force the victims to lie down on the ground. See Józef Słoma's testimony about the raid of March 1945 in Mirocin, the village where the perpetrators went after the crime in Kisielów: "they broke into the apartment and told the whole family that was at home to lie down on the floor, which is what we did (…) they told my mother, Anna, and father, Józef, to lie down next to each other, and once mother and father did what they were told, they fired about four shots at the aforementioned, hitting them in the backs of their heads" (AIPN, Rz_050_133, fol. 54).

43　AIPN, Rz 042_1024, fol. 7

44　AIPN, Rz 00141_1016_J, fol. 5

45　Józef Drabik, noms de guerre "Dziadek," "Świtalski," "Kruk," and "Pług," son of Michał and Józefa (née Świtalska), b. March 19, 1890, in Zarzecze; cavalry *wachmistrz* (sergeant), agronomist; before the war, manager of the Dzieduszyckis' manor farm at Zarzecze; during the war, member of the Union of Armed Struggle (*Związek Walki Zbrojnej*, ZWZ) and its successor organization, the Home Army (AK); company commander in the NZW (Radwan's group); from May 1945, communications officer at the NZW District Command (AIPN, Wr_0076_30); afterward, he moved to Jelenia Góra, and revealed himself to the authorities in Legnica in 1947; served as manager of the state-owned farms Mikluszowice and Janowice; died on May 29, 1965. His son Zygmunt mentions his uncle, Stanisław Nowosiad, son of Marcin, of Cieszacin Mały (AIPN, Rz 107_894, fols. 16, 20). There was another Stanisław Nowosiad, son of Tomasz and Katarzyna, b. January 15, 1911, in Kisielów (AIPN, Rz_0_43_502, fol. 69), who moved to Wola Rożniatowska in the 1960s. The latter was also in the vicinity at the time of the crime. He saw the perpetrators' wagon with a team of bay horses and heard about 14-15 shots fired while in his backyard.

46　Another spelling of his last name: Hałysz. Secret Collaborator "Jastrząb's" report from 1947 contains a statement that, in addition to Józef Machaj, Edward Zabłocki, and Bronisław Kudriański, the participants of the Kisielów raid included Kazimierz Hałysz, son of Ignacy; there is no information as to whether and how he may have been related to Katarzyna (AIPN, Rz_00_141_760, fol. 5).

47　This is not a direct testimony as Katarzyna Hałys died in 1961 and it was Józef Gaweł who relayed what he had heard from her to the investigators (AIPN, Rz 0_43_502, fol. 41). The participation of Józef Drabik in the crime is corroborated by the information supplied by Secret Collaborator "Liść," while sitting out his sentence in prison in Wrocław: "This is to inform you that, on July 27, 1948, Jan Boruń testified to me that in 1945 (…) seven Jews (…) were murdered in the village of Kisielów, Jarosław county, by the AK organization under the command of 'Radwan' and 'Dziadek.' To follow up, let me list the members of the AK organization who took part in the murder: Kurpiel, Zygmunt [of Zarzecze]; Michalak, Franciszek [son of Andrzej and Anna, b. 1922 in Zarzecze]; Baran, Stanisław ["Kosiba," son of Franciszek and Franciszka, b. February 7, 1920, in Nisko]; son of 'Dziadek' – Drabik [Zygmunt; see further on], who is reputedly residing in Legnica; Górski, Bronisław [son of Michał and Józefa (née Świtalska), b. February 6, 1920, in Pełnatycze], resident of the village of Pełnatycze (…); Drabik, Paweł, resident of the village of Pełnatycze (…); Kaduk, Bronisław, who is the commandant of the other AK outpost and currently resides in the village of Pełnatycze [see further on] (…); Henderscheder, Stanisław [see further on], resident of the village of Pełnatycze (…), at whose place the partisans used to gather: Witkiewicz, Jan (…), currently residing in Poznań Province, formerly of the village of Pełnatycze, where he was the grain mill manager; Kotliński, first name unknown [Stanisław; see further on], resident of Zarzecze (…), currently in jail, accused of theft. (…). Another man who took part in the murder is Michał Chował, resident of the village of Wola Rozwiennicka." Information submitted by Secret Collaborator "Liść," Wrocław, July 27, 1948, Prison No. 1 in Wrocław, ul. Kleczkowska 31 (AIPN, Wr 00141/10009/J, Bronisław Górski's file).

48 AIPN, Rz 0_43_502, fol. 41. The witness refers to Józef rather than Saul Schlaf, but the remaining part of the testimony indicates that the man was shot by the bandits, so this must be a mistake. The testimony given by Ewald Sroczyński (more on him will be said later in the text) includes a mention that already in the course of the raid "one of the household members said that one of the male Jews who lived in that house had left for Cieszacin and he was the one supposed to have dollars. Then I left, and before leaving I said I would go and look for that Jew in Cieszacin" (AIPN, Rz 0_43_502, fol. 268).

49 AIPN, Rz 042_1024, fol. 7; AIPN, Rz 00141_1016/J, fol. 5. Zygmunt Drabik, alias Świtalski, nom de guerre "Zabawa," son of Józef and Maria (née Świtalska), b. April 1, 1922, in Zarzecze, middle school in Kołomyja; "during the occupation, he signed the *Volksliste* in Jarosław county" (General Information Files, AIPN, Rz 00112/1); 1940, builders' school, subsequently ZWZ-AK and NZW: Ojciec Jan's detachments in the Janów woods and formations led by Radwan, under whom he was initially an arms master and then his deputy. Took part in the Kisielów killing. In 1946, he was head of the PAS intelligence unit called "Seret." He was in hiding, staying in Wrocław and Wilczyn Leśny near Trzebnica. As an NZW soldier, who participated in the killing of Red Army soldiers in the battle of Kuryłówka on May 7, 1945 (launched by the joint forces of Radwan, Lis, and Wołyniak's troops), he was sentenced to six years' imprisonment by the verdict of the Military District Court in Rzeszów on June 13, 1949 (AIPN, Rz 108_435, fol. 82). Via his wife, Henryka, Zygmunt Drabik became brother-in-law to Kazimierz Trojnar, who took over the NZW outpost in Cieszacin after its commandant, Ewald Sroczyński ("Dąb," "Rzeka") moved out of Podkarpacie.

50 See Surdej, *Okręg Rzeszowski Narodowej Organizacji Wojskowej*, p. 326, for more references on the subject.

51 Jerzy Zapalski, son of Kazimierz and Zofia, b. January 13, 1922, in Jarosław; school principal in Cieszacin Mały. His father, Kazimierz (son of Antoni), was a colonel in the command of the NSZ and NZW district (AIPN, Rz 0_43_502, fol. 131). Józef Kilisan testified in 1947, that during the winter 1945, Kazimierz Zapalski's home had been the hiding place of Józef Drabik's son, Zygmunt Drabik, nom de guerre "Zabawa" (AIPN, Rz 050_1850, fol. 65).

52 She was related to Stanisław Baran ("Kosiba"), a member of Radwan's group, son of Franciszek and Franciszka, b. February 7, 1920, in Nisko, a blacksmith by trade. Stanisław Baran took part in the murders of Jews in Kisielów and Kańczuga, among other places, and subsequently went into hiding (from 1947 to 1953), and he found employment in Warsaw. After being apprehended, he was sentenced to 12 years' imprisonment (AIPN, Rz 0_43_502, fol. 123). He married Jan Kaduk's daughter in Zarzecze (AIPN, Rz 0_43_502, fol. 167).

53 AIPN, Rz 0_43_502, fol. 67.

54 AIPN, Rz 0_43_502, fol. 139.

55 AIPN, Rz 0_43_502, fols. 60, 131. Kazimiera Mączyńska-Chmielowska, daughter of Filip (Ludwik) and Franciszka (née Drapała), b. February 18, 1917, in Zabłocie, Tarnopol county; allegedly the illegitimate daughter of General Mączyński of Lwów (AIPN, Rz 0_43_502, fol. 66); married to Adam Chmielowski, son of Jan and Władysława (née Muszyńska), b. January 15, 1923, electrical fitter and mechanic; during the war, he served in the NZW in Skawina under the command of Fr. Lelita; sentenced to 10 years' imprisonment. Mączyńska's mother was sister to Wincenty Stanowski's wife, at whose place the women lived after fleeing from Tarnopol (AIPN, Rz 0_43_502, fol. 58); in the village, Kazimiera was referred to as Jan Stanowski's cousin. At the time, Kisielów was also the place of residence of Michał Stanowski (probably Wincenty's brother), b. c. 1900, father-in-law to Marian Madera/Ossoliński (AIPN, Rz 0_43_502, fols. 51, 111). This relation by marriage may have made it even more difficult for Mączyńska to testify than her membership in the NZW.

56 AIPN, Rz 043_502, fols. 8-9. Mączyńska gave private lessons at home, i.e. in her apartment in the Stanowskis' house. That day, she walked the Schlafs' children home.

57 AIPN, Rz 0_43_502, fol. 73.

58 Kazimiera Mączyńska and Julia Płocica claimed that the Schlafs had been helping them, and that they were friends with them, AIPN, Rz 0_43_502, fol. 88.

59 See Joanna Tokarska-Bakir, *Bracia miesiące. Studia z antropologii historycznej Polski 1939-1945* (Warsaw, 2021), pp. 436-446. See also the spurious descriptions of neighborly situations in Kańczuga: "There were huge friendships here between the Poles and the Jews. My mom and grandma were on very good terms with them. Which is why this murder was a huge surprise to most Kańczugans. – I had Jewish

buddies; I shared a desk with one in school," Alfred Maksymowicz said. "Whoever was smart had good relations with the Jews. During the Corpus Christi processions, when the priest walked out of the church with a monstrance, the rabbi would walk out of the synagogue. They would meet at the first altar and exchange bows" (Piecuch, "Wielka noc w Kańczudze").

60 Lipiński, "Nikt ich nie tykał."

61 Władysław Machaj, son of Jan and Wiktoria, b. November 27, 1918, in Zarzecze, Jarosław county. Stanisław Machaj, son of Jan and Wiktoria, b. November 27, 1918, in Zarzecze, shoemaker; according to Piotr Lipiński, the latter served in the blue police (Polish Police under German rule) during the war, and joined the Polish Workers' Party (*Polska Partia Robotnicza*, PPR) after the war (Lipiński, "Nikt ich nie tykał"). In 1949 he was the first to provide the MO with a description of the Kańczuga killing and a list of the members of Radwan's detachment in Zarzecze (AIPN, Rz_050_86, fol. 35). They were both members of the NZW detachment headed by Tadeusz Kaduk. There was a third brother, Kazimierz Machaj, who was shot by the underground forces prior to 1949 (AIPN, Rz_0_61_411, fol. 7). Furthermore, the inquest documentation mentions a Józef Machaj (brother of little Edward), son of Jan, b. 1925 in Kisielów, who claims that he was near the Schlafs' house at the time of the raid, and that the perpetrators ordered him to lie down in the ditch to prevent him from identifying them (AIPN, Rz 043_502, fols. 47, 63; he revokes this testimony in fol. 67).

62 Helena Machaj, daughter of Jan and Wiktoria; no other data available.

63 Formal statement of Tadeusz Kaduk revealing himself to the authorities (AIPN, Rz 0_61_411, fol. 6). A crucial contribution to establishing the identities of the participants in the Kisielów killing was the denunciation by Kazimierz Trojnar, whom the Security Office (*Urząd Bezpieczeństwa*, UB, the common name for the Office of Public Security, the secret security police in early communist Poland) had recruited as an informer. The list of participants that he supplied included Ewald Sroczyński ("Rzeka," "Dąb"), Stanisław Baran ("Kosiba"), and Bronisław Kaduk ("Szpak"), among others (AIPN, Rz 061/539, fol. 57).

64 As indicated by Madera/Ossoliński's testimony, the assailants knew from the start that Stanisława Płocica-Nowosiad had recognized them (see AIPN, Rz 0_43_502, fols. 6, 106). In 1962, none of the perpetrators was in Kisielów anymore: some had moved to the west of the country (Józef Drabik and his son Zygmunt made their new homes in Legnica; Zygmunt Drabik also spent some time in hiding in Wrocław and Wilczyn Leśny near Trzebnica), others to an area near Gdańsk (Stanisław Machaj) or to Koszalin (Władysław Machaj and his brother-in-law, Eugeniusz Podbilski) (AIPN, Rz 0_43_502, fol. 224).

65 Stanisława Płocica-Nowosiad was related to Jan Płocica, son of Władysław, of Zarzecze, who liaised between the NZW commander Bolesław Usow ("Konar") and the commandant of the local outpost, Kazimierz Trojnar (AIPN, Rz_00_138_1261, fol. 34).

66 Bronisław Kaduk, nom de guerre "Szpak," son of Michał and Zofia (née Gernak), b. April 4, 1919, in Zarzecze; his father was an activist of the Polish People's Party (*Polskie Stronnictwo Ludowe*, PSL) faction called Liberation (*Wyzwolenie*); saddler at the Dzieduszyckis' manor; during the war, a member of the ZWZ-AK, subsequently an NZW platoon commander in Pełnatycze (AIPN, Rz 05_17, fol. 230). According to Eugeniusz Podbilski's testimony, during the raid in Kańczuga, Bronisław Kaduk shot three Jews from a submachine gun (AIPN, Rz_050_1850, fols. 39-40; Rz_00_138_1261, fol. 32; Kaduk's account: Rz 00_90_218, fols. 13-15). Arrested for this crime in 1949, he fled from jail in Jarosław and went into hiding until he turned himself in on April 17, 1953. He admitted to participating in the killing but not to shooting any Jews (AIPN, Rz 00_90_218, fol. 37). From April 18, 1953, under the code name Secret Collaborator "Szpak," he cooperated with the Third Department of the Provincial Office of Public Security (*Wojewódzki Urząd Bezpieczeństwa*, WUBP) in Rzeszów (AIPN, Rz 00_90_218, fol. 16; the file also includes his reports and confirmations of receipt of compensation, fols. 44-46), which led Tadeusz Górski and Stanisław Baran to reveal themselves, after living in hiding since 1947.

67 Tadeusz Kaduk, alias Kazimierz Paja, nom de guerre "Latawiec," son of Michał and Zofia (née Gernak), born in Zarzecze; served in the 3rd Legions' Infantry Regiment, trainee in the orchestra in Jarosław from 1934-1939; ZWZ-AK; In December 1944, he initially served in the Polish Army, then arrested by the NKVD as deputy commandant of the local AK outpost; spent six months in jail in Przemyśl. When the jail was busted in May 1945, he fled and remained in hiding until 1957, using the name Paja (AIPN, Rz_0_42_241, fol. 14). In addition to Bronisław and Tadeusz, there were two other Kaduk brothers, Stanisław (mentally ill) and Władysław, who moved to the Netherlands, as well as a sister, Stefania Kaduk-Kotlińska, the wife of Stanisław Kotliński, on whom more will be said later (AIPN, Rz 00_90_218, fol. 9).

68 For more on the Kańczuga raid see the interrogation of Bronisław Kaduk conducted in Jarosław on March 26, 1949: "After some time, we heard a series of shots in the Jews' apartment and a moment later those listed above, who were at home, came out with the stolen things, such as clothing, violins, and other things (…) and we all went to the wagon and drove away together from Zarzecze to the Machajs' place (…). I was given a violin" (AIPN, Rz 050_1850, fols. 8-9).

69 Testimony of Eugeniusz Podbilski: "During the raid in the town of Kańczuga, we murdered three whole Jewish families" (AIPN, Rz 050_1850, fol. 21).

70 Lipiński, "Nikt ich nie tykał."

71 Józef Skowron, son of Andrzej and Agnieszka (née Król), b. January 1, 1909, in Żurawiczki (AIPN, Rz 0_43_502, fol. 173).

72 AIPN, Rz 0_43_502, fol. 213. Stanisław Kotliński (son of Tomasz and Katarzyna, b. May 21, 1911; AIPN, Rz 0_43_502, fol. 137) was arrested in 1946 by the Jarosław PUBP and sentenced to five years' imprisonment (AIPN, Rz 00_90_218,

fol. 9). The interrogation of Kotliński is archived as AIPN, Rz 052_303, fol. 22. It was him that an opinion cited in Piotr Lipiński's article referred to: "Woman aged 83: 'Hated by everyone, he was. For various things. Stealing and everything. Not just in Zarzecze but all over the place. There was partisan activity here, but it also involved a whole bunch of irresponsible people. They were subordinate to Radwan to some extent, but then they would do some extra stuff on the side'" (Lipiński, "Nikt ich nie tykał"). Madera/Ossoliński claims that Stanisław Kotliński was the one who drove the wagon for the bandits that murdered the Jews in Kańczuga.

73 AIPN, Rz 00_90_218, fol. 9. At the age of 84, Tadeusz Kaduk, whom Piotr Lipiński found still alive in 2002, confirmed the relation by marriage and Stanisław Kotliński's bad reputation: "Yeah, my brother-in-law. A bandit and a thief, nothing more. And I beat him up, and my brother, the one who died, beat him up too. He was an adulterer, for one thing. My brother wanted to shoot him. He hit our sister in front of us. Flung her against the stove. He wasn't in my detachment; he used to force his way into things unrightfully, posing as a hero, because he'd done some pistol shooting someplace" (Lipiński, "Nikt ich nie tykał").

74 Stanisław Henderscheder of Pełnatycze, Rozwienica commune, Jarosław county, was also a sympathizer of Radwan's detachment (AIPN, Rz 0_43_502, fols. 206-228).

75 Władysław Skowron, son of Andrzej and Agnieszka (née Król), b. July 25, 1904, in Żurawiczki (AIPN, Rz 0_43_502, fol. 176).

76 AIPN, Rz 0_43_502, fol. 176.

77 Jan Kotliński (son of Tomasz and Katarzyna, née Szewczyk, b. December 12, 1902 in Żurawiczki) confirms that he dressed the animal, which was "still warm" (AIPN, Rz 0_43_502, fol. 181).

78 At some other place: "dropped down like sheaves" (AIPN, Rz 0_43_502, fol. 232).

79 Anna Skowron was the sister of Stanisław Kotliński, a member of Radwan's group (AIPN, Rz 0_43_502, fol. 213). As mentioned before, Stanisław Kotliński's wife, Stefania, was the sister of Bronisław and Tadeusz Kaduk (AIPN, Rz 00_90_218, fol. 9).

80 AIPN, Rz 0_43_502, fol. 193. Władysław Skowron adds that he saw at his brother's place "silver and gold spoons, expensive tableware (…) [and] suspected that the tableware and spoons had doubtlessly come from the robbery of the Jews in Kisielów" (AIPN, Rz 0_43_502, fol. 203).

81 AIPN, Rz 0_43_502, fol. 191.

82 AIPN, Rz 0_43_502, fols. 214-215.

83 AIPN, Rz_00_42_241, fol. 8.

84 AIPN, Rz 0_43_502, fol. 65.

85 Ewald Sroczyński, son of Józef and Wiktoria (née Grzęda/Grenda), b. February 11, 1917, in Delmendorf, Germany; noms de guerre "Dąb," "Rzeka," and "Obrazowski" (Surdej mentions the latter on p. 104). Before the war, his parents

ran a restaurant in Poznań. Before graduating from secondary school, he was in Cadet Corps No. 3 in Rawicz, then attended the officers' schools in Różan-upon-Narew and in Komorowo near Ostrów Mazowiecka (until 1939). In July 1939, he was assigned to the 56th Infantry Regiment in Krotoszyn (platoon commander with the rank of sub-lieutenant). After the German invasion in September, he saw action in Sokolniki and was wounded. Sought by the Gestapo, he moved from Pleszew in Jarocin county to Rozwadów and Stalowa Wola. From 1943, platoon commander in the detachment headed by "Ojciec Jan" (Franciszek Przysiężniak), where he operated under the pseudonym "Dąb." From July to December 1944, using the nom de guerre "Rzeka," he was the commandant of the NZW-AK outpost in Zarzecze near Przeworsk, and in close liaisons with the NZW district commandant, Kazimierz Mirecki ("Tadeusz," "Żmuda") and Bronisław Gliniak ("Radwan"). Toward the end of 1945, he returned to Pleszew, where first he dealt in foreign currencies and gold, and subsequently opened a beer bottling plant. In 1945, he revealed himself as a former partisan to the Ministry of Public Security (certificate no. 794) and had his military rank of captain verified by the Ministry of National Defense. He initiated cooperation with the Third Department of the Provincial Office of Public Security (*Wojewódzki Urząd Bezpieczeństwa*, WUBP) in Poznań (AIPN, Rz 0_43_502, fols. 171, 219-222) and, as Secret Collaborator "Halny," he helped in exposing Stefan Toczyński, Edward Błaszczak ("Grom"), and other members of the NZW (AIPN, Rz 0_43_502, fols. 223, 250; see his reports: AIPN, Po 8_579, fols. 137, 147, etc.). From 1956, he was a member of the Society of Participants of Armed Struggle (*Związek Uczestników Walki Zbrojnej*), and then ZBOWiD (AIPN, Po 8_579, fol. 36). In the late 1950s and early 1960s, he was called upon by the latter organization to provide clarification with regard to accusations of multiple murders and denied having been involved in any (AIPN, Po 8_579, fol. 39). The biographical note on fol. 41 in Sroczyński's file contains a (probably fictitious) statement that he spent some time with Soviet partisan forces under the command of Major Tsyganov (in the Janów woods?) and a reference to the Cross of Virtuti Militari awarded to him in 1944.

86 AIPN, Rz 0_43_502, fol. 168.

87 AIPN, Rz 0_43_502, fol. 230.

88 Statement, September 28, 1966, AIPN, Rz 0_43_502, fol. 238.

89 In the report of Secret Collaborator "Bocian" (at the time in Wrocław's Prison No. 1), dated August 2, 1948, we read: "In the village of Kisielów, Jarosław county, Commandant Ewald Dąb [Ewald Sroczyński ("Dąb," "Rzeka"); see further below] executed seven Jews by shooting. The Jews had been accused before Ewald Dąb by a farmer in that village (…) at whose place those Jews had been hiding throughout the period of German occupation, when they approached that farmer with a request for the return of some of the cash that they had given him for harboring them, explaining that they wished to start their own households. Being reluctant to give [it] back, and being an acquaintance of Dąb, he accused them before him, and Dąb executed them. The whole village of Kisielów can tell the name of that farmer

because everyone knows who kept those Jews in hiding. Stanisław Baran found out about it from Ewald Dąb, with whom he was in ongoing communication" (AIPN, Wr 024_226, Folder 2, fol. 78). Owing to the assistance of Alina Skibińska, who visited the Kisielów area on June 23, 2021, we can learn the names of the individuals who helped the Schlaf family during the war. They were supplied by a 92-year-old priest, Fr. Włodzimierz Nowosiad, son of Marcin and Maria (née Kudriańska), b. 1929, resident of the village of Sienno. Those who helped the Schlafs included his father, Marcin Nowosiad, the postwar head of Kisielów, and also his neighbors, the Kudriański and Hałysz families (see Note 46). The priest, who went to school with the Schlafs' children and claims that they were a well-liked family throughout the village, remembers that the two pieces of land left behind by the Schlafs were taken over by "the greatest enemies of the Jews."

90 In a subsequent testimony, he revoked his confession of shooting at the Jews (AIPN, Rz 0_43_502, fol. 263).

91 AIPN, Rz 0_43_502, fol. 239.

92 AIPN, Rz 0_43_502, fol. 219.

93 Surdej, *Okręg Rzeszowski Narodowej Organizacji Wojskowej*, p. 305. The authorities searched for Lubomirski, which was hardly difficult given how rare his name was. His personal data can be found on sheet 269 in the AIPN file marked Rz 0_43_502. However, it refers to Herakliusz (rather than Horacjusz) Lubomirski, son of Hubert and Teresa (née Radziwiłł), b. November 1, 1926, in Paris, France; in 1967 a resident of Ursus near Warsaw. The facts of his life prior to that date have been established: During the years 1944-1955, he was in the USSR (Krasnoyarsk), and came back to Poland in 1955 as part of the repatriation campaign. Lubomirski's photograph was shown to one of Radwan's soldiers, Stanisław Kotliński, who stated that "this person was unknown to him and he had never seen him." Nor was he recognized by any of the other eyewitnesses to the Kisielów crime (fol. 271). See also AIPN, BU_3936_220.

94 Surdej mentions this pseudonym, without stating the name, in the context of murders on Ukrainians returning from Germany (Surdej, *Okręg Rzeszowski Narodowej Organizacji Wojskowej*, p. 386; also includes a photo). The same nom de guerre features in the formal statement by which Tadeusz Kaduk revealed himself to the authorities, dated April 22, 1947, specifically on the list of his subalterns in Zarzecze (AIPN, Rz_0_61_411, fol. 6).

95 AIPN, Rz 0_43_502, fol. 242.

96 According to international terminology, any grave that holds more than three bodies becomes a "mass" grave by definition while any killing whose perpetrators are driven by the idea of exterminating a whole ethnic group becomes, by definition, a case of genocide. "What distinguishes genocide from murder, and even from acts of political murder that claim as many victims, is the intent. The crime is wanting to make a people extinct. The idea is the crime. No wonder it's so difficult to picture. To do so you must accept the principle of the exterminator, and see not people but

a people," Philip Gourevitch, *We wish to inform you that tomorrow we will be killed with our families. Stories from Rwanda* (New York, 1999), pp. 201-202.

97   AIPN, Rz_0_42_241, fols. 39-40.

98   AIPN, Po_0_8_579, fol. 208.

99   Letter from L. Beria to Stalin dated May 29, 1945 (Moscow), forwarding N. Selivanovsky's report on the activities of the Polish underground, in Tatiana Cariewskaja, Andrzej Chmielarz, Andrzej Paczkowski, Ewa Rosowska, and Szymon Rudnicki (eds.), *Teczka specjalna J.W. Stalina. Raporty NKWD z Polski 1944-1946* (Warsaw, 1998), p. 282.

100   AIPN, Bu_0644_374, Folder 2, fol. 44.

101   Karol Urban, nom de guerre "Lira," son of Maria Kłosowicz, b. February 27, 1914, in Jarosław; served in the 39th Infantry Regiment in Jarosław; deputy platoon commander in the detachment headed by Leut. Koba ("Rak"); remembered by his superior, Wojciech Szczepański ("Grzegorz"). Secret Collaborator "Liść" claimed that Karol Urban had also taken part in the Kisielów killing, and subsequently left Jarosław "because the Jews wanted to kill him" (AIPN, Bu_0644_374, Folder 2, fol. 163; AIPN, Rz 0_43_502, fol. 187).

102   AIPN, Rz_050_1850, fol. 187.

103   AIPN, Bu 0644_1, fols. 90-98. Other than Sroczyński ("Rzeka"), he also mentions the "heroes" that we know from Kisielów and Kańczuga – Bronisław Kaduk, "old Drabik" (Józef), his son Zygmunt, and others – as being the most dangerous bandits in the area.

104   Interrogation of Karol Urban, May 5, 1945 (AIPN, Bu_0644_1, fols. 90-98).

105   AIPN, Bu_0644_374, Folder 2.

106   Report of the Second Department of the Staff of the Warta Grouping dated May 30, 1945 (quoted in Surdej, *Okręg Rzeszowski Narodowej Organizacji Wojskowej*, p. 384).

107   National Archives in Kraków, Archive of the Freedom and Independence Movement, Folder 16, fol. 214, and Folder 7, fol. 127.

108   Letter from Wojciech Szczepański, document entitled "Grzegorz to Commander V, April 26, 1945" (AIPN, Rz_050_86, fols. 6-7). Szczepański was in danger of an attempt on his life by the NZW, which he testified about after being arrested; see also Surdej, *Okręg Rzeszowski Narodowej Organizacji Wojskowej*, p. 384.

109   Testimony of Stanisław Machaj (AIPN, Rz 050/86, fol. 33; Rz 00_141-934_J, fol. 10).

110   "In the Machajs' apartment I found the aforementioned [i.e. Władysław and Stanisław Machaj, Eugeniusz Podbilski, and an unknown individual] and their neighbor Stanisław Baran, who were drinking *samogon* vodka, meaning moonshine, together (…) While they were drinking, the Machajs' apartment was visited, among others, by Marian Ossoliński and another Stanisław Baran known as Kosiba, who drank the *samogon* with us. When we were pretty drunk, that

representative of the county announced to us that we were going to drive a wagon because we had a job to do" (AIPN, Rz_00_138_1261, fol. 36).

111 AIPN, Rz 00_90_218, fol. 3.

112 AIPN, Rz 0_43_502, fol. 262.

113 AIPN, Rz_107_894, fols. 65-7.

114 AIPN, Rz_0_61_411, fols. 97, 106; Rz_052_303, fol. 71.

115 AIPN, Rz 055_63, t.7, fol. 146 (quoted in Surdej, *Okręg Rzeszowski Narodowej Organizacji Wojskowej*, p. 322).

116 AIPN, Rz 055_63, t.7, fol. 146 (quoted *ibid.*, p. 321).

117 AIPN, Rz 055_63, t.7, fol. 146 (*ibid.*, pp. 321-322).

118 Surdej, *Okręg Rzeszowski Narodowej Organizacji Wojskowej*, p. 322.

119 AIPN, Rz 0_43_502, fol. 193: "The same night, around 12.00, the men who were at Józef Skowron's place subsequently drove to the PGR [state-owned farm] at Ożańsk, where they pilfered 3 sows, and brought them back to Mirocin, to Jan Kotliński's place. Kotliński dressed the pigs for them."

120 State Archives in Rzeszów, Fonds 108, ref. 150, Report of the "Złota" detachment, April 26, 1946, fol. 246 (quoted in Surdej, *Okręg Rzeszowski Narodowej Organizacji Wojskowej*, p. 387).

121 Surdej, *Okręg Rzeszowski Narodowej Organizacji Wojskowej*, p. 387 and footnote on p. 383.

122 See the materials on SN members held in the WiN archive which I describe in my article, Joanna Tokarska-Bakir, "The Polish Underground Organization Wolność i Niezawisłość and Anti-Jewish Pogroms, 1945-6," *Patterns of Prejudice* 48(2) (2017), pp. 111-136.

123 On the beliefs relating to Judeo-Belshevism and how they were combined with a modernized blood libel motif, see Joanna Tokarska-Bakir, "The Figure of the Bloodsucker in Polish Religious, National and Left-Wing Discourse, 1945-1946: A Study in Historical Anthropology," *Dapim — Studies on the Holocaust*, 27(2) (2013), pp. 75-106.

124 Józef Hajduk, son of Jan and Karolina (née Myśliwa), b. December 11, 1881, in Szymbark near Gorlice (AIPN, Rz, 0_42_241, fol. 17).

125 AIPN, Rz, 0_42_241, fol. 17.

126 AIPN, Rz 0_61_411, fol. 113.

127 AIPN, Rz 052/303.

128 Testimony of Bolesław Rusinek (AIPN, Rz_050_1083, fol. 12).

129 *Ibid.*

130 This refers e.g. to the bodies of 14 Soviet soldiers killed during the skirmish in the village of Szówsko on April 29, 1945 (AIPN, Rz_050_86, fol. 57).

131 Surdej quotes here a report by Edward Więcław ("Szczerba") of the Leżajsk PAS (Surdej, *Okręg Rzeszowski Narodowej Organizacji Wojskowej*, p. 312, Note 112).

132 Elżbieta Rączy, "Zabójstwa dokonane na Żydach w województwie rzeszowskim w latach 1944-1947 w świetle akt organów bezpieczeństwa," in Edyta Czop and Elżbieta Rączy (eds.), *Z dziejów stosunków polsko-żydowskich* (Rzeszów, 2009), Table 2.

133 AIPN, Rz 00_138_1261_J, fol. 32.

134 On the "black book" motif see Joanna Tokarska-Bakir, *Bracia miesiące. Studia z antropologii historycznej Polski 1939-1945* (Warsaw, 2021), p. 178.

135 Janina Dusiło, resident of Zarzecze, daughter of Jan and Katarzyna, b. June 24, 1914, in Szczytna.

136 AIPN, Rz 107_894, fol. 68. On the same sheet, Zofia Wojnar says: "In 1945 Zygmunt Drabik said to me that their group had murdered Andrzej Pecak, resident of the hamlet of Cieszacin Mały. Then he showed me a list, [meaning] that they had a list of all the people that they still had to shoot." See also AIPN, Rz 107_894, fol. 93; Rz 061_539, fol. 15.

137 Maksym Gorki, *Rosja*, trans. Małgorzata Buchalik (Kraków, 2016), p. V.

Introduction to Aharon Weiss's "The Jewish Police in Lwów, 1941–1943" — by Noam Leibman

This article on the Jewish police is a chapter from Aharon Weiss' ground-breaking and as yet unpublished doctoral dissertation entitled "The Jewish Police in the General Government and Upper Galicia during the Holocaust." Although almost 50 years have passed since its completion in 1973, it still serves as an important source for scholars exploring the Jewish police in these regions during World War II.

Although brief, the chapter in the dissertation about the Jewish police accurately depicts the general picture of what we know about them and their activity. Weiss' work on Lwów in this context is groundbreaking, no other scholar having investigated the topic. Likewise, even the memoirs, testimonies and documents he does not quote rarely offer further details or shed new light on the role of the Jewish police in Lwów. The Archive of the Jewish Historical Institute in Warsaw nonetheless holds sources neither Weiss nor more recent scholars adduce that may be of research value.

When reading the material, attention should be paid, *inter alia*, to two details that shed light on important aspects of Jewish police activity in Lwów:

a) In describing the relations between the Jewish police and the Judenrat, Weiss interweaves a thesis he had previously developed—namely, that the Judenrat's activities must be assessed in light of term of office—i.e., the first Judenrat established or the forum assembled in the wake of an earlier significant event, such as the dissolution of the Judenrat or the murder of its members. According to this theory, each Judenrat acted differently and must be identified accordingly. This is also true with respect to the Lwów Jewish police force.

b) Sources—like scholars—use the term "Jewish police" inconsistently. This fact is of great import in the case of Lwów, where four police frameworks operated. Weiss employs the term

"Jewish police" to refer to all of these, using OD (*Ordnungsdienst*) for the Jewish police—who were subject, at least structurally, to the Judenrat. The model of an additional police force to that subject to the Judenrat, effectively directly answering to the Germans, also existed in other ghettos. However, as Weiss notes, the distinction between the various frameworks became blurred in Lwów at an early stage, with serious consequences.

Over the last decade, research regarding Jewish Police during the Holocaust era has expanded extensively and provided profound insight into the organization's role and methods of operation. While never previously published, Weiss' study remains relevant and unique. Publishing Weiss' essay about the Jewish Police in Lwów in Yalkut Moreshet is an opportunity to give this study its proper place.

Notes to Introduction

1   Aharon Weiss, "The Jewish Police in the General Government and Upper Galicia during the Holocaust," doctoral dissertation, Hebrew University of Jerusalem, 1973 (Hebrew).

2   See, for example, Katarzyna Person, *Warsaw Ghetto Police: The Jewish Order Service during the Nazi Occupation* (Ithaca, 2018); Noam Leibman, "The Role of the Jewish Police in the Warsaw and Otwock Ghettos in Light of Survivor Memoirs," master's thesis, University of Haifa, 2019 (Hebrew); Neta Ehrlich, "The Image of the 'Jüdischer Ordnungsdienst' in the Warsaw Ghetto, November 1940 to July 1942," master's thesis, Tel Aviv University, 2020 (Hebrew). Weiss's research is also cited in studies of the Jewish police in other areas and contexts. See, for example, Dov Levin, "How the Jewish Police in the Kovno Ghetto Saw Itself," *Yad Vashem Studies* 29 (2001), pp. 143–85; Avihu Ronen, Hadas Agmon, and Asaf Danziger, "Collaborator or Would-be Rescuer? The Barenblat Trial and the Image of a Judenrat Member in 1960s Israel," *Yad Vashem Studies* 39(1) (2011), pp. 101–140; Samuel Schalkowsky (ed.), *The Clandestine History of the Kovno Getto Jewish Police* (Bloomington, 2014).

3   Cf., for example, the chapter on the Jewish police in Eliyahu Yones, *Smoke in the Sand: The Jews of Lvov in the War Years, 1939–1944* (Jerusalem, 2004), pp. 117–126. Yones views the police much more harshly than Weiss: "In contrast to the other Judenrat departments, which dealt with fulfilling the Germans' instructions with regards to the Jews' property or source of livelihood, the Jewish police delivered Jewish bodies and souls" (ibid., p. 117). Apart from this judgmental attitude, he

includes no new material, however. The same is true of the majority of the sources he notes: see ibid., p. 126 n. 29. See also Jakub Honigsman, *The Catastrophy of Jewry in Lvov* (Lviv, 1993).

4   See, for example, Abraham Goldberg, *Days Scorched in Fire* (Tel Aviv, 1987) (Hebrew); Joachim Schoenfeld, *Holocaust Memoirs: Jews in the Lwów Ghetto, the Janowski Concentration Camp, and as Deportees in Siberia* (Hoboken, 1985); Belah Guterman (ed.), *When Terror Came: The Jews of Lwów under the German Occupation: Testimonies* (Tel Aviv, 1991) (Hebrew). For information regarding the Jewish police, see primarily *Shmuel Czartkower's diary*, pp. 122–69; Zeev Rattner, Mami, *Do you Hear?!* (Tel Aviv, 2010) (Hebrew); reports and memoirs relating to the Lwów ghetto and Janowska camp in the Ghetto Fighters House Archive, Adolf Abraham Berman collection, 3171; Ben Z. Redner, *A Jewish Policeman in Lwów: An Early Account, 1941–1943* (Jerusalem, 2015); Zygmunt Hoffman, "Zteki lwowskiej," *Biuletyn Żydowskiego Instytutu Historycznego* 114–115 (1980), pp. 135–45; Renata Kessler, *The Wartime Diary of Edmund Kessler* (Boston, 2010).

5   Leon Weliczker, Archiwum Żydowskiego Instytutu Historycznego (AŻIH), 302/26; Irena Szajowicz, AŻIH, 302/56; Uri Lichter, AŻIH, 302/61; Janina Masłowska, AŻIH, 302/182; Kazimiera Poraj, AŻIH, 302/217.

6   For this theory, see Aharon Weiss, "The Policies of the Judenräte in Southeastern Poland," *Yalkut Moreshet* 15 (1972), pp. 122–59 (Hebrew); Weiss, "Jewish Leadership in Occupied Poland: Postures and Attitudes," *Yad Vashem Studies* 12 (1977), pp. 243–66.

7   See Leibman, "The Role of the Jewish Police," pp. 6–7; Ehrlich, "The Image of the 'Jüdischer Ordnungsdienst,'" pp. 15–16.

8   The most well-known was the "Office to Combat Usury and Profiteering and Price-Fixing" (Urząd do Walki z Lichwą i Spekulacją) in the Jewish Quarter of Warsaw. See Aharon Weiss, "The 'Thirteen' in the Ghetto Warsaw," *Yalkut Moreshet* 21 (1976), pp. 157–80 (Hebrew).

Aharon Weiss

The Jewish Police in Lwów, 1941–1943

The Germans captured Lwów on June 29, 1941, Jewish pogroms erupting the very next day. For three days, German troops and the local populace engaged in a killing spree, slaying around 4000 Jews, the market squares and streets becoming the scene of public butchery.

The massacre of Jewish public activists accused of sympathizing with the Soviet regime continued through July. Between July 25 and 27, almost a thousand were murdered by Ukrainians in what came to be known as the Petliura days, marking the fifteenth anniversary of the assassination of the former head of the Ukrainian National Republic by Szolem Szwarcbard on May 26, 1926 in Paris. The Jewish community were required to make a "contribution" of 20 million rubles.[1]

These conditions, of murder and theft, formed the backdrop against which the Judenrat was created. The Germans leant on well-known public figures to form a council, the position of chairman being offered, among others, to Dr. Moses (Maurycy) Allerhand, a Professor of Law at the University of Lwów.[2] When he declined it, they turned to Abraham Eliezer Kupfersztein, a Mizrahi leader and deputy chair of the community council. He, too, turned it down.[3]

Amongst the Jewish activists who sought an appropriate candidate for chairman of the Judenrat was Dr. Adolf Rotfield, head of the General Zionists in Galicia and Lwów. He persuaded Dr. Józef Parnas to accept the post.[4]

Although some of the attempts to assemble the Judenrat were made under German pressure, the leaders' attitude towards the issue indicates that political factors were in play up until September 1939, the elections thus being based on public considerations. This circumstance demonstrates that while the Soviet regime had intervened in the Jewish public sphere between 1939 and 1941, it had not completely destroyed it, with political leaders emerging and seeking ways to cope with the new problems facing the Jewish community in Lwów.

Dr. Parnas was a notable personage—a respected lawyer and former Austrian army officer. He accepted the position on the premise that it would enable him to aid the Jewish community in its distress. In this spirit, he set about organizing the council. From the very beginning, he stood firm against German pressure, paying for this resistance with his life (see below).

The Formation of the Police Force

The first official order for the establishment of the Jewish police in Lwów—to number 500—came from the SS and German police in Galicia on November 8, 1941.[5] In effect, however, preparations had already begun in August, the November order possibly merely confirming a process that had already been set in motion.[6]

Once the authorization had been given, a top-ranking captain from the Warsaw Jewish police force arrived to help organize the local Jüdischer Ordnungsdienst (JOD). Initially, a group of twenty was recruited, who immediately began training.[7]

Part of the German administration that pressured the Judenrat to set up a law enforcement unit was the Arbeitsamt. A separate police detachment was in fact established charged primarily with taking care of forced-labor issues.[8] These two cadres later merged, becoming the core of the Jewish police force. By the beginning of 1941, it numbered around 300, reaching 500 a few months later.

Recruitment

The Judenrat first sought to recruit those with military experience and an education. Responses to this call exceeded the places available.[9] Many were highly educated, lawyers being very well represented.[10] The force was directed by former Jewish military officers. Although it is difficult to accurately ascertain the social background of the Jewish police in the early period, the picture gained is that it was composed of respectable public figures who believed the force could play a positive role.[11] Even the youth groups debated whether to join the Judenrat, eventually deciding, after much deliberation, to stay out.[12] It may be assumed that, such being their attitude towards the Judenrat, they would have felt the same way towards the Jewish police.

Despite its positive elements, the Judenrat also consisted of dubious public and moral characters.[13] Those who applied to work therein were frequently motivated by benefits—exemption for themselves and their families from certain decrees (e.g., forced labor), extra food rations, greater freedom of movement and, in the ghetto, better accommodation.[14]

Organization

Geographically, the force was divided into four commissariats:

Commissariat 1 (Bernstein 11)

Commissariat 2 (Zmarstinowska 106)

Commissariat 3 (Kleparow 35)[15]

Commissariat 4 (Novoznisynska 33)[16]

Four frameworks also existed:

1. The JOD—the largest in size, forming division 10 of the Judenrat. A special division also worked next to the Judenrat's accommodation department[17]
2. The Kriminalpolizei (the Jewish Kripo)
3. The Jewish Sonderdienst or Spezialabteilung[18]
4. The Jewish gendarmerie[19]

The last three were unconnected to the Judenrat. Answering directly to the Germans, they contained large numbers of figures from the underground world.[20]

Police Commanders

Baruch Rojzen—Commander of the JOD, Captain (reserve) in the Polish army.

Dr. Abraham Rosenmann—Deputy commander of the JOD, Captain (reserve) in the Polish army.

Narzissenfeld—Second deputy of the JOD, Captain (reserve) in the Polish army.[21]

The Kripo and Jewish SD were headed by:

Max Goliger-Szapira—Son of a grain merchant and member of the Hashmonia sports club.

Krummholz—Goliger-Szapira's deputy, a refugee from Krakow.

Janek Scherz—Commander of the Jewish gendarmerie.[22]

These three special units were not clearly differentiated or delineated, with all of them falling under the command of Max Goliger-Szapira.

Uniform

The policemen wore flat dark-blue hats with a red band, and the officers' hats bore a silver Star of David. New recruits bore no distinguishing markings. On their left arms they wore a yellow ribbon bearing a Star of David and the words "*Judischer Ordnungsdienst—Lemberg*." Their service number was inscribed on a round metal badge worn on the left side of their chest. Apart from their hats and armbands, the uniform had no other elements.

Roles

Although a closed ghetto was only established in Lwów in September 1942, the Germans began separating and isolating the Jewish population even before then. Right from the beginning of the invasion, they began herding the Jewish communities into delimited spaces. The early tasks of the Jewish police included:

✦ Traffic warden duty, primarily of pedestrians

✦ Keeping the streets, squares, courtyards, and stairwells clean

✦ Clearing the snow from the streets

✦ Enforcing blackouts

✦ Fighting the black market and monitoring prices in licensed shops

✦ Enforcing the curfew and preventing assemblies[23]

Formally defined, some of these jobs were carried out. Others—some ordered directly by the Germans, others by the Judenrat—included:

✦ Keeping order in Judenrat offices, shops, and storehouses

✦ Accompanying the Besorgungsamt—the Judenrat division in charge of collecting items to fill German "orders." This often took the form of confiscation, the police using force to take what was demanded.

One report states that the police force set up a public council to help the poor in the Kleparów district: "The purpose of the council was to aid the poor and monitor the police commissariat in this region."[24] This initiative can be explained in several ways:

✦ As a way to improve its public image and balance the negative activity in which the police were forced to engage within the framework of their work.
✦ As a form of rivalry with the Judenrat and/or JSS.
✦ As a pure demonstration of public responsibility.[25]

The fact that the police force guaranteed that it would fully monitor the council's activities, however, indicates a wish to prevent the emergence of a body of whose character the police and Judenrat disapproved.

Although the police carried out these roles during the first weeks, as German policy consolidated their job began to change. These developments influenced the police force's relationship with the Judenrat and the Jewish populace's attitude toward the police, contributing to significant changes in the personal constitution of those employed.

Relations between the Judenrat and Police under Dr. Józef Parnas

Dr. Parnas only served a short while—until October 1941. As noted above, he valiantly withstood German pressure, the Judenrat trying to find ways to meet the Jewish population's urgent needs. Parnas received orders from the Germans to pay a contribution and provide people for forced labor. But when he was asked to give people to send to the work camp, which in time became the infamous Janowska camp, he put his foot down. This was a line he refused to cross, purportedly stating: "As long as I'm head of the Judenrat, not a single Jewish clerk or policeman will be given to meet this demand. I will not give people."[26] He was then arrested and murdered. While the majority of those who served in the Judenrat were held hostage, the Jewish police carried out the German order, assembling around 500 Jews and sending them to the camp.[27]

This was the first sign of the Jewish police carrying out German orders against the Judenrat head's explicit opinion—and apparently without coordination with the other members of the Judenrat.[28]

Dr. Adolf Rotfield

The second head of the Judenrat was Dr. Rotfield, Parnas's deputy. Rotfield was one of the leaders of the General Zionists. During his term of office—November 1941 to February 1942—the Judenrat sought to establish a branch of public activity to help weather the difficult conditions. Making fevered efforts to create jobs for thousands of Jews, solve the supply problems, and aid the poor, it even discussed the possibility of renewing the educational system.[29] At this stage, it still believed that it could play the role the Jewish Council had fulfilled before the war—and more.

During this period, however, new problems arose that highlighted fresh aspects of the Judenrat and Jewish police's activity. Towards the end of 1941, German "orders" for labor for the work camps in eastern Galicia increased. As young Jews began going into hiding, the quota could no longer be filled in the same way as before—i.e., people being summoned on the basis of pre-prepared lists given by the Judenrat to the JOD. The Jewish police now started taking people off the street. Those who could not prove that they worked in a known and approved place were assembled and sent to work camps. This was the first serious rift between the police and the Jewish public.[30]

In the wake of the seizures, the JOD became much more corrupt. The first sign of this was the acceptance of bribes to release people, others being taken in their stead. As a result, some members left the police force, being neither able nor willing to engage in such activity. These two trends—a drop in ethical standards and greater cooperation with the Germans on the one hand and the leaving/expulsion of the better elements from the police force on the other—later intensified.

With the exception of people who were seized for forced labor, sporadic killings, famine, and disease, the Lwów Jewish community experienced no major shocks between November 1941 and February 1942. During this period, the Judenrat's policy and relations with the Jewish police were thus put to no real test. Adolf Rotfield died of disease in February 1942—the only Judenrat head to die a natural death.

Dr. Henryk Landesberg

Rotfield was succeeded by Dr. Landesberg, a well-known lawyer and public figure. He was in office during the two big *aktion*s in Lwów. In March 1942, around 15,000 Jews were deported, another 50,000 or so following in August. When the

Judenrat was ordered to prepare lists for deportations to the "East" in March 1942, some members had reservations. Not wanting to take responsibility for such an act, they got prominent public figures involved.[31] Some public circles sought to dissuade the Judenrat from cooperating with the Germans in any way with respect to the deportations. A deputation of four was sent to Dr. Landesberg that asked him not to hand over any lists, basing their appeal on Maimonides' *Yoreh De'ah*, halakhah 2, §157, according to which no Jew is to be handed over to murderers.[32] Although Landesberg evaded giving a direct answer, he inclined towards the side of cooperation.[33] The central argument was that if the Judenrat did not collaborate, the Germans would conduct the deportation themselves and the consequences would be even worse. First and foremost, the deportations targeted "asocial elements."

The March *Aktion* and the Jewish police

The Jewish side of the *aktion* was coordinated by Józef Hoch, a top-ranking Judenrat official. Several accounts and evaluations exist regarding the part played by the JOD:

> On March 19, bands of five men belonging to the Judenrat and JOD began going out and looking for people whose names appeared on lists prepared beforehand for deportation. In the majority of cases, the houses were empty, the inhabitants having anticipated the visit and gone to ground … The police acted honorably in this *aktion*, the spirit of the police barracks not yet having yet affected them adversely and their conscience still coming to their aid. They thus gathered together at relatives' homes and spent the night drinking *hamin*, it being a terribly cold winter. At dawn, they returned to the council with a general report: most of the inhabitants have work permits. There were also some whose uniforms matched their bodies and spirits. Those arrested without work permits were taken to the Zobieski school.[34]

The Judenrat and Jewish police exhibiting clear reservations regarding this task, the quotas were not filled. The Germans thus convened an urgent meeting, attended by the Jewish police commanders and Dr. Jaffe, the head of the

Judenrat's accommodation division and one of the most prominent figures in the Judenrat, who had close contacts with the Germans. The latter announced that if the quotas were not filled, 100,000 Jews would be deported, each policeman being required to bring at least one person for deportation—otherwise he and his family would pay the price with their heads.[35]

Although this threat may be presumed to have worked, at a certain point in the *aktion*—which lasted around two weeks—the Germans and Ukrainians became directly involved.[36] While some testimonies affirm that the Jewish police and Judenrat officials did not provide the numbers demanded, others stress that some complied with the German orders.[37]

As noted above, the Jews were collected together at the Zobieski school. There, a committee comprised of Germans and Judenrat representatives conducted a *selektzia*. Those who had some skills remained; the others, around 15,000, were taken to Belzec and murdered.[38]

The Germans did not ignore the reluctance the Jewish police demonstrated in fully participating in the *aktion*, however, immediately after it ended they embarked on "purging" the ranks of the JOD. Several dozen policemen—according to certain sources, two hundred—were sent either to Belzec or the work camp at Jaktorów.[39]

After the March *aktion*, Dr. Rosenmann, the JOD deputy commander, resigned and disappeared from Lwów.[40] We cannot know for certain whether this was due to his inability to come to terms with the job imposed on the Jewish police or to the fear of being "purged." Other policemen also resigned when the nature of the work was made clear to them.[41]

Some members of the Judenrat recruited to participate in the *aktion* also vehemently opposed the delivery of people for deportation. Hoch ended their employment in the Judenrat.[42] The March *aktion* thus undermined the Judenrat's status and created a rift between the public and the police force.

Between March and August, the Lwów community continued to suffer and struggle to survive. During this time, people feverishly searched for work permits in the hope that these would save them from deportation. The Jewish police augmented its force, reaching 750 in number, those removed or who left voluntarily being replaced by men of less public and moral sensitivity.[43]

During this period, the Sonderdienst and Kripo units extended their operations, "taking care" of Jews suspected of collaborating with the Soviets between 1939 and 1941, those in possession of dollars, and black marketeers. Incarcerated in a Jewish jail and "interrogated," they were then handed over to the Germans. In many cases, they were able to gain their release with hefty bribes before they were sent to the ghetto.[44]

The Jewish Kripo and SD engaged in no activities that had any public orientation, nor made any pretence of doing so, playing an ignominious role in the community towards the end of their existence.

The August *Aktion*

By this time, German policy with regard to the Jews had become very clear. If in the March *aktion* the Germans had sought to disguise their intentions by declaring that they were "sending non-productive elements to the frontier regions," now the Jews had no doubts about their true fate. In this *aktion*, the Jewish police more directly answered to the Germans, some of the JOD also being more willing to collaborate. The change in character of those within the police force and the German terror both appear to have left their mark.

The *aktion* began on August 10, 1942, the Germans and Ukrainians laying siege to Jewish houses and streets and sending those they seized to the work camp at Janowska and then to the gas chambers at Belzec. The Jewish police took part in the search for those in hiding and helped assemble those found for deportation.[45] Around 50,000 were deported in this *aktion*. In some cases, the police helped the Jewish populace, primarily on a personal basis. Several witnesses report that the Jewish police saved them from being caught or informed them of an impending *aktion*.[46]

In its wake, the character of the police force changed once again, some resigning voluntarily because they could not reconcile themselves with the job they were called to do. The most prominent change, however, came after the German *selektzia*, many policemen being deported with the other victims, particularly those who refused to collaborate fully.[47] Whatever the cause, police numbers became greatly depleted and the JOD increasingly dominated by less desirable elements.

Under Dr. Landesberg's tenure, very few essential differences existed between the Judenrat and the Jewish police with respect to collaboration with the Germans.

At the end of the August *aktion*, the Lwów ghetto was closed off and the community experienced a new form of terror. In September 1942, a rumor spread that a Jew had killed a German soldier, one testimony stating that he was a Jewish policeman.[48] The SS and German police burst into the Judenrat and JOD offices, hauled off Dr. Landesberg and eleven policemen, and hung them above the balcony on the main street of the ghetto. Landesberg's rope broke and he asked for mercy on the basis of the tradition that if the rope broke the hanging should not proceed. The Germans ignored his plea and hung him again. Amongst the policemen who were executed was Dr. Tunis. A top-ranking officer, he noted that he had been a captain in the Austrian army and thus asked to be shot, as befitting an officer. The Germans acceded to this request.[49]

Dr. Edward Eberson[50]

These were the conditions under which Dr. Edward Abersohn, the fourth and final Judenrat head, began his term of office. Although not a prominent public figure before the war, he was known as a fair man and devoted to public affairs. Being no match for the Germans, however, he was thus joined by Józef Hoch. The latter—head of a Judenrat department—had made a name for himself by getting the members of the Judenrat to participate in the March *aktion*.

Another equally significant step, especially in relation to work, was the integration of the Jewish police commanders—Baruch Rojzen and Margolin, a Viennese Jew—into the Judenrat presidency.[51]

The end of 1942 was marked by letters indicating their degree of "usefulness" to the Germans. Others in the ghetto already had no right of existence. Dr. Ebersohn had no influence at all on what happened inside the ghetto. With the Judenrat not receiving any letters, its days were clearly numbered.

At the end of December 1942, the ghetto became a Julag (Judenlager) or work camp overseen by the SS. On January 30, 1943, all the members of the Judenrat presidency were summoned to the julag square with their families. Dr. Ebersohn and another six council members went. They were taken and murdered. Others decided to hide. The Germans left Dr. Jaffe, Józef Hoch and the Jewish police commanders alone.[52] This signaled the end of the fourth Judenrat term of office and the process that had lasted almost all through 1942—namely, the weakening of the ties between the Jewish police and the Judenrat, to the point at which the former replaced the latter.[53]

Jewish life in the julag changed beyond recognition; the role the Jewish police played during this final stage differed from that of the Judenrat, in particular in the first phases of its existence. Only workers in vital industries remained alive, the Germans classifying them according to their place of work. Food was distributed at the work place. One worker was appointed Oberjude, a team of Oberjuden forming a kind of supreme council that convened in the German commandant's building, where the Jewish police also had a station. Possessing no authority, its job was merely to pass on instructions and ensure that they were obeyed. The council was headed by the Jewish police commanders.[54]

During this period, the Jewish police were responsible for the cleanliness of the camp, checking attendance at morning roll call, accompanying workers to their work place, looking for "illegals," and helping with selections. They also participated in *aktions* in nearby towns due to the flight and scattering of the local Jewish police forces.[55] On February 13, 1943, a police *selektzia* was conducted, the Germans allowing 200 to remain in their posts, the remainder being deported with their families.[56]

In the meantime, personal competition and tension continued between the police commanders. In February 1943, the Germans deposed Baruch Rojzen, appointing Ruppert, another Viennese Jew, in his place.[57] That month, Margolin was also murdered by the Gestapo due to internal German frictions.[58] Each of the JOD commanders sought to establish his status on the basis of personal German contacts, falling victim to personal accounts amongst the latter.

Many believed that it was Max Goliger-Szapira, the Jewish SD commander, who controlled the camp alongside the Germans, placing responsibility on his shoulders for the discovery of many in hiding and their handing over to the Germans.[59]

The Jewish Police and the Underground

The organization and activities of the Jewish underground in Lwów still require investigation. Here, we shall relate primarily to areas linked to the Jewish police. The first evidence of organized underground activities in the city is relatively late, public Jewish frameworks having already largely been compromised under the Soviet regime (1939–1941). During these years, many members of the Zionist youth movements were arrested and put on trial, others being forced to flee the city.[60] While attempts at reorganization were made under the Germans, they never came to anything permanent.[61] Although ties appear to have existed amongst the Zionist youth movement members, these were insufficient to serve as the base for any extensive or continuous underground activity.

The pogroms and *aktions* also affected young organized groups, many perishing even before the idea of resistance had gained ground. In the August 1942 *aktion*, for example, one group of about forty suffered heavy casualties, around 70 percent being captured and deported.[62]

Although the A.K. operated in Lwów, it had no love for the Jews or Jewish resistance groups. The A.L. in the city and its environs, in contrast, was very weak, not being able to extend much help at all. Both Poles and Ukrainians harassed the Jews, only occasional cases of aid being known. The Bandera—national Ukraine units—killed all the Jews who sought refuge in the surrounding forests and fell into their hands. While these conditions clearly did not favor the organization of a Jewish resistance movement, after August 1942 revolt and resistance began assuming more concrete expressions. Various bands emerged rather than a general, overarching movement, however.

Towards the end of 1942, groups began forming to escape the ghetto for the surrounding forests. Not many succeeded, most being captured and falling into the hands of the Ukrainians and Germans. Only isolated individuals returned to the ghetto.[63]

Within the ghetto itself, people began looking for ways to acquire weapons and distribute fliers calling for resistance to the Germans. One of the most prominent figures in this regard was Abraham Wahrman (Shomer Hatza'ir).[64]

Several accounts of attempts to organize exist, some of which contain material relating to the Jewish police:

> A group of youngsters from the Judenrat acquired weapons and began organizing in the council's basement.[65] This source notes that they belonged to the Zionist movements. Some of the members of the latter were thus part of the Judenrat. No information exists regarding their fate, but they never became a military unit.
>
> Tadeusz Zaderecki: "Amongst the circles that sought to make contact with the Polish underground were Jewish

policemen, headed by a former Polish army chaplain (*rabin polowy*) of the rank of Captain, who was a decent fellow. But full-blown Jewish police collaboration with the Germans against their fellow Jews was not a good recommendation in the eyes of the Polish underground. They knew there were Jews on the German payroll roaming the ghetto. The traditional mistrust between Poles and Jews also played a part."[66]

"On a personal initiative, Goldberg, a Captain in the Jewish police, endeavored to set up a group of fighters comprised of five men. Goldberg was Ruppert's deputy. They bought weapons and began training. The Jewish SD immediately got wind of it, but because they were JOD officers, which could damage the Jewish police as a whole, Scherz and Szwadron [Goliger-Szapira's men] they made do with a warning and threat, telling Goldberg that if he did not disband the group right away and get rid of the weapons, he would inform the Gestapo."[67]

Another source states: "According to one testimony, Goldberg organized a group of young men from the Jewish police in Lwów that joined one of the partisan groups in the surrounding forest. When the ghetto became a julag, the partisan commander sent Goldberg to organize a rebel movement there, but he was caught and killed by the Germans."[68]

In the meantime, the Germans began increasing the level of terror in the julag, including targeting the Jewish police. On March 16, 1943, a Jewish worker killed an SS man. In response, the Germans burst onto the streets of the julag and hung a number of people, including some Jewish police officers.[69] This may have served as an opportunity to get even with those elements in the police force that opposed collaboration with the Germans—"one of them, the former 'Culture' director, Prof. Weinstein, consistently acted against the handing over of Jews, crying out 'On with the Nazis' when he was hung."[70]

In the fall of 1943, Dr. Balk, a JOD officer, informed the underground members that the police were intending to organize a resistance unit to fight the Germans during *aktions*. Balk stressed that some of the policemen had military experience that would certainly be helpful. The underground members, believing some basis for collaboration of some kind with the police existed, informed several JOD officers of the plans. On May 4, 1943, the Jewish police were stationed next to the fences at a short distance from one another. The ghetto was surrounded from outside and next to the gate a *selektzia* was conducted. The Jewish police promised the underground members that this was a routine check rather than an *aktion*. The latter thus decided to disperse and join the groups of workers that were about to leave the ghetto for work. The Germans immediately burst into the ghetto, however, and surrounded the groups of workers. Some of the young men tried to find a way out of the ghetto through the fences, other Jews following them, and some even succeeded in escaping. The Jewish police sought to stop the escapees, trying to catch those who fled. The Jewish underground viewed the police conduct as a betrayal and their attempt to cooperate with them as a mistake.[71]

Many of the policemen prepared bunkers for themselves, storing food and weapons as a form of self-defense for when the Germans began destroying the ghetto.[72] There was thus no basis for collaboration between them and the underground, which considered such behavior as a public problem.

The Wiping Out of the Ghetto and the End of the Police Force

The final destruction of the julag began at the end of May 1943, with the Jews putting up some resistance. The Germans burned down the houses, thereby razing the bunkers. The battle continued for over two weeks, the remnants of the ghetto burning until the end of June 1943.

Some of the Jewish police shared the fate of the populace, one testimony stating that they preferred not to surrender to the Germans and thus used their weapons to commit suicide.[73] Others continued to serve the Germans until the very end, preventing Jews from escaping the burning ghetto until the very last moment. The Germans promised them that they would send them to a camp. During the *aktion*, some of the police were killed on the spot. The last Jews of Lwów found their end in the ghetto ruins, some being murdered in the "Czolco" region near the city and small groups being transferred to the Janowska camp and liquidated there sometime later.

Endnotes

1   Filip Friedman, *Zaglada Zydów Lwowskich* (Lodz, 1945). The page numbers here refer to the Hebrew edition.

2   Tadeusz Zaderecki, *Lwów under the Swastika: The Destruction of the Jewish Community through the Eyes of a Polish Writer* (Jerusalem, 2019), p. 54. The page numbers here refer to the Hebrew edition.

3   Ibid.

4   Ibid., p. 404.

5   *Mitteilungen des Judenrats in Lemberg fur die Judische Gemeinde,* No. 1, 1/I/1942. These are appendices in ibid; "Judenrat announcement", YVA 06/21.

6   Jacob Maltiel, *Without Revenge* (Tel Aviv, 1946), p. 53 (Hebrew); "Trial of Nazi member F. G. Gebauer", YVA 04/20-52-2, p. 17.

7   Maltiel, *Without Revenge*, p. 53.

8   Ibid, p. 56; Sylvia Schapira, *Eine Jüdin, die als Assistentin des Direktors des Arbeitsamts,* Heinz Weber, tätig war, YVA M-9/10/11.

9   Mitteilungen des Judenrats, No. 1 1/I/42.

10   Z. Tramevska, YVA 03/1823, p. 8; Schenk, YVA 23-1-3/E, p. 13; Friedman, *Zaglada Zydów Lwowskich*, p. 617.

11   Ibid., p. 8.

12   Abraham Goldberg, YVA JM/91, p. 45. This decision did not apply to all the youth movements.

13   Tramevska, p. 8.

14   S. Levinter, YVA 03/2252, p. 12.

15   Editor's note: this appears to refer either to Kleparowska St. or Kleparów, a district of the city.

16   David Kahane, *Lvov Ghetto Diary* (Amherst, 1990) [YVA E/28-2, pp. 19–20] (the page numbers here refer to the Hebrew edition); *Mitteilungen des Judenrats,* No. 2, 1/I/42.

17   Maltiel, *Without Revenge*, pp. 134–135.

18   This unit was responsible for "political" issues, such as hunting down leftists and Soviet sympathizers, etc.

19   Maltiel, *Without Revenge*, p. 97; Zaderecki, *Lwów under the Swastika*, p. 77.

20   Dagobert Feil, YVA E/64-2-1, pp. 62–63; Zaderecki, *Lwów under the Swastika*, p. 77.

21   Dagobert Feil, 60.

22 Ibid.; Kahane, *Lvov Ghetto Diary*, pp. 19–20; Rubinsteinowa, "Pamiętnik ze Lwowa," *Biuletyn ŻIH* 1965, No. 61, 1967, p. 93; *Mitteilungen des Judenrats,* No. 1, 1/I/42. Nothing is known of his past.

23 *Mitteilungen des Judenrats,* No. 3, 1/III/4.

24 Maltiel, *Without Revenge*, p. 53; Zaderecki, *Lwów under the Swastika*, p. 76; *Mitteilungen des Judenrats* (all three numbers).

25 *Mitteilungen des Judenrats,* No. 3, 1/III/42.

26 Zaderecki, *Lwów under the Swastika*, 121. Other sources confirm Dr. Parnas's decency: Z. Radelcki, *Diary*, YVA B/37-2-2, p. 8; Kahane, *Lvov Ghetto Diary*, p. 43; Friedman, *The Destruction of the Jews of Lwow*, p. 614; Y. Levin, *I Immigrated from Spezia* (Tel Aviv, 1947), p. 39 (Hebrew); G. Marr, YVA 03/3381, p. 25. According to one source, Dr. Parnas's arrest and death occurred slightly differently: Dagobert Feil, who mediated between the Judenrat and the Germans, wrote that Parnas received an order from Emil Engels, "*der Hauporeferent der Judenabteilung der Gestapo (war) eine Liste anzufertigen mit 40 arischen und juduschen Prominenten: Rechtsanealte und Arzte…*" Parnas replied: "*dass er dem Herrn Kriminalkomisar Engels uberlasse, welche Namen er als prominent ansche…*" Objecting to Engel's "tone," he stressed that he was a reserve officer and unaccustomed to such treatment: Dagobert Feil, YVA E/64-2-1, p. 44.

27 Zaderecki, *Lwów under the Swastika*, p. 129.

28 Ibid.

29 Friedman, *Zaglada Zydów Lwowskich*, p. 646; Maltiel, *Without Revenge*, pp. 126–36; Schenk, "How the Jews of Lwow were Liquidated," *Davar*, November 5, 1946 (Hebrew); *Mitteilungen des Judenrats,* No. 1 1/I/42.

30 Tramevska, pp. 8–9; Kahane, *Lvov Ghetto Diary*, p. 20.

31 Maltiel, *Without Revenge*, pp. 88–89.

32 M. Terumot 8:12: "Similarly, if gentiles say to women, 'Give us one of you that we may defile her, and if not, we will defile you all,' then let them all be defiled rather than hand over to them one soul from Israel."

33 Kahane, *Lvov Ghetto Diary*, pp. 58–60; Zaderecki, *Lwów under the Swastika*, p. 198. On the opposition of social circles, see Friedman, *Zaglada Zydów Lwowskich*, p. 17.

34 Maltiel, *Without Revenge*, p. 90. See also A. Farber, YVA E/12-2-13, p. 4. The school served as the assembly point for everyone destined for deportation.

35 Trial of Rudolf Roder and others, YVA E/12-2-13, p. 4.

36 Friedman, *Zaglada Zydowskich*, p. 664; Kahane, *Lvov Ghetto Diary*, p. 61; Kahane, *Opinia* 20, June 30, 1947, p. 7.

37 Kahane, *Lvov Ghetto Diary*, p. 61; M. Radner, YVA E/64/2/1, p. 30.

38 B. Kirschstein, Ghetto Fighters' House Museum Archive, 0461, p. 2; Farber, p. 4.

39   Maltiel, *Without Revenge*, p. 124; Zaderecki, *Lwów under the Swastika*, p. 205; Roder trial, p. 55.

40   Zaderecki, *Lwów under the Swastika*, p. 205.

41   Tramevska, 10; Friedman, *Zaglada Zydów Lwowskich*, p. 617; Schenk, p. 13.

42   Zaderecki, *Lwów under the Swastika*, p. 442.

43   Friedman, *Zaglada Zydów Lwowskich*, p. 617; Schenk, p. 13; Tramevska, p. 8.

44   Maltiel, *Without Revenge*, p. 97; Friedman, *Zaglada Zydów Lwowskich*, p. 617; Zaderecki, *Lwów under the Swastika*, p. 232.

45   S. Levinter, YVA 03/2252, p. 12; S. Shapira, *Memoirs of a Convert* (Tel Aviv, 1953), pp. 36–37 (Hebrew); A. Rotenstreich, CZA S/26-1170, pp. 1–2.

46   L. Barb, Ghetto Fighters' House Museum Archive 0468, p. 3.

47   G. Gerash, "Zum 4-ten yahrtag von der August aktzia in Lemberg, Undezer wart," *Bamberg*, August 23, 1946, p. 6; Shapira, *Memoirs of a Convert*, p. 64.

48   Kahane, *Lvov Ghetto Diary*, p. 104.

49   Radelcki, *Diary*, p. 9; Radner, p. 9; anonymous testimony, CZA S/26-1159, p. 13; Rotenstreich, p. 2. According to Dagobert Feil (pp. 75–77), the Gestapo accused Dr. Landsberg of giving 100,000 złoty to the Polish underground. No confirmation of this claim exists and the information must be treated with caution.

50   Editor's note: this name is also sometimes spelled Ebersohn/Eberson in the sources.

51   Y. Farber, "Chronicles of a Lwower," *Reshumot* (new series) 1, p.15, (1946) (Hebrew).

52   Zaderecki, *Lwów under the Swastika*, p. 302, states that the police formed a sort of presidium (*nadprezydjum*) within the Judenrat.

53   Ibid., p. 305.

54   R. Ridner, CZA 016/270, p. 4; Manfred Reifer, *Death Journey* (Tel Aviv, 1946), p. 98 (Hebrew); Maltiel, *Without Revenge*, p. 235.

55   Zaderecki, *Lwów under the Swastika*, p. 305.

56   Tadeusz Zaderecki, *Erik Abglass: the Hangman of the Lwow Ghetto: A New Life*, February 18, 1949, p. 7.

57   Zaderecki, *Lwów under the Swastika*, p. 314.

58   Ibid.

59   Maltiel, *Without Revenge*, 236; Radelcki, *Diary*, p. 19; Stefan Szende, *Der Letzte Jude aus Polen* (Zurich, 1945), pp. 273–74.

60   *The Hashomer Hatzair Book* (Merhavia, 1961), Vol. 2, pp. 202, 212, 216–512 (Hebrew).

61   Goldberg, p. 45.

62   Ibid.

63   On the General Governorate, see the *Jewish Partisans' Book* (Merhavia, 1958), Vol. 2, pp. 222–23 (Hebrew).

64   Ibid., p. 222.

65   Friedman, *The Destruction of the Jews of Lwow*, p. 603.

66   Zaderecki, *Lwów under the Swastika*, p. 329. This is a single testimony, with all the implications for its content and interpretation.

67   Ibid., p. 330.

68   Ibid., p. 695.

69   Ibid., p. 696; Zaderecki, *Erik Abglass*, p. 7.

70   *Jewish Partisans' Book*, Vol. 2, p. 220.

71   Goldberg, p. 49.

72   Ibid.

73   D. Winter, p. 11.

Ronnen Harran

The Liquidation of the Jewish Communities of Eastern Galicia: A Systematic or a Random Process?

Introduction

On June 22, 1941, Germany launched Operation Barbarossa with the goal of conquering and destroying the Soviet Union. Within days, the German forces occupied the region of Eastern Galicia in southeastern Poland, which had been conquered by the Soviet army in September 1939 and annexed to the Soviet Union. On August 1, 1941, the region was proclaimed the District of Galicia (*Distrikt Galizien*) – the fifth district of the German General Governorate in occupied Poland (*das Generalgouvernement*). The head of the civil administration of the new district was Governor Karl Lasch, brother-in-law and friend of Hans Frank, Governor-General of the General Governorate. The SS and Police Leader in the district was Friedrich Katzmann.[1] Eastern Galicia was then home to 180 large and small Jewish communities with a combined total population of some 540,000 Jews. Within two years, by the summer of 1943, all the Jewish communities in the region were liquidated, and by the end of 1943 only a few thousand Jews remained.

This article concerns the attributes of the process of liquidation of the Jewish communities of the District of Galicia. The process was a complex one, consisting of several stages, which, for the most part, occurred over time and in parallel to one another. Schematically, the process consisted of the following main stages, each of which was actually constituted by a collection of separate events that occurred in different places and at different times:

◆ Local shooting *Aktionen* ("Holocaust by bullets")
◆ The establishment of ghettos and the isolation of the communities' Jews within them
◆ Deportation *Aktionen* in small communities and the concentration of their residents in nearby ghettos
◆ Deportation *Aktionen* to extermination camps ("Holocaust by gas")

Communities/ghettos were liquidated by means of deportation *Aktionen* to nearby ghettos (in the case of small communities) or by local shooting *Aktionen* and/or deportation *Aktionen* to extermination camps (in the larger communities). In some cases, shooting or deportation *Aktionen* were conducted not for the purpose of liquidating a community but rather to thin out its population (as occurred in the case of communities who were to be isolated in a ghetto that was allocated an area that was too small to contain its entire population). In other cases, liquidating a community required several shooting or deportation *Aktionen*, one after another, until it was completely liquidated. In some communities the Germans did not manage to kill or deport all the Jews during an *Aktion* since many Jews managed to hide or to escape the ghetto in time. The Germans would then establish "residual" ghettos (*Restghetto*) for the purpose of assembling and concentrating the Jews of the surrounding area, assuring them they could live there legally. These ghettos were also liquidated within just a few months or even weeks of their establishment, usually through shooting *Aktionen*.

The Jewish population in the District of Galicia was gradually liquidated based on clear priorities: first (already in the summer of 1941), members of the intelligentsia – that is to say, the elites of the Jewish communities – were executed by shooting in order to do away with the leadership strata and to prevent the possibility of organized resistance. Next (particularly in the second half of 1942), most of the population of the Jewish communities was liquidated, with a clear distinction between "productive" Jews – primarily artisans, who were shipped to labor camps after the liquidation of their communities (or remained in the ghettos, which were converted into labor camps) – and the others, who were deemed not fit to work: these children and toddlers on the one hand, and older and elderly Jews on the other hand, were shot to death or sent to be put to death in an extermination camp. Finally, in the course of 1943, after ideology (regarding the necessity of exterminating all the Jews) overcame pragmatism (regarding the need for working hands), the Jewish forced laborers who remained were liquidated as well.

This raises the following question: Was the liquidation of the Jewish communities, in its various stages, organized and systematic, or was it conducted in a random or arbitrary order that can be characterized only as chaotic? If we can identify order and method in the location and timing of the liquidation *Aktionen*, what were the priorities of the perpetrators, and what was the operational rationale that underlay this order and method?[2]

June 1941-February 1942: Shooting *Aktionen* and the Establishment of Ghettos

From the outset, Germany's invasion of Eastern Galicia was accompanied by anti-Jewish pogroms carried out by the local Ukrainian militias and by execution *Aktionen* of the *Einsatzgruppen* SS units. The pogroms carried out by the militias were usually conducted in accordance with the instructions of Reinhard Heydrich, chief of the Reich's Security Main Office (RSHA), to the commanders of the *Einsatzgruppen* to encourage and motivate the locals to carry out "self-cleansing efforts" leaving no traces of German involvement whatsoever.[3] These pogroms were only a partial expression of the mission, which was assigned to the *Einsatzgruppen*, of ensuring political and security calm in the newly occupied territories through the execution of Communist and Jewish officials and other hostile elements.[4] This policy escalated quickly, and as early as July 21, 1941, during a visit to Lwów, Heinrich Himmler, chief of the SS and the police, ordered Friedrich Jeckeln, commander of the SS and the police in "Russia South" (Ukraine), to kill all Jewish men, with the exception of those who could work as forced laborers.[5] In accordance with these instructions, the *Einsatzgruppe* C units (that were assigned to the southern front) began to execute Jewish men throughout Eastern Galicia in *Aktionen* they carried out themselves or with the participation of local militias and in some cases also soldiers of the Wehrmacht.[6] These shooting *Aktionen* were selective in nature, focusing on the "intelligentsia" of the Jewish communities in order to achieve two specific aims: to eradicate the Bolshevik leadership in every location, as Nazi ideology held that the Bolshevik regime in the Soviet Union had been established and was led by the Jews; and to neutralize the community leaders in order to prevent the possibility of organized resistance.[7] By the end of July 1941 (when the *Einsatzgruppe* C units left the Galicia region to follow the front eastward), some 20,000 Jews had been murdered in Eastern Galicia, including 7,000 in execution *Aktionen* conducted by units of the SS and the police. A few weeks later, German policy again escalated: on August 12, 1941, Himmler ordered that all Jews were to be killed, including women and children.[8] From that point on the Holocaust became a genocide.

Pogroms and Shooting *Aktionen*

Figure 1 represents the monthly distribution of shooting *Aktionen* that occurred in the District of Galicia between June 1941 and February 1942. The number of *Aktionen* conducted in July was unusually high in comparison to the other months (46 *Aktionen*, as opposed to a monthly average of 8 *Aktionen*). This exceptional number reflects primarily the pogroms that were carried out by the local Ukrainian militias and civilian population. This appears to have been a distinct expression of the Germans' success in inciting the Ukrainian militias and encouraging the local population to carry out as many anti-Jewish pogroms as possible. Between June and July 1941, improvised pogroms (and planned shooting *Aktionen*) were carried out in 43 different Jewish communities, representing almost one-quarter of the 180 larger Jewish communities in the District.[9] The following figures do not distinguish between shooting *Aktionen* (conducted by regular German units) and popular pogroms (conducted by local militias or an incited mob), for, as noted above, the pogroms occurred in accordance with German policy and, in many cases, the victims were subject to abuse by the local population but were shot to death by the Germans.[10]

Fig. 1

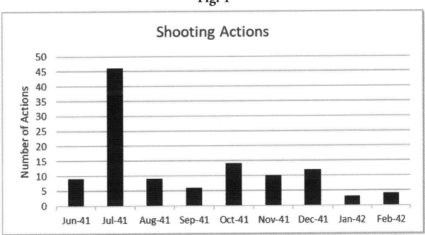

Considering the shooting *Aktionen* and the pogroms from a different perspective – that of the number of Jews who were murdered during them – tells a somewhat different story:

Fig. 2

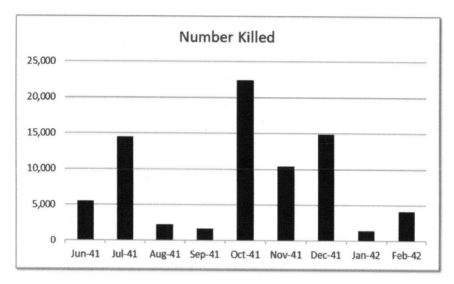

We can identify two distinct periods during which Jews were murdered: one in June and July 1941, and another between October and December 1941. Although shooting *Aktionen* occurred during each of the other months during this period, they were fewer and notably smaller in scope. During the first wave of *Aktionen* (June-July), some 20,000 Jews were murdered in 55 pogroms and *Aktionen* throughout the District.[11] The second wave of *Aktionen* (October to December) appears to have been less sporadic, more focused, and much more lethal, with approximately 48,000 Jews murdered in 36 *Aktionen*.[12]

Examining the spatial distribution of the shooting *Aktionen* and pogroms allows us to reach additional conclusions. Figure 3 indicates the geographical location of the *Aktionen* conducted in June-July 1941 and their relative scope (the number of Jews murdered during the largest *Aktion* at the location in question).

Fig. 3

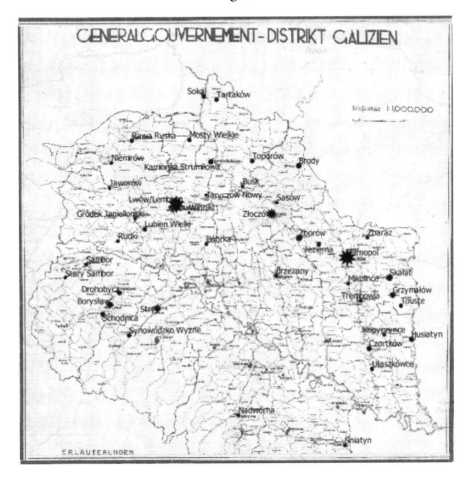

The *Aktionen* occurred throughout the northeastern half of the District, the largest in Lwów (where between 7,500 and 11,000 Jews were murdered in three *Aktionen*, the first of which occurred on June 30, 1941 and resulted in the murder of between 4,500 and 8,000 Jews) and in Tarnopol (where between 4,500 and 5,000 Jews were murdered on July 4, 1941). On the other hand, also noteworthy is the almost complete absence of *Aktionen*/pogroms in the District's southwestern region (with the exception of Nadwórna, where a few dozen Jews were murdered in mid-July 1941). This relative calm can be attributed to the Hungarian military government that controlled the area prior to the District's annexation to the General Governorate, which refrained from inciting the local population to carry out pogroms against the Jews and at times actively prevented it from doing so.[13]

In August 1941, following the addition of the District to the civil administration of the General Governorate, the execution *Aktionen* decreased significantly both in number and in the number of those murdered. However, in October 1941 a new, massive wave of execution *Aktionen* throughout the District got underway. The first significant *Aktion* occurred in the town of Nadwórna in Stanisławów County on October 6, when some 2,000 Jews were executed – "young and old, women and children."[14] But this massacre was only a prelude, a dress rehearsal of sorts, for the massacre that would take place in Stanisławów one week later on October 12, 1941, when between 10,000 and 12,000 Jews were executed in the local Jewish cemetery. This massacre, which later came to be known as "bloody Sunday" (*Blutsonntag*), was the largest massacre perpetrated in Galicia in particular and the General Governorate in general since the beginning of the war. The explanation for the massacre was the disparity between the limited area of the ghetto that the authorities had allocated to Stanisławów's Jewish community and the space required to house the number of Jews in the city. The authorities chose to bridge this gap, which they themselves created, by adjusting the size of the Jewish population to fit into the area of the ghetto by killing all "unnecessary Jews."[15]

During the three month period between October and December 1941, some 36 *Aktionen* were carried out in 26 Jewish communities throughout the district, as reflected in the following map in Figure 4.

Fig. 4

Most of the *Aktionen* took place in the District's southwest, with almost half (17 out of 36) occurring in just two southern counties (Kolomiya and Stanisławów). This wave of shooting *Aktionen* appears to have been the result of a series of meetings that Katzmann convened on the "Jewish Question" in the District of Galicia in September 1941, where it was decided to immediately begin liquidating the Jews in these counties. This occurred immediately following the deployment of the SS's Security Police (SIPO) in these counties after their transfer from the administration of the Hungarian military government (which controlled the area after its conquest by the Hungarian army in June 1941) to German control.[16] With the exception of the shooting *Aktion* in Lwów on November 15, 1941, which left 5,000 Jews dead (as a means of thinning out the Jewish population in order to move them into the ghetto that was allocated on the outskirts of the city, like in Stanisławów),[17] approximately half of the shooting *Aktionen* were indeed conducted in Stanisławów and Kolomiya counties in the southwest of the District of Galicia, resulting in the murder of at least 28,000 Jews.

During the first nine months of the German occupation (June 1941 to March 1942), 78,000 Jews were executed in the District of Galicia in 110 planned execution *Aktionen* and pogroms.[18] This, it should be noted, was just a prelude to a much worse impending future; after all, no matter how difficult and horrible they were, these *Aktionen* had a direct impact on only 64 Jewish communities – approximately one-third of the 180 Jewish communities that existed in the Galicia District at the time it was occupied.

The Establishment of Ghettos and the Concentration of the Jewish Population

In the summer of 1941, Frank still hoped that the new conquests in the East would enable an expansion of the territory of the General Governorate by incorporating additional areas in the east. This would enable them to solve "the Jewish problem" in the General Governorate by deporting the Jews "eastward," particularly to the vast areas of the Pripet Marshes in West Belarus.[19] Because he hoped that the Jews would be deported in the near future (on July 21 he spoke of the General Governorate's "imminent cleansing" of Jews), on July 17, 1941 Frank issued an order prohibiting the establishment of new ghettos in the General Governorate, as concentrating and isolating the Jews in ghettos was perceived as a measure that would perpetuate or at least acknowledge the Jewish presence.[20] However, the optimism of the summer quickly waned and was replaced by pessimism in autumn. At the beginning of October 1941, it sunk in that the Jews' deportation "eastward" would not be realized in the near future. Moreover, on October 13, Rosenberg categorically rejected Frank's proposal to deport the Jews of the General Governorate to territory that was under Rosenberg's responsibility.[21] As a result, local sporadic initiatives to establish ghettos got underway throughout the District of Galicia, apparently following the October 12 declaration by the General Governorate's interior minister Eberhard Westerkamp that "the isolation of the Jews from the rest of the population" needed to be enforced thoroughly and as soon as possible,[22] contrary to Frank's October 21 reiteration of his instruction to refrain from establishing additional ghettos in the District of Galicia, "in the hope that in the near future it will be possible to move the Jews out of the General Governorate," even though just one week earlier Rosenberg had clarified to Frank that the latter's hopes on the subject were mere illusions.[23]

Figure 5 depicts the monthly distribution of the number of ghettos that were established in the District of Galicia between July 1941 and March 1942.

Fig. 5

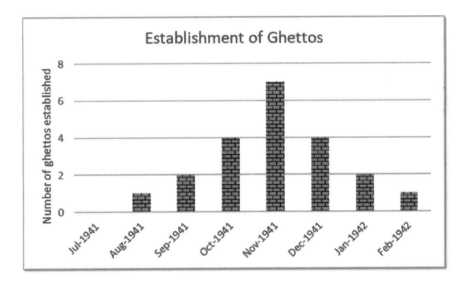

The figure clearly shows a single wave of ghettoization that began in August 1941 (with the establishment of a ghetto in Rohatyn, despite Frank's prohibition), peaked in November (with the establishment of seven ghettos in the District of Galicia), and declined until March 1942. Overall, only 21 ghettos were established during this period. Therefore, as of March 1942 (the onset of Operation Reinhard), most of the Jewish communities in the region had not been isolated within ghettos (only 12% of the 173 communities which existed in the District in February 1942 had been isolated). From this, we can conclude that the Jews' concentration in ghettos was neither a preliminary phase that preceded their physical liquidation, nor regarded by the Germans as a precondition for the extermination of the Jewish communities. It appears that ghettos were established as a result of local policies and perhaps also the whims of the governors of the various counties.

The establishment of ghettos was accompanied by a parallel process of concentrating the Jewish population that was dispersed among small settlements into a small number of larger communities.

Fig. 6

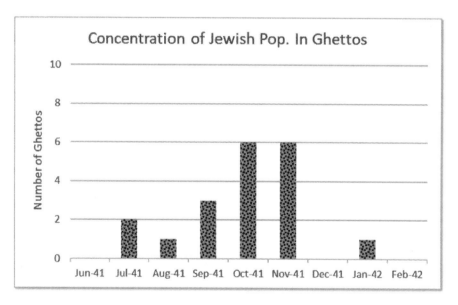

Only 19 transfer and concentration *Aktionen* were carried out until March 1942. The map in Figure 7 displays the spatial dispersion of the establishment of ghettos in the District of Galicia until March 1942 (squares) and the locations at which Jews from the nearby settlements were concentrated during this period (circles).

Fig. 7

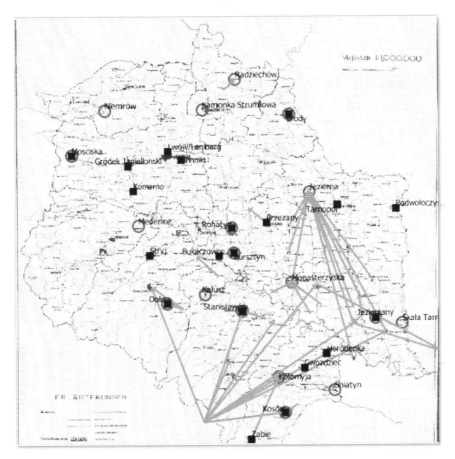

An examination of the map in Figure 7 reflects that there was not necessarily a connection between the establishing of ghettos and the concentration of Jews within them: although in eight cases the concentration locations were ghettos, in nine other instances Jews were concentrated within Jewish communities that had not been isolated as ghettos, and in 12 other instances the local Jews were isolated in ghettos without this being accompanied by the concentration within these ghettos of the Jews from the surrounding area.

An apparently abnormal event occurred in November 1941, when an unknown number of Jews were transferred from numerous communities in the nearby and more distant areas (including the Jewish community of Zaleszczyki on the district's southern border) and were concentrated in Jezierna in Tarnopol County. They were not, however, concentrated in a ghetto; rather, they were brought as forced laborers to a labor camp that had been established in Jezierna in October 1941 to pave the *Durchgangsstraße IV* from Lwów eastward toward the frontlines on the border between Ukraine and Russia. This strategic road, all along which labor camps were set up to facilitate its paving, passed close to Jezierna in its first segment between Lwów and Tarnopol.[24]

The process of the establishment of the ghettos in the District of Galicia was much more violent than that which had preceded it in the General Governorate over the previous two years. This may have been the result of an understanding that because it would not be possible in the near future to deport the Jews eastward out of the General Governorate, it was necessary to find a "final solution for the Jewish question" within the General Governorate itself. For example, on October 20, 1941, the governor of the Krakow District, Otto Wächter, asserted that "a radical and ultimate solution to the Jewish problem is inevitable, with no exceptions." At a conference of physicians held on October 16, the General Governorate's minister of health Jost Walbaum stated: "There are only two ways: either we condemn the Jews to death by starvation in the ghetto or we shoot them."[25] Walbaum apparently did not know that, at precisely the same time, a third path was being developed: death by asphyxiation using poison gas. On October 13, 1941, Himmler met with his friend Odilo Globocnik, SS and Police Leader in the Lublin District, to discuss Globocnik's proposal for "limiting Jewish influence through measures of the kind employed by the Security Police." During this meeting, Himmler charged Globocnik with the task of setting up an extermination facility, and approximately two weeks later the construction of a gas-extermination facility got underway near Bełzec, on the border between the Lublin District and the District of Galicia.[26] The operation to liquidate the Jewish communities in the General Governorate and to murder their inhabitants commenced.[27] It was named Operation Reinhard (*Aktion Reinhard*) (apparently already in June 1942), after Reinhard Heydrich. The operational activity of Operation Reinhard began in March 1942, with the completion of the first extermination camp within the General Governorate at Bełzec, and officially continued until October 1943.[28]

March-June 1942: The Onset of Transports to Bełzec Extermination Camp

In January and February 1941, almost no execution *Aktionen* were conducted. This may have been the result of a directive issued by Helmut Tanzmann, commander of the Security Police in the District of Galicia, that such *Aktionen* be temporarily suspended due to the difficulty of digging killing ravines in the frozen ground,[29] or of appeals by various county governors to Ludwig Losacker, the chief of staff of the governor of the District of Galicia (who opposed the shooting *Aktionen* due to their negative public reverberations in the Reich). Losacker contacted Himmler on the matter and asked him to restrain the SS and police commanders in the District. This, however, appears to actually have sparked Himmler to order the liquidation of the Jewish communities in the District of Galicia along with the communities of the Lublin District, by deporting their inhabitants to the Belzec extermination camp immediately after it began operating in March 1942.[30] In January 1942, upon assuming his post and as a preliminary measure for the anticipated deportations, district governor Wächter mandated an acceleration of the pace of ghettoization in the district, as well as the establishment of only closed ghettos from then on, to which the Jews would be sent. There, those who were fit to work were to be concentrated separately from those who were unfit to work. This separation stemmed from a recognition of the essential role of Jewish forced laborers in general, and of professional artisans in particular, particularly throughout 1942.[31] "Resettlement" (*Umsiedlung*) into ghettoes was set to be carried out immediately, and the liquidation of the ghettos of the Jews unfit for work and the "displacement" (*Aussiedlung*) of their inhabitants were planned to begin in the spring of 1942. On January 7, 1942 the authorities announced that Jews caught outside their declared area of residence would be punished by death,[32] and in February Katzmann informed the county governors within the District of Galicia of the planned "displacements."

Establishment of the Ghettos and Concentration of the Jewish Population

In March 1942, a second wave of ghetto establishment got underway with a drive to establish nine ghettos in that month alone. However, this second wave quickly subsided, and by June no more ghettos were established in the District, as reflected in Figure 8 (which also includes the first wave, for the sake of comparison). Hand in hand with the establishment of ghettos, a second wave of concentrating the inhabitants of the smaller nearby Jewish communities within a limited number of ghettos and/or large communities got underway.

Fig. 8

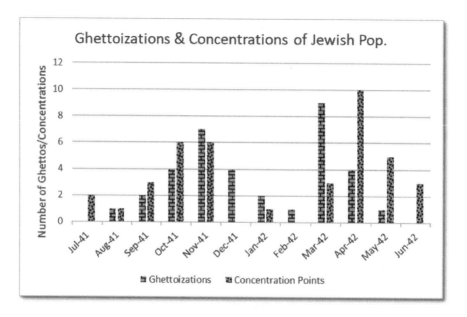

The map in Figure 9 represents the spatial dispersion of the ghettos that were established during this period, as well as the points of concentration of the small Jewish communities. Most of the ghettos (10 out of 14) were established in the southern counties of the District of Galicia, as were most of the points of concentration. Particularly prominent were the *Aktionen* that served to concentrate the nearby Jewish communities in Stanisławów and Kolomiya. As in the previous period, also prominent here was the non-overlap of these two processes: the establishment of ghettos without the concentration within them of Jews from the surrounding area, as well as the concentration of Jews from surrounding areas within communities with no ghettos.

Fig. 9

Aktionen for Deportation for Extermination

In parallel to the ghettoization and concentration that continued throughout this period, an altogether new process got underway: the deportation of Jews to the recently completed extermination camp at Bełżec. The first deportation *Aktion* occurred on March 15, 1942, just after the camp began operating. This deportation of 700 members of the Zółkiew Jewish community near Lwów was apparently the first deportation from the entire General Governorate for extermination at Bełżec.[33] The next deportations from the District of Galicia were from Brody on March 18 and from Rawa Ruska, from which approximately 1,000 Jews were deported on March 19. More massive deportations occurred during the second half of March 1942, when, within a two-week period, some 15,000 Jews were deported to their deaths at the extermination camp.[34] At least 18,000 Jews were deported for extermination at Bełżec in the second half of March 1942, mostly from communities in the northern section of the District of Galicia, near Bełżec.

The following month, the deportations focused on the Jewish community of Stanisławów and several communities in neighboring Kolomiya county. This measure was apparently intended to address complaints of the Hungarian government regarding the infiltration of Jews from these two counties, which bordered Hungary.[35] Figure 10 shows the monthly distribution of the deportations during this period (and, for the sake of comparison, from the beginning of the occupation) according to destination type: ghetto (or Jewish community), labor camp, or extermination camp (Bełżec).

Fig. 10

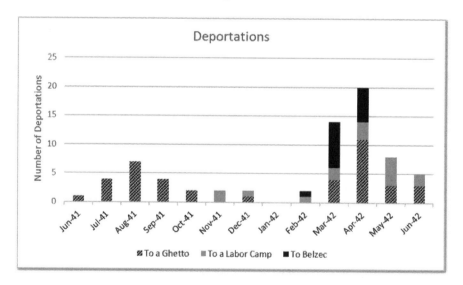

Figure 10 clearly reflects that the second wave of deportations (between March and June 1942) was more intensive than the one that preceded it, and that most of the deportations that occurred in March were to the extermination camp (Bełżec). However, by April the trend had already reversed itself, and most of the deportations conducted during this month were to other ghettos or communities. A cross-section of the number of deportees by destination type (Figure 11) reflects the exceptional scale of the deportations of March-April vis-à-vis both previous months and the months that followed (May-June).

Fig. 11

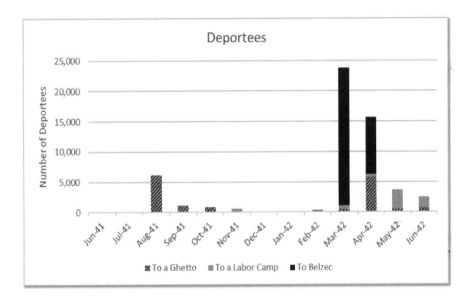

During these two months (actually, in the span of only four weeks – from mid-March to mid-April 1942), some 40,000 Jews were expelled from their homes, including at least 32,000 to Bełżec extermination camp.[36] The following maps reflect the spatial distribution of the deportations that occurred in March (top) and April 1942 (bottom). They show clearly that the first deportations to Bełżec in March 1942 were conducted in the northern part of the District of Galicia, whereas the deportations of the following month occurred in the southern part of the district. The maps in Figures 12 and 13 also highlight the phenomenon of local expulsions within the district itself, particularly from communities located close to Kolomiya to Kolomiya itself, just days before deportations from Kolmiya onward to Bełżec.

Fig. 12

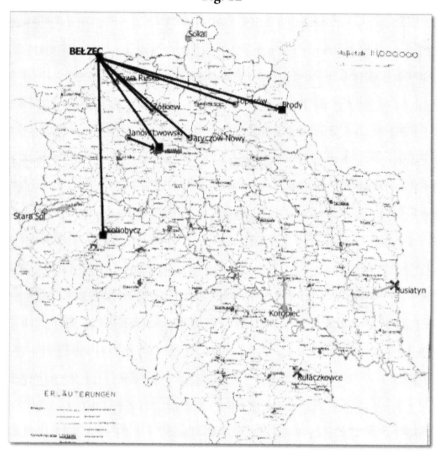

Fig. 13

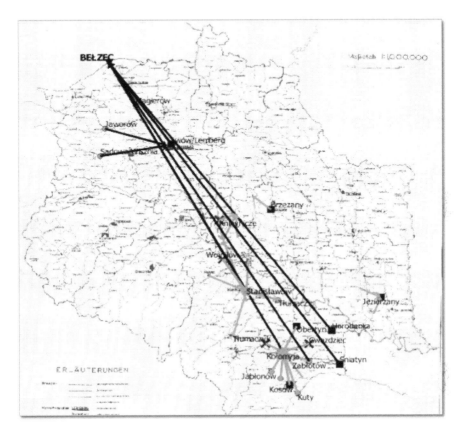

Shooting *Aktionen*

In parallel to the expulsions to Bełżec, this period also witnessed local shooting
Aktionen (in addition to the brutal killings of Jews during deportation *Aktionen*).
Figure 14 shows the number of shooting *Aktionen* that were carried out during
this period (in addition to the *Aktionen* that had been carried out since the
beginning of the occupation, for the sake of comparison). Although the
number of *Aktionen* during this period was lower than the number carried out
in the summer and autumn of 1941, a noticeable increase occurred in March-
April 1942, in parallel to the deportations to Bełżec. This becomes even more
prominent when we examine the number of those murdered in the shooting
Aktionen (Figure 15).

Fig. 14

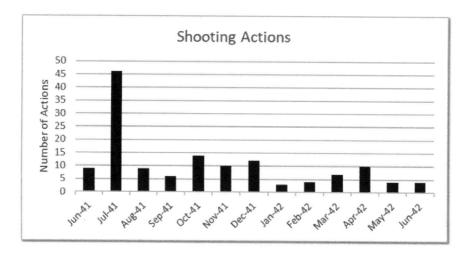

Fig. 15

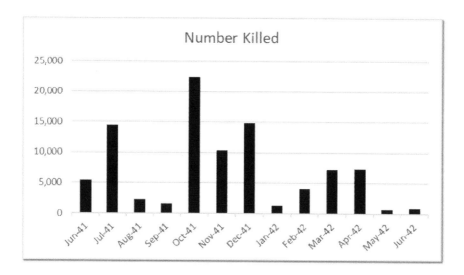

In March and April, the number of those murdered increased considerably in comparison to both the months that preceded them and the months that followed, even though it was already possible to eradicate Jews using the "cleaner" method of shipping them via train transport to an extermination camp.

During these two months, at least 16,000 Jews were executed, representing approximately half the number of Jews that were shipped to the extermination camp. The deportation *Aktionen*, it should be noted, were characterized by extreme brutality, with dozens if not hundreds being shot to death in the streets as deportees were being rounded up. However, among the thousands who were executed during these two months, only approximately 1,000 people were shot during deportation *Aktionen*; the rest were killed in shooting *Aktionen*.

Fig. 16

The map in Figure 16 illustrates the location and the relative scope of the shooting *Aktionen* during this period. The most severe shooting *Aktionen* occurred in Stanisławów (where several thousand Jews were executed in April 1942) and in Kolomiya (where some 4,000 Jews were executed in March 1942). The conducting of mass shooting *Aktionen* in parallel to transports for extermination to Bełżec was particularly notable in Stanisławów (a few weeks after the deportation of approximately 5,000 Jews to Bełżec at the end of March) and in Kolomiya (several weeks before the deportation to Bełżec of 2,000-5,000 Jews at the beginning of April). This may have attested to limited "supply" on the part of the Bełżec extermination camp in terms of its ability to receive transports from the District of Galicia (due to the priority that was given to transports from the Lublin District) in relation to Katzmann's "demand" that this new resource serve as a means of eradicating the Jews from the district. Moreover, by mid-April – just four weeks after they had begun – the exterminations at Bełżec had ceased and the camp's command staff, under the camp's commandant Christian Wirth, abandoned the camp and returned to Berlin (without reporting this to Globocnik, the commander of Operation Reinhard).[37]

Although the process of liquidating the Jewish communities of the District of Galicia and deporting their inhabitants to Bełżec for extermination began as soon as this was possible, and thus preceded the liquidation of the Jewish communities of the Warsaw, Radom, and Krakow districts, it appears to have been conducted sluggishly, as the transports to Bełżec ceased by mid-April 1942 – four weeks after the first transport. The process of concentrating the Jews in ghettos also appears to have progressed slowly, as only 35 communities had been isolated in ghettos by then.[38]

At the end of June 1942, there were still 413,000 Jews in the District of Galicia (including 86,000 in the Lwów Ghetto) living in the 164 communities that still existed, one-fifth of which had been isolated within ghettos, as reflected in the map in Figure 17.[39]

Fig. 17

July-December 1942: The Liquidation of Jewish Communities and the Transports to the Extermination Camp

The liquidation of the Jewish communities of the District of Galicia (and the General Governorate as a whole) shifted into high gear in July 1942, following Himmler's June 3, 1942 victory in his power struggle with Frank, when the authority to deal with all "Jewish affairs" in the General Governorate was transferred from the civil administration (the district governors) to Friedrich

Wilhelm Krüger, the Higher SS and Police Leader (HSSPF) in the General Governorate who reported directly to Himmler, and whose appointment as secretary of state for security matters in the General Governorate under his nominal authority alone Frank was compelled to accept.[40] On June 18, in accordance with his new powers, Krüger determined that "the resettlement" of the Jews required an urgent decision and that, after the moratorium on the non-military usage of trains (including the transport of Jews to extermination camps), it would be necessary to "accelerate the struggle against the Jews".[41] Indeed, one month later, on July 19, 1942, while on a visit to Lublin, Himmler ordered Krüger to complete the "evacuation" of the Jewish population of the General Governorate by the end of the year (with the exception of essential forced laborers, who would be concentrated in five large SS camps).[42] This was after Globocnik informed him that the Bełżec extermination camp was ready to resume operations after being upgraded (and the Treblinka extermination camp was ready to begin operations, after its construction). A few days later, massive transports to Bełżec (and to the two other extermination camps, at Sobibor and Treblinka) got underway from all over the General Governorate.[43]

Deportations to the Extermination Camp

The transports were also carried out in the District of Galicia. Within several days, deportation *Aktionen* for extermination got underway. In the final week of July, more than 3,000 Jews from four communities were sent to Bełżec, including approximately 2,000 who were deported from Rawa Ruska on July 27. This was only the beginning of a new wave of unprecedented extensive deportations. As represented in Figure 18, this new wave began in July 1942, reached its peak in September and October, and concluded in December. Considering it in succession to the deportations that occurred prior to it highlights its exceptional scale.

Fig. 18

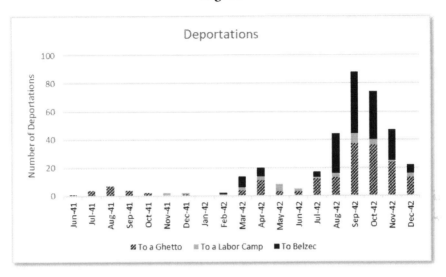

During the six-month period between July and December 1942, some 290 deportation *Aktionen* were carried out in the District of Galicia, including 140 to the Bełżec extermination camp (another 130 to other ghettos and approximately 20 to labor camps). The following series of maps (Figure 19) shows the geographical significance of the deportations that were carried out each month and the communities that were liquidated.

Fig. 19

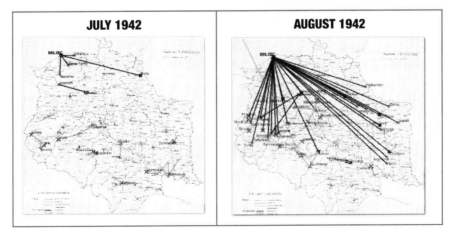

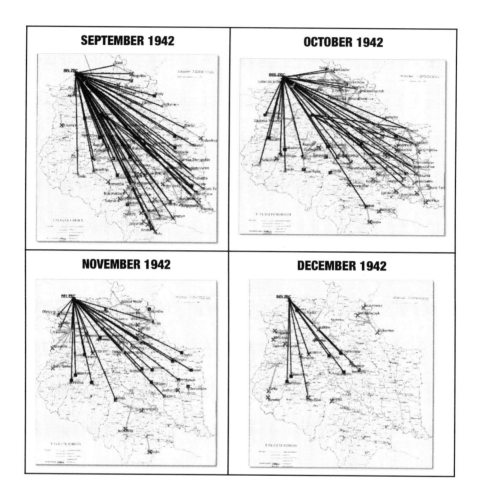

This series of maps does not enable us to identify clear priorities among the different counties, as during each month (except for July) deportations were implemented (and communities liquidated) in different counties. No focused effort could be identified in any one county at the expense of the others. The logical conclusion is that there were no spatial-administrative priorities, and that if there were, they were not significant.

An examination of the deportations with regard to the number of Jews deported (Figure 20) each month indicates that the wave began with substantial momentum, peaked in August 1942, shortly after it began, and gradually declined during the autumn.

Fig. 20

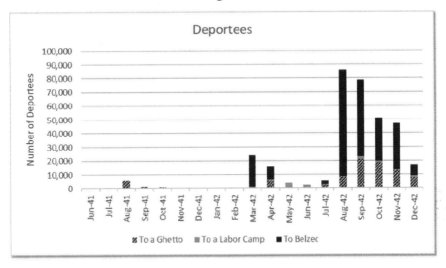

Fig. 21

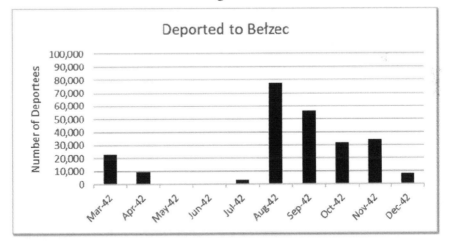

The peak months were August and September, with at least 77,000 Jews deported to Bełżec in August, and 56,000 in September. The following two months witnessed a decline in this number, with 32,000 Jews being deported to Bełżec in October, 34,000 in November, and 8,000 in December, before operations ceased on December 15 1942.[44] Figure 21 reflects the monthly distribution of the number of deportees to Bełżec. A comparison between the monthly number of deportations and the monthly number of deportees shows that more Jews were deported to Bełżec in August than during any other month, whereas the number of deportation *Aktionen* carried out in that month (28) was smaller than in September (44) and October (34). This is indicative of an initial preference for deportations from the larger Jewish communities, subsequently followed by deportations from smaller communities.[45]

All in all, at least 230,000 Jews were deported to Bełżec from the District of Galicia during this period, accounting for 56% of the 413,000 Jews who were deported to Bełżec from the General Governorate as a whole. We can conclude therefore that the Bełżec extermination camp primarily served the SS authorities of the District of Galicia.[46]

The map in Figure 22 represents the spatial distribution of the deportations to all the types of destinations during the second half of 1942. Overall, we can say that regional deportations to nearby ghettos (marked in gray), deportations to Bełżec (marked in black), and communities that were liquidated (marked with a black x) occurred throughout all parts of the District – without exception.

Fig. 22

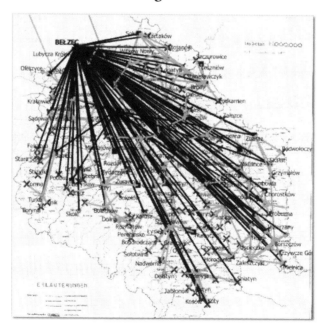

Shooting *Aktionen*

Hand in hand with the massive deportations to Bełżec, this period also witnessed the continuation of local shooting *Aktionen* (the purpose of which was to execute the local Jews). The graph in Figure 23 shows the number of shooting *Aktionen* that were carried out during this period (in continuation of the *Aktionen* that had been carried out since the beginning of 1942).

Fig. 23

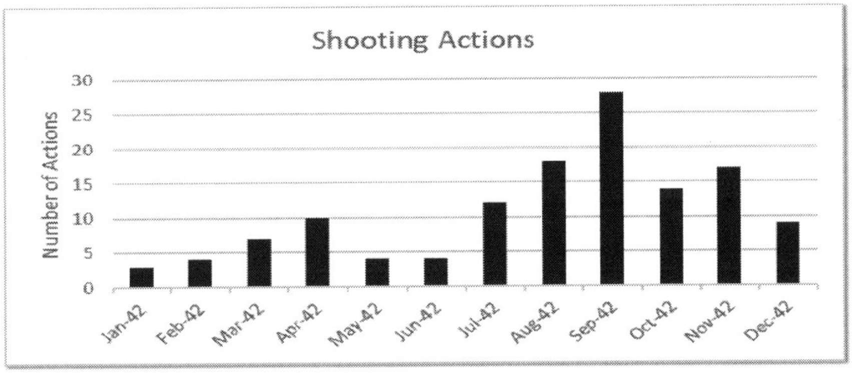

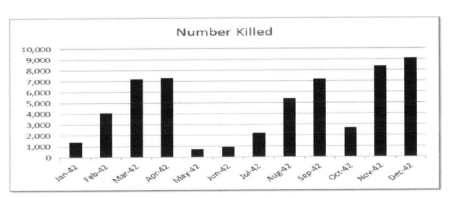

The graph indicates that the second half of 1942 witnessed a significant increase in the number of shooting *Aktionen*, in comparison to the first half of the year (over three times more), that occurred concurrently with the deportations to Bełżec. This is also evident in the number of victims that were killed each month (Figure 24).

Fig. 24

The second half of the year witnessed a marked increase in the number of those killed in comparison to the first half of the year (approximately 35,000 as opposed to 22,000). Even though the wave of deportations to Bełżec reached its peak during this period, and most of the murdered Jews in the District were put to death there, nevertheless local shooting *Aktionen* continued throughout the entire period, with an increasing number of dead each month (except for October), in an inverse trend to the number of deportees to Bełżec. This increase in the number of those killed is indicative of the determination of the SS authorities and their adherence to the task of liquidating all the Jewish communities in the District by the end of the year. It also reflected the fact that, with regard to the transports to the extermination camp, "demand" was exceeding the declining logistical "supply" (whether of the camp itself or the means of transportation to it). As a result, the SS authorities were forced to revert to the primitive methods of 1941. The marked decline in the number of Jews murdered in October 1942 is apparently related to the onset of the establishment of residual ghettos in order to assemble and concentrate the Jews who had managed to escape the deportation *Aktionen* to Bełżec.

Fig. 25

The map in Figure 25, which shows the location and the relative scope of the shooting *Aktionen* during this period, reflects the numerous shooting *Aktionen* that occurred throughout the District. The most severe was in Rawa Ruska in the north, where 5,000 Jews were executed on December 7, 1942, and yet again in Kolomiya in the south, with 6,000 executed on November 4, 1942. The shooting *Aktionen* took place following transports to Bełżec from the same communities or concurrently with them. For example, this was the case in Kolomiya after the deportation of 12,700 Jews to Bełżec in September and another 4,000 in October, and more so in Rawa Ruska, where 5,000 Jews were executed in the forest near the ghetto during the same period when some 2,500 were deported to Bełżec.[47]

The SS authorities appear to have reverted to the old method of local shooting *Aktionen* from the summer of 1942, because the logistical constraints only allowed the transport to Bełżec of a small (and continually decreasing) number of the Jews who were designated for death. They also knew that the possibility of using this "resource" would cease to exist in a few days, with no anticipated transports to the other extermination camps.

The Establishment of Ghettos

After an almost complete cessation of ghetto establishment between May and July 1942, a new campaign got underway. This third wave reached its peak in October with the establishment of 12 ghettos in the District of Galicia – more than any other month. The graph in Figure 26 shows the monthly distribution of the establishment of ghettos for the second half of 1942.

Fig. 26

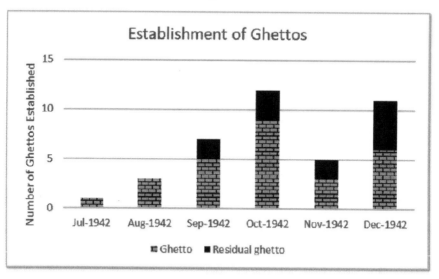

On November 10, 1942, Krüger issued an order mandating 32 "living quarters for Jews" (*Judenwohnbezirke*) in the District of Galicia.[48] The Jews who were residing outside of these locations were required to assemble in the designated ghettos, as

> beginning on December 1, 1942, it will be prohibited for Jews to be outside a Jewish residential quarter or to leave it without police authorization. Jews who violate the directives will be subject to punishment by death. All those who consciously provide refuge to such a Jew, especially those who provide overnight accommodations to, feed, or hide a Jew […] will be subject to similar punishment.[49]

The goal of the order appears to have been to entice the Jews who had managed to escape the liquidation *Aktionen* and to find refuge nearby into returning and concentrating within enclosed, defined locations to make it possible to liquidate them as well. Indeed, it appears that most of the Jews in hiding chose to assemble in places where they were permitted to reside, preferring the hope – no matter how slight – to continue living legally over the constant fear of being turned in or murdered. The residents of those ghettos tended to refer to them as "small ghettos," whereas historiography refers to them as "residual ghettos" (USHMM) or "return ghettos" (Yad Vashem).

The map in Figure 27 shows the spatial dispersion of the ghettos that were established during this period (black squares), as well as the residual ghettos that were declared by Krüger (larger gray squares).[50]

Fig. 27

The residual ghettos were scattered throughout the district but were almost completely absent from the district's southern counties, with the exception of the ghetto in Stanisławów (which was established in December 1941) and the ghetto that was established (though not declared) in Kosów.[51] In total, this period witnessed the establishment of 39 new ghettos (including 12 residual ghettos), more than the number of ghettos that Krüger had either approved or ordered to be established.[52]

The large number of residual ghettos that were declared in the District of Galicia (32) in comparison to less than ten declared in each of the other Districts in the General Governorate attests to the fact that at the end of 1942, the community liquidation process in the District of Galicia lagged behind the same processes in the other districts. The reality on the ground also reflects the extent to which the community liquidation process was far from over when Krüger ordered the establishment of residual ghettos. Indeed, at the beginning of November 1942, there were still 77 Jewish communities in the district, more than double the number of localities in which the Jews were officially permitted to live.

In tandem with the liquidation of the large communities and the deportation of their residents to Bełżec, the complimentary process of liquidating the small communities by removing their inhabitants and concentrating them in the ghettos of the larger communities continued. This involved a combined process of thinning out the population of the ghettos through *Aktionen* aimed at deportation to an extermination camp, on the one hand, and moving the Jews of the nearby communities into the semi-depopulated ghettos, on the other hand. This process (which began already in March 1942) continued with greater intensity during the second half of 1942 and reached its peak in October, when numerous *Aktionen* were conducted to concentrate Jews within ghettos that would be formally recognized several weeks later.

Fig. 28

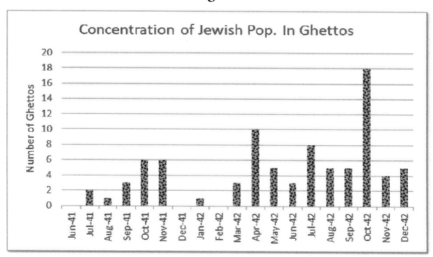

The map in Figure 29 presents the spatial dispersion of the concentration of Jews in ghettos and communities from July 1942 until the end of the year. It is evident that the concentration process during this period occurred throughout the District, once again with the exception of its southern counties, except Kolomiya.[53]

Fig. 29

Liquidation of the Communities

The massive wave of deportations to Bełżec extermination camp that began in July 1942, and the accompanying wave of shooting *Aktionen*, resulted in the complete liquidation of more than 140 communities within six months (in contrast to less than 20 communities that were liquidated during the first year of the occupation). At the beginning of November 1942, the JSS office in Nadwórna reported:

In Nadwórna, as in the entire area of our region [Stanisławów county], an *Aktion* is underway; its aim is to expel almost all the Jews from the region … As a result of this *Aktion*, it has become clear that the number of Jewish residents in the region has been reduced to approximately one thousand, whereas there were previously 18,000 Jews in the region.[54]

On the other hand, with a sense of satisfaction, county governor Heinz Albrecht proclaimed in a speech delivered on November 2, 1942, that: "In the course of this year, in the campaign in defense of the life of the Aryan peoples, European Jewry has been largely exterminated. In the near future, its last remnants will also disappear."[55] The graph in Figure 30 illustrates the scope of this wave of liquidations and reflects that its peak was reached in September 1942, when more than 30 communities were liquidated.

Fig. 30

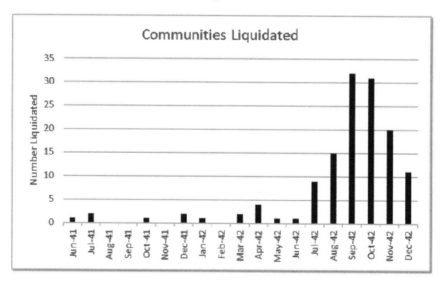

The liquidation of the communities occurred throughout the district, as reflected in the map in Figure 31 (liquidated communities marked by black x's). At the end of 1942, less than 50 Jewish communities were still in existence, virtually all in ghettos (marked by squares). On December 31, 1942, according to the statistical report on "The Final Solution for the Jewish Question" written by Richard Korherr, the chief statistician of the SS, the District of Galicia contained exactly 161,514 Jews.[56] If the District's Jewish population at the beginning of 1942 was still 85 percent of what it had been in June 1941, by the end of 1942 only 30% remained. Himmler's July 1942 directive to liquidate all of the Jewish communities within the General Governorate by the end of the year had not been fully implemented, especially in the District of Galicia, which now contained more than 50 percent of the Jewish population that remained in the General Governorate.[57]

Fig. 31

January-August 1943: Liquidation of the Ghettos and the Labor Camps

Just a few weeks after Krüger declared "legal" places for Jewish residence, and by December – with "the receipt of additional instructions [from Krüger] to now accelerate the removal of the Jews," as Katzmann wrote in the final report "On the Solution to the Jewish Problem in the District of Galicia" – *Aktionen* to liquidate these residual ghettos had gotten underway.[58] As the Bełżec extermination camp ceased operating in the middle of the month, Katzmann ordered local execution *Aktionen* – along the lines of the *Aktionen* that preceded the operation of the extermination camp – to liquidate the Jews remaining in the official ghettos and in the labor camps for Jews. In 1942, Jewish forced laborers were essential enough to delay the liquidation of a minority of the Jews – those who were considered to be "productive." In 1943, however, this orientation changed, when the ideological drive gradually overtook the economic considerations.[59] The shooting *Aktionen* became increasingly frequent during the first half of 1943 and reached their peak in June, apparently due to Katzmann's April 21, 1943 instructions to kill all the Jews in the District;[60] Himmler's subsequent May 10, 1943 directive (in light of the lessons learned from the Warsaw Ghetto Uprising) that "evacuating" the ghettos was "of supreme importance," as this was the main condition "for achieving comprehensive security calm in the region;[61] and Krüger's May 31 statement that "only recently had I received the order to complete the dejudification [*Entjudung*]."[62] Katzmann appears to have tried to meet Himmler's goal of completing the liquidation of the ghettos by June 30, 1943.[63]

Shooting *Aktionen*

With the cessation of transports to Bełżec, the shooting *Aktionen*, which had been conducted continuously from the beginning of the occupation, now became increasingly frequent, as reflected in the graph in Figure 32. We observe a general trend of escalation beginning in January 1943 (with fewer than ten *Aktionen*), peaking in June (34 *Aktionen*), and declining in the two months that followed. A similar pattern is evident when considering the monthly totals of those murdered in these *Aktionen*, as reflected in the graph in Figure 33.

Fig. 32

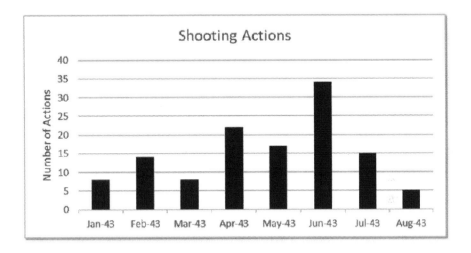

Fig. 33

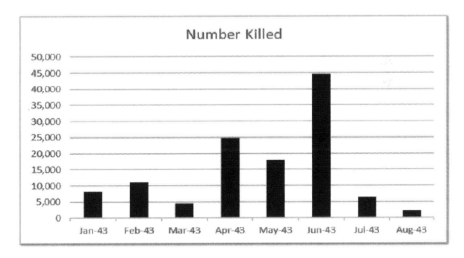

Marked escalation occurred between April and June 1943, when more than 87,000 Jews were murdered (in comparison to 24,000 during the preceding three months), including some 45,000 in June alone. This escalation was also manifested in the individual case of Buczacz: in a shooting *Aktion* conducted in early February 1943, 2,000 Jews were shot to death; in another shooting

Aktion in mid-April, 4,600 Jews were shot; and in the final *Aktion*, at the end of June 1943, the Jewish labor camp in town was liquidated, and approximately 1,800 of its inmates were executed.[64] More than 120 shooting *Aktionen* were conducted between January and August 1943, resulting in the murder of approximately 130,000 Jews.[65]

Fig. 34

The map in Figure 34 represents the spatial dispersion of the shooting *Aktionen* during this period. These *Aktionen* were conducted throughout the entire District, with the largest occurring in the Janowska labor camp in Lwów, where approximately 6,000 Jews were executed in mid-May 1943 and another 13,000 in June. In fact, during this period Janowska served as a central site for the murder of Jews, a substitute for the Bełżec extermination camp; the Jews who were sent there from throughout the District (see below) were executed in mass shooting *Aktionen*, either shortly after their arrival or after an extended period during which they engaged in forced labor.

Deportations

During the first half of 1943, the deportations from the few remaining communities and from the residual ghettos continued. As in the previous year, most of the deportation *Aktionen* were from small communities to the larger ghettos, both as a means of liquidating the small communities and for the purpose of concentrating the Jews in preparation for their shipment to extermination. In 1943, however, there were no deportations to extermination camps – neither to Bełżec (which had ceased operating) nor to the other General Governorate's extermination camps at Sobibor and Treblinka. The graph in Figure 35 shows the number of deportation *Aktionen* conducted during each month of the period in question. In the spring of 1943 (March to May), growth was evident in the number of deportation *Aktionen* to all types of destinations. The graph in Figure 36 reflects the number of Jews deported during the period in question.

Fig. 35

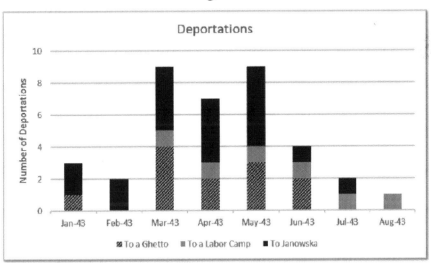

Fig. 36

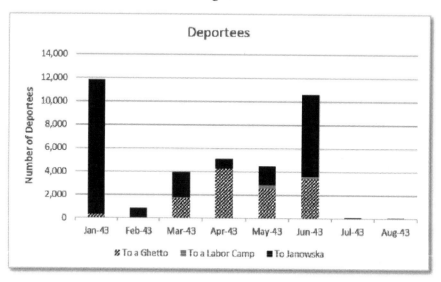

Deportees

Although only three deportation *Aktionen* were conducted in January 1943, the number of deportees was very high (approximately 12,000) – more than in any other month during this period. Each month between March and June 1943 witnessed deportations from small communities to larger ghettos and to the Janowska camp, particularly in June, when the wave of deportations came to an end. For example, the ghetto in Buczacz was liquidated in May 1943, and most of its residents were deported and dispersed among three nearby communities (as shown in the following map), whereas the rest (approximately 1,200) were transferred to a labor camp that was established there.[66] During the eight months from January to August 1943, some 24,000 Jews were deported to the Janowska labor camp in 20 deportation *Aktionen*, with most of the deportees (more than 18,000 of them) coming from the residual ghetto near Lwów.[67] The map in Figure 37 shows the spatial dispersion of all the deportations during the period in question. It also illustrates the fact that the Janowska labor camp served as a major destination of deportations from the entire District (although most of the deportees came from the nearby Lwów ghetto in deportations which cannot be represented on the map). In addition, two deportations conducted during this period were to a location outside the District: to the Majdanek concentration camp in the Lublin District.[68]

Fig. 37

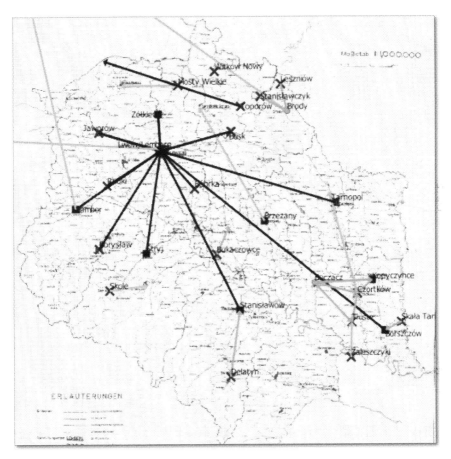

The Liquidation of Ghettos/Communities

By the end of June 1943, almost all the remaining Jewish communities and ghettos in the District of Galicia had been liquidated. Therefore, in his final report on "The Solution to the Jewish Problem in the District of Galicia," Katzmann could write that "all residential neighborhoods of the Jews" had been annulled, and that therefore "as of June 23, 1943, the District of Galicia became free of Jews (*Judenfrei*)."[69] This was not accurate, as at the end of June, four residual ghettos still remained in the District.[70] The map in Figure 38 shows the spatial dispersion of the Jewish communities and the ghettos that were liquidated in 1943.

Fig. 38

It is notable that all the residual ghettos that were declared in November 1942 (the large gray squares) were liquidated by August 1943.[71] Within the entire district, only approximately 21,200 Jews remained, almost all in labor camps.[72]

September 1943-July 1944: Final Liquidations

On June 19, 1943, Hitler ordered Himmler "to radically enforce the 'evacuation' of the Jews and to complete it within the next three to four months."[73] Since during this stage most of the Jews who remained in the General Governorate were forced laborers in labor camps, it was decided in September 1943 to convert all labor camps for Jews into concentration camps under the direct command of the SS Main Economics and Administrative Office (WVHA). In late summer 1943, only a few labor camps remained in the District of Galicia, including Janowska in Lwów. The final four months of 1943 witnessed a rapid decline in the number of shooting *Aktionen*, with no additional *Aktionen* in the autumn of 1943 (with the exception of two in November), as reflected in the graph in Figure 39. This is even more prominent in Figure 40, in the cross-section of the number of those murdered in the shooting *Aktionen* of 1943.

Fig. 39

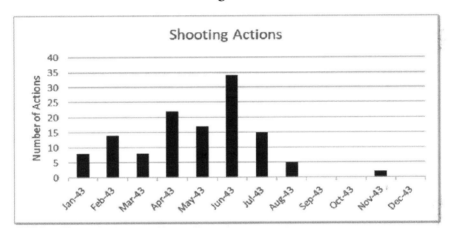

Fig. 40

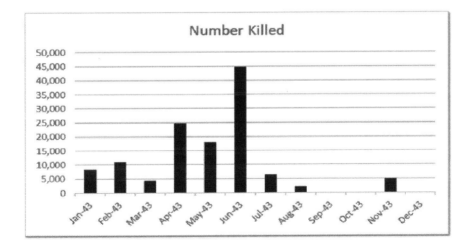

In contrast to the peak in June 1943 (when 45,000 Jews were executed), in November 1943 over 5,000 Jews were executed in two *Aktionen* at labor camps that were liquidated, mostly at Janowska. These irregular liquidations may have marked the tail end of the extensive *Aktionen* conducted in the Jewish labor camps in the neighboring District of Lublin in early November 1943, due to lessons learned from the Sobibor prisoner uprising of October 14, 1943.[74] At the end of 1943, no more than 6,000 Jews remained in the District of Galicia, with a minority in the two labor camps that were still in operation (in the oil fields of Drohobych County). The rest lived in hiding, persecuted by the German authorities and by the local Ukrainian population.[75]

During the final year of the German occupation, from the summer of 1943 through the summer of 1944, the authorities murdered thousands in an incessant hunt for individual Jews who were living in hiding.[76] In addition, at the beginning of 1944, a wave of pogroms, conducted by the Ukrainian militias and encouraged by the German authorities, got underway. This time, the pogroms targeted the rural Polish population with the aim of "cleansing" the District of its Polish minority. In the course of this ethnic cleansing, a few tens of thousands of Poles were murdered, as were hundreds of Jews who had been hiding in Polish villages.[77]

The two final labor camps were liquidated in 1944. In April, due to the Soviet army's spring Dnieper–Carpathian offensive in Ukraine (March 4 to April 17) and the conquest of the eastern regions of the District of Galicia, the labor camp in Drohobych was liquidated and approximately 1,000 Jewish forced laborers were evacuated westward to Plaszów concentration camp near Krakow. Finally, just a few days before the Soviet occupation of Lwów (July 26) and the completion of the conquest of the Galicia District, with the onset of the Soviet army's summer Lvov–Sandomierz offensive (July 13 to August 29), the Borysław labor camp was also liquidated, and all its forced laborers were hastily evacuated westward to the Auschwitz concentration camp.

Summing Up

Ghettos and Concentration in Communities

Although ghettoization in the District of Galicia had already begun in August 1941 (with the establishment of a ghetto in Rohatyn), it peaked at a relatively late stage – in the autumn of 1942, after most of the District's Jews had already been sent to the extermination camp. As reflected in the graph in Figure 41, between September and December 1942, 35 ghettos were established and were recognized after the fact in Krüger's directive regarding the concentration of the District's Jews in 32 official ghettos.

Fig. 41

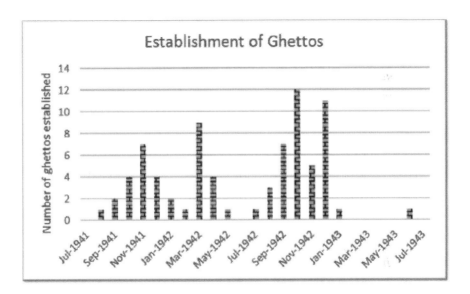

The ghettoization process was accompanied by a process of concentrating Jews from villages and small towns into the larger Jewish communities, ostensibly those that had been isolated in the ghettos. However, throughout almost the entire period, the number of concentration points was greater than the number of ghettos; that is to say, the establishment of a ghetto was not a precondition for concentrating the Jews of the surrounding area within a community. The ghettoization process concluded in December 1942, along with the conclusion of the transports to the extermination camp. In total, 76 ghettos were established in the District of Galicia, accounting for 42% of the Jewish communities that had existed in the District at the beginning of the occupation.

Fig. 42

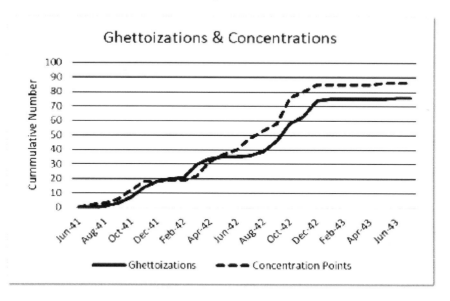

Killing versus Deportation

The District of Galicia was part of the General Governorate on the one hand, and part of the Soviet Union prior to its occupation by Germany in 1941 on the other hand. As a result, the two processes of ghettoization and concentration proceeded hand in hand with the mass shooting *Aktionen* ("Holocaust by bullets"), which were typical of the extermination of the Jews in the Soviet Union, and *Aktionen* for deportation to an extermination camp ("Holocaust by gas"), which were typical of the extermination of the Jews in the rest of Poland (and other occupied countries). For example, more than 85 percent of the Jews in Stanisławów county were shot to death, and only a minority of them were deported to an extermination camp.[78]

This combination of local mass murder and deportations to an extermination camp was, to a great extent, unique to the District of Galicia. However, these processes were markedly distinct from one another: whereas the shooting *Aktionen* went on continuously for two years, from June 1941 to June 1943, the deportation *Aktionen* (including deportation to Bełżec) of the second half of 1942 were extremely intensive, as reflected in the graph in Figure 43.

Fig. 43

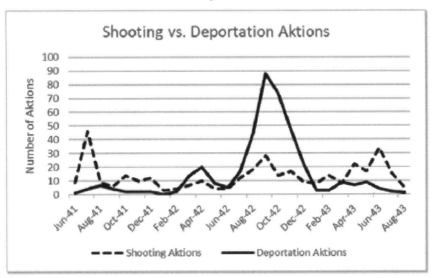

When we compare the number of those murdered in the shooting *Aktionen* to the number of deportees to the extermination camp, we see that from the moment the transports to Bełżec got underway, and as long as they continued, they constituted the primary means of murdering Jews, even in July 1942 (when the transports were renewed only during the last week of the month). Only in December 1942 (when the transports to Bełżec ceased mid-month) did the number of those murdered in the shooting *Aktionen* slightly exceed the number of deportees. The shooting *Aktionen* continued after the cessation of the transports to Bełżec, both locally and at the Janowska labor camp in Lwów, and reached their peak in June 1943. More than 111,000 Jews were murdered in shooting *Aktionen* throughout the District in the first half of 1943 (in contrast to the approximately 210,000 Jews – almost double the number – who were deported to Bełżec during the second half of 1942).

Fig. 44

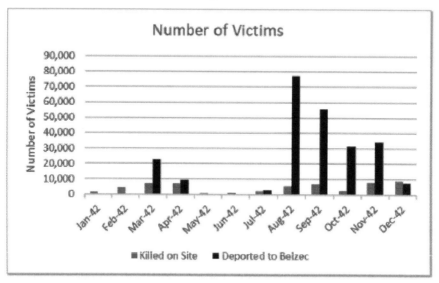

The graph in Figure 44 effectively illustrates the extermination camp's central role in the murder of the Jews of Galicia throughout 1942: the number of deportees to Bełżec was four times the number of those executed throughout the whole year, six times the number of those executed during the second half of 1942, and 14.3 times the number executed during the month of August alone.

Comparing the cumulative number of those executed with the cumulative number of deportees to the extermination camp, reveals that as early as August 1942, immediately following the beginning of the second and primary wave of transports to Bełżec, the number of deportees exceeded the number of Jews murdered in the shooting *Aktionen* during the entire first year of the occupation.

Fig. 45

The graph in Figure 45 reflects that approximately 256,000 Jews were sent from the District of Galicia to the Bełżec extermination camp to be put to death.[79] On the other hand, the shooting *Aktionen* in the District of Galicia resulted in the death of approximately 263,000 Jews, meaning that about half of the Jews in the District were murdered in shooting *Aktionen* (51%) and the other half through deportation *Aktionen* (49%).[80] The total number of Jews that were murdered in the District of Galicia from the beginning of the German occupation, then, can be estimated at 519,000 at the very least, representing some 96 percent of the 540,000 Jews who lived in the District in the summer of 1941.[81]

Bełżec, Sobibor

Bełżec, the first extermination camp in the General Governorate, was established beside the train station of the small village of Bełżec in the Lublin District of the General Governorate.[82] Therefore, the historiography of the Holocaust maintains that the camp, which was established at the initiative of Odilo Globocnik, commander of the SS and the police in the Lublin District, was located in the Lublin District.[83] However, careful examination reveals that the extermination camp was established exactly on the border between the Lublin District and the

District of Galicia, as is revealed by enlarging the northern part of the original map and superimposing it onto a current map (see Figures 46 and 47).

Fig. 46

Fig. 47

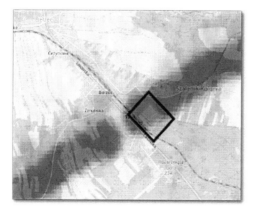

The black circle on the original map indicates the location of the camp. The black rectangle encloses the area of the camp (the grey rectangle) against the background of the thick border line between the Lublin District (above) and the District of Galicia (below).[84] Support for this assessment can be found in the words of Ferdinand Hahnzog, the commander of the gendarmerie in the

Lublin District, who testified after the war that the extermination camp was located "next to Bełżec, hidden deep in the forest bordering Galicia."[85]

Moreover, the extermination camp appears to have been affiliated with the District of Galicia more than with the Lublin District, as suggested by the following: (1) for the killing experiment that was conducted in February 1942, approximately 150 Jews were brought from nearby Lubycza Królewska, located in the District of Galicia; (2) the first "operational" transport to the camp, on March 15, 1942, was from Żółkiew, near Lwów;[86] and (3) the German civilians who lived in Buczacz, in the southeastern part of the district, were told that the Jews were being taken to be gassed to death in Rawa Ruska – the county seat at the northern border of which the Bełżec extermination camp was established.[87] Ultimately, Bełżec "served" primarily the District of Galicia, from which almost 60 percent of the Jews who arrived to the extermination camp were sent.

It seems that the ghetto-liquidation *Aktionen* that were carried out during 1943 involved no transports to any extermination camp, as Bełżec ceased operating on December 15, 1942.[88] Direct evidence of the cessation of transports to Bełżec can be found in a January 11, 1943 telegram sent by Hermann Höfle, the coordinator of Operation Reinhard, to Franz Heim, the deputy commander of the Security Police in the General Governorate (and apparently also to Eichmann). The telegram reports "B 0," meaning that during the last fortnight of December no Jews had arrived to Bełżec.[89] Although the two other extermination camps at Sobibor and Treblinka continued to operate until the summer of 1943, it appears that they received no transports from the District of Galicia.[90]

Bełżec's central role as the only camp to which the Jews of the District of Galicia were sent to be put to death was then replaced by the Janowska labor camp in Lwów. In the course of 1943, it was the destination or more than 24,000 Jewish deportees (over 18,000 from the Lwów ghetto), in comparison to approximately 7,000 Jews who were deported to the camp throughout 1942.[91] And still, Janowska was not a true substitute for Bełżec, as only a small percentage of the Jews were sent there (whether to be killed immediately or after being exploited as forced laborers), constituting less than a quarter of the number of Jews who remained in the district at the end of 1942.

We can therefore conclude that liquidating the ghettos in the District of Galicia in 1943 required the execution of the Jews who remained in the district, most through local shooting *Aktionen* and only a small fraction through shooting *Aktionen* at the Janowska camp. Although the other extermination camps in the General Governorate – Sobibor and Treblinka – continued to operate until the summer of 1943, they did not serve as a substitute for Bełżec and neither did Auschwitz-Birkenau. Once Bełżec stopped "serving" the SS authorities in the District of Galicia, they were forced to revert to the method of killing by shooting that had been used extensively in the District since the beginning of the occupation.

All of this raises two questions: (1) Why did Bełżec extermination camp cease operating at a time when the process of liquidating the Jews of the District of Galicia, which made extensive and exclusive use of the camp, was still far from complete?[92] (2) Why were the other extermination camps in the General Governorate not used later in the ongoing liquidation of the Jews of the District of Galicia in 1943?[93] It is difficult to come up with a logical explanation or an operational rationale for this state of affairs. Therefore, we may perhaps attribute it to bad personal relations between Krüger and Katzmann, his subordinate, against the background of a dispute between the two men following Krüger's order to set up residual ghettos in which Jews would be permitted to reside in the District of Galicia. Katzmann's response to Krüger's order betrays hints of a dispute in his assertion that "the HSSPF [Krüger] intervened once more in solving the Jewish problem with his order of November 10, 1942 regarding the establishment of residential areas for Jews," reflecting resentment at Krüger's intervention in the events in the District of Galicia, which he regarded as flagrant.[94] Moreover, Krüger's relationship with Wächter, the governor of the District of Galicia, was also strained due to Wächter's pro-Ukrainian policy (which peaked in April 1943 with the establishment of the SS "Galicia" Division through the conscription of Ukrainian volunteers).[95] We can therefore conjecture that Krüger decided to make things difficult for Katzmann and Wächter by ordering the Bełżec extermination camp to cease operations, despite the fact that it was still needed, and by prohibiting the transport of Jews from the District of Galicia to the two other extermination camps in the General Governorate, which continued to operate until the summer of 1943.

Liquidation of the Jewish Communities

The liquidation of the 180 Jewish communities in the District of Galicia began with the onset of the German occupation: on June 23, 1941, the small Jewish community of Ułaszkowce was liquidated. However, the major wave of community liquidation occurred in the second half of 1942, concurrent to the transports to Bełżec, and peaked in September and October (see Figure 48). The liquidation of communities ended on August 14, 1943 with the liquidation of the residual ghetto in Borszczów.

Fig. 48

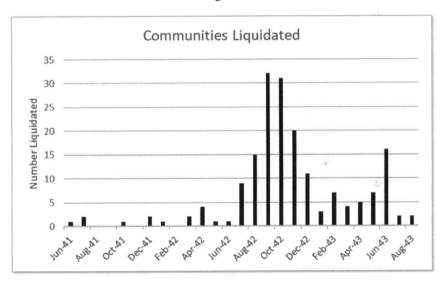

The graph in Figure 49 provides a summarizing mirror image of the liquidation of the communities by presenting the number of communities in the District of Galicia that were still in existence at the end of each month of the occupation. In June 1942, one year into the occupation, there were still 164 Jewish communities in the District (92 percent). Half a year later, in December 1942 following the period of the deportations to Bełżec, only 46 communities remained (26 percent). The cessation of transports to the extermination camp significantly slowed the pace of community liquidation: an average of five communities were liquidated per month, as opposed to a monthly average of 20 communities during the transports – a difference that illustrates the dependence of the SS authorities in the District on the transports to Bełżec, as well as the negative effect (in the eyes of the SS authorities) of their inability to continue using this resource. Nonetheless, the liquidation of the communities continued, albeit less intensively, and concluded in the late summer of 1943.

Fig. 49

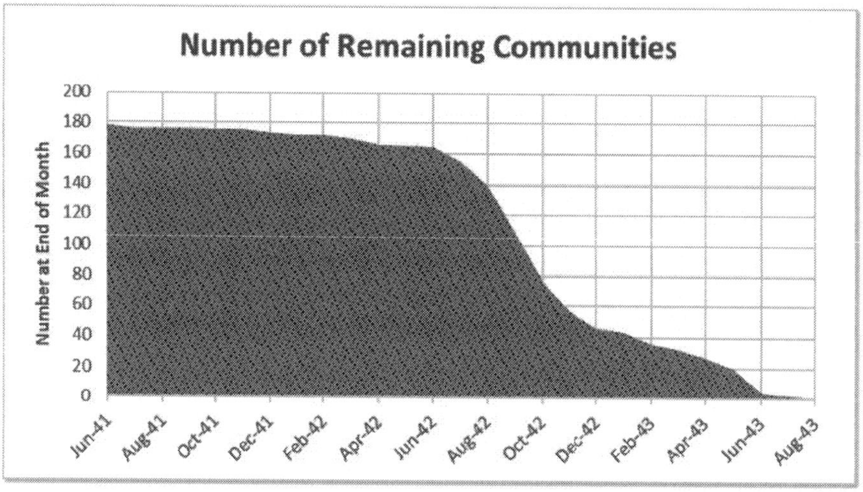

Number of Remaining Communities

Conclusion

This article addressed the following questions: Was the liquidation of the Jewish communities, at its various stages, organized and systematic, or were the communities liquidated in a random or arbitrary order that can be characterized only as chaotic? If we can identify order and method in the location and timing of the liquidation *Aktionen*, what were the priorities of the perpetrators? And overall, what was the operational rationale underlying this order?

The chronological order of the liquidation *Aktionen* vis-à-vis the geographical and administrative location of the liquidated communities, both during the massive liquidations that took place between July and December 1942 and during the periods that preceded and followed them, indicate two standing attributes that were not contingent on the duration of the period examined (one week, two weeks, one month, etc.): (1) During no period were communities liquidated in only one county; and (2) In no county were all the Jewish communities liquidated during a single period.

From this, we can conclude that the liquidations of the communities were not carried out in any systematic order, such as county by county, or from north to south; rather, they were conducted arbitrarily, wherever and whenever possible. As no order can be identified, there is no significance to the question regarding the priorities of the perpetrators, who worked to liquidate all the communities in the District so that it could be declared *Judenfrei* ("free of Jews") by the target date (June 30, 1943) – even if this declaration was not wholly consistent with the facts on the ground.

With regard to the operational rationale of the perpetrators, the arbitrary order of the liquidation of the communities may not have been the result of a lack of orderly planning but rather precisely the opposite – it may have been arbitrary by intention, in order to sow confusion among the Jews and prevent them from assessing when the wave of liquidations could be expected to reach their community. This would preclude them from preparing themselves for impending *Aktion*, whether by going into hiding in the ghetto, escaping from the ghetto, or organizing an active resistance.

Endnotes

1   Martin Winstone, *The Dark Heart of Hitler's Europe: Nazi Rule in Poland Under the General Government* (London, 2014), pp. 105-106.

2   Historian Yehuda Bauer has concluded that there was no clear method to the shooting *Aktionen* that were carried out in the eastern frontier regions of occupied Poland (including Eastern Galicia). See Yehuda Bauer, *The Death of the Shtetl* (Jerusalem, 2011), pp. 123 (Hebrew).

3   Christopher Browning, *The Origins of the Final Solution* (Jerusalem, 2004), pp. 249, 293, 300, 306 (Hebrew). This order was given orally on June 17, 1941 and in writing on June 29. On July 1, Heydrich again clarified that the cleansing actions needed to target "the Bolsheviks and the Jews." Kai Struve, "Rites of Violence? The Pogroms of Summer 1941," *POLIN Studies in Polish Jewry* 24 (2012), pp. 260-261. See also John-Paul Himka, "The Lwów Pogrom of 1941: The Germans, Ukrainian Nationalists, and the Carnival crowd," *Canadian Slavonic Papers* 53 (2011), p. 240.

4   Yitzhak Arad, Israel Gutman, and Abraham Margaliot (eds.), *Documents on the Holocaust: Selected Documents on the Destruction of the Jewry of Germany and Austria, Poland, and the Soviet Union* (Jerusalem, 1978), p. 301 (Hebrew); Browning, *The Origins of the Final Solution*, pp. 250, 293.

5   Alexander Kruglov, "Jewish Losses in Ukraine, 1941-1944," in Ray Brandon and Wendy Lower (eds.), *The Shoah in Ukraine: History, Testimony, Memorialization* (Bloomington, 2008), p. 274.

6   Sandkühler, "Anti-Jewish Policy and the Murder of the Jews in the District of Galicia, 1941/42," in Ulrich Herbert (ed.), *National Socialist Extermination Policies: Contemporary German Perspectives and Controversies* (New York, 2000), p. 130.

7   Bauer, *The Death of the Shtetl*, p. 117. For example, in the first Aktion, which was conducted in Buczacz on August 25, 1941, 400 Jews were executed. Most of them were men – "the cream of the crop of the Jewish shtetl." The artisans were released to their homes. See Omer Bartov, *Anatomy of a Genocide* (Tel Aviv, 2020), pp. 171-172 (Hebrew).

8   Kruglov, "Jewish Losses in Ukraine, 1941-1944," p. 275; Dieter Pohl, "Hans Krüger and the Murder of the Jews in the Region of Stanislawow Galicia," *Yad Vashem Studies* 26 (1998), p. 185 (Hebrew); Sandkühler, "Anti-Jewish Policy and the Murder of the Jews in the District of Galicia, 1941/42," p. 135.

9   Assessments of the number of pogroms (in Eastern Galicia and Volhynia combined) range from 35 to 140. See Struve, "Rights of Violence?" p. 268. In actuality, however, the proportion of the communities in which pogroms took place was very low. According to a thorough study, pogroms occurred in 126 of the 1,820 mixed localities (meaning, localities with Jewish, Polish, and Ukrainian populations), accounting for approximately seven percent of all the Jewish communities. Notable statistical variance was found between the Jewish communities that experienced pogroms and all the other communities: the

pogroms occurred primarily in locations with larger Jewish communities (the Jewish communities that experienced pogroms had a median population of 545, in comparison to a median population of 35 among those communities that did not experience pogroms), in locations where Jews constituted a larger percentage of the population (a median percentage of 24% versus a median percentage of only two percent), and in locations with a lower percentages of Ukrainian population (a median percentage of 24% versus a median percentage of 77%). Most surprisingly, the pogroms occurred primarily in Jewish communities in which there was massive support for equal national rights for Jews (as reflected in the local support shown for the General Zionists party in the general elections of 1928), giving the impression that they constituted a threat to Ukrainian nationalism: Jewish communities that experienced pogroms had an 81% median rate of support for the General Zionists, as opposed to 43% in other communities. See Jeffrey Kopstein & Jason Wittenberg, *Intimate Violence: Anti-Jewish Pogroms on the Eve of the Holocaust* (Ithaca and London, 2018), pp. 86, 95.

10 Kopstein and Wittenberg reference the pogroms of the summer of 1941 in the title of their book *Intimate Violence: Anti-Jewish Pogroms on the Eve of the Holocaust*. Indeed, the pogroms that occurred in the Polish frontier regions in the summer of 1941 must be understood as part of the Holocaust, even if they did occur in its (advance chronological) periphery, preceding the systematic mass murder carried out by the Germans (just as the "hunt for Jews" occurred in its rear periphery, after the Jewish communities were finally liquidated). "After all, this is not about 'pogroms' but about 'state-sponsored mass murder that envisaged totality'." See Dieter Pohl, "Dieter Pohl: 'At present, there are practically no comprehensive studies on the history of the Holocaust in the Ukrainian lands'," *Ukrainian-Jewish Encounter*, May 2021.

11 The differing assessments of the number of victims range from 12,000 to 35,000 (including Volhynia). See Struve, "Rites of Violence?" p. 268. The "popular pogroms" typically preceded the shooting *Aktionen* that were carried out by the *Einsatzgruppen*. For example, in Lwów, *Einsatzgruppe C* units began to shoot Jews to death after July 2, 1941, upon the conclusion of the pogrom that began on June 30, immediately after the conquest of the city. See Struve, "Rights of Violence?" p.269. Himka, on the other hand, maintains that Jews were shot to death during the pogrom by regular German forces. See Himka, "The Lwów Pogrom of 1941," pp. 239-240. In any event, the pogroms were carried out by an incited mob (civilians), members of Ukrainian militias, and German forces (*Einsatzgruppe C*), who shot most of the victims to death.

12 The numbers of victims of the pogroms and the shooting *Aktionen* must be treated with caution, as, in many cases, the exact number of victims is unknown or the assessments vary significantly. (For example, according to one assessment 4,500 Jews were executed in Lwów in June 1941, whereas a different assessment places the number at 8,000). Kruglov estimates that 19,000 Jews were executed in the first wave and 34,000 in the second wave. See Kruglov, "Jewish Losses in Ukraine, 1941-1944," p. 278.

13 For example, in July 1941, the Hungarian army prevented a pogrom against the Jews of Borszczów. See Dean, *USHMM Encyclopedia of Camps and Ghettos, 1933–*

1945: Ghettos in German-Occupied Eastern Europe, p. 753. In August, it prevented a massacre in Kolomiya. See Pohl, "Hans Krüger and the Murder of the Jews," p. 185.

14 This wording is taken from Esther 3:13 in reference to the planning of a massacre of the Jews. Winstone, *The Dark Heart of Hitler's Europe*, p. 151. This *Aktion* marked the beginning of the implementation of the Final Solution in the territory of the General Governorate.

15 Sandkühler, "Anti-Jewish Policy and the Murder of the Jews in the District of Galicia, 1941/42," p. 135; Christian Gerlach, *The Extermination of the European Jews* (Cambridge, 2016), p. 294; Winstone, *The Dark Heart of Hitler's Europe*, p. 151.

16 Dieter Pohl, "Hans Krüger and the Murder of the Jews," p. 186. Immediately following the conquest, the Hungarians deported thousands of Jews from the Ruthenia region, which, upon the eradication of Czechoslovakia in 1939, was annexed to Hungary, to the occupied territories in Eastern Galicia. On the other hand, the Hungarian military government did not initiate the execution of Jews and even took action to prevent pogroms in Eastern Galicia (June-August 1941).

17 Sandkühler, "Anti-Jewish Policy and the Murder of the Jews in the District of Galicia, 1941/42," p. 136; Winstone, *The Dark Heart of Hitler's Europe*, p. 152. The Jews' transfer to the ghetto was halted due to the spread of the Typhoid epidemic, leaving approximately 20,000 Jews living outside the ghetto.

18 Some 72,000 of them by the end of 1941. Gerlach estimates a total of 70,000 by the end of 1941, See Gerlach, *The Extermination of the European Jews*, p. 75.

19 Sandkühler, "Anti-Jewish Policy and the Murder of the Jews in the District of Galicia, 1941/42," p. 131. On September 19, 1941, Frank requested from Hitler's Chief of Staff that the Pripet Marshes be included in the General Governorate. His request was denied.

20 Winstone, *The Dark Heart of Hitler's Europe*, p. 107.

21 Peter Longerich, *Holocaust: The Nazi Persecution and Murder of the Jews* (Oxford, 2010), p. 293; Winstone, *The Dark Heart of Hitler's Europe*, p. 108; Browning, *The Origins of the Final Solution*, p. 374.

22 Gerlach, *The Extermination of the European Jews*, p. 293.

23 Bogdan Musial, "The Origins of Operation Reinhard: The Decision-Making Process in the Mass Murder of the Jews in the General Governorate," *Yad Vashem Studies* 28 (2000), p. 119 (Hebrew); Winstone, *The Dark Heart of Hitler's Europe*, p. 108.

24 Approximately 10,000 Jewish forced laborers were used to pave this road in 1942 (in addition to another 50,000 Soviet prisoners of war and another 50,000 Ukrainian forced laborers who had been mobilized from the settlements along the road). See Andrej Angrick, "Forced Labor along the 'Strasse der SS'," in *Forced and Slave Labor in Nazi-Dominated Europe: Symposium Presentations* (Washington, DC, 2004), p. 91

25 Gerlach, *The Extermination of the European Jews*, p. 293. Wächter was appointed governor of the District of Galicia in January 1942. See Winstone, *The Dark Heart of Hitler's Europe*, p. 53.

26 Longerich, *Holocaust: The Nazi Persecution and Murder of the Jews*, p. 294; Yitzhak Arad, *Bełżec, Sobibór, Treblinka: The Operation Reinhard Death Camps* (Jerusalem, 2013), pp. 44, 53; Pohl, "Hans Krüger and the Murder of the Jews," p. 186; Browning, *The Origins of the Final Solution*, pp 408, 413, 414; Musial, "The Origins of Operation Reinhard," pp. 96, 116.

27 At this point, the operation was apparently meant to liquidate only the Jews in the Districts of Lublin and Galicia. Longerich, *Holocaust: The Nazi Persecution and Murder of the Jews*, p. 296.

28 Longerich, *Holocaust: The Nazi Persecution and Murder of the Jews*, p. 332. Heydrich was assassinated on May 27, 1942 by British Intelligence. In a final report for Himmler, on November 4, 1943, Globocnik wrote: "On October 19, 1943, I concluded Operation Reinhard, which was under my command in the General Governorate, and I dismantled the camps." See Nuremberg Document NO-56.

29 Pohl, "Hans Krüger and the Murder of the Jews," p. 191.

30 Sandkühler, "Anti-Jewish Policy and the Murder of the Jews in the District of Galicia, 1941/42," pp. 136, 140; Winstone, *The Dark Heart of Hitler's Europe*, p. 155. The inclusion of the Jewish communities of the District of Galicia in the first deportations to Bełżec may have been related to the January 1942 appointment of SS official Otto Wächter, who cooperated closely with Katzmann, as governor of the District of Galicia.

31 For example, in 1942 it was argued that the Jews should not be killed immediately, as they were "extremely essential as professional workers and tradesmen." See Bauer, *The Death of the Shtetl*, p. 124.

32 Sandkühler, "Anti-Jewish Policy and the Murder of the Jews in the District of Galicia, 1941/42," pp. 140-141. In settlements without a ghetto (and settlements that were declared as designated residential area for Jews), the permitted area was the entire area of the settlement.

33 Dean, *USHMM Encyclopedia of Camps and Ghettos, 1933–1945: Ghettos in German-Occupied Eastern Europe*, p. 852. Arad maintains that this, indeed, was the first transport from the District of Galicia, but he dates it to March 25. See Arad, *Bełżec, Sobibór, Treblinka*, p. 144. This appears to reflect an error, as Arad also notes that the first deportees from the District of Galicia arrived from Lwów on March 19. See ibid., p. 124. Whereas the Holocaust historiography identifies the deportation of the Jews of Lublin to Bełżec as the beginning of systematic extermination in the General Governorate, this *Aktion* began on March 17 and continued almost non-stop until April 16. See, for example, Dean, *USHMM Encyclopedia of Camps and Ghettos, 1933–1945: Ghettos in German-Occupied Eastern Europe*, p. 676; David Silberklang, *Gates of Tears, The Holocaust in the Lublin District* (Jerusalem, 2013), pp. 283, 316.

34 Longerich, *Holocaust: The Nazi Persecution and Murder of the Jews*, p. 331. According to Arad, the deportations from Lwów began on March 19, 1942 and continued until April 1. Arad, *Bełżec, Sobibór, Treblinka*, p. 124.

35 Sandkühler, "Anti-Jewish Policy and the Murder of the Jews in the District of Galicia, 1941/42," p. 142. On March 31, 1942, in what was the largest transport to Bełżec up to that point, approximately 5,000 Jews were deported from Stanisławów to the Bełżec extermination camp. See Pohl, "Hans Krüger and the Murder of the Jews," p. 192. Between April 2 and 8, some 2,000 Jews were deported from Sniatyn; between April 3 and 6 some 5,000 Jews were deported from Kolomiya; on April 11, some 400 Jews were deported from Zabolotov; and on April 13, some 1,400 Jews were deported from Horodenka – all in Kolomiya County.

36 These figures do not include the number of deportees from Brody (which is unknown), which was home to nearly 7,000 Jews. Arad estimates that approximately 35,000 Jews were deported from the District of Galicia during this period. See Arad, *Bełżec, Sobibór, Treblinka*, p. 125.

37 Wirth returned to Bełżec in mid-May, after Globocnik asked Wirth's commanding officer Viktor Brack to have him return to the camp. The exterminations at Bełżec resumed at the end of May but were again halted in mid-June for one month in order to accelerate the pace of the killing. Arad, *Bełżec, Sobibór, Treblinka*, pp. 125, 145-146.

38 Sandkühler, "Anti-Jewish Policy and the Murder of the Jews in the District of Galicia, 1941/42," p. 142.

39 Each ghetto is represented by a black square, each liquidated community by a black x, and each remaining community by a small circle. Arad estimates the number of Jews residing in the District of Galicia at the end of April 1942 at between 472,000 and 487,000. See Arad, *Bełżec, Sobibór, Treblinka*, p. 126.

40 Gerlach, *The Extermination of the European Jews*, p. 127; Longerich, *Holocaust: The Nazi Persecution and Murder of the Jews*, p. 332. In January 1942, under Himmler's pressure, Frank was forced to remove Lasch as governor of the District of Galicia following the discovery of corruption (his own personal use of confiscated Jewish property). In the power struggle between Himmler and Frank, Himmler had the upper hand. Lasch was tried and executed in June 1942. See Winstone, *The Dark Heart of Hitler's Europe*, p. 53.

41 Longerich, *Holocaust: The Nazi Persecution and Murder of the Jews*, pp. 333, 358. The moratorium was instituted on June 19, 1942 and remained in place until July 7. Its purpose was to facilitate the massing of forces in preparation for the summer 1942 offensive against the southern portion of the Eastern front.

42 Arad, Gutman, and Margaliot (eds.), *Documents on the Holocaust*, pp. 219-220; Longerich, *Holocaust: The Nazi Persecution and Murder of the Jews*, pp. 335, 359.

43 Sandkühler, "Anti-Jewish Policy and the Murder of the Jews in the District of Galicia, 1941/42," p. 143.

44 Arad, *Bełżec, Sobibór, Treblinka*, pp. 210-211, 545. The last deportations to Bełżec from the District of Galicia were carried out on December 8, 1942, from Rohatyn (approximately 1,400 people) and Bóbrka (a few hundred people).

45 In August, some 42,000 Jews were deported from Lwów's Jewish community, which numbered 90,000 prior to the deportation. Himmler and Globocnik resided in the city during the deportation itself. See Longerich, *Holocaust: The Nazi Persecution and Murder of the Jews*, p. 337. A similar pattern was observable during the same period in the initial deportations to Treblinka, with most of the Jews coming from the large ghetto in Warsaw. On the other hand, the deportations from Hungary to Auschwitz in the spring of 1944 began in the satellite towns, whereas the Jews of the large community in Budapest "were left for last" (their deportation was averted due to pressure exerted by the Allies).

46 The total number of deportees to Bełżec in all the deportations after July 1942 regarding which we have quantitative data stands at approximately 210,000. However, the relevant information is not complete, as in 12 instances (of 138, or 9%) data (and even estimates) is missing regarding the number of deportees. Under the assumption that these instances would not significantly change the median number of deportees for the different deportations, the total number of deportees can be estimated at approximately 230,000. Arad estimates the number of deportees to Bełżec from the District of Galicia since July 1942 at approximately 240,000. See Arad, *Bełżec, Sobibór, Treblinka*, pp. 210-211. In an expert opinion at the Ganzenmüller trial, Wolfgang Scheffler placed the number of deportees at 232,400. See Pohl and Witte, "The Number of Victims of Belzec Extermination Camp," p. 21, fn 15.

47 Kolomiya offers an extreme example of the recurring shooting *Aktionen*: a few hundred were murdered in September 1941; 2,900 in October; more than 2,000 in November; 1,200 in December; 400 in January 1942; 4,000 in February; 4,000 in March; and 6,000 in November 1942. These actions were in addition to several deportation *Aktionen* to Bełżec, with 5,000 in April 1942; 8,700 in September; 4,000 in an additional *Aktion* in September; and 4,000 in October.

48 For one-third of the places on the list, the word "ghetto" appeared in parentheses, reflecting the existence of a ghetto in practice on the date of the list's publication.

49 See Document no. 98 from November 14, 1942 on the UMCS website (Maria Curie-Skłodowska University in Lublin); Arad, *Bełżec, Sobibór, Treblinka*, p. 217; Winstone, *The Dark Heart of Hitler's Europe*, p. 160.

50 The dark squares denote "regular" ghettos, and the light squares denote residual ghettos.

51 The ghetto in Kosów was established as a residual ghetto on September 28, after the liquidation of the community two weeks earlier, and was itself liquidated approximately one month later, on October 31.

52 The ghetto in Buczacz, which appeared on the list of declared areas, was established in practice in December 1942. See Bartov, *Anatomy of a Genocide*, pp. 200, 214.

53 In this context too, Kolomiya was an exception. In April 1942, immediately following the deportation *Aktion* of the same month, 5,000 Jews from the surrounding area were concentrated there.

54 Pohl, "Hans Krüger and the Murder of the Jews," p. 194. The JSS's report was received by the JSS office in Krakow on November 7, 1942.

55 Pohl, "Hans Krüger and the Murder of the Jews," p. 195.

56 Nuremberg Document NO-5194; Arad, Gutman, and Margaliot, *Documents on the Holocaust*, p. 266. It is interesting to note that Korherr offers an ostensibly exact figure for the District of Galicia, whereas the numbers in other districts are rounded up to the nearest hundred or thousand. Approximately 24,000 other Jews were held in dozens of labor camps throughout the district. Kruglov, "Jewish Losses in Ukraine, 1941-1944," p. 282.

57 The SS authorities intended on leaving only approximately 100,000 Jews alive in the General Governorate by the end of the year. In actuality, close to 300,000 Jews remained. Gerlach, *The Extermination of the European Jews*, pp. 91, 107.

58 Arad, Gutman, and Margaliot, *Documents on the Holocaust*, p. 266; Longerich, *Holocaust: The Nazi Persecution and Murder of the Jews*, pp. 376, 559.

59 Bauer, *The Death of the Shtetl*, pp. 125-127.

60 Ibid., p. 127. Bauer provides no documentation of such an explicit order.

61 Gerlach, *The Extermination of the European Jews*, p. 110; Winstone, *The Dark Heart of Hitler's Europe*, p. 160.

62 Nonetheless, Krüger maintained that it would be impossible to carry out Himmler's order to exterminate all the Jews working in the weapons industry due to the shortage of skilled workers. See Longerich, *Holocaust: The Nazi Persecution and Murder of the Jews*, p. 378.

63 In a speech he delivered at Heydrich's funeral in June 1942, Himmler stated that "we will complete the Jewish migration period (*Völkerwanderung*) within a year, and then Jews will not walk among us." Katzmann's report on "The Solution to the Jewish Problem in the District of Galicia" was issued on June 30, 1943, most likely in order to meet the deadline set by Himmler. Longerich, *Holocaust: The Nazi Persecution and Murder of the Jews*, pp. 332, 359; Gerlach, *The Extermination of the European Jews*, pp. 91, 107.

64 Bartov estimates the number of those killed in the April *Aktion* at 3,000. He also notes another liquidation *Aktion* that occurred in May 1943, but he makes no conjecture regarding the number of victims. See Bartov, *Anatomy of a Genocide*, p. 214.

65 The shooting *Aktionen* conducted during this period for which there are quantitative data resulted in some 120,000 murdered. However, the data is not complete, as in 18 cases (out of 123, or approximately 15%) we have neither data nor estimates regarding the number of those executed, which have therefore not been taken into account. On the assumption that these *Aktionen* do not significantly change the overall median number of the executed in all the *Aktionen*, we can estimate their overall number from January to August 1943 at 129,000. According to Kruglov,

during the year 1943 in its entirety, approximately 142,000 Jews were murdered in the District of Galicia. Kruglov, "Jewish Losses in Ukraine, 1941-1944," p. 283.

66 According to Bartov, the 200 "richest families" were sent to the local labor camp, whereas the rest of the population was deported to other cities. On the other hand, he subsequently notes that "the *Aktion* to liquidate" the ghetto consisted of the execution of masses of Jews in the local Jewish cemetery (*Anatomy of a Genocide*, pp. 164, 214). It should be noted that, unlike in the cases of the other shooting *Aktionen* (conducted in February, April, and June 1943), Bartov offers no evidence pertaining to the shooting *Aktion* of May 1943.

67 In addition to the 10,000 Jews who were deported from the Lwów ghetto at the beginning of January 1943, a few hundred were deported in February, approximately 1,000 in March, and 7,000 in June 1943, upon the final liquidation of the Lwów ghetto. According to Arad, the cessation of the deportations to Bełżec transformed Janowska to the main site of the murder of the Jews of Lwów. See Arad, *Bełżec, Sobibór, Treblinka*, p. 127.

68 Skepticism is in order regarding the veracity of the information on the deportation of 600-800 people from Lwów to Auschwitz extermination camp (on March 23, 1943), which was located within the borders of the Reich. This transport, if it occurred, would have been small in scale and an exception – the only deportation to Auschwitz from the General Governorate during Operation Reinhard. During the same period, the Lwów ghetto still contained at least 14,000 Jews, so this could have been neither intended to reduce the population of the ghetto nor a response to some urgent need for a few hundred forced laborers, when transports were arriving from Greece to Auschwitz on almost a daily basis. Furthermore, there is no mention of any transport from Lwów in the list of transports that arrived at Auschwitz during the period in question. See Danuta Czech, *Auschwitz Chronicle, 1939-1945* (New York, 1990).

69 Arad, Gutman, and Margaliot, *Documents on the Holocaust*, p. 270; Longerich, *Holocaust: The Nazi Persecution and Murder of the Jews*, p. 379. For example, the labor camp in Buczacz, which was established in May 1943 upon the liquidation of the ghetto, was liquidated in a shooting *Aktion* in June 1943, just a few weeks later, and the city was declared *Judenfrei*. See Bartov, *Anatomy of a Genocide*, pp. 195-196, 204, 214.

70 The Żółkiew and Kopyczynce ghettos were liquidated in July 1943, and the Tarnopol and Borszczów ghettos were liquidated in August.

71 The last residual ghetto was established in Borszczów only in June 1943 (although it was included in the list of ghettos that were declared in November 1942) and liquidated some two months later, in August 1943.

72 According to Katzmann's report, at the end of June 1943 the District contained 21,156 Jews distributed among 21 labor camps. Arad, Gutman, and Margaliot, *Documents on the Holocaust*, p. 270.

73 Longerich, *Holocaust: The Nazi Persecution and Murder of the Jews*, p. 379.

74 Ibid., p. 382.

75 More than 1,000 Jews were in hiding in the city of Lwów. See ibid., p. 381. Kruglov estimates the number of Jews in the District at the end of the year at between 4,000 and 5,000. Kruglov, "Jewish Losses in Ukraine, 1941-1944," p. 283.

76 Longerich, *Holocaust: The Nazi Persecution and Murder of the Jews*, p. 382. Kruglov estimates that approximately 1,300 Jews were murdered in 1944 before the Soviet re-occupation of the District was completed. Kruglov, "Jewish Losses in Ukraine, 1941-1944," p. 283.

77 Snyder, *Bloodlands*, p. 349.

78 Pohl, "Hans Krüger and the Murder of the Jews," p. 198.

79 This number includes approximately 242,000 people in 140 deportations for which numerical data or estimates are available, and another 14 deportations for which an estimate of the median of the other deportations was calculated. Kruglov estimates that some 251,000 Jews from the District of Galicia were sent to be put to death at Bełżec. See Kruglov, "Jewish Losses in Ukraine, 1941-1944," p. 288.

80 This number includes 253,000 people in 326 shooting *Aktionen* for which numerical data or estimates are available, and another 34 for which an estimate of the median of the other deportations was calculated. This result is remarkably consistent with the assessment of Pohl and Witte that just under half the Jews were murdered in extermination camps. See Pohl and Witte, "The Number of Victims of Belzec Extermination Camp," p. 20. On the other hand, Bauer concludes that the Jews in the District of Galicia were deported "to the Bełżec death camp…; elsewhere [on the Eastern frontier] the Jews were shot." See Bauer, *The Death of the Shtetl*, p. 130. Snyder offers the opposite thesis: that the Jews of Galicia were shot to death. He then explains that they were shot to death from the summer of 1941 through March 1942, when they started to be gassed to death. See Snyder, *Bloodlands*, pp. 280, 282. As noted, the data tells a completely different story with regard to both Bauer's argument and Snyder's two contradicting arguments.

81 Sandkühler estimates the number of those murdered at 530,000. Sandkühler, "Anti-Jewish Policy and the Murder of the Jews in the District of Galicia, 1941/42," p. 128. Kruglov estimates the number at 566,000 (out of the total of 656,000 Jews who were present in the District in 1939, or approximately 86 percent). See Kruglov, "Jewish Losses in Ukraine, 1941-1944," p. 284. According to the Katzmann report, 434,329 Jews were "removed" (meaning, murdered in one way or another) from the District between the spring of 1942 and the end of June 1943. Adding this number to the number of Jews who were murdered during the second half of 1943 yields an estimate of only 449,000. Arad, *Bełżec, Sobibór, Treblinka*, p. 270; Longerich, *Holocaust: The Nazi Persecution and Murder of the Jews*, p. 379.

82 Arad, *Bełżec, Sobibór, Treblinka*, pp. 65-66. On an administrative level, the village was part of Rawa Ruska County (*powiat*) in the District (*województvo*) of Lwów.

83 Bauer writes that the camp was established "just north of the border" of the district. See Bauer, *The Death of the Shtetl*, p. 130. For example, see Sandkühler, "Anti-Jewish Policy and the Murder of the Jews in the District of Galicia, 1941/42," pp. 136-137; Browning, *The Origins of the Final Solution*, p. 474.

84 The village of Bełżec is located in the upper left-hand corner. Also prominent is the railway that ran by the camp.

85 Musial, "The Origins of Operation Reinhard," p. 116.

86 Arad, *Bełżec, Sobibór, Treblinka*, pp. 68-69; Browning, *The Origins of the Final Solution*, p. 476.

87 Bartov, *Anatomy of a Genocide*, p. 210. Bartov explains that Rawa Ruska was the last stop before the extermination camp, although between the city and the camp there was another station at Lubycza Królewska.

88 Dabrowska, Wein, and Weiss's *Encyclopedia of Jewish Communities* refers to Bełżec twice as a destination of transports in 1943 – from Toporów in February and from Borszczów in March. This is clearly erroneous; Yad Vashem's *Encyclopedia of the Ghettos* indicates that the Jews of Borszczów were deported to Sobibor, and the USHMM's *Encyclopedia of Camps and Ghettos* indicates that they were deported to the Janowska labor camp in Lwów. With regard to the deportation from Toporów, we have no information from other sources.

89 Peter Witte and Stephen Tyas, "A New Document on the Deportation and Murder of Jews during 'Einsatz Reihnardt' 1942," *Holocaust and Genocide Studies* 15(3) (2001), p. 469; Arad, *Bełżec, Sobibór, Treblinka*, p. 545. According to this report, a total of 434,508 people were sent to Bełżec, and 60 percent of them were Jews from the District of Galicia.

90 Yad Vashem's *Encyclopedia of the Ghettos* mentions two deportations from the District of Galicia to Sobibor extermination camp: from Borszczów in March 1943 and from Brody in May. However, according to USHMM's *Encyclopedia of Camps and Ghettos*, the destination of these deportations were Janowska labor camp (from Borszczów) and Majdanek concentration camp (from Brody). See USHMM *Encyclopedia*, pp. 754, 759. Although Marek Bem maintains that we cannot rule out the possibility that transports from the District of Galicia were conducted in September-October 1943, the list of deportations from the General Governorate in his comprehensive work on Sobibor extermination camp contains no deportations from the Galicia District. See Bem, *Sobibor Extermination Camp, 1942-1943* (Warsaw, 2015), pp. 184, 363-368. According to Arad, several deportations to Sobibor from the District of Galicia occurred after Bełżec ceased functioning. He estimates the number of deportees at between 15,000 and 25,000 (p. 215) and also between 1,500 and 2,500 (p. 565), but the list of deportations from the General Governorate which his book contains does not include any deportations to Sobibor from the District of Galicia. Arad, *Bełżec, Sobibór, Treblinka*, pp. 215, 565. Longerich notes that between 15,000 and 25,000 people were deported to

Sobibor from the District of Galicia in 1943. He appears to be basing this conclusion on Arad, although this is not indicated in the text. See Longerich, *Holocaust: The Nazi Persecution and Murder of the Jews*, p. 379. Pohl and Witte, also not citing their source, maintain that there are only vague indications of deportations to Sobibor. Pohl and Witte, "The Number of Victims of Belzec Extermination Camp," pp. 19-20.

91 We can estimate that more Jews were murdered at Janowska than at Majdanek. See Winstone, *The Dark Heart of Hitler's Europe*, p. 168.

92 Arad explains the cessation of operations at Bełżec as a result of the abandonment of the plan to transport 200,000 Jews from Romania to be killed at Bełżec, as there were no more Jews left to deport. See Arad, *Bełżec, Sobibór, Treblinka*, p. 211

93 In 1943, approximately 11,200 people were sent to Sobibor (in contrast to the 121,900 who were sent there in 1942), indicating that the camp had no problem "receiving" deportees. See Bem, *Sobibor Extermination Camp, 1942-1943*, p. 368.

94 Arad, Gutman, and Margaliot, *Documents on the Holocaust*, p. 270; Nuremberg Document L-18. For a full translation into English from November 1945, see Harvard Law School Library, *Nuremberg Trials Project*, HLSL document #4404.

95 Winstone, *The Dark Heart of Hitler's Europe*, p. 204.

Grzegorz Rossoliński-Liebe

Ukrainian Nationalists and the Jews during the Holocaust in the Eyes of Anticommunist, Soviet, German, Jewish, Polish, and Ukrainian Historians: Transnational History and National Interpretations

Introduction

The participation of the Ukrainian nationalists in the Holocaust is one of numerous "blind spots" that at some point in time has appeared in many national historiographies. The German historians started to investigate the Holocaust only in the early 1990s and until recently have limited their studies to the German perpetrators. Polish historians omitted the subject of the Polish involvement in the Shoah until the publication of Jan Tomasz Gross' "Neighbors" in 2001. Similarly, they did not study the involvement of the Ukrainian nationalists in the Holocaust, although they studied the mass violence against the Polish population. After establishing the new restrictive politics of memory by the Polish Law and Justice Party in 2015, only few historians continued to research the Polish collaboration with the Nazis in the Holocaust. Ukrainian historians, with very few exceptions, never began to rethink the Ukrainian involvement in the Shoah because they considered the Ukrainian nationalists as a resistance movement.

Two important reasons why historians have avoided analyzing the role of the Organization of Ukrainian Nationalists (OUN, *Orhanizatsiia Ukraïns'kykh Natsionalistiv*) and the Ukrainian Insurgent Army (UPA, *Ukraïns'ka Povstans'ka Armiia*) in the Holocaust were firstly, the effects of Soviet propaganda, and secondly, a lack of research methods. While Soviet propaganda attacked Ukrainian dissidents and strengthened the anticommunist climate of the Cold War, the absence of appropriate research methods was related to the dismissal of documents left by the survivors. Historians, although in theory responsible for investigating and clarifying such difficult aspects of the past such as the violence of the Ukrainian nationalists, have, for various reasons, not investigated them, or have investigated only other aspects of the history of Ukrainian nationalism, such as propaganda, ideology, and resistance.

Given the fact that Ukrainian nationalists killed several thousand Jews on their own, were involved as policemen and members of the administration in the murder of 800,000 western Ukrainian Jews, and conducted an ethnic cleansing of the Polish population in Volhynian and Eastern Galicia in 1943 and 1944, it is a legitimate and important question to ask why the subject has not been researched for such a long time and why it has been eschewed. Because historians from different countries and various backgrounds written on the German occupation and the Holocaust in western Ukraine, the Polish-Ukrainian conflict, or the history of the OUN and UPA, there is a complex and manifold historiography of this field. To analyze several key pathways to this issue, I conceptualized a model that includes national (Jewish, German, Ukrainian, and Polish) and ideological (Soviet and Cold War) approaches to the subject. Like all models, this one simplifies the complex reality and puts together historians who may not feel they belong together. However, the impact of national narratives and politics on historiography and the biographical background of historians justify the use of this approach.

The first goal of this article is to show a broad range of historiography of this subject. The second is to analyze why different historians have avoided studying the subject, and when and why they began to investigate it. The third goal is to discover how it was possible to ignore this part of the Holocaust, while Jewish historians had written about it from the very beginning. The scope of historians and publications analyzed in this article is limited to some significant and representative examples. Although I included over twenty historians, this is only a part of all the scholars who have published about western Ukraine during World War II. The analysis concentrates on publications that appeared before the revolution against Yanukovych, the Russian invasion and annexation of the Crimea, changed the political situation in Ukraine. In April 2015, the *Verkhovna rada* passed Law 2538-1, which outlawed "disrespect" for "fighters for Ukrainian statehood in the twentieth century," and Law 2558, which "condemned the communist and national socialist (Nazi) totalitarian regimes in Ukraine and banned their propaganda and symbols."[1] These laws criminalized research on the Ukrainian perpetrators of the Shoah.

Ukrainian Nationalists and the Holocaust

Eastern Galicia and Volhynia were inhabited by Ukrainians, Poles, and Jews, for centuries. Although Ukrainians made up the majority of the population in these two regions, they were less present in cities such as Lviv than in villages and small towns. Before World War II, Jews in both regions accounted for about 10 percent of all inhabitants, Poles about 25 percent in eastern Galicia and 15 percent in Volhynia, and Ukrainians 60 percent in eastern Galicia and 70 percent in Volhynia.[2] As a result of the first and second partition of the Polish-Lithuanian Commonwealth in 1772 and 1793, eastern Galicia was incorporated into the Habsburg Empire and Volhynia into the Russian Empire which held also south, central and eastern Ukrainian territories and regarded them as parts of Russia. This geopolitical order changed only after World War I. In November 1917, Ukrainians proclaimed a state in Kiev and in November 1918 in Lviv, but they did not succeed in keeping either of them. In 1921 eastern Galicia and Volhynia were officially incorporated into the Second Polish Republic and almost all other Ukrainian territories constituted the Ukrainian Soviet Socialist Republic.[3]

During the interwar period, about 20 percent of all Ukrainians lived in the Second Polish Republic and 80 percent in the Ukrainian Socialist Soviet Republic. Poland was a multiethnic state which discriminated against Ukrainians and other minorities and treated them as second-class citizens.[4] In order to prolong the fight for a Ukrainian state, Ukrainian veterans of the First World War founded the Ukrainian Military Organization (UVO, *Ukraïns'ka Viis'kova Orhanizatsiia*) in Prague in 1920, and in 1929 the OUN in Vienna. The latter particularly attracted many young Ukrainians in Poland. The OUN ideology combined radical nationalism with racism, antisemitism, fascism, cult of war and violence, anti-democracy, and anti-communism. It collaborated with the Germans and other fascist movements such as the Ustaša and the Italian Fascists, and attempted both to establish a Ukrainian state and to turn it into a fascist dictatorship.[5]

In September 1939, eastern Galicia and Volhynia were incorporated into Soviet Ukraine. At that time several hundred OUN members left Ukraine and remained in the General Government, where they were trained by the Nazis and prepared a plan to establish a Ukrainian state after the German attack on the Soviet Union. In 1940 the OUN split into the OUN-B (leader Stepan Bandera) and the OUN-M (leader Andrii Mel'nyk). The OUN-B was more radical than the OUN-M and it found more support in the nationalist underground in western Ukraine. The leadership of the OUN-B decided to proclaim a state, although they did not have much contact with the Nazi leadership and did not have official approval for the proclamation of the statehood.[6] Instead they hoped that Hitler would accept the state as he had accepted Slovakia in March 1939 and Croatia in April 1941. The Ukrainian state was proclaimed on June 30, 1941, eight days after the German attack on the Soviet Union, in Lviv by the OUN-B leading activist Yaroslav Stets'ko who represented Bandera. Hitler, who had different plans for Ukraine than Slovakia and Croatia, did not approve of this political step and arrested the leadership of the OUN-B. As a result several leaders of the radical faction of the OUN-B, including Bandera and Stets'ko and several hundred other OUN-B members, were confined in German prison and concentration camps as special or ordinary political prisoners until the fall of 1944 and some even until the end of World War II.[7] The UPA resumed the collaboration with the Nazis in the spring of 1944.[8]

While some of the OUN-B leaders remained confined in Germany, the Jewish population of eastern Galicia and Volhynia was persecuted and annihilated by the German occupiers and their collaborators, including the OUN members. In early August 1941, the Germans incorporated eastern Galicia into the General Government as Distrikt Galizien and Volhynia became a part of Reichskommissariat Ukraine. Distrikt Galizien contained about 570,000 Jews and Volhynia about 250,000.[9] The annihilation of the Jews in Volhynia and eastern Galicia proceeded differently, although it began in both regions with pogroms, resulting in about 20,000 Jews being killed. The pogrom perpetrators were composed of the German invaders, OUN nationalists and locals, mainly Ukrainian. The spontaneous violent acts against Jews ceased a few weeks after the German invasion of the Soviet Union. In the following months the Jews were exterminated by the Einsatzgruppe C, which by the end of 1941 had killed about 50,000 Jews in eastern Galicia and 20,000 in Volhynia. At that time the Jews in both regions were also forced to move to the ghettoes.[10]

In the main part of the extermination, which in Volhynia had already concluded by the end of 1942, about 200,000 Jews were shot in front of mass graves by German perpetrators who were usually assisted by Ukrainian policemen.[11] In eastern Galicia about 200,000 Jews were deported to the annihilation camp Bełżec, while over 200,000 were shot or died in the ghettos and forced labor camps. The annihilation of the main part of the eastern Galician Jews ended in the summer of 1943. The shootings in eastern Galicia were conducted by the Germans assisted by Ukrainian policemen. The resolution of the ghettoes and deportations were carried out by Germans and Ukrainian policemen. The latter significantly outnumbered the German perpetrators. In both regions Jewish police was used to watch the ghettoes and search for hiding Jews.[12] Among the Ukrainian policemen involved in the Holocaust were many OUN members. The OUN sent its people to the police despite the conflict with the Nazi leadership and the arrests of their prominent members.[13]

About 10 percent, or 80,000 of Volhynian and eastern Galician Jews avoided the mass shootings and deportations while escaping from the ghettoes. These people tried to survive by hiding in forests and various hideouts in villages and cities, and others worked in slave labor camps. According to Dieter Pohl and Aharon Weiss, 10,000–15,000 (2–3 percent) of eastern Galician Jews survived the war. Shmuel Spector estimated the number of Volhynian survivors at 3,500 (1.5 percent).[14] Thus, about 60,000 of the Jews in hiding were killed by the Germans, Ukrainian police, the local population, and the UPA, which was formed by the OUN-B in late 1942. The UPA fought the Soviet partisans and from early 1943 massacred Polish civilians. It conducted an ethnic cleansing of Volhynia in 1943 and eastern Galicia in 1944 and killed between 70,000 and 100,000 Poles. At the same time, it murdered the Jews who hid in the woods or villages. The links between the nationalists and the Nazis were strong, even if they did not collaborate formally. In April 1943, as the mass violence against Poles escalated, 5,000 Ukrainian policemen, who had helped the Nazis to murder the Jews, deserted and joined the UPA.[15]

In the spring and summer of 1944, shortly before the Soviet Army returned to western Ukraine, several thousand Ukrainians — including Nazi collaborators, OUN members, and UPA partisans — left Ukraine together with the German occupiers. After the war, they stayed in West Germany, in camps for Displaced Persons, and in the late 1940s they were resettled in Australia, Canada, Great

Britain, and the the US.[16] The UPA opposed the Soviet authorities until the early 1950s. During a brutal conflict with Soviet authorities the Ukrainian nationalists killed about 20,000 Ukrainians who supported or were accused of supporting the Soviet authorities. The NKVD terror against people in western Ukraine was enormous. The Soviet forces, according to their own statistics, killed a total of 153,000 people, deported 203,000 into the interior of the Soviet Union, and arrested 134,000. Only some of them actually belonged to the UPA or actively supported the nationalist underground.[17]

Documents, Testimonies, and Perceptions

The OUN and UPA had already begun to destroy evidence of their involvement in the Holocaust during the war. In October 1943, leaders of the OUN and UPA issued orders to prepare documents that would indicate that the Germans persecuted the Jews without any help from the Ukrainian police.[18] During the Holocaust, the OUN and UPA publications mentioned the annihilation of the Jews very rarely, and in these sporadic cases identified the Germans as the sole perpetrators, suggesting that the Ukrainian nationalists were not involved in the Holocaust at all. The mass violence against Polish civilians was partially ignored in the OUN and UPA propaganda and partially portrayed as a Polish-Ukrainian war or a Polish aggression.[19] The killing and suffering of Ukrainians, on the other hand, was an important component of the official nationalist propaganda during the war. Especially important were the Ukrainian nationalists who were killed or imprisoned by the Nazis. These individuals were portrayed as soldiers who had fallen for Ukraine or suffered for their country.[20]

The destruction of documents by the Ukrainian nationalists and their propagandist publications was only one form of obstruction. In addition, historians were obstructed by Soviet propaganda, the general anticommunist climate of the Cold War, and the publications of the Ukrainian diaspora. During the Cold War, Soviet propaganda attacked the Ukrainian diaspora, which was composed both of veterans of the OUN and the UPA, as well as groups who were skeptical of ethnic nationalism, but who fought for a Ukrainian state and opposed the Soviet Union. The violence of the Ukrainian nationalists was an essential element of Soviet propaganda. Because the Soviet Union used it at length, people in the Western Block became suspicious of this claim, and generally disbelieved that the Ukrainian nationalists had collaborated with the Nazis, or that the OUN and UPA had murdered civilians or cleansed Ukraine of ethnic minorities during the German occupation.

Given the influence and quantity of Soviet propaganda and the counterpropaganda of the Ukrainian diaspora, it was not an easy task for a historian to study the Holocaust in western Ukraine before 1990. The documents of the Germans, who occupied western Ukraine from 1941 to 1944, did not hold much information about the involvement of the Ukrainian nationalists in the Holocaust and the murdering of the Poles by the UPA. The most appropriate source to study this form of violence and to comprehend its dimensions was the sources left by the survivors. Holocaust victims and survivors from Volhynia and eastern Galicia left various documents of mass violence which they experienced during World War II. The earliest ones were diaries written by individual victims and questionnaires collected by Jewish organizations. Some of them were written shortly after or even during violent events such as the pogroms in the summer of 1941, the liquidations of the ghettoes, or the mass killings in the woods. Contrary to the Ukrainians, Jews perceived the anti-Jewish violence as an essential aspect of the war and described it at length. Some of the accounts also provided relatively detailed information about the perpetrators.

The earliest accounts of the anti-Jewish mass violence in Volhynia and eastern Galicia were collected in late 1941 and early 1942 by the staff of the clandestine Jewish archives of the Warsaw ghetto headed by the historian Emanuel Ringelblum. These reports are composed of three parts: the Soviet occupation of western Ukraine, the German invasion, and the return to Warsaw. Some of them describe the pogroms and contain information about their perpetrators. Four main groups of perpetrators in these accounts are the Germans, Ukrainian nationalists, Ukrainian militia, and the local population, mainly Ukrainians. Some other details related to mass violence which appear in these accounts describe the joy of Ukrainians and Poles about the coming of the Germans to Ukraine in the summer of 1941, the presence of Ukrainian flags and other national symbols in public spaces, the massacres committed by the NKVD on the political prisoners, and the propagandistic abuse of the corpses of the NKVD victims by the Nazis and the OUN-B to incite the pogrom in Lviv.[21]

Diaries written during the war by Jews in Volhynia and eastern Galicia are more personal than the reports collected by the staff of the Ringelblum archives, but they hold similar information about the anti-Jewish violence and their perpetrators. Between 1942 and 1944, Edmund Kessler, a Jewish attorney from Lviv, kept a diary in which he described the Lviv pogrom and the ensuing events, such the force moving to the ghetto. Kessler wrote about the perpetrators of the Lviv pogrom: "The orchestrators here were the Germans. It is they who decided when to begin the pogrom, when to stop it, how long to torture the victims; whether until they lose consciousness or to slaughter them. They act capriciously toward their Ukrainian subordinates, even beating them when they are slow or overzealous in carrying out orders."[22]

Another diarist, Samuel Golfard, entered his observations from January 25, 1943 through April 14, 1943 while living in the ghetto in Peremyshliany, a town close to Lviv. He recalled how during the pogroms in the summer of 1941 the local perpetrators burned the synagogue and threw the son of the Rebbe of Bełż into the flames.[23] On March 6, 1943 Goldfard wrote in his diary: "The participation of Ukrainians in the murder of hundreds of thousands of Jews is beyond any dispute. To this day they carry out, often ruthlessly, the beastly Hitlerian orders. During the German invasion they themselves initiated terrible massacres compared to which even the cruelty of the Germans pales. It is a fact that the Germans took pictures of Jews being hurled into the flames of burning houses. In Peremyshliany the perpetrators of this were the Ukrainians. Had they been allowed, they would even today take apart the entire ghetto in their passion for plunder."[24] We did not find any entries in his diary about the killings of the Jews by the OUN and UPA, because Golfard did not know about the fate of the Jews who had escaped from the ghetto or lived outside of the labor camp. He knew only two types of Ukrainian Holocaust perpetrators: the policemen and the peasants. The first group killed Jews, assisting the Germans by mass executions or tracking down Jews hiding in the villages, and the latter denounced the Jews, refused to help them, and robbed them.[25]

Already before the end of World War II, in August 1944, Jewish survivors founded the Central Jewish Historical Commission (*Centralna Żydowska Komisja Historyczna*, CŻKH) in Lublin, which collected almost eight thousand reports from Holocaust survivors, including a number of survivors from Volhynia and eastern Galicia.[26] The members of the CŻKH used questionnaires to collect testimonies. One important point was to collect information about the anti-Jewish violence and the perpetrators.[27] Thus, in the testimonies of the survivors from western Ukraine we find much information about the eastern Galician and Volhynian perpetrators. In terms of the pogroms in the summer of 1941, alongside the Germans, the survivors interviewed by the CŻKH archivists identified the Ukrainian militiamen with yellow-and-blue armlets, and the crowd, which was composed of Ukrainians and to a lesser extent, Poles.[28] The survivors did not know that the militia was established by the OUN-B but they perceived OUN propaganda and noticed various forms of OUN activities during the pogroms.[29] These survivors, who had hidden in the woods and in the countryside, described at length how the Germans, OUN activists, UPA partisans, Ukrainian police and peasants hunted and killed Jews who hid in the woods alone, in small groups or in camps of different sizes. Some of them dug out bunkers and hoped to survive in them. Discovering a bunker or raiding a larger camp meant that the perpetrators could kill more than a hundred people at once.[30]

Similar descriptions of events as in the testimonies can be found in post-war memoirs written by survivors from eastern Galicia and Volhynia. Kurt Lewin, the son of the Lviv rabbi Jechieskiel Lewin, survived the war with the help of Andrei Sheptyts'kyi, the Metropolitan of the Ukrainian Greek Catholic Church. Lewin wrote his memoirs in 1945–1946 in Italy and Israel. He was a good observer and provided a very detailed and partially analytical description of the Lviv pogrom. During this event of mass violence, he was one of the Jews forced to carry out the decomposing bodies of the NKVD victims from the basement of the Brygidki prison. He identified the perpetrators as German soldiers, Ukrainian militiamen, and local civilians, mainly Ukrainians. All of them mistreated and killed the Jews in various ways.[31]

Eliyahu Yones survived the war in Lviv and in the slave labor camp Kurowice in eastern Galicia. He wrote his memoirs in 1954. During the Lviv pogrom Yones, like Lewin, was forced to work in the yard of the Brygidki prison. There he witnessed similar scenes as Lewin, but he managed to escape after a while.[32] In addition to the pogrom perpetrators, Yones described the extremely brutal behavior of the Ukrainian policemen in the Lviv ghetto, and the perpetrators in the slave labor camp Kurowice, where he was held until August 1943. The staff of this camp consisted of Germans and Ukrainians. The Germans held the leading positions in the camp and Ukrainian policemen worked there as guards and were sometimes mistreated and beaten by their German superiors. Both Germans and Ukrainians mistreated, beat, and killed Jews—the inmates of this slave labor camp—in various ways.[33]

The last massive collection of survivor accounts took place in the 1990s. Between 1994 and 1999, the Institute of Visual History and Education Shoah Foundation conducted and videotaped several thousand interviews with Holocaust survivors in dozens of countries. Among them were survivors from Volhynia and eastern Galicia. These survivors described the same and similar events of mass violence, and named similar types of perpetrators as survivors who had been interviewed by the CŻKH forty to fifty years earlier. Talking about the pogroms in 1941 the interviewees recalled that the perpetrators had been the Germans, Ukrainian militiamen with yellow-and-blue armbands, the crowd composed of Poles and Ukrainians, and remembered the victims to have been beaten, mistreated, and murdered almost exactly like the survivors who had been interviewed by the CŻKH and the survivors who had described their experiences of these events in their post-war memoirs.[34] The descriptions of the attempts to survive in the woods also very much resemble the accounts left by the survivors who had been interviewed by the CŻKH. Jews interviewed by the Shoah Foundation mentioned as perpetrators the Germans, Ukrainian policemen, OUN and UPA nationalists and peasants, and described horrifying murder scenes and acts of tracking them down similar to the Jews who had testified for the CŻKH.[35]

Jewish Historiography: Autobiographical Experience and Scholarship

Jewish historians began to research the Shoah while it was still happening, and published their first findings shortly after. They combined their academic training as historians with their own and very direct experiences of the subject, and they used observations of other survivors and other kinds of sources, including the perpetrator documents. The first short academic study of the Holocaust in western Ukraine was published in 1945 by Philip Friedman, a professional historian and the head of the CŻKH. Friedman was borne in 1901 in Lviv. He studied history and defended his PhD at the University of Vienna under the supervision of Salo Baron. From 1925 to 1939 he worked as a teacher at a high school in Lviv and Łódź. Friedmann's publication was a short brochure-like book of 36 pages titled "The destruction of the Lviv Jews." Friedman pointed out that the study was based on the author's own observations and observations of other survivors, and clarified that he was able to review only a few German administrative documents and documents of the Jewish Council in the Lviv ghetto because this material was partially destroyed and partially not accessible. The anti-Jewish violence of the Ukrainian nationalists did not play any major role in his narrative, but he mentioned it in several places. Describing the pogrom, Friedman mentioned as perpetrators the Germans, Ukrainian militiamen, Ukrainian nationalists, and local Poles and Ukrainians. He did not know about the connection between the Ukrainian militia and the Germans and mistook the date of arrival of the German and Ukrainian military troops to Lviv, but his description of the mass violence during the pogrom, although brief, corresponds with the current state of knowledge about this event. Also his descriptions and analyses of various other forms of mass violence after the pogrom and the perpetrators correspond with our current knowledge about the Holocaust in Lviv.[36]

Friedman described in more detail the conduct of the Ukrainian nationalists during the Holocaust and the involvement of other segments of Ukrainian society in the genocide against the Jews, in an article about Jewish-Ukrainian relationships during World War II, which was published in 1958 in Yiddish, and a year later in German.[37] Although he did not have any access to Soviet archives and could not know anything about some aspects of the history of the OUN and UPA, his analysis was very precise. He portrayed several types of Ukrainian perpetrators, and explained how Ukrainians murdered the Jews, either in collaboration with the Germans, for example as policemen, or without any direct help from the Germans, for example as partisans in the UPA. He was able to conceptualize such adequate analyses because alongside the German documents, he also used the testimonies of the survivors and other accounts left by the victims. He also personally interviewed survivors to verify that some of the documents had been forged by the Ukrainian nationalists, such as Stella Krentsbakh's autobiography *I Am Alive Thanks to the UPA*, which was published by the veteran and former head of the OUN propaganda division Petro Mirchuk.[38]

Other survivors, who after 1945 worked as historians, were Aharon Weiss, Shmuel Spector, and Eliyahu Yones. Their perspective resembled Friedman's approach to history. Not one of them questioned the leading role of the Nazis in the annihilation of the Ukrainian Jews, and no one analyzed the past due to anti-Ukrainian resentment, although some of them, like Yones, were mistreated, tortured, and almost killed by the Ukrainian nationalists. All of them mentioned the Ukrainian rescuers in their publications. They were critical of the characterizations of the OUN and UPA as national heroes by the Ukrainian diaspora, and analyzed how the Ukrainian nationalists killed Jews and other civilians during World War II.[39]

John Armstrong: Anticommunism, Cold War, and Bomb Shelter

Although Friedman's publications must have been indispensable to historians who studied World War II in Ukraine, in 1955 John Armstrong published a monograph about Ukrainian nationalism during World War II, without taking notice of Friedman's scholarship or any other publication by a Holocaust survivor.[40] Despite this essential shortcoming, Armstrong's monograph became the standard monograph on the OUN, UPA, and Ukrainian nationalism in general during World War II. As such it impacted on many other historians who relied on it and who quoted it at length, until recently. Armstrong was born in 1922 in St. Augustine, Florida. He began to study at the University of Chicago in 1942, but was conscripted and served at the Belgian front in 1944–45. After the war, he finished his studies and wrote his PhD on Ukrainian nationalism. In his later career he concentrated on the Soviet Union but irregularly published also on the OUN.[41] He was an anticommunist thinker who opposed the Soviet Union as a scholar. After his death in 2010 the Memorial Committee of the University of Wisconsin-Madison published a resolution in which we read that he was a "fierce opponent of Soviet regimes" who were "at odds with the liberal students and campus protests of the 1960s and 1970s," who erected a "bomb shelter … in his home" which he "kept fully stocked and proudly displayed to their frequent dinner guests" and who taught his three daughters "how to shoot."[42]

Although Armstrong's study of Ukrainian nationalism during World War II and Freidman's study of the Holocaust in Lviv were thematically closely related, they could not have been more different. Armstrong investigated the OUN in depth and provided an interesting, almost comprehensive and critical analysis of the ideology of this movement, which he understood as "integral nationalism." However, we find almost no information about OUN's and UPA's involvement in the genocide of the Jews and other atrocities committed by this movement during the war, such as the ethnic cleansing of the Poles in Volhynia in 1943 and in eastern Galicia in 1944. While investigating the subject Armstrong did not take any interest in the experiences recounted by the Jewish survivors. He did not work with the testimonies collected by the CŻKH, which were stored in the Jewish Historical Institute in Warsaw and must have been accessible to him. Instead he used and relied on German archival documents, Ukrainian nationalist publications, and also on interviews with the veterans of the OUN and UPA, of whom he met several in person. As a result he depicted the OUN as a radical nationalist movement and presented some aspects of its collaboration with the Nazis, but he left out the Holocaust and other forms of violence. In consequence, a reader of his book gets the impression that the OUN was not involved in the annihilation of Jews in eastern Galicia and Volhynia and did not conduct any other atrocities against civilians. The Jews are mentioned in his monograph eleven times. Two of them are very brief and casual references to their annihilation and one is to the Jewish doctors in the UPA. The pogroms in the summer of 1941 are not mentioned at all, although Armstrong explained and described the proclamation of the state on June 30, 1941 in Lviv, which happened at the same time and in the same place as the Lviv pogrom. Similarly, he did not write anything about the killing of the Jews by the UPA.[43] Armstrong did not alter his views on the role of the Ukrainian nationalists in the Holocaust during his academic career.[44]

Ukrainian Nationalist Historiography: Heroes and Freedom Fighters

Armstrong's apologetic narrative was based on publications of Ukrainian diaspora historians who had served in the OUN or UPA, before they became scholars. These historians derived their narrative directly from OUN and UPA propaganda, which some of them invented and distributed before they became historians. Immediately after the war, Ukrainian nationalists in exile published several short books and booklets about the war in western Ukraine, and also a number of brief memoirs in newspapers. One of such publications was authored by Mykola Lebed', who from the fall of 1941 until May 1943 had been the acting leader of the OUN-B. Lebed's book appeared in 1946 in Rome and was titled *UPA: Ukrainian Insurgent Army: Its Genesis, Rise and Deeds in the Struggle of the Ukrainian Nation for an Independent United State.* The former OUN-B leader portrayed the UPA as an army which bravely fought against Nazi Germany and the Soviet Union for an independent Ukrainian state. He did not mention in his book the vehement and racialist nationalism and antisemitism of the OUN, and characterized the ideology of the UPA as patriotism or love for its own country. Similarly, he did not mention the pogroms in 1941, the involvement of the OUN in mass violence against Jews as policemen, UPA's mass killings of the Poles and the killings of Jews by the Ukrainian police, UPA and local population. Describing Jewish doctors who stayed or were forced to stay with the Ukrainian insurgents, he stated that the UPA rescued them, although he knew that some of them were killed by the Security Service (SB, *Sluzhba Bezpeky*) of the OUN-B, OUN-B activists, and UPA partisans. It is also possible that he personally issued orders to kill them, before he left Ukraine. To substantiate the argument that the OUN-B and UPA did not collaborate with the Nazis, Lebed' described in detail every better-known Ukrainian nationalist who had been killed by the Germans, and published their photographs.[45]

Another intriguing early publication about World War II in Ukraine appeared in 1946 in Buenos Aires. Its author, Volodymyr Makar, used the pseudonym Marko Vira and called his book *Seven Years of Liberating Struggle*. Similar to Lebed', Makar forgot to describe the various kinds of mass violence practiced by the Ukrainian nationalists, the racist, antisemitic and other radical right elements of their ideology, and their collaboration with Nazi Germany. He victimized the Ukrainians even more than Lebed'. Before describing World War II, Makar strongly exaggerated the number of the Ukrainian victims of the Soviet policies while arguing that 20 million Ukrainians were starved to death and murdered by the Soviet regime. Describing the events after June 22, 1941 and the proclamation of the state on June 30, he did not mention the collaboration with Nazi Germany, but wrote about following the principle of independence. In describing the events of June 30, 1941, he noted how the OUN-B established a militia and attempted to establish a state but did not write anything about the Lviv pogrom or the role played by the OUN-B militia in this anti-Jewish act of violence.[46]

Next to heroism and the fight for independence, Makar made suffering a crucial component of his narrative. In his account, the Ukrainians are portrayed as the sole and principal victims of the Nazi terror in Ukraine. Every element of their suffering is exaggerated. Jews, on the other hand, are not mentioned at all. As a result, the reader gets the impression that the Ukrainians were the main victims of the Nazis in occupied Ukraine. Makar described, for example, how the Soviet POWs suffered in Ukraine because there were, according to him, many Ukrainians among them. Similarly, he explained in detail how the living conditions deteriorated during the German occupation and how the slave labor affected the life of the Ukrainians. The fate of any other group was not mentioned at all. Even describing the mass executions by the Einsatzgruppen, he maintained that the sole victims were Ukrainians.[47] The word "Jew" indeed did not appear even once in the entire publication.[48]

An element which appears in many Ukrainian nationalist publications about World War II is the motif of Ukrainian nationalist prisoners in Nazi concentration camps. Similar to the Ukrainian nationalists killed by the Germans, this fact has been used to argue that the Ukrainian nationalists opposed the Nazis, did not collaborate with them, were not fascist but fought for national independence and a free democratic state. Although Ukrainian nationalists were in the camps as special and ordinary political prisoners and although about 80 percent of them survived the camps due to this special treatment, they were presented as people who shared the fate of the Jews. These claims appeared in both the memoirs of the former Ukrainian political prisoners of the German concentration camps and in various historic books and articles about World War II. The fact that Bandera's two brothers Vasyl and Oleksandr died or were killed in Auschwitz was absolutely central for the nationalist narrative because it fortified the idea of a shared fate with the Jews. The question, if any of the Ukrainian nationalist prisoners had participated in the pogroms in the summer of 1941 was on the other hand not discussed in these publications.[49]

After the collapse of the Soviet Union, the narrative of the Ukrainian diaspora historians was adapted in Ukraine. Historians in independent Ukraine understood the OUN and UPA, similarly to the diaspora historians, as heroes and freedom fighters, and left out the OUN's and UPA's killings of the Poles and involvement in the Shoah, or relativized the role of antisemitism in the ideology of Ukrainian nationalism. There have been two groups of historians in post-communist Ukraine who have engaged with the history of the OUN and UPA. The first group are known in the academic community as "nationalists," and are associated with the person of Volodymyr Viatrovych, who has continued the apologetic narrative first composed by Lebed', Vira, and Mirchuk. With the financial support of the Ukrainian diaspora, they opened institutes in Ukraine which denied the involvement of the Ukrainian nationalists in the Holocaust.[50] The second group, known as "liberal" historians, is associated with Yaroslav Hrytsak, and challenges to some extent the nationalist narrative of Viatrovych. Nevertheless, due to the political situation in Ukraine, their research methods and political views, they do not rethink the history of nationalism or attempt to come to terms with the Holocaust.[51] Paradigmatic are the publications by Oleksandr Zaitsev, who studied the ideology of the OUN in depth and provided a complex analysis of it, but did not set it in relation to the violence practiced by the Ukrainian nationalists and their involvement in the Shoah.[52]

Two scholars of Ukrainian origins, who have challenged the nationalist narrative and rethought the history of the OUN and UPA during the Holocaust, are John-Paul Himka and Marco Carynnyk. Similar to the Ukrainian "liberal" and "nationalist" historians, Himka and Carynnyk relativized the role of antisemitism, racism and mass violence in the history of Ukrainian nationalism in the 1980s and early 1990s and apologized for the crimes committed by the Ukrainian nationalists. Perhaps the most important reason for not studying and instrumentalizing the history of the OUN and UPA on the side of Carynnyk and Himka, was their opposition to the Soviet Union and engagement in the intellectual fight for a Ukrainian state. The Canadian scholar David Marples also distorted the history of the Ukrainian nationalists and their involvement in the genocide of the Jews, portraying the UPA as a multicultural army. However, about a decade after the collapse of the Soviet Union, Carynnyk, Himka and Marples became critical of the apologetic and antisemitic narrative, rethought their positive attitude to Ukrainian nationalism, and published important studies on the pogroms in 1941, the role of antisemitism in the ideology of the OUN and UPA, and post-Soviet historiography.[53] In 2021 Himka published a monograph about the Ukrainian nationalists and the Holocaust.[54]

The Soviet Historiography: Instrumentalization of Terror and Sovietization of Victims

The Soviet historiography took very early notice of the mass violence conducted by the Ukrainian nationalists. However, the propagandist and ideological nature of Soviet historiography distorted the mass violence of the OUN and UPA. It was also antisemitic because it attacked "Talmudists," "rootless cosmopolitans," and other enemies of the Soviet Union who were Jewish. The readers of Soviet pamphlets were misinformed. They did not know what the Ukrainian nationalists fought for, nor did they learn of who they actually attacked and killed. This way of dealing with World War II puzzled and alarmed Western historians. Although the Soviet historiography described the violence of the Ukrainian nationalists at length and in very symbolic language, Soviet historians usually claimed that the victims of the Ukrainian nationalists were Soviet citizens. The nationality of the victims or the ethnic and political motivations of the killers were mentioned only rarely. The goal of the Sovietization of the victims was to strengthen Soviet nationalism and the Soviet identity.[55]

An important practical aim of the Soviet historiography was to discredit the Ukrainian nationalists and the Ukrainian diaspora. The OUN and UPA kept resisting the Soviet authorities until the late 1940s. From the summer of 1944 until the end of 1946, Soviet scholars and writers discredited the Ukrainian nationalists as "German-Ukrainian Nationalists," implying that the Ukrainian nationalists were an integral part of the German Reich, and that they did not stop targeting "peaceful citizens" even after the defeat of Nazi Germany. From early 1947, they were called the "bourgeois nationalists." This was related to the fact that parts of the OUN left Ukraine with the Nazis and remained in the Western Block, in which they lived the "capitalist" way of life and collaborated with the secret services of the Western states.[56]

The mass violence of the OUN and UPA and their collaboration with the Nazis played an important role in the Soviet historiography until the very end of the Soviet empire. However, the censorship determined how to present the subject. The fate or the suffering of the Jews was not a motif of the Soviet narrative about World War II or the Great Patriotic War. Soviet citizens usually did not know why the Jews were murdered during the war or if the Ukrainian nationalists had targeted and murdered them. Although Soviet historians had access to the archives and studied the documents concerning the history of the OUN and UPA, they wrote the history according to the rules of Soviet censorship, disregarding scholarly standards and archival documentations.[57]

Polish Historians and the OUN and UPA

Polish scholars and intellectuals conceptualized two different ways of dealing with the mass violence of the OUN and UPA. The first group, associated with Jerzy Giedroyc, viewed the OUN and UPA as a liberation movement and praised them for their resistance against the Soviet Union. This approach helped this group to reconcile with the Ukrainians. At the same time, it indicated that the exploration of OUN and UPA violence or their involvement in the Holocaust harmed the Polish-Ukrainian relationship and was political.[58] The second group researched the mass violence of the Ukrainian nationalists and viewed it as a central aspect of the history of the OUN and UPA, although it reduced the violence only to the anti-Polish terror. Both groups were not homogenous. Interestingly, the first group included many "liberal" historians and intellectuals who understood Ukraine as a "small sister country." They wanted to protect Ukraine from Russia, while not criticizing it for the murder of Jews and Poles. The second group was composed of two factions. The first were survivors of the OUN and UPA terror (*kresowiacy*) who were resettled to Poland after the war and who propagated nationalist, revisionist, and martyrological visions of the past. The second were professional, critical historians, such as Ryszard Torzecki and Grzegorz Motyka, who did not sympathize with the Ukrainian nationalists.[59]

Essential for the two ways of dealing with the mass violence of the Ukrainian nationalists in Poland was the censorship in communist Poland and the taboo of the subject by 1990. Historians of the *kresowiacy* community (Poles resettled from Ukraine) such as Edward Prus presented the subject in a nationalist and partisan manner. They exaggerated the number of the Polish victims of the Ukrainian nationalist violence, while ignoring the antisemitism in the OUN and UPA and their murder of the Jews. They also omitted the fact that Ukrainians were killed by the Poles in acts of reprisal and in other circumstances.[60] More valuable than this partisan historiography was the collecting of testimonies among the Polish survivors of the OUN and UPA violence. Two of the most prolific researchers who collected testimonies and published them were Władysław Siemaszko and Ewa Siemaszko. Their work enabled historians such as Motyka to analyze the mass violence of the OUN and UPA against the Poles, and to a lesser extent against the Jews.[61]

The ironic aspect of the Polish historiographical discourse about the violence of the Ukrainian nationalists during World War II was the fact that Polish nationalist and right-wing historians such as Lucyna Kulińska investigated the violence of the OUN and UPA at length, while the Polish liberal historians and intellectuals from the Giedroyc camp avoided researching and publishing on this subject, because they believed it would jeopardize the reconciliation process. One of the most prolific historians of the subject, who after World War II lived in Poland and Canada, was Wiktor Poliszczuk. He collected documents and published books in Polish and Ukrainian. In contrast to historians and journalists associated with the liberal papers *Gazeta Wyborcza* and *Krytyka Polityczna*, historians such as Poliszczuk and Kulińska published at length about the violence of the Ukrainian nationalists, even if the anti-Jewish violence was for them less important than the anti-Polish one.[62]

German Historians: Between *Nationalsozialismusforschung* and *Osteuropaforschung*

Although several German historians researched the Holocaust in Galicia, only a few analyzed the mass violence of the Ukrainian nationalists. An important reason for not investigating the conduct of the Ukrainian nationalists during the war and the Holocaust was the concentration on the German occupation of Ukraine and the German perpetrators, and also the ignoring of some types of documents. In contrast to the Jewish historians and the survivors, German historians believed that survivor testimonies should not be used to reconstruct history because they were not reliable. German historians viewed the documents left by the victims as "mystic," as opposed to the "reliable" and "factual" German documents. They assumed that the documents left by the victims were steeped in trauma, affected by anti-German resentment, and in general could not be used to reconstruct aspects of the past.[63] German historians also assumed that they were obliged to research the crimes committed by the National Socialists in the first place in order not to relativize the German responsibility for the Holocaust. The combination of these two factors, as well as the use of Armstrong's publications as a standard monograph on the subject of Ukrainian nationalism led to a marginalization of the agency of the Ukrainian nationalists and their role in the extermination of civilians in Western Ukraine.[64]

In 1993, the leading German expert of Ukrainian history, Frank Golczewski, published a volume with fourteen articles covering all epochs of Ukrainian history. The article about Ukraine during World War II was written by him. Golczewski, a careful and critical historian, opened with the disclaimer: "Until today huge parts of the Ukrainian context of the war have not been solidly analyzed in historiographical publications."[65] His article paid much attention to the OUN and UPA. He mentioned that antisemitism was widespread among Ukrainian nationalists and that the "Germans may have found for their annihilation of the Jews willing executioners" among them. He mentioned the OUN-B task forces, the militia, the Nachtigall battalion, the role which the corpses of the political prisoners left by the Soviets played in the pogroms, the mass shootings of the Jews by Einsatzgruppe C, the SD and the SS, and several other important aspects of the events in the first days after the German attack of the Soviet Union. Given the sources, Golczewski used, his analyses are astonishingly adequate, although we do not find any specific information about the involvement of the Ukrainian nationalists and ordinary Ukrainians in the mass violence against the Jews.[66] Similarly, we do not find any information about the murdering of Jews by the UPA or about the ethnic cleansing of the Poles in Volhynian and eastern Galicia.

The latter is even characterized by Golczewski as a "Polish-Ukrainian-Communist civil war" during which the Ukrainian nationalists fought "the Soviet partisans and the Polish colonists."[67] A look at the cited sources and publications provides an explanation of the nature of this narrative. Golczewski relied on and cited Armstrong and Mirchuk but he cited neither Friedman, nor any other Jewish historian who published on this subject, such as Aharon Weiss or Shmuel Spector or those who had studied the accounts of the Holocaust survivors. The only Jewish source quoted in this article is David Kahane's diary.[68]

Three years after Golczewski, two other German historians, Dieter Pohl and Thomas Sandkühler, published monographs about the Holocaust in eastern Galicia. Both provided an excellent analysis of the German role in the genocide of the Jews and Sandkühler also of the rescue of the Jews by Berthold Beitz, but both analyzed the role of the Ukrainian nationalists and the local population only marginally. Ukrainian perpetrators appear in these monographs mainly as German collaborators, in particular Ukrainian policemen. The murders committed by Ukrainians who did not collaborate with the Nazis are marginalized in both monographs. In consequence, the readers are not sufficiently informed about the fate of Jews, Poles, and Ukrainians killed by the OUN and UPA and about the different forms in which the Ukrainian nationalists were involved in the Holocaust. The concentration on the German actors substantially marginalized the agency of the non-German perpetrators and deprived the Holocaust of its complexity.[69] A similar description of events can be found in Frank Grelka's monograph, which was published in 2006. Yet, we do not find this Germano-centric and simplistic narrative in Franziska Bruder's monograph on the OUN, published in 2007.[70] Unlike Golczewski (in 1993), Pohl, Sandkühler and Grelka, Bruder did not exclude or marginalize the importance of the testimonies and other accounts left by the survivors from Volynia and eastern Galicia, did not assume that the German documents provided the most valuable sort of information, and did not limit their analysis to the role of the OUN and UPA in the German occupation of Ukraine.[71]

Bruder provided both a critical analysis of the ideology of Ukrainian nationalism and explained many facets of their terror against Jews, Poles, Ukrainians, and other ethnic groups. She achieved it due to two reasons. First, unlike Armstrong, she critically analyzed all documents of the Ukrainian nationalists, without being misled by the whitewashed accounts of the OUN and UPA veterans. Second, unlike Armstrong, Golczewski (in 1993), Pohl, Sandkühler, and Grelka, she explored at length the testimonies left by the survivors and regarded them as documents equally important to the documents left by the Germans and Ukrainians. Although she did not explore in depth the ethnic cleansing of the UPA against the Polish civilians in 1943–1944, the investigation of the survivor testimonies allowed her to achieve a more comprehensive and adequate study of the different forms of mass violence in Volhynia and eastern Galicia than the former publications.[72]

In the last few years, a number of papers about Ukrainian nationalism and the Holocaust in eastern Galicia and Volhynia have appeared, including an article by Frank Golczewski.[73] The authors of these publications, Omer Bartov, John-Paul Himka, Kai Struve, Grzegorz Rossoliński-Liebe, Per Anders Rudling, and many others, analyzed the victims' and survivors' accounts, did not marginalize the role which Ukrainian nationalists and ordinary Ukrainians played during the genocide of the Jews, investigated how fascism and racism impacted on the Ukrainian nationalism, and how the UPA conducted an ethnic cleansing against the Poles in 1943–1944. Finally, some of them also analyzed the attempts to deny the participation of the Ukrainian nationalists in the Holocaust and other forms of mass violence.[74]

Conclusion

Historians have viewed and depicted the attitude of the Ukrainian nationalists to the Jews during the Holocaust very differently. While Jewish historians, among them Holocaust survivors, viewed the killing of the Jews by the Ukrainian nationalists as an integral aspect of the Holocaust in western Ukraine, other groups understood the subject differently. The most vehement form of denial appeared in the early Ukrainian historiography. Some of the early Ukrainian historians or authors of historical publications about the OUN and UPA during World War II were prominent OUN members such as Lebed' or had worked for the propaganda apparatus of the organization, like Mirchuk. While some of them denied the involvement of the OUN in the Holocaust, others forged documents and published memoirs of fictive Jews rescued by the Ukrainian nationalists. This narrative was basically adapted by John Armstrong, a professional historian and political scientist who published the first standard monograph about the Ukrainian nationalists during World War II.

Although Armstrong did not eulogize the Ukrainian nationalists like Ukrainian diaspora historians and the OUN and UPA veterans did, he did not pay attention to the genocide of the Jews and other forms of mass violence conducted by the Ukrainian nationalists. He did not read Friedman's publications and did not use the survivor testimonies or other documents of the victims of the Ukrainian nationalists in his analysis. Researching the subject, he relied on German archival documents and on the testimonies of OUN and UPA veterans. His book pushed further research on Ukrainian nationalism and the Shoah in a particular direction.

An important reason not to research the violence of the Ukrainian nationalists before 1990 was the Soviet propaganda and the counter-propaganda of the Ukrainian diaspora. Both politicized the subject at length. Although the Soviet historiography paid a good deal of attention to the Ukrainian nationalists and their violence, it depicted the victims as Soviet citizens, and did not explain why the OUN and UPA used violence and who they targeted. The opposing narrative of the Ukrainian diaspora historians understood the OUN and UPA as an anti-Soviet liberation movement and followed Armstrong in terms of violence and involvement in the Holocaust. Although Polish historians were critical of Armstrong's narrative, they did not investigate the role of Ukrainian nationalists in the Holocaust, because they concentrated almost entirely on the violence against the Poles. A group of "liberal" Polish historians even declared the investigation of the mass violence of the OUN and UPA as illegitimate, because it harmed the reconciliation efforts between Poles and Ukrainians.

Although German historians paid much attention to the genocide of the Jews, they concentrated almost entirely on the German actors and the Nazi role in the Holocaust. Like Armstrong, they did not work with survivor accounts. Although they thoroughly examined the German occupation of western Ukraine and carefully analyzed the role of the Germans in the destruction of the Jews, they did not perceive the OUN and UPA as relevant actors and perpetrators. The dismissal of the accounts left by victims and survivors and also of the research done by Jewish historians, and an almost exclusive concentration on the German occupiers, did not allow them to write a comprehensive or transnational history of the Holocaust in western Ukraine.

Due to methodological, political, biographical, and ethical issues, many historians have until recently ignored the involvement of the Ukrainian nationalists in the Holocaust in western Ukraine. The only group of historians who did not omit or marginalize this subject from the very beginning were Jewish historians, such as Philip Friedmann, Eliyahu Yones, Shmuel Spector, and Aharon Weiss. Non-Jewish historians have changed their methods and have only recently begun to use survivor testimonies to research violence in western Ukraine. One of the first historians who used these types of documents to investigate eastern Galicia was Franziska Bruder. She published her monograph in 2007, and many others followed. Their publications can help Ukrainians come to terms with the Shoah and to write "integrated histories" of the Holocaust in Ukraine.

Endnotes

1 "Proekt Zakony pro pravovyi status ta vshanuvannua pam'iaty bortsiv za nezalezhnist' Ukrainy u XX stolittii," *Verkhovna rada Ukraini*, http://w1.c1.rada.gov.ua/pls/zweb2/webproc4_1?pf3511=54689 (accessed November 6, 2020); Law 2558 of April 6, 2015, "Proekt Zakonu pro zasudzhennia komunistychnoho ta national-sotsialistychnoho (natsysts'koho) totalitarnykh rezhymiv v Ukraini ta zaboronu propahandy ikh symvoliky," *Verkhovna rada Ukrainy: ofitsiinyi veb-portal*, April 6, 2015, http://w1.c1.rada.gov.ua/pls/zweb2/webproc4_1?pf3511=54670 (accessed November 6, 2020).

2 Christoph Mick, *Kriegserfahrungen in einer multiethnischen Stadt: Lemberg 1914–1947* (Wiesbaden, 2010), p. 10.

3 Frank Golczewski, *Deutsche und Ukrainer 1914–1939* (Paderborn, 2010), pp. 240, 264, 270–71, 414–21; Rudolf Mark, "Die gescheiterten Staatsversuche," in Frank Golczewski (ed.), *Geschichte der Ukraine* (Göttingen, 1993), pp. 177–179.

4 Jerzy Tomaszewski, *Ojczyzna nie tylko Polaków. Mniejszości narodowe w Polsce w latach 1918–1939* (Warsaw, 1985), pp.194–198; Joanna Michlic, *Poland's Threatening Other: The Image of the Jew from 1880 to the Present* (Lincoln, 2006), pp. 69–108.

5 Franziska Bruder, *"Den ukrainischen Staat erkämpfen oder sterben!" Die Organisation Ukrainischer Nationalisten (OUN) 1929–1948* (Berlin, 2007), pp. 32–51; Grzegorz Rossoliński-Liebe, "The 'Ukrainian National Revolution' of Summer 1941," *Kritika: Explorations in Russian and Eurasian History* 12(1) (2011), pp. 85–89; Alexander Prusin, "Revolution and Ethnic Cleansing in Western Ukraine: The OUN-UPA Assault against Polish Settlements in Volhynia and Eastern Galicia, 1943–1944," in Steven Béla Várdy and T. Hunt Tooley (eds.), *Ethnic Cleansing in Twentieth-Century Europe* (New York, 2003), pp. 518–520; Per Anders Rudling, "Eugenics and Racial Anthropology in the Ukrainian Radical Nationalist Tradition," *Science in Context* 32(1) (2019), pp. 67-91; Grzegorz Rossolński-Liebe, "Racism and Modern Antisemitism in Habsburg and Russian Ukraine: A Short Overview," in Raul Cârstocea and Éva Kovács (eds.), *Modern Antisemitisms in the Peripheries: Europe and its Colonies, 1880-1945* (Vienna 2019), pp. 133–159; Grzegorz Rossoliński-Liebe, "The Fascist Kernel of Ukrainian Genocidal Nationalism", *The Carl Beck Papers in Russian & East European Studies,* Number 2402, (Pittsburgh, 2015).

6 Rossoliński-Liebe, "The Ukrainian National Revolution," pp. 90–95.

7 Ibid., pp. 95–97; Bruder, *"Den ukrainischen Staat erkämpfen,"* pp. 140–145.

8 Grzegorz Motyka, *Ukraińska partyzantka 1942–1960. Działalność Organizacji Ukraińskich Nacjonalistów i Ukraińskiej Powstańczej Armii* (Warsaw, 2006), pp. 229–237.

9 For Volhynia, see Shmuel Spector, *The Holocaust of Volhynian Jews, 1941–1944* (Jerusalem, 1990), p. 11; Jeffrey Burds, *Holocaust in Rovno: The Massacre at Sosenki Forest, November 1941* (New York, 2016). For eastern Galicia, see Dieter Pohl, *Nationalsozialistische Judenverfolgung in Ostgalizien 1941–1944. Organisation und Durchführung eines staatlichen Massenverbrechens* (Munich, 1997), pp. 43–44, 385.

10　Alexander Kruglov, "Jewish Losses in Ukraine, 1941–1944," in Ray Brandon and Wendy Lower (eds.), *The Shoah in Ukraine: History, Testimony, Memorialization* (Bloomington, 2008), p. 278; Pohl, *Nationalsozialistische Judenverfolgung*, pp. 67–71; Spector, *The Holocaust of Volhynian Jews*, p. 79; Timothy Snyder, "The Life and Death of Western Volhynian Jewry, 1921–1945," in Brandon and Lower, *The Shoah in Ukraine*, p. 92.

11　Kruglov, "Jewish Losses in Ukraine," pp. 280–281; Spector, *The Holocaust of Volhynian Jews*, pp. 116–187; Snyder, "Life and Death of Western Volhynian Jewry," pp. 96–97.

12　Kruglov, "Jewish Losses in Ukraine," pp. 280–283; Pohl, *Nationalsozialistische Judenverfolgung*, pp. 139–262. For Volhynia, see Kruglov, "Jewish Losses in Ukraine," pp. 280–281; Spector, *The Holocaust of Volhynian Jews*, pp. 116–187; Snyder, "The Life and Death of Western Volhynian Jewry," pp. 96–97.

13　John-Paul Himka, "Former Ukrainian Policemen in the Ukrainian National Insurgency: Continuing the Holocaust outside the German Service," in *Lessons and Legacies XII: New Directions in the Holocaust Research and Education* (2017), pp. 141–163; Grzegorz Rossoliński-Liebe, "Ukraińska policja, nacjonalizm i zagłada Żydów w Galicji Wschodniej i na Wołyniu," *Zagłada Żydów. Studia i Materiały* 13 (2017), pp. 57–79.

14　Pohl, *Nationalsozialistische Judenverfolgung*, p. 385; Spector, *The Holocaust of Volhynian Jews*, p. 357.

15　On the killing of the Jews by the UPA, see Bruder, *Den ukrainischen Staat erkämpfen*, pp. 217–223; Omer Bartov, "Wartime Lies and Other Testimonies: Jewish-Christian Relations in Buczacz, 1939–1944," *East European Politics and* Societies, 26(3) (2011), pp. 491–498; Filip Friedman, "Ukrainian-Jewish Relations during the Nazi Occupation," in *Roads to Extinction* (New York, 1980), pp. 187–189; John-Paul Himka, "The Ukrainian Insurgent Army and the Holocaust," paper prepared for the forty-first national convention of the American Association for the Advancement of Slavic Studies, Boston, November 12-15, 2009. On desertion and the mass violence against Poles, see Motyka, *Ukraińska partyzantka, 1942–1960*, pp. 194, 298–400, 410–412, 523–525; Prusin, "Revolution and Ethnic Cleansing in Western Ukraine," pp. 523–35; Ewa Siemaszko and Władysław Siemaszko, *Ludobójstwo dokonane przez nacjonalistów ukraińskich na ludności polskiej Wołynia 1939–1945* (Warsaw, 2000).

16　Katrin Boekh, *Stalinismus in der Ukraine: Die Rekonstruktion des sowjetischen Systems nach dem Zweiten Weltkrieg* (Wiesbaden, 2007), p. 293; Howard Margolian, *Unauthorized Entry: The Truth about Nazi War Criminals in Canada, 1946–1956* (Toronto, 2000), pp. 131–132, 135, 146.

17　Motyka, *Ukraińska partyzantka*, pp. 536–537, 649. See also Boeckh, *Stalinismus*, pp. 366–367.

18　"Nakaz Ch. 2/43, Oblasnym, okruzhnym i povitovym providnykam do vykonannia," Central State Archives of the Supreme Bodies of Power and Government of Ukraine (Tsentral'nyi derzhavnyi arkhiv vyshchykh orhaniv vlady ta upravlinnia Ukrainy,

TsDAVOV) f. 3833, op. 1, spr. 43, 9. The translation is from Marco Carynnyk, "Foes of Our Rebirth: Ukrainian Nationalist Discussions about Jews, 1929–1947," *Nationalities Papers* 39(3) (2011), p. 345. See also Bruder, *"Den Ukrainischen Staat erkämpfen*, p. 222; Motyka, *Ukraińska partyzantka*, p. 290.

19 Motyka, *Ukraińska partyzantka*, pp. 295–296; Carynnyk, "Foes of our rebirth," pp. 344–345.

20 For an overview of nationalist newspapers and propaganda material, see Oleksander Stasiuk, *Vydavnycho-propahandyvna diial'nist' OUN* (Lviv, 2006). On the actual conflict and collaboration between the Ukrainian nationalists and the German army, see Motyka, *Ukraińska partyzantka*, pp. 187–237.

21 A collection of reports from the Ringelblum archives is reprinted in Andrzej Żbikowski (ed.), *Archiwum Ringelbluma. Relacje z Kresów*, Vol. 3. (Warsaw, 2000), pp. 516–923.

22 Renata Kessler (ed.), *The Wartime Diary of Edmund Kessler* (Boston, 2010), pp. 34–35.

23 Wendy Lower (ed.), *The Diary of Samuel Golfard and the Holocaust in Galicia* (Lanham, 2011), p. 53.

24 Ibid., p. 82.

25 Ibid., pp. 92–94.

26 On the CŻKH, see Natalia Aleksiun, "The Central Jewish Historical Commission in Poland, 1944–1947," in Jan Schwarz, Gabriel Finder, Natalia Aleksiun, and Antony Polonsky (eds.), *Making Holocaust Memory* (Oxford, 2008), pp. 74–97; Laura Jockusch, *Collect and Record!: Jewish Holocaust Documentation in Early Postwar Europe* (Oxford, 2012).

27 Laura Jockusch, "Historiography in Transit: Survivor Historians and the Writing of Holocaust History in the late 1940s," *Leo Baeck Institute Yearbook*, 58(1) (2013), p. 80.

28 On militiamen with yellow-and-blue armlets in the Lviv pogrom, see AŻIH, 301/4654, Henryk Szyper, 6; AŻIH, 301/1809, Janisław Korczyński, 1; AŻIH, 301/1864, Salomon Goldman, 1; AŻIH 229/22, Maurycy Allerhand, 1; AŻIH 301/3774, Salomon Hirschberg, 1; AŻIH, 301/1181, Lilith Stern, 2–3.

29 On the establishment of the militia by the OUN-B, see John-Paul Himka, "The Lviv Pogrom of 1941: The Germans, Ukrainian Nationalists, and the Carnival Crowd," *Canadian Slavonic Papers* 53(2-4) (2011), pp. 209–243, 220–221, 227–230; Rossoliński-Liebe, "The Ukrainian National Revolution," pp. 102–103.

30 On the discovery of the bunkers and the killing of their inhabitants by Ukrainian nationalists, see AŻIH, 301/1222, Izraela and Barbara Lissak, 6–7; AŻIH, 301/2193, Ignacy Goldwasser, 9–13; AŻIH, 301/808, Edmund Adler, 2; AŻIH, 301/1136, Lipa Stricker, 4; AŻIH, 301/3359, Edzia Szpeicher, 5; AŻIH, 301/6012, Leon Hejnysz, 2–4; AŻIH, 301/198, Leon Knebel, 5; AŻIH, 301/879, Kin Mojżesz, 2–4; Pohl, *Nationalsozialistische Judenverfolgung*, p. 377.

31 Kurt Lewin, *Przeżyłem. Saga Świętego Jura w roku 1946* (Warsaw, 2006), pp. 58–65.

32 Eliyahu Yones, *Die Straße nach Lemberg: Zwangsarbeit und Widerstand in Ostgalizien 1941–1944* (Frankfurt am Main, 1999), pp. 20–21.

33 Yones, *Die Straße nach Lemberg*, pp. 32–36, 60–61, 65, 71–72, 81–86.

34 Shoah Foundation, 29342 Wolf Lichter, 10–11; Shoah Foundation, 14797 Lusia Hornstein, 14–15; Shoah Foundation, 2991 Maria Gesiola, 10–13; Shoah Foundation, 51593 Tamara Branistky, 48–57; Shoah Foundation, 27779 Leszek Allerhand, 30–43; Shoah Foundation, 48148 Leopold Iwanier, 45–47; Shoah Foundation, 21303 Czeslawa Budynska, 30–43; Shoah Foundation, 12729 Edward Spicer, 17–19; Shoah Foundation, 9851 Rosa Moskowitz, 18–20; Shoah Foundation, 36104 Simon Wiesenthal, 141.

35 See for example Shoah Foundation, 1979 Milton Turk, 66–68; Shoah Foundation, 15542 Murray Bergman, 106–09; Shoah Foundation, 20586 Jack Glotzer, 13–15; Shoah Foundation, 26557 Aron Baboukh, 116–26; Shoah Foundation, 18287 Benno Noskovich, 100–02; Shoah Foundation, 11289 Leizer Roll, 39–41.

36 Filip Friedman, *Zagłada Żydów lwowskich* (Łódź, 1945), pp. 3, 6.

37 Friedman, "Ukrainian-Jewish Relations," pp. 176–208. The article was first published in Yiddish in *YIVO Bleter* 41 (1957-1958), pp. 230-263 and then in *YIVO Annual of Jewish Social Science* 12 (1958-1959), pp. 259-263.

38 On Mirchuk and Krentsbakh, see Grzegorz Rossoliński-Liebe, "Holocaust Amnesia: The Ukrainian Diaspora and the Genocide of the Jews," *German Yearbook of Contemporary History* 1 (2016), pp. 140–141; Per Anders Rudling, "The OUN, the UPA, and the Holocaust: A Study in the Manufacturing of Historical Myths," *The Carl Beck Papers in Russian & East European Studies,* Number 2107 (Pittsburgh, 2011), p. 25; Stella Krentsbakh, "Zhvu shche zavdiaky UPA," in Petro Mirchuk and V. Davydenko (eds.), *V riadakh UPA. zbirka spomyniv buv. voiakiv Ukrainskoi Povstanskoi Armii* (New York, 1957), pp. 342-349.

39 Aharon Weiss, "Jewish-Ukrainian Relations in Western Ukraine during the Holocaust," in Peter J. Potichnyj and Howard Aster (eds.), *Ukrainian-Jewish Relations in Historical Perspective* (Edmonton, 1988), pp. 409–420; Spector, *The Holocaust of Volhynian Jews*; Eliyahu Yones, *Smoke in the Sand: The Jews of Lvov in the War Years 1939–1944* (Jerusalem, 2004).

40 John Armstrong, *Ukrainian Nationalism* (New York, 1955).

41 John Armstrong, "Collaborationism in World War II: The Integral Nationalist Variant in Eastern Europe," *The Journal of Modern History* 40(3) (1968), pp. 396–410.

42 John Witte, David Tarr, and Crawford Young, "Memorial Resolution for Professor Emeritus John Armstrong - 1/18/2011," http://www.polisci.wisc.edu/news/default.aspx?id=71 (accessed April 13, 2013).

43 Armstrong, *Ukrainian Nationalism*, pp. 10, 17, 77–92, 156, 173, 222, 234, 238, 243, 256.

44 John Armstrong, "Heroes and Human: Reminiscences Concerning Ukrainian National Leaders dring 1941–1944," *The Ukrainian Quarterly* 51(2-3) (1995), p. 213.

45 Mykola Lebed', *UPA, Ukraïns'ka Povstans'ka Armiia: ïï heneza, rist i diï u vyzvol'nïï borotbi ukraïns'koho narodu za ukraïns'ku samostïïnu sobornu derzhavu* (n.p, Presove biuro UHVR, 1946). For the order to kill Jews who stayed in the UPA, see "Document, No. 44: Dovidka YShPR pro posylennia vyshkolu kadriv UPA, aktyvizatsiu diial'nosti zahoniv ukraïns'kykh povstantsiv proty partyzaniv i poliakiv," in P. Sokhan (ed.), *Litopys UPA*, Vol. 4 (Kiev, 2002), p. 126. On Lebed in general, see Per Anders Rudling, "'Not Quite Klaus Barbie, but in that Category': Mykola Lebed, the CIA, and the Airbrushing of the Past," in: Norman J.W. Goda (ed.), *Rethinking Holocaust Justice: Essays across Disciplines* (New York, 2017), pp. 158–187.

46 Marko Vira, *Sim lit vyzvol'nykh zmahan' (1939–1945)* (Buenos Aires, 1946), pp. 5, 14–17.

47 Vira, *Sim lit vyzvol'nykh zmahan'*, pp. 22–27.

48 Ibid.

49 See for example Petro Mirchuk, *In the German Mills of Death, 1941–1945* (New York, 1976); Stefan Petelycky, *Into Auschwitz for Ukraine* (Kiev, 1999).

50 Volodymyr Viatrovych, *Stavlennia OUN do ievreïv: Formuvannia pozytsiï na tli katastrofy* (Lviv, 2006). For an overview, see Rudling, "The OUN, the UPA, and the Holocaust," pp. 24–28; Grzegorz Rossoliński-Liebe, "Debating, Obfuscating and Disciplining the Holocaust: Post-Soviet Historical Discourses on the OUN-UPA and other Nationalist Movements," *East European Jewish Affairs* 42(3) (2012), pp. 206–222.

51 Grzegorz Rossoliński-Liebe, *Stepan Bandera: The Life and Afterlife of a Ukrainian Nationalist: Fascism, Genocide, and Cult* (Stuttgart/New York, 2014), pp. 474–480, 519–526. On the denial of parts of the Holocaust by Yaroslav Hrytsak and other Ukrainian historians, see Rossoliński-Liebe, "Debating, Obfuscating and Disciplining the Holocaust," pp. 214–222.

52 Alexander Zaitsev, *Ukrains'kyi integral'nyi natsionalizm (1920–1930-ti) roky: Narysy intelektual'noi istorii* (Kiev, 2013).

53 Himka, *The Lviv Pogrom of 1941*; Carynnyk, "Foes of Our Rebirth"; David Marples, *Heroes and Villains: Creating National History in Contemporary Ukraine* (Budapest, 2007). On Himka, Carynnyk, and Marples in the 1980s, see Rossoliński-Liebe, *Stepan Bandera*, pp. 435, 453–455. See also David Marples, "Ukraine during World War II: Resistance Movements and Reannexation," *The Ukrainian Weekly*, New Jersey, 53(41) October 13, 1985, pp. 7, 13.

54 John-Paul Himka, *Ukrainian Nationalists and the Holocaust: OUN and UPA's Participation in the Destruction of Ukrainian Jewry, 1941–1944* (Stuttgart, 2021).

55 Rossoliński-Liebe, *Stepan Bandera*, pp. 365, 373–374; Tarik Cyril Amar, "A Disturbed Silence: Discourse on the Holocaust in the Soviet West as an Anti-Site of Memory," in Michael David-Fox, Peter Holquist, and Alexander M. Martin (eds.), *The Holocaust in the East: Local Perpetrators and Soviet Responses* (Pittsburgh, 2014), pp. 158–184; Amir Weiner, *Making Sense of War: The Second World War and the Fate of the Bolshevik Revolution* (Princeton, 2001).

56 Rossoliński-Liebe, *Stepan Bandera*, pp. 365–388.

57 For historical publications by Soviet historians, see, for example, Vladimir Beliaev, *Formula iada* (Moscow, 1972); Vitalii Cherednychenko, *Natsionalizm proty natsiï* (Kiev, 1970); Ievhen Sheremet, *Ukraïntsi za fakhom* (Kiev, 1980); V. P. Troshchyns'kyi, *Naimantsi fashyzmu: Ukraïns'ki burzhuazni natsionalisty na sluzhbi hitlerivtsiv u mizhvoiennyi period 1921–1939 rr.* (Kiev, 1981); P. Shafeta, *People and Cains: Essays, Articles, Pamphlets* (Kiev, 1982).

58 One of the most active members of this group is Ola Hnatiuk. See, Ola Hnatiuk, *Pożegnanie z imperium: Ukraińskie dyskusje o tożsamości* (Lublin, 2003).

59 Grzegorz Rossoliński-Liebe, "Der polnisch-ukrainische Historikerdiskurs über den polnisch-ukrainischen Konflikt 1943-1947," *Jahrbücher für Geschichte Osteuropas* 57 (2009), pp. 54–85; Grzegorz Motyka and Cień Kłyma Sawura, *Polsko-ukraiński konflikt pamięci* (Gdańsk, 2013).

60 Rossoliński-Liebe, *Der polnisch-ukrainische Historikerdiskurs*, pp. 61–65.

61 Siemaszko and Siemaszko, *Ludobójstwo dokonane przez nacjonalistów ukraińskich*.

62 Lucyna Kulińska, *Działalność terrorystyczna i sabotażowa nacjonalistycznych organizacji ukraińskich w Polsce w latach 1922–1939* (Krakow, 2009); Lucyna Kulińska and Adam Roliński, *Kwestia ukraińska i eksterminacja ludności polskiej w Małopolsce Wschodniej w świetle dokumentów Polskiego Państwa Podziemnego, 1943–1944* (Krakow, 2004); Wiktor Poliszczuk, *Dowody zbrodni OUN i UPA*, Vol. 1-2 (Toronto, 2000).

63 Saul Friedländer, *The Years of Extermination: Nazi Germany and the Jews, 1933–1939* (New York, 1997), p. 2. On the debate between Friedländer and Broszat regarding Jewish and German documents, see Saul Friedländer, *Nachdenken über den Holocaust* (Munich, 2007), pp. 78–124.

64 Grzegorz Rossoliński-Liebe, "Survivor Testimonies and the Coming to Terms with the Holocaust in Volhynia and Eastern Galicia: The Case of the Ukrainian Nationalists," *East European Politics and Societies* 34(1) (2020), pp. 233-235; Grzegorz Rossoliński-Liebe, "Introduction: Conceptualizations of the Holocaust in Germany, Poland, Lithuania, Belarus, and Ukraine: Historical Research, Public Debates, and Methodological Disputes," *East European Politics and Societies* 34(1) (2020), p. 131.

65 Frank Golczewski, "Die Ukraine im Zweiten Weltkrieg," in Frank Golczewski (ed.), *Geschichte der Ukraine* (Göttingen, 1993), p. 241.

66 Ibid., pp. 251–252.

67 Ibid., pp. 252–257.

68 Ibid., p. 330, footnote 16.

69 Pohl, *Nationalsozialistische Judenverfolgung*; Thomas Sandkühler, *"Endlösung" in Galizien. Der Judenmord in Ostpolen und die Rettungsinitiativen von Berthold Beitz 1941–1944* (Bonn, 1996).

70 Frank Grelka, *Die ukrainische Nationalbewegung unter deutscher Besatzungsherrschaft 1918 und 1941/42* (Wiesbaden, 2005); Bruder, *Den ukrainischen Staat erkämpfen*.

71 Bruder, *Den ukrainischen Staat erkämpfen*.

72 Ibid., pp. 153–223.

73 Frank Golczewski, "Shades of Grey: Reflections on Jewish-Ukrainian and German-Ukrainian Relations in Galicia," in Brandon and Lower, *The Shoah in Ukraine*, pp. 130, 150.

74 See for example Kai Struve, *Deutsche Herrschaft, ukrainischer Nationalismus, antijüdische Gewalt: Der Sommer 1941 in der Westukraine* (Berlin, 2015); Jeffrey Kopstein and Jason Wittenberg, *Intimate Violence: Anti-Jewish Pogroms on the Eve of the Holocaust* (New York, 2018); Bartov, "Wartime Lies and Other Testimonies," pp. 486–511; Omer Bartov, *Anatomy of a Genocide: The Life and Death of a Town Called Buczacz* (New York, 2018); John-Paul Himka, *Ukrainian Nationalists and the Holocaust. OUN and UPA's Participation in the Destruction of Ukrainian Jewry, 1941–1944* (Stuttgart 2021), John-Paul Himka, "The Reception of the Holocaust in Postcommunist Ukraine," in John-Paul Himka and Joanna Beata Michlic (eds.), *Bringing the Dark Past to Light. The Reception of the Holocaust in Postcommunist Europe* (Lincoln, 2013), pp. 626–653; Per Anders Rudling, "Multiculturalism, Memory, and Ritualization: Ukrainian Nationalist Monuments in Edmonton, Alberta," *Nationalities Papers* 39(5) (2011), pp. 733–768; Rudling, The OUN, the UPA and the Holocaust; Rossoliński-Liebe, *Stepan Bandera*; Gzregorz Rossoliński-Liebe, "Der Verlauf und die Täter des Lemberger Pogroms vom Sommer 1941. Zum aktuellen Stand der Forschung," *Jahrbuch für Antisemitismusforschung* 22 (2013), pp. 207–243; Rossoliński-Liebe, Debating, "Obfuscating and Disciplining the Holocaust," pp. 199–241; Wendy Lower, "Pogroms, Mob Violence, and Genocide in Western Ukraine, Summer 1941: Varied histories, Explanations and Comparisons," *Journal of Genocide Research* 13(3) (2011), pp. 114–155; Snyder, "The Life and Death of Western Volhynian Jewry"; Kai Struve, "Rites of Violence? The Pogroms of Summer 1941," *Polin: Studies in Polish Jewry* 24 (2012), pp. 257–274.

Per Anders Rudling

'The Miracle of Sambir Harmony' or 'The Shame of Sambir'? The Story of the Crosses at a Jewish Cemetery in Western Ukraine

Introduction

On August 21, 2019 a number of religious, political, and community leaders gathered at the site of a mass grave of victims of the Holocaust in the city of Sambir in the L'viv oblast in western Ukraine. Among them were the heads of the Ukrainian Greek Catholic Church (UGCC), Metropolitan Epifanii, head of the recently independent Orthodox Church in Ukraine, but also representatives of Jewish organizations, including Rabbi Yaakov Dov Bleich.[1] The Ukrainian Greek Catholic Church, the largest and dominant church in Galicia, reported how "Father and Head of the Ukrainian Greek Catholic Church His Beatitude Sviatoslav participated in the consecration of a unique memorial complex for the victims of World War II in Ukraine 'Remember.' On the territory of the former Jewish cemetery in Sambir, L'viv region, a memorial cross was consecrated to OUN-UPA soldiers – victims of Nazism. This cross, the church stated, is the first element of a future memorial for the Ukrainians, Jews, Roma, and Poles who died here at the hands of the Nazis."[2] At the center of this memory conflict stands the far-right Organization of Ukrainian Nationalists of Stepan Bandera (1909-1959), known as OUN(b), an object of intense glorification in Western Ukraine.[3]

The inauguration of yet another nationalist monument in West Ukraine would normally not produce more than a notice in the local press. This monument to an organization which was a party to the Holocaust in the immediate vicinity of a Jewish mass grave would, however, turn an infected local conflict over memory into an international diplomatic row, involving Ukraine, Canada, and the Russian Federation over what one scholar referred to as "the rawest of nerves in Ukrainian Studies and the Ukrainian community: the legacy of the OUN and, more broadly, Ukrainian memories of the war."[4]

Using the small provincial city of Sambir in western Ukraine as a case study, this article sets out to outline how the meta-narrative has materialized on the micro-level, seeking to illuminate how an undigested past led to an international controversy – and a political liability.[5]

Soviet and Nationalist Massacres

The retreating Soviets were unable to evacuate their prisoners, and the NKVD shot many inmates in the prisons.[6] The most detailed study cites the total victims as numbering between 7,500 and 10,000, of about 400-500 victims in the Sambir prison on June 26, 1941 and between 116 and 120 the following day, and regards it as possible that over 800 people could have been killed by the retreating NKVD on June 26-27, 1941 in these two localities alone.[7] Though the majority of the victims had been killed by a bullet to the neck, the NKVD murders appear to have been particularly gruesome in Sambir. Local pro-Nationalist media was filled with stories on how the Soviets had tortured their inmates to death. The pro-Nationalist paper *Ukrains'kyi shchodennyi visti* alleged cannibalism in the local NKVD prison, depicting the Soviets as beyond the pale of humanity, connecting them to anti-Jewish imagery and blood libel, including unconfirmed claims that there were over 50 children among the victims.[8]

Immediately upon the capture of Sambir by units of the 444th *Sicherungsdivision* on the morning of June 29, 1941, a Ukrainian militia on the initiative of the OUN(b) was organized under the command of Ivan Poluiach. The following day a Provisional Ukrainian Committee, led by the priest Pleshkevych, was set up and recognized by the German *Ortskommendatur*. The Ukrainian Committee took control of the city, appointing a mayor and directors of various departments of the city administration.[9] On July 1 *Höhere SS- und Polizeiführer* Friedrich Jeckeln (1895-1946) entered Sambir, from which he ran the operation of the police and SS units.[10] The anti-Jewish mass violence initiated that day followed the pattern in other localities where prison inmates had been murdered; the Ukrainian militia forced Jews to the prison, beating and abusing them while forcing them to gather the putrefying corpses. According to the most detailed study to date, the Germans "took a relatively large part" in the process and controlled what transpired in the Sambir prison.[11]

The wave of anti-Jewish pogroms that swept western Ukraine in connection with the German invasion, and not least local perpetration, counts among the most sensitive issues of modern Ukrainian history.[12] At least 143 west Ukrainian localities saw violent pogroms which claimed the lives of between 7,295 and 11,309 people, or 1.35 to 2.1 percent of the Jewish population.[13] Micro-studies of Ukrainian Nationalist terror belong to the cutting edge of Holocaust research.[14] Holocaust researcher David Alan Rich concludes that "The 'Ukrainian militia,' according to most studies, initiated the rural pogroms and precipitated the worst spasms of killing in the cities. The affinities between OUN-B ideology and the maturing genocidal objectives of the German Einsatzgruppen also facilitated cooperation between Ukrainian militias and the Nazis on anti-Jewish policy."[15]

Ukrainian Nationalists took an active and violent part in the pogrom. A German member of the *Nachrichtenstaffel* of the Police Battalion testified during an interrogation by the GDR Ministry of State Security in November 1982 how: "Nationalists – today I do no longer recall which, forced a section of the Jewish population together, so that they could collect the corpses from the basements of the prison. I had seen these corpses lying in the prison backyard of Sambir. Their faces had already turned black. In the area of the prison the stench was unbearable. Here I saw how the nationalists armed with clubs (Knüppeln), but without other weapons, beat and forced the Jewish citizens in front of them."[16]

The survivor Herman Rieger recalled, "Two days after the Germans entered [...] the Ukrainian nationalists – they carried blue-and-yellow armbands – alone or with the Germans went through the houses and took Jews, men, women and children, with them to the backyard of the prison. Together with my wife and my five-year-old I was also brought to the prison. We were gathered in the afternoon around three. About one hundred Jews had already been forced to the prison. We had to clear the prison. As we were working, we were horrifically beaten by Ukrainians with iron bars."[17]

Another survivor, Dulek Frei, in a 1980 *Yizkor-bukh* for Sambor and Stari Sambir recalls the violent fury of the pogrom. "Around us were groups of wildly agitated Ukrainians, forcing and beating bloodied Jews in front of them." The

Jews were first brought to the city hall, where the Ukrainian leadership issued orders that the Jews be brought to the prison. "The prison gates were opened and closed behind us. In front of our eyes was an indescribable, hellish image: Ukrainians beat dozens of Jews with iron bars and rifle butts. At the end of the prison yard piles of corpses of Ukrainians, who had fallen victims to the retreating Stalinist murderers, were piled up. The swollen corpses gave off a horrendous stench, which literally took your breath away. The blood that flew from head and face from the strikes, shielded the view of what was transpiring around us."[18]

The estimates of the exact number of Jewish victims of the Sambir pogrom differ. *Ereignismeldungen UdSSR* nr. 24 of July 16, 1941 states that "in Sambir 50 Jews were beaten by the agitated," whereas Jewish survivors estimate the number of victims to between 100 and 150, and the Soviet Extraordinary Commission, tasked with the documentation of German crimes in October 1944, concludes that there were 120 Jewish pogrom victims.[19] The historian Kai Struve, author of the most authoritative study of the anti-Jewish violence in Galicia in 1941, concludes that between 50 and 150 Jews were murdered in Sambir on those days, and between 32 and 60 in Staryi Sambir.[20]

Collaborators into anti-Nazi resistance fighters

An independent Ukraine was not part of the New Europe envisioned by Hitler, who refused to recognize the state declared by the OUN(b), arresting, according to the organization, as many as 1,500 of its members.[21] Throughout 1941 and 1942, both OUN wings actively pursued a line of collaboration, encouraging its members to join the auxiliary police and militia. Within the ranks of the Ukrainian Auxiliary Police in Galicia and the stationary Schutzmannschaft in Volhynia these nationalist auxiliaries actively participated in the mass liquidation of the West Ukrainian Jewish population, becoming intimately involved in the murder of over 700,000 Jews in Volhynia and Galicia in 1942/43.[22] These local collaborators aided in the arrests and deportation of Jews, participated in "Jew hunts," guarded Jewish forced laborers, patrolled ghettos, and partook in mass executions.[23] The few Jews who managed to escape and hide with local peasants, historian Alexander Kruglov notes, "lived in constant fear of the Ukrainian policemen, who continued to search for them."[24]

The end of Sambir Jewry

The Sambir Jewish community was annihilated in stages. Between August and October 1942, four anti-Jewish *Aktionen* were carried out in Sambir. 5,000 of its Jews lost their lives in the Bełżec extermination camp; 600 were taken to the Janowska Street labor camp in Ľviv, and 400 were killed in Sambir. The following year, 500 Jews were shot in the forest near the village of Radłowice/Ralivka. On April 14, 1943 a second *Aktion* was carried out, in which about 1,200 people were jailed. About 300 people, mainly family members of the Jewish council and Jewish police were selected, following which, from one o'clock until sunset the remaining 900 were shot in the Jewish cemetery.[25] Sambir was declared *Judenrein* on June 7, 1943, although the last inmates of the Sambir ghetto were killed only on June 9. In all, about 2,000 Jews were killed by the security police and a commando unit of the Ukrainian auxiliary police. Many of those who managed to escape the clearing of the ghetto were later caught and shot.[26] The murder of the Jewish community in Sambir was near total; when the Red Army entered Sambir on August 7, 1944, almost all of its Jewish residents were dead.[27]

After Stalingrad, as it became obvious that Germany would not prevail in the war, the OUN(b) urged its men to defect from the ranks of the auxiliary police. These former auxiliaries came to form the backbone of the OUN(b) armed wing, the Ukrainian Insurgent Army, (UPA); 78 percent of the leading UPA and 66 of the OUN(b) cadres had a background in German or other Axis service.[28] The OUN and UPA carried out the systematic murder of Jews on their own initiative from 1943.[29] At the same time, in August 1943 the OUN(b) revised its program to increase its appeal with the Western allies. It abandoned fascist attributes, such as the raised arm salute, launched a systematic campaign to obfuscate its own immediate past,[30] and ordered the production and dissemination of propaganda, to the effect that "Nowhere does a Ukrainian police exist" and that, subsequently "People are beaten and robbed not by the Ukrainian police, but by German police with the help of the Schutzmänner."[31] Furthermore, it ordered the forging of "[l]ists that would confirm that the Germans carried out anti-Jewish pogroms and liquidations by themselves, without the participation or help of the Ukrainian police" along with "[m] aterials that would clearly confirm that Poles had initiated and taken part in anti-Jewish pogroms."[32] Jeffrey S. Kopstein and Jason Wittenberg argue that this "constitutes an important piece of evidence for the historians' equivalent of *mens rea* – evidence of a guilty mind in criminal law."[33]

OUN(b) and the Axis powers

Only months later, the OUN(b) resumed collaboration with Nazi Germany. Arrested OUN(b) leaders were released, negotiations about receiving weapons, military supplies and exchange of intelligence were initiated. In January 1944, the OUN(b) director of foreign affairs, Ivan Hryn'okh (1907-1994), met with *Hauptsturmführer* Bernhard Pappe in order to coordinate the UPA's anti-Soviet activities with the Germans.[34] From March 1944, UPA ceased any attacks on German occupation forces,[35] and the following month SS-*Oberstürmbannführer* Otto Skorzeny (1908-1975) met with Bandera and his deputy Iaroslav Stets'ko (1912-1986) in the vicinity of Berlin to synchronize OUN and Wehrmacht operations against the advancing Red Army.[36] The UPA received rifles, light and heavy machine guns, and 100,000 rounds of ammunition.[37] In August 1944, Bandera and Stets'ko were released from their *Ehrenhaft*.[38]

Nevertheless, reports from the Polish underground indicate that local relations between Ukrainians and Germans in May-June 1944 were periodically tense. In April, the Hungarian first army had been sent to East Galicia to prevent the Soviets from seizing the Carpathian passes. As to East Galicia, the Polish underground reported on June 2, 1944 about an escalation of the tension between UPA and the Hungarians and Germans, although it noted, "Obviously there is no reason to hope for a clean break between the Germans and Ukrainians,"[39] and, "In any case we are not talking about the same attitudes as of Ukrainians towards Poles."[40] Local tension and skirmishes were, to a significant degree, the result of the increasingly anarchic situation in connection with the retreat and impending collapse of the Axis powers. The Polish underground reported that "In the Sambor[Sambir] district, against the background of these killings carried out against Germans, the arrests among Ukrainians has increased daily. In the Turczański [Ukr. Turkivs'ki povit] district, a battle between the UPA and the Hungarian army has been lasting several days. In the area of the gmina Zawadka the Hungarians brought in the artillery."[41]

OUN and UPA supposed anti-Nazi activities were marginal. The number of Axis troops killed by the OUN and UPA probably counted in the hundreds, many of which consisted of members of auxiliary police formations, including those consisting of Poles and Soviet POWs.[42] To this number can be added over 300 uniformed Germans, mostly *Abwehr* and *Gestapo* officers, captured or surrendering to the insurgents. German personnel served in the OUN and UPA ranks until January 1947, when the OUN security service liquidated them in order not to compromise themselves in the eyes of the Western world.[43]

The veneration of OUN(b) and UPA as anti-Nazi resistance fighters became a cornerstone of the émigrés historical memory.[44] From the 1960s, the leaders of the exiled Ukrainian Greek Catholic Church Iosyp Slipyi (1893-1984) and Lubomyr Husar (1933-2017) took an active part in the sanctification of the OUN by inaugurating and blessing monuments in their honor.[45] In the 1990s, this memorial culture was re-exported to Ukraine.[46]

Sacrifical victimhood, grammar of martyrology

Harald Welzer argues that a milieu of memory is formed by families, local communities, interest groups, pedagogical settings, and the mass media.[47] Sambir is not an isolated case; museum exhibits across Galicia tend to be ethnocentric and exclude other historical residents of these lands, such as Poles and Jews.[48] Historian Yuliya Yurchuk refers to the cult of the OUN and UPA as a "space of sacrificial victimhood" and "grammar of martyrology," the key elements of which are "self-sacrifice for the noble cause," which "involves religious salvation as understood in the Christian tradition."[49] The clergy's quasi-religious references to sacrifice and holy devotion to the idea of the nation, complicates critical engagement with the past by creating an atmosphere in which one is "invited to take part in rituals that presuppose unanimous support and exclude questioning or debate."[50]

Historian Tarik Cyril Amar notes the stark contrast between the omnipresent veneration of the OUN(b) and UPA in Galicia with the absence of the Holocaust, which he refers to as an "anti-site of memory."[51] Former centers of Jewish culture have become what Pierre Nora refers to as places without memory (*lieux sans mémoire*).[52] To the extent the synagogues of Galicia have at all survived, they are often dilapidated ruins, or used as storage units, fitness centers, or schools.[53] In Sambir the former synagogue has been turned into a strip club.[54]

Absence of the Holocaust – Presence of Bandera

The cult of the OUN(b) and UPA is difficult to reconcile with an open and candid engagement with the Holocaust. Omer Bartov's *Erased: Vanishing Traces of Jewish Galicia in Present-Day Ukraine* (2007) documents the silence surrounding the Holocaust and the phenomenon of glorifying the OUN at sites associated with the destruction of the Jewish community. On the site of the former Drohobych ghetto the authorities erected an oversized Bandera statue in bronze, with "no indication anywhere in the park that this was a site of suffering and slaughter by fellow citizens."[55] In the city of Kosiv, the former residence of the rabbi of the murdered Jewish community now houses an exhibit to the OUN(b) and UPA.[56] Hundreds of localities across western Ukraine carry monuments to the OUN, the UPA, and its leaders. [57] In 2015, there were 100 streets, 50 monuments, 14 plaques, and five museums devoted to Stepan Bandera alone.[58] Along with the over-sized Bandera memorial in his birth village Staryi Uhriniv and the 3.5 meter tall Bandera statue in Ivano-Frankivs'k, many are the work of the sculptor Mykola Posikira (1946-2019). Towering above them all is his 4.20-meter-tall Bandera monument in Lviv,[59] provocatively erected in front of the former Roman Catholic St. Elżbieta cathedral.[60] Combining "monumental fascist and post-Soviet aesthetics," the oversized monument was accompanied by an enormous triumphal arch standing 28.5 meters tall, with Bandera's name in large golden letters.[61]

After Staryi Sambir erected a memorial to Stepan Bandera in 2008, on the initiative of the Congress of Ukrainian Nationalists (KUN), Sambir mayor Taras Kopylak and the Sambir city council contacted Posikira about getting a Bandera monument of their own.[62] This would be Pasikira's fourth, but not last, Bandera monument.[63] Regional authorities enacted local by-laws to facilitate the erection of eleven authorized copies of the L'viv memorial across the region. If the price for the Stepan Bandera memorial in Lviv reached UAH 7,683,916, the Sambir copy carried the more modest price tag of UAH 350,000. "The memorial to Stepan Bandera is only the first step towards the realization of the national idea. We plan to set up another 14 busts of national heroes," mayor Kopylak told the press in November, 2011.[64] Though the average passerby may have limited interest in the figures glorified by the new monuments,[65] their presence in the cityscape, their promotion in the classroom, in the army, through government agencies and memory laws, has had an impact on how they are perceived.[66] Approval of the legacy of the OUN, standing at 20 percent nationally in 2010, surged to 49 percent in 2017.[67]

A globally connected village

Today an ethnically homogenous west Ukrainian city of 35,000 residents, prior to the war Sambir was multi-ethnic and multi-confessional. The 1921 Polish census listed 19,417 residents, 6,068 of which were Jews. Poles constituted the majority population; according to the 1931 census 54 percent, whereas Jews and Ukrainians constituted 28.7 and 16.5 percent, respectively.[68] By 1939, Jews constituted around 8,000 people, almost a third of its 25,000 residents.[69] Whereas almost all Jewish residents were murdered, the Polish former majority population "was either massacred by Ukrainian nationalists or forced to move to western Poland."[70] Visiting Sambir in 2006, Bartov laconically noted how "Contemporary Sambir reveals no traces of the composition of its prewar population or of the events that unfolded there in the second half of the 1940s… Transformed into a homogenous Ukrainian town, Sambir has shed much of its past and memory."[71]

Yet, memory of the multi-ethnic past survived in emigration. A significant number of west Ukrainians were engaged in circulatory migration until 1939, and former Sambir residents, and their descendants, are scattered around the world.[72] Galicia remained the least Sovietized area of Ukraine. After 1956 cross-border contacts were re-established, in particular with Poland and Canada.[73] One of the people connecting Canada to West Ukraine was Jack Gardner of Victoria, British Columbia. Born Jakób Moiseevich Gertner (1914-2001), Gardner lost his entire family in the ghetto of the neighboring city of Staryi Sambir. For around 30 years, beginning already under Khruchshev, Gardner sought permission from the Soviet Ukrainian authorities to bring the local Jewish cemetery in order - in vain.[74] In the early 1990s Gardner visited Sambir for the first time since the war, and in November, 1993, he asked the Ukrainian ambassador to Canada for support to maintain the mass grave that was the final resting place of his murdered family.[75] In 2001, Gardner was able to arrange to have a fence set up around the cemetery and a new path to the cemetery paved. The renovated Staryi Sambir cemetery was re-opened in the presence of representatives, not only of the city council, but also of that of US and Israeli diplomats. This was an exceptional event.[76]

In the Soviet era many Jewish cemeteries had been destroyed, including the Jewish cemetery in neighboring Sambir. During one night in 1975 the cemetery of roughly five hectares was bulldozed. According to Bohdan Medvedik, Sambir's chief architect at the time, its destruction was part of an anti-Israeli campaign following the 1973 Yom Kippur War.[77] Though the Soviet authorities had removed the headstones, or *matzevahs*, the Jewish cemetery was well delineated; legal records predating the Habsburg era clearly established that the land had been purchased by the Jewish community, which received permission to set up a new cemetery in 1732. It is clearly depicted on the cadaster map of 1856.[78] Moreover, the records show it had been used exclusively as a Jewish burial ground.[79]

Encouraged by the example of neighboring Staryi Sambir, volunteers of the society Ukraine-Israel sought to enlist Gardner's aid to bring the Jewish cemetery in neighboring Sambir in order as well. In September 1991, the Jewish cultural society received permission from the Sambir city council to build a fence around the Jewish cemetery, but already by the turn of the century almost all of the metal fence that had been set up around the cemetery had been stolen.[80] What remained of the cemetery was an overgrown field over a mass grave and a somber brick wall with traces of bullet shots. In 2000, Mark Freiman, former Ontario deputy attorney general and president of the Canadian Jewish Congress 2009-2011 became involved in this project. To Freiman, this was a deeply personal matter. His grandparents, three aunts, three uncles, and a half-brother counted among the victims of the massacres.[81] His parents, who had managed to hide in a basement for 17 months, were among the only 100 Sambir Jews who had managed to survive the Holocaust. In the year 2000, Freiman obtained permission to erect a memorial in the shape of the Star of David on the cemetery;

there were plans to set up a memorial park in the form of a pathway in the shape of a six-pointed star in the lawn around the mass grave. The presence of a Jewish symbol was, however, unpopular among many local residents. No less than fourteen local "national-patriotic"[82] organizations protested, complaining that they had not been consulted about the reconstruction "of the territory of the former Jewish cemetery."[83] These "national patriots" took power into their own hands. Iosyf Zisel's (b. 1946) the head of the Ukrainian VAAD, the Association of Jewish Civic Organizations and Communities,[84] recalled how "A Greek Catholic priest, who has since passed away, went with a group of people to the Jewish mass grave, and, using a bulldozer, set up burial mounds (*kurgany*), on which he erected three large crosses. This happened spontaneously, Zisel's recalled - literally in one day. Local 'patriots' told the activists of the society Ukraine-Israel that 'here our boys are buried, and we will therefore not allow any Jewish symbols to be set up.' ... It was done out of spite, just in order to prevent Jews from creating a memorial space there."[85]

The crosses were erected on October 28, 2000, deliberately on the Jewish sabbath, blessed by both Greek Catholic and Ukrainian Orthodox clergymen, as symbols of Christian domination. Angry letters to the authorities stressed that the memorials were explicitly chosen to prevent "'Israeli and Jewish symbols' and to use 'Ukrainian and Christian symbols' instead."[86]

Visiting the site of the massacre in 2006, historian Omer Bartov noted the absence of any signs that this was a Jewish mass grave. "A small, hardly visible plaque, obviously dating back to the Communist period, commemorated 'the Soviet citizens' shot at the site by the Nazis. This was a typical Communist practice: no mention was made of the fact that these 'Soviet citizens' were murdered because they were Jews."[87] These nationalist activists added to the Soviet euphemisms a rivaling de-contextualization, this one seeking to appropriate the Holocaust for their own narrative of suffering, centered around ethnic Ukrainians.[88] The text on the enormous birch cross in the middle of the Jewish cemetery was just as cryptic: "At this site are buried victims of Nazi and Communist Terror, 1939-1950."[89] Bartov notes that "this is obviously an attempt to conflate Nazi and Soviet crimes and Jewish and Ukrainian victims by linking them to the very same site."[90]

Though hierarchs from both the Greek Catholic and Ukrainian Orthodox Churches supported removing the crosses, they were left in place and remained an irritant.[91] Zisel's and VAAD realized that the agreement would be respected.[92] Freiman envisioned a place of memory, in which existing memorials would be preserved, and all nationalities who had been subject to murder in Sambir would be represented. He set up a charity for the purpose and engaged the artists Miriam Husevych and Peter Miles of Washington, DC to turn the dilapidated grave site into a memorial park. From 2008 Freiman approached the Ukrainian authorities, seeking to convince them about the importance of commemorating the victims, yet was unable to reach an agreement.[93] He reached out to both Jewish and Ukrainian groups. In Canada he worked with Rabbi Reuven Bulka and the society "the friends of the Sambir Jewish cemetery," in Kyiv with Anatolii Shenheit, executive director of its Jewish community and from 2015 curator of the Ukrainian-Jewish Encounter project in Ukraine. He approached the Sheptytsky Institute in Toronto, and Oksana Wynnyckyj-Yusypovych, the honorary consul of Canada in Lviv,[94] but reached out also to the "national patriots" in Sambir, including Sviatoslav Chukhrai, a leading voice among the radical memory activists in Sambir,[95] and Stephen Bandera, the grandson of the late OUN(b) leader – and a stalwart promoter of his grandfather's legacy.[96] He met with moderately nationalist public intellectuals such as Myroslav Marynovych[97] and Taras Vozniak,[98] and the late cardinal Lubomyr Huzar.[99]

Freiman regarded the issue of the crosses as something akin to a litmus test for Ukraine's democratic maturity.[100] In the fall of 2016 a breakthrough appeared to finally have been reached: the mayor's office was ready to sign a memorandum agreeing to have the crosses removed, pending agreement of the hierarchs. On September 25, 2017, in an appeal to the residents of Sambir, the heads of the Ukrainian Greek Catholic and the Ukrainian Orthodox Church of the Kyiv Patriarchate, metropolitan Sviatoslav and patriarch Filaret endorsed the concept of a memorial park, and, in August 2018, expressed their support for the transfer of the crosses to what they described as a "deeply symbolic place – the cemetery of the Sich Riflemen."[101]

The 17 OUN anti-Nazi teenage martyrs

As the project was being finalized and discussed in the Sambir city council, there was a new turn of events. An old man showed up at one of the city council meetings. It was the above-mentioned Sviatoslav Chukhrai, who claimed that his older brother Mykhailo had been shot by the Gestapo at the gates of the Jewish cemetery in 1944, along with sixteen other young people, who, he asserted, were all members of the OUN. Chukhrai not only insisted on a memorial to these martyrs, but had already prepared a sketch for the monument, which he now presented to the council. This constituted a violation of the agreement between the Jewish community and the mayor's office, which stipulated that no "vertical objects" would be erected on the site. [102]

In addition to politics, economy appears to have played a role in the opposition. A key role in the opposition was played by former deputy mayor Iuryi Les'kiv, a local journalist, who "did everything he could to prevent the removal of the crosses."[103] Behind Lesiv stood former mayor Taras Kopyliak, who, according to *Khadashot*, had privatized real estate which once belonged to the Jewish community, including the old synagogue of Sambir, which he had turned into a night club and strip joint.[104]

In late 2018, Jewish groups approached local parishioners directly, distributing 11,300 leaflets to the households of Sambir, appealing to leaders of the Ukrainian Orthodox and Greek Catholic Churches to have the crosses removed. After the appeals were ignored by the parishioners,[105] in December 2018, Freiman conceded yet another compromise; half a million dollars was set aside to commemorate the two Jewish mass graves, but also for a memorial to the undocumented 17 OUN combatants, supposedly shot by the Gestapo in 1944.[106]

Dissent within the Jewish community

The attitude towards the legacy of the OUN divides the Jewish community. Zisel's is comfortable with the official mythology about the OUN and UPA as friends and rescuers of Jews,[107] has disputed the antisemitic legacy of the OUN(b) and dismissed critics as serving Russian interests.[108] Other Jewish public figures reacted strongly to Freiman's compromise. Eduard Dolinskyi

(b. 1969), General Director of the Ukrainian Jewish Committee, expressed outrage at Jewish groups funding a memorial dedicated to a group involved in the murder of Jews.[109] Meeting with Dolinskyi, Freiman disputed Dolinskyi's allegations that the monument honors perpetrators. As they were altogether fictional, Freiman argued, these teenagers could not have been complicit in the murder of the Sambir Jews.[110] Freiman told the *Canadian Jewish News*, "Local lore is a powerful reason for why crosses were erected at a Jewish burial site in the first place. One story has it that the Nazis executed and buried 17 members of a Ukrainian nationalist organization at the Jewish cemetery. It's a controversial, largely anecdotal narrative, but 'rather than fight that, we've accepted that story,' Freiman said. 'We're not going to contest it.'"[111] He assured *Khadoshot* "The monument will be erected to them not as OUN members, but as fighters for Ukrainian independence, murdered by the Gestapo. There is no information that they would have been involved in any sort of antisemitic actions. Thus, we are not talking about memorials to murderers of Jews and not about a memorial to the OUN. As far as Jewish money is concerned, this is also not the case, as the entire project is financed by the charitable organization UJE, at the head of which stands James Temerty, a well-known philanthropist of Ukrainian origin."[112] Freiman was nevertheless clearly troubled that veneration of the OUN had become a condition for having the crosses removed.[113] UJE curator Shenheit stressed the same point. "We emphasize: there is no single document (besides a single oral testimony) to confirm the claim that 17 OUN members would have been shot at that place. There is similarly no evidence about who these people were, the majority of whom – according to Mr. Chukhrai – had not yet turned eighteen."[114]

On July 24, 2019, the Sambir city council finally signed an agreement which entailed the removal of the crosses from the Jewish mass grave, but also the establishment of a memorial to the OUN, along the lines Sviatoslav Chukhrai had suggested, in the immediate vicinity of the Jewish cemetery. This monument also had the shape of a cross, but a very specific one – the black cross of the OUN(b)'s emblem, adopted in April 1941,[115] and a plaque with the text "On this site 17 young Ukrainians, members of the OUN, were shot by the German Gestapo in July 1944. Glory to Ukraine! Glory to the Heroes!"

(FIGURE 1) The inauguration of the monument was set for August 21, 2019.

FIGURE 1. Monument to 17 OUN martyrs, Sambir. In the public domain https://twitter.com/spacelordrock/status/1164763728635555841/photo/2 (accessed May 15, 2020).

The OUN Volunteer Battalion

On August 20, 2019, the eve of the event, the story took another turn, as militants from the OUN Volunteer Battalion (*Dobrovol'chyi Batal'ion OUN*, DB OUN), an ultranationalist militia organized in 2014 to combat separatists in eastern Ukraine, arrived in Sambir. A dozen of its vigilantes encircled the crosses, preventing their removal. As local police refused to get involved the crosses on the Jewish mass grave remained, and the agreement was violated. The DB OUN evoked an image of a beleaguered Ukraine: "We have lived to see how foreigners came to Sambir, how the Jewish minority, aided by local rabble…started…to destroy our Christian symbols, in particular the crosses which had been set up and dedicated on the burial site of people of various religious faiths, martyred by the Hitlerites and Bolsheviks. With the help of Sambir patriots the DB OUN managed to save the central cross. But for how much longer?"[116] At this point, Rabbi Dov Bleich now sought to opt out of the ceremony he had come to Sambir to attend, but when the protestors agreed to remove one of the crosses located directly on the Jewish mass grave, he decided to stay for the commemorative prayer.[117] The hierarchs from the two churches went ahead with the ceremony, now centered around the memorial to the mythical 17 OUN(b) anti-Nazi martyrs.

Canadian ambassador: Pay tribute to OUN members who fought the Nazi Regime

Roman Waschuk, the Canadian ambassador to Ukraine, was born in 1963 to a Toronto family of Galician Ukrainian Displaced Persons. Like many nationally conscious members of his generation, Waschuk was raised in the nationalist scouting organization Plast. He works closely with the Ukrainian Canadian Congress.[118] A trained historian, Waschuk holds an MA in the history of Central-Eastern Europe, and his first job was with the 1985-86 Commission of Inquiry on War Crimes in Canada. Waschuk has cautioned about the dangers of propaganda, arguing that these are best countered by "truthful information": "It would be an error to go down the same path as Russia, and get involved in counterpropaganda; then Ukraine would lose faith in itself."[119]

According to UJE chairman James Temerty,[120] (b. 1941) the Canadian ambassador had been invited by his organization.[121] The Canadian embassy in turn requested the participation of Canadian military servicemen at the ceremony.[122] Flanked not only by Canadian military personnel and the 1941 red-and-black OUN(b) flag,[123] (FIGURE 2) Waschuk consecrated the cross-shaped OUN(b) monument by a speech at the grave site. The Canadian ambassador described it as "a monument of one's motherland," stressing that it "must know how to defend itself so that it does not suffer again from waves of inhuman totalitarian terror as happened during World War 2."

Omitting any reference to the OUN(b)'s enthusiastic endorsement of Nazi Germany in 1941 and its role in the anti-Jewish violence in Sambir, Waschuk instead cast them as anti-Nazi resistance fighters and called for their veneration:

> "I am here with you as a representative of Canada, a multicultural and multifaith country where churches, synagogues and mosques co-exist on the same streets peacefully and amicably. ... I see that this particular memorial complex will symbolize, let us say, a common spiritual heart of the city of Sambir aiming at the present and the future, while respecting the multifaith and multiethnic history of this city. We should hear the voices of three and half thousand murdered innocent Jewish citizens of Sambir; of those Ukrainians who perished trying to help Jewish families; as well as those Ukrainians who fought against the Nazi regime as members of OUN-UPA. We should pay tribute and remember all of them."[124]

FIGURE 2. *Ambassador Roman Waschuk, James Temerty, Metropolitan Epiphanius, Major archbishop Sviatoslav Shevchuk, Rabbi Yakoov Dov Bleich and Mark Freiman. Sambir, August 21, 2019. From Sevunts, "Canada Accused," (Sambir municipal council/Facebook, in the public domain).*

FIGURE 3. Ambassador Roman Waschuk and Canadian military servicemen dedicating the monument to the OUN adjacent to the Jewish massacre site. Sambir, August 21, 2020. Image of the Sambir municipal council, posted on Facebook. In the public domain.

"Miracle of Sambor harmony" or "the shame of the Samborites"?

The Religious-informational service of Ukraine (RISU), an online portal dedicated to religious matters, reported that "On August 21, in Sambir in the Lviv oblast' in a solemn ceremony the memorial complex 'Remember' was inaugurated, in memory of the victims of the Second World War in Ukraine. On the territory of the former Jewish cemetery was dedicated a memorial cross to the warriors of OUN-UPA – victims of Nazism."[125]

The rhetoric of the religious hierarchs' combined truths stress "glory" and "memory": "Today we truly remember the tragic sides of our Ukrainian and Jewish history of the 20th century, as well as the glorious warriors who gave their lives for freedom and liberty. On this holy place we recall the peaceful citizens whose lives were taken. We have reached accord and unity, which is why we open this memorial jointly. Here Christians as well as Jews are honored," the head of the Ukrainian Orthodox Church Epiphanius I explained. Sviatoslav, the head of the Greek Catholic Church, emphasized the Ukrainian aspect of the event, stressing that it took place on the eve of Ukrainian independence day, which he placed into an OUN-centered teleological rendition of history.[126] "But someone had to pay a lot for it to happen. It is these killed 17 young fellows who speak to us today… And their words shatter any cliché of communist propaganda that still wants to distort the desire of Ukrainians to have their own state. The members of the OUN-UPA died at the hands of those killers who caused one of the greatest crimes of humanity – the Holocaust. And they are resting in an ancient Jewish cemetery here in Sambir."[127] Sviatoslav Shevchuk characterized the ceremony as "a miracle of Sambir harmony," and stated that "Today we want to show here in Sambir, in an ancient Jewish cemetery, that Jews are able to honor Christians and pray for their heroes, and Ukrainian Christians are able to worship religious sentiments of the late Jews."[128] Shevchuk refused to comment on the violation of the previously concluded agreement.[129] The communication department of the Ukrainian Greek Catholic Church developed the discourse further: "In April 1943, 1,200 Jewish men, women, and children were driven to this cemetery and shot. They were all buried in a huge mass grave. Some were buried alive. In 1944 seventeen Ukrainian OUN-UPA soldiers were shot by the Nazi fighters here. Jewish women and children who were hiding in this cemetery also found their last place of rest. They were found and destroyed, along with those Ukrainians who were hiding Jewish families. In addition, in this place were murdered and buried Poles and Roma people."[130]

The reporting gives no indication of the intense polarization which boiled to the surface during the ceremony. After the 95-year-old survivor Borys Dorfman from Lviv finished a short eulogy in Yiddish and recited *am yisra'el chai* – the people of Israel lives, Anatol Shenheit grabbed the microphone, shouting "*Pacta sunt servanda*,"– "treaties have to be fulfilled," three times. There was no reaction from the gathered audience, other than that from the local police chief, who briefly commented "Why do you have to provoke people?"[131]

The divisions ran through the Jewish community. If Dov Bleich tweeted that "It was indeed a very special and moving ceremony. I must mention that in my personal opinion this historic day was only possible in a Democratic Ukraine,"[132] the disillusioned Shenheit told *Khadoshot* "'This story … demonstrates, that even if you compromise, there are no guarantees that they won't cheat you, (…) This is the shame of the Samborites. It is they who will have to live with it."[133]

Other representatives of the Ukrainian Jewish Encounter sought to tone down the controversy. Interviewed by the *Canadian Jewish News*, an unnamed spokesperson of that organization stated, "OUN is not being memorialized, let alone glorified…" Rather, the spokesperson said, "There is a tombstone erected over the burial place of 17 young nationalists who were shot by the Nazis in a corner of the cemetery in 1944. This was a key compromise… In accordance with Jewish religious requirements, this area will be demarcated in a manner that will result in it not being considered part of the Jewish cemetery."[134] The Ukrainian Canadian Congress issued a triumphant statement that "Canada has been central in helping to resolve the issue of appropriate Holocaust commemoration in Ukraine." A similar argument was advanced by the Center for Israel and Jewish Affairs (CIJA), an advocacy agent of Jewish Federations of Canada, which insisted "This is not a monument to Ukrainian nationalists, it's a grave marker. It is part of a compromise in a much larger discussion that will lead to a Memorial Park dedicated to remembering the victims of the Holocaust."[135] It dismissed criticism as "a deliberate attempt by malign actors to destabilize a process by mischaracterizing it by very partially telling the story."[136]

From Local Conflict to International Political Scandal

The images of Temerty, Waschuk, and Canadian military personnel surrounded by black-and-red banners inaugurating a monument to the OUN(b) as Holocaust murder was soon picked up by news agencies across the globe. When The Jewish Telegraph Agency in Jerusalem first broke the story, the report carried the title "Rabbi helps dedicate a memorial to Ukrainian group that collaborated with the Nazis."[137] The reactions of the participants differed.

Dov Bleich defiantly challenged the critics to prove the mythical OUN teenagers' role in the pogrom: "I am not arguing or debating whether UNA [sic] participated in pogroms. We are talking about these 17 kids who were murdered in 1944. Anyone know if they participated in pogroms? If they were murderers?"[138]

Ambassador Waschuk and Temerty both declined to speak to Radio Canada International, whereas Global Affairs Canada turned down its correspondents' request for a copy of the ambassador's speech. On September 3 Radio Canada International published a long report on the Sambir controversy, entitled "Canada accused of promoting Holocaust revisionism with memorial in Ukraine."[139]

On September 11, VAAD issued a statement that cautioned that the agreement to have the crosses removed were reneged upon: "The ceremony was to seal the compromise achieved earlier: to move three crosses from the territory of the Jewish cemetery and to erect a monument to 17 young Ukrainians, OUN members, who were shot by the Nazi (sic) in July 1944. ... Unfortunately, the preliminary agreements were not executed in full, and two out of three Christian symbols were not moved from the Jewish cemetery to a place agreed upon earlier. We would like to emphasize the need to accomplish this process in full, in keeping with the earlier agreements."[140]

On September 12, 2019, the Canadian media corporation PostMedia followed suit with a long investigative report by well-known journalist David Pugliese, entitled "Canadian officials honour Nazi collaborators," a top news item in papers across Canada.[141]

Temerty now broke his silence, releasing a written statement on the website of the Ukrainian Canadian Congress protesting the reporting in Canadian media. Unlike Zisel's VAAD, Temerty and the UCC did not acknowledge problems in regards to the historical accuracy of the event:

> "A key element to reaching an agreement with the local community was incorporation into the Memorial Park of some recognition of non-Jewish victims killed by the Nazis, notably 17 young Nationalists killed in early 1944 in a corner of the Jewish cemetery. The process of finding a means for such recognition that respected the sensibilities of all the communities involved and was consistent with both Christian custom and Jewish religious requirements for a kosher cemetery." Temerty and the UCC did not register any problems with this narration. On the contrary, "Far from honoring radical nationalism or a legacy of collaboration, the opening ceremony was devoted to precisely the opposite ideas. Patriarch Sviatoslav Shevchuk explicitly declared that the Memorial Park project bore witness to the truth that radical nationalism is a dead end with no future."[142]

At this point, the Ukrainian embassy in Canada injected itself into the discussion, through an emotional tweet by ambassador Andrii Shevchenko.[143] "Disgusted by media attacks on a Canadian diplomat and soldiers, attending the remembrance ceremony at the Holocaust Memorial in Sambir, Ukraine. Grateful to [Canada] and Ambassador Waschuk for helping us to heal the WW2 wounds. We stay united in our fight against Kremlin-style propaganda."[144]

Shevchenko told the *Canadian Jewish News* that "the idea was to commemorate the victims of the Holocaust and the other victims of World War II. For us, we are looking for the best way to do so, with respect to the different cultural and religious traditions of the victims." Describing the OUN memorial as "a very good example of reconciliation," Shevchenko emphasized "We are grateful to those Canadians who are helping heal the wounds of World War II."[145] Shevchenko dismissed the critique of Waschuk as "an example of Kremlin-style, or Putin-style, propaganda of half-truths, half-myths on an industrial scale."[146] In response, Shevchenko circulated an editorial in the OUN(m)-affiliated *New Pathway/Novyi shliakh* by a long-term associate, the Edmonton-based journalist Marco Levytsky[147] which denounced Pugliese's article and Postmedia's reporting as "a grossly biased piece of Russian propaganda.'"[148] Levytsky's response contains a condensed version of nationalist rendition of the past.

"While OUN did initially co-operate with the Nazis when they invaded the USSR…this co-operation was very brief. Right after OUN leaders proclaimed Ukrainian independence on June 30, 1941, they were arrested by the Germans and sent to concentration camps. The Ukrainian Insurgent Army (UPA) was created two years later to fight the German occupiers and later continued the battle against Soviet Russian occupiers. There were many Jews who served with the UPA. ... The repeated attempts to besmirch OUN-UPA, as well as drive wedges between the Ukrainian and Jewish communities is a principal goal of Russian propaganda. One would hope that Postmedia and its respective member newspapers would practice much more journalistic responsibility and check the facts before they regurgitate such drivel, which comes from a source whose intension is to undermine democracies around the world."[149]

Canada and Ukrainian Long-Distance Nationalism

The Ukrainian Canadian Congress exercises considerable influence on Canadian policy towards Ukraine.[150] The Ukrainian Canadian Congress works closely with the Canadian government, which relies on its "expertise" in the field of historical memory.[151] In 2012 Canadian media has listed its president, Paul Grod, as one of the 80 top people in regards to influencing that country's foreign policy. Its current, Liberal, foreign minister refers to Grod as a "friend," whereas media reports in 2014 staged photo-ops of the UCC president flying in Conservative Prime Minister Stephen Harper's jet.[152] Since 1971, Canadian identity politics and normative multiculturalism has provided a fertile ground for Ukrainian nationalist mythology.[153] Canadian multicultural funding has underwritten the UCC and its member organizations' erection of monuments and buildings dedicated to OUN(b) leaders.[154] In 2010 the UCC enthusiastically endorsed the designation of Stepan Bandera an official hero of Ukraine and called for Canadian recognition and pensions for OUN and UPA veterans in Canada.[155] In the 2010s, the UCC sponsored Ukrainian revisionist scholars and arranged lecture tours to some of its most prestigious universities. As the Ukrainian diaspora historical memory is heavily centered around self-victimization, inquiry into atrocities committed by Ukrainians are perceived as a threat and elicit angry responses.

Russian instrumentalization

The failure to openly and critically engage in the legacy of the OUN and UPA is associated with political liability. As Canada has taken a clear stance on Russian aggression against Ukraine, Russia has responded by exposing – with some effect – its multicultural monuments to the OUN, UPA, and the Waffen-SS Galizien.[156] Accusations of Nazism and a fascist coup d'état against Yanukovych were leitmotifs of the intensive disinformation campaign which accompanied the Russian invasion of Ukraine in 2014. A Canadian ambassador opening an OUN memorial at a Holocaust massacre site appeared tailor-made for Russian propaganda.[157]

On September 26, 2019, the Russian News Agency TASS published the news release, "Moscow urges Kiev to abandon whitewashing of Nazi collaborators," in which the Russian Foreign Ministry lamented the "utterly outrageous incident" of erecting "a monument to the butchers on the tomb of victims." It continued: "The most scandalous part of this story is that the Canadian ambassador to Ukraine took part in the ceremony as well as Canadian military instructors who travelled to Ukraine to train Ukrainian Armed Forces' officers. ... Attempts to equate Nazi victims and their killers have nothing to do with tolerance and reconciliation. This is an abomination and disparagement of memory of those who lost their lives, which deserves resolute and universal condemnation,' the diplomatic agency stressed. 'We are calling on Kiev to abandon such untenable practice of whitewashing Nazi collaborators and mockery of history, while also urging their overseas friends to listen to the sound of reason and stand against such disgraceful events.'"[158]

Conclusion

In West Ukraine, Jewish survivors who seek to have the final resting places of their murdered family members honored in accordance with their culture and traditions have to reckon with a loud radical local opinion. The compromise survivors reached with local nationalists in Sambir to allow the removal of Christian crosses from a Jewish mass grave entailed accepting a revisionist narration that presented the OUN as anti-Nazi residence fighters and co-victims in the Holocaust. The inauguration, by a Canadian ambassador, of a highly controversial monument to the OUN at a Holocaust massacre site not only triggered an infected debate; it illustrates the political liabilities associated with the incomplete and selective engagement with the legacy of Ukrainian nationalist violence. The Sambir controversy underlines the difficulty of achieving reconciliation without an honest, open, and critical engagement with the issue of local collaboration in the Holocaust.

Endnotes

Acknowledgement ... The author wishes to thank Delphine Bechtel, Graciela Ben Dror, Anthony Dirk Moses, Moss Robeson, Nadja Weck, Barbara Törnquist-Plewa, Eleonora Narvselius, and Toman Sniegon, who have since read and commented on my text and two anonymous reviewers for critically reading the manuscript. Their suggestions did much to improve the final version of the article. The author is solely responsible for mistakes and errors in the text.

1 Jankel, or Jaakov Dov Bleich, is an American Karlin-Stolin Hassid, originally sent by rabbi Schneerson in Brooklyn to set up the United Jewish Community of Ukraine (*Obiedinenie evreiskikh (iudeiskikh) religioznykh organizatsii Ukrainy* (OEROU). Since 1992 Bleich refers to himself as the "main rabbi of Kyiv and Ukraine." Zvi Gitelman, *A Century of Ambivalence: The Jews of Russia and the Soviet Union, 1881 to the Present*, Second, expanded edition (Bloomington, 2001), p. 227; Aleksandr Burakovskii, *Istoriia i analiz vozrozhdeniia evreiskikh obshchestvennykh organizatsii i periodicheskikh izdanii v Ukraine v period 1985-2000 godov* (New York, 2008), p. 46; idem., *Khronika evoliutsii 'natsial'noi idei' Ukrainy i evrei 1987-2016 gody: Kniga dokumental'noi publitsistiki* (Boston, 2018), p. 379.

2 "Head of the UGCC at the inauguration of the memorial Remember: Killed young men speak to us… and destroy the cliché of communist propaganda," *Information Resource of the Greek-Catholic Church*, August 22, 2019, http://news.ugcc.ua/en/news/head_of_the_ugcc_at_the_inauguration_of_the_memorial_remember_killed_young_men_speak_to_us_and_destroy_the_cliché_of_communist_propaganda_87063.html (accessed October 3, 2019).

3 On the OUN, see Franziska Bruder, *"Den ukrainischen Staat erkämpfen oder sterben!": Die Organisation Ukrainischer Nationalisten (OUN) 1928-1948* (Berlin, 2007); Grzegorz Rossoliński-Liebe, "Der europäische Faschismus und der ukrainische Nationalismus: Verflechtungen, Annäherungen und Wechselbeziehungen," *Zeitschrift für Geschichtswissenschaft* 65(2) (2017), pp. 153-169.

4 Dominique Arel, "On Context, Comparison, and Dialogue," in David R. Marples (ed.), *Current Politics in Ukraine*, June 21, 2013, https://ukraineanalysis.wordpress.com/2013/06/21/on-context-comparison-and-dialogue/ (accessed March 19, 2020).

5 On the memory in Sambir, see Nadja Weck, "Geschichtspolitik und selektives Erinnern: Der Umgang mit dem Holocaust im westukrainischen Sambir," master's thesis, Universität Viadrina, Frankfurt an der Oder, 2006; idem., "European Holocaust Memory versus Local Practice in Western Ukraine: Dealing with the Holocaust in the Town of Sambir," in Nancy E. Rupprecht and Wendy Koenig (eds.), *Global Perspectives on the Holocaust*, (Newcastle-upon-Tyne, 2015), pp. 366-390.

6   Three major waves of terror swept through West Ukraine in 1939-41. In June 1941, the NKVD was in the midst of a wave of arrests, this time aimed at Ukrainian nationalists, who therefore constituted many of the prison inmates in late June 1941, "though many Poles and Jews were still imprisoned alongside them, especially in larger cities like Lviv." John-Paul Himka, *Ukrainian Nationalists and the Holocaust: OUN and UPA's Participation in the Destruction of Ukrainian Jewry, 1941-1944* (Stuttgart, 2021), p. 194.

7   Kai Struve, *Deutsche Herrschaft, ukrainischer Nationalismus, anti-Jüdische Gewalt: der Sommer 1941 in der Westukraine* (Munich, 2015), pp. 216, 434.

8   Ibid., pp. 435-436, citing "Iak shalily chervoni v Sambori," *Ukrains'ki shchodenni visti*, no. 5, (July 11, 1941), p. 3.

9   Ibid., p. 436.

10 Ibid., p. 437, citing Hgeb. Süd/Ia, Anlagen zum KTB Nr. 1, 2.7.1941-8.7.1941, Anlagenband 2, Bundesarchiv-Militärarchiv (henceforth BA-MA) RH 22-5, Bl. 16.

11 Struve, *Deutsche Herrschaft*, p. 437.

12 See Jeffrey S. Kopstein and Jason Wittenberg, *Intimate Violence: Anti-Jewish Pogroms on the Eve of the Holocaust* (Ithaca, 2018); Aleksandr Kruglov, Andrei Umansky, and Igor Shchupak, *Kholokost v Ukraine: Zona nemetskoi voiennoi administratsii, Romunskaia zona okupatsii, Distrikt 'Galichina,' Zakarpatye v sostave Vengrii (1939-1944)* (Dnipro, 2018), and Andrzej A. Zięba (ed.), *OUN, UPA i zagłada żydów* (Krakow, 2016).

13 Struve, *Deutsche Herrschaft*, p. 671. Earlier studies have listed 58 localities and a higher range of 13,000 and 35,000 victims in Western Ukraine. See Dieter Pohl, "Anti-Jewish Pogroms in Western Ukraine – A Research Agenda," in Elazar Barkan, Elizabeth A. Cole, and Kai Struve (eds.), *Shared History – Divided Memory: Jews and Others in Soviet-Occupied Poland, 1939-1941* (Leipzig, 2007), pp. 305-313 : p. 306

14 Christoph Mick, *Kriegserfahrungen in einer multiethnischen Stadt. Lemberg 1914-1947* (Wiesbaden, 2010); Grzegorz Rossoliński-Liebe, "Survivor Testimonies and the Coming to Terms with the Holocaust in Volhynia and Eastern Galicia: The Case of the Ukrainian Nationalists," *East European Politics and Societies* 34(1) (2020), pp. 221-240.

15 David Alan Rich, "Armed Ukrainians in L'viv: Ukrainian Militia, Ukrainian Police, 1941 to 1942," *Canadian-American Slavic Studies* 48 (2014), pp. 271-287: p. 272.

16 Struve, *Deutsche Herrschaft*, p. 437, citing "August F. Vernehmung Ilmenau 3. November 1982, Der Bundesbeauftragte für die Unterlagen des Staatssicherheitsdienstes der ehemaligen Deutschen Demokratischen Republik (BStU MfS) HA IX/11 AK 5235/73, Bd. 11, Bl. 289" and "Vernehmung 24. February 1983, Bl. 371."

17 Struve, *Deutsche Herrschaft*, p. 438, citing "Herman Rieger, Bericht vom 16. Jul 1948, Archiwum Żydowskiego Instytutu Historycznego (AŻIH), 301/3773, Bl. 1."

18 Struve, *Deutsche Herrschaft*, pp. 438-439. As noted in fn. 9 above, many of these were bodies of non-Ukrainian vicitms, and quite a few of the NKVD victims were Jewish. Himka, *Ukrainian Nationalists and the Holocaust*, p. 194.

19 Ibid., p. 441.

20 Ibid., p. 669.

21 Grzegorz Rossoliński-Liebe, *Stepan Bandera: The Life and Afterlife of a Ukrainian Nationalist: Fascism, Genocide, and Cult* (Stuttgart, 2014), p. 251.

22 Grzegorz Rossoliński-Liebe, "Ukraińska policja, nacjonalizm i zagłada Żydów w Galicji Wschodniej i na Wołyniu," *Zagłada Żydów: Studia i Materiały* 13 (2017), pp. 57-79: p. 74, 79. See also Jeffrey Burds, *Holocaust in Rovno: The Massacre at Sosenki Forest, November 1941* (New York, 2013); Jared McBride, "'A Sea of Blood and Tears': Ethnicity and Survival in Nazi Occupied Volhynia, Ukraine 1941-1944," doctoral dissertation, UCLA, 2014.

23 John-Paul Himka, "The Organization of Ukrainian Nationalists, the Ukrainian Police, and the Holocaust," paper prepared for the Seventh Annual Danyliw Research Seminar on Contemporary Ukraine, October 20-22, 2011, pp. 5-6; Rossoliński-Liebe, "Ukraińska policja."

24 Alexander Kruglov and Martin Dean, "Rudki," in Martin Dean (ed.), *The United States Holocaust Memorial Museum Encyclopedia of Camps and Ghettos, 1933-1945, Volume II, Ghettos in German-Occupied Eastern Europe, Part A* (Bloomington, 2012), pp. 823-824: p. 823.

25 Alexander Kruglov and Avinoam Patt, "Sambor," in ibid., pp. 824-826: p. 825; Dieter Pohl, *Nationalsozialistische Judenverfolgung in Ostgalizien 1941-1944: Organisation und Durchführung eines statlichen Massenverbrechens* (Munich, 1997), pp. 255, 296; Alexander Manor (ed.), *The Book of Sambir and Stari Sambor: A memorial to the Jewish Communities* (Tel Aviv, 1980), p. 39.

26 Pohl, *Nationalsozialistische Judenverfolgung*, 260.

27 On the murder of Sambir's Jewish population, see Manor, *The Book of Sambir and Stari Sambor*, pp. 64, 66, 224, 227, 240, 251-252, 255, 257; Thomas Sandkühler, *"Endlösung" in Galizien: Der Judenmord in Ostpolen und die Rettungsinitiativen von Berthold Beitz 1941-1944* (Bonn, 1996), pp. 115, 349, 353, 360, 370, 374, 377; Weck, "European Holocaust Memory," p. 370.

28 Ivan Katchanovski, "The OUN, the UPA, and the Nazi Genocide in Ukraine," in Peter Black, Béla Rásky, and Marianne Windsperger (eds.), *Mittäterschaft in Osteuropa im Zweiten Weltkrieg und im Holocaust* (Vienna, 2019), pp. 67-93: p. 78.

29 John-Paul Himka, "Former Ukrainian Policemen in the Ukrainian National Insurgency: Continuing the Holocaust outside German Service," in Wendy Lower and Lauren Faulkner Rossi (eds.), *Lessons and Legacies XII: New Directions in Holocaust Research and Education* (Evanston, IL, 2017), pp. 141-163.

30 Archiwum Wiktora Poliszczuka, Derzhavnyi Arkhiv Rivnens'koi oblasti (Henceforth: DARO), Rolka 15, number klatki 00059 – rozkaz komendanta Rejonu Wojskowego "Kostomarowa" z 1.09.44 o pozdiale ziemi po wymordowanych Polakach. "Rękopis

w języku ukraińskim" and "Nakaz komendanta raionu ['Iskra' Kostopil'skho rajonu VO "Zahrava"] "Kostomarova" (vid 1 veresnia 1943 r.)," DARO, f. R.-30. Op.2, Spr. 64, Ark. pp. 38-40. The author wishes to thank Wiesław Tokarczuk for bringing these documents to his attention.

31 Tsentral'nyi Derzhavnyi Arkhiv Vyshykh Orhaniv Vlady Ukrainy, (henceforth: TsDAVOVU), f. 3833, op. 2, spr. 1, Ark. pp. 246-247, as cited in Vitalii Nakhmanovych, "Do pytannia pro sklad uchasnykiv karal'nykh aktsii v okupovanomu Kyievi (1941-1943)" in V. R. Nakmanovych et al. (eds.), *Druha svitova viina i dolia narodiv Ukrainy: Materialy 2-i Vseukrains'koi naukovoi konferentsii m. Kyiv, 30-31 zhovtnia 2006 r.* (Kiev, 2007), p. 254.

32 Marco Carynnyk, "Foes of Our Rebirth: Ukrainian Nationalist Discussions about Jews, 1929-1947," *Nationalities Papers* 39(2) (2011), pp. 315-352: p. 345, and idem., "'A Knife in the Back of Our Revolution': A Reply to Alexander J. Motyl's 'The Ukrainian Nationalist Movement and the Jews: Theoretical Reflections on Nationalism, Fascism, Rationality, Primordialism, and History'," p. 27, citing Nakaz Ch. 2/43, "Povitnym i raionovym do vykonannia," October 27, 1943, TsDAVOVU, f.3833, op.1, spr. 43, l. 9. Website of the American Association for Polish-Jewish Studies, http://aapjstudies. org/manager/external/ckfinder/userfiles/files/Carynnyk%20Reply%20to%20 Motyl%202%20.pdf (accessed September 2, 2016).

33 Kopstein and Wittenberg, *Intimate Violence*, p. 92. *Mens rea* is Latin for "guilty mind," referring to the mental element of one's intention to commit a crime, or their awareness that one's actions would cause a crime to be committed.

34 Peter J. Potichnyj, "The Ukrainian Insurgent Army (UPA) and the German Authorities," in Hans-Joachim Torke and John-Paul Himka (eds.), *German-Ukrainian Relations in Historical Perspective* (Edmonton, 1994), pp. 163-177: p. 169. On Hryn'okh's negotiations, see Ivan Hrynokh, *Boh i Ukraina ponad use*, edited by Oleksandr Panchenko (Hadiach, 2007), pp. 72-73.

35 Dzheffri [Jeffrey] Burds, *Sovetskaia agentura: Ocherki istorii SSSR v poslevoennye gody* (New York and Moscow, 2006), p. 47.

36 D. V. Vedeneev and O.E. Lysenko, "Orhanizatsiia ukrains'kykh natsionalistiv i zarubizhni spetssluzhby (1920-1950-ti rr.)," *Ukrains'kyi istrorichnyi zhurnal* 3 (2009), pp. 132-146: p. 137.

37 Potichnyj, "The Ukrainian Insurgent Army (UPA)," p. 255; Dmytro V. Vedeneev and Genadii S. Bystriukhin, *'Povstans'ka rozvidka diie tochno i vidvazhno…': Dokumental'na spadshchyna pidrozdiliv spetsial'noho pryznachennia OUN ta UPA. 1940-1950-ti roky* (Kiev, 2006), p. 97.

38 Rossoliński-Liebe, *Stepan Bandera*, p. 285; Grzegorz Motyka, *Ukraińska partyzantka 1942-1960: Działalność Organizacji Ukraińskich Nacjonalistów i Ukraińskiej Powstańczej Armii* (Warsaw, 2006), pp. 227-237.

39 Document 30, "1944, 2 czerwca – Fragmenty meldunku tygodniowego Sekcji Informacji (krypt. '6005') Wydzialu Prasy i Informascji ODR we Lwowe, opracowanego przez Bolesława Stachonia (pseud. '870') i Kazimierza Świrskiego (pseud. '871'), Leona Kochańskiego (?) (pseud. '872'), i Kazimierza Świrskiego (pseud. '873'), dotyczącego ekterminacji ludności polskiej," in Lucyna Kulińska and Adam Roliński (eds.), *Dokumenty do dziejów stosunków polsko-ukraińskich 1939-1945 t. II: Kwestia ukraińska i eksterminacja ludności polskiej w Małopolsce Wschodniej w świetle dokumentów Polskiego Państwa Podziemnego 1942-1944* (Kraków, 2004), pp. 130.

40 Document 30, "Fragmenty," in ibid., p. 134.

41 Ibid.

42 Ivan Katchanovski, "The Politics of World War II in Contemporary Ukraine," *The Journal of Slavic Military Studies* 27(2) (2014), pp. 210-233: pp. 220-221.

43 Vedeneev, Lysenko, "Orhanizatsiia Ukrains'kykh Natsionalistiv i zarubezhni spetssluzhby (1920-1950-ti rr.)," p. 136.

44 Per Anders Rudling, "'Not Quite Klaus Barbie, but in That Category': Mykola Lebed, the CIA, and the Airbrushing of the Past," in Norman J. W. Goda (eds.), *Rethinking Holocaust Justice: Essays across Disciplines*, ed. (New York, 2018), pp. 158-187.

45 Taras Shchepaniak, "Svitloi pam"iaty Liubomyra Huzara," https://www.plast.org.ua/lubomyr-huzar/ (accessed April 2, 2020); Per A. Rudling, "Long-Distance Nationalism: Ukrainian Monuments and Historical Memory in Multicultural Canada," in Sabine Marschall (ed.), *Public Memory in the Context of Transnational Migration and Displacement: Migrants and Monuments* (Cham, Switzerland, 2020).

46 Rossoliński-Liebe, *Stepan Bandera*, pp. 459-529.

47 Harald Welzer, "Erinnerungskultur und Zukunftsgedächtnis," *Aus Politik und Wissenschaft* 25-26 (2010), pp. 16-23: p. 18.

48 Delphine Bechtel, "Le nouveaux héros nationaux en Ukraine occidentale depuis 1991," in K. Amacher and L. Heller (eds), *Le Retour des héros: La reconstitution des mythologies nationales à l'heure du postcommunisme* (Geneva, 2010), pp. 53-67: p. 65-66.

49 Yuliya Yurchuk, *Reordering of Meaningful Worlds: Memory of the Organization of Ukrainian Nationalists and the Ukrainian Insurgent Army in Post-Soviet Ukraine* (Stockholm, 2014), p. 201.

50 Ibid., p. 174.

51 Tarik Cyril Amar, "A Disturbed Silence: Discourse on the Holocaust in the Soviet West as an Anti-Site of Memory," in Michael David-Fox, Peter Holquist, and Alexander M. Martin (eds.), *The Holocaust in the East: Local Perpetrators and Soviet Reponses* (Pittsburgh, 2014).

52 Pierre Nora, "Between Memory and History: Les Lieux de Mémoire," *Representations* 26 (1989), pp. 7-24: p. 13.

53 Omer Bartov, *Erased: Vanishing Traces of Jewish Galicia in Present-Day Ukraine* (Princeton, 2007), pp. 41, 58, 59, 62, 102, 107, 120, 122, 130, 145; Delphine Bechtel, "Voir et représenter l'absence: paysages post-Shoah en Galicie," *Mémoires en jeu* 7 (2018), pp. 112-116; Jelena Subotić, *Yellow Star, Red Star: Holocaust Remembrance after Communism* (Ithaca and London, 2019), p. 215.

54 Mikhail Gold, "'Krestovyi pokhod' v Sambore kak mogil'shchik ukrains'kogo budushchego," *Khadashot: Gazeta assotsiatsii evreiskikh organizatsii i obshchin Ukrainy* 1 (January 2020), http://hadashot.kiev.ua/content/krestovyy-pohod-v-sambore-kak-mogilshchik-ukrainskogo-budushchego?fbclid=IwAR1xrC10svwfEdvFN-loiJKXJZdVhI31np_4ey8WQA6gs2NW7gt-5Uw1vbQ (accessed February 3, 2020).

55 Bartov, *Erased*, p. 52; Bechtel, "Le noveaux héros nationaux," p. 58.

56 Bartov, *Erased*, p. 93.

57 Delphine Bechtel, "De Jedwabne a Zolotchiv: Pogromes locaux en Galicie, juin-julliet 1941," *Cultures d'Europe centrale* 5 (2005), 69-92; Sofia Graczowa, "Oni żyli wśród nas?," pp. 861-875 and Marko Carynnyk, "Złoczów milczy," in Andrzej A. Zięba (ed.), *OUN, UPA i zagłada Żydów*, pp. 343-361.

58 Taras Kuzio, *Ukraine: Democratization, Corruption, and the New Russian Imperialism* (Santa Barbara, 2015), p. 180; Oksana Myshlovskaia and Andre Libikh, "Kul't Bandery do i posle Evromaidana: topograficheskii obzoe pamiatnikov i memorial'nykh praktik," *Forum noveishei vostochnoevropeiskoi istorii i kul'tury* no. 2 (2017), pp. 191-218: pp. 192-193, 201.

59 Marianna Popovich and Anna Mishchishin, "V Sambore ustanovili 'klon' l'vovskogo Bandery," *KP v Ukraine*, November 22, 2011, https://kp.ua/lvov/312152-v-sambore-ustanovyly-klonlvovskoho-bandery (accessed February 16, 2020). On Posikira, see Grzegorz Rossoliński, "Bandera und Nikifor – zwei Modernen in einer Stadt: Die 'nationalbürgerliche' und die 'weltbürgerliche' Moderne in Lemberg," in Lutz Henke, Grzegorz Rossoliński, and Philipp Ther (eds.), *Eine neue Gesellschaft in einer alten Stadt* (Wrocław, 2007), pp. 109-124.

60 Tarik Cyril Amar, "Different but the Same or Same but Different? Public Memory of the Second World War in Post-Soviet Lviv," *Journal of Modern European History* 9(3) (2011), pp. 373-396, and pp. 387-389 in particular; Eleonora Narvselius, *Ukrainian Intelligentsia in Post-Soviet L'viv: Narratives, Identity, and Power* (Lanham, MD, 2012), p. 347.

61 Rossoliński-Liebe, *Stepan Bandera*, p. 495.

62 "Vidkryttia pam'iatnyka Stepanovi Banderi u Staromu Sambori," *Sambirs'ko-Drohobyts'ka eparkhiia: Ukrains'ka hreko-katolyts'ka tserkva*, December 3, 2008, http://www.sde.org.ua/home/archive/item/1150-vidkryttya-pamyatnyka-stepanovi-banderi-u-staromu-sambori.html (accessed September 3, 2021).

63 "W Samborze poświęcono pomnik Bandery," *Kresy.pl*, November 28, 2011, https://kresy.pl/volgal/w-samborze-poswiecono-pomnik-bandery/ (accessed February 16, 2020).

64 Popovich and Mishchishin, "V Sambore ustanovili."

65 Yurchuk, *Reordering of Meaningful Worlds*, pp. 156-199.

66 In 2015, Poroshenko signed into effect Law 2538-1, criminalizing "disrespect" for the OUN and UPA. On the memory laws, see Tarik Cyril Amar, "Ukraine's Nationalist 'Decommunization' Laws of Spring 2015: Shielding Perpetrators and Excluding Victims," *Mémoires en Jeu/Memories at Stake. Dossier 'Illiberal Policies Regarding the Past* 9 (Summer-Fall 2019), pp. 99-103; David R. Marples, "Decommunization, Memory Laws, and Builders of Ukraine in the 20th Century," *Acta Slavica Iaponica* 39, (2018), pp. 1-22.

67 "For the defender of Ukraine Day," *Sotsiolohichna hrupa Reitinh*, October 5, 2017, http://ratinggroup.ua/en/research/ukraine/ko_dnyu_zaschitnika_ukrainy.html (accessed October 10, 2017); Vitalii Chervonenko, "Chym zakinchyt'sia 'istorychna kryza' mizh Ukrainoiu ta Pol'shcheiu?," *BBC Ukraina*, November 10, 2017, http://www.bbc.com/ukrainian/features-41934591 (accessed February 4, 2018).

68 Struve, *Deutsche Herrschaft*, p. 433, note 1.

69 Kruglov and Patt, "Sambor," in Dean, *The United States Holocaust Memorial Museum Encyclopedia of Camps and Ghettos, 1933-1945, Volume II, Part A*, pp. 824-826: p. 824; Struve, *Deutsche Herrschaft*, p. 433.

70 Bartov, *Erased*, pp. 43-44.

71 Ibid., pp. 43-44.

72 Alexander Clarkson, "Coming to Terms with Odessa Ukraine: The Impact of the Maidan Uprising on the Ukrainian Diaspora," in Timm Beichelt and Susann Worschech (eds.), *Transnational Ukraine? Networks and Ties that Influence(d) Contemporary Ukraine* (Stuttgart, 2017), pp. 115-136: p. 119.

73 Matthias Kaltenbrunner, *Das global vernetzte Dorf: Eine Migrationsgeschichte* (Frankfurt am Main, 2017).

74 Mikhalo Vitiai, "Strasti nad mogilami," *Argumenty i fakty v Ukraine* 36 (2000), p. 10. Thanks to Nadja Weck for sharing this material with the author; Gold, "Krestovyi pokhod."

75 Weck, "European Holocaust Memory," p. 374.

76 Gold, "Krestovyi pokhod." *Khadashot*, founded in 1991, is closely affiliated with Zissels' VAAD and is dependent on it for funding. Burakovskii, *Istoriia i analiz*, pp. 80-86, 133. Historian Nadja Weck notes that "by the summer of 2011, the Jewish cemetery in Stary Sambir was covered with so much brushwood that it was hard to see any of the gravestones. Instead of reconstructing the old synagogue, they erected a monument to Stepan Bandera." Weck, "European Holocaust Memory," p. 375.

77 Weck, "European Holocaust Memory," p. 372.

78 Ian Toporovski, "Pritiazaniia na evreiskuiu smert'," *OKNA*, February 15, 2001, p. 4. Thanks to Nadja Weck for sharing this material with author.

79 Gold, "Krestovyi pokhod."

80 Toporovski, "Pritiazaniia na evreiskuiu smert'."

81 Ron Csillag, "Canadian Lawyer Fights to Restore Ukrainian Mass Grave," *Canadian Jewish News*, January 9, 2019, https://www.cjnews.com/news/canada/canadian-lawyer-fights-to-restore-ukrainian-mass-grave (accessed October 3, 2019).

82 These included KUN, the Ukrainian Republican Party, the Social-Nationalist Party of Ukraine (SNPU, today VO Svoboda), the Narodnyi Rukh Ukrainy (NRU), the Revolutionary "Memorial," Brotherhood of OUN-UPA veterans, the Society of Political Prisoners and Repressed, but also Tymoshenko's party "Batkivshchina." "Dodatok do rozporiadzhennia holovy oblderzharministratsii vid," 2000; Undated letter to the head of the Lviv regional council, Laroslav Pitku, found in the private archive of Nadja Weck, Vienna.

83 Vitiai, "Strasti nad mogiłami."

84 On Zisel, see Burakovskii, *Istoriia i analiz*, pp. 132-147.

85 Gold, "Krestovyi pokhod."

86 Weck, "European Holocaust Memory," p. 381.

87 Bartov, *Erased*, p. 49.

88 Stephen M. Norris, "Inside L'viv's Lonsky Prison: Capturing Ukrainian Memory after Commuism," in Stephen M. Norris (ed.), *Museums of Communism: New Memory Sites in Central and Eastern Europe* (Bloomington, 2020), pp. 78-104; Per Anders Rudling, "Institutes of Trauma Re-production in a Borderland: Poland, Ukraine, and Lithuania," in Ninna Mörner (ed.), *Constructions and Instrumentalization of the Past: A Comparative Study on Memory Management in the Region. CBEES State of the Region Report 2020* (Huddinge, 2020), pp. 55-68; Subotić, *Yellow Star, Red Star*, pp. 174-204; Delphine Bechtel and Luba Jurgenson (eds.), *Muséographie des violences en Europe centrale et ex-URSS* (Paris, 2016).

89 Bartov, *Erased*, p. 42 contains an image of the monument from the summer of 2006.

90 Ibid., pp. 47, 49.

91 Csillag, "Canadian Lawyer Fights"

92 Gold, "Krestovyi pokhod."

93 Ibid.; Orysia Shyian, "Kanadiitsi zbuduiut' u Sambori memorial pam"iati zahyblym evreiam, ukraintsiam, poliakam i romam," *Zakhid.net*, May 3, 2018, https://zaxid.net/kanadiytsi_zbuduyut_u_sambori_memorial_pamyati_zagiblim_yevreyam_ukrayintsyam_polyakam_i_romam_n1455663 (accessed February 11, 2020).

94 A long-term *Plast* activist, Oksana Wynnycka-Yosypovych (b. 1957) also heads the World Coordinative Education Council of the Ukrainian World Congress. "Vydatni Plastunky: Oksana Vynnyts'ka-Iusypovych," https://www.plast.ca/seniory/vydatni-plastuny/wynnycka-oksana.shtml (accessed March 31, 2020).

95 "Memorial'nyi kompleks na mistsi kolyshn'oho evreiskoho kladovyshcha mae buty symvolom mudosti i pam"iati," *Sambris'ka mis'ka rada: Ofitsinyi sait mista*, April 27, 2018, https://sambircity.gov.ua/2018/04/27/memorialnij-kompleks-na-misci-kolishnogo-yevrejskogo-kladovishha-maye-buti-simvolom-mudrosti-i-pamyati/ (accessed December 8, 2020).

96 Gold, "Krestovyi pokhod." Stephen Bandera passionately dismisses claims that the OUN-B spearheaded pogroms in 1941 as "rehashing of misinformation." Stepan Bandera, "Rodynne prizvyshshe ochyshchene," in Tarik Syril Amar, Ihor Balyns'kyi, and Iaroslav Hrytsak (eds.), *Strasti za Banderoiu: statti ta esei* (Kiev, 2010), pp. 143-144; Rossoliński-Liebe, *Stepan Bandera*, pp. 504-509; Sam Sokol," Grandson of Ukraine's Stepan Bandera Reckons With Legacy of Nazi Collaboration," *Haaretz*, August 22, 2019, https://www.haaretz.com/world-news/grandson-of-ukraine-s-stepan-bandera-reckons-with-legacy-of-nazi-collaboration-1.7731876 (accessed April 6, 2020).

97 Myroslav Marynovych (b. 1949) was a co-founder of the Ukrainian Helsinki Group in 1976. Myroslav Marynovych, *Vsesvit za koliuchym drotom: Spohady i rozdumy dysydenta* (Lviv, 2016).

98 On Taras Vozniak (b. 1957), the publisher of the journal "*Ї*," is an active participant in discussions on historical memory in Ukraine, taking a moderately nationalist position. Eleonora Narvselius, "Tragic Past, Agreeable Heritage: Post-Soviet Intellectual Discussions on the Polish Legacy in Western Ukraine", *The Carl Beck Papers in Russian & East European Studies,* Number 2403 (Pittsburgh, 2015), p. 27.

99 Gold, "Krestovyi pokhod."

100 Csillag, "Canadian Lawyer Fights;" Dovid Katz, "On Three Definitions: Genocide, Holocaust Denial, Holocaust Obfuscation," in Leonidas Donskis (ed.), *A Litmus Test Case of Modernity: Examining Modern Sensibilities and the Public Domain in the Baltic States at the Turn of the Century* (Bern, 2009), pp. 259-277, and pp. 271-272 in particular; Tony Judt, *Postwar: A History of Europe since 1945* (London, 2005), pp. 803-804.

101 Gold, "Krestovyi pokhod." The Sich Riflemen (*Sichovi stril'tsi*) was the embryonic army of the short-lived Ukrainian People's Republic of 1918/1919, led by Evhen Konovalets' (1891-1938), who in 1929 would become the founding leader of the OUN.

102 Ibid.

103 Ibid.

104 Ibid., citing "Eks-mer Sambora Taras Kopyliak vidkryv nichnyi strip-klub u prymishchenni synahohy," *Forpost: Hromads'kyi portal L'vova*, November 8, 2018, http://forpost.lviv.ua/novyny/16191-eks-mer-sambora-taras-kopyliak-vidkryv-nichnyi-stryp-klub-u-prymishchenni-synahohy (accessed February 10, 2020).

105 Gold, "Krestovyi pokhod."

106 Boris Vainer, "V Sambore sovran proekt obustroistva memorial'nogo parka zhertvam natsizma," *Khadashot: Gazeta assotsiatsii evreiskikh organizatsii i obshchin Ukrainy*

12 (December 2018), http://hadashot.kiev.ua/content/v-sambore-sorvan-proekt-obustroystva-memorialnogo-parka-zhertvam-nacizma (accessed February 17, 2020).

107 John-Paul Himka, "The Organization of Ukrainian Nationalists and the Ukrainian Insurgent Army: Unwelcome Elements of an Identity Project," *Ab Imperio* 4 (2010), pp. 83-105: p. 95.

108 Burakovskii, *Khronika evoliuttsii 'natsial'noi idei'*, p. 427; Sam Sokol, "Ukrainian Jewish Leader Accuses 'Daily Mail' of Fabricating Holocaust Revisionism," *The Jerusalem Post*, August 27, 2015, https://www.jpost.com/Diaspora/Ukrainian-Jewish-leader-accuses-Daily-Mail-of-fabricating-Holocaust-revisionism-quote-413494 (accessed March 16, 2020).

109 Gold, "Krestovyi pokhod"; Vainer, "V Sambore sovran."

110 Gold, "Krestovyi pokhod." Freiman told the same to Radio Canada International. "My understanding is there [is] absolutely no evidence that they [the 17 Ukrainian nationalists] participated in any anti-Jewish activities, I haven't seen any such information." Levon Sevunts, "Canada accused of promoting Holocaust revisionism with memorial in Ukraine," *Radio Canada International*, September 3, 2019, https://www.rcinet.ca/en/2019/09/03/canada-sambir-monument-holocaust-revisionism-ukraine/ (accessed May 14, 2020).

111 Csillag, "Canadian Lawyer Fights."

112 Vainer, "V Sambore sovran."

113 Ibid.

114 Gold, "Krestovyi pokhod." On the absence of any form of archival documents on the supposed execution of these patriots, see Vitiai, "Strasti nad mogilami."

115 On the adoption of this symbol, see "Postanovy II. Velykoho zboru Orhanizatsii Ukrains'kykh Natsionalistiv," published in *Ukrains'kyi zdvyh: Zakerzonnia. 1939-1947. Vydannia druhe, dopovnene*, ed. Volodymyr Serhiichuk (Kiev, 2011), pp. 90-114: p. 106.

116 Gold, "Krestovyi pokhod."

117 Ibid.

118 In 2020, the UCC awarded Waschuk the Taras Shevchenko Medal "for his outstanding contribution to public service," "the highest form of recognition granted by the UCC." "Ukrainian Canadian Community Honors Roman Waschuk and Oksana Smerechuk," *The Ukrainian Weekly*, March 6, 2020, http://www.ukrweekly.com/uwwp/ukrainian-canadian-community-honors-roman-waschuk-and-oksana-smerechuk/ (accessed April 15, 2020).

119 Mykhailo Diakiv, "Roman Vashchuk," *The Plast*, January 16, 2015, https://theplast.org/story/diaspora/roman-vaschuk/ (accessed October 8, 2019).

120 Businessman and philanthropist James Temerty was born Konstantin Ilkovych Temerty to an ethnically Greek family in the village Koptivo in the Donbas area in 1941.

121 James C. Temerty, public statement to Rob Roberts, Editor in Chief of the *National Post*, September 19, 2019, available in Ihor Michalchyshyn, "UCC Statement on Misleading September 17 PostMedia article," *UCC Commuiques & News*, September 18, 2019, https://ucc.ca/2019/09/18/ucc-statement-on-misleading-september-17-postmedia-article/ (accessed September 24, 2019).

122 David Pugliese, "Canadian Officials Honor Nazi Collaborators in Ukraine, Angering Jewish Groups," *National Post*, September 16, 2019, https://www.msn.com/en-ca/news/canada/canadian-officials-honour-nazi-collaborators-in-ukraine-angering-jewish-groups/ar-AAHoeun (accessed October 3, 2019).

123 Sevunts, "Canada accused". On the flag, see Rossoliński-Liebe, *Stepan Bandera*, p. 179.

124 Roman Waschuk, speech in Sambir, copy provided to David Pugliese by Global Affairs Canada. I am grateful to David Pugliese for generously sharing this material with the author.

125 "Patriarkh UHKTs, predstoiatel' PTsU ta holovnyi rabyn Kyieva i Ukrainy vidkryly u Sambory memorial'nyi kompleks pam''iati zhertv II svitovoi viiny," *RISU: Relihiino-informatsiina sluzhba Ukrainy*, August 22, 2019, https://risu.org.ua/ua/index/all_news/state/national_religious_question/76907/ (accessed April 15, 2020)

126 Ibid.

127 "Head of the UGCC at the Inauguration of the Memorial Remember: Killed Young Men Speak to Us… and Destroy the Cliché of Communist Propaganda," *Information Resource of the Greek-Catholic Church*, August 22, 2019, http://news.ugcc.ua/en/news/head_of_the_ugcc_at_the_inauguration_of_the_memorial_remember_killed_young_men_speak_to_us_and_destroy_the_cliché_of_communist_propaganda_87063.html (accessed October 3, 2019).

128 "Head of the UGCC."

129 Gold, "Krestovyi pokhod."

130 "Head of the UGCC."

131 Gold, "Krestovyi pokhod."

132 "Chief Rabbi Bleich @Ukrainerabbi," Tweet of August 22, 2019, https://twitter.com/Ukrainerabbi/status/1164352131916279808 (accessed May 15, 2020).

133 Gold, "Krestovyi pokhod."

134 Paul Lungen, "Did Canada Honor Nazi Allies or Support a Jewish Cemetery?" *The Canadian Jewish News*, September 20, 2019, https://www.cjnews.com/news/international/did-canada-honour-nazi-allies-or-support-a-jewish-cemetery (accessed March 23, 2020).

135 Ibid. For additional information on the Memorial Park project, see the website "Pamiatai Sambir/Remember Sambir" at www.remembersambir.com (accessed September 3, 2021).

136 The Centre for Israel and Jewish Affairs (CIJA) is the advocacy agency of Jewish Federations of Canada – UIA, "CIJA @CIJAinfo," Tweet of September 17, 2019, https://twitter.com/CIJAinfo/status/1173985605149241346 (accessed May 15, 2020).

137 Sam Sokol, "Rabbi Helps Dedicate a Memorial to Ukrainian Group that Collaborated with the Nazis," *Jewish Telegraphic Agency*, August 26, 2019, https://www.jta.org/2019/08/26/global/rabbi-helps-dedicate-a-memorial-to-ukrainian-group-that-collaborated-with-the-nazis (accessed May 15, 2020).

138 Chief Rabbi Bleich @Ukrainerabbi replying to @WaschukCanUA and @Epifaniy on Twitter, August 26, 2019, https://twitter.com/WaschukCanUA/status/1164251733696139265 (accessed May 15, 2020).

139 Sevunts, "Canada accused."

140 "Statement of the Coordination Council of the Vaad of Ukraine in Support of the Initiative Group to Preserve Memory of Sambir Nazi Victims," Association of Jewish Organizations and Communities of Ukraine, September 11, 2019, http://vaadua.org/content/statement-coordination-council-vaad-ukraine-support-initiative-group-preserve-memory-sambir (accessed October 2, 2019).

141 Pugliese, "Canadian Officials."

142 James C. Temerty, public statement to Rob Roberts, Editor in Chief of the *National Post*, 18 September 2019.

143 Ukrainian diplomatic missions have played an active role in memory production, working closely with the UCC. When Ukraine opened an honorary consulate in Montreal in October 2020, it appointed Eugene Czolij (b. 1959), senior OUN(b) member and former President of the Ukrainian Canadian Congress (1998-2004), as honorary consul of Ukraine. "Ukraine Has Appointed an Honorary Consul in Quebec for the First Time in History," *Embassy of Ukraine to Canada*, October 16, 2020, https://canada.mfa.gov.ua/en/news/ukraine-has-appointed-honorary-consul-quebec-first-time-history (accessed October 28, 2020).

144 Andriy Shevchenko @AShevch, Sept 17, 2019, https://twitter.com/AShevch/status/1174023911392124929 (accessed September 26, 2019).

145 Lungen, "Did Canada Honour Nazi Allies."

146 Ibid.

147 In 1982, Marco Levytsky took over the editorship of the *Ukrainian News*, a publication of the Ukrainian Catholic Eparchy in Edmonton, from Fr. Nicholas Diadio (1909-1995) and Mykhailo Chomiak (1905-1983). He has served as director of the Ukrainian Canadian Congress – Alberta Provincial Council. "Who is Marco Levytsky?" *New Pathway*, November 15, 2017, https://www.newpathway.ca/who-marco-levytsky/ (accessed September 17, 2020). Levytsky's links to Andrii Shevchenko date back more than 20 years. Before becoming an MP for Iuliia Tymoshenko's party, "at the beginning of his media career in the 1990s,

Mr. Shevchenko worked as a Kyiv-based correspondent for the Edmonton-based newspaper *The Ukrainian News*." "Ambassador: Andriy Shevchenko," *Ukraine in Canada: Embassy of Ukraine to Canada*, https://canada.mfa.gov.ua/en/embassy/ambassador/cv (accessed September 26, 2019).

148 Marco Levytsky, "Setting the Record Straight about Sambir Memorial Complex," *New Pathway Ukrainian News/Novyi Shliakh Ukrains'ki visti*, September 24, 2019, https://www.newpathway.ca/setting-record-straight-sambir-memorial-complex/ (accessed October 3, 2019). Levytskyi has previously invoked this sort of rhetorical figures, dismissing evidence of OUN(b) involvement in the 1941 pogroms as a "Vladimir Putin-style ex-KGB style falsification." Marco Levytsky "Ukrainian Nationalists Played No Part in Massacre of 4,000 Jews," *Edmonton Journal*, February 9, 2010, A13. On *Novyi Shliakh*'s attitudes to Nazi Germany in the 1930s, see Orest Martynowych, "Sympathy for the Devil: The Attitude of Ukrainian War Veterans in Canada to Nazi Germany and the Jews, 1933-1939," in Rhonda L. Hinther and Jim Mochoruk (eds.), *Re-Imagining Ukrainian Canadians: History, Politics, and Identity* (Toronto, 2011), pp. 173-222.

149 Marco Levytsky "Opinion: Propaganda seeks to drive wedge between Ukrainian and Jewish communities," *Edmonton Journal*, September 24, 2019, https://edmontonjournal.com/opinion/columnists/opinion-propaganda-seeks-to-drive-wedge-between-ukrainian-and-jewish-communities (accessed October 3, 2019).

150 Aya Fujiwara, "Canada's Response to Euromaidan," in David R. Marples and Frederick V. Mills (eds.), *Ukraine's Euromaidan: Analyses of a Civil Revolution* (Stuttgart, 2015), pp. 199-215.

151 Bohdan S. Kordan, *Strategic Friends: Canada-Ukraine Relations from Independence to the Euromaidan* (Toronto, 2019), p. 151; John-Paul Himka, "The Lontsky Street Prison Memorial Museum: An Example of Post-Communist Negationism," in Klas-Göran Karlsson, Johan Stenfeldt, and Ulf Zander (eds.), *Perspectives on the Entangled History of Communism and Nazism: A Comnaz Analysis* (Lanham, MD, 2015), pp. 137-166.

152 David R. Marples, *Understanding Ukraine and Belarus: A Memoir* (Bristol, 2020), p. 139; Rudling, "Long-Distance Nationalism," pp. 109, 113.

153 On the distinction between descriptive and normative multiculturalism, see Per Bauhn, "Normative Multiculturalism, Communal Goods, and Individual Rights," in Per Bauhn, Christer Lindberg and Svante Lundberg (eds.), *Multiculturalism and Nationhood in Canada* (Lund, 1995), pp. 86-87; Grzegorz Rossoliński-Liebe, "Celebrating Fascism and War Criminality in Edmonton: The Political Myth and Cult of Stepan Bandera in Multicultural Canada," *Kakanien Revisited*, December 29, 2010, http://www.kakanien-revisited.at/beitr/fallstudie/grossolinski-liebe2.pdf (accessed October 18, 2020).

154 Per A. Rudling "Multiculturalism, Memory, and Ritualization: Ukrainian Nationalists Monuments in Edmonton, Alberta," *Nationalities Papers* 39(5) (2011), pp. 733-768.

155 John-Paul Himka, "Interventions: Challenging the Myths of Twentieth-Century

Ukrainian History," in Alexei Miller and Maria Lipman (eds.), *The Convolutions of Historical Politics* (Budapest, 2012), pp. 211-238: p. 227.

156 Rudling, "Long-Distance Nationalism," p. 96.

157 See, for instance, "Russian Media and the War in Ukraine," in Julie Fedor, Samuel Greene, Andre Härtel, and Andrey Makaryshev (eds.), special issue of *Journal of Soviet and Post-Soviet Politics and Societies* 1(1) (2015); Sanshiro Hosaka, "Welcome to Surkov's Theater: Russian Political Technology in the Donbas War," *Nationalities Papers* 47(5) (2019): pp. 750-773, and pp. 761-763 in particular.

158 "Moscow urges Kiev to abandon whitewashing of Nazi collaborators," *TASS – Russian News Agency*. September 26, 2019, https://tass.com/politics/1080058 (accessed 28 September 2019).

Nir Itzik

A Testimony of Gedaliah Lachman from Skała Podolska. Interview from 1946. From Moreshet Archive.

Introduction by Nir Itzik

Gedaliah Lachman (November 11, 1913–February 21, 1983) was an Israeli Holocaust survivor and educator. Born Gustav in the town of Skała Podolska, he established a branch of the Zionist Youth movement at the age of 16, heading it until the outbreak of World War II. Lachman lost all his family during the Holocaust, surviving despite being imprisoned in the Gestapo prison in Czortków, enduring a forced labor camp, and hiding for over a year. After the liberation of Poland, he became an underground Zionist activist, forming part of a group that clandestinely transferred child and youth survivors across the Czech and Polish borders to German DP camps.

Between November 1945 and 1946, he served as a youth group coordinator and instructor in German DP camps. As a member of the National Council of She'erit Hapleita, he also represented the latter at the Twelfth Zionist Congress. For the following two years (1947/1948), he operated in Europe on behalf of Eretz Israeli undergrounds, founding and working for the undercover Haganah school established on a farm near Föhrenwald, Germany, and secretly acting as the organization's information officer among the training groups in the camp and area. He was also active in the Aliyah Bet ("Irgun Habreicha") in Germany and France, laboring extensively to bring the training kibbutzim from Föhrenwald to Palestine.

In June 1946, at the age of 33, he was elected chairman of the board of Föhrenwald. He married another survivor, Amalia Weiss, born in Stryj, Poland, in the DP camp, his wife and son immigrating to Israel in October 1947 while he remained in Europe as a Breicha activist, spending six months in Germany and Marseille. In February 1948, he immigrated to Israel illegally, joining Kibbutz Ashdot Yaakov, participating in the War of Independence as a kibbutz member—the kibbutz being exposed to Syrian shelling. His daughter Ayala was born in the kibbutz in July 1948.

Between 1951 and 1952, he coordinated the boarding school at the Mikve Israel agricultural school, then becoming a history, geography, and social science teacher at the Katznelson High School in Kfar Saba. In 1956, he was appointed principal, remaining in that position until 1979. Lachman died in Kfar Saba on February 21, 1983.

Lachman testified about his experiences during the Holocaust on April 20, 1946. In the account below, he describes the harrowing events he survived between July 1941 and April 1943. This is the fascinating report of a man who suffered profoundly over a very short period of time. It provides information regarding the population in the territories described, in particular the situation of the Jews when the Soviet Union entered the war, as well as the authorities' attitude towards the Jews and the behavior of the local population, before and after the German occupation.

Continuing through to the German invasion of these areas and the stages of the persecution and murder of the Jews by the Germans and Ukrainians throughout Eastern Galicia, Lachmann also describes the actions of various Ukrainians gangs. He concludes with details of his joining of the partisan in the forests in 1943, his stay there, and liberation and move to Germany.

Collected shortly after the events, Lachman's extraordinary first-hand testimony, which opens another window onto the plight of the Jews during the Holocaust, was donated to the Mordechai Anielewicz Moreshet Archive in his memory: "When a Fire Burns: Gedaliah Lachman, 1913-1983—A file in his memory" (Testimony A. 1534).

Gedaliah Lachman, born November 11, 1913 in Skała Podolska (Eastern Galicia), delivered the following account:

When the Russians invaded and conquered Eastern Galicia, the Jews welcomed them as their deliverers from the Germans. During the German occupation, the Ukrainians had collaborated with the conquerors and attacked Polish captains and soldiers. When the Russians arrived, the Ukrainians changed their "orientation" and joined the communists, occupying high echelons of power on the basis of their view that the Red Army had liberated them from the Polish yoke. While Jews also gained such posts, they were second-class citizens. Some months later, attitudes changed, the Jewish refugees from the West being asked whether they preferred to remain in Galicia or return to Poland. Those who said they wanted to return were expelled to the East. Those who were not caught were not pursued, some even being given important posts.

The Soviet authorities fought antisemitic tendencies, viewing them as counter-revolutionary. This fact heightened Jew hatred in light of the protection they were given by the authorities. Like the Ukrainians, the Poles became increasingly rebellious. While the agrarian reforms[1] were implemented, the kolkhozy[2] were not established without rape.

Thinking that the Germans would return home, the Ukrainians were quick to enjoy the reforms. In Skała, 17 Jewish businesses were nationalized, the owners being expelled from their homes. Although they sent a telegram to Stalin about the matter, the authorities returned it, threatening to punish the Jews. It was the Jews who started the trials, on occasion even winning.

The Jews moved into manual labor. In Skała, for example, they worked in the stone quarry, some working in government offices. While there was food in abundance, in the winter, especially in the big cities, there was no coal and the cold was fearsome.

As a Zionist, I had to flee Skała, so I went to Lvov (Lwów). When the Germans invaded Russia, the Ukrainians left the underground and began attacking the

Russians. I then had to escape from the Germans. They caught me in Tarnopol on July 2, 1941; two days later, the mass killings started there.

The Ukrainian army was followed by a special unit devoted to exterminating the Jews. Mass killings also began around then in Złoczów Brzeżany: they stormed the Jewish quarter as they were going home, took all the men away, and shot them. Around the same time around 4,000 Jews fell in Tarnopol, apparently in retaliation.

I wandered around the streets and for some reason was not attacked. I saw the evil with my own eyes: Alter Kacyzne[3] and other Jews were caught, taken to the cemetery, and murdered.

After the city quieted down, I went to Lwów presenting myself as a Pole. When the Jews were being murdered in their thousands by the Ukrainians, R. Levin[4] and Advocate Leib Landau went to Metropolitan Szeptycki[5] for help. Szeptycki promised to issue a proclamation but cautioned them not to leave their homes because he couldn't guarantee their lives. Landau stayed inside, but Levin went out, claiming that his place was with the other Jews. When he returned home, the Ukrainians beat him to death.

After the pogroms, they imposed a contribution of 20,000,000 rubles on the Jews. The money was collected, even Poles giving; Szeptycki gave 100,000 rubles.

I stayed there until November 1941, when the ghetto was erected and all the Jews were forced into it. Then I went back to Skała. There, I started wearing the Jewish "sign."

At that time, the Hungarian Jews were passing through Skała in flight from the Germans. With the collaboration of the Ukrainian police, the Germans passed them on to Kamieniec Podolski, where they murdered them after forcing them to dig their own graves, shoulder to shoulder. Together with the Jews of Kamieniec, 17,000 were killed.

The German occupation can be divided into three periods:

1) The Jews were handed over to the labor bureaus and district authorities and forced to pay large contributions, forbidden to travel, and stripped of their possessions (fur coats in winter for the army, etc.) Some were sent to labor camps. Only in isolated

cases were they killed. But in Czortków, people say that Himmler ordered all the working intelligentsia (115 people) to be rounded up and shot. The same thing happened in Tarnopol, Buczacz, and other places. They also humiliated and persecuted the Jews. This period lasted until July 1, 1942.

2) The Jews were handed over to the Gestapo and the mass murders began. A special official was appointed for Jewish affairs. In Czortków, the Gestapo commander showed a secret order signed by General Katzman[6] in Himmler's name for the extermination of half the Jewish population. Then they began sending the Jews to Bełżec. This period lasted until the spring of 1943.

3) All the Jews of Galicia were exterminated.

During the first period, forced labor camps were set up in Michów, Tarnopol, Kamionka, Bogdanovka (Bogdanówka), Borki Wielkie, Stupki, Lwów, on Janowksa St., etc. In Stanislavov (Stanisławów), instead of being sent to labor camps the Jews were murdered in the surrounding cities by the Ukrainians and Huculi[7] with the help of the Gestapo. The survivors were put in the Stanisławów ghetto and then liquidated.

The Jewish labor camps also housed Red Army prisoners of war at first. Everyone died of starvation or was murdered. This made way for the Jews. The Germans were accustomed to demanding a precise list of Jews, men between 12 and 60, and on that basis the Jews were requested by the Labor Bureau. The Jewish councils had to deliver these lists and find the workers. The Labor Bureau officials were easier on the Jews. Some of them helped them, especially the Austrian Germans: these got presents or bribes and better conditions. Sometimes, they even released Jews.

On December 2, 1941, an initial group of young people—50 people from Skała—volunteered to work in Borki. In Czortków, they put them all in one building and then a Gestapo officer appeared and they began beating and abusing them. Some of the Jews escaped; 26 remained.

The Labor Bureau in Skała said that the Gestapo threatened to harass and kill the Jews. The Jews paid money and the threat was averted.

The Jewish workers were employed mainly in the stone quarry. The work was passed into private German hands and they used to beat and abuse the workers. Deaths were not uncommon. The councils sent food and medicine to the labor camps. In Skała, the Yiddische Sociale Hilfe was established, headed by Dr. Landvitz, who was appointed by General Governor Frank.

The councils collected money from the Jews in accordance with the demands made by the Gestapo. A workers' ransom fund was also set up—4,000 to 6,000 yellows—so that Jews could be released. The rich gave the money needed out of their own pockets and for the poor there was a council fund. Up until the end of February 1942, all the Jews from Skała who were in Borki were ransomed. Those who were sick and had a high fever were shot by the Germans. Anyone who tried to escape or was found stealing something to eat was hung in public.

During this period, they demanded around 50 Jews for work. The Gestapo head came to the council and threatened carnage if they didn't give him the number. The Jews, who knew very well the nature of the work, didn't want to go, so at first the council began looking for workers. The Jews hid and there was real danger of mass killings organized by the Gestapo. A meeting of all the inhabitants was called and it was decided that those who had been summoned had to go of their own free will. The head of the council, Mordehai Weidenberg (54, the Zionist chairman), announced that he would go, Avraham Bilogori (37, a Poalei Zion/Hitahdut member) was the second to volunteer, and I was the third. After us, around 30 others put their names down. The group left for Borszczów, where there was a Labor Bureau center. After the council paid a bribe, it was decided that there was no need for workers and everyone was released.

It was peaceful all winter, but the killings began again in April 1942. On the first day of Passover, all the men between 12 and 60 were summoned to Borszczów to register and get work permits. All the preparations were made; the Jewish intelligentsia were also included in the registration. Many of them doubted the truth of the German announcements but didn't have any way of evading them. All the Jews were rounded up from the surrounding towns. Then the Gestapo arrived, surrounded the Jews, and began snatching them for work. The elderly, children, and those already working for the Germans in regular jobs were let go. From Skała, they took 180 people in this way, who were sent to Borki and Stupki. Those who tried to escape were beaten and killed.

There was no food in the town. It was difficult to send food to the Jews working in the camps. A general kitchen was set up in the synagogue.

On May 14, 1942, the town commander again ordered the Jews to assemble in order to receive permits. After they had done so, the Germans surrounded them and chose about 20 people, including me, as hostages. We were taken to the Gestapo prison in Czortków and kept there from May 14 to June 3. The work was very hard and they also set dogs on us trained to jump and bite. The three prison heads were a German, a Ukrainian, and a Pole. I was put in charge in my cell and I imposed military discipline and order and thereby saved those in my cell. In other cells, Jews were beaten for any infraction. On the walls of our cell were lists of Jews who had been led to their deaths on April 24, 1942, including Shuval and his wife and daughter, Meizlin, Hanna Hollenberg, who was caught on the way with a piece of meat. There were similar lists in other cells.

When the Governor General came to Czortków, Jews were killed in his honor. Every time they took a number of Jews out, a Gestapo officer, Kuchman, doing this every morning before breakfast; he had a dog that would jump at people and tear out pieces of their flesh. Over time, the council managed to release all the hostages. It was all in vain, however, because eventually the Labor Bureau declared that it no longer needed Jewish workers. Influencing the officials, they succeeded in ransoming nine people, including two who were sick. Shortly afterwards, the Labor Bureau also released the others who had been ransomed with money, including me. They paid 4,500 rubles, which I gave them back afterwards.

After I got back to Skała, the Ukrainians helped the Germans organize a hunt for Jewish girls. They took their victims to work and released them in the autumn of 1942. On their way home, many of them were caught in *aktions*, however, at the beginning of July, awful rumors began circulating of *aktions* in Zaleszczyki, Buczacz, and other places. It was said that Jews were being sent to Volhynia (Wołyń) and Polesia. A Jewish area was set up there. Some Jews believed these rumors, but no one knew about the death camps around Lublin.

On August 27, 1942, the Germans organized the first big *aktion* in Czortków. Large numbers of the SD, gendarmerie, and Ukrainian police surrounded the Jewish quarter, going from house to house looking for Jews. Although the Jews had prepared bunkers and hiding places, the Germans were good at looking and found 2,500. Only two or three Jews attacked Germans, all of whom were killed. The weak who couldn't be moved were murdered on the spot, their corpses placed in orderly fashion on the ground and counted—how many captured dead and how many alive. Half the Jewish population was killed. Zvi Shomer, who had a wife and daughters and was head of the Zionists and served as the chairman of Ezra, was released because of his position. He waived this right, however, and went with everyone else. He didn't find his family. The group of 2,300 was put on a train in closed freight cars and taken in the direction of Lwów. In Lwów, the Germans let the young people out and those who could work and transferred them to the camp on Janowska St. The rest were sent to Bełżec.

Since then the name of Bełżec has become infamous. But then no one knew what went on there. All traces of those sent there have disappeared—including my relative Sonja Jegdendow-Zelcynger, a beautiful woman with a child of six, whose husband worked in a factory with a permit and was thus released. Together with others, including a Polish emissary, he embarked on a campaign to inform everyone of the fate of those sent to Bełżec. The Pole witnessed *aktions* and when he returned he told people that trains full of Jews stopped six kilometres short of Bełżec, went into a forest, and from there were passed into the hands of the SS. The workers and policemen came with the transport and then immediately left. He saw that the camp was surrounded by two barbed-wire fences, inside which were huts, masses of naked people being taken to barracks and not coming out. The information he collected made him aware that it was a death camp.

The camp had two methods of killing—electricity and gas, in a hut with a mesh strung over it through which an electric current was passed that killed hundreds in an instant. No one knows what happened to the corpses. With respect to the gas method, the Pole reported that people were forced into hermetically sealed barracks. These are detailed reports about Bełżec. The Jews of Galicia and abroad (France, Holland, etc.) were brought here and vanished. About a million Jews were exterminated here.

On September 25, 1942, *aktions* took place in Skała, Borszczów, Mielnica, Jezierzany, and Korolówka. Early in the morning, members of the SD and

Ukrainian policemen surrounded the towns. The Skała *aktion* was headed by an SS officer by the name of Franz Rozenhof, in Borszczów by Unterscharführer Kelner, who was appointed Secretary of Jewish Affairs in Czortków by the Gestapo. The day before the *aktion*, Kelner visited the towns and accepted a large amount of money from the Jewish councils, assuring them that there was no basis to the rumors of extermination, that he liked Jews and wouldn't allow anyone to harm them. In this way, he calmed everyone down.

Some weeks before, the Jews had been ordered to paint large Stars of David on their houses. At first, they were in every room. Then the district authorities printed the signs and sold them to the Jews, who had to put them in their windows so they could be seen.

Around the same time, the councils were ordered to deliver precise plans of the Jewish quarter. The Jews understood what was about to happen and hid in bunkers they had prepared. The Germans in Skała went from house to house, however, looking and taking Jews to barracks enclosed by barbed wire.

28 sick people were killed at this time. I hid my mother and she wasn't found. They found me with the help of Ukrainians, forcing me to reveal the rest of the hiding places. A Ukrainian policeman beat me the whole time, urging me to reveal the hiding places. We were on a hill on the banks of the Zbrucz River. I told him that I wanted to tell him something and he let me approach him. I attacked him and tried to push him off the hill. Not succeeding, he took me into town to hand me over to the SS. On the way, he continued beating me with the butt of his rifle. When we got close to the barracks, I managed to escape and hid in the attic of a house, where they didn't find me.

The *aktion* finished on September 26, at 12:00. Taking everything they could from the Jewish houses, the Germans enlisted 30 Ukrainians from a firefighting unit, giving them carts on which to load all the possessions, which they took to a storeroom next to the barracks. Another group of Ukrainians went with the Germans and showed them the hiding places they knew about.

A train was already waiting at the station. They separated the women and children, the men and young people, and loaded them onto special wagons. They caught 630 people and were missing 100, whom they couldn't find because they had to stop the *aktion* at 12:00. In punishment, they took a council member with them, R. Yehuda Dromer, the council head Eliezer Fisch, and Moshe Bilgori from the law and order division. They took all their money, bills, and jewelry. A couple of weeks later, reports were received from 60 people that they had been put in the camp on Yanovska St. in Lwów. The rest were taken to Bełżec and exterminated.

In Borszczów, an SS officer by the name of Laube, who conducted the *aktion*, took six elderly people out and ordered them to sing and dance. After photographing them, he shot them.

In Jeziarna, an SS driver by the name of Bretschneider killed 11 Jews.

On October 22, all the Jews in the surrounding towns were ordered to leave their homes and assemble in Borszczów, one of five towns in which they were permitted to live. In Skała, only a few Jews remained.

The border police unit (that operated between Galicia and Russia) had a farm on which Jews worked with Gestapo permission. They were about 30 in all. Another small group of Jews remained, 7 or 8 people, who worked for the Germans collecting skins, rags, and iron, etc.

Things calmed down over the winter and the Jews began returning to their towns, hoping to get good permits. They hid their possessions with the Ukrainians, promising them half in exchange. In this way, they aroused the Ukrainians' appetites, believing that they could save their lives in towns where there were no Jews. They inhabited houses other Jews had built for themselves, because all the buildings had been destroyed. When the towns passed into Ukrainian hands, a *modus vivendi* was established.

I escaped again from Borszczów and returned to Skała. The Ukrainians and Poles tolerated me, calling me "*chłopski Żyd*" because I worked my field. I lived in Ukrainian friends' houses in exchange for teaching their children. I also slept there when it was dangerous. Other Jews did the same, hiding with Ukrainians and Poles.

In the meantime, hope was growing stronger, especially after the battle of Stalingrad. Although the Ukrainians' mood fell a little, the Germans' didn't.

On April 6, 1943, the Gestapo ordered all the Jews, including those with permits, to assemble in the towns in which they had been allowed to live. At the same time, the Ukrainians were given broad license to act as they pleased. Most of them were openly hostile to Jews, being pleased with Hitler's acts of abomination because they wanted to be rid of the Jews.

Three Ukrainian parties were active during the war:

1) The Bandera group, named after Bandera, who demanded Ukrainian independence together with Russian Ukraine (whom the Germans helped set up a special army)

2) Melnyk's supporters—the successor of Colonel Konowalec who also depended on the Germans

3) Hetman Skoropadski's men, whom the Germans supported, thinking that they would put him back in power as in the earlier war.

The Communist regime rejected even the peasants, who were really frightened of the kolkhozy. They regarded the Ukrainian peasants, the members of the kolkhozy, as though they were all rebels. The terror also put off the Ukrainian masses: because of a speech against the kolkhozy or the Soviet regime they could be sentenced to 10 years. They deported the Ukrainians to remote places. The chasm between reality and the propaganda disappointed the Ukrainians, so they distributed fliers that referred to the Poles, Hungarians, communists, and Jews as the enemies of Ukraine.

In October 1941, rumors reached us that Bandera had been arrested and his legion disbanded. Bandera was said to have been killed. An Bandera underground was set up and bands were formed in the forests. When the Germans started seizing Ukrainians for work, they fled to the forests.

Ukrainian officials, the heads of the local authorities, incited hatred against the Jews. Most of their rhetoric was directed against the Jews on the grounds that they supported the Soviets. They celebrated Hitler's extermination of the Jews and benefitted from the plunder. The Poles also believed Hitler had liberated Poland from the Jews. But the Poles weren't involved in the *aktions* and pillage like the Ukrainians, except in isolated cases. This was due to the danger the Ukrainians posed to the Poles, as well as the fact that they became second-class citizens.

In 1942/3, the Borovets bands were set up under the pseudonym Taras Bulba. These began their activities in eastern Ukraine and then spread to Wołyń and Galicia. They killed Poles, their goal being to wipe them out without leaving any trace. 75,000 Poles were killed in Wołyń, which became "*polenrein*." The few survivors fled to Lwów and then Galicia, where the Germans left them alone. At that point, they weren't interested in the Jews. When they reached Galicia, there weren't any Jews left in the villages or towns; they'd all been put in camps.

In 1943, the Germans began the final extermination of Galician Jewry on Himmler's order. That's what they told the council members who were still working.

The work camps became death camps for the elimination of the Jews. The authorities in the villages and towns were delivered into the hands of the Ukrainian police. An order was given to look for Jews and kill them. Rewards were even offered. The Ukrainian police force carried out its task meticulously. In the large cities, like Lwów, the SS conducted *aktions* and the Ukrainian police helped them. Ukrainian civilians also participated, for various reasons, including fear that witnesses would remain who would inform the approaching Red Army about what they had done.

The camps and ghettos were liquidated.

On April 19, 1943, Borszczów was purified of Jews. They were taken to the cemeteries and murdered after digging their own graves.

A group headed by Yehoshua Zucker (Beitar) and Leon Jung (non-partisan/ assimilated) escaped from Borszczów to the forests. Many Jews escaped from the cities to the forests, where they built bunkers. Around Buczacz, groups of Jewish partisans attacked the Ukrainian police and Germans. On one occasion, they went into Buczacz and the army and commissar fled from them. Esther Wegdendorf was in this group and survived. In the Borszczów group, Żunia Augenblick was prominent and also survived. They had 22 rifles and five pistols, which they bought for a high price. They cooperated with the Kulpak group, which organized partisan groups between the Dnieper and Carpathian mountains.

In Borislav (Borysław), they set fire to the oil fields. With the help of the Kalpak groups, they conducted sorties into Borszczów and murdered the head of Cygany, who had handed Jews over to the Gestapo. The Germans organized a hunt and killed many of the Jews in the forests. Of 65 people in the group, 32 survived.

In January 1944, the Germans instigated a battle in which all the members fell apart from Yehuda Guttsman (Zionist Youth), who later attacked the Germans and died in a skirmish, and Wagner, who survived and today lives in Galicia.

In spring 1944, the Borszczów group numbered around 50, despite its heavy losses. As the Red Army approached the Złota Lipa, the Germans fortified their position and exterminated all the Jews in the forest. Only a few survived.

The slaughter continued ad intensified. In June 1943, the Germans threw hand grenades into the bunkers and killed all the surviving Jews in Borszczów in seven days of rampage. The Gestapo took those who were captured alive to the cemetery and shot them. Those who didn't die immediately were beaten to death with blows and rifle butts. At the end of June, there was only a small group of Jews left. These paid the Germans for the bullets they used to shoot the Jews—20,000 yellows. They were forced to dig a channel for the blood to run from the corpses onto the road.

Officially, there were no more Jews in Galicia at the end of June 1943. Only a few survived, hiding in bunkers in the forests or being hidden by Ukrainians and Poles, mostly for money. A small number hid as Aryans, but the Ukrainians recognized them and handed them over to the Germans.

The Ukrainians weren't satisfied with this but continued searching for Jews. On June 28, 1943, 30 Jews were taken from the bunkers and murdered. On August 10, 40 people. Hereby, the remnants of Galician Jewry were wiped out by Ukrainian policemen and youths.

Some of the Jews defended themselves and killed their assailants. The Ukrainian doctors didn't want to give medical attention to Jews. The only Jewish doctor who survived in Skała was killed at this time with his family.

In the summer of 1943, a lad who had been tortured for a long time told the Germans that some Jews were still in hiding, also naming me. A reward was put on my head because they said I was the head of the Jewish partisans and a communist. On September 30, they searched my friend the builder's house, whom they were told had built a bunker especially for me. They didn't find me—I was hiding with another friend, a communist. But eventually I had to escape to the forest.

Kulpak's partisans and other groups were in the forests along the banks of the Zbrucz that join up with the Wołyń forests. Kulpak's men did nothing, apparently just waiting for the Red Army. Bandera bands also hid in the forests without doing anything, only occasionally engaging in skirmishes with the

Germans. When they came upon Jews in hiding, they killed them. Taras Bulba gangs also came to the forests from Wołyń. They attacked and killed Poles. Only Kulpak's partisans helped Jews, also with food, which they had in plenty from the Ukrainian villages. Sometimes, they even gave weapons to groups who had very little ammunition. But they didn't allow Jews to join them.

I wanted to join the group led by Zucker and Jung but I couldn't find them because they were very few at that time. Two months later, the Soviet forces reached Skała. I stopped hiding at the end of March 1944. In December, the Russians conscripted me to the iron track army and I worked for half a year building the bridge over the San Rive near Przemyśl.

In 1945, I was liberated as a Polish citizen on the basis of the law of exchange. I came to Kraków and made contact with the Ichud group in Upper Silesia (Śląsk) – Zabrze.

In November 1945, I left with several kibbutzim for Germany.

It's difficult now to precisely determine how many Jews remained in Galicia. No one stayed in my town; everyone went to Poland. The law allowed not only Poles but also Jews to go to Poland and declare their Polish citizenship. Even the youths, who when the Red Army first arrived had different jobs in the government, left Galicia and went to Poland.

Endnotes

1   The agrarian reforms transferred ownership of the land by government order or with government support The kolkhozy were collective farms during the Soviet era. The notes are provided by the editor.

2   "Kolkhozy", meaning a collective farm at the URSS.

3   Alter Kacyzne was born on May 31, 1885 in Vilna, which was then part of the Russian Empire. A writer, poet, playwright, publisher, and chairperson of the Jewish branch of the International Writers Association, he was murdered, as depicted by Lachman's account, after being tortured and severely beaten in the Jewish cemetery in Tarnopol on May 7, 1941. See Sarit Yellov, "On Alter Kacyzne," *Davar*, June 7, 1985 (Hebrew); Rubik Rosenthal, "The Lost World of Alter Kacyzne," *Hotam*, June 7, 1985, pp. 18–19 (Hebrew).

4   Dr. Yehezel Levin was the Chief Rabbi of the Lwów Reform community. This reference to the Metropolite appears to be to Andrey Sheptytsky, Archbishop of the Ukrainian Greek Catholic Church. See Yossi Melman and Asaf Carmel, "The Ukrainian Schindler," *Haaretz*, September 6, 2005 (Hebrew).

5   "Szeptycki", Lachman is probably referring to the Ukrainian priest Andrei Szeptycki.

6   Fritz Katzman was a high-ranking SS officer and war criminal, responsible for the murder of Galician Jewry during World War II. When Operation Barbarossa began with the capture of a large swathe of the Soviet Union, the Germans established the district of Galicia, which was appended to the General Government. Katzman was promoted to the rank of Brigadeführer, being appointed commander of the *SS-und Polizeiführer* in Galicia on August 8, 1941, headquartered in Lwów. He served under the command of Higher SS and Police Leader Friedrich-Wilhelm Krüger in the General Government. After the war, he hid under the name Bruno Albrecht, his identity being discovered after his death in a hospital in Darmstadt.

7   The Huculi were a small ethno-cultural Ukrainian group whose members lived primarily in the southwestern Carpathian mountains of western Ukraine. Others resided on the northern regions bordering Romania in Marmoresh and Bukovina.

Father Patrick Desbois and Michał Chojak

"I saw them because I was pasturing the cattle"– Testimony of Petro A., a neighbor of the Lavrykivtsi Camp. From *Yahad In Unum Archive*

Introduction by Michał Chojak

Yahad In Unum, combining the Hebrew word *Yahad*, meaning «together,» with the Latin phrase *In Unum*, meaning "in one," was founded in 2004 by Catholic priest Father Patrick Desbois. The organization is dedicated to systematically documenting the mass executions of Jews and Roma perpetrated by German units in Central and Eastern Europe during World War II and identifying the execution sites of the victims. After in-depth research within the Soviet and German archives, YIU researchers enter the field. They travel from village to village to seek out local witnesses of Nazi atrocities, film interviews, document events, and locate the mass graves of Jewish and Roma victims. The objective of this work is to: record and document the "Holocaust by Bullets," or the mass executions of Jews outside of Nazi extermination camps, document evidence of mass killings to negate modern-day Holocaust denial, give dignity and respect to the victims' burial places and enable their preservation, and educate and disseminate information about the universal lessons of genocide derived from Yahad - In Unum's work.

The work being done by Yahad In Unum is based on the premise that the systematic mass killings of Jews perpetrated by the Nazis and their auxiliaries were not carried out in secret. Instead, these crimes were very often conducted in public, in broad daylight. Local inhabitants were almost always aware of what happened to their Jewish neighbors and, what is more, saw how, where, and by whom these victims were murdered. Yahad In Unum's ongoing research into the crimes against the Jews and Roma in Eastern Europe during World War II has uncovered the locations of more than 3,000 killing sites. These findings have been made possible through interviews with more than 7,300 witnesses.

The organization has conducted 185 investigation trips across 11 countries: Ukraine, Russia, Belarus, Poland, Moldova, Romania, Lithuania, Latvia, Estonia, Republic of Macedonia, and Slovakia[1].

In July 2019, a Yahad In Unum team traveled to the Ternopil *oblast* to interview the last witnesses of the Holocaust in that region. During the investigation, the organization's researchers explored different aspects of the Shoah in the region of Ternopil, Kremenets, and Chortkiv. One of the objects of study was the documentation of the fate of Jewish prisoners of the numerous labor camps, located in the vicinity of the *Durchgangstrasse IV* (*DG IV*), a strategic military road built by German authorities to supply the army at the southern sector of the Eastern Front. During the investigation, the team visited Lavrykivtsi[2], where one of these camps was located. Lavrykivtsi is a small village located 8 kilometers west of Zboriv. In autumn 1941, the occupation authorities created a forced labor camp for Jews [*Zwangsarbeitslager für Juden*] near a stone quarry for several hundred inmates[3]. The camp was run by German commander Paul Fox and his deputy, Holtkamp[4]. The inmates were tasked with extracting stones for the construction of the DG IV. The camp was liquidated in November 1942[5], and the forced laborers were taken to Zboriv.

During the investigation, a Yahad In Unum team led by Olga Kulbachna interviewed two Ukrainian witnesses living in Travolotoky, a village located near the former labor camp in Lavrykivtsi. With the sources on Lavrykivtsi being fragmentary, their testimonies bring more information to the existence and functioning of the camp and the local aspects of the genocide. The interview of Petro A., in particular, was interesting on any level. First, as the witness used to live in very close proximity to the quarry, his testimony is a first-hand account of the experience of the inmates. The interview seems to be the only source mentioning the murder of prisoners who were too weak to work. Moreover, the witness showed the team where the camp and the mass grave of the prisoners were located. The site had been forgotten until this interview. Not only is Petro testifying about the Jews brought from other places to work in the Lavrykivtsi camp, he is also providing crucial information about the names and the fate of local Jews from Travolotoky. Only one Jewish family was living in the village before the Second World War, the family of Yitsko, who had a wife and three children. The family hid in a forest near the village after refusing to go to the Zboriv ghetto. They were caught and killed in Travolotoky.

The testimony of Petro A. also highlights two important points. First, it shows the public nature of the genocide, which coexisted with a rural environment and a population who witnessed the persecution of Jews daily for almost a year. Indeed, the interactions between the camp and the inhabitants were numerous. The inhabitants of the villages were also requisitioned to bury the bodies of local Jews who were massacred. Secondly, the witness's account demonstrates, despite the precocity of the massacres in the Soviet territories, the necessity for the Nazi authorities to exploit the Jewish populations before exterminating them, especially in the context of the construction of DG IV, a decisive project for conducting their war in the East. Whether it was the execution of the only Jewish family in Travolotoky or one of the camp's prisoners in Lavrykivtsi, Petro's testimony gives an important insight about the local aspect of the genocide, allows the victims to be remembered, and contributes to the memory of the Holocaust in Eastern Galicia.

Yahad In Unum, Testimony 2605U

Testimony with Petro A., male, Ukrainian, born in 1929, recorded by Yahad In Unum on July 6, 2019 in the villages of Travotoloky and Lavrykivtsi (Ternopil oblast, Ukraine).[6]

Yahad In Unum: What year were you born[7]?

Witness: 1929th, February the 6th .

Y.U.: And where were you born?

Witness: Here in Travotoloky. […][8]

Y.U.: What did your parents do before the war?

Witness: Land. They had their land. There were no kolkhozes, but everyone had their own land.

Y.U.: Was the village of Travotoloky bigger before the war or smaller?

Witness: Maybe a little bigger. Right now we are rather smallish. There were 70 numbers, and now there are not. People are gone already.

Y.U.: Except Ukrainians, what other nationalities used to live in the village before the war?

Witness: Poles and Jews. […]

Y.U.: Were there more Ukrainian or Polish families?

Witness: Ukrainian. How many Polish there were (counts) one, two… three houses.

Y.U.: And how many Jewish families were there?

Witness: There was one Jewish house.

Y.U.: Do you remember this Jewish family? What were their names and last names?

Witness: His name was Yitsko (Їцко). He had daughters. Henka (Генка), Rida (Ріда) and Viika (Війка). And his wife was Baika (Байка). And the last name I just…

Y.U.: Do you remember what Yitsko, the father of the family, did for living?

Witness: What did he do for living? He had a field. He cultivated his land and he had his shop.

Y.U.: Where did you go to school before the war?

Witness: In Travotoloky. We had a school and 4 grades.

Y.U.: Did these Yitsko's children go to the same school as you?

Witness: Yes, they went to school. But they were younger, we didn't go together.

Y.U.: When the Soviet power came here in 1939, were you and this Jewish family able to keep your land and the shop? Or did the Soviets nationalize everything?

Witness: It was Poland… then… then they came, then there were kolhozes and they took all the land.

Y.U.: How about Yitsko's shop, was it also taken by the Soviets?

Witness: Soviets took, but then the Germans came. Then they… destroyed Jews and took everything.

Y.U.: Before the Germans came, do you remember if Yitsko's family was religious, if they went to pray in synagogue?

Witness: They had their own.

Y.U.: Where was this synagogue?

Witness: In their gathering. Because they didn't attend the church here.

Y.U.: Maybe you remember if Yitsko's shop was open on Saturdays?

Witness: It was open. I remember when we were boys we collected bags. We sold them and they bought them. And they gave us bread roll, if not money.

Y.U.: Do you remember if they worked on Saturday?

Witness: Every day you could come. Every day, that's it. They sold us these small knives, they called "small Jews". This was this shop. Later was organized our shop, so there was an Ukrainian shop. At the beginning they supplied everything.

Y.U.: Do you remember how the war started in 1941? […]

Witness: When the Germans came, and then that… and the war started.

Y.U.: Do you remember how you found out? Did you have a radio at home?

Witness: We didn't have anything. We found out when the planes were flying. They dropped one bomb, then another this is when we found out that it was the war. They dropped such bomb in the place where I lived, in the vegetable garden. We didn't have a radio, didn't have anything. It is now we have television and radio. At the beginning we lived like…

Y.U.: In 1939 when you say the war started, maybe you remember if there were any refugees, who came from Poland or..?

Witness: No, there weren't. I remember how those, how to say it… that those were taken to the war. Even my wife's father went to the war. […]

Y.U.: In 1941 when the war started, the Germans came and went on. Was it here the Germans who stayed? Or made local police?

Witness: They stayed here, it was 1941 – 1942.

Y.U.: Were there many of them here?

Witness: There were few. 2 Germans.

Y.U.: In which house were they here in the village?

Witness: They didn't live here.

Y.U.: So these 2 Germans, they based here and came to the village?

Witness: They came how to say it… They came to the village administration and gave the instructions. Why else would they come here?

Y.U.: And was the village local police here?

Witness: There wasn't. There wasn't anything. Everything was peaceful here. Now we have police.

Y.U.: When the war started and the Germans passed, do you remember what happened to the family of Yitsko?

Witness: They gathered them. There was such ghetto and they were gathered. And they escaped from home and made such pit and then they were … that… they dropped grenade and killed them.

Y.U.: Who drove them out of their home?

Witness: Who? They escaped by themselves because the Germans were rounding up to the Ghetto, to Zboriv (Зборов). And they didn't want to go and they escaped and were hiding in the village.

Y.U.: So the Germans came and..?

Witness: And they took away everyone right away to the Ghetto in Zborov. And they didn't go, they stayed here.

Y.U.: When the Germans came after the Yitsko's family, maybe you saw it or maybe you were told how it happened?

Witness: No, I didn't see it. I saw how they escaped and made a pit for winter to spend the winter there.

Y.U.: Do you remember where this pit was where they were hiding?

Witness: Why don't I remember?

Y.U.: Do you remember what they ate when they lived in that pit? Maybe people from the village brought something?

Witness: […] We were digging potatoes when they came. We gave them to eat and that's it. And this way everyone gave because they were ours. They didn't do to us anything.

Y.U.: So in the village everyone knew about this Jewish family?

Witness: They knew and also they had their own food because they had their household and everything. They had their own grain. Everyone had their own field and own sustenance.

Y.U.: Did Yitsko and his family come to you asking for food?

Witness: They didn't come. They came like there was a neighborhood field and they said: "Bring us food".

Y.U.: Can you tell us about the quarry where the Jews worked?

Witness: There was Bozhemski's (Божемський) barn uphill. Once someone else lived there (the name is not clear), then she was taken away. There was a barn and a house and they rounded up the Jews there to work in the quarry.

Y.U.: Maybe you know where those Jews were from?

Witness: They were taken from villages. Those who were caught at home had been rounded up. There were two Germans. There was such Fox (Фокс).

Y.U.: Maybe you know from which villages they were rounded up?

Witness: I didn't understand.

Y.U.: That's fine.

When did you see those Jews, when they were brought there, or when they were already working there?

Witness: I saw them because I was pasturing the cattle there. So I saw them when they had been brought to work because I was pasturing the cattle. They were working there and walking. They even sang "Our golden Hitler taught us how to work" [*nasz Hitler złoty nauczył nas roboty"*].

Y.U.: How many Jews were there, 20, 100?

Witness: There were around 200. This is how I think, or maybe less. That quarry was a big one. There was a German machine and they worked there crushing stone, sorting and taking away. And then they were taken to Zboriv and that was their end.

Y.U.: There were only men, or were women and children also there?

Witness: No, only men. Women weren't taken there. Why would they? It was a quarry.

Y.U.: Who guarded them?

Witness: The guard was the 2 Germans and they say there was Jewish police, which guarded them. They guarded themselves.

Y.U.: Did this Jewish police wear uniforms?

Witness: No, they didn't have anything. There were just 2 Germans and that's it. Other than that I haven't been inside and don't know what was going on there. They didn't let us.

Y.U.: Was it possible to distinguish those who just worked there and guards?

Witness: There was a bandage.

Y.U.: The Jewish police had a bandage?

Witness: Yes.

Y.U.: What was on this bandage?

Witness: Nothing was there, just a red bandage. And that's it.

Y.U.: How did they work there? They were brought in the morning and came back in the evening ?

Witness: It was not far. They were lined up near the house in the evening and also they were taken for lunch. They had to feed them.

Y.U.: Did they walk or they were taken by cars?

Witness: Why, they walked, because it was close. Like here to neighbors.

Y.U.: Was there a fence around the camp they stayed?

Witness: Nothing was there. Just a barn and a house where the food was prepared. And they slept in the barn. Nothing was fenced.

Y.U.: Did those 2 Germans live with them in the house?

Witness: They lived separately.

Y.U.: And where did they live?

Witness: I can't tell you for sure, I don't know.

Y.U.: Do you remember if those Jews came to the village to ask for food or just walked?

Witness: No, no they didn't come. They prepared food there. It was stone, so they were given food and everything. They were not allowed in the village.

Y.U.: Was this camp created at the very beginning of the war, in 1941, or later?

Witness: There was a household, owner was deported by Russians and it stayed, so they made that camp there. They rounded them up to crush that stone.

Y.U.: Were the Jews brought there at the beginning of the war or later?

Witness: When the Germans went further, came here and they mined stone and took it to Germany, so they worked.

Y.U.: You said that later they had been sent to Zborov and been killed, can you tell after what time when the camp was established?

Witness: They worked here almost a year and mined stone. And then after they were retreating they did their business.

Y.U.: During the year the Jews were working there, had you witnessed some violence from the Germans? Did they hit them?

Witness: They did whatever they wanted.

Y.U.: Maybe you saw something?

Witness: I could see them from above there. We pastured the cattle and we didn't come close because we were afraid.

Y.U.: Do you remember if you saw violence from the Germans, if they hit the Jews?

Witness: They escorted them to the quarry and they worked and that's it.

Y.U.: You told about decimation.

Witness: They told this, if someone was not able to work then… every tenth was shot and that's it.

Y.U.: Which moment did you see it?

Witness: They could do it at any moment. […]

Y.U.: Tell us how they did it?

Witness: How? They lined them up and counted: "One, two, three, four, five", "eins, zwei, drei… zehn".

Y.U.: And they lined them up in the quarry?

Witness: No, next to the house.

Y.U.: Next to the house. How far did you and your father graze the cows from there?

Witness: How far… 200 meters.

Y.U.: Did you see it once?

Witness: Once.

Y.U.: How many people did they decimate?

Witness: How many? How do I know how many?

Y.U.: So everyone was lined up and every tenth was..?

Witness: Yes.

Y.U.: And they shot them at the spot?

Witness: They shot them and buried them there in the garden and that's it.

Y.U.: Who buried them?

Witness: The Jews themselves.

Y.U.: Themselves. Where did they dig the grave, right by the barn?

Witness: There was a garden.

Y.U.: There was a garden and in that garden they dug the grave?

Witness: Yes.

Y.U.: And the Germans were standing and guarding?

Witness: No, no one was there. Those Germans who killed them, had given the order, and they [the inmates] buried themselves. That's it.

Y.U.: Could you see the place where they had been killed?

Witness: You could see it from the field up the hill. Now everything is outgrown. There's nothing there.

Y.U.: What happened to this garden now?

Witness: Then the Russians came, demolished everything, plowed and there's nothing there now. Only the pit where the quarry was is left now.

Y.U.: So the bodies are still there, no one reburied them?

Witness: Who would rebury them? Who knows, maybe they plowed everything and there's nothing left there.

Y.U.: Except for this case, have you seen or heard how the Jews had been killed?

Witness: I didn't go there all the time. […]

Y.U.: After they finished working and they had been rounded up to Zborov, do you remember if those 2 Germans or some other came for this?

Witness: Those were the same ones. They were those 2 Germans, they rounded them up and that's it.

Y.U.: Do you remember how it was? Were they lined up in columns maybe?

Witness: No, what columns, they just walked. As people walk, they walked. […].

Y.U.: Was the house empty till the end of the war after the Jews had been taken away?

Witness: It was empty till the end of the war, and was taken by pieces because no one was there.

And who did it, I don't know. There was a big barn there with a big household.

Y.U.: Let's go back to Yitslo's family, when they were hiding in the pit, you said that someone came and threw a grenade there. Who threw it, those 2 Germans?

Witness: No, no, the others did. After came the others. No one knew about them. If they hadn't come, then maybe they could keep hiding.

Y.U.: Do you remember how long this family had been hiding there, a week or a month?

Witness: They walked everywhere. They were here in the forest. And then when the summer was over and they were digging the potatoes, they made a pit and wanted to spend winter there.

Y.U.: When had they been killed? Was it the first year of hiding?

Witness: It was the whole year.

Y.U.: You said that it was the others who came and killed them. Who were they and where did they come from?

Witness: They came from Godovo (Годово). One German came. There in Godovo was a farm, a household and how to say, the German worked there.

Y.U.: Did the German from Godovo came by foot or rode a horse?

Witness: They drove here. And they walked going back. I didn't see how they drove to the village, I cannot tell you because I don't know.

Y.U.: How many Germans came from Godovo?

Witness: One German!

Y.U.: And how did this German know about Yitsko's family hiding ?

Witness: Someone told him.

Y.U.: And he purposely came to kill them?

Witness: And he purposely came with the grenade.

Y.U.: When did you see the German who came from Godovo, when he just came to the village or already by the pit?

Witness: I was digging the potatoes and he went and threw the grenade. Because that pit was right on our field. And I saw how he threw the grenade and how it exploded and that's it.

Y.U.: What distance were you from there?

Witness: Maybe 100 meters, maybe more.

Y.U.: The pit they were hiding in, what did it look like?

Witness: They took out the rocks, put some sticks and it was possible to live there. They took the rocks and it was a rather big pit.

Y.U.: Did this German tell them something before throwing the grenade?

Witness: He didn't tell them anything! He (shows) right away. And that's it. What would he tell them? He threw the grenade into the pit and that's it. They were killed right away and the girl Benka flew out. He told her to close her eyes. She closed her eyes and he killed her and that's it. The people, who were digging the potatoes, had been rounded up to bury the pit and that's it.

Y.U.: What language did the German speak to say to close the eyes?

Witness: German, but he could speak Ukrainian. I didn't hear it actually, maybe he showed. I didn't hear that. Why would I say that I heard if I didn't hear it?

Y.U.: Do you remember how old this girl Benka was?

Witness: Maybe 6 years old or 7, not more.

Y.U.: How did he kill her? With a gun?

Witness: He had a machine gun, German MP.

Y.U.: Do you maybe remember which uniform the German had? Black?

Witness: It was German green uniform.

Y.U.: You said that after he called people from the field to bury the pit, were there many people?

Witness: At every piece of field, they all dug at their piece and there were some people. For example, we dug with my mother, and further someone also was digging so you could gather some people.

Y.U.: Were you called as well?

Witness: No, we weren't called. Because they were closer, so they were called. There were 4 or 5 people. Why more? They covered everything and that's it.

Y.U.: Did the German call them in Ukrainian?

Witness: He said, "Komm" and gestured to cover it and that's it. He just gestured and that's it.

Y.U.: And Benka's body was also buried there?

Witness: Yes, they gathered all in the pit and buried and that's it.

Y.U.: What is now on this place of the grave?

Witness: There's nothing there. It was plowed, there's nothing there. Bulldozer evened everything up, so there's nothing there. It is many years passed.

Y.U.: So all the family, Yitsko, his wife and 3 children are all buried there?

Witness: Yes, all there.

On the site.

Y.U.: Tell us please, where are we now? What is this place and what is this hill?

Witness: They used to call it tranches.

Y.U.: Tranches. And there, those white rocks, that used to be the quarry?

Witness: (shows) The quarry was from here to there.

Y.U.: And those 200 Jews worked in the quarry? What did they do in the quarry?

Witness: They were stone mining.

Y.U.: What did they carry the stone with?

Witness: There were train wagons.

Y.U.: The train wagons? Were the rails here?

Witness: The narrow lane for trains was built here.

Y.U.: Did it exist before the war?

Witness: No, not before the war. It was made during the war.

Y.U.: The Germans built it?

Witness: Yes.

Y.U.: Where did this narrow lane lead?

Witness: (shows) There to Gostynets (Гостинець). There was a grinding machine for the stone.

Y.U.: So there was a special grinding machine. And what's after grinding?

Witness: They sent it to Gostynets and the rest to Germany.

Y.U.: What did they take it with?

Witness: Germans machines.

Y.U.: Those 200 Jews worked here in the quarry, where were those Germans, who had guarded them?

Witness: They were in that house (points).

Y.U.: They didn't stand next to them?

Witness: No, they didn't stand, they brought them to work. Why would they stand?

Witness: So they brought them to work and no one watched them?

Witness: No, no one watched. They gave them work and they were by themselves.

Y.U.: They were given a job and so they worked.

Y.U.: Where was the house where the Germans stayed?

Witness: There on the hill (points). Where those bushes are.

Y.U.: So there where the bushes are was the barn, where the Jews had been living?

Witness: The barn was there and the house.

Y.U.: Was the barn big?

Witness: It was rather big. There used to be 60 heads of cattle. It was a big barn.

Y.U.: And only men worked there?

Witness: Yes.

Y.U.: Was the kitchen outside or in the house?

Witness: In the house.

Y.U.: Did they go to lunch there or did someone bring it to them?

Witness: They went there. It was close, they were called and they went.

Y.U.: Where were you, when you saw how they had been killed?

Witness: I was on the hill there (points), where you left the car.

Y.U.: What did you do up there?

Witness: What did I do? I was grazing the cattle.

Y.U.: Where had they been lined up? Next to the barn?

Witness: Yes, next to the barn.

Y.U.: And how did it happen?

Witness: Those 2 Germans stood and counted them.

Witness: Well, how...“Eins, zwei, drei, vier... ” and that's it.

Y.U.: All 200 in one line?

Witness: Yes.

Y.U.: What did Germans shoot with?

Witness: MP

Y.U.: Did you hear single shots or burst of shots?

Witness: Single shots.

Y.U.: So it was seen when he was walking that they fell?

Witness: Yes. But we didn't come close, because we were afraid.

Y.U.: Where did they bury the bodies?

Witness: There in the garden (points), but there is a road now. Nothing left there.

Y.U.: Where is the pit related to that white rock?

Witness: There on the hill (points).

Y.U.: On the hill. There by the rock? On the left or right of it?

Witness: A little to the right.

Y.U.: Who buried them?

Witness: They did themselves.

Y.U.: Was there a pit already, or did they have to dig it?

Witness: They dug the pit for themselves.

Y.U.: Did you see that covered pit?

Witness: What did I see? They covered it and that's it.

Y.U.: Was it possible to see the outlines of the pit?

Witness: They covered it and that's it. They evened it and nothing could be seen.

Y.U.: When was it? Was it long before they had been rounded up Zboriv, or sometime in the middle?

Witness: They shot those who could not work anymore, those who were weak.

Y.U.: Could you hear the shots once or other times as well?

Witness: I saw it only once.

Y.U.: In what year did you say the Soviet government demolished everything here?

Witness: It was in 1945.

Y.U.: Right after the Soviet government came, they demolished it?

Witness: Maybe people took it apart.

Y.U.: And wasn't there any cross or a monument on that place?

Witness: No, nothing was there. They plowed it and that's it.

Y.U.: So they still lie there or have they been reburied?

Witness: They haven't been reburied anywhere.

Y.U.: And you say one day they had been taken to Zboriv, and when you came here nothing was left?

Witness: What was left? Nothing was here.

Y.U.: Did you see when the inmates were taken away?

Witness: They were gone and that's it. They told that they were taken away.

Y.U.: What year were they taken away?

Witness: In 1942. They were 2 years, 1941 and 1942. […]

Endnotes

1   State of research on September 1, 2021.

2   In prewar period, Lavrykivsti (Ławrykowce in Polish) was located in Poland in voivodship of Tarnopol. Between September 1939 and June 1941, following the Ribbentrop-Molotov pact, the village was located in the Soviet occupation zone in the Ternopol oblast. Following the Operation Barbarossa and the invasion of the Soviet Union by the troops of the Third Reich, the Ternopil region was occupied by the Nazis in early July 1941. From then Lavrykivtsi was part of the Galicia district [Distrikt Galizien].

3   Холокост на территории СССР: Энциклопедия / Гл. ред. И. А. Альтман. — Москва: Российская политическая энциклопедия (РОССПЭН): Научно-просветительный Центр "Холокост" (2-е изд., испр. и доп.), 2011, С. 237.

4   BAL / 162-2106, testimony of Paul Fox, former commandant of the labor camp.

5   Холокост на территории СССР: Энциклопедия / Гл. ред. И. А. Альтман. — Москва: Российская политическая энциклопедия (РОССПЭН): Научно-просветительный Центр "Холокост" (2-е изд., испр. и доп.), 2011, С. 237.

6   The duration of the interview is 61 minutes and includes a first part recorded in the house of the witness, and a second part recorded on the killing sites of the inmates of the forced labour camp of Lavrykivtsi. The interview was conducted in Ukrainian and French language by Olga Kulbachna and translated consecutively by Oksana Mirochnik. The written translation was done by Aleksandra Makovetska on the request of Yahad – In Unum. The signature of the interview is YIU/2605U.

7   As the interview was conducted in Ukrainian language, names of locations and individual were transcripted in Ukrainian.

8   Parts of the interview that are not relevant to the subject of the study have been removed to facilitate the reading.

Jan Burzlaff

Review of **John-Paul Himka, *Ukrainian Nationalists and the Holocaust. OUN and UPA's Participation in the Destruction of Ukrainian Jewry, 1941–1944,*** Stuttgart/New York, ibidem Press/Columbia University Press, 2021, 540 pp.

John-Paul Himka's assessment of his 2021 monograph seems too modest: writing that he does not "believe in definitive monographs," Himka nonetheless hopes to have "cleared some ground for future historians to work." Yet what he offers is in fact a groundbreaking study, one of the most thorough to date, of a non-German organization of perpetrators in the Holocaust, the Organization of the Ukrainian Nationalists (OUN) and its armed forces, the Ukrainian National Militia and UPA (*Ukrains'ka povstans'ka armiia*). Himka traces its prewar origins and interwar evolution, its heavy involvement in the annihilation of East European Jewry, and its postwar defenses. Several developments have facilitated the timing of this essential book, which eludes the dangers of pure condemnation and vain, politically motivated defense, let alone outright denial. Besides the recent turn to the "local" in Holocaust scholarship and the access to massive archives in Eastern Europe after 1991, the deep immersion in local languages and the consideration of non-German, non-Jewish populations, in the legacy of Jan T. Gross's *Neighbors* (2001), are crucial elements of this book about the OUN. But it is Himka's rejection of the nationalist narrative, much unlike the pro-OUN Center for the Study of the Liberation Movement, that helps produce an objective, and long-awaited, history of the Ukrainian nationalists' involvement in the Holocaust.

Any reassessment of OUN's wartime atrocities can only proceed by deconstructing the myths that nationalists and its defenders have been spinning, almost since the war's immediate aftermath. Himka peels back two of the most critical layers that have impeded a historical reckoning with OUN's role during the war. First, the silencing of Jewish (and Polish) voices, with authors simply writing histories based on self-flattering Ukrainian testimonies — often, these writers were themselves veterans of OUN. Instead, Himka considers an impressive number of Jewish memoirs, video testimonies, and other ego-documents gathered after the 1970s. Second, based on ideologically oriented material, previous accounts of OUN assigned any form of collaboration to supposedly morally depraved individuals — often depicted as the "scum" — or members of the lower social classes judged "unpatriotic." This narrative happened to fit well with published OUN veterans (to mention only Mirchuk, Herasymenko, and Shankovsky) and accessible records from Soviet interrogations, which highlight arrested nationalists who simply denied *individual* participation in the murder of communists, Jews, and other targeted groups. As a result, for almost fifty years, the topic has evolved in a vacuum. Himka's greatest merit is to puncture this bubble and, at last, to link it to the overall field of Holocaust studies. The widespread participation of OUN perpetrators alongside the German occupiers, as Himka notes, has yet to be distinguished both from the overall population of Ukrainians and individual rescuers, whom historians-turned-ideologues often like to cite. As Himka convincingly shows, one should not only avoid, as these "historians" propose, conflating an organization (OUN) with an ethnic group (Ukrainians); but one must also single out different stages *within* OUN's history, such as the Ukrainian National Militia in 1941 and the Ukrainian Auxiliary Police after 1942.

Three core elements of OUN's ideology, then, emerge from Himka's excellent study: its vision of a monoethnic Ukrainian state that guided the organization's wartime behaviors; the pervasiveness of antisemitism; and its intricate relationship with fascism, the object of an impassionate debate among specialists. First, at the onset of the twentieth century, the bitter and ultimately unsuccessful fight for an independent state increasingly radicalized the promoters of Ukrainian nationalism, such as Mikhnovsky and his ten commandments in 1903. The 1930s, in particular, with its Stalinist purges and political persecution, came to add an acid anti-communist flavor to the already deadly cocktail of eugenics, exclusionary nationalism, and race, particularly in Galicia, which Himka coherently defines as the oblasts of Ivano-Frankivsk, Lviv, and Ternopil. Three groups were particularly attracted to OUN's call for a monocratic state without Jews and Poles: nationalists from across Europe, Galician POWs returning from camps in Poland and Czechoslovakia, and students having come to age during the 1920s. Antisemitism, second, proved another glue among these groups that increasingly solidified during the 1930s. Here, Himka provides an important corrective to some of his own studies, which, because they resorted to a limited source base, had undervalued the extent of OUN's antisemitism. Third, Himka opts for a middle ground between those affirming (Rudling and Rossoliński-Liebe) and those denying OUN's fascist nature (Motyl and Zaitsev). For Himka, "it is not a mistake to label OUN as fascist, if one proceeds from an appropriate definition or from the family resemblance classification." He has convinced me that "nationalist" offers a more appropriate description based on OUN's self-understanding.

After many insights into OUN's prewar developments, Holocaust historians will be particularly interested in chapter 4 on the Soviet occupation, which shaped how the subsequent Nazi persecution unfolded. By pulling together topics that have often been studied in isolation — consider the impact of Soviet rule, and the NKVD, on OUN within the broader cultural and socio-economic changes in the annexed territories after 1939 — Himka ably demonstrates that despite several public trials and political persecution, OUN "became the only Ukrainian political organization to survive into 1941." This resiliency, which they had gained through underground experiences stretching back to 1920, would again prove important in the guerilla warfare after 1944. Based on estimates provided by Taras Hryvul, OUN had grown from 7000-7500 members in 1940 to about 20,000 members, in addition to some 30,000 sympathizers in June 1941.

Chapters 5, 6, and 7 will become standard readings for students of the Holocaust and East European Jews, ranging from the Ukrainian National Militia's involvement in the bloody summer of 1941 in Galicia, Bukovina, and Volhynia; the nationalists' more stable commitments to the Ukrainian Auxiliary Police in Galicia and the *Schutzmannschaften* in Volhynia from early 1942 to mid-1943; to the ethnic cleansing of Poles and other non-Ukrainian victims, including Jews, in Volhynia, and later Galicia, and the hunting down of Jewish survivors until 1944. For experts of these groups and regions, it is not so much the matter of the OUN persecution itself, with its almost unbearable violence and horror, than the painstakingly reconstructed timeline that makes Himka's book so novel and valuable. Thanks to his attention to detail and sensitivity to victims' and survivors' voices, the conclusions are clearer than ever before: OUN was not only involved in the murder of thousands of Jews but also directly responsible for round-ups and hunting down hundreds of thousands of Jews. Embedding this wartime violence within a longer history of anti-Jewish attitudes within OUN, Himka also argues, rightfully in my opinion, that the Nazis "taught genocide by example."

The thoroughness of Himka's study also results from an impressive array of documents, from survivor testimonies and Viktor Polishchuk's collection of wartime activities of OUN and UPA in Volhynia, Soviet interrogations and trials of members of OUN and UPA in the archives of the Security Service of Ukraine (SBU), the Extraordinary State Commission for the Establishment and Investigation of the Crimes of the Fascist German Invaders and Their Accomplices, to OUN-UPA archives in Ukraine and newspapers and periodicals of the 1930s and 1940s, including postwar periodicals from DP camps in Germany and Rimini, Italy.

Many questions remain, paving the way for further in-depth studies of Ukrainian-Jewish relations and wartime behaviors. In my reading, the inclusion of Jewish accounts is particularly insightful because Himka suggests a more fine-grained framework for such testimonies. The fact that Jews speaking about pre-1939 Soviet Ukraine are more explicit about local non-German perpetrators indeed confirm my own research; the stability of such stories told over five decades call for more attention regarding non-German violence. Recently, historians have also emphasized the weight of individual actions and behaviors. To rethink the complicated issue of 'collaboration' through different scales of organizational, communal, and individual agency will certainly prove helpful. One should also follow Himka's hint at various and distinctive visual cultures, which could shed more light on local and regional networks. No German photographers recorded cruelties committed by the nationalists, but the dominant OUN culture valued individual and, above all, collective portraits. As Himka indicates, the largest repository of Polish materials, that is, the Eastern Archive (*Archiwum Wschodnie*) of the Karta Center, Warsaw, still awaits its historians as well.

With Himka's monograph, we can now embrace the third generation of the venerable perpetrator history (*Tätergeschichte*). Whereas Raul Hilberg barely mentioned OUN, the second generation around Thomas Sandkühler and Dieter Pohl tackled the new sources during the 1990s and early 2000s. With Himka, we have now finally begun to understand non-German perpetrators, similar to what Jan Grabowski, and the broader Polish school of the Holocaust, have so far accomplished for the Blue Police and Polish-speaking lands. At times striking a personal voice that guides the reader through the terrible history of OUN, at times providing nuance to his own work, Himka has written a landmark piece at the peak of the field's abilities. At a time when right-wing ethno-nationalism firmly grips the academy in those very countries where the Holocaust unfolded, trying to conflate yet again "OUN" with "Ukraine," Himka's book should and certainly will receive the attention it deserves after years, if not decades of work. Ultimately, the book is a clear indictment of OUN's role in the Holocaust, but it is more than that. If not OUN's definite account, Himka proposes many ways to examine non-German perpetrators in Eastern Europe.

Havi Dreifuss

Review of **Wendy Lower, *The Ravine: A Family, a Photograph, a Holocaust Massacre Revealed.*** Boston/New York: Houghton Mifflin Harcourt, 2021. 272 pp.

The photo that lies at the heart of Wendy Lower's *The Ravine: A Family, A Photograph, A Holocaust Massacre Revealed* brilliantly exemplifies the saying "A picture is worth a thousand words". A leading Second World War and Ukrainian Holocaust scholar, Lower has spent the past several years analyzing a singular image. Presented to her by two Czech journalists, this is a rare record of the murder of a Jewish family in Miropol, a town in Zhytomyr Oblast, Ukraine, on October 13, 1941. The desire to identify all its elements—animate and inanimate—led Lower on a gripping cross-continental journey to archives where she discovered written and visual historical sources.

The importance of this book lies in its integration of two areas of research that have contributed greatly to the broadening and deepening of Holocaust studies in recent years: micro-history and visual history. Alongside monumental essays, comprehensive historical surveys, and discussions of the fate of the Jews in large communities, the analysis of a single military unit or transport or a defined geographical area reveals unknown aspects of the period, provides new insights, and elucidates the complexity of the events that took place at any given location.[1]

For example, Christopher Browning's examination of the actions of the "ordinary men" who comprised Reserve Police Battalion 101, a unit of the German Order Police in Poland, has demonstrated that a variety of German units participated in the murder of Jews and presented a complex figure of the murderers of the Jews as "ordinary people".[2] The *Night without End* also places the actions of those who murdered Jews in their local context, thereby disclosing the involvement of various factors in the persecution of the Jews, the amorphous division between murderers and bystanders (with all the latter's limitations), and illustrates the way in which Jews adopted diverse survival strategies, such as hiding, assuming false identities, and escaping to the forest.[3] Inevitable in interpersonal interactions, these complexities are often missed in broader and more comprehensive discussions.

While in the past historical research has focused primarily on the analysis of written and oral sources, including official documents, diaries, testimonies, etc., in recent years researchers have drawn on more diverse sources—such as setting, archaeological finds, and visual documentation.[4] A number of studies have even placed these non-written sources center stage, using them to verify the existing sources. In some cases, these are well-known visual-history documents—the photograph of the young boy from the Warsaw ghetto or the so-called "Lili Jacob's 'Auschwitz Album'," for example. In others, the analysis is of documentation that only came to light decades after the war.[5]

The photograph that came into Lower's hands is just such an instance. Immortalizing the murder of a Jewish family at the mouth of a death pit, it also attests to much more, to the discovery of which Lower dedicatedly devoted herself.

Security Services Archive, Historický fond StB (H), arch. č. H-770-3 (i.e. Historical Collection of the StB, archival no. H-770-3). [6]

The photograph is appalling in its detail: the smoke from the guns rising in the center of the picture, the group of murderers—including men in different uniforms—the Jewish family at the mouth of the death pit, the deep ravine on whose edge the murder takes place, the objects scattered on the ground, the wooded area, and the sun shining through the trees. Lower's detailed research includes cross-referencing the Slovak photographer's interrogation file (1958) with West German (1969) and Soviet Union (1986) interrogations, analysis of testimonies, and a variety of other sources that enabled her to tell the story of the picture, and to present much beyond that.

As she demonstrates, the photo was taken by a Slovak soldier named Lubomir Škrovina on the outskirts of Miropol on 13 October, 1941. That morning, Škrovina got wind of the fact that the Germans were rounding up Jews and murdering them nearby. With the approval of his commanders and accompanied by two friends, he went to the site, carrying his portable Zeiss Ikon Contax camera (which he later donated to the Bratislava Jewish Community Museum). Standing about 20 meters away and in full knowledge of those present, he took several pictures—as he later testified, to document the process. Five of the photographs he took were developed: one of bodies lying by the roadside, three of murders taking place, and one of a victim lying in the pit. According to Škrovina, he was deeply shocked by the sight and hoped that his photographs, which he secretly sent to his wife, could be used in the service of future anti-Nazi activities. In practice, they sat on a shelf for many years. Moreover, upon his return to Slovakia, Škrovina became a member of the Slovak underground, which, among its other activities, also helped to rescue Jews.

As Lower demonstrates, although Škrovina took the photographs as evidence of atrocities, he was aware of their explosive content, fearing that they might even implicate him in the murder. He thus hid them for years, finally reluctantly handing them over to the Czechoslovak State Security Service (a KGB-like authority in Soviet-controlled Czechoslovakia) on his re-interrogation in 1958. On this occasion, Škrovina provided further details about the event that fill dozens of pages.

Although taking pains to absolve himself and his Slovak friends of any complicity, he stated that the murder was not carried out by SS soldiers, the Gestapo, or the Order Police (as verified by a close examination of the German uniforms). The Germans in the photograph were Custom Border guards (*Zollgrenzschutz*) recruited specifically to assist in the murder of Jews in the town. The Ukrainians, he stated, were locals, who knew some of the victims, calling them by name during the massacre and taunting them.

These phenomena were not unusual and point to two important aspects of the murder of Jews in Eastern Europe during the Holocaust that emerge clearly from Lower's book. In remote regions, the Germans often lacked professional forces to exterminate Jews, thus recruiting a variety of local units. In contrast to the prevailing image, the German presence in many small and remote locations in Eastern Europe was sporadic, and various local German forces were often in conflict with one another. Despite their differences of opinion, however, they appear to have united when it came to murdering Jews, as did the Custom Border guards in Miropol.

At the same time, Lower's presentation and analysis of Škrovina's testimony highlights the "intimate murder" that marked small communities (and not only them). The locals recruited to help the German occupiers often actively participated in the murder of their Jewish neighbors. Under such circumstances, personal tensions, past conflicts, and jealousies led to outbursts of physical, sexual, and emotional violence.[7] Some locals claimed in retrospect that the Jews had supported the Soviets, their antisemitic views thus taking the form of anti-Judeo-Communism. In this photograph, however, the local collaborators are dressed in Red Army overcoats, suggesting not only that Ukrainian militias were recruited but also that the collaborators were often servants of two masters, working for the Red Army and Nazi Germany with the same enthusiasm and dedication.[8]

According to Lower, Škrovina was not the only one who was haunted by these sights. In 1969, one of the Customs Border guards filed a complaint at his local police station in West Germany against two of the members of his unit who took part in the murder—Erich Kuska and Hans Vogt. Despite the fact that a formal investigation was opened and numerous testimonies collected, Vogt was never located. The charges against Kuska were likewise dropped in 1970, allegedly due to lack of conclusive evidence of his involvement. The Soviet courts were less forgiving, however. Following the intensive work of a KGB investigator, three Ukrainians were identified in 1986 as taking part in the murder of Jews in Miropol. Two—Ivan Les'ko and Dmitri Gnatyuk—were executed; the third, Nikolai Rybak, a minor at the time, was sentenced to hard labor.

Significantly, the three separate investigations never shared their findings—written or visual. They are thus dovetailed for the first time in the book. Lower also conducted a field study with Father Patrick Desbois' "Yahad In Unum" organization. Additional testimonies were collected from local residents still living in Miropol who remembered the events. Some recollected Jews being rounded up and were able to identify the murder site; others were among those forced to help dig the ravines before Jewish men were brought in to replace them.

Having identified the killers, Lower faced the most challenging task of all— uncovering the victims' faces and stories. As she notes, although identifying about half of those murdered, she was unable to confirm the woman's identity with certainty, suggesting the names of Dina Rapaport and her baby and Khiva Brontzovskaya Vaselyuk. The fate of the Jewish victims can still be told however – as Lower shows - with the story of the Miropol community during the Holocaust taking center stage in the book, accompanied by a detailed discussion of the murder of the Jewish family as a central pillar of German Jewish policy.

When the Germans occupied the town on July 6, 1941, hundreds of Jews were living in Miropol, mostly women and children.[9] When the occupation mechanisms began operating, the Germans mobilized local auxiliary forces. These took an active part in the measures against the Jews, including registration, yellow-badge and forced- labor enforcement. After the ghetto was established at the end of July or the beginning of August, living conditions rapidly became intolerable. As early as September 28, 1941, *Einsatzgruppe* C began operating in Miropol and the nearby settlements, and during October close to 250 Jews were murdered in two ravines dug for this purpose between the municipal park and the river, on the border of the forest.[10] The approximately 100 remaining Jews—mostly craftsmen and their families—were shot by Ukrainian police on February 16, 1942. Most of the attempts of Jews who sought shelter amongst the local population and in nearby forests ended in their murder.

The impossible task of identifying all of the victims led Lower to coin the phrase the "missing missing"—those victims with no one to attest to their existence (Chapter 7). The circumstances of their deaths, as also the story of their lives, names and ages, are largely unknown, lying beyond reconstruction or commemoration. As Lower stresses, this absence is conspicuous not only with respect to Ukrainian Jewish history but also the Soviet Union as a whole. Erasing whole families, the "Holocaust by bullets" often left just a few identifiable individuals out of entire communities and prosperous towns are often known by only a handful of names. While the murderers in the photograph have been named, their victims remain anonymous.[11]

Nevertheless, Lower's efforts to tell the story of the Jewish family—its life and death—during the Holocaust are not fruitless. Despite not succeeding in conclusively identifying the woman or her child, her meticulous research revealed the presence of another child in the photo. On close examination, the woman leans over another body in front of her, whose feet appear to be stuck in the ground. The mother? / grandmother? / aunt? stands right on the edge of the death pit, her left hand holding the boy's as he slips onto his knees and her right hand embracing another child in her lap. Although the resolution of the photo in the book does not allow this detail to be discerned, Lower proposes that the last photo of Škrovina's shows the woman still holding the hand of one of the dead children.

Lower also highlights the presence of additional murderers throughout the book. The thick smoke, bullet casings on the ground, and coat and shoes lying on the edge of the pit all show that the photo was taken in the midst of the massacre, the previous victims not being visible. They also indicate that it is ultimately only a single detail from one scene in a protracted event. One of the most important chapters of the book thus adduces not only what is in the photo but also what is not: the young Ukrainian girls forced to dig the pit while the Jewish men were being brought out; the abuse the Jews had suffered up until this point; the murder of the men before the women; and the groups of Jews brought to the pit and forced to watch before being killed themselves.[12] Lower also reveals the identity of others present but not captured by the camera lens—Germans, Ukrainians, and Slovaks, contending that numerous people are required to kill many people.

In this sense, the study's zoom-in does not impinge on the importance of its zoom-out and the broader picture arising from Lower's research. More than three Customs Border guards and three Ukrainians participated in the slaying at Miropol and the local Jews—a hundred in number—were killed in groups. The massacre was also a complex operation, requiring aid from various sources. The enclosure of the ghetto, the guarding of its confines, the concentration of the Jews and their guarding at the assembly points, their transfer to the murder site, and the shooting itself demanded the participation of large numbers of helpers, even in the small ghettos.[13]

Other elements that formed an integral part of the *aktions* are also missing from the photo, including the deliberate depravity towards the Jewish community and the plundering of Jewish property and possessions. Despite the vastly differently ways in which the *aktions* were carried out, these elements existed in most cases, and had a destructive significance on both Jewish individuals and the collective.

The deliberate cruelty was exemplified by the specific targeting of parts of the community, a task frequently laid upon the shoulders of the local leadership. In Miropol, for example, after the October 1941 *aktions*, people working in required professions and their families largely remained. One can assume that other Jews were forced to help classify the community, either by threatening their most loved ones or by sowing seeds of hope and then crushing them. The institutionalized cruelty also carried private, personal aspects: the assembly of the Jews in the town square, leading them to the park, and their subsequent murder being accompanied by destruction, suffering, and abominations that shocked the Jewish public and its members.

The *aktions* were also accompanied by the massive plunder of Jewish property and possessions, a subject Lower does not directly address in the book. In addition to providing an opportunity for stealing jewelry and money and demanding bribes, the deportation of the Jews also served as a method of organized plunder. Lower's book thus raises questions regarding who got the coats and shoes visible in the photo and what happened to the property that was left behind in the town—houses, furniture, clothing, eating utensils, etc. The pillaging was not merely an economic issue but also directly affected the Jews' plight, heightening their efforts to buy their way out of deportation, etc. The fact that Jewish goods could be stolen made people far less inclined to become "paid rescuers", since apparently it was possible to win Jewish property even without the burden of saving Jewish lives. The flooding of the market with Jewish property also made the local civilian populace much more willing to help the Germans. These aspects, which are not visible in the photo, formed a concrete element of the murderous acts, shattering Jewish lives and spirits.

Another absent element in the photo is the more distant past, to which Lower makes almost no reference. Although the pre-war religious, economic, ethnic, and national tensions between Jews and Ukrainians; the Holodomor years that so devastated the inhabitants, Jews and non-Jews alike, of Miropol; and German-

Ukrainian relations might not necessarily provide a better explanation of what the photograph immortalizes, they would certainly add another layer to it.[14]

At the same time, it is difficult to underestimate the book's importance and its contribution to the broader Holocaust discourse. Holocaust scholars have focused for decades on the murder of the Jews in the death camps, yet in recent years it has become increasingly clear that many Jews perished by other means—most prominently in the death pits. Lower's detailed analysis of a specific dimension of Ukrainian Jewish Holocaust history shifts the focus back to the Jews of the Soviet Union. For years, these communities have suffered from a double form of silence: the Soviet authorities had no interest in discussing Jewish deaths within Soviet territory during the Great Patriotic War, the Western powers being similarly disinclined. The studies published in recent decades by Lower and others evinces that significant phenomena occurred in these regions that also shed light on the general picture of the Holocaust of European Jewry in general. The nature of the ghettos erected therein, the Jewish responses, their attitude towards their environs (whether multi-ethnic or primarily Soviet), all break the prevailing Holocaust mold with respect to the terms bystanders, Jewish existence in the forest, etc.

Despite the difficult content, Lower succeeds in providing an all-encompassing, fascinating demonstration of the essence of the work of the historian. She consistently refers to the photo and what arises from it in order to discuss broader questions, including visual documentation, the Jewish family, and the Ukrainian Jewish Holocaust. Some of this material is relegated to the endnotes, however, which are referenced according to page numbers. While this aids smooth reading, it impinges on the impressive frame: the wide-ranging scientific apparatus and broader intriguing discussions. The reader who manages to consult the notes while immersed in the text cannot but be impressed by how much this research is rooted in the up-to-date research and the scope of the aspects it addresses.

While the book is dedicated to a single family, photo, and massacre, it goes far beyond that. It not only presents the murder of the remnants of one Jewish family in Miropol by German Customs Border guards with the help of local Ukrainians, but also shifts the focus back onto a form of murder that took the lives of around two million Jews, highlights the fact that the murder was perpetrated not only by Germans and presents the vast void of the "missing missing".

Endnotes

1 Claire Zalc and Tal Bruttmann (eds.), *Microhistories of the Holocaust* (New York, 2019).

2 Christopher R. Browning, *Ordinary Men: Reserve Police Battalion 101 and the Final Solution in Poland* (New York, 1992).

3 Barbara Engelking and Jan Grabowski, *Night without End: The Fate of Jews in Selected Counties of Occupied Poland* (Warsaw, 2018) (Polish).

4 See, for example, Julia Brauch, Anna Lipphardt, and Alexandra Nocke (eds.), *Jewish Topographies: Visions of Space, Traditions of Place* (London/New York, 2008); Tal Bruttmann, Stefan Hördler, and Christoph Kreutzmüller, *Ein Album aus Auschwitz* (Darmstadt, 2019); Yoram Haimi and Wojciech Mazurek, "Uncovering the Remains of a Nazi Death Camp: Archeological Research in Sobibór," *Yad Vashem Studies* 41(2) (2013), pp. 43–78.

5 See, for example, Dan Porat, *The Boy: A Holocaust Story* (New York, 2011); Ofer Ashkenazi, "A Jewish Memory of a German Past: Jewish Amateur Photography in Nazi Germany," *Zion* 82(2) (2020), pp. 263–94; Martin Cüppers et al., *Fotos aus Sobibor: Die Niemann-Sammlung zu Holocaust und Nationalsozialismus* (Berlin, 2020); Nadine Fresco, *On the Death of Jews: Photograph and History* (New York, 2021).

6 Security Services Archive, Historický fond StB.

7 See, for example, Jan Tomasz Gross, *Neighbors: The Destruction of the Jewish Community in Jedwabne, Poland* (Princeton, 2001); Jeffrey Kopstein and Jason Wittenberg, *Intimate Violence: Anti-Jewish Pogroms on the Eve of the Holocaust* (Ithaca, 2018).

8 Juergen Matthaeus, "What about the 'Ordinary Men'?: The German Order Police and the Holocaust in the Occupied Soviet Union," *Holocaust and Genocide Studies* 10(2) (1996), pp. 134–50; Martin Dean, "The German 'Gendarmerie,' the Ukrainian 'Schutzmannschaft,' and the 'Second Wave' of Jewish Killings in Occupied Ukraine: German Policing at the Local Level in the Zhitomir Region, 1941–1944," *German History* 14(2) (1996), pp. 168–92.

9 In the 1926 census, there were 1,143 Jews in the town. By mid-1941, however, the number had dropped to about 600. When Operation Barbarossa began, some (probably mostly men) managed to escape to the forest, an estimated 70 percent of the pre-war Jewish population remaining: see Geoffrey P. Megargee and Martin Dean (eds.), *Encyclopedia of Camps and Ghettos, 1933–1945. Vol. 2: Ghettos in German-Occupied Eastern Europe* (Bloomington, 2012), p. 1545.

10 According to USHMM Encyclopedia, these were two *aktions*: in October, 157 Jews were murdered in the park, including 29 men, 66 women and 62 children; And on October 13, 1941 – the event that was documented by the photograph - 94 more Jews were murdered, including 14 men, 31 women and 49 children.

11 See, for example, Zvi Gitelman, "History, Memory and Politics: The Holocaust in the Soviet Union," *Holocaust and Genocide Studies* 5(1) (1990), pp. 23–37; John Klier, "The Holocaust and the Soviet Union," in Dan Stone (ed.), *The Historiography of the Holocaust* (London, 2004), pp. 276–95; Thomas C. Fox, "The Holocaust under Communism," in Stone, *The Historiography of the Holocaust*, pp. 420–39.

12 Deposition of Gustav B (b. 1906), member of Police Battalion no. 303: B162-6673, p. 35. According to Lower, they mocked the Jews by addressing them by them by their first names, shattered children's heads against tree trunks, and brutally murdered a disabled woman. Mykhailo T. similarly testifies that while the pits were being dug people were tied to barbed wire fences and children's heads pulverized: https://www.yahadinunum.org/in-evidence

13 See, for example, Yehoshua Büchler, "The Nazi Sicherheitspolizei and the Deportation of the Jews of Tarnów," *Yalkut Moreshet* 43 (1986) (Hebrew); Browning, *Ordinary Men*, pp. 54–65. See also the descriptions of the *aktions* in Engelking and Grabowski, *Night without End*: Vol. I: Alina Skibińska, "Powiat biłgorajski," pp. 262–98; Jan Grabowski, "Powiat węgrowski," pp. 416–44; Anna Zapalec, "Powiat złoczowski"; Vol. 2: Dariusz Libionka, "Powiat miechowski," pp. 64–91.

14 See, for example, Shimon Redlich, *Together and Apart in Brzezany* (Beersheba, 2005) (Hebrew); Omer Bartov, *Anatomy of a Genocide: The Life and Death of a Town Called Buczacz* (New York, 2018).

Oded Heilbronner

Review of **Omer Bartov's** *Anatomy of a Genocide:*
The Life and Death of a Town Named Buczacz
(Am Oved, 2020), 352pp. [Hebrew]

Today, the town of Buczacz is located in Ukraine. Like many parts of Eastern Europe in recent centuries, it has been part of a number of national and super-national entities: Poland, the Ottoman Empire, the Austro-Hungarian Empire, Nazi Germany, the Soviet Union, and Ukraine, as already noted. Indeed, the upheavals of the past may suggest that the last word has yet to be said regarding the town's geopolitical location. The town was home to a number of well-known Jews, including Hebrew writer S.Y. Agnon, Nazi hunter Simon Wiesenthal, and Warsaw Ghetto historian Emanuel Ringelblum.

Personal considerations are what sparked the curiosity of historian Omer Bartov, who teaches in the United States. His mother was born in Buczacz but immigrated to Mandatory Palestine prior to the Holocaust. In the 1980s, as a scholar specializing in genocides and in the genocides of Eastern Europe in particular, he was one of the first to uncover the involvement of the German army in the war crimes on the Eastern front. His book on Buczacz, which was initially published in English a few years ago, combines a personal perspective with a research perspective, fuelling the originality and daring of his research and the resulting book. *Anatomy of a Genocide* is a micro-history, and unlike many studies that pertain to genocides and their circumstances and that deal with a short period of time, it covers hundreds of years and is deserving of praise.

Far-off Buczocz received world acclaim as a result of Agnon's novel *A City in Its Fullness*. Agnon describes Buczacz as a mini Garden of Eden and a small piece of heaven. However, according to Bartov's book, Buczacz was actually a little piece of hell: a meagre, impoverished, dirty, and violent town, from the short period of Polish-Lithuanian rule in the seventeenth century, where Bartov starts his story, to the post-Soviet era at the beginning of the twenty-first century.

Nostalgia bursts forth again and again from excerpts from the memoirs and interviews that Bartov conducted with Jews from the town and from travelogues, tour guides, and promotional books pertaining to that part of Eastern Europe. Still, a reading of his book leaves the impression of an ill-fated town that was already on the verge of its demise even before the outbreak of World War II and that was dealt a death blow by the violent Soviet occupation at the beginning of the war; the subsequent brutal German occupation, which resulted in the extermination of the town's Jews in 1943; and the ruthless population exchanges that were imposed by the Communists following the war.

Bartov's book belongs to the genre of the genocide studies of recent decades, as well as to the intricate politics of the field and its international implications. Today, the genre is one of the foci of historical research for a number of reasons. First, interest in the subject was sparked by the traditional debate regarding whether the Holocaust as unique or a certain type of genocide sparked interest in the subject. A second factor has been the political discussion regarding the classification of the murder of the Armenians during World War I; regarding the murders of other national groups carried out by the Communists under Stalin's leadership; and regarding the genocides that occurred in Cambodia under the Khmer Rouge in the 1970s, in former Yugoslavia, and in Rwanda in the 1990s. All of these factors, as well as genocides of the distant past (such as the genocide that was carried out by the Germans in Africa before World War I – the holocaust that preceded the Holocaust – and the White Americans' genocide of the Native Americans) have contributed to the high standing of the genre of genocide studies in both the world of academic research and world politics.

Unlike many studies from recent years and to his credit, Bartov, it should be noted, makes room for questions regarding issues such as the uniqueness of the Holocaust and the burdensome theoretical discussions on the difference between genocide and the mass killing sprees that have always occurred throughout the world. Bartov engages in a micro-historical study of Buczacz, adding notes to illuminate the broad processes that were underway in Eastern Europe from the seventeenth century onward and that help us understand what occurred in the town during each period. In this way, Bartov produces the wretched story of Buczacz as an anatomy of mass violence that was intertwined with the effort to create ethnic or ethno-religious homogenization as part of the establishment and the fall of empires in recent centuries. A broader view situates Buczacz within a vast region that, over the centuries, experienced violent population exchanges, murders, and genocides – among Poles, Ukrainians, and Jews alike – and indicates that the fate of Buczacz was apparently no different from that of hundreds of other villages and towns in Eastern Galicia in recent decades and a comparable number of localities in the "bloodlands" (Timothy Snyder) that stretched from the Baltic Sea in the north to the Black Sea in the south, and from the Oder River in the west to twentieth century western Russia, or the Eastern European "rimlands" (Mark Levene), in the east.

Bartov's book, then, is an original multi-layered study that covers centuries and tells the story of Buczacz from the view of its Jewish, Polish, and Ukrainian inhabitants. Their stories are told using photographs, official documents, tourist books, travelogues, and memoirs that reflect a number of social, ethnic, and religious groups that in some cases lived beside one another and in other cases lived intermingled. According to Bartov, the relationships between these groups were usually characterized by violence, persecution, suspicion, betrayal and deportation, and, ultimately, extermination, "as well as flashes of altruism and kindness" (p. 18). In response to Agnon's well-known book, Bartov shows that the Jews of Buczacz did not live in the "splendid (or sordid) isolation" (ibid.) that has characterized the writing on the Eastern European Jewish shtetl. The Jews' integration was almost complete and from the outset was accompanied by violence. Although Bartov does not advance a clear argument to this effect, an uninterrupted reading of his book suggests that the extermination of the Jews of Buczacz was a shocking but natural conclusion to centuries of persecution.

"The gathering storm" referred to in the title of Bartov's first chapter had already taken shape in the seventeenth century in the form of the major Cossack and peasant rebellion known as the Khmelnytsky Uprising. Tens of thousands of Jewish inhabitants of the eastern portion of the Polish-Lithuanian Commonwealth, including the inhabitants of Buczacz, were mercilessly slaughtered. Over the three centuries that have passed since the massacre, the town and its surrounding area have experienced severe episodes of murder and killing, especially during the eighteenth and the twentieth centuries, of which Bartov provides a detailed account. Women and children were brutally slaughtered (the lacerated, bleeding bellies of women and children are recurring features of the descriptions), and men were executed en masse both during the Khmelnytsky Uprising and the Turkish conquest of the late seventeenth century, and of course during the German occupation of 1942-1944. But almost daily violence and cultural tension were not the lot of the Jews alone. Turks, Ukrainians, Rusyns (Eastern European Serbs), Poles, Russians and Communists, and finally Germans clashed with one another over the course of centuries. Only after the violence and the mass expulsions that occurred during the years immediately following World War II, it appears, did Buczacz finally quiet down. The blood-stained story of Buczacz has another feature — the polluted nature of the town, to which Bartov makes repeated reference. He does not spare us the disturbing descriptions of the neglect and filth that prevailed in Buczacz, especially among its largely illiterate non-Jewish inhabitants. Also almost always rampant in the town was poverty and economic want. This is how the German army found the town when it conquered it in the summer of 1941.

As was the case throughout Europe from the beginning of the nineteenth century until the outbreak of World War I, especially after the Revolutions of 1848 (known also as the "Springtime of Nations"), the violence in the town was relatively low-intensity. During this period, the town and its environs appears to have been given a "rest" from being a site of perpetual killing. The interethnic tensions, particularly between the Ukrainian Rusyn peasantry and the Polish elite groups, only increased with the rise of nationalism and ethnic nationalism in the second half of the nineteenth century, but they did not reach the state of wide-scale violence. Bartov emphasizes the building and the development that occurred in the region, and during Agnon's childhood Buczacz appears to have enjoyed relative peace, economic prosperity, increasing literacy, and cultural and political development among the different ethno-national groups: the Rusyns, the Jews, the Poles, and the Ukrainians. But the religious and national tensions did not dissipate; hatred, and sometimes waves of violence, continued to simmer both beneath the surface and in plain sight. In this context too, Bartov does not spare us the difficult accounts. "Most of the former serfs remained wretchedly poor, illiterate, and the target of ruthless exploitation by landowners," he explains. "Ruthenian peasants associated their landlords with Poles and associated merchants, traders, shopkeepers, and tavern owners with Jews (p. 32)." Accordring to Bartov,

> The starkest symbol of alleged village venality was the village tavern, perceived by Polish and Ukrainian nationalists as the cause of the peasants' chronic alcoholism, indebtedness, and transfer of property to the Jews…Peasants learned to blame their own drunkenness on the Jews. One correspondent wrote, "You go into the tavern for tobacco, and the Jew…begins to praise his liquor and make fun of society…Before you know it you've had one drink, and then another."

Finally, the peasant "sells his boots for his liquor and pays double for whatever he drinks," whereas "Iudka just puts his hands in his pockets, jingles his money, laughs, and makes fun of the drunk" (p. 33).

After considering the countless different tensions among the social, national, religious, and ethnic groups and minorities, as well as the ideologues (including the Zionists, with their different nuances) on the eve of the war, Bartov cautions that "all three ethnoreligious groups were turning inward…in a more aggressive, resentful, accusatory manner…The trigger was finally pulled in 1914" (p. 46).

The Thirty Years War that was fought in Europe and other regions of the world between 1914 and 1944 also impacted Buczacz and its environs. During this period, regions of Central and Eastern Europe became "bloodlands" until they were liberated (or conquered, depending on the perspective of the locals) by the Soviet Union at the end of World War II.

In 1920, Buczacz became part of Poland and Polish nationalism reemerged, doing equal injury to the town's Jewish and Ukrainian residents. The Zionist movement had established a number of branches in the town and in Eastern Galicia prior to World War I, and a few dozen of its young residents immigrated to Palestine in the war's aftermath in the hope of finding mental and economic relief in a new land. However, in the new country many faced difficult living conditions that were similar to, and in some cases even more severe than what they had experienced in their hometown. Like many immigrants of the Third and Fourth Aliyah (two waves of Jewish immigration to Palestine), they too returned to their hometown just a few years later.

In Buczacz, those who returned were met not only by their families, who were struggling with notable economic difficulties, but also by Polish antisemitism, which combined religion and nationalism to create "an ideological and psychological climate ripe for widespread violence." The Poles viewed Jews as "an alien, inassimilable, and a potentially subversive element…" (p. 113). They regarded the Ukrainians as a threat to the new Polish state. Thus, for three decades, in addition to attempts to rehabilitate the region and the endless economic crises, all the town's inhabitants – more than 50 percent of which were Jews – experienced innumerable violent conflicts. This dynamic reached its height during the Soviet occupation in 1939 and the German occupation in 1941.

Half the book deals with the period of World War II, with an emphasis on the German occupation, the impact of Jewish-Polish and Jewish-Ukrainian relations, and, of course, the extermination of the Jews of Buczacz. Even earlier, the town experienced waves of violence during the Soviet occupation to which Eastern Galicia was subject following the division of Poland between Nazi Germany and the Soviet Union. The Ukrainians took revenge against the Poles and were among the last to suffer at the hands of their Polish brethren, who suspected them as Communist agents or supporters of Stalin and his associates in a "Jewish-Ukrainian conspiracy." Thousands of Polish inhabitants were deported to the eastern Soviet Union, whereas others were "'killed with knives and scythes' by their Ukrainian neighbors" (p. 144). During these years, the town experienced "unremitting fear and suspicion" (p. 147) and violence.

The tension and violence that characterized the Soviet occupation were dwarfed by the atrocities committed by the Germans during their three year occupation of the town. In addition to murdering Jews they also abused and murdered Poles. But the town's residents who suffered most were, of course, the Jews, and Bartov skillfully and painfully recounts the normalization of the everyday lives of the murderers. This process corresponded with the Jews' removal from the public sphere, the slave conditions in which they lived, and, ultimately, their extermination. The most shocking sections of the book are those into which – in addition to their abuse of the Jews – Bartov incorporates the everyday lives of the Ukrainian murderers, the military men, the German staff of the civil administration, and, most significantly, the members of the Nazi security forces (the SS and the Gestapo). As already noted above, Bartov also provides similar accounts from earlier periods in the history of Buczacz, although the brief period of the German occupation, the intensiveness of the atrocities, and the ultimate extermination of the Jews in death pits around the town and at Belzec extermination camp create a distinct sense of unease, especially in the chapter "The Daily Life of Genocide." This chapter, which depicts the way in which the Jews experienced the genocide, consists of anatomical descriptions of the murder of children, as well as of the women and cut-out organs that are reminiscent of the accounts of the atrocities in the book's initial chapters that deal with the seventeenth and the eighteenth century. "…we saw dismembered bodies, bodies without heads" recalled one witness (p. 224). "He went under the bed," recounted another. "His wife and two little boys panicked as she went to the door, and they just split their heads with axes, all three of them" (p. 230). To this end, Bartov consults countless local sources, German archives, newspapers, and, most notably, the testimonies and memoirs of locals and of Jewish survivors. All of this is accompanied by numerous photographs of victims and of German criminals. Bartov even follows the lives of the German criminals after the war, noting that most were not punished.

The title of the book's final chapter, "Neighbors," corresponds with the well-known book by Jan Gross, who researched the massacre carried out by Poles against the Jews of the town Jedwabne in 1941. This chapter, in which Bartov describes the reciprocal Polish-Ukrainian killings of 1944, is important in its highlighting of the broader local context of the murder of the Jews and of the fact that in the eyes of the Polish and Ukrainian nationalists, the difficult experience of the period was not the Holocaust but rather their mutual massacre of one another. Later in the chapter, Bartov depicts the attempts of the Soviets, who reached the area in the summer of 1944, to impose order in Eastern Galicia by changing the make-up of the population and deporting hundreds of thousands of Poles into Communist Poland and approximately half a million Ukrainians into the Soviet Union. Bartov takes advantage of this chapter to provide accounts of the efforts undertaken by a small number of Poles and

Ukrainians to assist and rescue their Jewish neighbors during the war, although he acknowledges that those who did so were few and far between.

After the war, Buczacz became a Soviet town, remaining grey, remote, impoverished, neglected, and depressed into the post-Soviet era. Under the Germans, the centuries-old Jewish study hall (*beit midrash*), described by Agnon as the "lifeblood of the local community," became a granary and was used in this manner until the 1990s when it became a shopping center.

In addition to this study's pioneering-historical value, we also note a number of elements addressed by the book that contribute to research on the definition of genocide, the Jewish shtetl, "wars of memory," and other subjects around which countless debates continue to revolve.

Bartov's book is titled *Anatomy of a Genocide*, and it can be assumed that this is a reference to the Germans' extermination of the Jews of Buczacz. This part of the book is most likely what will attract most of the attention of Holocaust researchers. However, as I have noted on more than one occasion, mass murder was also characteristic of the earlier history of the location, though not on the same scale as in the 1940s. The "gathering storm" that continued to intensify over the town, was indicative of what would occur there centuries later. From Bartov's book, genocide researchers can learn not only how to weave together a micro-history of genocide, which is something that many refrain from doing, but also how to integrate it into long-term history to show a predetermined fate.

Bartov's Buczacz is a distinct example of a Jewish shtetl – the traditional Eastern European form of Jewish settlement, which, on the one hand, has been subject to substantial criticism for the meagre living conditions of its inhabitants, and, on the other hand, has been the subject of longing for a rich and authentic Jewish experience. Although Bartov does not refer to Buczacz as a shtetl, it seems to me that it was one. In recent decades, an attempt has been made to restore the prestige and the presence of the Jewish shtetl. Bartov is not party to this effort, and to some extent his book presents the paucity and the suffering of the world of yesterday that no longer exists, which is a good thing – although it is a shame that its disappearance occurred under such circumstances.

Finally, Bartov skillfully describes the "war of memory" that continues to be waged over the bloody legacy of the region. Toward the 1940s, Buczacz became calm after centuries of violence; political, ethnic, and cultural upheavals; and countless rivalries of all kinds. The Soviet occupation, and especially the transformation of the previously multiethnic areas into one area that was completely homogenous due to genocide, ethnic cleansing, and a policy of population exchange, brought relief to the ill of the town and the surrounding area. However, Bartov effectively describes the physical and cultural struggles over memory. At the end of the book he considers the contemporary "war of memory" between Poles and Ukrainians, which is rooted in the period of "The Gathering Storm" – the name of the book's opening chapter – which reached its height during the war. In Bartov's words:

> The three ethnic groups who lived in Buczacz endured extreme suffering, although their hardships reached their heights during different periods and, often at the hands of different victimizers, as their willingness to collaborate with the occupiers depended on different factors and changing circumstances. Still, at the end of the war and for a long time afterward, each group strived to portray itself as the main victim of both the occupiers and of its neighbors (p. 267).

Bartov notes how the Poles, and especially the Ukrainians, yearned to emphasize their suffering, to prevent the genocide that was perpetrated by the Nazis from overshadowing their own victimization. The Poles described the Ukrainians as savages during the war, but the Ukrainians viewed themselves as saints who sacrificed their lives for the liberation of their homeland (p. 274). Even today, the members of the Ukrainian underground are still described "as the harbingers of the nation" (ibid.), and in 2016 their black and red flag was once again waving over the remnants of the medieval Polish castle overlooking the town. History stacks up. Or in the words of Bartov, "History was back to its old tricks" (p. 275).

Nicolas Dreyer

Review of Father Patrick Desbois, *In Broad Daylight: The Secret Procedures behind the Holocaust by Bullets.*
New York: Arcade Publishing, 2018. 312 pp.

Father Desbois' book *In Broad Daylight: The Secret Procedures behind the Holocaust by Bullets* is much more than a publication of enormous historical research on crimes committed by the local Eastern European population in aiding the German Shoah. In his work, Desbois ultimately pursues the question of what turns human beings, specifically neighbors, into willing cogs of an inhumane killing machinery. His research asks specific questions: they concern the roles these neighbors played in the Nazi genocide, the reasons that possibly made them collaborate or refuse collaboration with the Nazis, and the organization, routines, and schedules of an average execution day. Based mainly on interviews with local collaborators, his book is an outstanding work in illuminating such contexts and in providing very detailed insight into the dimension of local collaboration as well as into the technical operation of countryside executions in ditches and similar places. The overarching question, however, is that of moral judgment, or the predominant absence thereof, by locals in their individual decisions to help the Nazis, or less frequently to help Jews: why and how are village residents turned into murderers of their own Jewish neighbors, even friends, of the same village? A secondary overarching question asked by the book is that of memory and amnesia, collectively and individually, busting the "myth" of secrecy that has enveloped the massacres in the participants' recollections.

The monograph consists of 26 chapters, two introductions, a conclusion, and an afterword. The first introduction is a historical one, offering a general location of the work concerning the Shoah and its research. The second introduction is a very personal one and retraces Father Desbois' exposure, since his childhood, to the Second World War and the Shoah in Eastern Europe. The main chapters are mostly relatively short and are titled according to the activities or functions which local residents fulfilled and which are described in the respective chapters. The chapters are grouped into five sections that lay out the typical chronology of an execution day, beginning from "The Night Before," covering "The Morning," "The Day," and "The Evening," until "The Day After." Most chapters are dated and begin with some recollection or personal reflection by Father Desbois on the chapter's subject matter, the circumstances or people whom he and his team met in the course of conducting interviews with locals represented in the chapters, or taking recourse to depositions from German or Soviet archives. The book represents about eight years of research conducted by Father Desbois and his team of international and local researchers, driven by the question of what exactly took place, how a typical day of mass murder at a local site could unfold, and which factors may have facilitated the local population's participation in it.

The work is introduced by Andrej Umansky, sketching out the distinctiveness of the Shoah in occupied Soviet Eastern Europe. He describes the scope of the so-called "Shoah by bullets": its geographical expanse, as well as time, nature, and quantity. Over 80 percent of the murdered Jewish population of Russia, Ukraine, and Belarus was executed by firing squads, often at sites in the vicinity of their own village or town. Umansky introduces brief post-war testimonies by German perpetrators that revealed only their interest in the mechanical efficiency of the extermination of the Jewish population, and in the detrimental psychological effects on the shooters themselves: they proved oblivious to the fact that they had committed manifold murder and genocide. Above and beyond pointing out the Nazis' absence of normal moral categories, in that they conceptualized the killing of the Jews and others as an ideological and racial necessity, he emphasizes another distinct feature of the Shoah in occupied Soviet territories: the killings were not conducted in secrecy, as was the case with the deportation of Jews to the concentration and death camps and their extermination there. Instead, the "Shoah by bullets" took place in "broad daylight," to explain the book's main title: it took place in plain sight of the local population and other German military personnel and, in fact, required the local population's participation in the crimes at practically all stages of the executions. Umansky concludes by highlighting that even though both Soviet and post-war German judicial investigations have collected testimonies of survivors, executioners, and neighbors concerning the destruction of almost all Jewish communities, and that these testimonies document that the execution took place for everyone to see, they are not explicit about the daily routine and organization of the executions.

In his very personal and autobiographical "Introduction," Desbois sets the narrative tone for the whole book. He reminisces about his childhood and upbringing in rural France, where he experienced social division, and where earlier his family had been involved with the French Resistance. He encountered the silence of his beloved grandfather Claudius there, when he would ask him about his experience as a prisoner of war in the French internment camp at Rawa Ruska in Ukraine, where 25,000 Soviet prisoners were murdered. In Rawa Ruska, 15,000 Jews were also shot. It was this silence which he also experienced when first visiting Rawa Ruska himself and many other sites of mass murder since, that set him on his journey of founding the work of "Yahad – In Unum." Subsequently, a certain dimension of this secrecy concerning the genocide against the Jews in rural and municipal occupied Soviet territories could be lifted: more than four thousand interviews were conducted and statements by witnesses were cross-referenced with archives, allowing the presentation of a certain narrative explaining crucial aspects of this "Shoah by bullets," aspects which had hitherto not been understood in such detail. The "aggregated" or cumulative contents of many testimonials offered the "Yahad" researchers the opportunity to identify and "distill" an astounding general reality and rhythm of the killings: "it became clear that the Shoah by bullets in Eastern Europe was not the secret we have been led to believe for so long. Rather, many people – Ukrainians and Poles, especially – saw it all with their own eyes and sometimes did more" (p. 11). The local residents were the constant "helping hands" of the killers and were involved in building the ghettos, rounding up the victims, and digging and filling the graves. *In Broad Daylight* takes the reader on a journey of gradual discovery of the public nature of these executions and the local population's involvement in them.

Each chapter contains excerpts from testimonials, descriptions of individual historical and local contexts, a narration of Father Desbois and his team's approach in dealing with local witnesses, as well as Desbois' reflections on the encounters with the local witnesses and their actions and behavior. Gradually, as the book progresses, the veil of secrecy is lifted and specific dimensions of a typical day of killing are added, so that eventually, a largely complete picture emerges of how the killings were organized and to what extent locals were engaged in them, be it forcibly or voluntarily. As has been suggested above, the author often shares his own questions as to what may have motivated the neighbors' individual moral choices; sometimes such moral judgment is expressed rather explicitly by the neighbors, sometimes it is only implicit in their narration of their participation in events. Often, given his own biographical familiarity with rural life in the mid-twentieth century and its cyclical nature, the author meditates on his perception of the role which the social situation of rural communities in Soviet Russia, Ukraine, and Belarus with their specific structures, customs, habits, routines, and experiences – some of which go back to Tsarist Russia, others imposed by the Soviets – may have played in the executions and may have been purposely exploited by the Nazis. Certain groups of Ukrainians of German descent, so-called *Volksdeutsche*, were a rare and distinct example of the local civilian population participating in the actual executions by killing local Jewish populations themselves.

Rather than reviewing the book chapter by chapter, the present discussion will first outline the book's cumulative lessons concerning the organization of mass executions and the extent of local participation. Following that, some of the author's thoughts responding to such lessons will be summarized. First of all, the executions at each site of mass murder took place regularly within less than twenty-four hours and were carefully thought through and organized. The activities involved, such as the preparation and the carrying out of executions at provincial or municipal sites as well as the concluding work, were manifold. In all of these auxiliary roles, the local population participated; often they were requisitioned by the Germans, sometimes they participated voluntarily. The activities contributing to the executions included the locating of a site appropriate for mass execution and burial, the measuring out of the needed space in the earth, the digging of such ditches. Furthermore, they included the planning and organization of transportation, the sealing of Jewish neighborhoods and ghettos, the readying of local *polizei* forces for the next day, food provisions, the digging of the ditches, the laying of planks across the ditches, the filling of the mass graves with lime, and their subsequent closing. In addition, it meant the transporting of clothes and other material possessions of the murdered Jews, as well as their preparation for further use and their "marketing" at auctions. Also involved was the documentation by the Germans for official propagandistic or private home consumption; German soldiers photographed and filmed the genocide.

Such auxiliary preparations began the night before the executions took place, in the vicinity of the locality from which the Jewish population would be extracted the following day. While a German architect or surveyor would measure out a prospective site of mass murder ahead of time, logistical requisitions for the next day would be set into motion by the regional German headquarters. At the same time or somewhat later during the night, Germans and the police would encircle the ghetto, restrict the movement of its residents, and often allow the police to rape, and subsequently shoot, women of the ghetto, as well as to steal their property: "It was as though nothing held these men back because the Jews were going to be killed the next day. [...] The extermination machine is not just for killing. It authorizes all forms of cruelty so long as they don't interfere with the strict timing on the day of the genocide" (p. 69).

During the following morning, several things took place simultaneously. The ditches had to be dug precisely as had been calculated and measured out before to provide the right space for the planned number of human bodies. Food was ordered from a local dining hall for the day. Local vehicles, carts, and sledges had to be readied by the population (or sometimes transport companies) by the morning. The Jews were deported from the ghetto or rounded up in their houses by local police. Perhaps long before the deportation to an execution site, the ghetto was physically sealed off, often by local residents. Lime was requisitioned from the village to fill the blood-soaked mass graves, in order to sanitize them. For all of these activities, the support and services of the local population were requisitioned. The police established two cordons, one directly at the site of murder around the ditch, to prevent attempts at flight, and a second "outer" cordon to seal off traffic as well as, effectively, to separate "the space of the crimes from that of ordinary villagers" (p. 81). It was a perimeter separating life from death – even offering the local non-Jewish population a sense of safety that the genocide was not directed against them, but against the Jews exclusively. All the way and time from the ghetto to their execution, Jews would be subject to abusive treatment. In some instances, local residents perceived the column of Jews as they were taken to their execution site as "Judgment Day," as "Jews going up to Golgotha," as a kind of "religious procession" and divine retribution for what Christianity had taught about the Jews for many centuries: the Christian accusation of deicide. Some spectators even made the sign of the cross in response to such scenes (pp. 88-92). The persecution of the Jews by the Nazis reverberated with a Judeophobia that was transported by traditional Christian beliefs and customs, which to some extent continued underneath the superimposed Soviet ideology.

During the daytime shootings, the executioners often took turns or breaks, during which they ate and drank and reloaded their weapons. The food had been requisitioned from the local population. Neighbors of those Jews who were being shot, as members of the *polizei* or ordinary requisitioned helpers, were present at the executions as people who dug the ditches, as those who helped round up and transport the Jews to them, as people who moved the planks on the ditches on which the Jews had to stand to be shot, as people who filled the ditches with lime, as those who provided meals to the Germans, and as those who removed the clothes and valuables while others back in the village or town roamed the Jewish homes, killed individuals that had occasionally managed to hide, and stole their abandoned property. Meanwhile, often, local residents who did not participate could still watch securely from some distance. The killing operation itself was mostly over by midday. While the locals who helped or watched returned to their communities, now emptied of Jews, the German murderers returned to their regional headquarters, celebrated with a party in the evening, and conducted execution de-briefings, evaluating their genocidal efficiency.

Desbois' research describes this execution "process" in great detail, furnishing information from many individual testimonies concerning a great number of mass executions. In doing so, he reveals the immense extent to which these crimes were embedded in local communities. Many individuals from a community were involved in single or even in several stages of the genocide of their Jewish neighbors, either as participants, or as spectators. Effectively, the whole community knew what was happening, before, during, and after the crime. Desbois' presentation also makes space for neighbors who either refused to participate in the local genocidal acts or who actively engaged in helping their Jewish neighbors, while seeking to understand their motivations. However, reflecting on the magnitude of the willingness of non-Jewish neighbors to support the killing of the local Jews, Desbois makes several suggestions which are certainly worthy of further contemplation and research. First of all, he enquires into the moral breakdown that made it possible to suppress human feelings and sympathy with one's neighbors. Secondly, he suggests that certain social and communal structures, as well as sets of beliefs, were already in place, that the Germans were able to consciously use. These include the specific rural and municipal government institutions of the Russian Empire and the Soviet period. Such structures had also served the Soviet requisition policies, with which the Soviet population was therefore well acquainted. Also, antisemitism, specifically Christian Judeophobia, and racism were likely prevalent among the provincial population, as outlined above. In addition, life in the villages and small towns was adapted to the daily, weekly, monthly, seasonal, and yearly individual and communal routines of an often agricultural – and perhaps, to a lesser extent, also artisanal – cyclical life. Also, without justifying this morally, the abject poverty of the provincial population, worsened by the war, the German occupation generally but also by preceding Soviet policies, makes it conceivable that residents may have considered money, an item of clothing or of food, something that suddenly became accessible through the death of a neighboring Jew, more valuable than his or her life. The author considers it possible and likely that the German genocidal machine "tapped into" such local paradigms of social behavior and that the specific routines of the genocide in Soviet Eastern Europe may have been developed to fit in with them.

In the "Afterword," the author summarizes his reflections concerning individual moral responsibility in the Shoah in particular and in genocide more generally. He suggests that above and beyond the specific totalitarian and genocidal ideology and the rhetoric and discourse of racial purity, genocide is ultimately not enacted by ideologues who follow their own rules of purity, but by "mere" criminals, by individuals who are offered the opportunity to "extract themselves on a personal level from the usual criminal motivations. […] Genocide masquerades as a moral act" (p. 259) in that it provides an ideological justification for murder, rape, theft, and related genocidal crimes. For Desbois, the "unmasking of the killer, wiping away the lie" (p. 261) of ideology of racial or religious superiority, may be the first step in combating the perpetration of genocide and in examining the true extent of complicity in genocidal crimes.

In conclusion, *In Broad Daylight* is a fascinating and very readable, albeit (and for obvious reasons) shocking, account of a specific aspect of the Shoah in Soviet Eastern Europe, which is a dimension of the Shoah that for many decades and for well-known historical reasons had not been properly researched. Father Desbois and his team's work of breaking through barriers of silence and secrecy – barriers often motivated by the desire to hide one's personal involvement in a specific act of the genocidal process – makes an important further contribution to research in this field, with which he has already been associated, owing to the precursor of his present book, *The Holocaust by Bullets: A Priest's Journey to Uncover the Truth Behind the Murder of 1.5 Million Jews* (2009). Above and beyond discovering certain and important historical facts, his personal story and relevant reflections offer conclusions and suggestions that may provide the impetus for further research concerning the Shoah in Soviet Eastern Europe, be it through the lenses of psychology, social anthropology and social studies, theology, church history, and antisemitism studies, in order to better understand actions of the local population in the context of the Shoah in Soviet territory. Ultimately, his book is also a call to the reader to consider the question that confronts all Shoah and genocide researchers alike, the question of what makes a human being disregard the humanity of his or her fellow man or woman.

List of Contributors

Prof. Omer Bartov is the John P. Birkelund Distinguished Professor of European History at Brown University. He is the author of eight monographs, including *Erased: Vanishing Traces of Jewish Galicia in Present-Day Ukraine* (2007) and the award-winning *Anatomy of a Genocide: The Life and Death of a Town Called Buczacz* (2018). His many edited volumes include *Shatterzone of Empires: Coexistence and Violence in the German, Habsburg, Russian, and Ottoman Borderlands* (2013), *Voices on War and Genocide: Three Accounts of the World Wars in a Galician Town* (2020), and *Israel/Palestine: Lands and Peoples* (2021). Bartov's new monograph, *Tales from the Borderlands: Making and Unmaking the Galician Past*, is forthcoming with Yale University Press in 2022.

Prof. Yehuda Bauer is the (Emeritus) Professor of Holocaust Studies at the Hebrew University in Jerusalem. Born in 1926, he is the Academic Adviser of Yad Vashem, the Israeli Holocaust Remembrance and Educational Institution, Member of the Israeli Academy of Science, and Hon. Chairman of the Intergovernmental International Holocaust Remembrance Alliance. He has authored 22 books, mainly on the Holocaust and Genocide (and its prevention), and about 100 refereed articles and chapters in books and journals. He has spoken to the German Bundestag (1998), the Stockholm Fora on Holocaust Education (2000) and Genocide Prevention (2004), the UN General Assembly (2007), and has advised on a number of films and documentaries, including Claude Lanzman's "Shoah". He is the recipient of the Israel Prize (1998) and of the Emet Prize (2017).

Dr. Graciela Ben Dror has been the editor of *Moreshet, The Journal for the Study of the Holocaust and Antisemitism*, since 2011. She has served as a researcher at the Stephen Roth Institute for the Study of Antisemitism at Tel Aviv University, a lecturer at the Departments of Universal and Jewish History, University of Haifa, and Director of Moreshet, Mordechai Anielevich Memorial. Her books include: *The Catholic Church and the Jews: Argentina, 1933-1945* (2000) (Hebrew), which was awarded the Israeli Ministry of Culture's Prize for the year 2000 and was published in Spanish (2003) and English (2008); *La Iglesia Católica ante el Holocausto. España y América Latina 1933-1945* (2003); *Radical Socialist Zionism on the Banks of Rio de La Plata: The Mordechai*

Anielevich Movement in Uruguay, 1954-1976 (2016) (with Victor Ben-Dror); *Christianity without Grace* (2018) (Hebrew). Her articles have been published in: *Handbook des Antisemitismus, Kirchliche Zeitgeschichte-Contemporary Church History, Revista de Historia Contemporánea, Historia Sacra, Yad Vashem Studies, Moreshet Journal, Dapim, Antisemitism Worldwide, Kesher, Zmanim, Judaica Latinoamericana, EIAL, Jewish Latin American Studies* and elsewhere.

Dr. Jan Burzlaff is the William A. Ackman Fellow for Holocaust Studies at Harvard University, a graduate of the École Normale Superieure, Paris, and the 2016–17 Jane Eliza Procter Fellow at Princeton University. He is currently completing his dissertation, the first transnational history of Jewish survival during the Holocaust. Further areas of interest are interdisciplinary approaches with the social sciences, comparative genocide, and global histories of violence. His most recent work is published in Holocaust and Genocide Studies and Contemporary European History.

Michał Chojak has worked with Yahad In Unum since 2010, when the organization began its research in Poland. In the ensuing 11 years, Mr. Chojak has participated in 50 research missions in Eastern Europe and interviewed hundreds of eyewitnesses of the Holocaust by Bullets. Director of Yahad In Unum Research Center since 2020, he has specialized in the research of the Holocaust in Poland, Ukraine and the Baltic States. He is also involved in Yahad In Unum's research projects in Guatemala and Iraq. A graduate from the Université Paris IV Sorbonne, his research focuses currently on the Baudienst, a forced labor service for young Poles created in German occupied Poland.

Father Patrick Desbois, a Professor at Georgetown University, who has devoted his life to confronting antisemitism and furthering Catholic-Jewish understanding. In 2004, he founded Yahad In Unum, an organization dedicated to documenting, identifying and commemorating the sites of Jewish and Roma mass executions in Eastern Europe during World War II. Father Desbois is also the author of *The Holocaust by Bullets: A Priest's Journey to Uncover the Truth Behind the Murder of 1.5 Million Jews*, winner of the National Jewish Book Award, *In Broad Daylight: The Secret Procedures behind the Holocaust by Bullets*, and *The Terrorist Factory: ISIS, the Yazidi Genocide and Exporting Terror*, based on his investigation of the Yazidi genocide in Iraq. Former director of the Episcopal Committee for Relations with Judaism (1999-2016), Father Desbois serves as a consultant to the Vatican, and was a personal aide to the late Archbishop of Paris, Cardinal Jean-Marie Lustiger. His work through Yahad In Unum has been recognized through numerous awards, including the Medal of Valor by the Simon Wiesenthal Center, the Humanitarian Award of the U.S. Holocaust Museum, the Tom Lantos Human Rights Prize from the Lantos Foundation, and honorary doctorates from The Hebrew University and Bar Ilan University in Israel.

Prof. Havi Dreifuss is a professor of Jewish History and head of the Institute for the History of Polish Jewry, as well as, Israel-Poland Relations at Tel Aviv University and director of the Center for Research on the Holocaust in Poland at the International Institute for Holocaust Research, Yad Vashem. Her research deals with various aspects of everyday life during the Holocaust, including the relationship between Jews and Poles, religious life in light of the Holocaust, and Jewish existence in the face of extermination. Her latest book, *The Warsaw Ghetto – The End (April 1942 - June 1943)* was awarded the Shazar Prize for the Study of Jewish History and will be published in English.

Dr. Nicolas Dreyer is a postdoctoral researcher and adjunct lecturer in Slavic and Jewish Studies at the University of Bamberg, Germany. His research focuses on the transculturality of Haskalah literature and press in Russia and Germany. In 2020 and 2021, he published contributions on Jewish and non-Jewish Russian-German transculturality. He holds an MA (Hons) in International Relations and Russian Studies (2004), and a Ph.D. in Russian literature (2011), both from the University of St. Andrews, Scotland. From 2011 to 2015, he did charitable work in Germany with Holocaust survivors from Russia and Ukraine. Following this, he researched and published on Soviet and post-Soviet Holocaust memory politics. In 2020, his monograph on post-Soviet Russian fiction, entitled *Literature Redeemed: 'Neo-Modernism' in the Works of the Post-Soviet Russian Writers Vladimir Sorokin, Vladimir Tuchkov, and Aleksandr Khurgin,* was published by Böhlau Verlag Cologne.

Ronnen Harran has been a Ph.D. candidate at The Department of Jewish History, Haifa University since 2017. He gained his M.A. Degree in 2015 in Holocaust Studies and was placed on the Dean's list of merit at the University of Haifa. His

B.Sc. in 1983 was in Mathematics and Computer Sciences, with distinction at Ben-Gurion University. Among his publications: "The Sonderkommando Uprising in Birkenau – The Destruction of Krematorium IV". *Yalkut Moreshet*, Vol. 15, 2018; "The Jewish Women at the Union Factory, Auschwitz 1944: Resistance, Courage and Tragedy", *Dapim, Studies on the Holocaust*, Vol. 31, Issue 1, 2017.

Prof. Oded Heilbronner is a Senior Lecturer at the Shenkar College for Design and Art in Ramat Gan, Israel, and a lecturer at the Reichman University Herzliya and the Hebrew University, Jerusalem. His latest publications include: *Popular Liberalism in South Germany* (Routlede 2016); *Suicide and Mentally Ill in Young Israel* (Hebrew, Carmel publishing 2020); "Towards a Global History of Israel", *Asian Review of Global History,* July 2021; "Großraum Europa: The Nazi Concept of 'Greater European Space'", *English Historical Review*, October 2021.

Dr. Tamir Hod is an expert historian on the topic of the Second World War, the Holocaust and Holocaust remembrance in Israel. His research on the Demjanjuk affair in the United States and in Israel, was published as a book titled: *Rembember to Forget*, is considered a pioneering and groundbreaking study on the subject. Dr. Hod also served as a consultant for the Netflix documentary "Ivan the Terrible" that has garnered millions of viewers worldwide. As part of his academic activities, Dr. Hod teaches at Tel-Hai College and Western Galilee College and is a member of the Spiegel Fellows Forum, a member of the Polish Forum on Holocaust Studies, and a member of the Ghetto Fighters' Museum Scientific Committee.

Nir Itzik is the Guiding Department Director in the Ghetto Fighters House Museum. He was previously the research director of the Ethiopia Jewry Heritage Center in Israel and before that worked as a researcher and archivist at Moreshet, Mordechai Anielevich Memorial. In addition, he worked for many years as a research assistant for Prof. Havi Dreifuss of the Department of Jewish History at Tel Aviv University. His master's thesis, written in the Department of Jewish History at Tel Aviv University under the guidance of Prof. Havi Dreifuss, dealt with the testimonies of Yitzhak (Antek) Zuckerman about the Jewish Fighting Organization in the Warsaw ghetto. An article based on the thesis was published in Moreshet Journal for the Study of the Holocaust and Antisemitism, volume 16, English version, titled, "The Testimonies of Yitzhak (Antek) Zuckerman from Wartime to *Those Seven Years*: A Reassessment."

Noam Leibman is a Ph.D. candidate in the Jewish History Department at the University of Haifa, under the supervision of Prof. Marcos Silber and Prof. Guy Miron. He holds a master's degree from the University of Haifa's Department of Jewish History, for which he was awarded *summa cum laude*. Leibman has been awarded scholarships and prizes from Yad Vashem and the Inter-University Program in Russian and East European Studies. He has been working at the Education Department of Moreshet – Mordechai Anielevich Memorial Holocaust Study and Research Center, since 2008, and is currently the Head of the Educational Center. His article "Merely a description of the events" or something deeper? The Memoirs of Jewish Warsaw Ghetto Police Officer Stanilaw Gombinski as a Model from Hermeneutic Analysis" was published in Vol. 18 of *Moreshet Journal*.

Prof. Alina Molisak, Ph.D, is Assistant Professor in the Department of Polish Literature of the Twentieth Century in Warsaw University. She previously taught at Humboldt University in Berlin (2007/2008). She was guest lecturer in the winter semester 2015/16 (Gastdozentin) at the University of Hamburg. She is a member of Gesellschaft für Europäisch-Jüdische Literaturstudien and the Polish Society of Yiddish Studies. Her published books include: *Judaizm jako los. Rzecz o Bogdanie Wojdowskim* (Bogdan Wojdowski — Judaism as Destiny); *Żydowska Warszawa — żydowski Berlin. Literacki portret miasta w pierwszej połowie XX wieku* (English version – 2021, *Jewish Warsaw — Jewish Berlin. A Literary Portrait of the City in the First Half of the 20th Century*). She is also the co-editor of several books, including: *Stosowność i forma. Jak opowiadać o Zagładzie* (Decorum and Form, How to Tell about the Holocaust); *Pisarze polsko-żydowscy XX wieku, Przybliżenia* (Polish-Jewish Writers In the Twentieth Century: Approximation); *Polish and Hebrew Literature and National Identity; Nach dem Vergessen. Rekurse auf dem Holocaust in Ostmitteleuropa nach 1989; Ślady obecności* (Traces of Presence); *Galician Polyphony. Places and Voices; Pomniki pamięci. Miejsca niepamięci* (Memorials. Places of Non-Memory); *The Trilingual Literature of Polish Jews from Different Perspectives; Tożsamość po pogromie. Świadectwa i interpretacje Marca '68* (Identity After the Pogrom. Testimonies and Interpretations of March '68). She is interested in Polish-Jewish literature, literature of the Holocaust, questions of identity, and the poetics of urban spaces.

Prof. Yuri Radchenko is the director of the Center for Interethnic Relations Research in Eastern Europe (Kharkiv, Ukraine) and associate professor at the Institute of Oriental Studies and International Relations "Kharkiv Collegium" (Kharkiv). He is currently working on his project "Andriy Melnyk: the OUN Leader's Life History and the Memory of Him and His Movement". Yuri was a post-graduate student (aspirant) at the Department of the History of Ukraine of the V. Karazin Kharkiv National University. His dissertation dealt with "Nazi Genocide of the Ukrainian Jews in the Military-Administered Area (1941-1943)". He has been the recipient of many fellowships: Saul Kagan Claims Conference Fellowship for Advanced Shoah Studies, L. Dennis and Susan R. Shapiro Fellow, Center for Advanced Holocaust Studies, United States Holocaust Memorial Museum, Fellow in Zentrum für Holocaust-Studien, Institut für Zeitgeschichte (Munich, Germany), Yahad In Unum Research Fellow, Yad Hanadiv/Beracha Foundation post-doctoral fellowship, Post-doctoral fellow of The Israeli Inter-University Academic Partnership in Russian and East European Studies, and Ben-Gurion University of the Negev. Yuri has recently finished his monograph titled "Hilfspolizei, Self-government and the Holocaust in Ukrainian-Russian-Belorussian Borderland: Motivation, Identity, Collective Portrait and Memory" (forthcoming). His academic interests include the history of the Holocaust, Ukrainian-Jewish relations in 1920-1940-th, collaboration with Nazis in Eastern Europe and the history of right radical movements in Europe in 1920s-1940s.

Prof. Grzegorz Rossoliński-Liebe is an historian at the Freie Universität Berlin and a lecturer at the Zentrum für Antisemitismusforschung. He specializes in the history of the Holocaust, fascism, antisemitism, and multiethnic cities. He is a fellow of the Gerda Henkel Stiftung, Alfred Landecker Stiftung and an Honorary Research Fellow of the Alexander von Humboldt Stiftung at the Center for Holocaust Research at the Polish Academy of Sciences. He published the first scholarly biography of Stepan Bandera (*Stepan Bandera: The Life and Afterlife of a Ukrainian Nationalist: Fascism, Genocide, and Cult, 2014*), several articles on the Holocaust in East Central Europe, and has edited volumes about antisemitism at European universities, transnational fascism, and multiethnic cities. Currently he is finishing a collective biography of Polish mayors in the Holocaust.

Prof. Per Anders Rudling is an Associate Professor of History at Lund University, and is a Wallenberg Academy Fellow, funded by the Knut and Alice Wallenberg Foundation. He holds a Ph.D. in History from the University of Alberta, Canada (2009) as well as MA degrees in history from San Diego State University, US (2003) and Slavic studies from Uppsala University, Sweden (1998). Following postdoctoral fellowships at the universities of Greifswald and Lund, he was a visiting professor at the University of Vienna and Visiting Senior Fellow at the National University of Singapore. He is currently leading a research project on memory and long-distance nationalism in Central and Eastern Europe. In 2015, his book *The Rise and Fall of Belarusian Nationalism, 1906-1931* (Pittsburgh UP, 2014) won the Kulczycki Book Prize in Polish Studies from the Association for Slavic, East European & Eurasian Studies (ASEEES).

Prof. Marcos Silber is an Associate Professor at the Department of Jewish History, the University of Haifa and its former chairman. Silber also serves as chairman of the Gotteiner Institute for the History of the Bund and the Jewish Labor Movement, University of Haifa, as well as Director of The Interdisciplinary Unit for Polish Studies. At the core of his academic interest is the relationship between citizenship and ethnicity. He has written on Jewish Diaspora Nationalism in Poland, Lithuania, and Russia in the early 20th century; on Yiddish and Polish mass culture in inter-war Poland, and Polish-Israeli relations and mutual migrations. His major publications include *Different nationality, Equal citizenship! The Efforts to Achieve Autonomy for Polish Jewry during the First World War* (Hebrew, Tel Aviv 2014) and with Szymon Rudnicki: *Polish-Israeli Diplomatic Relations, a Selection of Documents (1945 -1967)*, (Polish version Warsaw 2009, Hebrew version Jerusalem 2009). His articles have been published in: *Galed, Michael, Journal of Baltic Studies, Journal of Israeli History, Polin, Simon Dubnow Institute Yearbook, Shvut, Tzion, Iyunim be-Tekumat Yisrael, East European Jewish Affairs* and elsewhere.

Prof. Kai Struve is a Privatdozent at the Institute of History at Martin Luther University in Halle, Germany. He received his Ph.D. at the Free University of Berlin and held previous positions at the Herder Institute in Marburg and the Simon Dubnow Institute of Jewish History and Culture in Leipzig, as well as visiting fellowships in the US, France, and Poland. Among his publications are the books *Deutsche Herrschaft, ukrainischer Nationalismus, antijüdische Gewalt. Der Sommer 1941 in der Westukraine*, München: DeGruyter-Oldenbourg 2015; *Bauern und*

Nation in Galizien. Über Zugehörigkeit und soziale Emanzipation im 19. Jahrhundert, Göttingen: Vandenhoeck & Ruprecht 2005; and the edited volumes (with Michael G. Müller): *Fragmentierte Republik? Das politische Erbe der Teilungszeit in Polen 1918-1939*, Göttingen: Wallstein 2017; and (with Elazar Barkan, and Elizabeth A. Cole): *Shared History – Divided Memory. Jews and Others in Soviet- Occupied Poland, 1939 – 1941*, Leipzig: Leipziger Universitätsverlag 2007.

Prof. Joanna Tokarska-Bakir is a Cultural and Historical anthropologist, and Professor at the Institute of Slavic Studies of the Polish Academy of Sciences in Warsaw, Poland. She specialises in the anthropology of violence and is the author of, among other publications, a monograph on blood libel *Légendes du sang, Une anthropologie du préjugé antisémite en Europe* (Albin Michel, Paris 2015), *Pogrom Cries. Essays on Polish-Jewish History, 1939-1946*, Peter Lang 2017), *The Kielce Pogrom. A Social Portrait* (Czarna Owca 2018), and *Jewish Fugitives in the Polish Contryside 1939-1945* (Peter Lang, 2021).

Dr. Aharon Weiss received his Ph.D. from the Hebrew University of Jerusalem in 1973. His thesis deals with the Jewish Police in the Generalgouvernement and in Upper Silesia during the Holocaust. His research deals with the Jewish leadership in Eastern Europe during the Holocaust, and also with the attitude of the Ukrainian Nationalist Movement against the Jews during the Holocaust. He was one of the writers and editors of the *Pinkasei HaKehilot* (Encyclopedia of Jewish Communities) and former editor of *Yad Vashem Studies* (1984 -1990). Dozens of his articles have been published in the most important Holocaust journals, such as *Moreshet Journal for the Study of the Holocaust, Yad Vashem Studies*, and elsewhere.

Prof. Anna Zapalec is an Associate Professor at the Department of Modern History at the Institute of History and Archival Studies at the Pedagogical University of Kracow. She studies the problems of the Second World War in the context of the history of Poland. Her research focuses in particular on repressions and crimes committed in Poland by the occupying forces from the period of the war. Selected publications: *Ziemia tarnopolska w okresie pierwszej okupacji sowieckiej (1939-1941)* (Kraków, 2016); *Druga strona sojuszu. Żołnierze brytyjscy w Polsce w czasie II wojny światowej* (Gdańsk 2014); *Powiat Złoczów, in: Dalej jest noc. Losy Żydów w wybranych powiatach okupowanej Polski,* (ed.) B. Engelking, J. Grabowski (Warszawa, 2018).

INSTRUCTIONS FOR CONTRIBUTORS

MORESHET, THE JOURNAL FOR THE STUDY OF THE HOLOCAUST AND ANTISEMITISM

1. *Moreshet Journal,* a **peer reviewed publication,** invites researchers to send us scholarly articles and/or review essays relating to topics dealing with the Holocaust and Antisemitism.

2. Articles have to be original, and not published in other publications.

3. Manuscripts should not exceed 10,000 words including notes, and including a short abstract of 150 words. The articles must be sent by email. Manuscripts must be typewritten, double-spaced, and all pages should be numbered consecutively. Two typewritten, double-spaced copies of the article on A4 paper should be sent to the address of the *Moreshet Journal.*

4. Details of the author's institutional affiliation, degree, short CV for the list of contributors (6-8 lines), address, phone number and email must be added.

5. To be accepted for publication the articles will pass both internal and external peer review and, if accepted, the author may be requested to make revisions.

6. Articles may be sent in English, French, German, Polish or Hebrew, but in some cases other languages will also be considered.

7. The author will receive a copy of the volume in which the article was published.

Please send the articles to the following address and e-mail:
Dr. Graciela Ben Dror, Editor
Moreshet, the Journal for the Study of the Holocaust and Antisemitism
Givat Haviva, Doar Na Menashe, 37850
Israel
graciela.moreshet@gmail.com

AN ANTHOLOGY
OF MORESHET JOURNALS
VOL. 1-9 ARE AVAILABLE
in an eBOOK Collection*

MORESHET JOURNAL for the STUDY
of the HOLOCAUST and ANTISEMITISM
The English Language Collection

www.amazon.com
or on Apple's iBook Store
*Individual volumes of the Moreshet Journal
volumes 10 (2013) – 17 (2020) can also be purchased
on Amazon.com or the iBook Store

MORESHET

JOURNAL FOR THE STUDY OF THE HOLOCAUST AND ANTISEMITISM

14 2017

- Graciela Ben-Dror
- Yehuda Dvorkin
- Sharon Geva
- Aviva Halamish
- Liat Meirav
- Dalia Ofer
- Avinoam J. Patt
- Na'ama Seri-Levi
- Zipora Shehory-Rubin
- Ada Schein
- Bilha Shilo
- Yfaat Weiss
- Yechiel Weitzman

MORESHET

JOURNAL FOR THE STUDY OF THE HOLOCAUST AND ANTISEMITISM

15 2018

MORESHET

JOURNAL FOR THE STUDY OF THE HOLOCAUST AND ANTISEMITISM

16 2019

- Nava T. Barazani
- Tammy Bar- Joseph
- Graciela Ben-Dror
- Yaakov Borut
- Robert Cohen
- Sharon Geva
- Lior Inbar
- Nir Itzik
- Yvonne Kozlovsky-Golan
- Daniel Nadav
- Dina Porat
- Dov Schidorsky
- Margalit Shlain
- Eli Tzur
- Amit Varshizky

MORESHET

JOURNAL FOR THE STUDY OF THE HOLOCAUST AND ANTISEMITISM

Historiography of the Holocaust

17 2020

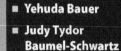

MORESHET

JOURNAL FOR THE STUDY OF THE HOLOCAUST AND ANTISEMITISM

18 2021

- IRIT BACK
- JUDY BAUMEL-SCHWARTZ
- GRACIELA BEN DROR
- IRITH CHERNIAVSKY
- SHARON GEVA
- DAVID GOLINKIN
- AVIVA HALAMISH
- NIR ITZIK
- MENACHEM KEREN-KRATZ
- LEA LANGLEBEN
- NOAM LEIBMAN
- DALIA OFER
- MICHAL SHAUL
- ELI TZUR
- MOSHE VERED
- YECHIAM WEITZ
- EFRAIM ZADOFF

Routledge
Taylor & Francis Group

THE ISRAEL JOURNAL
of Foreign Affairs

A publication of the Israel Council on
Foreign Relations under the auspices
of the World Jewish Congress

Visit the *Israel Journal of
Foreign Affairs* website at
www.tandfonline.com/rifa to:

· Register for table of
  contents email alerts

· Find out how to submit
  an article

· Access the latest journal
  news and offers

· Find pricing and ordering
  information.

www.tandfonline.com/rifa

Made in the USA
Columbia, SC
01 September 2022

65922723R00267